Understanding educational psychology

Irma Eloff & Estelle Swart

Understanding educational psychology

First published 2018

Juta and Company (Pty) Ltd
First Floor, Sunclare Building, 21 Dreyer Street, Claremont 7708
PO Box 14373, Lansdowne 7779, Cape Town, South Africa
www.juta.co.za

ISBN 978-1-48510-247-2

All rights reserved. No part of this publication may be reproduced or transmitted in any form or by any means, electronic or mechanical, including photocopying, recording, or any information storage or retrieval system, without prior permission in writing from the publisher. Subject to any applicable licensing terms and conditions in the case of electronically supplied publications, a person may engage in fair dealing with a copy of this publication for his or her personal or private use, or his or her research or private study. See section 12(1)(a) of the Copyright Act 98 of 1978.

Project manager: Deidré Mvula
Editor: Annette de Villiers
Proofreader: Willemien Jansen
Cover designer: Nicole de Swardt
Typesetter: Lebone Publishing Services
Indexer: Sanet le Roux

Acknowledgements of tables and figures: Figure 10.1: Adapted from: Gordon Dryden and Jeanette Vos. 2005. *The New Learning Revolution*. Network Continuum Education. Used by permission of Bloomsbury Publishing Plc.; Chapter 12 case study: *Yazilaya imbila* (*The rock rabbit/dassie learns the hard way*) Canonici, Noverino N. 1993: pp 3–5 *Izinganekwane: An anthology of Zulu folktales*. © and permission of the Zulu Language and Literature Dept., University of Natal; Figures 35.1, 35.2, 44.1 – Claudia Eckard; Figure 36.2 – photograph taken by David Lurie; Figure 47.1 – illustration by Jana Slabber

Typeset in Minion Pro 11.5 pt

The author and the publisher believe on the strength of due diligence exercised that this work does not contain any material that is the subject of copyright held by another person. In the alternative, they believe that any protected pre-existing material that may be comprised in it has been used with appropriate authority or has been used in circumstances that make such use permissible under the law.

Contents

Contributor information xvii

Preface xxvi

Part 1: Introduction 1

Chapter 1: Educational psychology as science and profession in South Africa 2
Estelle Swart & Irma Eloff
Introduction 2
History 3
What do educational psychologists do? 4
Where do educational psychologists work? 5
How to become an educational psychologist 5
The science of educational psychology 6
The way forward 9

Chapter 2: Educational psychology as the intersection between philosophy and psychology and education 10
Johnnie Hay
Introduction 10
Why is it important to know about this intersection between philosophy and psychology and education? 10
The major debates about the relationship between education and psychology 15
How is knowledge of the intersection between philosophy and education and psychology relevant for South African schools and classrooms? 18
Conclusion 18

Chapter 3: The role of educational psychologists in teaching and learning 19
Motlalepule Ruth Mampane
Introduction 19

The relevance of educational psychology to South African schools and classrooms 21
The role of an educational psychologist in the education process 23
Major debates within the field of educational psychology 27
Conclusion 27

Chapter 4: Children's rights in South Africa: Implications for educational psychologists 29
Jace Pillay & Lucia Munongi

Introduction 29
Importance of children's rights 30
Major debates about children's rights 31
Relevance of children's rights in South African schools and classrooms .. 32
Implications for educational psychologists 33
Conclusion 34

Part 2: Teachers 35

Chapter 5: Becoming a teacher 36
Mariechen Perold

Introduction 36
Why is the process of 'becoming a teacher' important? 38
Some theories and debates about teacher identity 38
The meaning of 'becoming a teacher' for schools and classrooms in South Africa 40
Conclusion 44

Chapter 6: Teachers as role models 45
Moeniera Moosa

Introduction 45
Why is modelling important? 46
What is modelling? 46
What is observational learning? 47
Teacher modelling 48
How is teacher modelling relevant to South African schools and classrooms? 50
Conclusion 51

Chapter 7: The emotionally intelligent teacher 52
Elma Fleischmann

Introduction 52
Why is the study of emotional intelligence (EI) important for teachers? 53
History of the concept emotional intelligence 54
Emotions and the brain 55
Feeling, thinking and doing 55
The use of emotions 56
Defining emotional intelligence 56
Emotions and learning 58
Conclusion 60

Part 3: Teaching and learning 61

Chapter 8: Teaching for learning in South African schools: A sociocultural approach 62
Joanne Hardman

Introduction 62
Why is a sociocultural approach to teaching for learning important and what major debates does it address? 63
Vygotsky and pedagogy: Teaching for learning 65
From mediation to scaffolding: Neo-Vygotskian approaches 66
Relevance to South African schools and classrooms 68
Conclusion 68

Chapter 9: Learning theories and the use of technology in the classroom 69
Geesje van den Berg

Introduction 69
Why is knowledge about learning theories important? 70
Major debates within the field of learning theories 70
Conclusion 76

Chapter 10: Learning styles and intelligences in diverse classrooms 77
Kamleshie Mohangi

Introduction 77

The importance of learning styles and intelligences in diverse classrooms 78
Debates within the field of learning styles and intelligences in diverse classrooms 82
How are learning styles and intelligences in diverse classrooms relevant to South African schools and classrooms? 83
Conclusion 84

Chapter 11: Simultaneous multisensory instruction to advance children's academic achievement 86
Annelize du Plessis

Introduction 86
Challenges we have to face in the classroom 87
Why is simultaneous multisensory instruction important? 88
The major debates within the field of simultaneous multisensory instruction 91
How is simultaneous multisensory instruction relevant to South African schools and classrooms? 92
Conclusion 93

Chapter 12: Indigenous stories and games as approaches to teaching within the classroom 94
Patrick Mweli

Introduction 94
Description of indigenous knowledge systems 95
Indigenous languages as cultural artifacts 96
Indigenous stories as an approach to teaching in the classroom 97
Indigenous games in classroom teaching 99
The implication of using indigenous stories and games to teach within South African schools and classrooms 100
Conclusion 101

Chapter 13: Whole child development through formal teaching and learning 102
Trevor Moodley & Colleen Gail Moodley

Introduction 102
What is holistic education? 102

The relevance of holistic education 105
The relevance of a holistic education approach to South African schools and classrooms 107
Conclusion 109

Part 4: Cognition 110

Chapter 14: Cognition in the world of action 111
Bruce Brown

Introduction 111
Why is it important to link cognition and action? 113
The major debates within the field of cognition 118
How are systems of cognition relevant to South African schools and classrooms? 119
Conclusion 119

Chapter 15: Piaget, mental networks and learning to act in the world 120
Bruce Brown

Introduction 120
Why is Piagetian learning theory important? 121
The major debates within the field of Piagetian learning theory 127
How is Piagetian learning theory relevant to South African schools and classrooms? 128
Conclusion 129

Chapter 16: Vygotsky, regulating alignment with tools, people and the world 130
Bruce Brown

Introduction 130
Why is mediation and alignment important? 131
Some major debates within the field of mediation and sociocultural learning theory 137
How is Vygotsky relevant to South African schools and classrooms? 137
Conclusion 138

Chapter 17: Knowledge of neuroscience for the classroom 139
Lara Ragpot

Introduction	139
A brief history of 'mapping' learning acts in the brain	140
Knowledge of neuroscience for language in the classroom	142
Knowledge of neuroscience for reading in the classroom	143
Knowledge of neuroscience for classroom mathematics	144
Knowledge of neuroscience for creativity in the classroom	146
Implication for South African educationists	148
Conclusion	149

Chapter 18: Cognitive psychology: Post-Piagetian notions of childhood conceptual change 150
Lara Ragpot

Introduction	150
Conceptual change: Stage general or domain specific?	152
Cognitive developmentalist Susan Carey: Concepts, beliefs, theories and conceptual change	154
Alison Gopnik: The '*Theory* theory' and children as 'little scientists'	159
Conclusion	162

Chapter 19: Identity, motivation and achievement 163
Salomé Human-Vogel

Introduction	163
Why is this theme important?	164
Major debates	166
How is the theme relevant to South African schools and classrooms?	167
Conclusion	168

Part 5: Language 169

Chapter 20: Understanding language development and learning 170
Funke Omidire

Introduction	170
Importance of understanding language development and learning	171
Commonly accepted stages of language development	171

Process of language development 174
Relevance of language development and learning in South African
schools and classrooms 177
Challenges associated with language development 178
Strategies for enriching language development 179
The role of educational psychologists in school settings 181
Conclusion 182

Chapter 21: Communication across the curriculum 183
Hanlie Dippenaar & Candice Livingston

Introduction 183
Defining language proficiency 184
Defining teacher language proficiency 185
Language proficiency and the roles of the teacher 187
Conclusion 189

Chapter 22: Individualised learner support 191
Annalene van Staden

Introduction 191
Reading 192
Conclusion 201

Part 6: Health and well-being 202

Chapter 23: Teacher well-being and the role of positive
psychology 203
Beverley Feldman

Introduction 203
The importance of teacher well-being 204
Prominent theories of well-being and the role of positive psychology 205
Relevance to South African schools and classrooms 209
Conclusion 210

Chapter 24: Promoting psychosocial well-being in teaching
and learning environments 212
Cheryl Ferreira, Connie Haasbroek, Beverly Feldman, Monkie Moseki &
Chantel Weber

Introduction 212

Understanding the term 'psychosocial well-being' 213
Bronfenbrenner's ecological systems theory of human development 213
Learners' psychosocial well-being 215
Legal support for psychosocial well-being in learners 216
The importance of the teacher's psychosocial well-being 217
The teachers' role in creating a safe psychosocial environment 218
Promoting psychosocial well-being within diverse teaching and learning contexts 219
Conclusion 220

Chapter 25: A relationship-focused approach to the optimal development of learning and well-being 221
Ansie Elizabeth Kitching

Introduction 221
Why a relationship-focused approach? 222
The critical role of relationships in the optimal development of learning and well-being 222
What does a relationship-focused approach to the optimal development of learning and well-being encompass? 223
Why is the application of a relationship-focused approach relevant in a South African context? 227
Conclusion 228

Chapter 26: Positive psychology and diversity: Accumulation of strengths 229
Fumane Portia Khanare

Introduction 229
A socio-educational context 230
Positive psychology perspective 231
The influence of positive psychology on diversity 232
Ways of enhancing positive diversity in the classroom 232
The benefits and challenges of positive psychology in a diverse society: Thinking forward 235
Conclusion 235

Chapter 27: School-based championship of resilience 237
Linda Theron

Introduction 237
Beating the odds versus changing the odds 238
Which matters more: Children's contributions to the resilience
process or those of the social ecology? 239
Championing resilience in relevant ways in the South African classroom 242
Conclusion 246

Chapter 28: The role of self-talk in self-regulation 247
Rienie Venter

Introduction 247
Why is it necessary to take note of self-talk in educational psychology? ... 248
Clarification of self-talk and related constructs 249
Educational implications of the quality of self-talk in schools in South
Africa 253
Conclusion 254

Part 7: Inclusion 255

Chapter 29: Inclusive education: The global movement 256
Mirna Nel

Introduction 256
Understanding inclusive education in a global context 257
Historical global conventions 259
Conclusion 262

Chapter 30: Inclusive education in the South African context 263
Mirna Nel

Introduction 263
Background to inclusive education in South Africa 264
Defining inclusive education within a South African context 265
The use of appropriate terminology within the South African context ... 266
Challenges in implementing inclusive education successfully 268
Conclusion 269

Chapter 31: Learning support in South Africa 271
Mirna Nel

Introduction	271
Understanding learning support	272
Support structures	273
Conclusion	277

Chapter 32: Teacher collaboration and working with school-based support teams 279
Jean Fourie

Introduction	279
School-based support teams	279
The importance of collaborative teacher teams	280
Goals of collaboration	281
A collaborative theoretical framework	283
Conclusion	285

Chapter 33: Disability and inclusive employment through the lens of educational psychology 286
Maximus Monaheng Sefotho

Introduction	286
Social construction of disability	287
The relevance of inclusive employment for South African schools and classrooms	289
Teaching about the psychosocial aspects of disability	290
Conclusion	291

Part 8: Schools 292

Chapter 34: Considering school-based interventions: What do you need to think about? 293
Surette van Staden & Vanessa Scherman

Introduction	293
Theoretical insights on maximising the implementation quality of interventions	297
Conclusion	298

Chapter 35: Strengthening parental partnerships 299
Debbie Cilliers

Introduction 299
Theoretical background 300
The importance of parental partnerships 300
The different types of parental partnerships 302
Getting and keeping parents involved 303
Parental partnerships in South African schools 305
Negative influences on parental partnerships 306
Conclusion 307

Part 9: Educational psychological support 308

Chapter 36: Educational psychology and aesthetic learning 309
Karlien Conradie

Introduction 309
What does the aesthetic disposition look like? 309
Why are aesthetical learning experiences important? 310
How can we practise aesthetic openness to stimulate deep learning? 314
Conclusion 315

Chapter 37: Sexuality education 316
Nicola Jearey-Graham & Catriona Ida Macleod

Introduction 316
Why is sexuality education important? 317
The major debates within the field of sexuality education 318
Recommendations for school-based sexuality education 321
Conclusion 322

Chapter 38: 'Teenage pregnancy' or early reproduction 323
Tracey Feltham-King & Catriona Ida Macleod

Introduction 323
Why is 'teenage pregnancy' important? 324
The major debates 325
Conclusion 329

Chapter 39: Exploring the complexity of aggression and violence within the school context ... 330
Lynne Damons

Introduction ... 330
The changing socio-educational landscapes of schools ... 331
The link between aggression and poor academic performance ... 332
Responses to challenging behaviour ... 333
Conclusion ... 336

Chapter 40: Gender and violence against women and girls ... 337
Naydene de Lange

Introduction ... 337
'The personal is political' ... 338
Discourses around patriarchy and violence against women and girls ... 340
What has violence against women and girls got to do with schooling? ... 343
Conclusion ... 344

Chapter 41: Giftedness ... 345
Marietjie Oswald

Introduction ... 345
Why is a focus on giftedness important? ... 346
The major debates in the field of giftedness ... 347
The relevance of giftedness to South African schools and classrooms ... 351
Conclusion ... 352

Chapter 42: Attention deficit hyperactivity disorder and the role of the educational psychologist ... 354
Ramodungoane Tabane

Introduction ... 354
Diagnosing attention deficit hyperactivity disorder ... 355
Why is understanding attention deficit hyperactivity disorder important? ... 357
Major debates within the field of attention deficit hyperactivity disorder ... 358
What causes attention deficit hyperactivity disorder? ... 358
Intervention ... 360

How is attention deficit hyperactivity disorder relevant to South African schools and classrooms? 361
Conclusion 363

Chapter 43: Assessment and support of learners with autism spectrum disorders 364

Rina Lemmer

Introduction 364
Why are assessment and support important for learners with autism spectrum disorder? 365
Current debates within the field of assessment and support of learners with autism spectrum disorder 366
How is assessment and support of learners with autism spectrum disorder relevant to South African schools and classrooms? 372
Conclusion 373

Chapter 44: The brain, cognition and neuro-physical impairment 374

Deirdré Krüger

Introduction 374
Why is basic knowledge of brain functioning important? 375
Major debates within the field of cognitive neuroscience 379
How is cognitive neuroscience and neuropsychology relevant to South African schools and classrooms? 380
Conclusion 381

Chapter 45: Efficacy of the student support services 382

Mandla Morris Hlongwane

Introduction 382
Why are student support services important? 384
What then are functions of student support services in universities? 385
Coordination and provisioning of student support services 385
Office of the Dean of Students 385
Major debates 389
Conclusion 391

Part 10: Careers 392

Chapter 46: Life design: The essence of helping people live successful lives and make social contributions 393
Kobus Maree

Introduction	393
Why is life design important?	394
Major debates in the field of life design	396
How is life design relevant to South African schools and classrooms?	397
Conclusion	399

Chapter 47: A map to career paths within educational psychology 400
Carla Feenstra & Mariechen Perold

Introduction	400
Why it is important to think about career paths in educational psychology	401
Some of the major debates and paradigm shifts in educational psychology	403
Aspiring to enter the South African education scene	405
Conclusion	409

Chapter 48: Pathways to technical and vocational education in the school curriculum 411
Boitumelo M Diale

Introduction	411
Why is technical and vocational education (TVE) important in the school curriculum?	412
Trends in technical and vocational education	414
Relevance of TVE to South African schools and classrooms	416
Conclusion	418

References 419

Index 473

Contributor information

Chapter 1

Irma Eloff is a professor of educational psychology, a registered educational psychologist and a rated social scientist. She was the seventh dean of the Faculty of Education at the University of Pretoria and also the first woman to hold this position. She is a past President of the Education Association of South Africa and Chair of the SA Akademie vir Wetenskap en Kuns. She serves on the UNESCO International Task Team for Teacher Education.

Estelle Swart is a professor in the Department of educational psychology at Stellenbosch University, which she chaired for several years. She is a registered educational psychologist and was a member of the HPCSA Board for Psychology and chair of the PsySSA Division for educational psychology. She is a NRF-rated researcher with an interest in childhood disability, professional learning and support practises in inclusive education.

Chapter 2

Johnnie Hay is an associate professor at North-West University, Potchefstroom Campus, and an educator, educational and clinical psychologist. His research focuses on education support services within inclusive education, educational psychological issues of learners and the teaching of Life Orientation. He is the 2018 Chairperson of the Education Association of South Africa.

Chapter 3

Ruth Mampane is the Head of Department of educational psychology and Associate Professor at the University of Pretoria. Her research focuses on resilience research, specifically in disadvantaged communities. She also serves as Council member of Umalusi and is the 2017 Chairperson of the Education Association of South Africa (EASA).

Chapter 4

Jace Pillay is a South African Research Chair in Education and Care in Childhood at the University of Johannesburg. His research focuses on orphans and vulnerable children, children's rights, and children affected by HIV/AIDS. He is a member of PsySSA and chairs the National Task Team for educational psychology.

Lucia Munongi is a Post-Doctoral Research Fellow at the University of Johannesburg. Her research focuses on children's rights and responsibilities, and vulnerable children.

Chapter 5

Mariechen Perold is an educational psychologist and lectures in the Department of educational psychology at Stellenbosch University. The focus of her teaching is the education of teachers, counsellors and educational psychologists. Research activities include the topics of teacher identity, and counsellor identity for relevant psychological practice in South Africa.

Chapter 6

Moeniera Moosa is a lecturer at the University of the Witwatersrand. Her research focuses on bullying and aggression, teacher education and social psychology. She serves as a member of the UNESCO Chair in Teacher Education for Diversity and Development as well as on the Governing Council of the Sunshine Association.

Chapter 7

Elma Fleischmann is a lecturer at the Cape Peninsula University of Technology. Her research focuses on soft skills and emotional intelligence. She passionately taught children for many years, believing their full potential is unlocked by teaching with heart.

Chapter 8

Joanne Hardman is an associate professor at the University of Cape Town. Her research focuses on child development, cultural historical activity theory and teaching/learning. She also serves as African exco member of the International Society for Cultural Historical Activity research and African secretary for the International Association for Cognitive Education and Psychology, and received the distinguished teachers award at UCT in 2015.

Chapter 9

Geesje van den Berg is Head of the Department of Curriculum and Instructional Studies at Unisa. Her research focuses on open distance learning and the integration of technology in teaching and learning. She also serves as a member of the International Council for Distance Education and the International Association for the Advancement of Curriculum Studies.

Chapter 10

Kamleshie Mohangi is a full professor and an educational psychologist at Unisa. Her research focuses on positive approaches to learning and learning support, child, adolescent and family well-being, and inclusive education. She serves on college level committees at UNISA and is a member of PsySSA.

Chapter 11

Annelize du Plessis is a lecturer at the University of Pretoria. Her research focuses among other on simultaneous multisensory instruction in the classroom. She is an active member of the Department of Higher Education's initiative, called the Teaching and Learning Development Capacity Improvement Programme (TLDCIP), which mainly focuses on the implementation of a new programme to strengthen and assist with capacity development in selected areas of teacher education.

Chapter 12

Patrick Mweli is a lecturer at the University of KwaZulu-Natal. His research focuses on Inclusive education, Indigenous knowledge systems (IKS), and languages.

Chapter 13

Trevor Moodley is a senior lecturer at the University of the Western Cape. His research focuses on factors influencing teaching and learning. He is a registered educational psychologist with the HPCSA.

Colleen Gail Moodley is a lecturer at the Cape Peninsula University of Technology. Her research focuses on sexual practices in emerging adulthood, coaching and factors influencing teaching and learning. She is also a certified executive leadership coach.

Chapters 14, 15 and 16

Bruce Brown is a senior lecturer at Rhodes University. He has lectured at both the Department of Mathematics (Pure and Applied) and the Department of Education. At the Department Education, he has served two terms as Head of Department. His research focuses on the learning of mathematics for effective mathematical thinking, rational number learning and teaching, psychological approaches to thinking, learning and practice, and self-sustaining change processes in teacher education and professional development. Much of his research is oriented to dynamical processes and to understanding the systems of interaction involved in these processes.

Chapters 17 and 18

Lara Ragpot is an Associate Professor at the University of Johannesburg. Her research focuses on childhood cognitive development and learning, and multimodal learning in higher education. She also serves on the editorial board of the South African Journal of Childhood Education, is a member of PsySSA, has won the UJ Vice Chancellor's Award for Teaching Excellence, and a national HELTASA commendation for teaching excellence in higher education.

Chapter 19

Salomé Human-Vogel is Associate Professor in educational psychology and Deputy Dean of Teaching and Learning in the Faculty of Education, University of Pretoria. Her research focuses on self-regulation, commitment, and academic achievement. She is a member of PsySSA, and also serves on the Education, Training, and Registration Committee of the Board of Psychology.

Chapter 20

Funke Omidire is a lecturer in the Department of educational psychology, University of Pretoria. Her research interests centre on multilingualism in education and its challenges, and issues of psychological well-being of affected students and teachers and parents. She is a member of the World Education Research Association (WERA) and Psychological Society of South Africa (PsySSA).

Chapter 21

Hanlie Dippenaar is a senior lecturer at the Cape Peninsula University of Technology, and subject head of English (GET), based on the Wellington campus. She has been working in the field of Education for the past 30 years and holds a PhD in language teaching. She has received the Top Laureate Award for Teaching and Learning from the University of Pretoria, and was awarded a commendation for the HELTASA National Teaching Award. Her research focuses on language teaching and learning, service-learning and curriculum development.

Candice Livingston is a senior lecturer and research coordinator at the Wellington campus of the Faculty of Education at the Cape Peninsula University of Technology. Her research focuses on critical cultural competence, digital literacy and the teaching of language in a decolonised context. She serves on the Executive Committee of the English Association of Southern Africa and is currently the convener of the Percy Fitzpatrick Prize for Youth Literature. She also serves as a reviewer for Umalusi, where she reviews the English Home Language examination questions for the National Senior Certificate (NSC) and the Senior Certificate (SC).

Chapter 22

Annalene van Staden is a senior lecturer and researcher at the University of the Free State. Her research focuses on psycho-linguistics and literacy development.

Chapter 23

Beverley Feldman is an educational psychologist, lecturing at Unisa. Her research focuses on positive psychology, well-being, and creating enabling school environments.

Chapter 24

Cheryl Ferreira is a lecturer at Unisa. Her research focuses on spiritual intelligence (SQ) and adaptive functioning in adolescents, and the cultivation of values within educational contexts.

Connie Haasbroek is a senior lecturer in the College for Education, Department of Psychology of Education at Unisa. She is specialising in the field of mental health. Before joining Unisa in 2013, she was self-employed as a mental health practitioner and education consultant for 14 years. During this time, she served on the Mental Health Review Board of Gauteng. Her passion is the well-being of teachers and learners in schools, as well as student support in an ODeL environment.

Beverley Feldman (see Chapter 23).

Monkie Moseki is a lecturer in the Department of Psychology of Education at Unisa. She focuses on teacher professional development and curriculum development broadly in her academic work. She is an expert on adolescent self-regulated learning and social cognitive theory. In private practice, she works with behavioural challenges in children and adolescents, as well as career counselling.

Chantel L. Weber is a lecturer at Unisa. Her research focuses on resilience, fragile X syndrome and developmental impairments.

Chapter 25

Ansie Elizabeth Kitching is an associate professor at the North-West University. Her research focuses on the development of an integrated, multilevel approach to the promotion of holistic well-being in South African school communities. She is a member of the Educational Psychology Association of South Africa and the South African Educational Research Association.

Chapter 26

Fumane Portia Khanare is a senior lecturer in the School of Education Studies at the University of the Free State. Her research focuses on psychosocial support of vulnerable children, child agency, HIV and AIDS education and inclusive education, with particular emphasis on using participatory visual arts-based methodologies and asset-mapping.

Chapter 27

Linda Theron is a professor at the University of Pretoria. Her research focuses on the resilience of South African adolescents made vulnerable by structural disadvantage. She is an associate editor of *Child Abuse & Neglect*, as well as *School Psychology International*, and a member of PsySSA. She received an Education Association of SA Research Medal in 2013 and the NWU Vice-Chancellor Award: Service Excellence in Community Engagement (Applied Research Results) in 2014.

Chapter 28

Rienie Venter is an associate professor at Unisa. Her research focuses on the impact of social and religious authority on the identity development of children.

Chapters 29, 30 and 31

Mirna Nel is a research professor in the Optentia Research Focus area at North-West University. Her research focuses on teacher education for inclusion and high performance learning. She is the leader of a sub-programme within Optentia called Holistic Learner Development in Diverse Contexts and the vice-president of the International Association for Cognitive Education South Africa (IACESA).

Chapter 32

Jean Fourie is a lecturer at the University of Johannesburg. Her research focuses on inclusive education, schools as networked systems, and supporting children with neurodevelopmental disorders. She is a supervising educational psychologist and a member of PsySSA.

Chapter 33

Maximus Monaheng Sefotho is a senior lecturer at the University of Pretoria. His research focuses on inclusive employment. He is a member of the Scientific Committee (Comité científico 2016–2018) of the *Journal: Revista Latinoamericana de Orientación y Desarrollo Humano: 'OrientAcción'*, and has won an Honorary award for career guidance from Universidad de la Marina Mercante – Buenos Aires.

Chapter 34

Surette van Staden is a senior lecturer at the University of Pretoria. Her research focuses on reading literacy, large-scale assessment, and school-wide reform interventions. She also serves on the Suid-Afrikaanse Akademie vir Wetenskap en Kuns Onderwyskommissie, and she is the international research network coordinator for the World Education Association's network on reading literacy and associated interventions for at-risk students. She has received the Dean's Award for Excellence in Education Research in 2015.

Vanessa Scherman is an Associate Professor at Unisa. Her research focuses on psychometrics, school climate, and bullying in schools. She also serves on the board of the Mixed Methods International Research Association as governance chair and is NRF-rated researcher.

Chapter 35

Debbie Cilliers is a lecturer at the Cape Peninsula University of Technology, Wellington campus. Her research focuses on parental involvement in schools and learner support. She leads an outreach programme for learner support by BEd-4 students in primary schools.

Chapter 36

Karlien Conradie is a lecturer at the Stellenbosch University and an educational psychologist. Her research focuses on aesthetical ways of meaning-making in professional development concerning both psychotherapy practice and curriculum design.

Chapter 37

Nicola Jearey-Graham is a PhD candidate with the Critical Studies in Sexualities and Reproduction Unit at Rhodes University. Her research focuses on interventions, which aims to improve sexual and reproductive outcomes. She has recently received an Emerging Researcher Award from the South African Association of Child and Adolescent Psychiatrists and Allied Professionals, and the Dr K. Gillis Prize from Rhodes University for academic achievement. She is also a registered as a counselling psychologist in private practice.

Catriona Ida Macleod is a professor of Psychology and SARChI chair of Critical Studies in sexualities and reproduction at Rhodes University. Her research focuses on feminism, sexualities, and reproduction. She also serves as a steering committee member of sexual and reproductive justice coalition, and has received numerous awards for her research and community engagement.

Chapter 38

Tracey Feltham-King is a lecturer and research coordinator in the Department of Psychology at the University of Fort Hare. Her research focuses on the ways in which the label 'at risk' is used to deny stigmatised individuals and groups access to reproductive and sexual justice. She was awarded the Wilf Malcolm Institute of Educational Research Doctoral Award in 2016.

Catriona Ida Macleod (see Chapter 37).

Chapter 39

Lynne Damons is a lecturer at the Stellenbosch University. Her research focuses on marginalised youth, safer learning spaces and youth empowerment. She also serves on the Senate Committee for Social Impact at Stellenbosch University.

Chapter 40

Naydene de Lange is Professor Emeritus at the Nelson Mandela University. Her research focuses on gender violence, HIV and AIDS education, inclusive education, using participatory visual methodologies. She serves as one of the editors of the *Educational Research for Social Change Journal*, is NRF-rated researcher and has received the DST Distinguished Woman in Science, Runner-up Award.

Chapter 41

Marietjie Oswald is an extraordinary senior lecturer at Stellenbosch University. Her research focuses on teacher training, inclusive education, transformation of schools and educational support for the gifted learner. She employs cultural-historical activity theory as lens in her research. She is a registered psychometrist.

Chapter 42

Ramodungoane Tabane is a senior lecturer at Unisa. His research focuses on attention deficit hyperactivity disorder (ADHD), child and neurodevelopment, innovative qualitative research methodology, cross-cultural and educational psychology. He serves as the chairperson on the Society of educational psychology of South African (SEPSA) Board, and is a member scholar for the International Institute for Qualitative Methodology (IIQM).

Chapter 43

Rina Lemmer is a lecturer at AROS. Her research focuses on the assessment of children with autism spectrum disorder, and teaching practice of students in the Foundation Phase. She has presented papers at conferences of teaching practice.

Chapter 44

Deirdré Krüger is an associate professor at Unisa. Her research focuses on movement therapy and post trauma art therapy. She is a member of the national research group, Schools as Enabling Systems.

Chapter 45

Mandla Morris Hlongwane is the head of the Department of educational psychology at the University of Zululand, previously having served as the dean of students and the head of student support services. The foci of his research is in psychological assessment, the self, adolescents, young adults and the application of psychotherapy in a complex African multicultural context. He is a member of the Psychological Society of South Africa (PsySSA) as well as the Community of Practitioners (CoP); the latter playing a significant role in the integration of the HIV and AIDS curriculum in the academic and professional training programmes of institutions of higher learning in South Africa.

Chapter 46

Jacobus Gideon (Kobus) Maree is a professor at the University of Pretoria. He is internationally acknowledged for his work in career counselling and life design. A council member of the Psychological Society of South Africa, he has a B1 rating from the NRF.

Chapter 47

Carla Feenstra is a lecturer at the Stellenbosch University and an educational psychologist. Her research focuses on the scholarship of teaching and learning, with a specific focus on educating registered counsellors and educational psychologists. She is also interested in career pathing in educational psychology.

Mariechen Perold is an educational psychologist and lectures in the Department of educational psychology at the Stellenbosch University. The focus of her teaching is the education of teachers, counsellors and educational psychologists. Research activities include the topics of teacher identity, and counsellor identity for relevant psychological practice in South Africa.

Chapter 48

Boitumelo M Diale is the head of department in the Department of educational psychology and a senior lecturer at the University of Johannesburg. Her research niche areas are in the fields of career construction across the life span, technical and vocational education in the Intersen Phase (Grades 4–9) of education and violence and bullying issues in schools and workplace systems. She also chairs the Transformation Committee of the Faculty, serves as the section editor for the *South African Journal of Childhood Education* and executive member of SEPSA, an educational psychology division of PsySSA.

Preface

The word 'understanding' seems to presuppose reciprocity. It denotes a dynamic interplay between two or more entities, where communication takes place, and where a heightened awareness and deepened collective knowledge can be the result. Understanding is usually associated with synonyms like 'comprehension', 'cognisance' or 'grasping'. It is a word that has many positive connotations such as 'discernment' and 'appreciation' and it is often connected to harmony.

Yet, at the same time, 'understanding' is not necessarily synonymous with comfort or with being *comfortable*. Because in order to truly 'understand', it often means that we need to extend ourselves beyond that which is familiar. Often we can only broaden our understandings of a phenomenon by embracing uncertainty and by opening up avenues for new understandings to emerge within us.

With this book, we took a number of deliberate decisions in order to optimise the potential for a book that would grow current understandings of educational psychology in South Africa. As registered psychologists and active researchers in educational psychology, we identified a fissure in the field. On the one hand, we saw superb research being conducted in educational psychology. We knew about exceptional educational psychological interventions that were yielding results that were contextually relevant and pioneering. For two decades we saw high levels of responsiveness by both practitioners and researchers in educational psychology to the substantial challenges we are facing. We saw a new generation of educational psychologists accepting the challenges with enthusiasm and a previous generation being extraordinarily generous with their time and expertise. We saw tremendous interdisciplinary work and we saw new theoretical paradigms growing. When we visited schools, we noticed that the concerns of teachers, parents and principals were inescapably linked to the context in which we were living and working.

Yet, somehow, we did not see this work being adequately reflected within a collective book that would mirror what educational psychology means in South Africa at the moment. Frequently, we would find work by researchers and practitioners in educational psychology that has not been disseminated, purely because the current work to be done at grassroots level did not allow for adequate writing time. We were worried that if this work was not captured, good work may be lost into perpetuity. When it came to classrooms and lecture halls, this also meant that scholars and students in educational psychology often had to rely on texts that were conceptualised on other continents and in different countries. Despite the fact that empirical work from the global South was increasingly showing world-wide impact, and the fact that we knew about remarkable indigenous voices in the field, we still noted a need for more representation in scholarly publications. Yes, there were a number of excellent texts for educational psychology in South Africa, but most were developed at the birth of our new democracy and in the years shortly thereafter. We wanted to capture the here and now. We wanted to seize the contemporary *zeitgeist* in educational psychology in South Africa.

So how did we go about doing it?

- ***Invited content.*** The first decision we took was *not to be prescriptive in terms of the potential contributions* that potential chapter authors could make. We were interested to learn what researchers and practitioners were doing. So, rather than spending time as editors to craft a tentative table of contents that would cover the broad fields within educational psychology from our perspective and then asking different authors to contribute within those prescribed fields, we sent out open invitations to scholars in the field. We gave the broad background to the book, but we asked potential authors to send us *their ideas*. What were they working on? What were the aspects of educational psychology that they just hadn't gotten around to writing down? The response was overwhelmingly positive. 'Thank you,' said many authors, 'I have been meaning to write about this particular project,' or 'One of my students is doing very interesting work, can we perhaps do a collaborative chapter?' Interestingly enough, the broad themes that we would have liked to see in the book were covered after we had received the ideas from the invited authors, eg, teaching and learning, health and well-being, cognition, language, inclusion, schools, educational psychological support and the work of educational psychologists in career psychology. In retrospect, there could perhaps have been more work on families, teacher learning, learning in schools or the social-emotional side of educational psychology, or even the role of educational psychologists to support the sustainable development goals. We have also not focused on some of the exciting research methodologies that are being used in educational psychology— where South African educational psychological researchers are international leaders in some of the research methodologies. But this open invitation approach with a strong focus on the science and the profession had served our broad mission of capturing the status quo of educational psychology in South Africa, in that it provided glimpses of ongoing work.
- ***Contributions from scholars in related fields.*** We are acutely aware that the work of educational psychologists continuously overlaps with researchers

in related fields. It was, therefore, our intention to also invite contributions from scholars in related fields. This volume thus includes contributions from language experts, education specialists and a variety of psychologists from registration categories other than educational psychology. They present new voices and fresh ideas to the field.

- ***Keep it short.*** Rather than asking for voluminous chapters, we subscribed to the notion that the essence of a phenomenon, project or theme could be captured within the confound of a few thousand words. The reason for this strategy was two-fold: it increased the chances of a positive response from leading scholars, who may not have had the time for writing a lengthy chapter, but it also allowed us to widen the scope of invited authors to institutions across South Africa. In the end, some chapters, by virtue of its focus, extended slightly beyond the original intent, but the majority of the chapters present a clear, synoptic view of the chapter theme.
- ***Terminology fluidity.*** Terminology changes in education and it is constantly adapted in psychology too. In South Africa, we have seen extensive terminology fluidity with words like 'teacher', 'educator', 'children', 'learners', 'students', and 'pupils'. In line with the open and flexible approach we took when we invited chapter contributions, we decided to also remain equally flexible about terminology. Different chapter authors therefore are using terminologies of their choice, rather than editorial prescription. In some instances, the same author/s may even be using fluctuating terminologies within their own chapter. This changing conceptuality reflects, in our view, the shifting parameters of the field of educational psychology, and it also presents the complexities that are palpable in the field.
- ***The scientific discipline and the profession of educational psychology.*** Educational psychology is a scientific discipline that leads into the profession of becoming and being an educational psychologist. In this book, the discipline and the profession of educational psychology are explored together. We did not ask for contributions to either the discipline or the professional knowledge base specifically. Often the discipline and the profession intersect. Even more frequently, it can be quite indistinguishable. This book embraces this integration between the theoretical scientific discipline and the applied science within the profession. Educational psychology is also an integral part of foundational learning in teacher education. Teachers need a solid grounding in educational psychology, because they work with the whole child. So in addition to providing the science to educational psychologists, educational psychology also provides foundational science to the teaching profession.

The book was written for scholars and researchers in educational psychology who have a specific interest in the field as it presents in South Africa. But it was written in a style that also makes it accessible to undergraduate students—on the assumption that 'scholars' in a particular field are not confined to those who have degrees. We believe that the community of current and future researchers are enriched when interest in a field is encouraged early on, and when we share our work inclusively.

There is also an adjectival meaning to the word 'understanding', eg, where 'understanding' can refer to a certain level of thoughtfulness, tolerance or compassion. In this regard, it is our hope that this book will contribute to increased thoughtfulness, tolerance and compassion for those who work tirelessly in educational psychology and its related fields.

Irma Eloff & Estelle Swart
20 July 2017

1 Introduction

1 Educational psychology as science and profession in South Africa

ESTELLE SWART & IRMA ELOFF

The purpose of psychology is to give us a completely different idea of the things we know best. (Paul Valery)

Introduction

Educational psychologists play an important role in education and more specifically educational support in South Africa. The vision for educational psychologists working in schools is to make a meaningful difference to the lives of children as individuals as well as schools, families and communities that are in close interaction with them. As an introduction to this book, we consider, in this chapter, both the profession of educational psychologists and the scientific field of educational psychology as it pertains to the South African context.

Educational psychologists are registered with the Health Professions Council of South Africa (HPCSA) that regulates the training, role and practice of psychologists. Educational psychologists employed by the Department of Basic Education are also registered with the South African Council for Educators (SACE).

The Health Professions Act No. 56 of 1974 makes provision for five registration categories for psychologists namely Educational Psychology, Counselling Psychology, Clinical Psychology, Research Psychology and Industrial Psychology (two new categories might soon be added, namely Forensic Psychology and Neuropsychology.). The core services that all psychologists provide include the assessment, diagnosis and treatment of behaviour, mental processes, emotions, personality or social adjustment. However, the scope and focus of every category differ. What makes educational psychology unique is the focus on learning and development.

History

The earliest traces of psychology and guidance and counselling in South African schools date back to the beginning of the 19th century. In fact the first psychometric testing was introduced in 1912 to determine the extent of intellectual disability in schools and identify children who required special schooling and classes. The first batteries for psychological testing were applied in 1922 and programmes for career guidance in primary and secondary schools followed in 1927. Before psychology was established as a profession, different services were provided under the name of school psychology, for example by teacher psychologists, clinical school psychologists (orthopedagogue), clinical school psychologists (remedial teacher or orthodidactition), school guidance counsellor and sociopedagogue (school social worker) who acted as education advisors (Van Niekerk, 1986).

During the apartheid years between 1948 and 1994 the education system and educational support services began to be divided along racial lines. This led to unequal provision of resources and services. The system of support for children with disabilities and emotional, behavioural and learning difficulties at the time was based on a medical deficit model of thinking which is a model of diagnosis and individual treatment. Professionals mainly followed a 'find-out-what-is-wrong-and-cure-it' paradigm. This paradigm or model of thinking therefore framed the roles of professionals, their education and the segregated support structures created.

Educational psychology was formally established as HPCSA registration category around 1980. The training of educational psychologists, then often referred to as the 'clinical' programme, was traditionally housed in faculties of education. Their role was described as assessing, diagnosing and intervening in order to facilitate the psychological adjustment and development of children and adolescents within the contexts of family, school, social or peer groups and communities (HPCSA Newsletter, 2002). Educational psychologists were therefore trained to play a central role in assessment, placement and support of individual children with learning difficulties and disabilities before the first democratic elections in 1994. These services were not equally available for all children. The criteria used to label children for placement and the effectiveness of the practices of educational support services were also questionable.

The South African socio-political landscape has since changed dramatically. In the attempt to address imbalances of the apartheid past, major educational reform followed with the purpose of creating quality educational opportunities for all. In addition, changing philosophical views of learning and children, and theoretical paradigm shifts in the discipline of educational psychology served as catalysts for exciting developments in both theory and practice in education and educational psychology. One such innovation is establishing an inclusive education system that accommodates the full range of learning needs in South African schools and educational institutions (see Chapter 30). Developing such a system cannot be successful without supporting the diverse learning needs of all children, teachers, schools and education systems. To make a relevant contribution, the nature of educational support, including the role and practices of educational psychologists needed to change.

What do educational psychologists do?

The core practices of educational psychologists are outlined in the policy of the Department of Health (Department of Health, 2011). The Task Team for educational psychology in South Africa summarised the role as follows:

Educational Psychologists assess, diagnose, prevent and intervene, utilising psychological knowledge and theory derived from research and practice to optimise psychological functioning related to learning and development. Their professional activities are aimed at assisting the development— learning, cognitive, mental, neuropsychological, behavioural, social and emotional—of children, youth, adults, families and communities. The acts of educational psychologists are undertaken within their individual areas and levels of training and expertise and with due regard to ethical and legal standards. (Task Team, 2012)

Educational psychologists therefore:
- Assess and diagnose individual cognitive, mental, social, personality, behavioural, emotional, and neuropsychological functioning in relation to learning and development using psychological and educational instruments and techniques (including career development);
- Identify, diagnose and address psychopathology in relation to learning and development;
- Conduct family, group and community based assessments or investigations in order to inform preventative and intervention strategies;
- Intervene with individuals, families, groups and communities to address difficulties and to promote psychological well-being;
- Conduct psycho-legal assessments;
- Design, manage, conduct, report on and supervise psychological and educational research;

- Advise on policy development based on psychological and educational theory and research; and
- Design, manage and evaluate educational and psychological programmes.

To address the need for educational support in schools and make support more accessible, educational psychologists and other professionals had to redesign their roles. In an inclusive education system they use and 'give away' their knowledge and skills by supporting schools to effectively develop protective processes and prevent and address barriers to learning. This, among others, entails collaboration and consultation with teachers, principals, schools, communities and other professionals in transdisciplinary teams, teacher development and mentorship, whole-school development, multilevel assessment, prevention and intervention. A consultative role positions an educational psychologist as a change agent and the members of school communities as experts and partners. The redefinition of the role of educational psychologists is therefore an exciting work in progress.

Where do educational psychologists work?

Educational psychologists work in different contexts. They may work in private practices, in the education department (district-based support teams or inclusive teams), private schools, student support services in higher education, public schools (appointed by governing bodies), non-governmental organisations or the corporate sector. In this book, Chapter 47, Career paths within educational psychology, provides more details.

The term 'school psychologist' is not a registration category, but is used in education to refer to those who provide psychological services to schools. These professionals are registered with the HPCSA as educational, clinical or counselling psychologists or at least registered counsellors (Daniels, Collair, Moolla & Lazarus, 2007). They can work in education districts, at special schools or at education department head offices.

How to become an educational psychologist

To practice as an educational psychologist, a person must have completed a Master's degree in educational psychology accredited by the HPCSA. The entry requirements for the Master's programme include a Bachelor's degree majoring in Psychology (BA, BEd or BPsych) and an Honours degree in educational psychology or psychology. Most universities also require a teaching qualification, which could either be a BEd or a Postgraduate Certificate in Education (PGCE). Only a limited number of students are selected per year due to the intensive nature of the training and supervision required. The duration of the Master's programme is a minimum of two years full-time or three years part-time including a 12 month full-time internship. After completing all the requirements, students have to pass a Board for Psychology exam before they can register as an educational psychologist. In education it therefore takes at least seven years to become an educational psychologist. The professional learning that follows after qualifying as an educational psychologist is a lifelong process. All practitioners registered with the HPCSA must therefore fulfil minimum requirements for continued professional development every year.

These are the qualification pathways to the profession of educational psychologist. More options are considered in the chapter on career paths later in this book. But what is understood by the 'science' of educational psychology?

The science of educational psychology

The profession of educational psychology and the science of educational psychology go hand in hand. In fact, educational psychologists and educational psychological researchers often find themselves simultaneously immersed in both the profession and the scientific field of educational psychology. The cyclical nature of theory informing practice, and practice then, in turn, informing theory in educational psychology has meant that the boundaries are often blurred. Some leading scholars in educational psychology (Woolfolk, 2016; Seifert & Sutton, 2009) pro-actively merge theory and practice (eg 'science and profession') when educational psychology is presented in textual format. In this way, the close ties between the scientific discipline and the profession are reiterated.

Yet, these 'blurred lines' between the science and the profession can also present challenges. Educational psychology, as an applied science for instance, is constantly changing and developing. In South Africa, the field of educational psychology has seen particularly acute changes in both its theoretical approaches, as well as its scope of practice (Eloff, 2015).

There are numerous ways in which the discipline and the profession of educational psychology have impacted on each other. As educational psychologists have had to expand their roles in the latter part of the 20th century, the development of the discipline has seen similar significant growth in the first two decades of the 21st century. Theory had to keep up with practice, and practice needed to adjust to the huge advances in the theoretical understandings in the field.

In many instances, theoretical 'developments' did not necessarily entail the 'development' of former theories. Instead, deep questioning of existing theories in educational psychology became more and more evident. It affected the way in which students were educated, publications were positioned and the way in which policies were developed.

The work of the National Commission on Special Needs in Education and Training (NCSNET) and the National Committee on Education Support Services (NCESS), in the late 1990s, for instance, catapulted the thinking about children with special needs into a whole new conceptual realm. Rather than defining children with special needs in terms of 'inherent' disability, the NCSNET and NCESS spearheaded the use of terminology such as 'barriers to learning', and it pragmatised the way in which inclusive education were to be understood in the emerging democracy of South Africa. These policy signifiers stimulated numerous scientific publications that manifested the bridge between what was needed in the profession, and what was known in the scientific discipline (Engelbrecht, Green, Naicker & Engelbrecht, 1999; Oswald & Swart, 2008; Dalton, McKenzie & Kahonde, 2012). Gone were the days of a singular focus on support at the individual level by educational psychologists. While individual support remained important, holistic approaches at the systemic level were fast gaining ground. Educational psychologists responded by embracing systemic interventions that could reach higher numbers of children, teachers and schools (some examples include Engelbrecht, 2004; Donald, Lazarus & Moolla, 2014). Inclusion remains a challenge (Donohue & Bornman, 2014), yet the landscape for supporting children with disabilities have become more responsive to diverse needs.

But the movement towards inclusive education was just one of the ways in which the work and science of educational psychology were impacted upon. At the same time several other developments were also taking place. Globally, psychologists were moving away from the strong focus on 'disharmonious dynamics', or what was known as 'deficit-approaches' within the helping professions. Some researchers were exploring more strength-based approaches and starting studies on phenomena such as resilience, hope, wisdom, emotional regulation and 'flow' (Kashdan, 2007; Larsen & Stege, 2010). They wanted to find out more about happiness in children, how technology could be used in diverse classrooms, how to build partnerships with parents and how teachers could be supported in all the different roles they were fulfilling at school. At the same time, the changing nature of families meant that researchers in educational psychology were conducting studies on the role of caregivers, same-gender families and the experiences of children during a variety of life transitions. Educational psychologists had to find innovative ways to support families in a world where the challenges that children and youth are facing remain complex.

Some researchers were even critiquing the emerging systemic approaches as an expansion of the 'deficit-approach', in that it still had a strong pre-occupation with deficits and failure. These researchers promoted the use of 'asset maps', empowerment evaluation or strength-based assessment practices (Ebersöhn & Eloff, 2006; Lubbe & Eloff, 2004; Ebersöhn, 2017). The 'illness ideology' served as a departure point for a counter-revolution. In the words of Maddux (2012) there was a need to emphasise 'wellbeing, satisfaction, happiness, interpersonal skills, perseverance, talent, wisdom, and personal responsibility'. The study of what makes life worth living, while emphasising social context, became more and more important. In South Africa, this movement resonated with many scientists who were trying to find ways to provide support in thoughtful ways that were sensitive to contextual realities (Theron & Donald, 2013; Ebersöhn, 2008; Dunbar-Krige & Pillay, 2010; Ferreira, 2016). Educational psychologists also played a leading role in redesigning career psychology and education (Maree, 2011).

Another way in which the science of educational psychology has shifted in the last two decades relates to the blurring boundaries between different professions. To start with, educational psychology spans the two disciplines of Education and Psychology. As will be shown in Chapter 2, it also has strong roots in Philosophy. Yet, within the professional domain, the work of educational psychologists can easily overlap with that of teachers, counsellors, social workers, occupational therapists, audiologists or speech therapists. When it comes to career counselling, it can be similar to the work of counselling psychologists or industrial psychologists. When working with families, it can become very difficult to decide where the work of an educational psychologist, working with adult parents, ends and where the work of a clinical psychologist starts. Again, these challenges within the 'profession of educational psychologists', has echoed in the scientific sphere of the field.

What is the field of educational psychology, when the intersections and connections with other professions are so significant? How do we forge an identity that is distinct? A predominant focus on learning and instruction and the creation of positive learning environments (Snowman & Biehler, 2006) is still key to the field, but the range of educational psychology as a scientific field extends far beyond.

Becoming a competent teacher requires the acquisition, integration and application of different types of knowledge. Educational psychology is one of the disciplinary subjects that form the foundation of the initial teacher education curriculum. With its focus on learning and development, it also informs both pedagogical learning and practical learning in this curriculum. This is reflected in the topics about being a teacher, learners, and learning and teaching in the context of South African classrooms and schools. Learning support is one of the specialisation areas in both the undergraduate and postgraduate teacher education curriculum.

The way forward

Educational psychology in South Africa is well-aligned with global movements in education and psychology. It is deeply connected to the contexts in which it 'lives', but at the same time it remains relevant within the global milieu.

In many ways, the development of the science of educational psychology in South Africa has serendipitously benefited from the socio-political transitions and the birth of a new democracy. Some may argue that a dynamically evolving society allows opportunities to reconsider both a science and a profession at a deeper level than what would otherwise be afforded. Much of the development in the field has been self-propelled, but some of the developments have been due to external factors. For instance, the reactivation of the 'student voice' within the tertiary sector in South Africa was evidenced in student protests in recent years. Apart from calling for greater access to tertiary education, students were also indicating a need to 'decolonise the curriculum'. This has implications for both the science and the profession of educational psychology. While it creates avenues for new knowledge to emerge and existing indigenous knowledge to be foregrounded (as was done by numerous authors in this book), it is also important to acknowledge the substantial progress that has been made in a relatively short period of time.

2 Educational psychology as the intersection between philosophy and psychology and education

JOHNNIE HAY

Educational psychology has fought a tiring battle over the last one hundred or so years, substantiating itself as a scientific discipline while maintaining weak linkages to its disciplinary forebearers (i.e. philosophy or psychology).
(Murphy, 2003:137)

Introduction

The discipline of educational psychology is at the same time 'one of the most exciting, fast-growing and dynamic fields' (Eloff & Ebersöhn, 2004:4) of study, internationally and in South Africa today, but also no 'stranger to the quest for identity, importance, and heritage' (Murphy, 2003:137). Despite these seemingly divergent sentiments, educational psychology has been part of teacher education curricula in the USA (Fendler, 2013) and various other countries (such as South Africa) for more than a hundred years, claiming to contribute to the training and development of effective teachers.

Educational psychology represents a complex discipline comprising of elements of philosophy and psychology (as Murphy stated in the citation above) and, of course, education.

Why is it important to know about this intersection between philosophy and psychology and education?

I will argue that it is important for you as undergraduate student to know about the intersection between philosophy and psychology and education that has

Educational psychology as the intersection between philosophy and psychology and education

eventually led to the discipline of educational psychology as we know it today. I will always make an effort to enlighten students—at undergraduate and Honours level—about this relationship, as I believe it is crucial to understand the foundations of your discipline. You are surely aware of the importance of a good foundation when you build your own (and perhaps first) home: it almost guarantees that your home would not show cracks later on in its life, and provides a safe basis from which you can operate. In the same vein, I suggest that you will develop a solid foundation in teacher education from which to teach if you understand the origins of educational psychology.

Illustrations of the importance of having a grasp on the history and development of educational psychology that you may have, or will come across, are the following questions that are often posed: 'Why do we have to study educational psychology when we want to become teachers? Why do some universities, such as Unisa and the University of the Free State, call their discipline 'psychology of education', while most other universities term the field 'educational psychology'? As education is such a practice-oriented profession, could an academic discipline, such as educational psychology, really add value? And why do some of the older teachers speak of psycho-pedagogics? Is it true that philosophy also played a part in the development of education and psychology? Is educational psychology still part of the so-called 'foundational' or base disciplines of education? And finally, is educational psychology not only important if you want to become an educational psychologist?' I trust that these (and other) questions will be answered once you have worked through this chapter.

Let us delve somewhat deeper into the reasons for having to develop a grip on the origins and timeline of educational psychology. Aligned with the sentiments of historians, I would argue that it is almost impossible to understand the present and chart the future without having an understanding of the past. Your present and your future as teacher or as registered counsellor or as educational psychologist will be unlocked if you understand where the discipline of educational psychology comes from, and how it is viewed today.

Philosophy as foundation of education and psychology

Both education and psychology originated from the so-called 'mother discipline' of philosophy (adjusted from Alexander, 2003; Leadbetter & Arnold, 2013). In fact, philosophy is often viewed as the ultimate foundational discipline from which many disciplines have developed, especially those in the humanities. Why do we say that? A literal translation from the Greek combination of the words *philos* and *sophos* is 'love of wisdom'. Philosophers thus loved seeking wisdom through logical reasoning and rhetorical questioning (Ornstein, Levine, Gutek &

Vocke, 2017). This represents the beginnings of scientific studies and academic disciplines.

Consider the following: the Greek philosopher Plato is credited to have developed the first and ground-breaking philosophy of Idealism, according to which a human being is capable of producing ideas in the mind, independent of the environment. Through these latent ideas, eternal truths and the reality can be uncovered. Knowledge also resides within these latent ideas of the human mind. The way through which these truths, reality and knowledge could be uncovered, was via the Socratic method (Socrates was Plato's teacher and developed the Socratic method to influence people). This was done on the market plains of ancient Greece, where Socrates pretended to know little of a subject, and through asking the appropriate (and seemingly naive) questions, developed insight into people's minds by uncovering their latent ideas.

Plato's pupil, Aristotle, developed the second significant philosophy in the contestation of Plato's focus on inner ideas: he believed that reality exists objectively and outside of the human mind—and can only be accessed through the senses. Truth and knowledge thus reside in the outer world. Aristotle's philosophy came to be known as Realism.

Before I explain the relationship of these two philosophies to education and psychology, an interesting fact related to the Greek and Roman era is that Greeks that were captured during the time of the Roman Empire, and utilised as teachers of Roman children, were called *pedagogues*. Apparently this was preceded by rich Greeks who also called one of their slaves, who had the responsibility of teaching their children, a *pedagogue*. Obviously, our well-known term in education today, namely 'pedagogy', derives directly from the term for these first teachers of the young (Ozmon & Craver, 2012).

I have concisely discussed the first two philosophies that developed (in the Western world), namely Idealism and Realism, and now wish to demonstrate how these formed the foundations of education and psychology.

Education

Plato's Idealism suggested that learning is the uncovering of latent ideas that are present in the learner's mind. A pedagogue's teaching is thus focused on discovering and rediscovering truth, reality and knowledge through the Socratic method. The mind is much more important than the body, and ideas are more valuable than anything we can touch, smell, taste, see or hear. From idealism, modern-day education derived a number of principles: that a focus on the mind is paramount, that academic learning may be more important than practical learning (currently still so rife in South Africa, where university learning is

Educational psychology as the intersection between philosophy and psychology and education

viewed as much more important than becoming an artisan), that learners have the latent capacity, in the form of ideas, to excel, and that a well-rounded person possesses academic learnedness.

Aristotle's realism, on the other hand, posited that truth, reality and knowledge can only be uncovered through learning about the objective, outer world via the senses. Education by a pedagogue would, therefore, focus on experiencing the physical world through touching, smelling, tasting, seeing and hearing. Knowledge and the truth cannot be obtained through engaging with the inner ideas of a person, as these are not a source that can be trusted as being real and true. From realism, modern-day education derived a number of principles: that experiential learning represents true and effective learning, that learners should be trained to utilise their senses to the full, that the focus should be on the real world outside of the human being and that practical, experiential learning will bring real rewards for the learner (inferred from Ornstein, et al, 2017; Ozmon & Craver, 2012).

Psychology

Idealism and Realism can also be seen as the forerunners of two of the so-called 'big thrusts' in psychology. Idealism, with its focus on the inner ideas of a human being, is often viewed as the forerunner of cognitive psychology, with its focus on inner thinking and beliefs, and the power to change from within. Realism, on the other hand, is seen as the forerunner of behaviourist psychology, with its focus on the overt (outer) behaviour of a person, and the thesis that people are conditioned by stimuli from the external world.

With this short exposition, I have tried to demonstrate how philosophy really is the 'parent' discipline (Leadbetter & Arnold, 2013), from which both education and psychology originated. Of course there are many more philosophies and many more links that can be drawn between these and educational theory and psychological approaches: other chapters for example refer to the links between educational psychology and pragmatism as philosophy, critical and learning theories (such as information processing and constructivism), and the psychological approaches of behaviourism and connectivism. It is recommended that you are attentive to these links in the following chapters, and also focus on these connections in further studies; in addition, remember to focus on the contribution from the African continent in terms of a philosophy, such as ubuntu.

I now would like to turn to the importance of understanding the relationship between education and psychology.

The relationship between education and psychology

It is crucial to realise that educational psychology/psychology of education represents the confluence of two distinct and powerful fields of study, which both originated from the love of wisdom or philosophy.

Many commentators in the field describe education as an art or craft which needed experimental psychology to strengthen its scientific standing (Crozier, 2011; Depaepe, 2013; Norwich, 2002). This is partially true, but as Norwich (2002) correctly indicates, it was not only education which needed psychology, but also psychology which needed education. Towards the end of the 19th century, education, or more specifically teaching, was viewed as an art or a practical activity (craft), with so many unforeseen variables involved that the field could hardly be described as scientific. With the dramatic rise in psychology during this period and its focus on experimental work in laboratories (and later classrooms), educational practitioners looked to the field of psychology to strengthen the scientific status of teaching. In this way the discipline of educational psychology evolved to both strengthen the scientific basis of education and came to serve as one of the foundational (or contributory) disciplines of education (together with philosophy of education, history of education and sociology of education).

A number of substantial contributions to education were made by educational psychology: learning theories were developed to support the learning process, special needs education emerged as educators soon realised that children are unique and different—and realising that psychologists could be of help with their psychometric assessment—and developmental psychology brought new insights to the understanding of child development. However, as psychology supported education, education also extended the range of psychology: psychologists were initially interested in understanding human experience and human behaviour in a general theoretical sense, but needed specific fields of application to test out these theories and insights. Education was one of those fields where psychological theories could be tested and researched. And as Norwich (2002:16) furthermore aptly states:

> *By associating with education, psychology also comes into contact with the applications of other disciplines such as sociology, history and philosophy, which can offer alternative, and often rival, perspectives on education. In addition, the interdisciplinary contact is especially valuable for understanding the internal theoretical differences in psychology.*

Psychology has thus helped education to move from an art or craft to become a more scientific endeavour; and education has helped psychology to move from a developing theoretical science to an applied science, and to link up better with the other foundational disciplines of education.

Is the terminology *educational psychology* thus the best way to describe the confluence of education and psychology? Although most books make use of this description, I favour the use of *psychology of education* (supporting Thomas, 2007); this is aligned with the terminology of the other foundational disciplines (eg, history of education/sociology of education) and indicates that we are primarily dealing with the influence of psychology in education. In my view, the term educational psychology describes a branch of psychology—and as educators we are primarily concerned with education. Psychology of education also offers university departments the option to be encompassing in appointing all directly related professionals (apart from educational psychologists), such as learning support educators, specialist inclusive educators, Life Orientation educators and specialist psychological educators (my own terminology for those not registered as psychologists, but specialised in psychology of education). Psychology of education is a later version of the earlier *psychopedagogics* (Depaepe, 2013), where the emphasis is also on the contribution of psychology to pedagogics or teaching the young.

The confluence of education and psychology into educational psychology/psychology of education has been a tiring battle: in the process an identity had to be carved out and the importance of the new discipline constantly defended (Murphy, 2003). Today educational psychologists and psychological educators reap the fruits of this struggle over especially the last 150 years, by being respected as one of the indispensable components of effective teacher education programmes.

The major debates about the relationship between education and psychology

A number of debates have been and are currently still raging within the discipline, of which some have been alluded to already:

- Is psychology or education the dominant force in educational psychology/psychology of education?

    The sentiments expressed earlier in this chapter about terming the confluence of these two substantial fields of study, allude to this debate: whether it should be educational psychology (where education only forms the adjective to psychology) or psychology of education (where psychology really supports education). This debate is still ongoing today and has not been resolved. However, most academics and practitioners probably realised that this is a matter of terminology; what really matters is that both fields have had major influences on each other (Norwich, 2002). Furthermore, most people have also grasped that educational psychology is not only the domain of educational psychologists, but also of specialist psychological educators.

- Is educational psychology a pure scientific discipline, such as biology or chemistry?

This debate has been ongoing for decades—not only in educational psychology, but also in education and psychology. Despite huge strides that have been made in developing educational theory through research to strengthen the art or practical craft of teaching, some commentators are not convinced that education has reached the stage of a fully fledged science (inferred from Smeyers & Depaepe, 2013). In the same vein, the diverse theories in psychology (eg, about personality) create the impression that psychology still has not reached the scientific stage of being well-integrated and coherent. If doubt still exists about the scientific status of the two constituting disciplines, it goes without saying that certain commentators still have reservations about the scientific status of educational psychology—it may be best to refer to the field as a developing discipline, which still has some way to go to be viewed as developed. However, as disciplines and professions, both education and psychology enjoy worldwide scientific recognition. It is constantly being developed and also studied and practiced by millions on a daily basis.

- Is educational psychology really essential to the teacher-training project?

Fendler (2013) summarises the debate about this matter excellently by positing four possible reasons why educational psychology is part of teacher-training programmes: efficacy, professionalisation, management and habit. Under efficacy it is understood that educational psychology helps to train more effective teachers; for this claim, she reasons, no conclusive evidence exists. Under professionalisation it is understood that the more scientific discipline of psychology helped to raise the professional status of teaching.

Her verdict is that:

... it is plausible that psychology remains as a requirement in the curriculum of teacher education because psychology has helped to raise the professional status of university-based teacher education ... However, at the same time, it is important to note that the professionalisation of teacher education through affiliation with psychology (and/or learning sciences) may be occurring at the expense of the professionalisation of teachers. (Fendler, 2013:60)

The issue of management refers to the fact that psychological research:

... renders the unruly practices of teaching more predictable, rational, and manageable; the language of psychology gives teacher educators a voice in educational policy making. (Fendler, 2013:60)

Educational psychology as the intersection between philosophy and psychology and education

She further states that 'psychology serves to frame educational problems in ways that seem amenable to rational management'. Policymakers seem to take education more seriously when problems are framed in psychological terms. The last issue of habit that she discusses, relates to the possibility that educational psychology is included in teacher education curricula out of habit. She concludes that:

> ... *it is possible to affirm that psychology persists in the curriculum of teacher education because of habit; however ... we do not know if it is a good intelligent habit or a bad thoughtless habit.* (Fendler, 2013:63)

She finally concludes her argumentation on the matter by quoting Norwich's nuanced position (2002:203):

> *Whatever contribution psychology makes to education is also one of many contributions from allied fields. Its links with education provides it with a constant reminder of its place among the network of connected social sciences relevant to education.* (Fendler, 2013:66)

- How can educational psychology as an original Western discipline be translated to make sense on other continents, such as Africa?

This debate has gained momentum since 2015 in South Africa with the #FeesMustFall movement that included a call for the decolonisation of the curriculum. Academics in the field of educational psychology/psychology of education have, for the last two decades or longer, acutely been aware of this matter, namely that (educational) psychology predominantly originated in Western Europe and the United States of America, and that many psychological theories were developed with white middle class males as focus (Donald, Lazarus & Moolla, 2014; Stead & Watson, 2017). Efforts to make educational psychology more relevant to the context of (South) Africa have been ongoing for a number of years. From numerous initiatives, two examples of these efforts are the work of Sechaba Mahlohaholo (WSU) into sustainable learning environments and Liesel Ebersöhn (UP) that focuses on community educational psychology in deep rural schools. This is a debate that needs urgency and agency—but a good start to this is to make educational psychology as relevant and applicable to the African context as possible.

How is knowledge of the intersection between philosophy and education and psychology relevant for South African schools and classrooms?

Norwich (2002) states that some educators believe that teaching is such a practical craft that its activities and procedures can be learned without having any theoretical basis. In this chapter, I tried to convince you that knowledge of the history and philosophical foundations of both psychology and education (and the other foundational disciplines) are not only essential, but also highly enriching for educators—to eventually know and be able to make a difference in the learning, development and individuation of their learners.

Conclusion

Educational psychology, as we know it today, represents the confluence (and complex intersection) between psychology and education—both built on the love of wisdom that is called 'philosophy'. I trust that you will work to understand these foundational developments of this exciting discipline, that will—in my opinion, and contrary to Fendler's somewhat pessimistic view—contribute substantially to unlocking your understanding of what a good teacher should be.

3 The role of educational psychologists in teaching and learning

MOTLALEPULE RUTH MAMPANE

Education is what survives when what has been learnt has been forgotten.
(B.F. Skinner)

Introduction

Educational psychology is a scientific field which deals with the psychology of learning across all phases of life, contexts, cultures, and human development. Skinner (1953) refers to educational psychology as a specialist psychology in the field of education. Shuell (1996:6) sees educational psychology as a multifaceted discipline focused among others on the 'study of the child, counselling, guidance, special education and reading'. Anderman (2011:185) defines educational psychology as a 'bountiful body of knowledge about how individuals learn, and how school contexts can be organized to facilitate learning'. The cognitive, socio-emotional and behavioural domains are the core domains of human development included in the psychology of teaching and learning across a lifespan. Whilst straddling both, educational psychology can present a clear distinction between the processes of teaching and learning as presented by teachers in the classroom as well as the psychology of learning in human development.

This chapter will clarify the significant role educational psychology plays in teaching and learning by highlighting the science and psychology of learning. Literature has aligned educational psychology with the scientific field and has identified it as key to teaching and learning (Elliot & Travers, 1996) and psychoeducational issues that influence academic and scientific growth (Berliner, 1993). On the other hand, O'Donnell and Levin, (2001:73) also commend educational psychology for its significant role in the 'development and application of psychological principles to education, as well as the adoption of psychological perspectives on education'.

The roots of educational psychology trace back to Edward L. Thorndike, a psychologist accredited for originating the psychology divisions of the American Psychological Association (APA) (Bernliner, 1993; O'Donnell & Levin, 2001). However, it is the seminal works of Johann Friedrich Herbart (1776; as cited by Berliner, 1993:3) on Herbartians, which, through the science of psychology, provided the current structures which pave the path of the fields of educational psychology. According to Berliner (1993:3):

It was the Herbartians who first made pedagogical technique the focus of scientific study, pointing the way, eventually, to the field of research on teaching, a very fruitful area of research in educational psychology.

Somr and Hruškova (2014:414) argue that, the science and education theory of Herbart focused on guaranteed outcomes expected from applying pedagogical ideas in educational practices. The work of Herbart influenced the scientific field of philosophy, psychology, and pedagogy with the focus on 'pedagogical causal relationship' (Somr & Hruškova, 2014:417). Herbart formalised teaching and learning through the five steps of teaching. The following five steps of Berliner (1993:3) became the basis of education, teaching and learning in human development across the lifespan:

1. Preparation (of the mind of the student).
2. Presentation (of the material to be learned).
3. Comparison.
4. Generalisation.
5. Application.

Educational psychology thus is able to offer insight regarding comprehension, learning and instruction (Jones, 1985). The above steps show the application of the science of learning. Educational psychology as applied science is reflected in addressing the what, how, why and when of knowledge and information acquirement. The role an educational psychologist plays in teaching, learning and human development in the broad education system cannot be underestimated. The science of teaching and learning within the education system can be highly expanded and enriched when educational psychology is recognised and afforded the fundamental role it deserves.

Educational psychology has a significant role in education of 'translating psychological theory into suggestions for educational practitioners' (Shuell, 1996:6). Educational psychologists have specialised training in learning, development, motivation, classroom management, and assessment, which is core to teacher development and training (Patrick, Anderman, Bruening & Duffin, 2011). Every school should have an educational psychologist and every learner (student) should have access to an educational psychologist across a lifespan. The training of educational psychologists focuses on the social context of learning and human development, with special attention on counselling, development in the areas of career, the domains of cognitive, socio-emotional behaviour and overall assessment (see Figure 3.1).

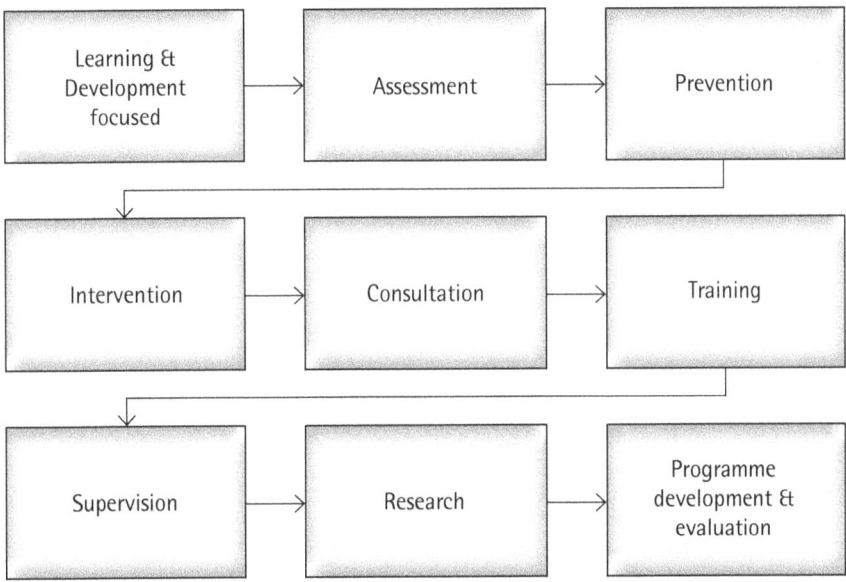

FIGURE 3.1 Representation of higher education focus on the training of educational psychologists programme

The education system should cater to the educational, social, emotional and physical well-being of every learner. The priority of an educational psychologist within the education system is to enhance well-being and wellness in human development, social, behavioural and mental health of a learner.

The relevance of educational psychology to South African schools and classrooms

In South Africa, the focus of educational psychology training programmes in higher education is on the assessment, teacher training and education, support and intervention in learning and somewhat less on preventative strategies. Knowledge and understanding of the educational context and the functioning of the school system is core in the training of educational psychologists (Burden & Taylor, 2014). Currently, South Africa has 22 private and 26 public universities (see Table 3.1). Of the 48 universities, only 18 offer psychology programmes, of which only 13 focus on educational psychology programmes.

TABLE 3.1 Public and private South African universities with accredited psychology programmes according to the Health Professions Council of South Africa (HPCSA) register

HPCSA record of universities in South Africa with Psychology programmes	Educational psychology programmes Honours & Masters	Other Psychology programmes
Nelson Mandela University		X
North-West University	X	X
Midrand Graduate Institute	X (Hons)	X
Rhodes University		X
Stellenbosch University	X	X
University of Cape Town		X
University of Free State	X (Hons)	X
University of Fort Hare	X	X
University of Johannesburg	X	X
University of KwaZulu-Natal	X	X
University of Limpopo		X
University of Pretoria	X	X
University of South Africa		X
University of Venda	X	
University of Zululand	X	X
University of Western Cape	X	X
University of Witwatersrand	X	X
Walter Sisulu University	X	X
Total Programmes	13	17

Total number of public universities in South Africa	Total number of private universities in South Africa	Total number of universities
26	22	48
Number of public universities with Psychology programmes	Number of private universities with Psychology programmes registered with HPCSA	Total number of universities with Psychology programs (AQ)
18	1	19

Source: Health Professions Council of South Africa, nd

The Health Professions Council of South Africa's (HPCSA's) definition of the scope of practice for educational psychology is on intervention:

> ... *alleviating: emotional, learning, academic, intellectual, behavioural, social and developmental difficulties...* (Health Professions Council of South Africa, 2017)

South African literature on educational psychology often focuses on inclusive education and the continuum of support for learning disabilities or barriers to learning (Lomofsky & Lazarus, 2001; Engelbrecht, 2006; Oswald & Swart, 2011). The focus on inclusive education in educational psychology is not unique to South Africa. International researchers in the United Kingdom (Kershner & Farrel, 2009; Lindsay, 2003 & 2007), and the USA (Artiles & Kozleski, 2016; Kozleski & Siuty, 2016) and Australia (Forlin, 1995) for example, have seen the significance of educational psychology in the face of learning disabilities and for special needs education and inclusive education.

Higher education institutions that prepare educational psychologists are usually housed in the faculty of education where teacher education also resides. This move is strategic in that educational psychology as a discipline and science should be closely linked to teacher education. Similarly, educational psychologists can then be exposed to working in schools for their internship wherein they provide psychological services to learners, parents and teachers in schools. However, it can be argued that more needs to be done to integrate the work of educational psychologists in the education of pre-service teachers.

The role of an educational psychologist in the education process

Skinner (1953:402) defines education as the acquisition or 'establishment of behaviour which will be of advantage to the individual and to others at some future time'. Since the beginning, the profession of educational psychology has focused on the role of teacher education. Teacher education programmes in South Africa fall under the Department of Higher Education and Training (DHET). Educational psychologists are often referred to as school psychologists in other contexts (HPCSA, 2017). However, currently, it seems specifically in South Africa, the focus has shifted towards community and private practice rather than teacher education (see Figure 3.2). On teacher education, the focus of educational psychology is mostly identifying and preventing learning problems, motivation and support for learning and acquiring knowledge of human development and theories of development.

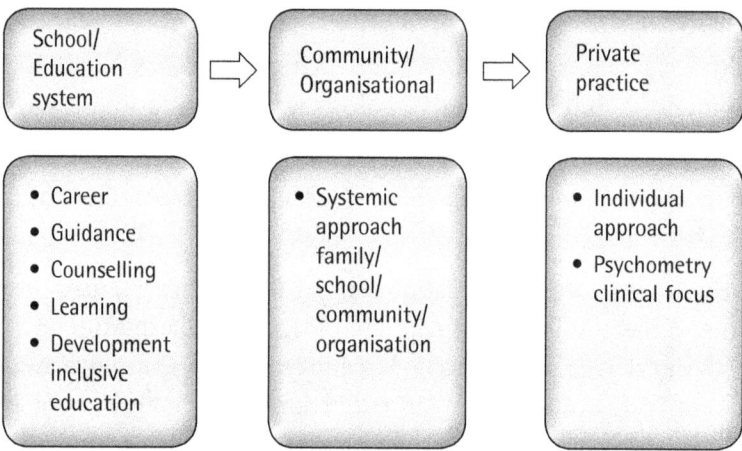

FIGURE 3.2 Representation of three-tier higher education training focus of educational psychologists

The scope of practices defined by HPCSA states that the role of educational psychologists is concerned with:

> ... alleviating: emotional, learning, academic, intellectual, behavioural, social and developmental difficulties in children and young people within the systems in which they function including families, schools, peer groups etc., thereby providing extensive support and psychological services to any role-player which may support clients' optimal functioning. (Health Professions Council of South Africa, 2017)

Teacher education and training is not clearly defined by this scope of practice definition, but it can perhaps be seen under the umbrella of 'within the systems in which they function'. Most teacher education programmes do include modules on educational psychology and its related fields. The role of educational psychologists in teacher education in South Africa can, however, be made more explicit. Educational psychologists are well-positioned to impact and contribute to the science of teacher education, training, and development within the discipline of education as stated in the APA. This can include educators and lecturers at higher education institutions.

Educational psychologists are integral to the school system and teacher education. To ensure that they remain relevant to the education system and teacher education, they in turn need to have knowledge and understanding of the education context and how the school system functions (Burden & Taylor, 2014). Shuell (1996:9) posits that the goal of educational psychology in teacher education is to expose pre-service teachers to basic knowledge of teaching, to help them comprehend the psychological understanding of the teaching profession, and to provide them with strategies to solve problems using psychological knowledge and methodologies.

Anderman (2011:185) acknowledges the significant role educational psychologists have played over the years in developing the body of knowledge on learning and how school contexts can be organised to facilitate learning. Even with the developments on the science of knowledge and how learning occurs, mainstream education and curriculum have not mastered the skills of specialised differentiation in learning based on the diversity of learners. Mainstream education is structured to cater for the needs of an average person with the assumption that all learners can and have the ability to learn the same. The process of learning is, however, complex and closely aligned to human development, especially when systemic, cognitive, socio-emotional, and behavioural theories are considered. Learning is an interactive process, with De Houwer, Barnes-Holmes and Moors (2013) stating that it entails change in behaviour as a result of the individual's experience. Learning and cognitive development theories frequently explain intellectual development based on intelligence quotient (IQ) scores and measurements ranging from average, below and above average, as explained by normal distribution curve. This form of classification of ability used to be common in classrooms and teachers were familiar with it. Florian and Black-Hawkins (2011) confirm that the actions and decisions of teachers about learner ability are sometimes informed by the naturalised 'bell-curve theory', which is highly contested. Accordingly, learners who fall 'below average' may require specialised forms of support from educational psychologists as well as other specialists such as, physiotherapists, speech therapists, occupational therapists and teachers with specialised training to provide learning support.

In some extreme cases, special school education is preferred so that the learner can be included within the broad learning and education system. In situations where teachers are not able to teach across all learning diversities and needs, the role of an educational psychologist is significant, for their specialised training enables them to support the learner and teacher by enhancing learning to best match the learner's ability. However, when questions are asked on the preparedness of pre-service and in-service teachers on early identification, support and referral of learners with learning problems, the focus is often on the training they received and thus the critical role of educational psychologists in teacher training is brought to light.

Teacher education programmes and curriculum development can benefit from the knowledge and expertise of educational psychologists to foster awareness of diversity in human development, and create a disposition to teach all learners and to develop relevant teaching strategies. Educational psychologists can assist pre-service and practicing teachers with knowledge to educate all learners, irrespective of their ability (Hanich & Deemer, 2005).

Burden and Taylor (2014:342) declare that, all learning is the result of:

> ... *dynamic interactions between teachers and students by means of a mediational process, involving psychological tools such as language and other symbol systems, around a series of activities usually referred to as the curriculum.*

Learning does not happen in a vacuum and is the result of active interactions or an interactive process between the learner and the environment. The learning process occurs as an outcome of specific interaction and contribution of the following five factors (Burden & Taylor, 2014:342):

1. Teacher (teachers are subject specialists who mediate, interpret and facilitate learning; implement policy and curriculum; they research and assess the process of learning, leading to support when required).
2. Learner (learners are important participants in learning, they mostly mirror the competence, relevance and process of learning in their lives, they provide feedback on learning and inform policy through assessment feedback).
3. Curriculum (formal and informal: curriculum is the signpost of the department's mandate on teaching and learning, it is part of a policy directive and core to the quality of teaching and learning; educators are key to the implementation of curriculum).
4. Activity (teaching activities are interpreted from the curriculum and meant to operationalise the curriculum and educate the learner).
5. Context (learning occurs in all contexts of development eg, home, school, universities; community, work, etc).

Major debates within the field of educational psychology

There is more criticism on the relevance of educational psychology content to pre-service teacher education (Patrick, Anderman, Bruening & Duffin 2011; Shuell, 1996). This concern arose due to emphasis and focus of the discipline on theoretical (factual) knowledge while ignoring the focus on practical application of theory (applied knowledge) in teacher education. Shuell (1996) contends that in educational psychology both science and practice are significant. The new curriculum for teacher education in South Africa aims to address this issue (Department of Higher Education and Training, 2015).

There are concerns and criticisms of educational psychology's frequent lack of differentiation between science and practice, where dominance of science often overshadows the significance of practice in teacher education and training. According to Patrick et al, (2011:72), educational psychology in teacher training was criticised for:

> *... contributing abstract, decontextualized, and universal content that did not help students see the relevance of the theories that were taught or make meaningful and practical connections with real educational situations.*

Thus, there is a need for educational psychology to deconstruct theories and assist pre-service teachers in understanding the what, why, when and how of educational psychology knowledge in teaching.

Uncertainty over the profession of educational psychology and the scope of practice is one of the concerns raised by Cameron (2006) who cites rifts within the profession of psychology about professional training. This concern is experienced in South Africa especially with the current uncertainty regarding the scope of practice of educational psychologists. As such, the role of educational psychologists in teaching and learning remains critical at schools and institutions of higher learning. When Thorndike expanded the field of Psychology by highlighting the importance of the scientific study of the pedagogical domain, the foundations were laid for teaching and learning to be integral to the role of educational psychologists.

Conclusion

Educational psychology is significant to teacher education specifically and the field of teaching and learning broadly. However, more needs to be done regarding understanding the context of teacher education, the school education system and the post-school education system in order to fully utilise the contributions of educational psychology as a science and a profession. Currently, the role of educational psychology in the teacher education training is not highly emphasised and valued. This is mostly seen in the fact that higher education institutions that train educational psychologists do not have compulsory and mandatory internship programmes within the school system where the role of educational psychology within the schooling system and teacher education and training can be emphasised and operationalised.

Children's rights in South Africa: Implications for educational psychologists

JACE PILLAY & LUCIA MUNONGI

There can be no keener revelation of a society's soul than the way in which it treats its children. (Nelson Mandela)

Introduction

The United Nations Convention on the Rights of the Child (UNCRC) in 1989 placed children's rights on the agenda of governments worldwide (Ludbrook, 2000; Smith, 2002) but its definition remains a contentious issue since it means different things to different people. For example, for those in the legal profession, it would entail children's involvement in the criminal justice system and their representation in civil and political structures (Arts & Popvoski, 2006). For social workers, children's access to state resources is essential, while educational psychologists emphasise the psycho-social and educational well-being of children (Pillay, 2014). The large variety of civil, cultural, economic, social, and political rights further compounds the issues around children's rights. Despite the complex issues around children's rights one would contend that the central focus would be on the empowerment and protection of children (Mangold, 2002), which is embedded in three specific categories, namely: provision, protection, and participation. Provision refers to the right to access relevant services such as education and health (Freeman, 2000). Protection endorses the right of children to be protected from all forms of abuse, neglect, and discrimination (Hodgkin & Newell, 2007), while participation promotes the notion of children being involved in decision-making processes which affect them (Viviers & Lombard, 2013). Taking all of the above into consideration, we adopt Nikku's (2013:1) definition of children's rights, which emphasises 'the human rights of children with particular attention to survival, development, protection and participation rights.' While we believe that government should take the lead in promoting children's rights, we acknowledge it is not the sole responsibility of government. It should, in reality, be a joint endeavour of all stakeholders who care for and render support to children. Educational psychologists will be important stakeholders since their core responsibility is the psycho-social and educational well-being of children. Hence, this chapter highlights the importance of children's rights. The aim is to point out some of the relevant debates around children's rights and how it could be infused in the classroom taking the implications for educational psychologists into consideration.

Importance of children's rights

Children as rights holders are a special case because they are vulnerable and need adult protection, which depends on their age and stage of development. Their safety is paramount as without adult protection they are vulnerable to the harmful practices and actions of adults. For example, African countries are mesmerised by various inhuman practices that infringe on children's rights. These include, among others, child trafficking and child labour (Kisirye, 2007), use of child soldiers (Coalition to Stop the Use of Child Soldiers, 2008), stigmatisation of children as witches (Secker, 2013), genital mutilation and male circumcision (Twum-Danso Imoh, 2011) done in the respect for culture. Although some of the practices are viewed as necessary cultural processes, they potentially violate the rights of children. These practices are initiated by adults who are supposed to be the protectors of children, hence, in the absence of children's rights, children are prone to being abused. Thus children's rights are an integral aspect of protecting children. The state, non-governmental organisations, and adults have the duty to fulfil children's rights, namely the rights to survive, to be safe, to belong, and to develop (Pillay, 2016).

In South Africa, children's rights are violated on a daily basis. For example, children are being raped and killed. The rape and murder of Courtney Pieters, aged three, from Cape Town on 4 May 2017, which made news headlines (De Villiers, 2017), is just one example of the infinite number of cases of gruesome child abuse cases in South Africa. According to a National Prosecuting Authority spokesperson, 19 children were killed from January to May 2017 in the Western Cape alone (De Villiers, 2017). Such incidents emphasise the need to promote children's rights to be safe and protected.

Childhood is supposed to be a period that every child should enjoy, and this can be realised by fulfilling children's rights. These rights are important as they protect children from undignified practices that can affect their physical, psychological, and emotional being. They also ensure children are provided with basic needs for their survival and are recognised as active members of society. Children should be viewed as individuals who have the capacity to contribute towards the decision-making process (Alderson; as cited in Kosher, Ben-Arieh & Huebner, 2014) rather than being passive participants in an adult world. Therefore, respecting children's rights also implies recognising them as valuable members of society. If the state and adults uphold children's rights, then children can be assured of enjoying their childhood in environments that provide them with the opportunity for maximum development, socially, politically, democratically, physically, emotionally and economically.

Rights should ensure access to education, health care, nutrition and secure environments, which are all crucial for the full development of children. If children know their rights, they are more likely to become aware of and respect other people's rights (Howe, Covell & McNeil, 2008). Teaching children about rights tends to help with seeing the link between rights and responsibilities (Howe, Covell & McNeil, 2010). Therefore, rights are important in promoting social and moral responsibility in children.

Major debates about children's rights

Debates within children's rights have centred on whether children should be given full rights as adults. For Archard (2011), giving children too many rights erodes the value of rights, hence, the notion that inflation of rights talk devalues their currency. This viewpoint has been criticised for treating children as non-humans and denying children their human dignity (Freeman; as cited in Ferguson, 2013).

Other debates have raised concern over the imbalance created by teaching children only about their rights without mentioning responsibilities. This has led to the South African government coming up with a Bill of Responsibilities for the Youth of South Africa. The Bill defines the rights that children have and the corresponding responsibilities that accompany those rights (Bill of Responsibilities for the Youth of South Africa, 2011). This has also raised concern with the fact that imposing responsibilities can be interpreted as an attempt to place conditions on the rights of children. The Convention on the Rights of the Child (CRC) is not explicit about children's responsibilities as it advocates the unconditional granting of children's rights. However, responsibilities are not always seen as burdens by children as they are progressively given and age related (Nsamenang, 2005). They are viewed as a way of incorporating children into social responsibilities that they will face in their adult lives (Twum-Danso

Imoh, 2009). Therefore, the debatable issue is how society defines rights and responsibilities.

Other debates on children's rights focus on children not being accorded participation rights, which include the freedom of expression, movement, association, beliefs and expression, access to information, privacy, liberty, and development towards independence (UNESCO, 2007). Children are often viewed as being incapable of decision making due to their age and level of cognitive development. This has led adults to be more responsible for deciding on children's issues rather than promoting equal participation. This has created resentment and resistance from children in some cases as they feel that adults prescribe solutions for them without considering what children feel about matters that affect them. The CRC on the other hand promotes the best interest of the child in the issues that concern them. The CRC wants children to be treated as active agents, who have the capacity to contribute towards such issues. Thus opportunities for participation should be provided depending on the cognitive development of the children. Children's ideas should therefore be considered when making decisions on matters that affect them.

Relevance of children's rights in South African schools and classrooms

South African school curriculum specialists have worked hard to integrate the teaching of children's rights in school subjects. However, this was criticised as it was happening to a minimal extent especially in subjects like Mathematics (Carrim & Keet, 2005). Munongi (2016) found that children lacked knowledge of their rights and that the teaching of rights was only happening to a large extent in the subject of Life Orientation and to a low-to-moderate extent in the rest of the subjects. Education is a vehicle for change and as such could be instrumental in promoting children's rights. Children's rights must be integrated across the curriculum as many children in South Africa still do not know and enjoy these rights in practice (Munongi, 2016). Classrooms must be the starting points for promoting the realisation and fulfilment of children's rights. Learners spend most of their time at school where their rights could be upheld or violated by authorities (Deba & Mathews, 2012). The classroom is, for this reason, a strategic and crucial platform where rights should be taught. Since teachers are influential in children's lives, they could make a significant difference to learners if they teach them about their rights (Firat, 2013). The South African government recognises the relevance of children's rights, hence their inclusion in the curriculum. There is a need to infuse the teaching of children's rights in every subject so as to promote the maximum education of this topical issue in schools to ensure that policies on children's rights are implemented.

Implications for educational psychologists

Educational psychologists deal mostly with children regarding therapy, assessments, advocacy, and research, hence knowing children's rights is of paramount importance so that they could protect children from abuse. During their engagement with children, educational psychologists need to promote children's rights and be able to identify if other stakeholders do the same. Their role should be to protect children from harmful situations (Pillay, 2014c) and this can be achieved if they know children's rights. They need to promote children's rights and equip children with the knowledge of their rights since they are custodians of children's rights (Detrick; as cited in Pillay, 2014a).

Educational psychologists need to be aware of the debates surrounding children's rights and how they should be engaging with them. They should be involved in having discussions and workshops in schools and education districts with teachers and education officials to address the different debates around children's rights. According to Pillay (2014b), educational psychologists working in Africa have to be aware of the different cultural, racial and ethnic contexts when working with children. Given that South Africa has various racial groups, which have diverse differences within and between them regarding how they view the issue of rights, educational psychologists need to be conversant with such differences to accommodate everyone when teaching about rights. Pillay (2014b) further points out that if they are not properly trained, educational psychologists could face difficulties in working with such diversities. However, at the same time, this could be an opportunity for them to learn to be flexible when working with individuals and groups from a variety of cultures. Educational psychologists are therefore expected to be competent enough in human rights education as well as dealing with different racial and cultural groups.

The fact that children should be accorded participation rights implies that educational psychologists have to assist in creating opportunities for children to exercise their democratic rights in decision-making (Lake & Pendlebury, 2009) in preparation for adult life. This can be done by allowing children to contribute to classroom and school rules, suggesting how they should go about various activities in the school, participating in awareness campaigns to teach others about and to promote their rights. Given the extent of violation of children's rights in South Africa, educational psychologists should also facilitate the extension of this into children's families and communities (Bartolo, 2010) by teaching adults about children's rights so that they may learn to value and protect children from abuse. Additionally, schools must have strong mechanisms that protect children from violation of children's rights. Educational psychologists can help to educate all school authorities about children's rights so that they can be able to teach and or promote them to create a society which protects children in all areas.

Given the minimum integration of rights in the curriculum, educational psychologists should be involved in structuring the school curriculum and assist with integrating children's rights in all subjects and extra curriculum activities so that such programmes are in line with children's developmental needs. They could act as mentors in educating school management teams, school governing bodies and teachers on how to promote children's rights in the classroom and the school at large. As such, educational psychologists should also strategically position themselves (Pillay, 2014a) to become influential through teaching children about their rights. This can be done by having individual or group sessions at school to talk about children's rights.

Pillay's (2012) study found that educational psychologists need both internal and external support from teachers, learners, school management teams, parents, district officials, NGOs, and so on, for their role to be meaningful in schools. Although support cannot always be available due to various reasons such as different cultural beliefs, lack of funds or human resources (Pillay, 2012), educational psychologists need to stand in the gap and do as much as they can to both educate and promote children's rights.

Conclusion

This chapter focused on the importance of children's rights in South Africa, the major debates surrounding such rights as well as their relevance in South African classrooms. The strong point of contention in this chapter is the notion that educational psychologists should be fully aware of children's rights and the role that they should play in safeguarding, as well as promoting these rights, especially within the context of schools. For this to occur, educational psychologists must take an active role in educating children, as well as all other stakeholders, about children's rights.

> **NOTE**
> This work is based on research supported by the South African Research Chairs Initiative of the Department of Science and Technology and National Research Foundation of South Africa. South African Research Chair: Education and Care in Childhood, Faculty of Education: University of Johannesburg, South Africa, Grant no. 87300.

2

Teachers

5 Becoming a teacher

MARIECHEN PEROLD

One of the tasks of the progressive educator, ... is to unveil opportunities for hope, ... hope as an ontological need demands an anchoring in practice, in order to become historical concreteness. (Paulo Freire, 2004)

Introduction

Most people have attended twelve years of school, and have met and spent a considerable amount of time with many different teachers during that period in their lives. Some teachers have been loved, some may have been hated and some generated indifferent feelings about them. However, all those professional teachers influenced learners in profound ways, and in many cases still do to this day. So, who are teachers? How can a teacher's identity be described? Can a teacher be described in any definitive way? What is a teacher thought to be? How do students in education think about themselves as teachers? Who are student teachers and who are they supposed to be? What made students decide to become teachers and what might be the perceptions of the content of studies in education? What might students expect of this process of becoming teachers, of the preparation for and access to the teaching profession?

All the above-mentioned questions, and many more in the same vein, can be asked to ascertain the ideal identity of a teacher. Sociocultural theories do not view identity as fixed, but as an ongoing process of 'becoming'. These theories claim that multiple sources and processes contribute to identity development, in whichever way. Traditional views of identity hold that the construct is something each person has in him/her, and are focused more on biographical components or on cultural memberships to determine who we are. A current understanding of identity and identity construction, however, would emphasise multiple intrapersonal, ecological, experiential and relational or interpersonal factors that play roles in this process of 'becoming'. Within a posthuman school of thinking, relationships between human beings and the material world would be included as well. This demonstrates a move away from essentialist and context-independent notions of identity towards the notion of identity development as a continuous and lifelong process.

Theorists from the cultural-historical activity theory (CHAT) point of view declared their efforts to 'render an account of the self as a profoundly social phenomenon, yet at the same time as real, agentive and unique' (Stetsenko & Arievitch, 2004:476). They state that the self, a presentation of who a person is, of his/her identity, cannot only be shaped by historical, cultural, personal and environmental influences, but is ultimately dependent on the goal-directed activities in which the person engages (see Chapter 19). According to CHAT, regardless of all the possible influences of and interactions among these influential factors, human activity remains the principal foundation of human life. This implies that an individual, like a teacher, is simultaneously formed by society and informs society, that she is created by history, but that she also creates her own history, and that she is the 'author and actor of her own drama' (Stetsenko, 2005:85). These possibilities for agency emphasise the importance of identity and identity processes in the working life of a teacher.

Another view of identity as proposed by postmodern social constructionist thinkers includes the assumption that language constitutes reality and meaning (Freedman & Combs, 1996). This implies that the words we use, as well as the words used by others, contribute to how we think about ourselves and to our constructions of our identities. Language used may therefore also determine who or what is thought of as a teacher, or maybe who or what an effective teacher is. Policy documents, theorists, academic literature as well as popular media may convey descriptions of teachers and of the teaching profession that could have a major influence on how individuals think about what teaching is and about what is expected of a teacher. These documents may also influence how a person thinks about knowing, learning, and teaching.

Being aware of all the potential influences on who a person is as a teacher implies also that a person has agency in this process of becoming as an individual, as well as in a chosen profession. It seems important to stay cognisant of the language used, and of own individual meaning making, and of the tellings, and retellings, of experiences.

Why is the process of 'becoming a teacher' important?

In this process of becoming a teacher, of developing a professional identity, a student will have to learn certain skills, and will have to do certain thinking in relation to current theoretical conversations, as well as in relation to own worldviews. Certain relationships with the community of teachers of which it is hoped to become part, will have to be formed. The development of a professional identity, becoming a teacher, involves fostering self-descriptions consistent with the performance of the values and skills of teaching practice.

Moments may arise for descriptions and narratives that can support a sense of who students are and who they want to be as teachers, and provide the evidence for it (Winslade, 2003). These moments range from lectures, to exercises in class, to role plays, to mid-year interviews, to practising basic skills, to meetings with supervisors, to participation in group supervision sessions, to reading, to assignments and other forms of assessment, to trying to get their heads around new and different ways of thinking, and many more. Teaching practice could be a fertile part of the 'training' and may present many of these moments, affording opportunities for self-descriptions that align with who they want to become (Winslade, 2003).

As someone enters a programme preparing to become a teacher, that person brings to the process certain historical experiences, certain cultural influences, certain personal dispositions, certain knowledges or paradigmatic assumptions, which may all play a role in interacting with the teacher education programme. Experiences whilst studying will add influential factors. Engagement with these influences will lead to individual construction of meaning and with certain behaviours following. These individual activities will contribute to and have constitutive effects on identities as persons, and as teachers.

In the following section, some of the theoretical assumptions or debates that influence current thinking about the identity of a teacher and about the process of becoming a teacher, are discussed.

Some theories and debates about teacher identity

Some theorists and educationists tend to describe a teacher by the different roles he/she needs to fulfil. In 2000, the South African national education authorities described the teacher as fulfilling seven important roles (Department of Education, 2000). These roles were not intended to present a checklist for being a successful teacher, but rather indicated important functions that a teacher was expected to fulfil. The roles were those of a learning mediator, an interpreter and designer of learning programmes and materials, a leader, administrator and manager, a scholar, researcher and lifelong learner, a community, citizenship and pastoral role player, an assessor; and then also a learning area/subject/discipline/phase specialist.

Currently, a teacher is described by the Department of Basic Education (Department of Basic Education, 2017) as a person who has the following attributes: passion, commitment, tolerance, perseverance, character and the dedication to make a difference in the lives of a diverse group of children.

In the National Policy Framework for Teacher Education and Development in South Africa, a teacher is defined as a person who studied theoretical approaches to teaching, with the aim of leading others to insight and understanding of specific topics, as required by the schools where they might be appointed as teachers (Department of Basic Education, 2017). These descriptions seem to be technical in nature, focusing mainly on formal descriptions of the functions of a teacher, as found in policy documents. They do not consider, however, the teacher as a whole person. As previously argued, the language used to describe a teacher can contribute to what the teacher does, how she thinks about herself, which values she may attach to herself, as well as to the sense of self-efficacy that she develops. As an aside, Woolfolk (2014) cites research that indicates that the stronger a teacher's sense of self-efficacy, the harder she will work and the longer she will carry on trying out new, supportive teaching strategies. A lack of self-efficacy on the other hand may contribute to teachers viewing themselves as solely carrying out directives, and not as realising their own agency and resources.

Conley, et al (2010) draw attention to teachers as reflective practitioners, caring professionals, educational theorists, curriculum designers, mediators of learning, assessors, users of media, classroom managers, agents of inclusivity and agents of transformation. These are not presented as roles, but more as attributes indicating different activities in which teachers would engage. The collection of activities implicitly assumes specific sets of values and norms that teachers should adhere to in their practice.

These roles, attributes or activities introduce the following themes in the development of an identity as a teacher that are deemed important: teaching as a way of being; teaching as doing (as cognitive, behavioural but also—importantly—as emotional labour) and then, flowing into the last theme, namely teaching as specific ways of communicating.

Questions are voiced regarding the way this identity developmental process of 'becoming' a teacher can be facilitated in students in teacher education programmes. What theories do students need to be exposed to? How can such theory be applied in practice? Might this lead to different ways of being, of knowing and of teaching and communicating? In the international literature, debates on the relationship between theory and practice started as early as in

1904, when John Dewey wrote an essay deconstructing this relationship. He argued strongly for a balance between theory and practice (Dewey, 1904). Davis, Sumara and Luce-Kapler (2008:8) employed the metaphor of a rhizome to visualise the interconnectedness of theory and practice in education in the following words: '… seemingly distinct (and opposing) ideas can be deeply intertwined, even if their associations remain hidden from view'.

Within teacher education, 'training' models comprise a variety of interpretations of so-called best practice. Classroom observations and opportunities to teach formal lessons most commonly form the pattern of practical experience in most teacher education programmes. This often leads to students finding it difficult to develop a deep understanding of the interconnectedness of theory and practice. One often hears students saying that the theory being taught by lecturers at university has very little relevance in the 'real world out there' in classrooms and schools. Faulstich Orellana, et al (2017) argue in favour of opportunities for pre-service teachers to also join, observe and engage with children in informal settings, for instance in after-care settings, during sports activities and in other extracurricular environments. They argue that such observations and interaction with children might allow students to gain an understanding of child behaviour, insight into how children learn and into children's meaning-making. They advocate for reflective journaling and discussions about their reflections with more knowledgeable others who can mediate the intertwining of theory and practical knowledge gained in this way.

To link with CHAT, as mentioned earlier, there has been a shift from viewing teaching as merely the transfer of knowledge into the minds of children, to seeing teaching as facilitating active engagement with new knowledge and '…situat[ing] [this learning] in the sociohistorical and cultural practices of a community' (Faulstich Orellana, et al, 2017). This thought is based on Vygotsky's (1978) theory of learning and human development (see also Chapters 8 and 16). According to Donald, Lazarus and Moolla (2014:77), Vygotsky's theory contains '…the idea that cognitive development takes place through social interaction…', and therefore interaction, as activity, plays a major role in the learning process (see Chapter 16).

The meaning of 'becoming a teacher' for schools and classrooms in South Africa

In South Africa, with its history of inequities among different sociocultural and ethnic groups, a focus on the relevant preparation of student teachers seems to be of utmost importance. This especially becomes the case when the different roles and attributes that are expected of teachers, as stated in official documents, are taken into consideration. Dominant negative discourses among teaching professionals about the diverse needs and demands in classrooms, inclusive pedagogies, large classes, too little time, curriculum expectations, too many administrative duties, the resultant high stress levels and lack of appropriate training, may create a very bleak picture of teaching as a profession (see Chapter 30). This eventually may have the effect that the picture becomes bleaker every year, as fewer students may want to enter the profession and more teachers may want to leave the profession.

It seems critical that young people who want to make a difference in children's lives within the teaching profession are supported in meaningful and exciting ways. This could happen by engaging them in dynamic processes of their own personal learning and development towards a way of being, towards an identity as a teacher. This can make them realise their own agency and their own resources. It will also imply a process of becoming aware of factors that have influenced, and still influence, their own values and norms, and their own worldviews, and of critically revaluing these, discarding what they do not agree with any more and adopting and trying out new ideas.

Popular beliefs in general, but also specifically in education, have traditionally included '… precise definitions, unambiguous classifications, unimpeachable foundations and irrefutable logic' (Davis, Sumara & Luce-Kaplan, 2008:5). 'Universal truths, accurate measurements, context-free methods and predictable outcomes' (Davis, Sumara & Luce-Kaplan, 2008:5) constituted the foundations of education. This can contribute to a feeling of not being connected to the children a person is teaching. Children may not respond in ways that are expected of them. It is therefore important during students and teachers' 'becoming' processes to consider the ways of thinking about life in general, and to also consider the validity of the above-mentioned ideas regarding the absolute and inflexible nature of life (and teaching). Does *knowing* refer to having clearly defined collections of facts in memory? Does the complexity of the world we live in not counter such a safe position? Emerging ideas seem to come out of nowhere, and continuous change or transformation has become part of all the respective levels of everyone's lives. Because of the interdependence of phenomena it would seem as though almost everything depends on many other things at the same time, seeming to refute the possibility of simpler, more regular and more expected patterns in life. And in education! *Knowing* is therefore dependent on taking a contextual approach, and accepting diverse positions or diverse understandings. 'Knowing this has to do with noticing correspondences and relations—and with being able to appreciate one's position within' (Davis, Sumara & Luce-Kaplan, 2008:12). So, if knowing is not fixed, what does that say about *learning*?

When considering wat *learning* means to a teacher-to-be, it might be helpful to be aware of a rather superficial, but useful, way of describing some learning theories as correspondence theories, and others as coherence theories. Correspondence theories are underpinned by finding a match between what happens inside the mind of a child and the outside or objective world (see Chapter 18). Although the foci of respective correspondence theories may differ, they are similar in respect of relying on a relationship between intrinsic models of reality and external reality. An example would be behaviourist learning theory, which includes classical and operant conditioning processes.

Coherence theories, on the other hand, reject the notion that divisions exist between knowers and knowledge, between individuals and others, and between humans and things that are not human. These theories focus on individual constructs of meaning within social groupings and within cultural groups. The integrity of the environment is given high regard. Therefore, coherence theories present a wide variety of foci. Commonalities include metaphors related to the physical and biological world, like systems theory and evolution, rather than cause-effect descriptions. Examples of these theories would include constructivist theories, constructionist theories and cultural and critical theories of learning (see Chapter 8).

How would a young teacher then decide to plan her *teaching* strategies? In which learning theories would she ground her pedagogical plans? An interesting definition of *teaching*, proposed by Davis, Sumara and Luce-Kaplan (2008:158), is the following: '… any event or experience that prompts *learning* can properly be called *teaching*. *Teaching* is not about what the teacher does, it is about what happens to the learner.' It is therefore important to remain aware of what is believed about *knowing*, about all the possible ways of *learning*, and to know what is aimed for and which outcomes are envisaged resulting from *teaching*, rather than to apply simple, taken-for-granted teaching recipes. By adopting a correspondence view of learning, teaching might involve a well-controlled curriculum that is linear, carefully ordered, step-by-step, and punctuated by regular assessments, thus ensuring that it is possible to keep record of the exact way that learning progresses. The word *teaching* can be replaced by terms such as *explaining, telling, instructing* or *directing*, for example. Coherence theories, on the other hand, assume that knowing cannot exist in isolation in an individual; it exists in contextual, relational ways and is ever-evolving, even if in established terms (Davis, Sumara & Luce-Kaplan, 2008). *Teaching* can therefore be interpreted as creating opportunities for learners to seek and find coherence among themselves, in their contexts, in relationships between individuals, between individuals and the environment, as well as in relationships among other beings. Put in a different way, *learning* in these theories refers to children making sense and meaning of themselves and their world, and *teaching* is making that possible. Examples of words in this view of *teaching* would be *mediating, mentoring, modelling, initiating* and *enculturating*. In addition, critical theorists emphasise the ethical responsibility to *empower* and *liberate*.

The above-offered views of *knowing, learning* and *teaching* have bearing on teaching as a way of being, as being ever aware of multiple possibilities, as seeing theory and practice as two sides of a coin, metaphorically as a rhizome. It also addresses teaching as a way of doing, acting cognitively (thinking), planning strategies and executing them in the classroom (behavioural activities), and responding dynamically according to the aims and needs of the environment. There is another dimension of doing, the affective component of being a teacher, and this refers to what Carl Rogers called ways of relating (Rogers, Lyon & Tausch, 2014). Rogers is the father of person-centred psychotherapy. This model of psychotherapy assumes that all human beings have an inborn self-actualisation tendency. Provided that the core conditions of empathy, unconditional positive regard and congruence or authenticity can be experienced, this tendency to strive towards self-actualisation, towards the highest form of fulfilment, will be lived and will make transformation possible (Corey, 2009). Rogers transferred his theory of psychotherapy to the field of education and called it person-centred education (Rogers, Lyon & Tausch, 2014). The responsibility for working towards change therefore is on the person seeking change, and is this not what can be called *learning*? In the case of person-centred education then, the facilitator of the ideal circumstances for such change to happen in the learner would be the teacher. This implies that part of 'becoming a teacher' would involve acquiring the skills of listening empathically, and being able to resonate with the thoughts and feelings of another. Skills of keeping judgement out of communications with learners, and being able to accept unconditionally, would address the second condition necessary for change, or learning. The third condition of authenticity or realness refers to developing the ability to be yourself, to be genuine, without any pretence or role playing; not to put on a teacher's hat, but just to be the teacher.

Rogers relates the following about listening attentively and really hearing another person (Rogers, Lyon & Tausch, 2014:69):

When I truly hear a person and the meanings that are important to him at that moment, hearing not simply his words, but him—and when I let him know that I have heard his own personal meanings, many things happen. There's first of all a grateful look. He feels released. He wants to tell me more about his world. He surges forth with a new sense of a sort of freedom. I think he becomes more open to the process of change. I've often noticed, …

> *in classrooms that the more deeply I can hear the meanings of this person, the more there is that happens.*

This sounds like a hugely satisfying experience of being a teacher, does it not? Listening in this active and attentive way to learners, resonating with their feelings and points of view or thoughts without judgment, mirroring this deep understanding back to them in authentic ways, can prepare a space where change can happen, where learning can happen and where a student will have become a teacher.

Conclusion

Concluding, it seems important to once again consider the process of 'becoming a teacher'. This process would include developing an awareness of a person's own paradigm or worldview, vigorously critiquing it, embracing what is valued, being open to new experiences, living it in mindful ways and engaging with the process enthusiastically. This dynamic process does not only happen during a discrete 'training' period whilst at university studying to be a teacher. It implies in fact, a lifelong process of 'becoming', that defines a person on an ongoing basis, by continuously constructing an identity as a teacher.

> *[T]he issue that presents itself for teaching is not how to control what happens, but how to participate mindfully in the unfolding of possibilities. It is about maintaining an awareness that we, individually and collectively, are constantly enacting our knowing and always learning.*
>
> *That is, teaching isn't something that is done. Teaching is lived as one encounters self and other, individual and collective, past and future, actual and possible.* (Davis, Sumara & Luce-Kaplan, 2008:226)

6 Teachers as role models

MOENIERA MOOSA

Children are great imitators. So give them something great to imitate. (Anon)

Introduction

Social learning theory (Bandura, 1977, 1986), also referred to as observational, model or imitation learning, proposes that humans learn largely through interaction or observation of others. It can thus be claimed that individuals' behaviours are guided by social learning with regard to societal norms, values and beliefs, which will equip them to adjust successfully into society. According to this theory, learning by observing and imitating others can be regarded as an effective way of learning as well as a meaningful method of teaching (Davis, 1983:144). Teaching can be considered as one of the oldest and most important professions in the world. Children spend most of their day in a school environment; it is within this environment that they are constantly interacting with and observing various teachers. Therefore teachers have the responsibility to model certain occurrences to children and must recognise their responsibility in setting an example (Department of Education, 2001:4) to children. Teachers play a particular role in a child's learning processes because children have the ability to reproduce observed behaviours without attempting any other substitutes (Flynn & Whiten, 2008; Hopper, Flynn, Wood & Whiten, 2010; Horner, Whiten, Flynn & De Waal, 2006).

An educator can be viewed as someone who strives to enable children to develop a set of values consistent with those upheld in the Bill of Rights as contained in the Constitution (Republic of South Africa, 2000). The Code of

Conduct of the South African Council for Educators (SACE) clearly stipulates the role that teachers are expected to fulfil. These include that teachers commit to:

> *the noble calling of their profession to educate and train the learners of their country ... uphold and promote basic human rights ... act in accordance with the ideals of their profession ... not bring the teaching profession into disrepute.*

What these expectations indicate is that teachers have a responsibility to act as positive role models to children not just academically but also socially and morally. Hence teachers can be regarded as powerful role models for children. It is imperative to note that a teacher cannot act like a role model if they do not understand what it means to be a role model. This chapter will be deliberating the importance of teachers as role models to children by discussing why modelling is important and then defining what modelling is. This will be followed by a discussion of how teachers act as models of acceptable values, academic growth and development.

Why is modelling important?

It is within the school environment that children are exposed to various skills needed to master the content they are taught and also to what can be regarded in society as acceptable behaviour, values, skills and healthy relationships. These two aspects can be demonstrated to children by their peers but also by their teachers. Teachers are important role models to children with regard to being able to demonstrate specific skills needed to master various subjects. Thus teachers would need to demonstrate to children how to, for example, write sentences, read, and solve mathematical problems.

What is modelling?

Modelling is a critical component of social cognitive theory (Bandura, 1977), which refers to the behavioural, cognitive and affective changes that occur from observing one or more models (Rosenthal & Bandura, 1978; Schunk, 1987; Zimmerman, 1977). Eggen and Kauchak (2001: 236) define modelling as 'changes in people that result from observing the actions of others'. The main focus of modelling is learning by observing others (Hill, 1985:154). Modelling can thus be viewed as a strategy used by teachers to demonstrate a new concept that children learn by observing. Modelling should not be confused with imitation as has been done historically because modelling is a more inclusive concept. Imitation involves actions that are elicited by an instinctive drive, actions that fit existing cognitive structures and behaviours that are reinforced through shaping and reinforcement (Schunk, 2012:124). For a child to learn complex skills there would need to be a combination of observation and performance. Thus what a teacher does is equally important to what they say as children are continually learning by observation.

What is observational learning?

According to social learning theorist Albert Bandura (1977:22):

> *Learning would be exceedingly laborious, not to mention hazardous, if people had to rely solely on the effects of their own actions to inform them what to do. Fortunately, most human behaviour is learned observationally through modelling: from observing others one forms an idea of how new behaviours are performed, and on later occasions this coded information serves as a guide for action.*

Observational learning can be seen as an ongoing and continuous process. Children have the ability to spontaneously imitate behaviour, both consciously and unconsciously, simply by watching their parents, teachers, peers, and others. Thus teachers need to note that almost every action has the potential of being modelled. Teachers should capitalise on this modelling process by making every effort to be desirable models to children (Schau, Phye, Hudgins, Theisen, Arnes & Ames, 1983).

Observational learning through modelling occurs when children display new patterns of behaviour that they would not have been able to perform prior to the exposure to the modelled behaviour (Bandura, 1969). Observational learning comprises of four processes namely attention, retention, production and motivation (Bandura, 1986).

Children cannot imitate someone unless they pay attention to what the model is doing and saying, as well as to the consequences of the model's actions. Models often attract children's attention because they are distinctive, successful, prestigious, powerful or have other winsome qualities. Television is particularly successful at presenting models that draw children's attention. The process of attention is followed by retention. It is at this stage that children need to mentally organise, rehearse, code and transform the information that they observed in order to store it in their memories. The information can be stored in the form of an image or in a verbal form or both. Following this the observed action needs to be produced in an overt manner because complex behaviours cannot be learned solely through observation. It is not only through observing others that children learn but also by doing. Thus children learn enactively by actually doing or vicariously by observing models perform (Schunk, 2012:121).

Observing others allows children to be able to gauge what is possible without actually performing the task themselves. This form of learning also protects children from experiencing any direct personal negative consequences for actions. Lastly, the consequence of the modelled behaviour informs children about the value and acceptability of these behaviours. If the outcomes align with the child's expectations, they are more likely to enact that behaviour. Children are constantly observing various behaviours but they may or may not choose to perform certain observed behaviours themselves. Thus children's decisions are governed by various factors other than mere observation.

Factors that impact on observational learning and performance

There are various factors that teachers need to consider that will have an impact on children's observational learning and performance outcomes. These include the child's developmental status as children's ability to learn from models is affected by their developmental level. Children are able to make judgements about the usefulness of modelled behaviours. Modelling competence is therefore a significant factor in children's learning. Teachers can be regarded as high-status models to children as they have the task of not only developing children's intellect but can also be influential with regard to social behaviours, educational attainment, dress and mannerisms. Motivation is also an important factor with regard to observational learning. Children's goals, expected outcomes, values and self-efficacy all play an important role in their willingness to perform observed behaviours. Lastly, if children place value on the consequence of the observed behaviour they are more likely to repeat that behaviour (Schunk, 2012:136). This leads to the question of how teachers can act as models to children.

Teacher modelling

Teachers have a responsibility towards children to model acceptable values, attitudes, skills and behaviours. Teachers should also see themselves as models of academic growth and development for children. The types of modelling that teachers engage in, which will be discussed, are those proposed by Coffey (nd), namely disposition modelling, task and performance modelling, metacognitive modelling, modelling as a scaffolding tool and student-centred modelling.

Disposition modelling

Teachers are in a position to model personal values and ways of thinking to children. According to Duplass (2006:204), 'teachers who are creative, diligent, well-prepared, and organized model the kinds of strategies needed to succeed in the workforce'. At the Saamtrek conference in 2001, Nelson Mandela stated: 'One of the most powerful ways of children and young adults acquiring values is to see individuals they admire and respect exemplify those values in their own being and conduct.'

However, teachers need to be careful that the types of values and ways of thinking that they model do not exclude anyone. By acting with integrity, empathy and setting high expectations teachers are able to model desired characteristics to children. Furthermore, children can learn about 'cleanliness, slovenliness, altruism, selfishness, self-discipline and disorganisation' (Mwamwenda, 2004: 198) from their teachers. Children observe teachers' behaviours. For example, a teacher chewing gum whilst presenting a lesson, but who then does not want children to chew gum in class, creates conflicting messages to children. It is imperative for teachers to tell their learners how to behave, but it is more effective if a teacher acts as a living example of what is acceptable. Teachers' attitudes towards their subject or other subjects also impact on how much effort children will be willing to put into mastering the content of the subject.

Metacognitive modelling

According to Tonjes (1988), metacognitive modelling can be described as the way in which teachers demonstrate reading and comprehension strategies to children. She further argues that teachers who use this approach should concentrate on modelling mental processes rather than simple procedures. In this way children are able to apply what they have learnt across various situations. This type of modelling can also be very useful in Mathematics when teachers guide children through multiple mental processes to solve a problem.

Task and performance modelling

Task modelling occurs in the form of a teacher doing a demonstration of a task that children are expected to perform afterwards on their own. So, for example, a teacher would read a short story or paragraph aloud to demonstrate pronunciation, tone and pace to children. Teachers would model specific skills solving mathematical problems, writing topic sentences, or using specific computer programmes. A more explicit form of task modelling is for teachers to show children examples of completed projects to enable them to design their own. This will also allow children who feel unsure of what to do, to get a better understanding of what is expected of them. Teachers also need to model to children how to do oral presentations, as this will assist them in becoming more confident. This strategy is used to give children an opportunity to first observe what they are expected to do at a later stage.

Modelling as a scaffolding tool

Teachers need to be able to demonstrate the 'how to' component of a lesson. Children will observe what the teacher is doing and then would attempt to do it themselves. The teacher would take cognisance of children who have not grasped what needs to be done and provide support to those children by assigning tasks to them that they can complete at their own pace.

Student-centred modelling

Children's learning styles are sometimes affected by how they perceive their teachers as role models (Marshall, 1991; Shein & Chiou, 2011). In order to ensure that all children can benefit maximally from a learning experience, it is occasionally necessary for teachers to move away from a teacher-centred learning approach. In this form of modelling, teachers move away from a teacher-centred approach and get children to model behaviours or processes that they have mastered to their peers. Children find it particularly effective if they see their peers being able to master a task as this lessens their self-doubt (Woolfolk, 2010:353). Within a South African context, teachers have a specific role to play regarding modelling values and skills to children.

How is teacher modelling relevant to South African schools and classrooms?

Teacher modelling is vital in a South African context as it should be used as a tool to improve children's academic performance, but also to impact on possible moral and social decisions that children need to make. With regard to children's academic growth, the South African education system has been in the spotlight for low literacy and numeracy levels. Teachers have a responsibility to make use of metacognitive tools and also demonstrate and perform academic tasks for children in order to assist them academically. Furthermore, teachers should assist children to set realistic academic goals. In this way children will believe that they are able to achieve these goals, which will promote children's level of self-efficacy. Learning is based on mental processes by which children take in, interpret, store and retrieve information. Teachers need to explain and demonstrate concepts and skills to children because this allows them to be in a position to learn and believe that they are capable of further learning. Since there is a connection between the performance of previously learned behaviours and new learning, a teacher needs to be aware of what children are able to do and build on that when new skills and information are introduced. In this way teacher modelling will include scaffolding of content. Teachers must have the necessary skills and knowledge about the content they teach in order to model tasks effectively to children. In the absence of academic modelling, children will possibly find the process of mastering certain skills more arduous.

At a social and moral level, dispositional modelling is imperative for children and teachers have an important role to play in this regard. A study done by Cooper, De Lannoy and Rule (2015) identified sexual and reproductive health, youth pregnancy, HIV, violence, substance abuse and mental health as the major challenges facing young people in South Africa. Although the origins of the aforementioned social and moral issues do not necessarily find their roots in schools, teachers are often the ones who have to deal with the impact of these issues in their classrooms. Teachers need to take cognisance of the fact that children are more influenced by actions than verbalisations and hence need to ensure that their instructions to children (eg, 'bullying is not acceptable') are consistent with their own actions (teachers do not bully and victimise children). It is thus imperative that teachers play a role in directing children towards becoming responsible citizens. In this regard, social learning theory has numerous implications for classroom practice.

Conclusion

Teachers are responsible for imparting knowledge to children, creating stimulating learning environments, preparing children for future career selections, moral and social choices as well as preparing them to become useful and honourable citizens who will be able to contribute to society in a meaningful way. Observing teachers gives children cues of what is appropriate and acceptable. Teachers are important role models to children not just in the attainment of academic results, but also in the development of social responsibility.

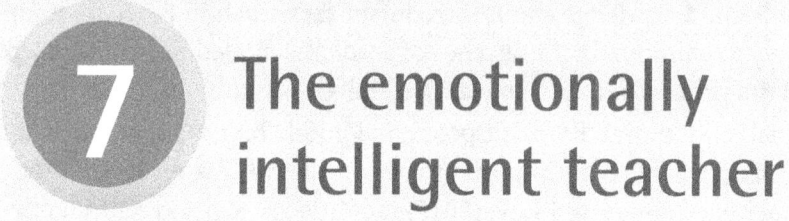

7 The emotionally intelligent teacher

ELMA FLEISCHMANN

Teaching is a work of heart. (Coetzee & Jansen, 2007)

Introduction

Teachers are said to be one of the main indicators that play a role in the effectiveness of learning in the classroom. For a teacher to be deemed a good or even an exceptional teacher, many different competencies are needed. These competencies are in a unique combination as all teachers are different people. This chapter explores a competency which is often undervalued in teacher training, but plays a determining role. This competency is emotional intelligence (EI)—a relatively new concept, which is widely seen as an indicator of happiness and success. The chapter attempts to define and explain EI while clarifying the concept with a practical example from the life of a teacher.

> **SCENARIO**
>
> Rosalin is a Grade 10 Mathematics teacher. Her Grade 10 class wrote a test the previous day and she was excited to mark the test and see the results. She really likes the Grade 10 class. Although they are not the strongest academically, they are 40 lively, creative and engaging teenage boys and girls, who come from different backgrounds and cultures (but some teachers say they are 'naughty' and undisciplined). While marking the tests at home, she realises that the learners did not grasp some of the basic concepts of the topic. As she is marking, she feels her heart pounding. Immediately she feels angry—she is sure the learners did not study. She knew it was a difficult topic and therefore she worked really hard during the holiday to prepare the lessons.

The emotionally intelligent teacher

> She created diverse learning environments to make sure the learners grasp the concepts. She set extra exercises. It was a lot of hard work—why did the learners not do their part? There is still a lot of work left for the rest of the term ... there is no time to revise the previous topic. They have to move on!
> - Can you identify the feelings that this teacher is experiencing?
> - How does she feel?
> - What does her body feel like?
>
> Teachers have to cope with what they are feeling about what happens in their classrooms every day.
>
> What is important in this scenario is that Rosalin has certain feelings, and fortunately she is aware of what her feelings are, but she also has certain options in dealing with the feelings. Some of the things she can do are:
> - Ignore what has happened and just hand out the tests and carry on with the work;
> - Express her anger and frustration with the learners the following day about them not studying; or
> - Feel incompetent as a Mathematics teacher.
>
> Furthermore, when Rosalin hands out the tests to the learners, how do they react, and what do they feel? Chances are that some will be angry, others might be sad, and still others might even be frightened of the consequences of their test results. There will undoubtedly be some learners that will be excited because they achieved good marks and some might have feelings of guilt because they might have achieved better marks than they feel they deserved.

Why is the study of emotional intelligence (EI) important for teachers?

Freedman (2017) quotes Plato 2000 years ago saying, 'All learning has an emotional base.' Ultimately teachers want learners to learn from them. For a teacher to be effective, many different skills are required. If you ask any person which skills a good teacher possesses, there are a wide range of requirements that are defined. Broadly speaking they can be classified into two categories: personal skills and professional skills (Vesely, Saklofske & Leschied, 2013). The personal nature of skills needed by teachers is emphasised in literature and even in the seven roles identified in the *Norms and standards for educators* (Department of Education, 2000), echoed by the *Revised policy on minimum requirements for teacher qualifications* (Department of Higher Education and Training, 2015). According to the classification of roles, personal skills help a teacher to fulfil at least three of these roles named:

1. Leader, administrator and manager.
2. Scholar, researcher and lifelong learner.
3. Community, citizenship and pastoral role.

The *Revised policy on minimum requirements for teacher qualifications* goes further and names basic competences of a beginner teacher and these competences echo the importance of personal skills. Many of these competences place emphasis on the ability of the teacher to take the individual needs of learners into account, communicate effectively, be mindful of diversity of learners in their classrooms and reflect critically on their own practice (Department of Higher Education and Training, 2015). All of these competences are personal competences without which a teacher will struggle to be a good teacher.

In the training of teachers, great emphasis is placed on professional skills, but this chapter is about personal skills, and because of the highly interpersonal nature of teaching, these skills are really important (Vesely, Saklofske & Leschied, 2013; Coetzee & Jansen, 2007). These personal skills are vital because they impact on how a teacher copes, but they also impact on how learners identify with the teacher and how effectively they learn from the teacher. Learners also identify with teachers and thus pick up these personal skills from the teacher.

In the life of a teacher, the kind of situation Rosalin is facing—a situation which evokes strong emotions—will probably occur on a daily base. Situations that evoke emotions are not only academic in nature, classrooms are sometimes full of undisciplined learners that come from diverse and often emotionally unstable homes. This puts a lot of pressure and stress on a teacher and ultimately burnout can become part of the everyday life of many teachers (Hassan, Hayati, Som, Hami & Azizam, 2015; Vesely, Saklofske & Leschied, 2013). This is not only a South African occurrence. All over the world teachers are leaving the profession because of stress and burnout. Emotions play a major role in the management of stress. Emotions can be a powerful motivator and energiser, if they are put to use in a constructive way. Otherwise, the emotions can also drain and demotivate a teacher. The study of emotions and the management thereof is very important so that a teacher can cope and persevere.

Another reason why the study of emotions is relevant in the life of teachers, is that a considerable amount of research shows that emotions and ultimately emotional intelligence (EI) play a role in the process of learning. Teachers are supposed to be facilitators of successful learning, and research has shown that teachers are one of the greatest indicators of effective student success (Vesely, Saklofske & Leschied, 2013; Coetzee & Jansen, 2007). Thus, it is important for a teacher's well-being and effectivity to be aware of the role emotions play in their work life.

History of the concept emotional intelligence

The working of emotions and the influence it has on a person's well-being and learning capacity is a topic that has only received detailed attention in the last twenty years, but as early as the 1950s the 'Human Potential' movement believed that people could develop their emotional, physical, spiritual and mental strength. Other concepts that laid the foundation for EI were those of social intelligence (Zeidner), and multiple intelligences (Gardner).

During the 1990s, more serious work was done on the topic of emotions. Joseph LeDoux (a neuroscientist) did research about the mechanisms that are processed in the brain regarding emotions. These researchers paved the way for research about emotions and intelligence.

It was Peter Salovey and John Mayer who first used and defined the term 'emotional intelligence'. Daniel Goleman published a book, *Emotional Intelligence*, which popularised the term 'emotional intelligence' (Goleman, 1995). In 1995, *Time* magazine published an article about Goleman's book, and that was the beginning of the popularisation of the term.

Some popularised versions of EI is said to be too wide, including too many characteristics that do not necessarily involve emotions, or the management thereof. Mayer, Salovey and Caruso (2008) stress that the correct use of the concept 'emotional intelligence', involves the 'ability to engage in sophisticated information processing about one's own emotions and other's emotions and the ability to use this information as a guide to thinking and behaviour'. This chapter focuses on the importance of EI while keeping this warning in mind.

Emotions and the brain

LeDoux identifies two constructs when referring to emotions or feelings: first, 'the feeling that makes itself known to consciousness when we are in a situation facing a challenge or an opportunity' and second, he refers to 'survival circuits' and argue that they 'did not evolve to make emotions, but to give organisms the tools to stay alive' (LeDoux, 2014).

The relevance of the work of LeDoux for this chapter is that emotions are triggered when a person is facing a situation (which evokes these feelings) and there is a physical reaction to this situation. LeDoux (2014:319) further remarks that:

> ... *nonemotional ingredients: sensory activation of a survival circuit that produces arousal in the brain, and body responses that feed back to the brain; retrieval of relevant implicit and explicit memories; cognitive processes such as attention, monitoring, appraising and prediction, work together to form an emotion.*

Feeling, thinking and doing

For Rosalin in our case study, what she is feeling about the test results, influences what she is thinking and how she is acting. If she has time to digest her feelings about the results of the test, she might make choices of how she is going to react wisely, but in some situations that teachers are faced with, they do not have that advantage. If the teacher is faced with what she perceives as a 'naughty' class that is rowdy and objectionable on a day that she is tired or has a headache, her emotional control might not be so effective. Then it is not so easy to digest the feelings she has before she reacts, and this will definitely have an influence on her well-being and her relationship with the learners. Ultimately, it will impact on whether and how effectively the learners learn from her.

Even though considerable work has been done about the working of emotions since the 1990s, many mysteries still exist in terms of understanding emotions. The work of Freedman (2017) show how the constructs of 'feeling', 'acting' and 'thinking' are closely interlinked. These three human actions cannot be separated and have an influence on each other. This relates back to the story of Rosalin.

Because teachers (like all people) get these inputs that evoke feelings many times on a daily basis, it is important to reflect on the influence of emotions for a teacher. In the training of teachers, great emphasis is placed on the nurturing and stimulation of their professional skills, but very little attention is given to their personal skills. This is why the study of EI could fill that void.

The use of emotions

A teacher is a human being and a human being is an intricate combination of body, mind and emotion. Any incident can evoke emotions, and these emotions are an integral part of a human being. For many years cognitive processes were seen separate from emotional processes, but with the work of Mayer and Salovey in the 1990s and the consequent work done by other researchers, the influence of EI (sometimes called EQ) was recognised. Daniel Goleman in turn stressed the importance of EI in the workplace in his book *Working with emotional intelligence*. Research on EI blossomed in the following years, more and more research shows that high EI is an indicator of achievement, productivity, leadership and personal health (Mayer, Salovey & Caruso, 2008; Cooper & Sawaf, 1997; Freedman, 2017; Coetzee & Jansen, 2007).

Defining emotional intelligence

There is more than one definition for EI. These definitions have slightly different emphasis, but broadly have the same thrust. For the purpose of this chapter, the definition of Goleman will be used.

Goleman (1998) defined EI as 'the capacity for recognising our own feelings and those of others, for motivating ourselves, and for managing emotions well and in our relationships'.

This definition has five distinctive parts:
1. Recognising your feelings.
2. Those of others.
3. Motivating yourself.
4. Managing emotions well.
5. In our relationships.

In the following paragraphs this definition is explained by relating it to the story of Rosalin.

Recognising your feelings

While Rosalin is marking, she feels uncomfortable. Her heart is pounding. It is important for her to recognise that she is upset, and why she is upset. Otherwise her daughter might come into the room where she is marking and ask for a glass of milk and she might respond impatiently that she is busy, and although that is true, the reason for her impatient reaction is not that her child is disturbing her, but because she has been upset by the test results.

Recognising the feelings of others

Handing out the tests to the learners is a make-or-break moment for Rosalin. She sees the learners' faces when she hands out the test, and some look happy, some sad, some angry, some perplexed. These emotions influence how they will function the rest of the day. It is important for Rosalin to use this as a moment of positive growth and learning.

Motivating yourself

For a teacher, the success of the learners becomes her success. Therefore the feelings she had while marking and reflecting, motivates her to plan a course of action. The recognition of the emotions in herself and the learners motivate her to make a new plan to help learners to understand the topic better.

Managing emotions well

Even though Rosalin had certain feelings during the marking, by the time she reaches the class, she is calm and can settle the learners. She will be able to choose the wisest words to say to motivate the learners not to give up, but to work harder.

Positively impact relationships

The learners will feel affirmed because Rosalin takes their feelings into consideration when she hands out the tests. This plays a role in the positive relationship between the learners and Rosalin, and has a positive influence on the trust that the learners has in Rosalin and how they learn from her.

Apart from the definition, it is also useful to study the competences of EI as listed by Mayer and Salovey (1997). These competences also illustrate the progression from merely recognising emotions to using emotions to grow intellectually. These competences are:

- Perception, appraisal and expression of emotion;
- Emotional facilitation of thinking;
- Grasp and analyse emotions; employ knowledge; and
- Regulating emotion promotes emotional, intellectual growth.

Emotions and learning

Emotions influence performance and ultimately emotional intelligence influences effective learning. This is apparent from what Gasque (2016) states in an article: 'Emotions influence not only the way we perceive, view and react to environmental stimuli, but also how we learn and create new memories'.

For the teacher that means that he/she will learn more effectively with high EI. Emotionally intelligent teachers have the capacity to create emotionally intelligent classrooms, which creates a space conducive to learning. For the learners, it means that if they have an emotionally intelligent teacher (who nurtures emotionally intelligent learners) they should learn better. A further benefit is that learners do not only learn cognitive skills from teachers. They learn behaviours and skills that are of a personal nature.

It is useful to study the competences of EQ as listed by Goleman (1998). Goleman divides these competences into two groups, namely the personal competences and the social competences.

Personal competences are derived from the first three parts of the definition of EI:

- Self awareness:
  - Emotional awareness;
  - Accurate self-assessment; and
  - Self-confidence.
- Self regulation:
  - Self-control;
  - Trustworthiness;

- Conscientiousness;
 - Adaptability; and
 - Innovation.
- Motivation:
 - Achievement drive;
 - Commitment;
 - Initiative; and
 - Optimism.

Social competences explain the last two parts of the definition:
- Empathy:
 - Understanding others;
 - Developing others;
 - Service orientation;
 - Leveraging diversity; and
 - Political awareness.
- Social skills:
 - Influence;
 - Communication;
 - Conflict management;
 - Leadership;
 - Change catalyst;
 - Building bonds;
 - Collaboration and cooperation; and
 - Team capabilities.

How does a teacher learn to be emotionally intelligent?

The good news is that emotional intelligence is not stagnant. Emotional intelligence can be learnt. The ways in which EI can be learnt can take a multitude of forms, many of which are easy, but it can make a profound difference in the personal and professional life of the teacher, and ultimately also in the life of learners.

> **NOTE**
> A few tips—it is worthwhile to spend time on EI:
> - Be aware of your own feelings—without being aware, feelings cannot be managed.
> - Create space between the feeling and the reaction—count to 10! There is actually an organisation called Six Seconds where the name is derived from creating space between your emotion and your reaction.

> - Try to read the feelings of others, but check your observations. Do not assume you are right in your deduction. Different people show what they feel in different ways.
> - Affirm your own feelings (and those of others)—it does not help to ignore what you are feeling.
> - Make sure that you make space to debrief your own (and other peoples') feelings. Create space to talk, play sports or do activities with the goal of debriefing.
> - Creating an emotionally intelligent classroom might go a long way to solve issues of lack of discipline, bullying, and disrespect for anyone.

The value of being emotionally intelligent is personal, but it definitely flows over to relationships at home and in the workplace.

Scenario

> When Rosalin has digested the emotions she experienced initially after marking the tests, she can choose to guide learners through the process of understanding their emotions when they receive back their tests. She can explain how emotions work, and ask learners what they are feeling. Instead of just carrying on without pausing, she can spend time on helping learners to react in an emotionally intelligent manner. This diffuses the emotions and opens up 'mindspace' for learners to digest their emotions, and renew their energy levels to try again—a process which is vital for effective learning.

Conclusion

The current situation in South Africa and across the world is that teachers are under pressure—different kinds of pressure. Many teachers struggle to cope with various challenges. These challenges include heavy academic and administrative workloads, the implications of various socio-economic influences on learners and parents, which results in disciplinary problems in classrooms, and possible under resourcing. This often leads to stress, depression, health problems and ultimately teachers either leaving the profession or doing only what they have to do.

'Teaching is a work of heart' is the name of the first chapter in the book *Emotional Intelligence in the classroom* (Coetzee & Jansen, 2007). As such, EI training should have a high priority in the training of teachers. Some writers even say that the most important variable in the creation of an effective classroom environment is the emotional intelligence of the teacher (De Klerk & Le Roux, 2003). The combined advantages of the teacher personally being happier and the classroom environment being more effective make it worthwhile for teachers to familiarise themselves with the notion of emotional intelligence (EI).

3

Teaching and learning

8 Teaching for learning in South African schools: A sociocultural approach

JOANNE HARDMAN

Pedagogy must be oriented not to the yesterday, but to the tomorrow of the child's development. (Lev Vygotsky, 1978)

CASE STUDY

Read the extract below and answer the questions.

MR ABEL [*children learn*] through concrete examples. They need to be able to see something, hold it, use it, then they begin to understand it. So in the class today, they had to actually use shapes to draw a person. Then I can ask them, what is this shape? And then I go on and I ask them more difficult things like, why is this a triangle? What are its properties? So, first start with the practical group work and then do exposition.

1. What is Mr. Abel's theory of how children learn?
2. What kind of pedagogy does he suggest you use for learning?
3. What is your theory of how children learn?
4. How do you think you should teach for a student to learn?

Introduction

The extract above is drawn from an interview with a teacher. In it he describes how he thinks children learn best. In this chapter, we will be looking at what kind of teaching leads to effective learning. You will be introduced to the work of Vygotsky (1978; 1986), a Russian educational psychologist who was most famous for his work around teaching/learning (see Chapter 16). While we will be drawing heavily on Vygotsky, we will also utilise the work of Wood, Bruner and Ross (1976) carried out in the West, which adds to some of Vygotsky's theorising. Vygotsky's work is referred to in the East as cultural historical theory but this has been taken up in the West as sociocultural theory. For our purposes in this chapter, we will refer to Vygotsky's work as sociocultural theory. The reason for selecting this theoretical framework is three fold:

1. On the one hand, Vygotsky's work is incredibly influential in educational debates on teaching/learning. In fact, it is probably the work that most informs current pedagogical practices in schools that have largely become known as 'constructivist' practices. In general, what these practices share is an acceptance that children learn through being actively engaged in a pedagogical setting. That is, children actively construct knowledge through interacting with the world.
2. Vygotsky views teaching and learning as *dialectically* entailed: one cannot have teaching without learning and vice versa. Further, his theory provides a pedagogical structure that shows one how to teach for optimal learning.
3. Finally, Vygotsky's work is incredibly useful in multicultural settings, such as South Africa. Vygotsky was interested in how to develop diverse students' cognitive functions through structured pedagogical practices and, in our multicultural milieu we can learn much from his work.

Before we begin this chapter, it is important that we have a definition of what exactly we mean by 'pedagogy'. Hardman (2007) defines pedagogy as:

A structured process whereby a culturally more experienced peer or teacher uses cultural tools to mediate or guide a novice into established, relatively stable ways of knowing and being within a particular, institutional context, in such a way that the knowledge and skills the novice acquires lead to relatively lasting changes in the novice's behaviour; that is, learning.
(Hardman, 2007:5)

We will keep coming back to this definition as we go through the chapter. What is important to note for the moment is that this definition implies:

1. That a teacher is *necessary* for teaching; so a teacher is not a guide on the side but an essential aspect of the teaching/learning dyad.
2. That tools are used when teaching.
3. That learning implies relatively lasting changes in the learner's behaviour.

Why is a sociocultural approach to teaching for learning important and what major debates does it address?

South Africa continues to underperform internationally in terms of mathematics and science, which are gateway subjects to higher education. Many studies have sought to understand why South African students lag behind their international counterparts and one of the key findings relates to the nature of pedagogy in schools. Simply put, teaching in our schools is not equipping students with the requisite knowledge to succeed in core subjects. What is needed, then, is an approach to pedagogy that actually leads to learning. This chapter will argue that Vygotsky's work does precisely this.

The call for a novel approach to pedagogical practices in South African schools comes against the background of a debate about how children learn optimally and against the introduction of new curricula in schools. Launched in March 1997, Curriculum 2005 (C2005) signalled a departure from content based to outcomes-based learning. This marked a break with the past and a move from fundamental pedagogics to progressive pedagogy underpinned by a learner-centred approach to teaching and learning. Here 'learner-centred' refers to a curriculum that focuses on acquisition rather than transmission (Chisholm, 2004; Brodie, 1997). However, largely because of its attempts to integrate school subjects and 'real world' material without explicitly outlining learning requirements, C2005 failed sufficiently to articulate the pacing, sequence and progression requirements in subjects, which resulted in poor student performance. The Review Committee into Curriculum 2005 Report (Chisholm, et al, 2000) indicated that C2005 was understipulated and overdesigned, disadvantaging the teachers and the students it was aimed to assist (Jansen, 1997). Crucially, the Review indicated that under present South African school conditions, evaluation and learning requirements need to be made far more explicit than C2005 allowed for. This explication of learning and evaluation requirements is embedded in the Curriculum Assessment Policy Statements (CAPS) curriculum. So, initial attempts to impact on performance in schools were addressed through changes in the curriculum, from outcomes-based education (OBE), through Curriculum 2005 to the new CAPS curriculum, these debates situate underperformance at the level of the curriculum. The implementation of new curricula, of course, has seen a consequential change in pedagogical practices with teachers moving from an almost entirely didactic, passive approach to teaching prior to OBE to a more active and interactive approach to teaching under CAPS. Some commentators refer to this as a move from teacher-centred to learner-centred pedagogy. In this chapter these terms will not be used, as all teaching is both teacher- and learner centred and it is rhetorically hollow to suggest that teaching can be centred only on the teacher or vice versa. The content that follows will demonstrate how teaching is centred, necessarily on the learner, by investigating Vygotsky's notion of mediation.

Vygotsky and pedagogy: Teaching for learning

Writing at the turn of the 20th century, Vygotsky's theoretical position challenged firmly held ideas that children were blank slates, or passive vessels, into which knowledge could be 'poured' or transferred. According to him, children actively construct knowledge through interacting with those in their environment. The fact that learning, and hence development, require the intervention of another is summed up below in his general genetic law that states that:

> [e]very function in the child's cultural development appears twice: first, on the social level, and later on the individual level; first, between people (interpsychological), and then inside the child (intrapsychological). This applies equally to voluntary attention, to logical memory, and to the formulation of concepts. All the higher functions originate as actual relations between human individuals. (Vygotsky, 1978:57)

Pedagogically, what this means is that a student needs a more knowledgeable other (generally a teacher) in order to develop cognitively and that this is done during interaction between the knowledgeable other and the novice before being internalised by the novice. The process by which knowledge is jointly constructed is theorised in the concept of 'mediation'. Mediation refers to the structured guidance of a more knowledgeable other who assists the student to accomplish something with help that they cannot do alone (Hardman, 2011). That is, mediation guides the student from a space of not knowing, to a space of knowing. The social space in which this happens is referred to by Vygotsky as the zone of proximal development (ZPD). This is a unique space that is opened up between the culturally more knowledgeable teacher/other and the student/novice during a problem solving activity and is defined by Vygotsky as:

> ... the distance between the actual developmental level as determined by independent problem solving and the level of potential development as determined through problem solving under adult guidance or in collaboration with more capable peers... the actual developmental level characterises mental development retrospectively, while the zone of proximal development characterises mental development prospectively. (Vygotsky, 1978:86–87)

Crucially, what this points to is that a child can do more with the help of a more competent other than they can do on their own. While it may seem obvious to us in the 21st century that children can accomplish more with assistance than they can on their own, it is worth noting that even today we continue to test students based on what they have already learnt, rather than on what their potential to learn is. The ZPD is also a developmental principle in that it suggests that one can develop a student from a space of not knowing to one of knowing. It is also important to note that in any given class children may have different ZPDs depending on their backgrounds and prior schooling. The ZPD tells us what the child's potential to learn is, rather than testing what the child already knows. Summative testing that continues in schools, however, tests only what the student has already learnt and tells us nothing about what they can learn. So it is from this notion of the ZPD that we get the understanding of formative assessment, or assessment that guides students during problem solving activities. Significantly, what is learnt in the ZPD cannot be learnt in the absence of a teacher because the nature of the concepts learnt, what Vygotsky referred to as 'scientific concepts' are abstract and require instruction to be learnt. Vygotsky notes that:

> [t]he development of the scientific ... concept, a phenomenon that occurs as part of the educational process, constitutes a unique form of systematic cooperation between the teacher and the child. The maturation of the child's higher mental functions occurs in this cooperative process, that is, occurs through the adult's assistance and participation. ... In a problem involving scientific concepts, he must be able to do in collaboration with the teacher something that he has never done spontaneously... we know that the child can do more in collaboration than he can do independently. (Vygotsky, 1987:168, 169, 216)

Note in the quote how Vygotsky stipulates that the development of scientific concepts requires cooperation between teacher and taught. Scientific concepts, however, must not be confused with science concepts. Scientific concepts refer to all knowledge that is school based and has to be taught (Hedegaard, 1998). So teaching verbs, for example, in English is regarded as teaching scientific concepts. Vygotsky distinguishes between scientific and everyday concepts; everyday or spontaneous concepts are learnt through empirical interaction with the world. For example, when it is cold, I know to put my jersey on and I do not have to be explicitly taught this. However, knowing what cold feels like, tells me nothing about the scientific concepts of temperature or indeed thermal dynamics. For this, I will need to be explicitly taught these concepts. It is important to note that scientific and everyday concepts are dialectically entailed: you cannot really separate them because you need both to learn. Our everyday concepts help us to make abstract scientific concepts meaningful and scientific concepts help to make our everyday knowledge conscious.

From mediation to scaffolding: Neo-Vygotskian approaches

While Vygotsky's notion of mediation provides an intriguing introduction into how one can teach for optimal learning, he died relatively early at the age of only 37 and therefore did not fully develop exactly how one can mediate in a classroom environment.

> *Vygotsky never specified the forms of social assistance to learners that constitute a ZPD …. He wrote about collaboration and direction, and about assisting children "through demonstration, leading questions, and by introducing the initial elements of the task's solution." … but did not specify beyond these general prescriptions.* (Moll, 1990)

In the above quote, we can see that while giving a general idea of how to teach using mediation this was not specified by Vygotsky. In the West, Wood, Bruner and Ross (1976) developed the notion of scaffolding which echoes well with Vygotsky's conceptualisation of mediation. Scaffolding, as its name suggests, requires that the teacher provide a structure for a/the student to learn and gradually withdraw this structure as the student progresses, much like scaffolding functions when building a house. They suggested the following strategies for scaffolding:

- *Recruitment:* In the recruitment phase one must gain the students' attention. Let's say, for example, that you are teaching calculus to a senior school class. What is an effective way to grab their attention? A good way to get them interested might be to play a YouTube link showing how base jumpers jump off Table Mountain. Without a sense of calculus, a base jumper would not be able to calculate his/her trajectory and would meet a rather bad end!
- *Reduction in degrees of freedom:* This requires simplifying complex task into smaller tasks. So if the challenge is to teach the addition of 4-digit numbers, one might simplify this by breaking the large numbers up into thousands, hundreds, tens and units. So 4 650 + 2 345 becomes (4 000 + 2 000) + (600 + 300) + (50 + 40) + (5) = .
- *Direction maintenance:* Here the teacher provides verbal guidance about how to reach one's goal, helping the child to maintain their direction on the task.
- *Marking critical features:* This requires that you pick out critical issues and interpret discrepancies. One way of highlighting what is important, for example, is to underline it.
- *Frustration control:* It is impossible to learn if you are frustrated. Students are not merely cognitive beings, they have feelings too and a teacher must be sensitive to any frustration a student might have.
- *Demonstration:* Demonstrating how to arrive at a correct answer is one of the most important pedagogical techniques a teacher can use. If for example, one is teaching addition of fractions, demonstrating how to add fractions with the use of concrete examples such as a pizza or cake can help the student to achieve the desired goal.

Relevance to South African schools and classrooms

South Africa's history has been indelibly coloured by the apartheid policies of the past. Arguably, the greatest impact of the apartheid system was the under education of people of colour in our country. While democracy has seen the fall of apartheid, unfortunately our education system continues to feel the impact of this discriminatory system in both human and material resources with many schools in poorer areas not having access to basic resources. What this has led to is underperformance on a large scale in South African schools, with children presenting as unable to even read at a Grade 6 level. The vastly different levels of performance seen in classrooms are often interpreted as some children being 'unable' to learn. However, if we take Vygotsky's notion of the ZPD, as that space in which teaching and learning happens optimally, we can begin to see the importance of his work (see Chapter 16). As noted in the chapter, the ZPD is unique to individual children; all children may have different ZPDs and may benefit to greater or lesser degrees from assistance. The transformative principle regarding the ZPD is that a teacher can effectively mediate to different children, with different levels of performance, in order to develop the child. We noted that the ZPD is a developmental principle. What this means is that teaching/learning in the ZPD actually leads to cognitive development through the process of mediation. So, if a child is not performing in school, working in the ZPD does more than merely teach the child, it actually develops that child cognitively. Meeting the needs of the diverse students we face in South African schools requires a pedagogy like that outlined by Vygotsky where a culturally more competent teacher can cognitively develop the student through the process of mediation in the ZPD.

Conclusion

This chapter introduces a way of thinking about pedagogy as a developmental tool that can cognitively develop students. Vygotsky's (1978) work provides the foundation for this view of teaching/learning as inextricably linked through a structured process called mediation in each child's unique ZPD. Mediation sees the role of the teacher as absolutely essential in teaching the kind of concepts one learns in schools, namely scientific concepts. Vygotsky's theory provides for a view of pedagogy that actually leads to cognitive development. Especially in South Africa where the education system is plagued by persistent underperformance in schools, this theory provides for a transformative pedagogy that can develop students to their full potential.

9 Learning theories and the use of technology in the classroom

GEESJE VAN DEN BERG

In the end, I can't see how a discussion of learning theories can be avoided. Unless teachers have this basic understanding of the different views of learning, they will not be in a good position to make choices, especially regarding the use of technology for teaching and learning. (Tony Bates)

Introduction

Technology is becoming increasingly more important, not only in South African classrooms, but in both formal and non-formal educational settings all over the globe. In their daily lives, learners use texting, emails, WhatsApp, and they participate in social networks such as Facebook, Twitter and Instagram. Likewise, they can search for content on Google, save and share content in the Cloud, access wikis and blogs, and watch videos on YouTube. They can access all kinds of information on the internet using different devices such as computers, smartphones and tablets. Information has become accessible at anytime, anywhere. While the internet and mobile communication change the way in which both learners and teachers communicate, we need to change the way we think about teaching and learning. An education system that fails to take the pivotal role technology plays in education into consideration, is failing our next generation: a generation who is growing up with technology and who needs to be prepared for their future careers in a digital world.

Teachers have to adapt their traditional didactical practices to online learning environments. This means that they have to be proficient in using the technology. The challenge is then to set tasks that allow, among others, creativity, critical thinking and a variety of answers, both for individual and collaborative tasks. Although adapting to online environments happens in all spheres of life, teachers most probably have the biggest responsibility because this shift is about learning: learning new knowledge and skills, learning how to adapt to new contexts and ultimately to be successful in life. Harasim (2012) mentions a need to reflect on our theory of learning and to rethink teaching practices and pedagogical approaches, keeping in mind the opportunities online technologies have to offer.

Why is knowledge about learning theories important?

Learning theories help teachers to understand how learning takes place, and how theory translates into practice. To be able to apply learning theories, they need to understand them as tested principles that have the power to explain how things work in the classroom. Teachers have to be aware of the different learning theories when adopting a learning approach: considering the learner, the context as well as the nature of the content.

In order to understand current ways of learning, it is necessary to discuss where learning theories come from, and how they have developed over time. A brief account of major debates within the the field of learning theories can be useful to serve as a basis for current and new ways of thinking about teaching and learning. This chapter also discusses possible ways in which different technologies could support learning.

Major debates within the field of learning theories

Before we discuss some of the major learning theories of the 20th and 21st centuries, it is necessary to explain what we mean by a learning theory. A learning theory can be described as a research-based explanation of how learning takes place: how individuals acquire, retain and recall knowledge. Learning theories aim to help us to understand how people learn, which is an extremely complex process, as we all know. Over the years, many theories have attempted to explain how people learn, and in this chapter, four major theories and how each provides a lens to look at how teaching and learning takes place, are discussed. Keep in mind that these theories should be seen as building on one another, and that they are not the only theories that exist. Furthermore, theory serve as explanations of how and why we teach the way we do.

We will discuss the following theories:
- Behaviourist learning theory;
- Cognitivist learning theory;

- Constructivist learning theory; and
- Connectivist learning theory.

Behaviourist learning theory

Behaviourist learning is about change in learner behaviour by using repetition and reinforcement from the environment. It focuses on what is objectively observable and measurable. Behaviourism, which was developed from late in the 18th century by theorists such as Watson, Pavlov, Thorndike and Skinner can be considered as one of the first examples of the use of scientific methods to explain learning. From the behaviourist point of view, teaching is an activity of the teacher, who knows what learners need to learn, often using the textbook as a resource of information. Educational activities are executed from a teaching perspective and focus on the strong points, preferences and teaching styles of the teacher (Brown, 2006). It is a teacher-centred approach to teaching and learning. Behaviourists maintain that all behaviours can be learnt and reinforced and that learning takes place when a stimulus receives the required response (Ertmer & Newby, 2013). Behaviourists also posit that when a behaviour becomes unacceptable, it can be unlearned and be replaced by an acceptable one.

Behaviourist learning in the classroom

In the classroom, behaviourism can be seen when teachers do drill and practice exercises, use flashcards in their teaching to teach concepts, use rewards or punishments, and when they provide prompt feedback to their learners. Teachers evaluate learners based on the same criteria for all.

Behaviourism and technology

Computer-aided instruction using games, drill and practice, tutorials, simulations, educational games and problem-solving programmes based on behaviourist principles are still used today to teach facts, patterns, information and skills associated with subject-related material (Dede, 2008). In this process, the learner has to interact with certain activities until the desired response is demonstrated.

Criticism

Limitations to behaviourist learning began to be recognised in the early 1920s, mostly because researchers were unable to explain social behaviours, problem solving, language learning and critical and creative thinking. Behaviourism does not take the mind's thought processes, learners' learning styles or their feelings, intentions and opinions into consideration. Psychologists working in the field of learning began to realise the significance of the power of the mind to influence decisions that were not directly related to external stimuli. These developments led to the rise of the cognitivist learning theory.

Cognitivist learning theory

As a revolutionary reaction to behaviourism, the cognitive learning theory gained support since the mid-1900s. It is based on thought processes, rather than merely on responding to external stimuli and was driven by research in both linguistics and computer science (Stravredes, 2011). With Gagné and Bruner seen as the main contributors to the cognitive learning theory, it focuses on mental processes, on opening the 'black box' of the mind in order to understand how people learn. Cognition refers to the learner's thoughts, feelings and ideas, and knowledge and understanding of the self. The learner plays an active role in seeking ways to process new information and to link it to his/her existing body of knowledge. Although the theory is very different from behaviourism, the focus of the learning process is also on the teacher, and the learner has to make sense of whatever the teacher is teaching. Teachers therefore have to find the best and most relevant educational strategies to promote learner understanding. Like behaviourism, it is therefore also a teacher-centred approach to teaching and learning.

Based on cognitive development, taxonomies or classifications of learning are considered to be important. Benjamin Bloom (1956) developed one significant example of such a taxonomy. He worked on the notion of how objectives could be achieved based on different cognitive levels of complexity. His taxonomy, which is still widely used as a basis for student assessment, consists of six levels, namely, knowledge, comprehension, application, analysis, synthesis and evaluation. They are listed according to levels of difficulty, with the prerequisite that the first level must be mastered before moving to the next.

Cognitivist learning in the classroom

Cognitive learning activities are geared towards pushing learners through problem-solving activities. The goal is to make learners think and apply problem-solving strategies, using their logic and creativity. Learning activities that enable learners to advance through the different developmental stages as specified by Bloom is an example of cognitive learning. Several cognitive games are designed to stimulate the brain, promote critical thinking and help learners learn. These games can for example be used to learn a foreign language or memorise new material. Using board games and puzzles further promote learners' cognitive development.

Cognitivism and technology

Several technologies that are readily available can improve long-term memory, enabling learners to connect new knowledge with what they already know. Using software programmes for concept maps and mindmaps to organise material and for note taking can improve learners' understanding. Various websites and software programmes can be used for concept maps, which can be seen as a physical representation of cognitive processes. Internet games involving virtual journeys can further contribute to learners' understanding of places and this can contribute significantly to problem-solving processes (Orey, 2012).

Criticism

During the 1970s, cognitive learning theory came under criticism, mainly because educational researchers started to reject the idea that humans could be programmed like computers. Furthermore, there was very little emphasis on the development of the affective domain as well as on individualism. Constructivist learning theory, which can be regarded as a counter theory of cognitivism and behaviourism, began to recognise aspects not accounted for before.

Constructivist learning theory

The constructivist learning theory states that learners construct their own knowledge and understanding, based on their prior knowledge and experiences. Constructivism puts the learner in the centre of the learning process while the teacher acts as a facilitator. Piaget (1983), who can be regarded as the father of cognitive constructivism, suggested that learners can acquire knowledge by experiencing things and linking them to what they already know, in terms of developmental stages. In this process, new knowledge is constructed by either associating it with what is already known, or creating new information, leading to a broader understanding. This reminds us that because of prior knowledge and experience, learners learn in different ways, and at a different pace.

Vygotsky's introduction of social constructivism can be seen as a variation of cognitive constructivism, in which learning is seen as a social process during which learners interact with the environment to gain new knowledge (Vygotsky, 1978). Social constructivism implies cooperative and collaborative learning. Working with co-learners implies real-life experience of working in a group, and allows learners to develop their metacognitive skills as they reflect upon their own learning. This means that learning is seen as an active process during which learners make intellectual sense of the material during a process of problem solving until the knowledge and skill is mastered to ensure self-regulation and independence.

Constructivism is a learner-centred approach to teaching and learning. The teacher is not the only source of information, but rather fulfils the roles of facilitator, coach and motivator. However, it means that the teacher has to carefully plan and structure learning activities.

Constructivist learning in the classroom

Several activities support constructivist learning, for example, a class discussion based on a film or a field trip. Group discussions based on individual experiments is another example, as well as reporting to the class or group on small research projects. Learners are not seen as the so-called blank slates, but can be asked to formulate questions, come up with their understandings of tasks, concepts or problems. Another important learning activity in the constructivist classroom is reflecting on activities and learning.

Constructivism and technology

Through the use of the web, learners are exposed to vast amounts of information, and they can choose what they want to learn. Web surfing, learning management systems, emails and the use of the internet create a terrain for networked, collaborative and social learning. In this way, learners learn as individuals as well as from each other, with the possibility of constructing rich and sophisticated ideas. In a constructivist learning environment, networks are used to facilitate interaction between spatially separated learners, using electronic mail and online discussions to share information and solve problems.

Criticism

Like all other learning theories, constructivism also received its criticism, including concerns that the emphasis is more on the acquisition of knowledge than on learning. Furthermore, learners have different learning styles and preferences and not all learners are comfortable with constructivist learning. Another point of criticism lies in the fact that constructivism did not cater for learning impacted through technology and 21st century learning. A paradigm shift was needed, which led to the rise of connectivism.

Connectivist learning theory

Connectivism, a fairly new learning theory, was developed by Downes and Siemens in 2004, in response to society's connectedness within a digital network. It is a theory for the digital era, during which learners learn in a connected world: connections between learners themselves and between learners and information and communication technology (ICT) (Siemens, 2005). The ability of ICT to transcend geographical boundaries and allow information flow increases the capacity to know more than what was previously possible. Connectivism builds on previously known learning theories such as perceiving knowledge as transmitted facts, the need for unique cognitive skills to process information successfully, and collaboration in distributing the information (Bell, 2011). The connectivist learning theory has had an impact on teaching and learning since ICT provides the social media for networking and information distribution to all network members to gain knowledge. This applies to both teachers and learners. The nature of having network members from all over South Africa, and even over the world, having access to information from various sources implies that in connectivism, learning and knowledge rest in a diversity of opinions. With such an overwhelming amount of available information, the challenge lies in obtaining quality, accurate, current and trustworthy information. Teachers should know what to teach and also direct their learners. Furthermore, teachers' competencies in the use of technology, as well as their attitude towards its use, determine the success of the use of technology in the classroom. At the end of the day, in a learner-centred approach, the learner will be instrumental in determining the content of learning, the levels of communication as well as who participates (Kop & Hill, 2008).

Connectivist learning in the classroom

Since connectivism is a theory for the digital age, technologies are involved to support learning. Learners can use technologies such as WhatsApp, Skype or emails to share information, solve problems or discuss content. Learning management systems such as Moodle or Sakai can be used for threaded discussions on certain topics. Blogs can further be created to share experiences with others. However, in connectivism, it is not about the technology, but about the democracy of the learners' voices; about fundamental ways in which knowledge is created, distributed and shared.

Connectivism and technology

Twenty-first century technologies, such as Web 2.0 tools enable the formation of networks and discussion forums. Since connectivism relies on connections and sharing, any form of technology that allows for sharing could be used. For this reason, social media such as Twitter, Facebook, and wikis could all be used to share knowledge. Videos and lectures can be posted online before classes start to enable learners to prepare for the class. They can also revise the work at their own time after class. By doing so, they learn for themselves and by themselves at their own homes, flipping the classroom.

Criticism

Although connectivism is widely acknowledged worldwide, criticism exists about it as a learning theory. One is that it is not regarded as a different or new learning theory, but rather it is adapting to the technological environment (Kop & Hill, 2008). Further critique is that the role of the teacher may become obsolete since learners can access, share and distribute knowledge using their own networks.

Conclusion

The theories described in this chapter differ in their perspectives on how learning takes place, though each one has influenced and shaped instructional methods and practices. The rapid development of technologies to support learning makes constructivism and connectivism more relevant than theories that focus on knowledge transmission. However, behaviourist and cognitive learning theories are needed for tasks when, for instance, facts, patterns and certain sets of information need to be taught. On the other hand, constructivist and connectivist approaches to learning are of the utmost importance in organising and constructing new knowledge and tasks that need deeper thinking. Because of its complexity, no one learning theory can fully explain how learning takes place. Therefore, a balance of approaches is needed. (Other chapters in this book elaborate on some of these approaches, eg, see Chapters 8 and 16.) The teacher needs to act as a guide and facilitator, but on occasion also as an instructor, or to explain and teach concepts and content. While different learning theories may have different principles, they all focus on the learning process and the attainment of educational goals.

In our rapidly changing world, different new learning theories and new technologies to support learning will keep on being developed. In fact, the use of technology to support teaching and learning will become more and more prevalent. The role of teachers might even be more multifaceted than ever, since they have to stay abreast of these new developments that can assist them in their teaching and their learners' learning, in order to prepare them to be competent citizens in the world they have to live in.

Learning styles and intelligences in diverse classrooms

KAMLESHIE MOHANGI

It's not how smart you are; it's how you are smart. (Howard Gardner)

Introduction

The aim of this chapter is to emphasise that not all learners learn in the same manner and that every learner has distinct and unlimited potential in different ways. The intent of educationists and teachers in contemporary classrooms is to plan and deliver lessons so that all children can fully engage in learning and flourish in a mentally and psychologically empowering, diverse sociocultural environment. Yet, many teachers find it challenging to design appropriately effective teaching approaches that are grounded in sound insight into the ways that children play and learn. Heterogeneous classroom environments embrace learners with different needs from varied backgrounds who learn together. Diversity and similarity abound in classrooms where personal and social factors including cultural, ethnic, economic, and even geographic backgrounds, are central to learning.

This chapter provides perspectives to South African teachers who are sensitive to the need to engage with learners, to deepen their understanding of and to improve their response to the learning needs of individual learners and the learner body in general.

The importance of learning styles and intelligences in diverse classrooms

According to Dryden and Vos (2005:353), every person has 'a different lifestyle and a different workstyle', 'yet many of our schools operate as if each person is identical'. Learners differ in many ways, both individually and as groups and thus, the dilemma confronting teachers is, namely, how to accommodate the diverse needs of learners in order to teach more effectively.

If learners repeatedly fail to understand the teacher or to engage and participate in the classroom lessons, they are likely to disengage from learning and amuse themselves by playing games, sleeping, eating, distracting others, or fooling around. In addition, teachers, who are unaware of diverse learning styles among learners, will likely teach in a manner that precludes learners from showcasing their strengths.

One of the critical tasks of a teacher is creating a classroom climate that embraces not only differences but also commonalities in an atmosphere of positivity and acceptance. However, to conceive ways of addressing individual learning styles and different learning needs in a diverse classroom is daunting, given the large learner numbers in South African classrooms. The following questions may aid teachers in focusing their thinking towards formulating effective approaches:

- What are my learners' interests?

  As individuals, for example, some learners might be interested in mathematics and natural sciences, whereas others might be interested in languages and history.

- What are my learners' abilities?

  Differences in general individual abilities are a human trait that need to be assessed and accommodated.

- Does my teaching style fit my learners' learning styles?

  Consonance between teachers' individual teaching styles and learners' learning styles is essential since learners tend to lose focus when classroom instructional strategies do not match their learning styles. Teachers may have life experiences that are dissimilar to those of many of the learners they are teaching, for example, because of culture (language and beliefs) and/or economic circumstances (affluence and poverty).

- How do my learners think and learn?

  Close attention to the differences between learners' ways of thinking and learning will aid towards deciding upon the most appropriate strategies for accommodating both individual and group cognition.

By encouraging a range of styles of learning, teachers can teach to a wider variety of learners—irrespective of their backgrounds or those of the teachers themselves—thereby fostering more effective instruction. Teachers' knowledge of constructive teaching strategies could enable them to select approaches that are most responsive to the strengths and needs of their learners. Such flexibility allows teachers to support learners' individuality and avoids the danger of stereotyping learning needs based on background knowledge (Seifert & Sutton, 2011:79).

Increasing numbers of teachers and educationists contend that teaching to specific learning styles may hold value in increasing learner motivation and engagement, and they have therefore come to use specific learning-styles strategies to increase learner interest.

Learning styles in the classroom

Owing to its complex nature, learning style as a concept has been defined variously by researchers. For example, Dunn, Dunn and Price (1984) explain learning styles as being visual, auditory, and kinaesthetic ways by which individuals learn whereas Allinson and Hayes (1996) distinguish between intuitive and analytic thinkers. Recently, Willingham, Hughes and Dobolyi (2015:266) described learning styles as 'differential preferences for processing certain types of information' or 'for processing information in certain ways'. These views have value in providing theoretical perspectives on learning styles as a phenomenon, but teachers should, in particular, be mindful of whether learners engage in individual learning (singly) or cooperative learning (groups). They should also bear in mind that learning styles do not refer to differences in ability among learners but to the varying ways in which they process information.

Dryden and Vos (2005:372) provide a particularly convenient guide to identifying learners' learning styles as reflected in their body language:
- Visual learners may sit up straight and follow the teacher with their eyes;
- Auditory learners softly repeat to themselves words spoken by the teacher, or nod their heads frequently when the teacher is speaking;
- Bodily-kinaesthetic learners tend to slump down when they listen; and
- Tactual learners love to play with objects while listening, for example, by flicking a pen, fiddling with stationery, or squeezing a ball.

Intelligences in the classroom

Similar to learning style, the term 'intelligence' is a multifaceted concept and scholars hold different views on its representations. In general, different forms of intelligence should not be seen as reflections of emotions, personality, or sensory awareness, neither should intelligence be viewed as a single, delimitable entity. It is best approached and understood as multiple manifestations of the ability to process different kinds of information when solving problems or engaging in any creative process. Howard Gardner, who introduced the multiple intelligences theory in the book *Frames of Mind*, published in 1983, pioneered this approach.

In Gardner's (2006:27) writing, the term intelligence is defined as the 'bio-psychological potential to process specific forms of information in a particular way'. Gardner initially posited seven different forms of intelligence each of which functions independently of the others. Later he included an eighth, and has recently propounded the possibility of a ninth (see Table 10.1). However, research has indicated that individuals have a mix of all eight or nine abilities in varying quantities, which helps to constitute their individual profile. For example, Szpringer, Kopik and Formella (2014:353) state that 'each person possesses a range of all intelligences and uses them in accordance with their preferences and tasks performed'. Nonetheless, everyone has natural tendencies towards particular types of intelligence traits.

In an educational context, a multiple intelligence framework can be tabulated as described in Table 10.1.

TABLE 10.1 Intelligence type and identifying characteristics

Intelligence type	Some identifying characteristics
Linguistic	The ability to speak and/or write well. Shows an interest in the world of spoken and/or written words.
Logical–mathematical	The ability to reason, calculate, and apply logical thinking. Shows an interest in the world of objects, symbols and/or numbers and mathematical calculations.
Visual–spatial	The ability to draw, paint, sculpt, compose photographs, and read maps easily. Shows an interest in the world of images and spatial forms.
Bodily–kinaesthetic	The ability to use hands or body. Shows an interest in the world of movement and physical contact.
Musical	The ability to compose songs, sing, and play musical instruments. Shows an interest in the world of sound, rhythm, and melody.
Interpersonal	The ability to relate to others as a form of social intelligence. The ability to understand, communicate and interact well with others.
Intrapersonal	The ability to access inner feelings and to adopt an introspective and self-reflective attitude.

Intelligence type	Some identifying characteristics
Naturalist	The ability to note patterns in nature. Shows an interest in the natural environment and surroundings.
Existential	The ability to be sensitive to a spiritual dimension.

Source: Adapted from Dryden & Vos, 2005:352–366; Seifert & Sutton, 2011:67; Szpringer, Kopik & Formella, 2014:353–354

The multiple intelligence theory is particularly valuable for meeting these classroom objectives:
- To match how teachers teach to the ways by which learners learn;
- To encourage learners to expand their abilities;
- To develop learners' potential as fully as possible; and
- To embrace diversity.

It is not common for learners' potential gifts or talents to become immediately noticeable in the classroom. Instead, each child has a unique potential and it is usually up to the teacher to nurture and develop this potential further so that it may become a talent or special gift, or even develop into a special intelligence.

From this perspective, it is clear that traditional approaches to intelligence and learning have contained misapprehensions that have over time, become regarded as truths. In fact, many tenets of such views are misconceptions (untruths) that require clarification, as illustrated in Figure 10.1.

Misconception	Truth
Learning occurs in an identical manner for all people.	We all have a personal learning style, working style, and thinking style. We might have commonalities with others, but essentially we are each different.
The intelligence you are born with remains static throughout your life.	We all have individual strengths and talents that we may use at different times in our lives. Teachers, parents, and other significant adults help children make the most of their strengths to overcome weaknesses.
There is only one type of intelligence.	There are many types of intelligence and one can also have different traits and talents.
One's intelligence is gained mainly through one's genes.	Nature and nurture work together to determine your strengths and talents.
Everyone can be successful in everything.	People have different aptitudes that help them excel in different ways. A single person cannot always succeed in everything.
School is the main or best place to learn.	Learning takes place in different and multiple settings and environments.

FIGURE 10.1 Some misconceptions and truths about learning and intelligence

Source: Adapted from Dryden & Vos, 2005:144–149

Debates within the field of learning styles and intelligences in diverse classrooms

While an increasing number of educationists have found the learning styles and multiple intelligences theories compelling enough for formulating new teaching strategies, debate among researchers on the accuracy of these theories continues. Researchers such as Farkas (2010), Gardner and Moran (2006) as well as Burke and Dunn (2010) have suggested evidence for a positive correlation between teaching to specific learning styles and intelligences and increased learner scholastic achievement. Others, such as Waterhouse (2006) and Willingham, Hughes and Dobolyi (2015), hold contrary views.

The main critique is that these theories lack theoretical, empirical, and pedagogical rigour. For example, Waterhouse (2006), as well as Willingham, Hughes and Dobolyi (2015), claim that despite the principles of these theories being widely accepted and used in the field of education, they lack adequate scientific support to justify their utilisation as the basis for classroom teaching or general educational purposes. The strategies to assess learning styles have also been criticised as not sufficiently reliable (Coffield, Moseley, Hall & Ecclestone, 2004). The researchers claim that if learning styles and multiple intelligences are to have teaching value, the following aspects must be taken into account:

- A person's fundamental learning style should be constant across situations. Thus, for example, an auditory learner would consistently learn best through auditory processes regardless of the situation. In other words, a predominantly auditory learner today cannot be a predominantly visual learner tomorrow. Nonetheless, the argument proposed is that a fundamental learning style does not preclude learners from availing themselves—to a greater or lesser extent—of other learning styles that may be more appropriate to changing situations.
- Cognitive function should be more effective when it is consistent with a person's preferred learning style. This means that a visual learner should remember better (or problem solve better) with visual materials than with other forms of learning (Gardner & Moran, 2006).

One way of encouraging success in the classroom is to use differentiated instruction according to learners' needs and talents, which requires recognising and teaching according to different learners' talents and learning styles. Such methods encourage learner responsibility, peer tutoring, flexible grouping, and learner choice. This approach involves modifying instruction so that all learners can be successful (Morgan, 2014).

How are learning styles and intelligences in diverse classrooms relevant to South African schools and classrooms?

Learners in South African classrooms may be racially, linguistically, culturally, and geographically diverse from or similar to each other and their teachers. The country's 11 official languages, by illustrating the extent of linguistic diversity, serve as a prime example of the scope of sociocultural differences.

Dryden and Vos (2005:353) state that:

> ... in order to transform the world's high schools, find out each learner's combination of learning styles and talents and cater to it—and at the same time encourage the well-rounded development of all potential abilities.

In South African classrooms, however, in which more than 40 learners per class are not unusual, it may not be easy for teachers to notice individual learners' interests and abilities. Schools and the curriculum are driven by policies in terms of which learners are expected to become proficient in certain subject matter and then demonstrate their competency to be promoted to the next grade. The Curriculum and Assessment Policy Statements (CAPS) guides the South African education system, and teaching is conducted accordingly with little latitude for pursuing the vision of multiple intelligences and learning styles.

Contemporary teachers need to have up-to-date knowledge to create supportive learning conditions for all learners. Additionally, teachers are required to take cognisance of their individual learning styles and how these may influence their teaching. The ideal for classroom success is that teaching styles match the learning styles of today's learners. For example, teachers, who are usually 'digital immigrants' (or late-life technology users), tend to neglect using digital resources in their classes for the learners, who are 'digital natives' (or early-life technology users), and consequently run the risk of disengaging learners (Hicks, 2011). The misfit between teaching styles and learning styles may create teaching and learning gaps that give rise to frustration on both sides.

Teachers need to be aware of some of the layered circumstances of South African learners and their families:

- *Migrant learners:* The children of migrants or immigrants are often linguistically, culturally, and ethnically different from their South African counterparts. Socialisation and environmental experiences shape the way children learn and the impact of emotional well-being on learning process must be considered.
- *Schooling in rural conditions:* Large parts of South Africa are rural, and limited resources in rural schools are a common challenge for teachers,

parents, and the schooling community. Nonetheless, educational research in rural areas show that accessed resources and community support networks help to buffer against the impact of social issues (Ebersöhn & Ferreira, 2012).
- *The political climate of the country at any point in time:* Television and newspaper images depicting political instability, xenophobia, and unrest create anxiety and uncertainty among learners, especially when such conditions affect their parents and families. In such cases, successful teaching and learning are affected.

Regardless of the perpetuating narrative of challenges facing our schools and learners, there are examples of school-based interventions aimed at developing schools as safe havens that foster resilience and create 'enabling spaces' (Ebersöhn, 2016:1) for learning and development. Furthermore, there seems to be a combination of factors that one can consider (Dryden & Vos, 2005:375–359) to enhance teaching and learning:

- In the way that learners perceive information most easily;
- How learners organise and process information;
- How learners retrieve information; and
- The conditions that need to be met to help learners absorb, store, and retrieve information.

Teachers can incorporate multiple intelligences perspectives into the classroom. They can, for example, develop the study of a particular topic by applying different media and encouraging learners to express their understanding of the topic through different methods such as story or essay writing, 3D-model construction, music, dramatisation and role playing, and sculpting, drawing or painting. Such approaches could make it possible for learners to find ways of learning that are commensurate with their intelligence predispositions and therefore increase their motivation and encouragement in the learning process. Use of these approaches also increases the likelihood that each learner will gain new perspectives on the topic being discussed.

Conclusion

Teaching and learning dynamics in contemporary classrooms are as multifarious and nuanced as the characteristics of the teachers and learners who are challenged with the tasks of teaching and learning. While much of the focus of this chapter has been on classroom diversities encapsulated in different learning styles and multiple intelligences, it is necessary to remain mindful of the similarities in how children learn. Attention to individual differences among learners is essential, but it does not mean that common group characteristics should be neglected.

The latter may indeed carry the risk of stereotyping, but they remain part of teachers' array of instruments for reaching large numbers of learners. Embracing a wider application of learning styles and multiple intelligences theories to South African classrooms may be the way forward.

11 Simultaneous multisensory instruction to advance children's academic achievement

ANNELIZE DU PLESSIS

What lies behind us and what lies before us are tiny matters compared to what lies within us. (Ralph Waldo Emerson)

Introduction

Being passionate about teaching implies changing lives, building relationships and capacity, as well as nurturing in children's minds the 'art of possibility'. The teacher awakens creative possibility and silences the voice within that tells the child he/she cannot become who they were meant to be. In doing so, the teacher creates something out of nothing. Michelangelo once suggested that we each have a piece of marble with a beautiful statue inside. All we need is a hammer and chisel to get rid of the excess material that stands in the way of uncovering the real piece of art within. If we were to apply this visionary concept to our own teaching practices, we shall find ourselves busy chipping away all the barriers that prevent the awakening possibility within the child. Successful teaching is therefore not an expectation to live up to, but rather a possibility to *live into*—a stance that creates opportunities for transformation in both children and teachers (Zander & Zander, 2000).

In order for us as teachers to bring about change and awaken possibilities in children, we need to rethink the way we teach—we need to allow our teaching to be transformed, thus conceding to a total paradigm shift. Teachers often teach from a paradigm of downward spirals that suggest 'you must', 'you should' and 'you need to'; such an attitude is demoralising, competitive, pressured and always measured against something, thus a state of constant comparison. But what if we allow ourselves the opportunity to radiate possibility outwards—for instance the 'what ifs', 'how about', 'what are we looking for?' and 'what's next'? (Zander & Zander, 2000). Such an attitude will allow shared commitments and involvement, development, curiosity, creativity, contribution and open-heartedness. It will further enable us to create a vision full of passion and potential that will leave no child behind.

Challenges we have to face in the classroom

The overall poor academic performance of children in South African schools is well researched and reported on and it paints a grim picture. In South Africa there are children who, by the end of Grade 3, cannot yet read a single word. Furthermore, 58% of Grade 4 children are not properly taught how to read and write, despite having been in school for four years (Howie, Van Staden, Tshele, Dowse & Zimmerman, 2012). Besides the above issues, we also face the challenges of an inclusive education system where teachers now have to teach in such a way that they also teach children with special needs, such as attention deficit hyperactivity disorder, dyslexia, autism and many more (see also Chapters 29, 30, 31, 42 and 43).

All of the above may be considered impossible challenges, but if we radiate possibility and consciously allow ourselves to make a paradigm shift in the way we teach, these difficulties may well prove to be solvable and to be hurdles and problems that can be overcome (see Chapters 24 and 26).

There are many research reports that focus mainly on the so-called inabilities of children and why they cannot be taught successfully (see Chapter 29). Is this really true or should we seek answers elsewhere? Perhaps we should also investigate the teaching practices of teachers, which include the teaching methods and strategies that they use to teach reading and writing skills, for instance. Evidence-based teaching practices and prescriptions should be consulted to learn more about what it is that teachers should do in their classrooms to cope with the challenges experienced especially here in South Africa with our constantly evolving nature of schools and classrooms.

Some teachers seemingly do not know how to teach to address or satisfy the diverse learning needs of children. They lack the necessary knowledge and skills on how to design and present the curriculum in ways that meet the diverse needs of the children in their classrooms (see Chapter 31). Teachers tend to embark on a unisensory way of teaching (focusing on one or two senses only) or can even adopt a one-size-fits-all approach that expects children to adapt to a rigid curriculum. The latter approach to teaching could invariably leave some children behind. Hence, it is imperative that teachers should be properly trained to embrace a variety of teaching approaches and methods to support and acknowledge children's strengths, and to address their diverse learning needs (Townsend, 2007).

Why is simultaneous multisensory instruction important?

The Education White Paper 6 (Department of Education, 2001) clearly states that the education system, including teachers, should acknowledge the fact that any child has the right to learn and be supported to succeed academically. It further argues that teachers should change their attitude, behaviour and teaching methods to meet the diverse needs of our children, especially in the inclusive classroom. This is a direct call to change the current methodologies that may hinder our children to achieve academically, and as such the following questions are posed:

- If what we have done thus far caused the majority of children in South Africa to fail the mastering of basic academic skills, should we not seriously rethink the way we teach?
- What if we could open ourselves as teachers to different ways of thinking and teaching on how we could possibly meet the diverse needs of our children?

The good news is that there is evidence of approaches that have been utilised successfully to accommodate the diverse learning needs of children and that allows for active and collaborative (engaged) learning, as well as for a learner-centred rather than a teacher-centred approach (see Chapter 8). One such approach is simultaneous multisensory instruction (SMI). SMI challenges both teachers and children; it allows teaching and learning to be creative and active, extremely satisfactory and most enjoyable; and it engages all children in the learning process, thus keeping their attention and boosting achievement (An & Carr, 2017).

Advocates of the SMI proclaim that it increases children's engagement and overall achievement, as well as improves their attitude towards learning. Furthermore, a greater capacity for learning is generated and children seem to recall knowledge far more easily.

The significance of this approach is that it does not emphasise a specific learning style for a specific child. Simultaneous multisensory instruction is an eclectic approach that teaches all the children at once, regardless of their preferred perceptual modality (Farkus, 2003). Chances are that if SMI is properly planned and delivered in every lesson, no child might be excluded.

Many teachers tend to use a single technique to teach children the same information and in the same manner. Teaching is frequently presented through direct instruction, and the children are expected to learn mostly from listening and observing, which leaves them inactive and not part of the learning process. Thus, the majority of teaching methods utilised focus on unisensory teaching (visual or auditory) and therefore make inadequate provision for learners to use all their perceptual modalities (visual, auditory, tactile and kinaesthetic) to process information. Teachers must ensure that children see, say, hear and manipulate the things that they have to learn during the learning process, since we encode and represent any given information by using these five sensory-based modalities (Barsalou, 2008). The process known as simultaneous multisensory learning involves immediate, intensive and continuous interaction between what we see, hear and feel. Kinaesthetic (movement) and tactile (touch) stimulation are also harnessed in this type of learning (Borek & Thompson, 2003). (The reader should however not confuse perceptual modalities, through which information is sensed and processed, with Gardner's theory of multiple intelligences. The latter focuses more on how a child demonstrates ability (see also Chapter 10)).

If our senses are the way by which human beings gather information, why then do we limit learners during the learning process to use only two senses, ie, vision and hearing? Many children struggle to perceive information unless it is imported simultaneously through several sensory channels—a technique that helps learners to organise and retain what they have learned (Shams & Seitz, 2008). The more children are exposed to new information that was taught via all the senses, the stronger their ability to learn more easily and faster will be. They will also better retain the knowledge they gained and apply it more readily to future learning over a longer period of time (Mayer, 2014). Neuroscientists are of the opinion that if the neurons in the brain are 'fired together, they will wire together' (Sousa, 2006:1). This means that if we teach in such a way that we utilise all the senses at once and allow enough repetition of information, 'pathways' are formed in the brain. Neurons linking up with each other to create neural networks that allow the brain to store and retrieve information in the myelin much more effectively. Neurons convey information to one another by utilising a special signal. Some of these signals bring information to the brain from outside of one's body, such as the things we see, hear, touch and smell, while other signals convey instructions straight to the organs, glands and muscles (Dispenza, 2016).

As teachers, it is important to have a 'toolbox' ready with a variety of ways to present any given content to the children in our class, so as to improve their learning experiences. One of the tools in our toolbox should be to employ a variety of SMI methods that will address all the senses simultaneously in one lesson, for instance role play, dancing, rapping, making a collage, building models, debating, watching a video, making a presentation, doing group work and discussions, and using the playground. If a child cannot learn in the way we teach, we must remember to use the tool that requires us to be flexible enough to change our teaching to the way in which this child learns. We have the responsibility to provide children with multiple ways of accessing content so that their learning may be improved—even if it means teaching outside the classroom (Hattie, 2011).

Another tool for our toolbox is the inclusion of different activities that will address the diverse learning needs of children. Teachers may sometimes experience a kind of hopelessness due to not knowing how to reach some of the children in the classroom. Instead of giving up on them, why not present the content of the lesson in a completely different way, or why not provide them with new options? Before doing so, one obviously has to understand the kind of activities that are needed to present to all the senses. Activities such as listening to music, clapping and saying rhymes, body movement and tasting and touching enhance the processing of information through the senses (Fleming & Mills, 1992). The specific activities will naturally differ, depending on the subject taught.

Using the following resources may stimulate visual reasoning and learning: any text, handouts and pictures on paper, colourful posters, diagrams and flow charts, notes, films and video clips, flipcharts, computers, highlighted text. Children could also create art or images and be asked to draw to explain ideas. For auditory learning and listening, the teacher may use activities such as talking through ideas, peer explaining, debating, discussions, reading aloud, audio recordings, music and lectures. To enhance the children's tactile-kinaesthetic senses, one may consider hands-on activities such as touching of real letters or numbers, building with blocks such as Lego® and jigsaw puzzles, writing in the air, drawing in sand trays, using finger paints and modelling materials such as clay and sculpting materials, body movement such as clapping hands, rapping, role play and dancing, as well as building models and acting out processes, concepts and practical tasks. It is envisaged that all of the above activities may assist in the building of pathways in the brain to capture newly acquired information for future utilisation.

Against this background, one may ask who will benefit from SMI. The answer will be potentially almost each and every one—irrespective of whether a child has learning inabilities, learning disabilities or no barriers to learning, are children belonging to any race, gender, nationality or culture, and are children from any learning environment, whether a private school, public school or rural resource-constrained school. However, it is important to take cognisance of the fact that there might be children who are overresponsive to sensations of touch, movement, sight or sound, and who might suffer from epilepsy and autism too. In such instances, precaution should be taken not to traumatise or harm these children in any way since there might be an overstimulation of the senses. In such instances teachers should adapt the utilising of some activities through the senses. One example will be to focus more on visual activities for autistic learners rather than an overstimulation through touching and hearing. In cases where learners are suffering from tactile defensive disorder, teachers should avoid activities involving the touching of different materials such as sand paper.

Simultaneous multisensory instruction can also be used on a tertiary teaching level and during facilitation of the development of adult learners. Typical activities may include critical group discussions and debating, the building of models, poster presentations, YouTube clips and online e-learning activities such as wikis and discussion board activities as well as videos. These SMI activities will most definitely increase the learners' active engagement and meaningful deep learning of content which include critical thinking skills, problem solving skills and the creation and application of knowledge stimulating lifelong learning.

One may also ask if SMI can only be applied successfully when teaching a structured subject such as a language. The answer is no. Simultaneous multisensory instruction may be utilised in any subject including mathematics, science, geography, art, computer skills, business studies and many more. It is also applicable to any grade or level of schooling as well as on a tertiary level.

The major debates within the field of simultaneous multisensory instruction

The utilisation of SMI where senses are used to process and represent information are gaining ground. However, criticism has been raised pertaining to the application of SMI in classrooms which may include children with autism, epilepsy and sensory processing disorder as well as the possibility of not being sensitive enough in the application thereof, overseeing these children's needs. Both opponents and proponents validate their arguments and provide substantial evidence in support. Furthermore, it has become evident that researchers' understanding and interpretation of the terms 'learning styles' and 'perceptual modalities' differ from each other. Many researchers mistake learning preferences for learning styles. Based on the latter, there are four important issues that provoke criticism among academics:

1. The first issue of criticism pertaining to the utilisation of learning styles is that they describe and categorise behaviours rather than give an in-depth explanation of the developmental processes and causal mechanisms that underlie these behaviours.
2. The second issue is that learning style measures seem to rank one learning style higher or lower than the others, thus labelling the different teaching/learning styles.
3. The third point of criticism seems to be the lack of reliability and validity of the learning styles instruments.
4. Lastly, opponents of SMI doubt that academic achievement is a given when one adapts teaching methods and strategies to suit children's preferred modality of learning through which they process information.

How is simultaneous multisensory instruction relevant to South African schools and classrooms?

Many of the academic challenges that we are trying to meet in South Africa are related directly to elements of the human information processing system. The latter refers to aspects such as attention, perception and memory, which entail processes and operations such as the integration and retrieval of new information (see Chapter 14).

Simultaneous multisensory instruction is very relevant to South African schools and classrooms since it can easily be applied to any educational setting. It does not matter whether teaching occurs under a tree or in a classroom, whether it is in an inclusive classroom, in a school teaching children with learning disabilities, or in a resource-constrained school (of which there are many, especially in rural areas).

One example where SMI has been successfully used in our local educational context is the Venter Multisensory Reading Programme (VMRP). It was implemented in four resource-constrained schools in South Africa for a short period of time. The programme had a significant effect on the literacy skills of children in Grade 3—of whom some were 14 years old and could not read a word—but they were granted the opportunity to successfully obtain literacy skills via the VMRP (Venter, 2007). The programme has also been used with great success in private practice over a period of more than 17 years, where pre-schoolers among others were taught how to read and write.

Conclusion

Albert Einstein once referred to learning as an experience, and stated that everything else is just information. In order for the learning process to be an experience, one needs to see, hear, feel, touch and taste to perceive and process information. The more of our senses we simultaneously utilise, the more successful our learning process will be. Human beings learn through all of their senses. They also learn by doing. Combinations of seeing, hearing, smelling, tasting, touching and doing can enhance their opportunities for optimal learning. Teachers can experiment with SMI in the classroom, reflect on their own and the learners' experiences, and adapt the way in which they create learning environments in creative ways.

# Indigenous stories and games as approaches to teaching within the classroom

Patrick Mweli

Language, any language, has a dual character: it is both a means of communication and a carrier of culture. (Ngũgĩ wa Thiong'o)

Introduction

This chapter deliberates on indigenous stories and games as approaches to teaching within the classroom. Addressing diversity within the classroom is crucial in promoting inclusive education. Indigenous games and stories bring an element of educational activity where learners from different cultures learn and understand each other's values and belief systems. In the process, they develop a sense of tolerance and unity and healthy living together. Further, core competencies learnt through indigenous stories and games cut across all cultures. Moreover, this section describes briefly what indigenous knowledge systems are and highlights the centrality of indigenous languages in storytelling and games within the context of Africa, more particularly the South African context, and present one indigenous story *Inganekwane* as an example and how it can be used to teach in the classroom. The section presents one indigenous game and how it can be an asset in teaching within the classroom.

Finally, it discusses the implications of using indigenous stories and games within the South African classroom. These implications relate to indigenous children in South African schools. In the context of this chapter, indigenous children refer to children who come from families with an existing wealth of knowledge such as folktales, games and stories, culture and belief systems. These children are often 'vulnerable, marginalised and left behind as the result of disparities linked to poverty, gender, ethnicity, and language' (UNESCO, 2010). They come from communities that occupy a particular geographic area sharing the same history, culture, wealth of knowledge and belief systems (Dondolo, 2005). In this sense, the classroom is a conglomeration of diverse cultures and prosperity of knowledge. Teachers teaching in this classroom should tap into this wealth of knowledge by using culturally relevant educational strategies. Indigenous stories and games are part of the cultural richness inherent in indigenous communities.

Description of indigenous knowledge systems

There is no umbrella definition for indigenous knowledge systems. Indigenous knowledge is defined and understood relative to its context and perspective. For the purpose of this chapter, indigenous knowledge is defined as comprehensive knowledge that covers technologies and practices that have been and are still used by indigenous and local people for existence, survival, and adaptation in a variety of environments (Mosimege & Onwu, 2004). Internationally, within a Western context, indigenous knowledge has often been associated with the notion of primitive, the wild and the natural (Semali & Kincheloe, 2011) in favour of western knowledge systems as the 'authentic' sciences and ways of knowing. For example, Loubser (2005) elaborated that the term 'indigenous' is understood by most Europeans as a synonym of 'African,' 'black,' 'aboriginal,' 'traditional,' and 'native American.' In Africa and nationally in South Africa, the phrase 'indigenous' refers to a specific group of people occupying a particular geographic area sharing the same culture, knowledge and belief systems (Dondolo, 2005; Masonga, 2005).

In this regard, indigenous knowledge systems incorporate rich knowledge and skills that have been treasured and used by indigenous people for many years. Further, indigenous knowledge systems are 'the knowledge' embedded in cultures and used by individuals to construct their worlds and sustain their living. These knowledge systems have been passed on from generation to generation by word of mouth, and by demonstration, observations and implementing the skills learnt in real-life situations. Hence, the latter is of paramount importance in educating indigenous children within the classroom, as it incorporates the ways of knowing (epistemologies) of indigenous people. 'Indigenous', in this case, refers to belonging to an indigenous community, occupying a particular geographic area, sharing the same language, culture, ethnicity, and history. More particularly, South Africa is a multilingual and multicultural society with a wealth of knowledge to tap into to boost students' academic achievement. Language, storytelling, original games and folk songs are some of the most relevant indigenous practices for teaching and learning within the classroom. In a diverse South Africa, 'indigenous knowledge' accounts for multiple indigenous knowledge systems which are emanating from a broad spectrum of indigenous people.

Indigenous languages as cultural artifacts

Research across the globe and in Africa (Alidou & Brock-Utne, 2006; Fakaye & Sonyika, 2009; Skutnabb-Kangas & Dunbar, 2010) indicate that indigenous language is becoming more important in education. Mother tongue instruction promotes educational success (Nyika, 2015), and in a country such as Tanzania, they use Swahili as a medium of teaching everywhere. In this sense, it is imperative to understand what language is and how it is used in society and within the classroom during the learning and teaching process.

Language is a system of representation that enables us to encode and convey meaning through a combination of signs (Christy, 2013). Words (symbols) have no meaning by themselves unless they are attached to the shared values and cultures. Hence, what exists in any particular society is represented in one's cognitive domain as mental concepts. Mental concepts are meaningful within a shared language. For instance, when the group shares the same language, this means they share the same mental concepts and, by understanding a particular language, access to mental concepts (Ghassemzadeh, 2005) is gained. For example, the word 'table' is meaningless without its mental concept, characteristics and the manner it is used by members of the society. In other words, a 'complete table' is the combination of the physical object and the shared meanings attached to it by society.

Effective learning and teaching of indigenous children are likely to take place if their education is culturally connected and uses indigenous languages as the language of learning and teaching. Learners construct knowledge through encoding and decoding information; interactions and communication with knowledgeable others within the classroom. Language, in this case, is a social tool that connects societal meanings with higher mental functions of the learner and promotes deep learning. Furthermore, the use of indigenous languages taps into the ways of knowing, belief systems and cultures of indigenous children and optimise learners' understanding of the concepts and increase meaningful participation in academic activities within the classroom. Storytelling and original games are part of the most relevant indigenous activities that can be used effectively to promote interest and active participation of learners in learning activities.

Indigenous stories as an approach to teaching in the classroom

Historically, within the African context, knowledge has been passed on from one generation to the other orally. Legends and folklore have been traditionally used to teach children skills and appropriate behaviour. Magliocco (2010) concurs that there is a correlation between language, culture, and identity. Hence, culture and identity are part and parcel of the language that is used to tell stories. The incorporation of storytelling within classroom learning and teaching is of great importance and an asset to promote deep learning and high academic achievement. For example, the use of riddles as brain teasers have the potential of engaging young minds to higher levels of thinking (Banda & Morgan, 2013). Learners through the use of folklore and oral narrative can identify themselves and make sense of the academic subject content. It is important to note that indigenous children in olden days normally gathered around the fire to listen to stories that were told by elders. The reason for telling stories was to equip youngsters with skills needed to survive and to sustain their lives within their environment. Furthermore, it is crucial to explore how original stories can be used effectively to teach in the current classroom for example, *Izinganekwane* (isiZulu) legends and folktales. To illustrate, here is one fireside story as a case study.

CASE STUDY

Story: *Izinganekwane* (isiZulu)

Yazilaya imbila (The rock badger (dassie) learns the hard way)

Kwasukasukela (isiZulu) (Once upon a time (English))

Cosi (Little by little)

In the ancient times, all the animals were without tails. Dogs had no tails, cats had no tails, and horses had no tails, and oxen, donkeys, pigs, hares, lions, elephants, had no tails. All domestic and wild animals had no tails. The creator looked at the animals and realised that they did not look nice. He then made many tails. He made long ones and short ones; big ones and small ones. When he had finished, he sent out a proclamation that all the animals should come and fetch their tails. The horse set off. When he arrived he admired the tails: he liked the bushy one and chose it. He thought it would help him chase the flies away. He took it and fixed it on; as soon as a fly would come, up sprang a lash. The horse was extremely happy. The pig set off too. He saw a little curly tail and liked it. He thought a big tail would be too cumbersome and warm, while he wanted to feel cool. All the animals set off to go and fetch their tails. Their path passed by the home of the rock badger (dassie). Now, the rock badger was very lazy: he just liked to sit on the rocks basking in the sun.

> He saw the hare coming and called out to him: 'Hallo cousin!' 'Yes, Hello cousin!' answered the hare. The rock badger went on: 'You must help me cousin!' and he sobbed as if crying. The hare replied: 'How should I help you, cousin? Why do you weep?' 'It is my child,' answered the rock badger. 'He is not well. Last night I did not sleep at all, I have not slept a wink. I do not know sleep: I am just sitting. I cannot fetch my tail. Do help me, my cousin: bring one for me, please!' The rock badger was lying: his child was not sick at all'. I hope your baby gets better!' and the hare went off.
>
> There appeared the donkey. It was walking and plucking grass at the same time. The rock badger reflected that perhaps his cousin the hare might forget: it would be better to also ask the donkey. He stopped the donkey saying: 'Hallo, uncle Big Ears.' Moreover, again he sobbed as if he was crying. The donkey answered: 'Hallo, child of my sister. What is wrong with you that you are crying?' The rock badger repeated the same story he told the hare. All the animals went by, and the dassie was giving them the message to bring one tail for him because he is unable to go. All the animals came back with their tails, and the rock badger was admiring the beauty of their tails. When the hare came back, the rock badger said, 'Your tail is very nice. You must be pleased. The rock badger started feeling apprehensive at not seeing his tail. Said the hare: 'It is nice indeed, cousin. I am glad you like it. Yours too is coming, cousin. It is very nice. It is coming with your uncle the hyena.' The hare went off. All the animals came back with their tails. The rock badger was appreciating them, and the animals were telling the rock badger that yours is coming with so and so until the last animal appeared. The rock badger was now disheartened, he was shaking with apprehension. 'Hallo, Shaky One!' said the rock badger, greeting the chameleon. 'Yes, hello, you Giver of Commissions,' answered the chameleon, laughing. The rock badger was deeply upset and said: 'To whom are you saying that? Where is my tail? They said it was coming with you.' The chameleon said laughing: 'Sorry, not a single tail is left. The pig took even the smallest one.' The rock badger was deeply disappointed. In his sorrow he went into the cave, his heart was heavy with grief. He realised that giving messages had been his downfall. He wished he had gone himself, like the other animals, to fetch his tail. This is why the rock badger has no tail.
>
> *Cosu cosu iyaphela!* (little by little it has come to an end)
> *Siyayibonga! Yamnandi!* (Thank you for it. What a nice story)

Source: Canonici, 1993:3–5

The lesson of the story is 'do not procrastinate, be diligent and do things yourself to achieve the desired outcomes that you can be proud of'. In this case, the rock badger was lazy and persistently asking other animals to bring him a tail. The symbolism of all animals returning home with their tails indicated that those who toil and labour in time would sing when they reap the fruits of their labour. However, the badger without a tail was embarrassed, ashamed and was forced to hide under rocks and resided there for the rest of his life.

This story can, for example, be used to teach Life skills and Literacy in the classroom. There are many more stories like this example. When telling the story, the teacher can ask the learners to sit in a circle to simulate sitting around the fire. While listening to the story, the learners will empathise with the characters in the story. They may feel like they are part of the events in the story, thereby engaging their higher mental activities and internalising (Wertsch, 2007) the appropriate behaviour that is being taught through the story.

Using stories in teaching literacy could develop various skills including attention skills, remembering, listening skills, voice control, and correct use of the language, creativity, and imagination skills. When the teacher tells a story to develop listening skills (while retelling the story and debating issues related to the story), the learners also develop thinking and oral language proficiency. The teachers can also develop writing skills by asking the learners to write down how they feel about certain characters in the story. In this manner, learners also learn discerning expertise and a sense of appreciation while identifying with the values imparted in the story.

Indigenous games in classroom teaching

Games play a significant role in the socialisation of children (Potgieter & Malan, 1987). Several researchers (Honeyford & Boyd, 2015; Martlew, Stephen & Ellis, 2011) have documented the significant role of learning through play for children especially in the lower grades. Games can be adapted to suit a variety of social, cognitive and affective needs of children. For example, the *masekitlane* game has been successfully used as a therapeutic tool (Dipale, 2013). In the African context, indigenous games are symbolic representations of cultural expression from a specific society and children are bearers of cultural expression through these games (Burnette & Sierra, 2003). However, the school curriculum in many African countries and more specifically in South Africa has been dominated by Eurocentric knowledge, and most of the games used for learning and teaching also followed suit. Indigenous games were marginalised and resulted in a devastating effect on indigenous cultures and knowledge. Effective education and learning could be facilitated, transmitted and expressed through these games. The incorporation of indigenous games into learning and teaching in the classroom could be a great asset in the development of self-confidence, identity and in accelerating active participation, healthy living and higher academic achievement of indigenous children in most school subjects especially Mathematics and Physical Education. The following case study illustrates one indigenous isiZulu game that can be useful in classroom teaching.

> **CASE STUDY**
>
> **Game: *Amagende***
>
> This game is played in pairs, mostly by girls. To play the game, you need small stones (called *amagende*). The number depends on how many *amagende* the players can manage to pull and push.
>
> The players need to draw a circle on the ground called *isibaya* (kraal). *Amagende* are placed inside the *isibaya*. Each player will have her special stone called *ingede*, which she holds in her hand and will use during the game. The game is played as follows: the first player starts by throwing her *ingede* in the air and simultaneously grabbing a handful of *amagende* out of the *isibaya*. She then needs to catch the *ingede* as it falls back down. The player then throws the *ingede* in the air again while pushing the *amagende* back into the *isibaya* (at the same time), but making sure she leaves one outside the *isibaya*. The one left outside now belongs to her. The same process continues until the first player collects all the *amagende*. If the *ingede* falls on the ground, the player is out and has to give the next player a chance. When the second player completed taking out *amagende* one by one, the game continues with two, three, and four, and so on.

This game develops many skills such as hand–eye coordination, concentration, balancing, measurement, counting, accuracy, cooperation, observation, and competitiveness. These skills are essential for learners' holistic development especially in the early years of development. More particularly, the game develops children's mental strengths and facilitates their thinking processes. Teachers can use this game in any subject to reinforce the skills mentioned above. For example, in Mathematics, it can be used to teach counting (in ones, twos, threes and so forth). An innovative teacher can use a poster and draw *isibaya* and use plastic bottle lids as *amagende* and *ingede* and orally give instruction on how to play the game. Finally allowing the learner to explore the game and develop skills through play. Learners encounter the world at an experiential level through play. In the play, children confirm their existence and affirm their worth (Kekae-Moletsane, 2008).

The implication of using indigenous stories and games to teach within South African schools and classrooms

Most African countries inherited Eurocentric education systems through colonialisation. More particularly in the South African context, education emerged predominantly from missionary, colonial and Afrikaner ideology (Gelderblom, 2003), with the inadvertent consequence that indigenous children had to approach and learn new concepts from a worldview other than their own. Therefore it became challenging for most indigenous children to acquire new concepts, think abstractly and engage meaningfully in the learning process. The latter is likely to hinder epistemological access to the curriculum and knowledge production for these learners (Morrow, 2009). The use of indigenous stories and games in the learning process has the potential to align learners' cultures, epistemology, values and belief systems with the knowledge imparted in a Eurocentric manner within the classroom (Henslin, 1997). It can also provide prominence to new ways of knowing and learning.

Conclusion

Indigenous stories and games are vital in the education of indigenous children and can be used to develop key skills and knowledge during teaching and learning. One of the critical aspects of storytelling and games is the use of language; considering language is a gateway to cognition (Vandeyar & Killen, 2006). The use of indigenous languages during storytelling and in playing indigenous games connects children with the cultures, values and belief systems held by their communities. Further, they promote critical thinking skills, physical development, healthy living and command of the language.

13 Whole child development through formal teaching and learning

TREVOR MOODLEY & COLLEEN GAIL MOODLEY

Education means all-round drawing out of the best in child and man—body, mind, and spirit. (Mahatma Gandhi)

Introduction

Education happens throughout life, both formally and informally. It is also clear that education in the form of formal schooling has increasingly been the focus of attention in many countries. There is almost unanimous agreement all around the world about the importance of education in preventing and addressing many of the problems faced by contemporary societies. There are, however, divergent views about what it means to educate a child. So what do we mean when we claim that we are educating a child? One possible response is that (formal) education prepares the child for the future. For most children it is anticipated that the future will entail living in an increasingly globalised and diverse world with a growing world population, and competing for limited resources and work opportunities. This chapter focuses on the formal education received at school with the aim of making teachers aware of their role in developing the 'whole' child. The chapter therefore sheds some light on a form of education known as holistic education.

What is holistic education?

There are various conceptions of holistic education since it has different meanings for the various proponents of this approach. We will explicate a few ideas of different scholars that together contribute to the paradigm of holistic education. For example, Rudge (2016:170) states that holistic education 'incorporates principles of spirituality, wholeness, and interconnectedness along with those of freedom, autonomy, and democracy'. The purpose of holistic education is the nurturing of the development of the whole person in relation to the physical, social, emotional, intellectual, and spiritual domains (Miller, 2005:2). Miller (2000) defines holistic education as a 'philosophy of education based on the premise that each person finds identity, meaning, and purpose in life through connections to the community, to the natural world, and to humanitarian values such as compassion and peace'. Nakagawa (2000) and Forbes (2003) maintain that the ultimate aim of holistic education is transforming the self.

The origins of holistic education are found in the educational practices of indigenous societies (Arrows & Miller, 2012:45). Similar to indigenous world views, holistic education emphasises respect for nature, the interconnectedness of people to nature and the universe and the spiritual aspect of human beings (Mahmoudi, Jafari, Nasrabadi & Liaghatdar, 2012).

The philosophy and principles of holistic education are reflected (to a greater or lesser extent) in the pedagogical practices of different alternative (to mainstream) formal schooling systems such as Montessori, Waldorf/Steiner, Krishnamurti, Democratic/free, Quaker/friends and Reggio Emilia schooling systems (Rudge, 2008). Montessori schools focus on the development of the whole child by nurturing the physical, mental and spiritual qualities of the child (Miller, 1997:160). Waldorf schools emphasise the importance of nurturing the spiritual and creative aspects as a means of developing other aspects of the child. Krishnamurti schools emphasise that education should lead to the freeing of the mind and self-discovery. They also emphasise the importance of nurturing inquiry and critical thinking in learners. Democratic/free schools as well as Open schools emphasise democracy, autonomy and independence as well as the freedom of learners to make choices about their learning. Quaker schools are known for their spiritual and humanistic orientations, but also reflect other characteristics of holistic education such as respect and cooperation. Reggio Emilia schools emphasise most of the holistic education principles except for spirituality since these schools subscribe to a social constructivist view of human identity (Rudge, 2008). Transdisciplinary and/or interdisciplinary approaches to teaching and learning are characteristic to some of these schools (Rudge, 2008).

Holistic education is utilised worldwide. Japanese holistic teachers, for instance, believe that a teacher's main responsibility is to help children to grow as human beings so that they are able to think for themselves and treat others with fairness and kindness. Japanese schools focus on holistically integrating activities such as mindfulness, respect, kindness and oneness with nature, into the curriculum. Children are taught to respect each other, nature and the world by caring for animals, plants and trees (Miller, 2007). Holistic education can be seen as part of a process of reclaiming the ancient vision of wholeness (Miller, 2006).

Education is important for the integration of separate entities. Bhardwaj (2016) found that the Indian education system is in dire need of developing learners holistically. He found that the formal education system develops the child's physical and mental capacities, which are important to produce professionals such as teachers, doctors, and engineers. However, the formal education system does not always focus on developing character. He advises that a value-based education system be adopted which develops the child through three aspects: physically, mentally and through improving character, as a means of developing a holistic student and a well-rounded human being. Physical and mental strengths are considered important but can be vices without character. Value-based education is perceived as instilling character, humility, honesty, strength, spirituality, morality and integrity in an individual. It therefore develops better citizens, people with high ethical values, who are willing to cooperate with others and enjoy a happier life while improving the lives of others (Bhardwaj, 2016).

Holistic learning environments are intentionally structured to:
- Address the educational needs of individual learners;
- Promote positive relationships; and
- Nurture social, physical, emotional and creative development, while promoting academic success among learners.

This approach emphasises the application of what is being learnt to real-life situations, such as applying knowledge about economics to solving ecological problems (Badjanova & Iliškon, 2015).

Different scholars of holistic education have identified different sets of principles representing holistic education. One set of ten principles or goals of holistic education was outlined by the leaders in the field at a conference in 1991 by Global Alliance of Transforming Education (Global Alliance of Transforming Education (GATE), 1991). These principles provide information about what holistic education entails, its components and how these components relate to education, schools and the curriculum. These components are:

1. Educating for human development: Education should develop the human as a whole and instil and develop human values such as honesty, love, cooperation, peace and equality.
2. Honouring learners as individuals: Each learner should be accepted as valuable and unique, considering their strengths and different learning styles.

3. The central role of experience: Education should provide a perfect environment for learners to experience life and the natural world.
4. Holistic education: All educational institutions including educational policies should consider wholeness as part of the educational process.
5. New role of teachers: Teacher training programmes should consider the new roles required for teachers and encourage awareness, inner growth and creativity in their programmes.
6. Freedom of choice: Throughout the education and learning process, individuals should be able to exercise their own choice.
7. Educating for a participatory democracy: Education provided, should be democratic enough to include all citizens in various ways and from different races, cultures and communities.
8. Educating for global citizenship: Every person should be educated to be a global citizen.
9. Educating for earth literacy: Education should have respect for life at its basis and promote literacy where individuals are able to identify their roles and responsibilities.
10. Spirituality and education: Education should support the development of a healthy spiritual life. Individuals should be recognised as spiritual beings able to express themselves through their knowledge, skills, talents, etc.

A succinct summary of the content of holistic education is offered by Badjanova and Iliškon (2014:23) who identified the following content considerations:

(1) interrelatedness, interaction, cohesion and integration; (2) biological, physical, ecological, spiritual, social, moral, aesthetic, intellectual and other aspects of human life and personality development; (3) conscious inclusion in education of knowledge, insights and perspectives from other disciplines; (4) development of the learner as a whole and their active participation in the global community; (5) critical perspective on dominant worldviews and practices within an alternative educational paradigm.

One could conclude that the diverse conceptions of holistic education are integrally connected by its primary aim, which is to develop the whole child. This aim embraces the fact that 'whole' might have multiple interpretations by different holistic education scholars.

The relevance of holistic education

Different aspects of holistic education resonate with well-known theories of learning and development such as Vygotsky's sociocultural theory which emphasises the role of culture and society in providing the contexts that learning begins in (see also Chapters 8 and 16). Similar to holistic education goals, Feuerstein's theory of mediated learning experiences also highlights the importance of social interaction and importance of bridging knowledge learnt to other contexts. Like Erikson's theory of psychosocial development, holistic education also considers how both academic as well as non-academic experiences influence personality development. Bronfenbrenner's ecological systems theory resonates with holistic education considerations by highlighting the different factors (interacting systems, people, processes, contexts and time) that influence human development and learning. Gardner's theory of multiple intelligences is reflected in the holistic education principle of considering individual learner characteristics (see Chapter 10). The focus of holistic education on 'whole child' development thus incorporates the consensus among child development scholars that the different developmental domains (cognitive, physical, social and emotional) are interrelated and development in one domain affects the development in other domains. We are also aware of the influence that quality early childhood education plays in mitigating potentially adverse factors such as impoverished (non-stimulating) home backgrounds. Research also indicates that brain development in young children is negatively affected by maltreatment and overwhelming stress experiences (De Bellis, Keshavan, Clark, Casey, Giedd, Boring, Frustaci & Ryan, 1999). To summarise, holistic approaches recognise learners' social contexts and how these influence learning.

Holistic education is especially important since society is constantly changing and we require an education system to adapt accordingly. For example, employers now stress that apart from academic acumen (as was the main requirement for jobseekers in the past); individuals entering the workplace should also possess certain essential non-cognitive skills such as: professionalism, work ethic, critical thinking and problem-solving skills, collaboration and teamwork skills, and oral communication skills (Garcia, 2014). In fact, beyond the workplace, these skills are also essential for the effective functioning of a society. However, it is concerning that development of these non-cognitive skills is largely neglected in current formal education systems (Oberle, Domitrovich, Duncan, Meyers & Weissberg, 2016).

Research has also established the positive influence of social and emotional learning (SEL) on academic outcomes. Durlak, Dymnicki, Taylor, Weissberg and Schellinger (2011) found that learners receiving SEL programmes together with the regular classroom curriculum achieved higher academic outcomes in comparison to those who had not received additional SEL in their classrooms. Furthermore, in the school context, there is a reciprocal relationship between early achievement of academic success and later success with social emotional skills (Welsh, Parke, Widaman & Neil, 2001).

Non-cognitive skills assist individuals to live fulfilling lives, including their involvement as family members, and being good neighbours and responsible citizens. Furthermore, non-cognitive skills promote trust and increase the likelihood that individuals will participate in democratic voting while decreasing the likelihood of divorce (Heckman, Humphries, Urzua & Veramendi, 2011). These skills also correlate with improved life satisfaction (Hofmann, Luhmann, Fisher, Vohs & Baumeister, 2014).

The relevance of a holistic education approach to South African schools and classrooms

It is common knowledge that the South African basic education system (pre-tertiary education) has been found wanting by international indicators measuring numeracy and literacy skills. Though there has been improvement, South Africa falls below international mathematics and literacy standards as respectively measured through the International Association for the Evaluation of Educational Achievement's (IEA) Trends in International Mathematics and Science Study (TIMSS) 2015 results and the Progress in International Reading Literacy Study (PIRLS) 2011 results (Mullis, Martin, Foy & Drucke, 2012). The annual national assessments (ANAs) conducted by the South African Department of Basic Education also indicate low performances in Mathematics and Literacy. This situation exacerbates the skills shortages within the South African workforce because many learners complete formal schooling without the requisite matric subjects (Mathematics and Physical Science) to pursue tertiary studies in scarce-skills fields such as the mathematics and science fields, thereby not addressing the skills shortages in the country. This is a worrying prospect given the high unemployment rates and widespread poverty in the country.

Consequently, there has been an intense response to address poor literacy and numeracy rates by the South African Government including the revision of the Basic Education Curriculum from Outcomes-Based Education to the Curriculum, Assessment and Policy Statements (CAPS) (Department of Basic Education, 2012). Unfortunately, the focus on the literacy and numeracy fields seems to be an over-compensation for the problems in our education system. Consequently the current education focus may be criticised as narrow and an impoverished attempt at educating children. This situation is worse for the many South African learners who come from impoverished communities to schools that offer impoverished education. Many traditional 'non-cognitive' subjects such as Art, Music, Health Education, Guidance and Physical Education have been grouped together under the banner of the subject, Life Skills or Life Orientation.

With the rapid changes occurring in South African society, Life Orientation (LO) is viewed as a suitable means to prepare learners for making informed choices, taking suitable actions to achieve success and meaning in life (Department of Basic Education, 2011:9; Theron & Dalzell, 2006). Post-apartheid South African education policy statements consider environmental and social concerns as extremely important. The National Curriculum Statement Grades R-12 (NCS) includes in its aims the need to address these environmental and social concerns (DBE, 2011). Suitably skilled teachers are required to provide knowledge, skills and values embedded in the environment to adequately prepare learners to become more environmentally aware, responsible and competent individuals (Nsubuga, 2011:106).

However, both learners and teachers responsible for LO, have in the past and currently not accepted the subject well. Teachers find difficulty in providing learners with suitable life skills knowledge, attitudes and values to deal with real-life situations. Jacobs (2011) found that learners' enthusiasm for LO was reduced because of their teachers' poor attitudes towards the subject. Teachers are often ill-equipped to teach LO content because they lacked appropriate epistemology and skills (Van Deventer, 2009; Christiaans, 2006; Rooth, 2005). Life Orientation therefore enjoys a 'Cinderella' status currently and as a stand-alone subject, it does not seem to be making the impact that is required to address the many social challenges faced in society.

A holistic education approach in our education system has the potential to balance the economic imperatives with the social requirements of our society—a society which was built on a violent historical context and still experiences high crime rates, high rates of violence, and many forms of discrimination. The focus of this approach is to develop in learners the 'social glue' required for the country to succeed at nation-building, respecting democratic principles and the promotion of equity and equality.

When analysing our country's context from a holistic education perspective, it is important and appropriate that the South African basic education curriculum includes social and emotional learning (SEL) given the high rates of school violence, sexual abuse, rape, pregnancy rates, dropout rates, poverty, and poor academic performance. South African children also experience high rates of physical and sexual abuse, neglect and rejection which impacts on mental health causing stress, depression and post-traumatic stress (Centre for Justice and Crime Prevention [CJCP], 2015). This in turn, results in behaviours such as: disengagement, defiance, violence and disruption in schools, leading to poor academic achievement (Roffey, 2016). Durlak et al's (2011) meta-analysis provides evidence that the teaching of social and emotional skills through SEL can have a direct positive influence on mental health, pro-social behaviour and academic outcomes. However, a school's cultural context should be taken into account when implementing SEL (Roffey & McCarthy, 2013). Researchers have found that schools that are most effective at promoting mental well-being and positive behaviour include the following basic principles in their daily practices: positive relationships, community connection, high expectations, and social and emotional learning (SEL) which in turn promote resiliency (Noble, McGrath, Roffey & Rowling, 2008).

The inclusive education policy, as espoused by Education White Paper 6 (Department of Education, 2001) has had challenges of implementation (see Chapter 30). Perhaps a holistic approach, with its focus on individual learner needs within a systemic context of living, learning and interacting, may strengthen the implementation of inclusive education in South Africa. Its philosophy of whole child development resonates with the aims of inclusive education to provide learners with the skills and knowledge that minimise and/or prevent barriers to learning, both academic and non-academic.

Conclusion

A holistic approach to education compels the different role players in formal education to reflect on what it means to be educated. It addresses the complexity of teaching and learning by highlighting different but not necessarily competing educational considerations for the learner as an individual whole being but also as a member of society (see Chapter 25). Holistic education offers the opportunity to design formal education systems that promote much more than skilled individuals that satisfy economic demands (though also important). It encourages richer forms of education with the promise of fuller human experiences for both the individual and society.

Cognition

14 Cognition in the world of action

BRUCE BROWN

I think, therefore I am. (René Descartes)

Introduction

Have you ever thought, on a lovely summer day, how wonderful it would be to be a sunflower? To stand in one place, enjoy what the day brings and just turn your face to follow the sun. Not to think, just to be …

So why do we need to think? Because we are not flowers. We are animals, with bodies that move in complex ways. And if we use our bodies well, we can take advantage of the possibilities that the world offers. To do this, we need to be able to regulate and coordinate our movements. So that all the different parts of the body work together—the core, legs, arms, feet, hands and faces. If we do this well, we can place ourselves in a good space in the world and do things there that will be good for us. We act to coordinate ourselves with the world, changing it for ourselves where we can and to adapting to the world when it moves us. To regulate ourselves in all this complexity requires a powerful controller—this is the brain, one of the most complex structures in the universe.

Let's look in a bit more detail at what we are talking about. But first, we must decide where to start looking—at the world, the body, the brain? Luckily, it doesn't matter where we start, because if we follow the effects, we will pass through every part of this system and come right back to the start.

So, let's start with the brain (Society for Neuroscience, 2012). It is generally accepted that the thoughts we are aware of involve some coordinated pattern of firing of the neurons in the brain. This pattern of firing will activate many other neurons because of the particular connections between the neurons in the brain at that specific time. If we think to make some action happen, then this thinking will activate some specific motor neurons and these will cause some muscles to contract, which will move the body in some way. This movement of the body will impact on the world in some way—either physically, by pushing against something in the world, or socially, when another person notices the movement (often both). But the act doesn't stop there, because the world usually pushes back: physically, for each physical influence, and socially, through the response or non-response of the other, for each social influence. These changes in the world result in a changed effect on our senses. That is, we sense this change in the world. If we are paying attention, then we perceive that change and this changes our thinking in some way. This makes a 'causal loop', as shown in Figure 14.1. A cycle of cause and effect, where any change in one part of the system spreads through all the other parts and eventually returns in some way to influence itself. We see from this loop that we think in order to activate and regulate our actions in the world and also that our actions and the activity of the world influences our thinking.

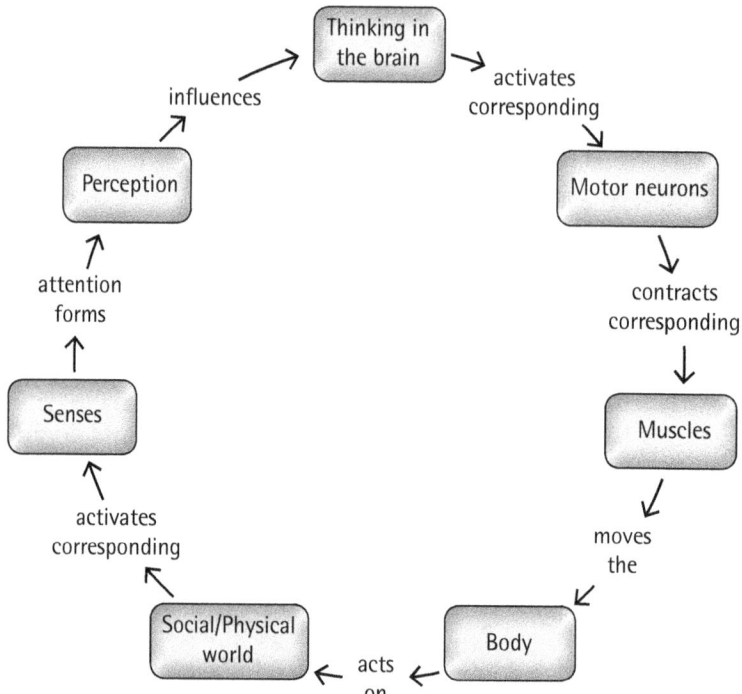

FIGURE 14.1 Loop of cause and effect relating thinking and action

Why is it important to link cognition and action?

If we wish to understand people, we need to understand their thinking (cognition) and their actions. To understand our actions, we need to understand the thinking that initiates and regulates these actions, and to understand our thinking, we need to understand our actions within the activity of the world, which influence this thinking.

If we leave out any of the parts of the loop, we will get an incomplete picture. What is more, we will miss the powerful effect of feedback, as the influence of each part returns (moderated by the other parts) to influence itself. If we cut the loop at any part, we will get a linear chain of cause and effect and it will be easy to see the first part of this chain as causing everything else. Two of the many ways of doing this are shown in Figure 14.2.

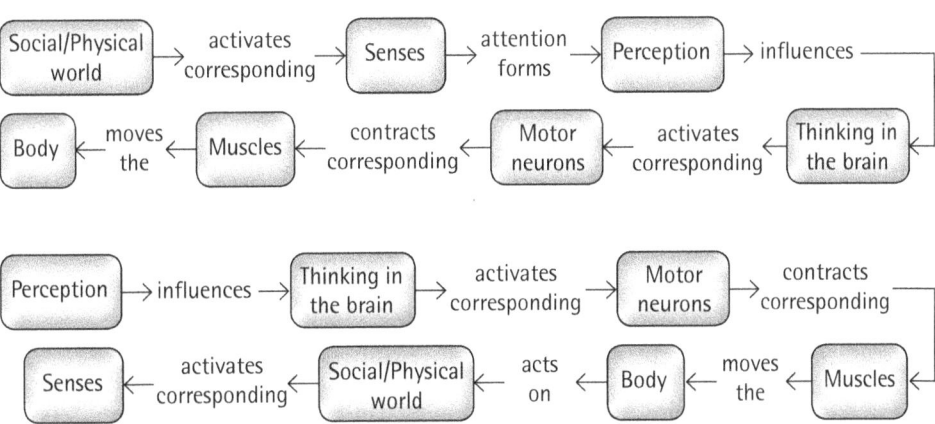

FIGURE 14.2 Two different linear chains from the same causal loop

In these linear chains, the influence of the first part is shown to spread through the chain to all the others. But if we stop there, we will get a biased understanding from this incomplete picture because we will miss the way the influence of all the other parts loops back to influence the first part. Cutting the loop in this way is useful for analysing each part—to clearly understand the influence of that part on the others. But once we have analysed each part, we need to put all these pieces together—carry out a synthesis—so that we build a full understanding of how all these influences work together. In this section, we will briefly analyse some of the important components of cognition (Atkinson & Shiffrin, 1968) and also provide some ideas of how each component fits in the loop of thinking in action. We will look at the four major components: working memory, long-term memory, perception and attention.

Understanding educational psychology

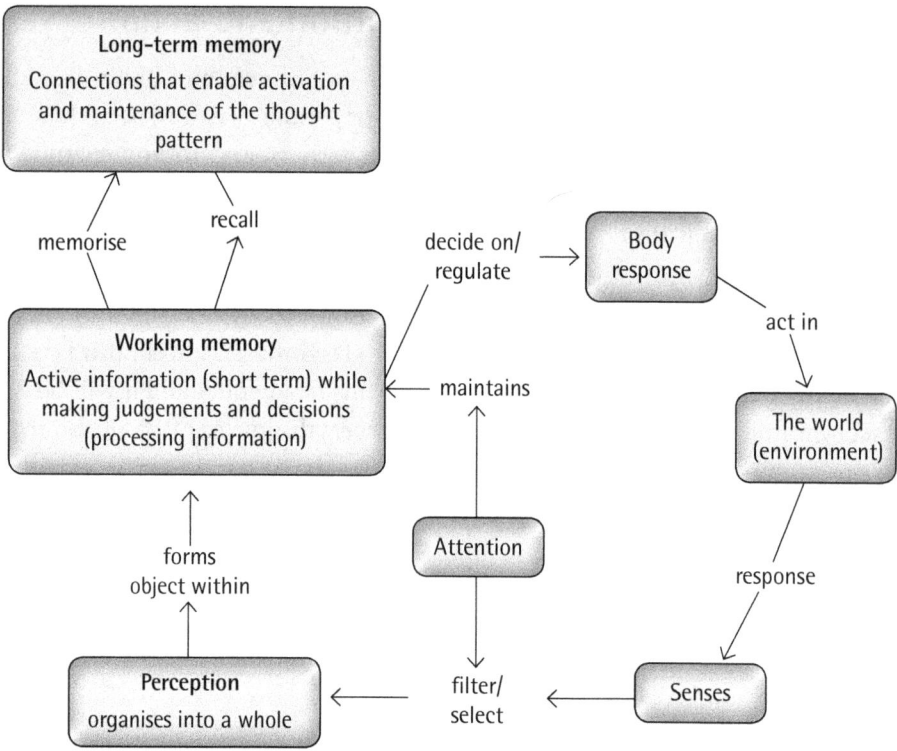

FIGURE 14.3 Components of the cognitive system and the loop through the world

Working memory: awareness and reasoning

We can think of working memory (Baddeley, 2000) as a structure, a collection of areas in the brain that are active when we are using it. This is useful, but it is not the whole picture, because the concept of working memory also captures the idea of 'work'. To do this, we also need to think of it as a function that relates to active thinking—the deliberate processing of activation patterns in the brain that we perceive as representing something in the world. We are aware of this active information in the working memory and we use this information to make sense of our world and to make decisions for action. We also use our working memory for self regulation—deciding how best to use our own resources (mental and physical) as we act to achieve our goals in the world.

The working memory has limited capacity—we can't keep many items active in our mind at the same time. Earlier research suggested that most adults could keep approximately seven items active at one time. The exact number is not particularly important, most important is that this number is rather small. Another limitation is that without actively working on them, items do not stay active in the working memory for long. From 15–20 seconds without any active work, to up to 20 minutes if we are actively working with the information.

Cognition in the world of action

The working memory functions are spread throughout the brain and they make it possible to think about things in the world. It is these patterns of active firing of neurons in the working memory that generate our awareness of what we are thinking about. When we think about things, we are able to perceive these things as they appear to us. So our working memory is closely linked to our sensory systems because these are what we use to show us the world. But we also relate each thing we think about to how we remember it from our past experience. So our working memory also works closely with our long-term memory.

Looking at the different ways we can view things in the working memory and at what we do with these things, we can identify four components of working memory:

1. **The visuo-spatial sketchpad**

   This part of working memory links to our sense of sight ('visual'—from 'vision') and of movement ('spatial'—from movement in space). It allows us to mentally build up images and to mentally manipulate (work with) them, or move them around. Even though we haven't seen these images in the world, we can construct them in our thinking by linking in with the parts of the brain that deal with sight and movement. Visual images are a very powerful way of thinking because one image can carry a lot of information. Also, very complex relationships can often be captured in images and diagrams, and so images give us a powerful way of thinking about complex relationships.

2. **The phonological loop**

   This part of the working memory deals with sound (for 'phono', think 'telephone'). It is linked to the parts of our brain that deal with sound and allows us to build and manipulate sound. It is interesting that this is also linked to the parts of our brain that deal with speech. This makes sense because, particularly in our early years, our learning and use of language is very strongly related to the sound of the words. The ability to talk to ourselves in words 'in our heads' gives us a powerful way of thinking that we develop from about the age of three. The phonological loop is the working memory structure that allows us to do this. Another similar function of the phonological loop is the ability to mentally repeat a sequence of words and keep these in our memory in this way. Also, to make sense of sound, and of language, we need to work with how different sounds follow each other and with the rhythm of the sounds. So this part of the working memory is very important for working with sequences and sequencing (placing things in order).

3. **The episodic buffer**

   An important part of being a person is that we live through experience in time. We remember these experiences as episodes of our lives. The episodic buffer is a part of our working memory that allows us to reconstruct and manipulate such time-related episodes in our thinking. This allows us both to experience what this would be like to 'live through' such experiences and also to tell ourselves stories (narratives) of the experience. Telling stories allows us to make sense of such episodes in many different ways, putting ourselves in different roles and exploring different goals and capabilities.

4. **The central executive**

   The last part of the working memory is not directly related to sensation or lived experience. Rather it relates to organising the work we do with these mental constructions. This is the central executive and involves those parts of the brain that are concerned with decision making, coordination and conscious self regulation. As such, its function is to coordinate and regulate the work done in the other parts of the working memory.

Long-term memory

One of the important learning mechanisms in the brain is that when a connection between neurons is involved in transmitting activation, then the connection is strengthened. So the activation of a pattern of firing also increases the chance of that pattern of firing being activated again. So the consistent activation of patterns of thought in working memory also changes the connections in the brain so that these thoughts are more likely to occur in future. It is this structure of connections in the brain that forms our long-term memory—the connections across all the neurons in a pattern of activation that contribute to keeping the pattern active (Martindale, 1990). For this reason, long-term memories are not pieces of information stored in one place in the brain, rather each memory is widely distributed through the brain. The number of different patterns of connections distributed throughout the brain is huge and so the number of long-term memories that we can store is almost unlimited. Long-term memory is important to allow us to repeat skilful actions (procedural memory) and also to understand the world by remembering our perceptions and experiences (declarative memory, which includes episodic memory and semantic memory—memory of meanings and words).

Storing the memory (memorising the thought) is setting up connections, but not activating the thought structure. So having a long-term memory does not mean that we are aware of the memory. To become aware of the memory, we need to activate the neurons that form the pattern—this is the process of recalling the memory. We recall the memory (reactivate the pattern) by thinking thoughts that relate in some way to the memory—either through similarity, or through known links. Organising and setting up these links so that we can recall our long-term memories is very important when memorising information, because laying down the memory and not being able to recall it is not useful. We can do this by relating the new information to concepts or experience that is already known, or by organising the information into themes or categories. Another way is to code the information in some way, for example, to make a sentence using the first letter of each word to be remembered.

Perception

Perception provides the link between the impulses generated by our sense organs and the coherent objects that we perceive and think about in our working memory. These objects are activated on the basis of our sensory impressions, but they are completed and further detailed through recall of corresponding objects in long-term memory. This makes it possible for us to recognise whole objects in the environment, even though our sensory information is incomplete and unclear. Examples are shown in the shapes with missing parts in Figure 14.4. Do you see the rectangle and the triangle as complete shapes? Or does the right hand shape look like an arrow pointing down, because the base is a bit too long to be perceptually completed?

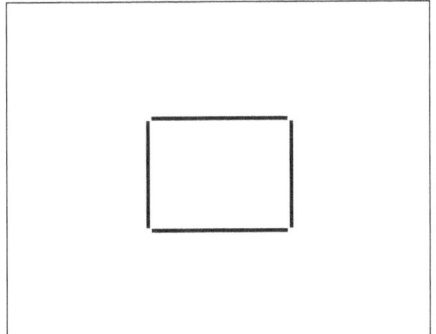

FIGURE 14.4 Some simple shapes with missing parts

Perceived objects are generally multimodal, in that they integrate and evoke impressions from multiple sensory modes. As well as these sensory impressions, they are also linked to the meaning that these objects have to us. In this way, they carry our awareness and conceptualisation (understanding) of the objects in our environment. The process of perception itself is automatic, operating out of conscious awareness. But it does depend on our current episodic experience and awareness of context. For example, if we are cooking in a kitchen and hear the sound of the word 'flour' (or 'flower') we will generally perceive the meaningful concept of 'flour'.

Attention

Attention relates to our capacity to focus our senses and our thinking on a particular aspect of the environment, or our thinking on a particular chain of thought. This is termed 'sustained attention'. Recently, it has become evident that sustained attention may be achieved mainly through the process of inhibitory control. Inhibitory control refers to the capacity to deliberately (wilfully) not respond to stimuli which would normally attract our attention. Inhibiting this response makes it possible for us to keep our current focus of attention.

Reactive attention is an automatic process (which may, in certain cases, be inhibited through inhibitory control) that causes us to shift our attention to a new sensory stimulus. This makes it possible for us to respond immediately if we sense something that may be threatening or dangerous in the world.

The major debates within the field of cognition

It is possible to identify two different ways we mentally control our actions (Kahneman, 2003). Automatic processes (sometimes termed type II processes) are quick and efficient, but not flexible and need little attention (so giving us space to think of other things at the same time). More deliberately controlled processes (type I processes) are slower and less efficient, but much more flexible and need our attention to control them. The distinction between these processes and the manner in which they interact in our thinking, our acting and our learning, is currently an active area of research in the field of cognition.

Although there is general agreement that our thinking relates to patterns of firing of neurons in the brain, as yet there is no consensus on the structure and dynamics of these patterns and even on how it may be possible to identify and distinguish such active patterns. Currently there is a great deal of research that studies the energy traces produced by our brains, as we carry out specific tasks that involve certain types of thinking and action. These traces provide good information about how these patterns spread throughout the different parts of the brain and from this we now understand that much of our thinking involves the coordination and integration of many different areas in our brain (Society for Neuroscience, 2012).

When we examine thinking for acting in the world, we may identify a number of important characteristics of our thinking. These include:
- That thinking is embodied, about and influenced by the functioning of our body.
- That thinking extends to physical structure in the world and to other people we interact with—in this way, thinking is distributed and communal.

- That we may use our ideas of words and symbols to organise and manipulate our thinking and in this way our brains are like mechanisms for manipulating symbols.

Many current debates play these ideas off against each other, while other research attempts to integrate and combine them. With all these technologies, the field of cognition is currently an exciting one to be involved in.

How are systems of cognition relevant to South African schools and classrooms?

School is fundamentally about learning—mental, physical and social learning. And ultimately, everything a person learns is carried in the long-term memory in the brain. For this reason, an understanding of long-term memory and how we may help learners to develop and organise their memory is vitally important for teachers.

But knowing something is never enough. If we can't use what we know to make decisions and act effectively in our lives, then all this learning will be a waste of time. Making sense of the world, making decisions and regulating and controlling our actions all require us to use our working memory. The working memory is powerful and flexible, but it also has some strong restrictions (we can only hold a few items in our working memory and these only for a short time). Teachers need to understand how to interact with learners so that they take advantage of the power of working memory without overloading it. Being aware of their learners' thinking and all this involves, including perception, attention, working memory and long-term memory and how these influence and are influenced by their interactions with the world, will help teachers to interaction with learners in ways that are appropriate to the learners and learn as effectively and efficiently as possible.

Conclusion

In this chapter, we have seen how our thinking, our action and the world all interact with each other and together form a closed loop system. And each thought, action and happening in this system is both an effect and a cause of others. Our brain also forms a system with different structures and functions that influence each other and act together to form our thinking. To make sense of these systems we need to understand these structures and processes and how they may act together to either achieve lasting learning and more powerful action, or to achieve learning that is only temporary and has little effect on action.

15 Piaget, mental networks and learning to act in the world

BRUCE BROWN

The goal of education is not to increase the amount of knowledge, but to create the possibilities for a child to invent and discover, to create men who are capable of doing new things. (Jean Piaget)

Introduction

A person's brain is the most complex system that we know of in a human being. It is an interconnected network containing hundreds of billions of neurons (cells) and other cells and hundreds of trillions of connections. What is more, the working of each connection is a complex chemical process that responds to the chemical state of the surrounding region of the brain, as well as the recent activity of the connection. Our awareness and thinking relates to organised patterns of coordinated neural activity in the brain—patterns of 'firing'.

The brain does not exist on its own. It is highly integrated with our body, with nerve fibres spreading through every part of the body to collect information about the body and from the senses and to send impulses to act, to all of the muscles in the body. As well as being linked through the 'firing' activity of neurons, the chemical state of the body also determines the chemical state of the brain. So the brain should not be seen as the executive of the body, sitting in safe separation and telling the body what to do. Rather it is part of a complex brain-body system where the body influences the brain as much as the brain influences the body. The functions may be different, with the brain looking after the high-level thinking and organisation and the body looking after the low level and largely unconscious details of living. But if you have ever tried to think and plan for an important and stressful meeting when you are tired and hungry and needing to get dressed and find food for yourself and those you live with, you will appreciate the influence that the body and low-level demands of living have on our high-level thinking in the brain.

What is more, our brain-body system does not live on its own. It is a tightly integrated part of the world that we live in—both social and physical. As well as setting goals (low level and high level) for what we want to achieve in the world, our brain helps us to regulate our emotions and actions so that these may align with the demands and opportunities of the world in order to achieve our goals as best as is possible in our situation. That is, we and the world form part of a closed system where the world is continually influencing us and we are continually influencing the world. As we live, we act on the world, so that it becomes better adapted to us. But at the same time, through our learning, we change our brain so that we adapt better to the world. Both of these processes are always happening (they are continuous), but they are also slow and effortful, so that any substantial change (in ourselves and the world) takes time and effort.

In his work on learning, Piaget researched the thinking and learning of children as they took part in this active process of acting in and adapting to the world (Flavell, 1996; Wadsworth, 2004). In this chapter, we will explore some of his insights and how they may be related to closed systems of interaction between body, brain and the world and also between multiple layers of functional elements (activation patterns) in the brain.

Why is Piagetian learning theory important?

Piaget's thinking provide a number of very useful insights about the processes of thinking and learning. These insights will be explored in this chapter.

Structures, stability and layering

A fundamental idea that Piaget used, was that of a mental structure (he called this a schema, but in this chapter we will use the term 'mental structure'). We will be thinking of mental structures as particular patterns of activation in our mental system. But, if we think of the meaning of the word 'structure' in the physical world, it generally is reasonably solid and lasting. To fit with this, we require that to function as a mental structure a pattern must be stable. But what does stability mean? We know that most activation patterns in our working memory do not last long. They stay active while they are being used and then they fade away. So how long it lasts when activated is not important for a pattern to be seen as a mental structure. By stability, we mean that some important properties of the pattern must remain similar over a long period of time (months or years). Two important properties that need to be stable are the coherence and distinctiveness of the pattern. Coherence in that in activating some parts of the structure will generally result in the whole structure being activated and suppressing any part of the structure will generally result in the whole structure being suppressed. So the structure is coherent because it will generally be active or inactive as a whole. Distinctiveness in that the boundaries of what is part of the pattern and what is not will generally be reasonably clear, particularly when comparing it to a different pattern.

If the coherence and the distinctive properties of an activation pattern remain stable over a reasonable period of time (months or years) then we see this pattern as a mental structure. A pattern that is not coherent or distinctive over a reasonable period of time is transient (it does not last long) and so should not be considered as a mental structure. As an example, let's consider the activation pattern that forms our idea of a cow. If we think of part of a cow (say the horns), or of something that we do involving cows (like herding them) the idea of one or many whole cows will generally be part of our thinking—the cow pattern is coherent. Also people who know cows and donkeys will also know what makes a cow a cow and not a donkey—the cow pattern is distinctive in relation to the donkey pattern. It follows that the idea of a cow may be considered to be a mental structure. As another example, for most Grade 2 children, the idea of the fraction 2/3 is not stable—they know that this is a number of some sort and they may know that it relates in some way to sharing and to cutting into parts, but just what it is as a complete object and just how it is similar to and different from other fractions and any whole number is not clear. Also, if they do not work with fractions for a period of time, they may find it difficult to think about 2/3 again. This idea is not yet stable—it is transient—and so shouldn't be seen as one of their mental structures. The children need more experience and learning for it to become stable.

Viewing mental structures as activation patterns allows us to consider how these structures interact in layers. Within a layer, the different structures generally do not activate each other, in fact, similar structures in a layer may inhibit each other (so that the chance of many of them being active at the same time are small). The structures in a layer may function to activate structures in a different layer and themselves may be activated by the structures in that different layer. That is, activation effects occur both ways between layers. The layers form a hierarchy in terms of their level of coordination and integration of signals from and to the world. Lower layer structures may generally be seen as identifying and carrying information about particular details of the objects identified by higher level structures. For example, if we think about how we make sense of what we see when we look at a cow, the 'cow' object will be activated in our thinking, but so too will objects at a lower level in the hierarchy that correspond to the features: a tail, an udder with four teats, a large, solid body, two back legs, two quite different front legs, a large head, two big eyes, horns, and so on. This way of thinking allows us to make sense of Piaget's stages of development as well as his two fundamental concepts relating to the process of thinking and learning.

Piaget's stages of development

Piaget spent a great deal of effort carefully observing children of different ages as they worked on different tasks. Based on these observations, he came to the conclusion that children's stable ways of thinking (global mental structures) seemed to change over long periods of time (Piaget, 1968). He identified four different stages, each corresponding to a general and stable way of thinking displayed by children in that stage. These four ways of thinking may be seen as four layers of mental structuring, each one building on the previous layer and forming a necessary foundation for the next layer. Because they build on each other, these stages occur in a fixed order. Also, the ways of thinking in each stage become developed and organised to form parts of the more complex and more effective thinking of the next layer. But the ways of thinking of a previous stage are not lost when the next stage is established—in appropriate circumstances the person will still use prior ways of thinking. If the ways of thinking of a previous stage are not properly developed, it will not be possible for the child to develop the next stage of thinking. So, understanding Piaget's stages of development gives us some insights into tasks that may, or may not be appropriate at any stage.

The four stages of thinking are:

1. **The sensori-motor stage (approximately 0–2 years)**

    The main developmental task of the child at this stage is to organise and coordinate all the different sensory input it receives together with all the output activation it sends to the motor (muscle) system. In doing so, it constructs an identity for itself as a coherent object that exists in a reasonably consistent world of other coherent objects. This understanding of object permanence is a major achievement of this stage.

2. **The pre-operational stage (approximately 2–6 years)**

    In this stage, children work to identify and label the many different objects in their world. They build mental models (structures) that allow them to think about objects even when they are not present. They also physically explore what different objects can do (often, in imaginative play, they use other things to stand for the object they are exploring—like using a long wooden block to stand for an aeroplane that they pretend to fly). In this way they learn to act on objects, and label these actions. But they do need to use physical objects to think about such actions and responses. The development of words to label objects and actions and to communicate with other people about them sees a massive development of language at this stage.

3. **The concrete operational stage (approximately 6–12 years)**

   In this stage, children have the mental structures that allow them to mentally model their actions on physical (concrete) objects, the consequences of these actions and even of reversing, or undoing these actions. Stable mental structures that allow children to think about both doing and reversing an action are called operations and in this stage, children build up a large number of such operations that focus on concrete objects (hence the concrete operational stage). So children in this stage become able to reason mentally about their concrete actions in the world and no longer need to use concrete objects to do this. Also, they build experience with reading and writing and so become able to represent objects and actions symbolically through their writing (formally). But they are not yet able to use such formal systems mentally to direct their thinking and reasoning.

4. **The formal operational stage (from approximately 12 years)**

   In this stage, children have enough experience with reading and writing formal systems, and have developed the mental structures to be able to reason formally and to explore the implications of 'what if' situations that can be described symbolically even though they do not exist. This is the final stage, in which children are now able to think as flexibly and effectively as adults.

Assimilation

Assimilation is the process that involves fitting an experience of the world, to a mental structure that allows us to make sense of and regulate that experience. In this way, assimilation makes it possible for us to use our existing mental structures (that carry our knowledge and expectations of the word) to guide and regulate our interactions with the extremely complex world we live in, in a way that is quick and easy. As long as the world fits our knowledge and expectations (our prior knowledge) reasonably well, assimilation provides a simple and effective structure for our interaction. How does this work?

Let's first look at assimilation in perception—at the process of object perception. To keep things simple, we will refer to only two layers of mental structures (even though object recognition involves many more): the lower layer of visual features and the upper layer of physical objects. The interaction between these two layers and the sensory visual input is shown in Figure 15.1.

Piaget, mental networks and learning to act in the world

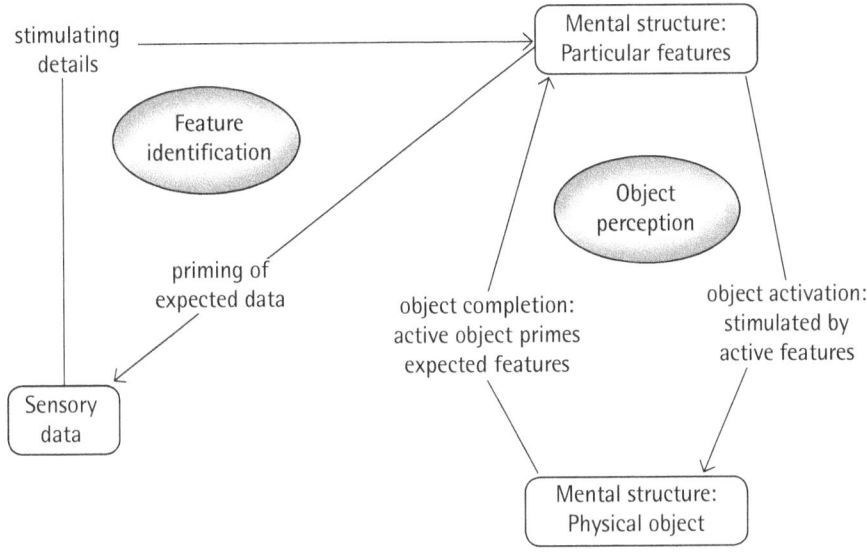

FIGURE 15.1 Assimilation in perception (shown using two layers)

Let's discuss this process together with our example of looking at a cow. To make the role of both layers clearer, let's assume that the cow is standing looking out of the door of a dark farm stall and we are looking from the side so we can only see its front part. Cows have a distinctive shape and so the visual sensory data will stimulate the activation of the particular features: cow head, neck, shoulders and front legs. As each of these features is activated it will stimulate the activation of the 'cow' object structure. If the combined stimulation from all these features is high enough, the cow object structure will be activated. But the process doesn't stop there. The active cow object structure will also stimulate the other visual features expected for a cow that we have not yet seen. So, even though we haven't yet seen them, very little additional stimulation from our visual system will be sufficient to activate these features—our visual system is 'primed' to see them. If a flash of light gives us a very brief sight of the rest of the cow, the rest of these visual features could become active, even though we would not have seen them clearly enough to be identified without this priming. In this way, the priming from an activated object structure, automatically fills in the gaps in what we see. This happens without us even being aware of doing it—we think that we have seen the whole object, even if we haven't. Filling in the gaps in this way is very useful, because it allows us to recognise and respond to even vague and indistinct stimuli. And in general, if our expectations are reasonable, what we recognise will be appropriate. (This happens a lot in talking where we can generally recognise and make sense of very indistinct spoken language.) But sometimes, we expect something different from what we get and when this happens, our perceptions may be quite inappropriate. For example, in our brief sight of the animal, we may perceive a cow, even though the animal is really a bull.

Assimilation in action is similar. In this case the higher level mental structure is an action procedure that we wish to implement to carry out a certain action. Carrying out this action will require us to perform a number of different component tasks. Each task expects a certain state of readiness in our body and the world and is then implemented to generate a different state in the body and the world. The tasks are arranged in a sequence but there may be points where different tasks are selected based on different final states of the task before. If we wish to carry out the action, then we activate the action which at each point in time stimulates the activation of the current and the next possible tasks in the sequence. The current state of the body and the world also stimulates these tasks and the task that is carried out is the one with the highest level of stimulation (although if this level of stimulation is not enough, then no task will be activated and the action will not be completed). In this way (generally on many levels) we assimilate our experience of the conditions of the world into our activated action structure.

Accommodation

Accommodation is the dual process to assimilation. It involves adapting our mental structures in order to fit the world as we experience it. Accommodation occurs when our experience of the world does not fit with our expectations. Note that for accommodation to make sense, we need to have expectations of the world (which will be based on active mental structures) and then we need to interact with the world in a way that allows us to see whether or not these expectations work. That is, accommodation requires both expectations and action. These can be seen in Figure 15.2.

If the misalignment between expectations and experience is minor, then the priming of our perception by our active mental structures will result in the world being experienced as expected and so there will be no need to change our thinking. But if the misalignment is more extensive, then priming will not be sufficient to overcome it and we will perceive a conflict (cognitive conflict) between our thinking and the world. In such cases, we will often not achieve our goals and so will also experience failure. These negative experiences will motivate us to put in the effort that is needed to change the way that we think and so we will adapt our mental structures. This is the process of accommodation, in which the failure of our expectations leads to learning. Small changes (minor accommodations) will occur in response to small mismatches—an example of this is when we get ourselves used to specific conditions during our initial practice in preparation for a game of sport or for playing a musical instrument.

Larger changes (major accommodations) occur when the mismatch is more extreme and in these cases the experience of failure and frustration could be quite notable.

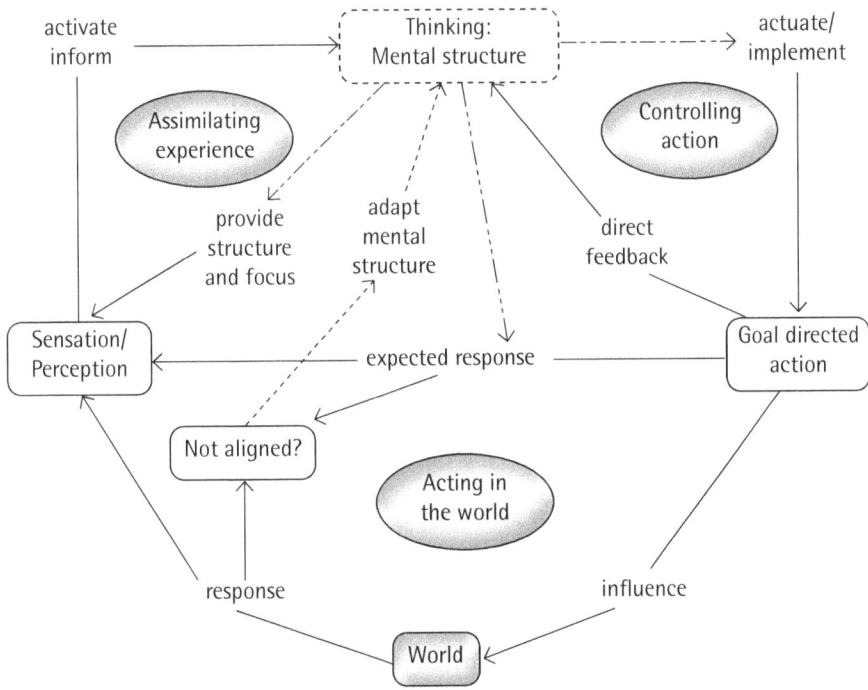

FIGURE 15.2 Accommodation results from expectations and action

The major debates within the field of Piagetian learning theory

Even though it is generally acknowledged that Piaget saw children as far more capable than most developmental psychologists of his time, a number of researchers have criticised him for not fully recognising the extent of children's capability. This is due to the fact that the way he questioned children was not necessarily child appropriate (Donaldson, 1978).

Piaget is also often only seen as a stage theorist—providing a rigid sequence of structural stages that constrain children's thinking at every age. This constraining theory of stages has been, and is still being, extensively criticised. Critiques of his stage theory relate to: the precise details of the constraints on thinking at each stage; the precise age boundaries between each stage; and whether the ways of thinking in each stage supplant those of earlier stages or whether instances of thinking related to prior stages may be noted.

This chapter follows other readings of Piaget (Wadsworth, 2004) that focus more on the continuous process of learning in order to make sense of and adapt to experience, and the gradual nature of the transitions, described by Piaget. In these readings, stages may be seen as emergent and transient, but long lived, commonalities in ways of thinking within a continuous and gradual evolution of thought. Here the primary variable is experience and not age, and the fundamental concern is not constraint, but rather learning and adaptation with assimilation and accommodation the prime mechanisms regulating thinking and adaptation.

How is Piagetian learning theory relevant to South African schools and classrooms?

Piaget's theory provides a number of insights into the processes of thinking and learning, which have important implications for teaching in South African schools. At the most basic level, his understanding that learning is an active process of making sense of the world we live in. Effective learning then requires learners to be active and not passive in schools, and teachers need to ensure that learners make sense of what they learn and not just passively memorise information. Learners need to consistently engage in and make sense of appropriate experiences in order to change and develop the way they structure their thinking and acting. Learning is not a one stop shop, but rather a gradual process of change in which learners adapt to consistent experience.

The process of assimilation demonstrates the importance of prior knowledge for schooling in that learners will automatically perceive their experience in terms of their existing knowledge structures—their prior knowledge. This perceptual structuring is good, because it allows learners to respond efficiently and effectively to their world. But at times learners will not hear what teachers expect them to hear, or see what teachers wish them to see, because this automatic structuring will not fit with the knowledge structures the teacher wants them to develop. When faced with such misperceptions, it is up to the teacher to draw their attention to the particular features that will help the learners change their ways of seeing.

Learning occurs through the process of accommodation and this happens when there is some conflict between what the learners expect and what they experience. In this way, learning follows on failure. It is important for our learners to understand that, even though it is uncomfortable, failure is not a bad thing, but rather, it is a normal and natural part of learning—failure provides the opportunity to learn. An important part of teaching is helping learners to cope with failure and develop the resilience to use failure as an opportunity for further learning. Learners who fail must not be punished, but must rather be supported to learn.

Conclusion

Piaget sees learners as scientists—actively working to make sense of their world, working through failure time and time again until they eventually develop ways of thinking that work. This needs experience, adaptability and resilience, as well as support and encouragement from their teachers. The closed loop, multilayered models of assimilation and accommodation discussed in this chapter provide useful insight into the mental processes involved in this learning and may be used to guide the teaching and learning interaction at a fine level of detail.

16 Vygotsky, regulating alignment with tools, people and the world

BRUCE BROWN

Through others we become ourselves. (Lev Vygotsky)

Introduction

The world is not an empty place. It is filled with things and even more so with people. Living in the world is all about being with people and doing things together. So a lot of our thinking will be about how to get along with people and how to do things together. Working with people allows us to do much more than we could on our own. Another thing that enables us to do so much is the fact that we make and use tools. On our own, we can't do much. But we make and use tools that give us power and strength (from hammers, to bulldozers to massive mining diggers), speed (bicycles, cars, express trains, aeroplanes and rockets), protection (shoes and clothes, houses, concrete bunkers) and precision (scalpels, dentists drills, microscopes and laser cutters). We also make things that help us plan, think and judge better: some of these are physical, like road signs, books and computers, and others are relational, like symbols and symbol systems, for example, words and language, or scientific terms and theories.

Lev Semyonovich Vygotsky was very interested in how we interact with people and use tools to help us live better. But he was even more interested in how working with people, tools and signs, shapes and changes the way we think about ourselves and about the world and in this way helps us to develop and become more fully human—more complex, complete and creative people.

For Vygotsky, all the ways of thinking that are what make us fully human (higher psychological functions) develop from our social interaction with other people. He states this clearly in his essay titled 'The genesis of higher mental functions'. Here are two quotes from page 11 of this work:

> *We can formulate the general genetic law of cultural development as follows: every function in the cultural development of the child appears on the stage twice, in two planes, first, the social, then the psychological, first between people as an intermental category, then within the child as an intramental category. This pertains equally to voluntary attention, to logical memory, to the formation of concepts, and to the development of will.* (Vygotsky, 1931)

and

> *Every higher mental function was external because it was social before it became an internal, strictly mental function; it was formerly a social relation of two people. The means of acting on oneself is initially a means of acting on others or a means of action of others on the individual.* (Vygotsky, 1931)

Based on this idea, Vygotsky worked to understand how the development from social to psychological, from external to internal occurred. He was also very interested in schooling and in understanding how the social interactions between teacher and child and between child and child in school contributed to this learning and development, as well as how teachers could better enable and facilitate this process. His work could help us to deepen our understanding of teaching and learning and to improve our practice of teaching in schools (see also Chapter 8).

Why is mediation and alignment important?

Mediation

To understand the process of interaction when we work together or use a tool to do something, we need to consider three elements: first, the thing we are trying to achieve—the object (or goal) of our activity. Second, the person who wants to (and is actively working to) achieve that object—the subject. Third, the tool that is being used or the person who is helping the subject—the mediating tool or person.

Using the tool, or working with the mediating person, allows the subject to achieve a lot more than they would if they worked unaided. That is, the tool or mediating person extends the range of action of the subject, making it possible to effectively achieve the object. This allows us to describe the mediated action of the person on the world in order to achieve their object. But in performing this mediated action the subject also gains experience and so learns: learning either how to effectively use the tool and what may be done with the tool, or what the mediating person did to contribute to the process and how this was done. In this way the person learns by internalising the mediated process. This interaction, that includes both performing and internalising the mediated action, is shown in Figure 16.1.

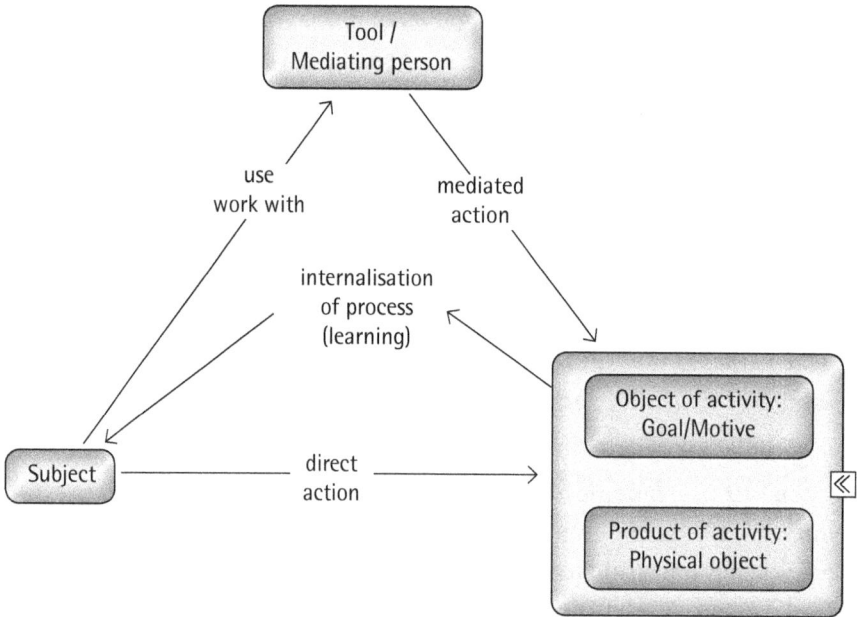

FIGURE 16.1 The triangle of mediation, with internalisation

Social mediation

In most cases, we work with both people and tools—working together to achieve a common objective. Then we will have many of these mediating processes happening all together at the same time. If we draw a diagram of this, it will include many different triangles of mediation. But these processes are not all separate and so we need to understand the links between these component processes. For a simple example which does explore some of these links, let's look at two people working with different tools, where one person is also mediating the action of the other. Looking at the classroom, this would describe a teacher working with a single learner to help them solve a specific problem using pens and paper. In this case, they would each have a pen (possibly different colours) and would be writing on the same (or possibly different) pieces of paper—the pens and paper would be the tools they are using. The object of their activity would be to solve the problem and this would normally be shown by producing a drawing or a written explanation of the solution—the product. A diagram that shows this process is shown in Figure 16.2.

Vygotsky, regulating alignment with tools, people and the world

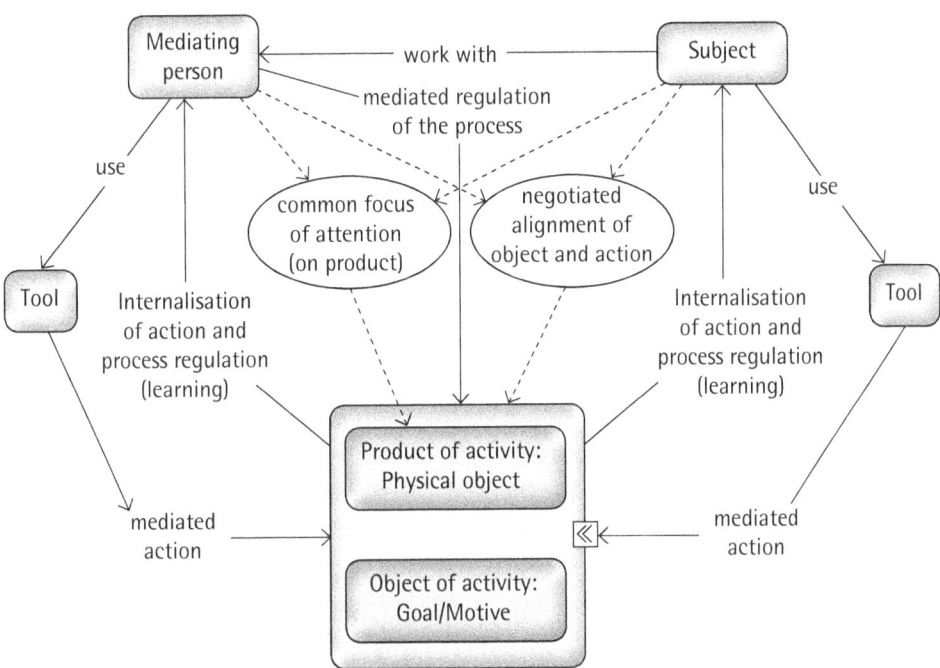

FIGURE 16.2 Social mediation by a single person

The diagram shows the tool mediated action (writing) of the subject (the learner) on the right hand side. And the tool mediated action (writing) of the teacher (the mediating person) on the left. Across the top and down the middle, it shows the teacher (mediating other) regulating the learner's (subject's) action—because they are working with different tools, the teacher mediates the way the learner regulates the action (process regulation). The return arrows to the subject (learner) and the teacher (mediating person) show their learning through internalisation of this action—note that both the teacher and the learner learn, even though what they learn is different.

Lastly, the dotted lines show how these different component actions are linked. The teacher and learner talk to each other about what they are doing and why. In this way, they negotiate their alignment (lining up) of what they are trying to achieve (the object) and also how they are trying to achieve this (the action). But talk on its own is not enough—to be sure that they both understand each other, they physically focus their attention on the same product and even on the same part of the product. To show what they are focusing on, they will often point physically to the part of the product they are looking at. This act of pointing (indicative act) is very important because it allows them both to look at the same thing and so think of this together as they talk. Having the same mental focus makes it possible for them to make sense of their talk in a similar way and so they will communicate effectively through their talk. It is this shared focus during their talk that allows them to use their talking to effectively negotiate alignment about their goals and actions. And this alignment is necessary for them to be able to work together to achieve their goals.

Communication, mediation and egocentric speech

As we can see from this diagram and discussion, the process of social mediation is complex, because it requires proper communication, so that the two people can align their goals and actions. Proper communication needs both a shared language and shared attention, which requires working closely together. This is particularly important in the case of a teacher–learner interaction, where the mediating person is a lot older and knows (and can do) a lot more than the subject. In this case, it is very easy for them to understand each other's words differently and so they need the shared physical focus to ensure that their interpretations of the language align.

Talk during social mediation is often about what to do, when and why. That is, through talk the mediating person helps the subject to regulate the process. For example, when starting to work with a learner to solve a problem, the teacher may ask: 'Read the question carefully. What does it say? What is the story of what is happening?' If the learner is still uncertain, the teacher may suggest: 'Should we draw a picture?' By responding to the teacher's suggestions, the learner will gradually move towards a solution. But the learner is not just solving the problem, he is also learning from the teacher what to do at each stage of the solution.

After some experience when the learner works on his own to solve these problems, you may hear him say at the start: 'Read the question carefully', 'What is the story?' or even 'Should I draw a picture?' Here the learner is talking to himself and so this is called egocentric speech (because the speech is centred on the self—the ego). This talk is useful, because he is using it to help himself decide what to do next—how to regulate the process. Also, he is using the words of the teacher. It is almost as if he plays the part of the teacher to help him regulate the process. Here we see that process oriented egocentric speech is the first step when internalising the teacher's social mediation. For later problems, we may still see him using egocentric speech, but now it has become quieter and greatly shortened. Something like: 'Read carefully' or 'story'. As he does more, his talk will become less and less and quieter and quieter, until he won't be talking at all. By this time, the mediation has become completely internalised and the learner regulates his own process mentally.

The zone of proximal development (ZPD)

Does mediation always lead to learning? And is it always helpful? The answer to both these questions is: No. The reasons are given by the idea of the zone of proximal development (ZPD). The ZPD is a spatial metaphor (zone) that describes the conditions needed for learning to occur during the process of mediation (Veresov, 2004). According to Vygotsky, the ZPD is:

the distance between the actual developmental level as determined by independent problem solving and the level of potential development as determined through problem solving under adult guidance or in collaboration with more capable peers. (Vygotsky, 1997:33)

The first condition is that learning will not occur if the mediation is not needed. If the learner can successfully complete the task on her own without any mediation, that is, the learner can solve the problem independently, then the task is outside the ZPD and learning will not occur. Here the task is too easy for the learner. The condition that the mediating interaction occurs within the 'level of potential development' is a little more difficult to formulate precisely. Roughly, if learners are not able to incorporate the mediation into their performance and use it to progress appropriately, then the task is outside the ZPD and mediated learning will not occur. For example, if the task is too difficult so that even when mediated, the task is beyond their range of action, then learning will not occur. Also, if the mediation of the task does not align with the motives of the child for engaging in the activity, then the child will not attempt to coordinate his/her activity with that of the mediator and so will not learn from the actions of the mediator. In these cases, the task is again outside the ZPD and mediated learning will not occur.

On the other hand, if learners have the motive to engage in the activity and are not able to complete the task unassisted and are able to align their actions with those of the mediator, then they will learn from such a mediating interaction that enables them to successfully complete the task. In this case, the mediated task is said to be within the ZPD and learning will occur.

Language and tools for thinking

In his work, Vygotsky (1986) underlines the importance of language and in this section we will look briefly at some of the important implications of literacy and of theory building. These both provide us with powerful tools for thinking that we can use by aligning the processes of internalisation and externalisation. We have seen that internalisation refers to the process of taking something in our external world, physical and social, and incorporating it into our internal, mental world. Through this, we become able to mentally represent and work with this thing—to think about it. Externalisation is the opposite process. It involves taking some of our thinking and representing it in our external world. This representation may be some writing, a drawing, or even a physical object—let's call it an artefact (something we have made). But when we interact with this representation, we do not interact with it as it is (marks on paper for writing or drawing, or the physical object in itself). Instead, we use it to guide our thinking by reactivating the thinking that it represents—we use it as a sign indicating something else, not as itself.

The great thing about artefacts is that, once they are made, they stay made without any effort on our part. Thoughts don't work this way—we have to work to keep them active and when we stop working on this, they fade away and are no longer part of our thinking. So, one easy way to keep hold of a thought is to write it down. The words serve as external memory and it no longer matters if we now think of anything else. If we want to get back to the thought, all we need to do is look at the writing and it will remind us—as long as we can read it, reading it will reactivate the thought. One of the powerful functions of writing is that it provides us with a reliable and easily accessible external memory.

But that is not all. By writing down a number of thoughts, we can explore different ways of inter-relating these thoughts, by simply rearranging what we have written. In this way, we can use writing to manipulate our thinking. This can be very powerful if we need to work to make sense of a lot of ideas. We can form and reform them into different stories, until we find a story that works well and makes good sense. This story then organises these ideas into a bigger whole that makes sense. Here we are using writing and reading to synthesise our ideas (combine them into a meaningful whole). On the other hand, we can also use writing to help us with a vague idea that we are not quite sure about, or with an idea that we wish to understand in more detail. To do this, first write down the general idea in a sentence or two. Then look for the words that identify important parts of the idea and try to write down an explanation of each one of these parts. If you need more detail and clarity for this component, then do the same for this—identify and write down an explanation for each important part of this component. In this way, we can use and expand our writing (our externalisation of the original idea) to generate a more detailed understanding of each component of the idea. This is the process of analysis. We could then follow a process of synthesis as discussed above to organise and relate our detailed understanding of each part to form a good understanding of the original idea. Reading and making sense of the explanations and stories that we have generated leads us to form and structure our thinking in ways that align with these formal, written texts. Through this internalisation of the externalised formal structure, we change, organise and develop our thinking. In this way, literacy forms an extremely flexible and powerful tool for thinking.

Some major debates within the field of mediation and sociocultural learning theory

The idea of mediation and mediating learning in the classroom is important. An important focus of recent research on mediation has been to develop useful analytical frameworks that teachers could use to analyse the teaching and learning in their classrooms so that they can improve their regulation of this process. Teaching techniques that make mediation more noticeable and provides specific ways and means of mediating learning in the classroom are also being developed.

A number of sociocultural approaches to thinking and learning have grown out of Vygotsky's work. Many of these, such as the dialogical approaches to learning (Wertsch, 1991) have further developed our understanding of the important role of communicative language, voice and dialogue (both external and internalised) in developing our thinking and our view of ourselves. Others include a much wider range of social influence in their picture of learning. Two examples are: First, the view of situated learning, that learning is always situated in a community of practice (Lave & Wenger, 1991) and so is at least as much about becoming a member of the community, as it is about knowledge and skills. Second, activity theories (Engeström, 1999) take their basic unit of analysis to be a social activity system, which focuses its analysis on the complex elements that interact to form an activity system and on the way activity systems develop and interact.

How is Vygotsky relevant to South African schools and classrooms?

Vygotsky's ideas about alignment between learners, tools and language have many important implications for teaching in South Africa. One of the most fundamental implications arises from the understanding that learning occurs through internalisation of one's experience of mediated tasks. It follows that learners need sustained and extensive experience of such tasks (within their ZPD) in order to effectively do this—learning takes time and extensive experience.

Second, learning is not the simple memorisation and reproduction of words and procedures. Rather, learning involves becoming able to carry out tasks that achieve a significant object, using appropriate tools (physical and textual). Learners need to work together with these tools and with the teacher, focussing on and discussing specific aspects that they need to complete the task, in order to develop a meaningful and useful understanding of the words, the tools and the task. The teacher needs to be present and prepared to provide appropriate mediation (keeping to the ZPD)—enough so that learners may successfully complete the task, but not too much, so that learners are continually needing to develop their own capacity and take up their independence.

Vygotsky's understanding of language and literacy also provides some important guidelines for teaching. Learners need to write things down and then read them later, to allow effective recall and building on what has been learned. Also, writing things down when planning or problem solving, gives us things to think about, to work with and to check, so that we can engage deeply and flexibly with possible solutions. Finally, we see that developing reading and literacy is critical for learning because learners need to work with text to structure, organise and make sense of their thinking and to develop their capacity for analysis and synthesis.

Conclusion

This chapter provided a short overview of some of Vygotsky's ideas and showed how they involve the continual interplay and alignment of our thinking, our acting on the world with tools and our social interaction with others. We saw how we use the world for thinking and learning, and also how we use thinking to regulate our activity in the world. Teaching our learners to become comfortably powerful in this interplay has some important implications for our teaching.

17 Knowledge of neuroscience for the classroom

LARA RAGPOT

[N]urturing the cross-fertilization of ideas and paradigms and refining our vision of the Educational Neuroscientist ... can revolutionize education. It's not a bridge too far if it is built by properly trained engineers. (J.N. Zadina)

Introduction

The former view that neuroscience has unequivocal custodianship of the study of brain biology and function, that exploring the cognitive processes involved in learning belong only to psychology, and that the research of pedagogy is under the proprietorship of the discipline of education, has slowly transformed during the past three decades. These disciplines have now unified in a new field of study known as 'Mind, Brain and Education' or MBE (Fischer, Daniel, Immordino-Yang, Stern, Battro & Koizumi, 2007)—thus the interface of mind (cognitive psychology), brain (neuroscience) and education (pedagogy), to espouse effective learning outcomes in the classroom.

The cognitive neuroscientist, Stanislas Dehaene, states that because of the great strides made in understanding brain processing, the application of cognitive neuroscience to education is no longer a 'bridge too far' (Dehaene, 2011:278). Modern educationists need to have a working knowledge of brain structure and functioning, understand how brain anatomy and operations underlie behaviourally observed acts of learning, as well as the know-how to support learning with effective educational practices (the term 'educationists' will be used in this chapter as an all-encompassing term for classroom teachers, learning support specialists and educational psychologists). Furthermore, they should ensure that teaching strategies espouse conceptual understanding which takes into consideration the developmental level of the child being taught, as well as new ideas proposed by conceptual change theorists. A foundational understanding of brain processing that underlie learning events, should thus form one of the core components of every educationist's knowledge toolkit (Uitzinger & Ragpot, under review).

This chapter will focus specifically on the interface of neuroscience and education, also known as educational neuroscience. As the research in the field of educational neuroscience is rapidly expanding, this chapter serves as merely an introduction to encourage further in-depth reading on the different topics. This chapter will start with a short introduction on the history of educational neuroscience and how it affords us new insights into human learning; then give some examples of current research areas in educational neuroscience. Lastly, it will follow a discussion on possible implication for the South African educationist.

A brief history of 'mapping' learning acts in the brain

To gain a better understanding of learning on a more biological level, as processing happens in the brain, it is important to explore the neurological research that has been done in this field. A study of neuroscientific research could teach the educationist much about the brain structures involved, and functional processing in the brain, whilst individuals are learning. What we now know about how learning happens in the brain originated with the development of technology to scan and 'map' processing in the brain by determining an increase in blood flow at distinct brain locations.

In the 1980s, the main method to develop these 'brain maps' were single photon emission computed tomography (SPECT) and positron emission tomography (PET) scans (Posner, 2010). PET scans focuses on cell activity; where an increase in cell activity generates increases in localised blood supply to the cells. These PET scans were called functional brain imaging as they showed which areas of the brain were active at a given moment, as the blood flow was directed to that specific area, when the individual performed a task. The PET 'mapping' was first employed to show how, during tasks such as reading or listening to music, much of the brain, but not the whole brain, exhibited increased blood flow (Lassen, Ingvar & Skinhoj, 1978).

The next major development in the 1990s was the use of magnetic resonance imagining (MRI) to measure localised changes in blood oxygen in the brain (Ogawa, Lee, Kay & Tank, 1990). Following onto that *functional magnetic resonance imaging* (fMRI) was introduced, which could show a picture of brain activity whilst performing actions or functions, such as for example reading or singing. fMRI was an improvement on PET scans as it could reveal much more localised activity than PET thus making it more accurate, and did not use any radioactivity, thus making it less invasive. This meant that it could be used with children and could examine changes that occur with learning and development, as an individual could be scanned repeatedly with fMRIs without harm (Kelly & Garavan, 2005). Researchers were now able to combine trials of different types of functioning. In this way it was discovered that for example, listing nouns and then generating verbs associated with these nouns within the same series of trials, language activity differs across brain functions dependent on what the activity asked the individual to perform (McCandliss, Cohen & Dehaene, 2003). Language was thus not located only in certain areas of the brain like Wernicke and Broca's areas as believed before, but could be mapped across brain areas related to functionality of tasks (Williams, 2010). Much subsequent work has confirmed and elaborated the meaning of brain area activations, particularly with respect to reading (McCandliss, Cohen & Dehaene, 2003) and mathematics (Dehaene, 2011; Butterworth, 2010; Spelke, 2012).

An important aspect of the way we learn explained by neuroscientific research is *plasticity* in the brain, which means that the brain is highly adaptive (Singer, 1995; Squire & Kandel, 1999; Banks, 2016). Individuals' brains continuously adapt to their environments—this includes the settings and conditions of their contexts, where they spend their daily work and their leisure time. Although there are specified areas of the brain, which will always relate to certain activities (like the pre-frontal cortex that directs executive functioning (Blair & Raver, 2015)), learning events in different settings and circumstances continuously shape the architecture of the brain, due to neural connectivity modification. Leisman, Mualem and Mughrabi (2015:79) argue that the brain has:

> *... networks of interconnecting nerve cells called neurons and supportive glial cells. Learning experiences are translated into electrical and chemical signals that gradually modify connections among neurons in certain areas of the brain.*

This implies that as time passes, these modifications in neuro-connectivity could accumulate to noteworthy restructuring of the brain areas which are engaged in specific types of learning (Leisman, Mualem & Mughrabi, 2015). The study of individuals with brain injury has also shown that entire brain functions could be adopted by other areas of the brain, if injured brain tissue can no longer support certain functions (Posner, 2010). Apart from specific linguistic areas of the brain, almost all other functions could be adopted by supportive brain areas because of brain plasticity. This is an important discovery for educationists as individuals who struggle with certain aspects of learning, could be supported by incorporating other areas of brain function.

What researchers have also learned from studies of brain activity is that several neural areas are sometimes needed to work together to carry out a specific task, for instance reading. This is known as *connectivity* (Posner, 2010) of involved neural networks which could also be further developed and enriched with practice (McNamara, Tegenthoff, Hubert, Buchel, Binkofski & Ragert, 2007). When individuals go through learning experiences, some connections are initiated, while others are not. As time passes, the connections which are used more in relation to others are reinforced, while the less active ones are diminished or removed (Squire & Kandel, 2009). This is obviously a very important discovery for educationists, as there was proof that learning and repetition could make stronger neural pathways and there is often a reduction in the number and extent of activations when a task is practised (Fair, Cohen, Poer, Dosenbach, Church, Meizin, et al, 2009), which proves that the task becomes easier and more automatic, thus utilising less brain energy.

From the research mentioned, we have learnt that certain brain areas dominate certain learning processes, that brain processing is adaptable, and that one activity could be the combination of various connected brain regions and processes. With the continued advances in neuroscientific research in specific areas of focus, the contemporary educationist can draw upon a wealth of knowledge about human learning. Certain subfields of educational neuroscientific research have developed, which each seek to understand the functions and processes which underlie specified learning in the brain. Insights gained from these subfields could broaden educationists' knowledge on various aspects of learning and development—some examples are briefly mentioned in the section that follows.

Knowledge of neuroscience for language in the classroom

Neuroscientific research has led to greater awareness of the brain bases of speech and language. The left-hemisphere dominance for language has been confirmed (Dehaene-Lambertz, Dehaene & Hertz-Pannier, 2002), but there is also proof that the right hemisphere contributes greatly towards the processing of more demanding language tasks, for instance meaning in language, which includes prosody, humour, inferences, metaphors etc (Monetta & Joanette, 2003). An important finding for educationists is that school-age children do not have fully developed language systems and their spoken language skills continue to grow throughout their school career. This is not just because they are exposed to more complicated vocabulary and grammar at school, but also because of the underlying changes in neural structure and function (Williams, 2010).

When teaching children in the Foundation Phase, teachers must take into consideration that the child is learning many new skills (like letter formation, phonemic awareness and spelling rules) that take up much cognitive resources and the child might not have the maturational readiness to use a specific language for a learning task. Children may also not always be able to coordinate listening to language and writing language at the same time. These two activities involve different language processing demands in the brain and coupled with learning new skills, such as the technicalities of letter formation, there may be an overload of cognitive processing demands.

Neuroscience has also proved what teachers have long observed, that it requires less effort to learn a second language when one is younger. It is because it is easier for the brain to learn a second language before school-going age, as the language processing involved is more automated (Kovelman, Baker & Pettito, 2008). Learning additional languages after that is doable, but necessitates the use of more controlled cognitive processes, such as cognitive flexibility, working memory and inhibitory processing (Wartenburger, Heekeren, Abutalebi, Cappa, Villringer & Perani, 2003). What neuroscience affords us to understand about language development, is that it is not just a tool that children apply to the learning process, but that it involves intricate processing and is an evolving skill well into adulthood.

Knowledge of neuroscience for reading in the classroom

Neuroscience investigation have revealed the functional organisation and development of reading in the brain. Gabrieli and colleagues noted that reading is a prevailing threshold to knowledge and changes from an initial '*focus* in formal education (learning to read)' to the '*medium* of formal education (reading to learn)' (Gabrieli, Christodoulou, O'Loughlin & Eddy, 2010). Reading is, however, a recent cultural invention and our brains are not wired through evolution to read. This means that when we are born, we do not have an innate (inborn) knowledge to be able to read, but because of the brain's capacity to create new capabilities through incorporation of older abilities (connectivity), humans are able to learn how to read. Because there are no specific areas in the brain for reading as there is for spoken language, the brain must recruit certain regions to recognise written text—one such a region is the 'visual word form area (VWFA)' (Dehaene & Cohen, 2011:254). When learning to read, the brain must balance two goals:

1. Relating printed words to sounds of words.
2. Matching the printed words as fast as possible to meaning.

For these two goals to be attained, readers use two different neural routes. The first, the *phonological route*, which relies on left hemispheric posterior temporal brain regions, is used to decode a string of letters, translate it into some pattern, and then access meaning of the word or sound pattern (Gabrieli, et al, 2010). This route is specialised for words that are regular, rare, or novel; on this neural route, the typical rules for translation from letters to sounds can or must be applied. Then there is another *direct route* to bypass sound-pattern stage and attempt to match a printed word directly with meaning (Gabrieli, et al, 2010). This route is ideal for frequently encountered words, also called 'sight words' which have irregular, but memorised pronunciation and meaning.

Through a process of phonological awareness children who begin to learn to read learn to relate the words that they hear (auditory language) to the words in print. They thus become aware that spoken words comprise of specific sounds (phonemes) that can be represented by letters or syllables (graphemes). Ziegler and Goswami (2005:4) found that 'phonological awareness in prereaders predicts later success in learning to read in both alphabetic and non-alphabetic languages'. Functional neuroimaging studies identify a circuit that is engaged during phonological analysis of reading, which typically includes several left-side brain regions in frontal, temporal, and parietal lobes where graphemes (print) are matched to phonemes (sounds).

Functional brain imaging could also assist in the early identification of pre-reading children who may be susceptible to developing reading difficulties later on, as studies show that early identification correlate highly with their reading and general language scores years later (Guttorm, Leppänen, Poikkeus, Eklund, Lyytinen & Lyytinen, 2005). Evidence furthermore shows that an increase in phonological decoding abilities were similarly predicted by behavioural and fMRI measures, but that the combination of the two, envisaged improvements notably better than either measure alone (Hoeft, Ueno, Reiss, Meyer, Whitfield-Gabrieli, Glover, et al, 2007). Functional brain imaging could thus play an important part in the prediction of future achievement or difficulty in reading. However, combined with genetic and familial information, it will add even more to the educationist's support toolkit to facilitate preventative intervention and allow more children to experience success at learning to read.

Knowledge of neuroscience for classroom mathematics

Developments in knowledge regarding the neural bases of numerical cognition has led to increased research in this field, and educationists' engagement with recent developments in the expanding field of mathematical cognition has been described as 'overdue' (Gillum, 2012:288). A growing number of studies have investigated how numbers are represented in the brain, what brain regions underlie calculation abilities, and how these brain regions develop (Ansari, 2010). Starting with Karen Wynn's breakthrough discoveries at MIT in the 1990's (Wynn, 1992) and continuing with works of Stanislas Dehaene (1997, 2011), Brian Butterworth (1999, 2010), Keith Devlin (2010), and Daniel Ansari (2010, 2017), these studies have revealed many new facts about the way in which the brain learns mathematics.

We now know that there are certain areas in the brain which regulate all maths functions, whether seeing a quantity, a number symbol, or when doing arithmetic (Dehaene, 2011). Studies using fMRI also reveal that mathematical capacities in the brain appear to be localised, specifically in an area known as the horizontal intra-parietal sulcus or *hIPS* (Dehaene, 2011). Neuroscientific studies of maths in the brain also show that all humans are born with two innate or 'core-knowledge systems of number' onto which many other mathematical skills build (Henning & Ragpot, 2013:74). These two systems are known as:

1. The *approximate number sense* (ANS) which is an analoge sense of relative sizes of collections.
2. The *object tracking system* (OTS) which has to do with the ability to precisely track small numbers of distinct objects (Feigenson, Dehaene & Spelke, 2004).

The ANS is inherited from our evolutionary past and denotes the child's later competence for doing arithmetic which is grounded on a foundational representation of approximate number (Dehaene, 2010). Humans of all ages (even newborn babies) have the ability to instinctively detect the estimated number of objects in a specific set presented to them (Piazza, 2010), and is active anytime someone uses or even thinks about numbers, not only when doing formal maths (Mazzocco, Feigenson & Halberda, 2011). The OTS as a mental system of quantification which shows in infants where they can represent an exact distinction among small numbers and that 'their sense of number is not dependent on numerical ratio, but on individual object tracking with an "upper bound" of three' (Feigenson, Dehaene & Spelke, 2004:310; Henning & Ragpot, 2013:74). Numbers and arithmetic beyond the quantity three, require the use of language (Devlin, 2010).

Some controversy surrounding mathematics education involves the need for rote learning, which denotes learning the facts of maths. Some researchers show that mathematical education should rely entirely on conceptual understanding, others argue that rote learning of the basic number facts and practice of procedures is best, as the Hindu-Arabic system is difficult to learn and use efficiently (Devlin, 2010). Bezuidenhout (2017) argues that mathematical competence relies on the child utilising three sets of knowledges namely, factual, procedural, and conceptual—a point of view which is supported by evidence from neuroscience. Devlin (2010) furthermore states that arithmetic development relies to a large extent on the ability to connect the quantity representation with other representations of linguistic and Arabic symbols for number, as well as on the recycling of nearby cortical regions involved in representing space. The importance of language in learning mathematics is proposed by both Elizabeth Spelke (2012) and Susan Carey (2009), as they argue that 'language serves as combinatory agent in assembling knowledge to form concepts once children learn through language and other symbols' (Fritz-Stratmann, Balzer, Herholdt, Ragpot & Ehlert, 2014:120). The goal of educationists should be to support the development of fluent and automised interactions between these representations and symbols, so that it frees the all-purpose working memory resource of our prefrontal cortices for other purposes in the building of mathematical concepts (Devlin, 2010).

Knowledge of neuroscience for creativity in the classroom

For many years, myths sparked by laterality studies of the brain have propagated the idea that hemispheric lateralisation exists in a person's 'learning style'. This promoted the popular idea that some people are 'right brained' and thus more creative, and others are 'left brained' and thus more logical (Fischer & Heikkinen, 2010). Fortunately, these myths have been debunked by studies of creativity in the brain. What we have now learned from *neuroart* (neuroscience focusing on the study of creativity), is that creative activities are not localised in one hemisphere, but promotes connectivity across brain regions. In fact, multiple neural connections which would not ordinarily be made, are sparked by creativity. Winner and Hetland (2007) proved that in order to think creatively, for example envisioning mental images to perceive in novel ways, support learning across multiple domains.

An interesting study to show that multiple brain regions are involved when one performs creative acts was done with an artist performing lyrical improvisation. Siyuan Lui and colleagues did fMRI on a hip-hop, free style rapper, while he was practicing his craft (Liu, Chow, Xu, Erkkinen, Swett, Eagle, Rizik-Baer & Braun, 2012). This was a novel study as it was the first time 'in action' creativity, as opposed to 'imagined' creativity could be studied in real time. This is because fMRI requires as little as possible movement of the body to get an accurate scan of the brain. Creative activities usually ask for movement, such as painting or dancing, thus to be creative in an fMRI machine was almost impossible as movement is very limited. Former neuroscientific studies of creativity relied on the person 'imagining' the creative process (Schlegel, Kohler,

Alexander, Konuthula & Tse, 2013) for example of doing a dance routine (Calvo-Merino, Glaser, Grèzes, Passingham & Haggard, 2006), which would cause similar neural activity as during real performance. In Lui's study, the artist (rapper) was able to lie still, but do 'freestyling'—thus lyrical improvisation in the hip-hop genre on any given topic. Findings showed the rapper's brain processes bypassed normal mechanisms of executive control of what he was saying; he was thus less inhibited by what he should or should not say allowing sudden insights, seemingly unbidden, to emerge. Lui et al (2012) noted that 'these functional reorganizations may facilitate the initial improvisatory phase of creative behaviour'. The brain's language processing centre was also more highly active than during normal conversation, because of the intricacy involved in choosing words, rhyming, and maintaining a cohesive idea. The attention of the freestyling rapper was furthermore defocused, as though he were drawing on many thoughts and experiences to create his craft—this may be the 'zoning-out' many artists refer to when they are deeply involved in their creative acts.

Another landmark discovery which explains much about the learning process during creative activities, especially those that involve movement, was the discovery of mirror neurons. Giacomo Rizzolatti and his colleagues (Rizzolatti & Craighero, 2004) found neurons, which respond in the same way when a person performs an action and when that person witnesses someone else perform the same action. They subsequently dubbed these 'mirror-neurons'. These mirror neurons take in an observation by processing it as if you were actually doing the action, and the next time you are able to replicate the action it is as if you have already done it once. Mirror neurons might thus be the answer as to why we learn through mimicry and proves why children learn better and easier when a teacher explains and demonstrates what needs to be done, instead of just verbal instruction.

Studies such as the aforementioned prove that the brain utilises different activations of neurons during creativity, which could be advantageous for classroom learning. Heilman, Nadeau and Beversdorf (2003), argue that creativity includes the demonstration of divergent thinking, which involves coactivation and communication among brain regions that are not ordinarily connected during activities that are non-creative. Including creativity in classroom activities could transform children's learning and foster divergent thinking skills, such as imagination and innovation. Stevenson and Deasy (2005) detected learning capabilities that the arts foster—these include: longer periods of sustained concentration, focused attention to given tasks, and abstract understanding by using multiple modalities to communicate ideas. This proves that pedagogy should focus on an increase of classroom learning activities, which include among others, visual arts, theatre and dance.

Implication for South African educationists

Much emphasis is placed on importance of context and environmental issues when it comes to teaching and learning in South African classrooms. Even though one cannot negate the significance of the influence of the environment on children's learning (as proven in epigenetic studies by Peckham, 2013), neuroscience also proves that brain structure and functions are pretty much uniform across all human beings (excluding perhaps those with injury and/ or some disabilities) during specific developmental stages. This knowledge of universal traits shared by all children compels South African teachers to take cognisance of the developmental level of the children whom they teach. Knowledge of the age in which certain processes in the brain show optimal development such as executive functions which develop lifelong, but peak during the ages between four to seven years (Röthlisberger, Neuenschwander, Cimeli, Michel & Roebers, 2011; Carlson, 2005) affords the teacher the necessary awareness to design and differentiate lesson outcomes according to the learners' age, and needs at that age.

As neuroscientific discoveries are made continuously the onus also lies with the teacher to update her knowledge regularly. Dissemination of new research findings are readily available on social media, the internet and YouTube, and relevance to classroom practice are made by educationists worldwide. But the explosion of availability of findings from neuroscientific research made brain images persuasive—and pervasive—in popular media (McCabe & Castel, 2008). Thus, a cautionary note, as educationists need to critically question many of the educational approaches and materials that claim to be 'based on neuroscientific research'. The educationist needs to always ensure that the presented research has been peer reviewed, as facts that are presented as 'simple truths' about the brain, are often oversimplifications to serve a specific purpose, such as selling a so called 'brain-based' product (Pickering & Howard-Jones, 2007).

Apart from vigilance in the study of presented material, educationists have much to gain from continuously updating their knowledge on neuroscientific research and learning. Moreover, they should not only be passive recipients of knowledge from scientists, but should become researchers of their own practice, thereby adding the necessary educational input to the neuroscientific research in the field of educational neuroscience. Together researchers and practitioners can lay the groundwork for a true 'science of education' (Fischer & Heikkinen, 2010:321).

Conclusion

This brief introduction to the field of educational neuroscience has highlighted the significance for the modern educator to have cognisance of 'self in science' beyond the discipline of pure pedagogy. Long gone are the days where the teacher can prepare a lesson based on 'good methods', walk into a classroom and teach, and expect that learning has indeed taken place. The 21st century educator should study neuroscience and pedagogy in tandem, to afford learners optimal learning opportunities, intervention and support. Even though cautions had been raised about making arbitrary associations between neuroscience and education (as strongly advocated by Bruer in the 1990s (Bruer, 1997)), educationists could learn much about improving pedagogy based on ideas proposed in neuroscience. The usability of educational neuroscience to inform everyday pedagogy lies in its potential to be used in combination with developmental, cognitive and other leaning sciences to provide a novel perspective on daily educational practices (Ansari & Coch, 2006).

18 Cognitive psychology: Post-Piagetian notions of childhood conceptual change

LARA RAGPOT

Conceptual change is a particularly profound kind of learning—it goes beyond revising one's specific beliefs and involves restructuring the very concepts used to formulate those beliefs. (State University Education)

Introduction

Everyday educationists (the term 'educationists' will be used in this chapter as an all-encompassing term for classroom teachers, learning support specialists and educational psychologists) teach individuals at various stages of development with different abilities. Much energy and time is spent on lesson planning, methodology and the teaching of facts and procedures. Yet, immaterial of how well the educationist 'performs', learning often does not take place for the individual(s) being taught. Knowledge of pedagogy thus does not hold the only key to attaining the envisioned learning outcome, and cannot provide the only answer as to why, and when, some children learn and others not. To gain a better comprehension of what encompasses childhood learning and how to fully support it, educationists thus need to gather insights from other disciplines in the social sciences.

Cognitive psychology, as a subfield of psychology, focuses on describing and deconstructing the cognitive processes involved in human learning. According to Lu and Dosher (2007:2769) cognitive psychology focuses on investigating human cognition scientifically, thus converging on 'our mental abilities—perceiving, learning, remembering, thinking, reasoning, and understanding' (Lu & Dosher, 2007:2769). Essentially, cognitive psychology investigates how individuals attain and employ information and knowledge. It has grown as a research field and is now seen as part of the more all-encompassing interdisciplinary cognitive sciences, which values the hard sciences as well as the social sciences, thus incorporating ideas from, among others, biology, physical sciences, linguistics, philosophy, neuroscience, computer science and even artificial intelligence.

A brief historical overview of cognitive psychology shows that it was at first overshadowed by behaviourism, which focused on studying the laws relating to apparent behaviour to objective, discernible stimulus conditions, with no or little consideration of mental processes within (Watson, 1913; Boring, 1950; Skinner, 1950). With this lack of insight into and little appreciation of internal mental processes involved in learning, behaviourists could neither provide a distinction between memory and performance, nor could they describe complex learning adequately (Chomsky, 1959). These limitations led to the waning of behaviourism and its dominance of scientific psychology, which brought about the 'cognitive revolution' (Price, 2011:26) when researchers in several fields developed *theories of mind* based on more multifaceted representations (Miller, 1956; Broadbent, 1958; Chomsky, 1959; Newell, Shaw & Simon, 1958). Only during the 1960s did cognitive psychology gain prominence as an independent field (Tulving, 1962; Sperling, 1960). With his publication of the book *Cognitive Psychology* (1967), Ulrich Neisser (often seen as the father of cognitive psychology), unified research ideas relating to perception, attention, problem solving, pattern recognition, and memory. From these beginnings, cognitive psychology today continues to be a growing field of study of the human mind and learning. One sub-branch of research and interest within the field of cognitive psychology, which focuses particularly on childhood developmental processes of learning, is known as cognitive developmental psychology. This subfield should be of particular interest to all involved in the education of children and adolescents.

The main protagonist of cognitive developmental psychology has been Jean Piaget (1955, 1977), whose ideas still holds merit, but are no longer seen as the quintessential epitome of describing childhood cognitive development. Piaget's theory has two main tenets: 'the process of coming to know; and the stages we move through as we gradually acquire this ability' (Huitt & Hummel, 2003:1). Piaget believed that biological development and maturation drives progress from one cognitive stage to the next. Experimental and correlational studies have supported some of his ideas, but others have also disproved what Piaget held as truth (Huitt & Hummel, 2003). Nevertheless, the vast impact Piaget's ideas had on our construction of how children develop cognitively (see Chapter 15), is evident in its constant incorporation in most undergraduate and post-graduate child development courses and child development books (Bergen, 2008).

With the development of neuroscience and insights into the biological basis of brain structures and functions, many new ideas on cognitive development and human learning have emerged over the past 30 years. These insights showed the need for a shift beyond Piagetian stage generalised understanding of childhood cognitive development. In the past, cognitive theorists, such as Piaget, had to depend on behavioural observations to determine children's learning; but contemporary cognitive psychologists can for example, use functional Magnetic Resonance Imaging (fMRI), to give empirical evidence that infants show memories and mental combinations at a much earlier age than what Piaget proposed (Graham, Pfeifer, Fischer, Lin, Gao & Fait, 2015; Gaillard, Grandin & Xu, 2001); and '(n)euroscience techniques provide an open window previously unavailable to the origin of thoughts and actions in children' (Arsalidou & Pascual-Leone, 2016:1). The insights which neuroscience affords are thus an addition to classical interactive behavioural observations, thereby giving a more comprehensive and holistic 'picture' of cognitive development, which incorporates core or innate, as well as acquired ideas, of conceptual development and learning. The ideal is thus to identify the heuristic importance of constructivist-developmental ideas (such as proposed by Piaget) in combination with, and as complimentary to, contemporary cognitive developmental neuroscience (Arsalidou & Pascual-Leone, 2016; Evans, 2011; Scherf, Sweeney & Luna, 2006) to give comprehensive insights into the ways in which children learn.

One very specific approach to delineate the processes involved in learning and the development of concepts is known as conceptual change. Childhood conceptual change is of particular importance to educationists, as it gives insights into ways to facilitate and/or support optimal development and intervention of children's learning in educational settings (Agianse, Williams, Dunnamah, Tumba, 2015; Davis, 2001). The rest of this chapter will focus on explicating *learning* in terms of conceptual change theory. The first discussion will establish a central definition and understanding of 'conceptual change', then the chapter will spotlight two contemporary post-Piagetian theorists of conceptual change, Susan Carey and Alison Gopnik. Attention to their insights contribute to an alternative view of childhood conceptual change that incorporates, but goes beyond, former notions suggested by theorists, such as Piaget. The insights they afford thus build a progressive bridge from Piaget's descriptions of how children develop and modify conceptual understanding (and thus learn), to a more up-to-date view.

Conceptual change: Stage general or domain specific?

Conceptual change is a specific approach to defining learning of new concepts and according to Jonassen (2006) conceptual change is the mechanism underlying meaningful learning. In the early 1980s, Posner and his colleagues (Posner, Strike, Hewson & Gertzog, 1982), who included researchers of science education and science philosophers, proposed a theory of conceptual change. This theory is grounded in Piaget's ideas of disequilibration and accommodation, but was furthermore hugely influenced by the work of Thomas Kuhn (1962) in his pursuit of explaining thinking and paradigms in science. Science has long been the predominant proponent of conceptual change theory (Vosniadou, Vamvakoussi & Skopeliti, 2008). In developmental psychology, conceptual change as a term, derived from the awareness of development that involves *qualitative shifts* in children's ideas about physical qualities, time, space, number and life in general (Ragpot, 2013). Most of these shifts were seen to be happening in the progressive construction of powerful *domain-general thinking structures* as proposed by Jean Piaget (1955). A domain general view means that the changes in course of cognitive development is described in generalised periods which are essentially free of content and culture, and based on innatist (inborn), maturational (growing with maturity) stages. This domain-general description of cognitive developmental proposes, for instance, that the child will *always* be egocentric in the pre-operational stage—regardless of the specific domain (area of development) in question.

Unlike domain-general developmental changes, contemporary research on cognitive development attribute conceptual change to collections of innate domain-specific knowledge systems (Spelke & Kinzler, 2007). Some of the systems may include knowledge of language, physical objects and number (Chomsky, 1980). Each system of knowledge pertains to a definite set of phenomena and entities (Carey & Spelke, 1994) and will be structured according to specific fundamental principles. In the domain of number concept, for instance, they might include the tenets of one-one correspondence and ordinal number concept (Feigenson, Dehaene & Spelke, 2004). Domains can team up when they centre on the same core principles—for example, knowledge of language and knowledge of numbers can do this when they attempt to describe collections of objects.

Domain-specific knowledge systems also require of human reasoning to be able to identify and categorise entities belonging to a specific system in a particular domain. For example, a sophisticated system of knowledge of psychology (a theory of mind—how to read people and interact with them) is of little use unless individuals who are doing the (mindful) reasoning can establish when they are faced with other persons, in interaction. Reasoning, in this instance, thus depends on the mechanisms within the domain (of the theory of mind) which single out entities of this domain—something Carey and Spelke (1994:170) refer to as 'domain-specific perception.' In infancy, these researchers propose that a single knowledge system direct reasoning and perception in no less than three domains: psychology (theory of mind), physics and number (Carey & Spelke, 1994; Ragpot, 2013). Knowledge also grows via a process of enhancement, when central principles become further ingrained, when the child is learning from action, observation, or from social interchange (Carey & Spelke, 1994). Knowledge in specific domains contributes to overall cognitive development. Ideas put forward on domain specificity of cognitive development, could assist the educationist in identification of the specific domains (such as mathematics) in which a child seems to be lagging and is in need of support; in the same vein domains which are developmentally advanced (such as verbal development) could be incorporated into pedagogy as assets in support of weaker domains.

These general ideas about conceptual change serve merely as an introduction and the focus of discussion will now centre around two contemporary conceptual change theorists who have done much research in the field and their ideas pose some interesting insights into how children develop and change conceptual understanding.

Cognitive developmentalist Susan Carey: Concepts, beliefs, theories and conceptual change

Since the 1970s, Susan Carey conveyed her ideas of conceptual change to the developmental psychology community (Smith, 2010), and she has been identified as one of the most highly influential cognitive psychologists whose work is significant for psychology, philosophy and linguistics (Barner & Baron, 2016). A main tenet of her work is her view of what is meant by 'conceptual change' and this is expansively described and discussed in her seminal book *The Origin of Concepts* (Carey, 2009). The discussion following is merely a brief summary of her ideas, but may nonetheless be insightful as her views pose an alternative to stage generalised maturational thoughts of childhood conceptual change. Furthermore, even though she is not an educationist per se, Carey's ideas about conceptual change have many educational implications in general classrooms and for intervention specialists, who support children individually.

Conceptual change

Carey questions 'conceptual change' as it is referred to in the fields of psychology and education to denote knowledge enrichment and belief revision, as she sees it differently (Carey, 2009:364). Carey (2009) notes that conceptual change does not happen suddenly and that there is not a sudden moment of gestalt shift, but that it may take years in the child engaged in knowledge restructuring. This view is contrary to a Piagetian view of specific stages in cognitive development, which are age-related in all children, and where children make sudden leaps in their cognitive development when they exit a former and enter a new specific stage. Carey argues that she would rather refer to conceptual change as the term is used in the philosophy of science (Carey, 2009). In this sense, conceptual change is not the same as changing one's mind, acquiring new knowledge, or changing one's beliefs, but rather, generating *new concepts* not expressible in terms of previously available vocabulary. In this vein 'conceptual change' requires incommensurability of the two different concepts, or, conceptual systems (Carey, 2009:364).

Incommensurability

The notion of commensurability was first suggested by Kitcher and Kuhn (Carey, 2009:267):

> *Kitcher outlines (and endorses) Kuhn's thesis that there are episodes in the history of science at the beginnings and ends, of which practitioners of the same field of endeavour speak languages that are not mutually translatable.*

They have become incommensurable. This means that the explanations, beliefs, and laws, that are explicable in the terms and phrases used at the onset, in language l (L1) of conceptual system 1 (CS1), cannot be articulated in terms of the terms and phrases used at the end, in language 2 (L2) of conceptual system 2 (CS2) (Carey, 1988). Conceptual change is thus a considerable state of change brought about by learning, development, insight, research, theorising, and so forth. According to Carey, incommensurability entails 'the relation between conceptual systems such that one contains concepts that are not merely absent from the other, but are actually incoherent from the point of view of the other' (Carey, 2009:359). For instance, once young learners grasp that air takes up space and has volume, it is no longer possible to refer to air as 'nothing' and they can never go back to fully believing that the air is 'nothing'.

The conceptual system of understanding within which one functions, is also very closely related to the language one uses (as referred to in Kitcher's reference previously). Adults who work with children should keep in mind that their conceptual system on a specific idea/content may not always be the same as the child's conceptual system and therefore their use of language in the adult conceptual system might be incompatible in meaning to that of the child's, even if exactly the same words are used. Children may learn use and meaning of language from adults, but conceptually they are not blank slates. As they learn new words and expressions of their language, they have to 'map' these onto the ideas and concepts they already know and then use the signs of language to develop the concepts further. They thus create probable hypotheses about word meanings based on the knowledge available to them in their conceptual system. Thus the way in which they use words and develop language is constrained by their knowledge of the actual words, but also by the way they understand the world around them (Carey, 2009). Thus when a preschool child says that the sun is alive or that buttons are alive because they keep your shirt closed, the child is making true statements that have been formulated with regard to different concepts from those expressed by adult use of the same word 'alive'. The child uses these terms as 'undifferentiated concepts that no longer play any role in the adult conceptual system' (Carey, 1988:180)—they have become incommensurable.

Incommensurability and education

The notion of *incommensurability* asks of the educationist to be more cognisant of child's understanding of the content in a specific domain, thus the child's conceptual system (conceptual system 1—CS1) and the language the child uses to express that conceptual system (language 1—L1). The adult might be functioning and using terms of expression in a more sophisticated conceptual system (conceptual system 2—CS2), which might be far removed from the child's understanding and might use language differently in meaning (language 2—L2). If the educationist wants to teach the child a new understanding of a concept, she needs to facilitate a change in the child's understanding from the current conceptual system CS1 expressed in L1 to a new extended and enriched understanding in conceptual system CS2, with new expression or understanding of language used to express ideas in that conceptual system—L2.

A proficient educationist takes cognisance of the child's conceptual system and language (CS1 and L1) and 'returns' to *that* conceptual system in order to facilitate the child to further understanding towards the conceptual system and language expression in that system envisioned (CS2 and L2). This brings to mind the Vygotskian idea of zone of proximal development (Kozulin, 1990) (see Chapters 8 and 16), but goes further in asking greater pedagogical proficiency from the adult, as it does not just entail 'meeting the child half way', but actually asks of the adult to 're-think' the phenomenon within the understanding of the child's conceptual system (CS1), and also use the language of *that* conceptual system (L1). For example, when asking the child to think of the number five (5), don't just assume that the child will think of the Hindu Arabic symbol (5), but have cognisance of the child's conceptual level within the domain. The child might still only think in terms of quantities and had not yet moved to a symbolic ascription of the quantity five to the symbol '5'. Thus, when the teacher refers to five as a Hindu Arabic symbol (5), the young child might be envisioning 'five' puppies playing on the ground and might struggle to follow why five plus one make six. In 'rethinking' herself back into the conceptual system of the child (CS1), the teacher will use language of that conceptual system (L1) to guide the child to new understanding in CS2 with L2. Using our example of five, the teacher could for instance use objects to count out five, relate that to the number-word five, and then only explain that it could also relate to the Hindu Arabic symbol '5'.

Cognitive discontinuity

Cognitive discontinuity explains why when a child has gained development in understanding a concept, some of the previous beliefs about the concept cease to exist. There is thus an incompatibility between CS1 and CS2. An example could be when the child who believes that the Easter bunny leaves chocolates eggs in the garden (CS1), one morning sees her dad hiding the eggs in the garden. Her former unequivocal belief in the existence of an 'Easter bunny' can never exist again. The child has moved in her understanding and belief from CS1 (the Easter bunny is real) to her new understanding (CS2) that the Easter bunny is fictional.

Domain specificity

Conceptual change is *domain specific*, and when we analyse children's thinking structures, we should rather look at domain-specific changes linked to content than at domain-general stages. Carey shows that children's thoughts are controlled by domain specific structures, which are inherent instinctive theories in which daily expounding concepts are entrenched and which guides models of conjecture and problem solving.

Bootstrapping

Apart from being domain specific, conceptual change also often rests on a 'multi-step, iterative *bootstrapping* process' (Carey, 2009:21). In terms of conceptual change, to pull oneself up by one's bootstraps will mean that children often create new 'representational resources that are not entirely grounded in forerunner representations' (Carey, 2009:20) as explained previously in terms of incommensurability and cognitive discontinuity. Bootstrapping is thus a process where 'the phenomena in the domain, represented in terms of whatever concepts the child has available, in terms of the set of interrelated symbols in the placeholder structure' (Carey 2009:245).

Placeholder structures

By *placeholder structure*, Carey means both existing knowledge and language or other representations that prepare a 'space' for cognitive development. In other words, a child may already know that a certain word/phrase exists, but has not yet 'mapped' it semantically and syntactically, thus comprehend the full meaning. The word/phrase itself serves as a partially interpreted *placeholder*, which 'holds a place' for the meaning and which will come with time, waiting to be filled with richer meanings (Carey & Sarnecka, 2004:487).

An example could be to learn the drawing, and name, of the 'number line', before really understanding what it means in terms of successive numbers which will always be in a specific order. Another example of a placeholder idea could be when a child is told by an adult that she needs to eat her food to grow and stay alive, but she does not yet fully comprehend what the biological processes are which underlie this statement. The child will repeat this statement, but without full comprehension, as it is just a repetition or rote learning of new networks of symbols at this stage. After this initial process of mere repetition, the next step is when the child starts to interpret the placeholder idea and gain understanding of the knowledge which underlies the statement. With development and exposure to different learning situations and content, the child uses a selection of non-deductive modelling processes (for example through analogies and inferences which offers the most suited explanation) to interpret the placeholder idea in a new way. So, after the initial nonsensical repetition of the adult's statement, the child gains a new understanding of the uttered phrase in terms of the biological world in which they exist.

Intuitive theories

Lastly, Carey (2009:478) maintains that even pre-schoolers 'have *implicit intuitive theories* in which their everyday explanatory concepts are embedded and play a role'. They use these intuitive or naïve theories to direct the way in which they extrapolate knowledge and do problem solving. These theories are also constantly revised when they are faced with additional information from their environment. Carey (2009) argues that many aspects of childhood conceptual change are the same whether the individual who is doing the learning act is a small child or a highly educated adult scientist. Children and scientists both use clear symbolic representations to devise placeholder structures. They then infuse the placeholder structures with meaning via modelling devices such as analogies, inductive inference and thought experiments.

The notion of similarities of theory changes in young children and adult scientists, is explored further in the next section, which focuses on the work of another contemporary conceptual change theorist—Alison Gonik—who with her colleague Andrew Meltzhoff, developed the '*Theory* theory' of conceptual development.

Alison Gopnik: The '*Theory* theory' and children as 'little scientists'

Alison Gopnik is an internationally acclaimed scholar who investigates the way in which children learn and develop. She unequivocally holds that children's minds could assist us in comprehending profound philosophical questions (Gopnik, 2003). This section of the chapter focuses on a particular aspect of Alison Gopnik's work, where she proposes a theory of childhood cognitive development and conceptual change, referred to as the '*theory* theory'.

According to the *theory* theory, childhood conceptual development is analogous to cognitive development in adult scientists as viewed from the history of science. Just as scientists' theory change involves radical knowledge restructuring, conceptual development in children also requires radical theory changes that involve conceptual change. Children can furthermore be compared to scientists in the way in which they change theories as described by Thomas Kuhn in his work on paradigm shifts (Kuhn, 1989). One theory can replace another when it is better suited to the empirical evidence and permits one to make better forecasts, conduct more thorough interpretations, and explain phenomena more clearly. Evidence that contradicts a theory is disregarded except when it persistently presents itself. Theories stand until there are replacements that explain, interpret and predict phenomena more forcefully. They have to be defeasible and also, thus, falsifiable, otherwise they do not enjoy the status of a theory.

According to Viale (2001:11) the 'methodological criteria of theory change in big and little scientists are not the guarantee of truth and representational success'. These criteria may initially lead to the invention of false hypotheses, but when these predicted theories prove to be untrue, the child will look for other theories which will explain their experiences in the world more accurately. If the child does not generate theories which could be defeasible (thus proven to be false), they would not present with growth and change and would be stuck. As children develop, they will only replace existing theories with alternative ones if the alternative theory does a better job at *interpreting*, *predicting* and *explaining* the presented evidence. Conceptual learning is thus guaranteed when the child makes errors, as these inaccuracies generate alternative theories better suited to fit their newfound understanding of the world.

Gopnik and her colleague Andrew Meltzoff (1997:10) argue that 'children's conceptual structures, like scientists', are theories and that their conceptual development is theory formation and change'. Gopnik and Meltzoff (1997:32–40) assert that most of the characteristics of theories, such as abstractedness, coherence, causality, ontological commitment, prediction, interpretation, and explanation, ought to be viewed as relevant for children's initial cognitive structures as these structures are really theoretical. Thus, children's theories involve appeal to abstract conceptual ideas, which show coherence and causality. As they form theories they learn characteristic patterns of predictions—these include extensions to new groups of evidence and inaccurate predictions. They make mistakes like scientists do. Children's theories also lead to idiosyncratic clarification of evidence, thus two children with two different theories will interpret even elemental facts differently. Children's theories invoke typical explanations couched in terms of abstract ideas and laws.

The '*theory* theory' has been successfully applied to explain children's developing understanding of the *physical world* (Smith, Carey & Wiser, 1985), the *biological world* (Gelman & Wellman, 1991), and the *psychological* world (Gopnik, 1993). It has been used to explain adults' learning (Murphy & Medin, 1985), learning of children at school (Keil, 1989), pre-schoolers (Gelman & Wellman, 1991), and even infants' learning (Gopnik & Meltzoff, 1997). Gopnik and Meltzoff (1997) furthermore suggest, that infants come into this world with innate/inborn theories and that even during infancy they already start revising these theories. Hence infants have an inborn set of beliefs or principals that facilitate their initial interaction with the world around them. Viale (2001) argues that one such a core set of principals is the underlying understanding of the interactions amid physical events. Researchers have proved that a six-month-old infant can already:

> ... *apply the principle of cohesion (a moving object maintains its connectedness and boundaries); the principle of continuity (a moving object traces exactly one connected path over space and time); and the principle of contact (objects move together if and only if they touch).* (Spelke, Phillips & Woodward, 1995:48)

Children are also able to distinguish theories of biology and psychology (Viale, 2001). Thus, children have intuitive/inborn theories of what distinguishes living beings from objects or artefacts.

Gopnik and Meltzoff (1997) suggest that their research proves that children use their innate principles to start understanding abstract entities which they come across in their development, how these entities are coherently organised, and have connecting interactions. In this way children are able to formulate ontological predictions and maintain counterfactuals. They keep options for change open and so they learn to use what is made available for explaining phenomena, predicting possible outcomes and even making interpretations.

At first, children often simply overlook counter-evidence to what they believe as true; then they justify possible opposing evidence with supplementary hypotheses; the next step is if they start using this new supplementary hypothesis or theoretical awareness in restricted contexts (testing the waters to see if new idea might hold); the last step is when they restructure their knowledge and the newly accepted theoretical entities perform dominant roles. In this way, they observe and test their environment. While they are constructing a new theory, they will test it extensively to gather empirical truth that it holds true. If educationists understand this type of reasoning, they will think about the way they teach. As much as they will explain, tell, and inform and demonstrate, they will at least be in a position to consider the role of children's own theorising and not only provide data (instruction) but also challenges to 'test theories' of, for example, cardinal number in mathematics learning. They may also wonder about their own theorising along these lines.

According to Gopnik and Meltzoff (1997) there are three distinct sets of problems which are at the heart of the children's cognitive and semantic development in the period between late infancy and early childhood. They suggest that there is a continuous development that bridges these core areas or domains from the time of early recognition and object manipulation to later naming and classifying objects of 'kind' understanding when they are able to utilise language. This natural progression is 'reflected in the child's non-linguistic problem solving, in their spontaneous language and later in their verbal performance tasks' (Gopnik & Meltzoff, 1997:74). They also argue that in this continuity there is deep conceptual change that takes place in children's grasp of each of these three domains of:

1. Children's theory of appearances.
2. Children's theory of action.
3. Children's theory of kind.

Children's early conceptions in these three domains are different from later conceptions and their ideas about the domains change in a way that is like theory change—on the basis of new 'data' from the world. These specific domains (unlike Piagetian domain-general stages) are relatively independent of each other in development, though there are some similarities. In all three domains, the child's understanding of the world is accomplished through continuous hypothesising and testing of relevant evidence, rather than theory-independent maturational or information processing changes.

The '*theory* theory', presents educationists with an alternative view of childhood conceptual development to the confines of the Piagetian stage theory that leaves little space for recognising the value of individual experimental learning. If the educationist understands that children's minds are constantly weighing options and testing hypotheses, thereby creating conceptual change, they may learn to move away from teacher-centred lessons, to classrooms where children explore and learn through (guided) trial and error. In this vein, educationists should keep in mind that children need action and appropriate language to learn to categorise and manage their worlds and so generate conceptual change. In this way, they can engender classroom activities based on movement and communication and the use of evidence children can find around them. This proposes a move away from theory-independent maturational or information-processing views of children's learning and conceptual change.

Conclusion

Carey and Gopnik's work have brought further insights into the study of children's cognitive development and conceptual change since the onset of the cognitive revolution. Although there are some caveats in both these authors' premises, they stand tall in the estimation of reviewers of their work, such as Shea (2011) and Xu (2011) for Carey, and Gutheil (1999) and Davids (2010) for Gopnik.

What this chapter aimed to do was to encourage a move away from a purely constructivist, maturational, stage generalised view of childhood cognitive development. With the discussion of new ideas about childhood conceptual change and learning, the chapter aimed to highlight the importance for the contemporary educationist to utilise insights afforded by cognitive psychology, developmental psychology, and cognitive developmental neuroscience, to inform practice.

19 Identity, motivation and achievement

SALOMÉ HUMAN-VOGEL

Motivation is what gets you started. Commitment is what keeps you going.
(Adapted from Jim Ryun)

Introduction

Teachers fulfil an important role in the development of children and young people. They are entrusted with the cognitive, emotional and social development of the learners in their class. We can assume that teachers want the best for the learners in their classes, and that they want their learners to be happy about learning, and also be successful. Apart from being experts of their subject and the science of teaching and learning, literature tells us that the best teachers are also knowledgeable about the cognitive, emotional, and social development of the learners in their class, they are fair and just, and they are able to motivate learners by meeting their needs for autonomy, competence and support in the classroom. Effective teachers are also effective in their approach to classroom management and how they manage discipline. Learners who, through the support of their teachers develop autonomous forms of motivation are more likely to be happy about their learning experiences, and they are more likely to work hard to achieve in school. This is true not only for school learning, but across the lifespan, and continue into young adulthood when learners have to adapt to the demands of higher education. In this chapter, we will discuss what we know about the importance of identity and motivation to academic achievement, and the factors that make it more likely that learners can succeed. Knowing how to support the identity development of learners in your class can help you to be more effective in your teaching and learning, and will help you to support learners to be successful in school.

Why is this theme important?

As a teacher, you will play a central role in shaping and facilitating the educational experiences of the learners in your class. At school, teachers act *in loco parentis*, meaning that they take over the role of the parents during the time that the child is at school. This is not a task to be taken lightly. We know that children respond better to teachers with whom they have positive and supportive **relationships**, and who are able to create a positive and supporting environment to learn in. It is important for learners that their teachers accept them, and treat them fairly and justly. As with parents, teachers stand the best chance of creating a positive and responsive learning environment when they take the time to get to know their learners, establish a relationship of trust with them, and learn how to establish an authoritative relationship with them.

Apart from establishing a relationship with learners that are conducive to learning, teachers are also confronted with finding the most effective ways of supporting learners to develop their learning potential, and to find ways of fostering their **motivation** to want to learn and achieve. Not all learners are equally motivated to expend the time and effort to engage with schoolwork, and understanding how teachers can play a role in influencing learners' motivation positively, is an important skill that teachers need to develop.

Most teachers are familiar with the concept of intrinsic and extrinsic motivation that describes motivation that is essentially internally or externally determined. Fewer teachers are aware that motivation is really about how teachers are able to support learners' three basic psychological needs, namely autonomy, competence and relatedness. What these three needs tell us, is that learners are motivated to succeed when teachers are able to help learners understand that they can participate in choices that affect them (autonomy-supportive), that it is important for teachers to help learners develop a sense that they are able to do things for themselves (competence-supportive), and that learners feel that they can develop a supportive relationship with the teachers (support for relatedness). This theory of motivation is known as self-determination theory (Ryan & Deci, 2006). In addition to the three basic psychological needs, it is also important to understand that learners are motivated when they feel that schoolwork is meaningful. Most people feel more motivated to do something, when they feel that what they are doing, is personally meaningful to them. This is where identity is relevant, because personally meaningful, essentially means that people want to connect their goals in life to who they are—or how they know themselves.

How well learners know themselves—their sense of identity—determines what kind of life goals they choose. For example, if a learner does not really know him/herself very well, it is very typical for that learner to not know what they want in life, or what goals are important to them, and they are more likely to choose many different—but incoherent—goals as they are trying to get to know themselves. Alternatively, they restrict themselves to doing only a few things they know they are good at. If a learner decides early on—possibly based on feedback from parents and teachers—that they are just not good at schoolwork, they will most likely not do well at school, and will not set goals that are related to school. Hence, their motivation for doing schoolwork will be very low. It is a significant challenge that faces teachers everywhere, to develop in their knowledge of how to support learners to develop their sense of self, their motivation, and their ability to set meaningful goals for themselves.

Research tells us that not all learners approach a learning situation in the same way, and that their approach to learning is very much dependent on how they regulate their learning. **Self-regulation** of learning refers to the way learners set learning goals, and what they do to ensure that they meet their learning goals, all the while monitoring whether they are achieving them, or not. While self-regulation in a sense relates to personal choices that learners make, it can be greatly influenced by the learner's teacher. Also, as we have mentioned, a learner's sense of self—how well they know themselves—determines the kind of life goals that they consider to be personally meaningful. Since we know that a great deal of self-regulation is about setting goals and monitoring the attainment of those goals, it follows that identity also provides a significant constraint on self-regulation of behaviour in general. This is why, as a teacher, you may find that you do not get very far if you attempt to assist learners who struggle by teaching them to set academic goals, and to break down those goals into tasks. Such goals can be thought of as behavioural goals, and while most learners—and people in general—can learn to set behavioural goals and attain them, their motivation to do so continuously will be affected by how coherent those behavioural goals are with their life goals, and how personally relevant their life goals are in terms of their identity.

Related to self-regulation, is the very popular conception that all learners have different **learning styles** (see Chapter 10), and that a part of a teacher's success in mediating learning in the classroom, is about the extent to which a teacher is able to adjust his/her teaching style to accommodate various learning styles in the classroom. Many teachers worry about how to do this in the large classes that are so typical of South African classrooms, and with educational resources that are not freely available in all South African educational environments. Whenever one discussed learning styles, we need to take cognisance of brain development and functioning. As a teacher, it's a good thing to know what the brain is capable of and how it will affect the learning that happens in a classroom (see Chapter 17). Current knowledge of brain functioning does not empirically support the theory that it is helpful to teach according to various learning styles. As a teacher, you are much better positioned to approach teaching and learning in a fashion that allows learners to process complex information by drawing on a range of modalities supported by visual, auditory and motor processing.

Major debates

The most important educational debates in South Africa are focused on issues of access and success in learning. Access debates deal with problems related to fairness and equity around the fact that not all learners are able to access institutions of learning, or quality learning in quality schools. While this is an important problem in its own right, it is outside the scope of the present chapter, so the focus will centre on factors related to success in learning, assuming that a learner has gained access to an institution of learning, which is assumed to be a school (see Chapters 29, 30 and 31).

The most important debate therefore is how to ensure success in learning. Much of the research focus on engagement, which relates to understanding what students need to do to be successful. Literature tells us that those who are more engaged, ie, those who spend more time and effort on their learning, tend to be more successful. While this seems like a very simple fact, it belies much complexity. What are the factors that determine whether a learner will spend time and effort on their learning? Are these factors related to the learners only (such as in the case of being motivated or not)? What external factors in the environment contribute to whether learners are motivated (such as the characteristics of the learning environment or the home environment)? Again, it is important to consider how well learners know themselves, and how their self-knowledge impacts on their motivation to set goals that will support academic achievement. In terms of motivation, it is also important to consider what teachers can do to support learners' needs for autonomy, competence and relatedness to create a positive and responsive learning environment in which learners would want to achieve.

Motivation and academic achievement is a well-researched area in education, and most teachers are aware that some learners are motivated more by internal conditions, whereas others are motivated more by external rewards, such as certificates of merit or public recognition. In recent years, this theory, called self-determination theory (Ryan & Deci, 2006), has developed to the extent that scholars now realise that teachers can motivate learners by creating a learning environment that supports learners' basic psychological needs, which include a need for autonomy, competence and relatedness (Ryan & Deci, 2006).

In terms of the self-regulation of behaviour, researchers know that understanding the process of self-regulation, even teaching learners how to set learning goals, and how to monitor their progress towards them, are not enough to guarantee that learners will engage in these steps. Simply having knowledge of a process, does not guarantee that learners will:

1. Know under which circumstances it is necessary to use that knowledge.
2. When to use that knowledge.
3. How to use that knowledge in different contexts.

These problems are known as knowledge transfer problems. Another reason why teaching self-regulation behaviours is not enough to make a difference to academic achievement, is that learners only tend to carry out actions that are meaningful to them. If they do not experience learning or academic achievement as personally relevant or meaningful, they are not likely to show the kind of behaviours that communicate the importance of academic achievement. Learners who know themselves well and perceive academic achievement as personally meaningful are much more likely to be proactive in their learning by setting learning goals for example (Human-Vogel & Rabe, 2015).

How is the theme relevant to South African schools and classrooms?

To be an effective teacher, it is not enough to be a subject-knowledge expert. You also need to get to know the learners in your class on a personal level and build a relationship of trust that will facilitate a positive learning environment. How the learners in your class view your discipline style and whether they perceive you to be fair and just make a difference as to how they participate in the class (Human-Vogel & Morkel, 2017). In addition to perceptions of justness, there are also other factors that influence how learners perceive their learning environment. Some of these factors are related to the teacher, others are related to the learners, and others to the accessibility of the learning environment (Human-Vogel & Mahlangu, 2009). Academic achievement depends not only on a repertoire of behaviours that learners must show to be successful, but they also need to develop a future orientation that includes goals that are personally relevant and meaningful to them. As a teacher, you can help learners to get to know themselves better, so that they are better able to develop a personally meaningful picture of their future. We know that learners who develop a good understanding of what kind of future they are striving for, are more likely to choose goals that will help them move closer to that future, and consequently, they will develop a better idea of what kinds of actions and behaviours they must choose to help them accomplish their goals.

One way in which you, as a teacher, can help the learners in your class to achieve this, is to develop their self-awareness and self-knowledge (Human-Vogel, 2008). By creating opportunities for learners to develop their identity through self-reflection, they will be better able to understand who they are and what they want for their future. Researchers in South Africa, as well as internationally, have learnt that learners who explore and reflect on their personal values and try to learn as much as they can from life, develop identity styles that can facilitate academic achievement. Learners who never reflect on their values, or question them to come to an understanding of their personal significance, tend to develop a diffuse identity style that is negatively associated with academic achievement (see Chapter 28). This is because learners, who don't know themselves and do not understand and commit to their personal values, generally do not find learning meaningful. As a result, they often don't know what they want to achieve in life one day, making it even more difficult to understand the relevance of learning to their future.

Conclusion

Teachers straddle fields of knowledge that ranges from human development and learning, learning science, the facilitation of teaching, pedagogy, psychology, cultural knowledge systems, classroom practice and management to name but a few. Teaching is one of the most advanced professions that exists, and requires great maturity, expertise and responsibility. In this chapter, we only focused on how some basic fields of psychology could be relevant to the teaching profession, and to support you to be an effective teacher. No doubt, as you will see from other chapters, there are other equally important topics to master, but all of them will require you as a teacher to also grow on your identity—your self-knowledge—as a teacher so that your life goal of teaching can be personally meaningful to you. When it is, you will find that you will be better able to take actions that support the kind of teacher you wish to be. In turn, you will be able to facilitate the same process of identity formation, motivation and achievement for the learners in your school and classroom.

5

Language

20 Understanding language development and learning

FUNKE OMIDIRE

The limits of my language are the limits of my world. (Ludwig Wittgenstein)

Introduction

An important aspect of educational psychology is the active engagement of practitioners with the assessment of the cognitive, personality, emotional and neuropsychological functions of individuals in relation to learning and development. The necessary next step is the identification and diagnosis of barriers to learning and development, and subsequently applying the appropriate psychological intervention to address the barriers identified in order to promote optimal learning and development. Aspects of language play an important part in this process.

Language development is the process that supports an individual's ability to communicate their thoughts, opinions and wishes to others. Language supports a child's ability to express ideas and emotions to others. Language also plays a part in a child's ability to process and understand information received from others. The role of language in learning cannot be overstated. This chapter aims to discuss the relationship between language development and learning. It gives an overview of global issues surrounding language development and learning, as well as language as a barrier to teaching and learning. The chapter goes on to discuss language development and learning within the South African context. It concludes with key strategies for the effective support of learners.

Importance of understanding language development and learning

Language appears in several forms, which are linked through an underlying integrated language system. These forms are:
- Spoken language (listening and speaking);
- Reading; and
- Writing.

The primary language system refers to the oral skills of listening and speaking. These are developed first. The secondary language system refers to reading and writing. Language systems are categorised into input and output:
- Input: receptive language modes (listening and reading are receptive skills); and
- Output: expressive language modes (speaking and writing skills).

The interrelationships between these forms of language serve to build the core of the language system. Early experiences in listening and talking provide the foundation for reading and writing. What the child learns through oral language provides a knowledge base for reading and writing, which in turn improves reading and spoken language. When a child exhibits language difficulty in one form, the underlying language deficit often appears in other forms. Through experience with oral language, children learn the linguistic structures of language, they expand their vocabularies and they become familiar with different types of sentences—hearing stories, songs and rhymes (Lerner & Johns, 2015).

Language is the means by which we process our thinking, refine ideas and process information received through our senses. Language development is critical to cognitive development, which is important for learning. Language therefore plays a significant part in our ability to learn. The various forms of receptive and expressive language, including listening, speaking, reading and writing, have stages of development and function through an integrated, interdependent system. Challenges experienced in the process of language development can have devastating effects on learning if not properly addressed. It is critical that trainee educational psychologists, pre-service teachers and other trainee specialists who work with children understand the role language development performs in the learning process. For learning challenges to be effectively addressed, the possibilities of delays in language development must be adequately and timeously explored and identified.

Commonly accepted stages of language development

Schunk (2012) states that the period from birth to five years is critical for language development. This is the period when the brain develops a significant proportion of language functions. Parts of the brain that deal with visual and auditory perception work together as the coordination between these is required for proper language development. There is also an undeniable interaction between heredity and environment that impacts on language development. This is in line with Piaget's stages of development, which puts full language development at the pre-operational stage (see also Chapters 15 and 17).

Receptive language development involves those aspects of language development that relate to the process of learning to listen to sounds and associate meaning to them. Expressive language development involves the stages of learning to speak and make use of language to communicate. The commonly accepted stages of language development from birth to five years for both the receptive and expressive domain are stated below. From five years onwards, children begin to receive language instructions that lead to proficiency in speaking, reading and writing, as well as the development of extended listening skills. Table 20.1 displays the age range for the development of receptive and expressive language and indicates signs of problems and which actions to take when identified.

TABLE 20.1 Receptive and expressive language development

Age	Receptive language development	Expressive language development	Signs of problems	Action
Birth to 3 months	Sound awareness. Reacts to noise. Distinction between sounds. Turns towards the direction of sounds (familiar voices). Appears to pay more attention to unfamiliar voices and sounds. Soothed by comforting tones.	Makes sounds to express needs (crying). Makes sounds to express contentment or recognition. Repeats and uses sounds to differentiate needs.	Makes no other sounds apart from crying. Does not respond to familiar and/or unfamiliar voices.	General check-up of the sight and hearing – paediatrician.

Understanding language development and learning

Age	Receptive language development	Expressive language development	Signs of problems	Action
4–12 months	Responds to changes in tone. Responds to objects and toys that make sounds. Responds to their names. Listens when being spoken to. Recognises familiar names. Responds to yes/no questions.	Able to communicate by using sounds and gestures. Able to use different sound to get attention for different purposes. Sounds change towards the 12-month mark as speech develops. Imitates sounds heard.	Does not respond to different sounds. Unaware when being spoken to.	Possible referral to clinical audiologist.
1–3 years	Understands familiar names and body parts. Understands brief instructions and short questions. Enjoys listening to short stories and rhymes. Excited about some sounds. Begins to understand more complex instructions.	Progressively accumulates more words. Words spoken become clearer. Begins to form sentences. Vocabulary increases.	Spoken words are unclear. Uses the same words for everything. Vocabulary not increasing.	Possible referral to clinical audiologist or speech therapist.

Age	Receptive language development	Expressive language development	Signs of problems	Action
3–5 years	Understands and responds to simple 'W' questions. Can hear you when you are not in the same space and out of the line of sight. Hears and understands speech clearly within the context of the home, playgroup and pre-school. Proper development hearing and understanding of speech established.	Sentences start to become longer. Describes interesting events at pre-school or on the way. Speaks clearly. Can tell stories and communicate well. Other people outside the family can now also clearly understand what the child says. Stuttering can be detected from this stage.	Inability to hear and respond to sound. Lack of comprehension of speech.	Possible referral to a clinical audiologist or speech therapist.

Process of language development

The process of language development starts with that of brain development at the pre-natal stage. Critical to language development is the nature versus nurture debate. In this instance, the interaction between what nature provides and the nurture received is essential. There has to be proper early brain development and the environment has to be enriching from infancy for optimal learning to occur.

The first five years of a child's life are critical for language development. Language development is dependent on the development of all the senses and, at the initial stage in particular, the auditory system. Children (infants and toddlers) listen to sounds from the speech of others and repeat these sounds,

Understanding language development and learning

trying to model what they hear. Learning a language and language competence depends on the interplay of the child's ability to listen, speak, read and think about the information from the other modalities. An environment where children are exposed to rich linguistic interactions and resources for language development is best for the development of language functions and competence (Dednam, 2011).

The functions and features of language facilitate our understanding of the importance of language to learning. The functions of language include being:
- A vehicle of thought;
- A means of communication and socialising;
- A means of transmitting culture; and
- A means of storing and retrieving information.

Table 20.2 displays the features of language and provides a brief explanation.

TABLE 20.2 Features of language

Feature	Description	Challenges
Communicative	We transmit and receive messages through language.	Inability to communicate what has been learnt, results in poor academic achievement.
Abstract	It is a system of signs and meaningful symbols that represent something.	Difficulties in recognising signs and symbols, and appropriately identifying what they represent could result in delayed reading and excessive rote learning.
Rule-governed	Rules determine the order of sounds and words in sentences.	Inability to master the rules of a language affects the ability to communicate effectively in that language.
		Children learning in a second language often transfer the rules of the L1 to the L2 or sometimes mix the rules together thereby producing grammatically incorrect sentences in the L2.
Social	It enables a person to interact with other people.	Problems that could arise on the social level could involve children being ostracised or bullied for their lack of basic communication skills.

Feature	Description	Challenges
Versatile	It can be arranged and combined limitlessly and used to communicate future information.	The versatility of language needs to be embraced more to support children who experience language related learning difficulties.

The points above demonstrate that language is critical for understanding learning, as well as the disabilities and challenges associated with learning. Leading theorists such as Chomsky, Skinner, Vygotsky and Bruner delineate the importance of language development and its role in learning (see Chapters 8, 16 and 17). Although each of these theorists has varying views, these views are not diametrically opposed to each other and there is something to be learnt from each. For Chomsky, nature plays a pivotal role and human beings have an inherited innate ability to acquire language, using what he refers to as the language acquisition device (LAD). Skinner's postulation is that language is learnt from repetition and the imitation of sounds and words. He believes that practice and the reinforcement of correct speech lead to the proper development of language. Both Vygotsky and Bruner believe that social interaction is pivotal to cognitive development and learning; and language is a tool that plays a major role in this (Schunk, 2012).

Most children acquire language, and understand and respond to the language of others in a meaningful way before they reach school-going age. However, about 8% of children exhibit deviations and delays in language development. These children require additional time and teaching to internalise the language system. Several views of how children learn language, featured in Table 20.3, are as follows:

- Imitation and reinforcement;
- Innate factors; and
- Social factors.

As indicated in Table 20.3, the consensus is that both heredity (nature) and environment (nurture) influence language development and learning. Interaction with parents and other individuals, proper exposure to the target languages, and environments that are rich in materials that could build vocabulary raise the interest of children in reading and writing. This is exasperated in environments where the child has to learn in a second or additional language. The process continues once the child enters the schooling system. Here teachers have the responsibility to ensure that learning takes place.

Table 20.3 Acquisition of language

Acquisition of language

Imitation and reinforcement	• Young children imitate the sounds that they hear and are reinforced for their language attempts. • Children begin to learn language when adults reward them for their attempts with attention and praise.
Innate factors	• The task of learning a language is very complex and some important aspects of language cannot be learned, but are innate within the brain, and children are biologically predisposed to learn to use language.
Social factors	• Children acquire language through social interactions within interpersonal relationships with more knowledgeable language users.

Relevance of language development and learning in South African schools and classrooms

Language development and the ability to communicate are critical for effective learning. The process of language development and communicative skills can be facilitated through different methods of instruction. The process of learning is an intricate one that requires the use of all the senses, different parts of the brain, the cognitive processing of information, memory and well-developed language skills. Sight, hearing, speaking and thinking needed for language learning are also required for learning, as individuals need to read, write, listen, think, speak and make associations. In classrooms, care must be taken to distinguish between learning challenges and identifying the source of the problem. Identification becomes more difficult for teachers in multilingual classrooms such as we have in South Africa. South Africa has 11 official languages, excluding South African sign language. The majority of the schools have at least three to four of these languages represented in the classrooms, while English is used as the language of teaching and learning. Lack of proper development of the home language (L1) creates challenges for learning across the whole curriculum (Nel, 2011; Neiman, 2006; Phatudi, 2015).

Multilingual classrooms are linguistically diverse settings. Additional complexities and sometimes challenges are thus introduced to the teaching and learning situation. Linguistic diversity in a classroom refers to the situation where two or more home languages and cultures are represented in a single classroom. Teachers and learners in multilingual and multicultural classrooms face the task of distinguishing between language-related achievement issues and other obstructive factors, such as genuine learning disabilities (Camilleri & Law, 2007:313; Lidz & Macrine, 2001:77). It could be taxing for teachers to establish whether or not the objectives of the lesson have been achieved if the learners are not proficient in the language of teaching and learning at an academic level of proficiency. Linguistic diversity in the classroom could also make it easy for misclassification and labelling of learners to occur, contributing to motivational, emotional and behavioural challenges to learning.

In instances where the first language (L1) is not well developed, the challenges are more pronounced in the linguistically diverse classroom, since an alternative language of learning/instruction may be used. The language of learning may be the second language (L2) of the learner, but it may also be the third or fourth language. In addition, the language of learning can be the second, third or fourth language of the teacher. This practice directly impacts on the development of both first and second languages. On the one hand, L1 development is limited, and on the other, this affects learning of L2. It is therefore evident that the application of learning across the curriculum requires academic proficiency in the language of learning. This has been shown to be facilitated by the adequate development of L1. However, there are still children who experience challenges with speech, language and social communication (Dednam, 2011; Nel, 2011; Neiman, 2006; Phatudi, 2015).

Challenges associated with language development

Classifying communication disorders, the fifth edition of the *Diagnostic and Statistical Manual of Mental Disorders* (DSM-5) (American Psychiatric Association, 2013) identifies language disorder, speech sound disorder and social communication disorder as being characterised by deficits in development. Many children with learning disabilities and related mild disabilities have speech and language difficulties. Speech and/or language disorders are common co-occurring conditions for older students with disabilities, which result in poor oral language and communication skills. Speech disorders include the following:
- Articulation difficulties, eg, a child who cannot produce certain sounds;
- Voice disorders (a very hoarse voice);
- Fluency difficulty (stuttering); and
- Cluttering.

Language disorders are much broader and encompass the entire spectrum of communication disorders, which include difficulties in learning and using language. Other conditions indicated are childhood-onset fluency disorder (stuttering) and other specified or unspecified communication disorders. The manifestations of these disorders are displayed in Figure 20.1.

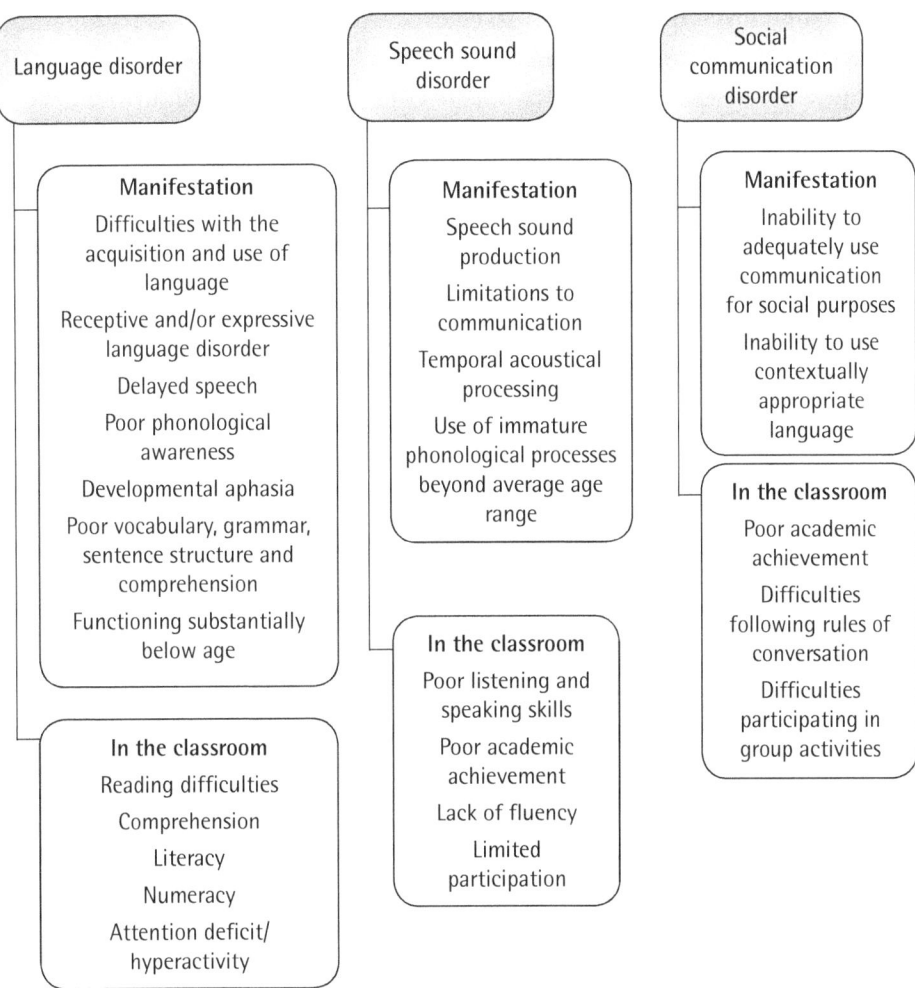

FIGURE 20.1 Communication disorders and effects on learning

Multilingual, culturally and linguistically diverse learners who learn in a language other than their home language often get labelled and classified as having learning disabilities. While learning disabilities cannot always be ruled out, the classification is often due to the learners' lack of proficiency in the language of teaching and learning. It is therefore important for educational psychologists to rule out additional language proficiency as a barrier to learning at an early stage in assessment and intervention.

Strategies for enriching language development

The social environment has a significant influence on learning, and theorists such as Vygotsky stress the notion of interaction between teachers and learners, and between learners (see Chapters 7, 9, 16 and 17). Learning, being a dynamic process, should not only focus on learner-centred individualistic activities, but should embrace learning as an interpersonal collaborative series of events. With these underlying assumptions, attempts to enhance learning and further develop language skills should incorporate social interaction.

Home

- From the early months of life, children have to be spoken to, and should be encouraged to speak to others and to verbally express themselves.
- Promote early literacy by:
    - Engaging children in oral language activities;
    - Surrounding young children with a literacy environment;
    - Introducing concepts about print;
    - Using word and sound games;
    - Building alphabet knowledge;
    - Making children aware of letter-sound correspondence;
    - Encouraging early writing; and
    - Helping children build a beginning reading vocabulary.
- Listening skills are also developed from the early years. Parents have to be aware of this and make a concerted effort to engage with children to ensure that these basic skills are acquired.
- The physical environment should be such that it fosters the development of vocabulary in L1.
- The parental attitude to L1 has to be a positive outlook.
- Books, creative and writing material should be available.
- Parents should read to children where possible. Where parents are unable to do so, stories could be related to children orally to develop their interest in reading.
- Children should be encouraged to play with others.

School

- Teachers' attitudes to the various languages have to change. Value has to be placed on the development of L1.
- Efforts should be made to change the attitude of learners to their home languages and culture.
- Interventions for the development of self-efficacy in terms of language use should be implemented.
- Teachers should have basic skills to distinguish between poor academic achievement resulting from language challenges related to L2 learning and possible learning disability. Professional intervention should be sought as soon as possible.

- Collaborative learning should form part of the strategies used in class (group work, peer tutoring, discussions and debates).
- Efforts should be made to develop learners' independent thinking skills.
- Strategies such as reciprocal questioning should be used to build the learners' thinking and question-formulation skills.
- Material used should be relevant to the learners' life experience. It should also be interesting to promote the motivation to learn.
- Differentiated instruction should be used to cater to the needs of diverse learners.
- A special effort should be made to develop learners' vocabulary.
- Communication should take place between the home and the school. Collaborative efforts between parents and teachers will enable teaching and learning strategies to be sustainable.
- Different components of language (listening, speaking, reading and writing) should be consciously taught.
- Language should be taught across the curriculum.
- Reading for leisure should be promoted.

Community

- Opportunities should be created to learn within the community through the organisation of family events.
- Libraries and other resources should be provided to create enabling environments for learners, especially those without the necessary family support.
- Value placed on learning could be portrayed through community functions that promote culture, heritage and education.

The role of educational psychologists in school settings

The educational psychologist cannot always prevent limited language development and other factors like socio-economic status, and behavioural and emotional challenges from constituting barriers to learning (Mwamwenda, 2004). Educational psychologists can, however, develop and maintain a portfolio of proactive preventative interventions for use within their areas of influence on a regular basis. These interventions could include the following:

- Being familiar with appropriate assessment tools, recommended practices and acceptable accommodations;
- Raising awareness of the complexities of language development;

- Encouraging and organising school-based pre-emptive tests of the visual and auditory systems of learners, particularly at primary school level;
- Advocating for proper school support for language development;
- Promoting a reading culture;
- Advocating for a change in attitude towards home languages;
- Instituting weekly reading programmes;
- Encouraging functional school libraries;
- Establishing classroom libraries; and
- Holding workshops to support parents.

Conclusion

Language development and learning are intricately interwoven. The extent of language development can have an effect on the cognitive processes required for learning. The fact that receptive (listening and speaking) and expressive (reading and writing) forms of language are interrelated through an integrated system means that challenges with one form of language will very likely affect another form.

Learners in a multilingual setting often stand the risk of being labelled as having learning disabilities because of their inability to master the language of learning at an academic proficiency level. It is the responsibility of the educational psychologist to distinguish between the two and recommend the appropriate support and interventions. It is also the responsibility of the educational psychologist to constantly remind the teachers within their frame of reference of the signs for the identification of those who might require intervention. For educational psychologists who work within school environments, it is important to proactively organise workshops for teachers and parents on how to support learners.

21 Communication across the curriculum

HANLIE DIPPENAAR & CANDICE LIVINGSTON

Only dialogue, which requires critical thinking, is also capable of generating critical thinking. Without dialogue there is no communication, and without communication there can be no true education ... (Paulo Freire)

Introduction

Language is the essence of communication in any area of human life. This is especially true of the field of psychology, which deals with the holistic experience of being human. The role and importance of language in any educational sphere, is reiterated in the ideas of Paulo Freire, who believed that dialogue is the essence of communication, and without communication, there is no education (Freire, 2005). Freire points out that dialogue implies love, humility, and faith, and all of these exist in a 'horizontal relationship of mutual trust'. If there is no dialogue, education becomes a 'banking method' (Freire, 2005:77) of knowledge transfer only. He describes mutual trust as the essence of dialogue and a precondition for true communication. Trust is reciprocal and coincides with actions. Within these elements lies the essence of being human. Freire (2005:90) further states that true dialogue 'cannot exist unless the dialoguers engage in critical thinking' which leads to a process of transformation. Future teachers have to take cognisance of the fact that *every teacher is a language teacher* and that communication inside and outside of the classroom is the most important tool any teacher has.

This chapter focuses on the importance of language as medium of instruction and investigates ways in which teachers could enhance communication in the classroom. Neeta and Klu (2013:255) propose that teachers' professional knowledge includes the role of language in facilitating learning. They point out that content discipline teachers expect learners to engage on various topics but do not necessarily provide the language tools necessary for the task.

Teachers in South Africa face many challenges in classrooms where English as the medium of instruction within the classroom dominates as the lingua franca (see also Chapter 20). When considering language in the South African classroom, it is imperative to clarify the fundamental importance that teachers' English language proficiency plays in the teaching and learning environment. The question that is raised focuses on what language proficiency entails and what levels of language proficiency is required of teachers.

According to the South African Census (Statistics South Africa, 2012), English as a home language is spoken by only 9.6% of the population; yet 81.4% of learners in Grade 12 are taught through the medium of English. Afrikaans constitutes 12.8% and the other official languages comprise 5.8% (Department of Basic Education, 2010). English is still the dominant medium of instruction at most educational institutions (Uys, Van der Walt, Van den Berg & Botha, 2007:71, Singh, 2009:282). Consequently, most learners are taught in a language that is not their home language and often teachers are not adequately prepared to teach through the medium of English themselves (Evans & Cleghorn, 2010:147, Heugh, 2009:97).

Defining language proficiency

Language proficiency is a relative concept which refers to the ability one has to communicate in the target language and to 'display a sense for appropriate linguistic behaviour in a variety of situations by using and processing language' when reading, writing, listening and speaking (Dippenaar, 2004:7). Cummins (2000:58) distinguishes between Basic Interpersonal Communication Skills (BICS) and Cognitive Academic Language Proficiency (CALP), where BICS refers to the mastery of language in a social context and CALP as the language used in academic contexts but which must be explicitly taught. CALP cannot be acquired without BICS in a target language. BICS may take approximately 3–5 years to acquire and CALP may take an additional 10 years to acquire (Cummins, 1999:2).

The importance of English in the classroom implies that teachers must have a very good command of the medium of instruction (English) to ensure that effective teaching and learning take place (Mafisa & Van der Walt, 2002:23). Elder (2001:152) points out that the language proficiency required by teachers includes both formal and informal communication, as well as a range of specialist subject proficiency. This has an impact on teacher training programmes, as teacher language proficiency requires a strong foundation in general language proficiency before interpersonal and subject specific competencies in the medium of instruction may be developed (Uys, 2006:58).

Defining teacher language proficiency

Defining the language proficiency requirements for teachers is not a straightforward task. Teacher language proficiency goes beyond general language proficiency and includes specialist skills, subject specific language and a command of interpersonal language, which includes language used to create a social climate within the classroom in order to facilitate tasks (Dippenaar, 2004:20; Elder, 2001:69; Uys, 2006:33). As subject knowledge is mediated through a teacher's use of language, an understanding of language encompasses both an understanding of the subject specific knowledge as well as a teacher's general language ability.

In a study, which focused specifically on English language teachers, Richards (2010:103) argues that there are certain language-specific competencies that a teacher requires. These include skills such as text comprehension, maintaining correct and fluent language in the classroom, providing clear explanations and instructions and providing correct feedback to learners regarding their use of language. Richards (2010:103) states that in addition to this, the teacher should also display other discourse skills which relate to classroom interaction, such as the monitoring of their own language to provide learning input, avoidance of unnecessary colloquialisms and providing learners with a high level of spoken language. Richards' identified competencies are applicable to all teachers in the South African context.

Central to effective communication in the medium of instruction is an expert command of the linguistic features of the language of instruction, knowledge of the subject specific language and terminology and adequate knowledge of second language acquisition (Uys, 2006:33). When a teacher has not achieved adequate language proficiency in the medium of instruction, there is an increased tendency for teachers to become over reliant on teaching resources and less inclined to engage with the learners (Richards, 2010:103). In order to be proficient in the medium of instruction, teachers need a clear understanding of the basic constructs of language in order to be able to correct their own and learners' language, where necessary. A teacher must be proficient in subject specific jargon, register, syntax, semantics and pragmatics of the medium of instruction (Uys, 2006:56).

Language proficiency is not static but continues to develop throughout a person's lifetime. Proficiency also does not develop at the same rate within the four skills (reading, writing, speaking, and listening). Evans (2005:161) states that for many second language speakers, receptive skills (reading and listening) are more developed than their expressive skills (speaking and writing) but this is not to say that this does not change as language proficiency develops. Therefore, a continuum to explore teacher proficiency would make sense as it allows for areas with differing proficiency levels to be evident.

A teacher's language competence in the medium of instruction could compromise learners' success. Successful teachers have effective communication skills and are aware of the importance of language in their classrooms. Teachers require three types of language proficiencies in classroom language. These are interpersonal language, which creates the interactive social climate within the classroom, pedagogical language proficiency to transmit knowledge, skills and attitudes, and general language proficiency regarding the rules of using a language effectively (Elder, 2001:152; Uys, 2006:54).

Interpersonal language proficiency enables a teacher to manage a class, create a social climate and control, organise and motivate learners (Uys, 2006:56). It includes the ability to communicate with colleagues, participate in meetings and liaising with parents, beyond the classroom environment. Uys (2006:57) identifies typical teaching activities which require interpersonal language skills such as establishing and maintaining relationships, exchanging ideas and information, getting things done inside and outside the classroom; exchanging messages such as letters, reports and circulars, motivating learners, participating in scheduled meetings and maintaining order and discipline. How a teacher uses interpersonal skills will greatly influence the students' willingness to learn. Dippenaar (2004:20) states that an enthusiastic, confident teacher will serve to enhance the learning situation. A teacher who perceives him/herself as weak in the target language will have reduced confidence and a lesser sense of professional legitimacy (Richards, 2010:104).

Pedagogical language proficiency refers to the use of 'subject-specific language', which is the teacher's ability to demonstrate subject specific terms, pronounce terms correctly, using of specialist terms, making clear connections between ideas, explaining concepts clearly and explaining models and diagrams appropriately (Elder, 2001:169). General proficiency (ie audibility of utterances, stress, pitch and tone; enunciation; facial and body movements; fluency, accuracy, flexibility, comprehension and range of expression) underpins interpersonal proficiency and pedagogical proficiency in that it requires knowledge of the rules embedded in language use (Uys, 2006:58). Without general language proficiency, a teacher cannot have the basic language structure to develop interpersonal and pedagogical language proficiency. Further aspects of general proficiency include the quality of grammar usage, written questions which are clearly formulated, and use of spelling, which includes demonstrating an understanding of an intended sender's message as well as seeking clarity from the message when necessary (Elder, 2001:167). It includes an understanding of the rules of a language, which is necessary for assisting learners in their own language usage (Uys, 2006:58).

Central to language usage in the classroom and vital to successful teaching is the use of the teacher's voice, as learners spend up to 80% of the school day listening to their teachers (Morton & Watson, 2001:23). Uys (2006:59) states that interpersonal, pedagogical and general language proficiency cannot be separated from the way voice skills are used in the classroom. She identifies seven paralanguage aspects namely: loudness, pitch, rate, variation, articulation, fluency and tone.

Uys (2006:59) reports that a common complaint regarding new teachers is that they speak too quickly, which could be a result of excitement and nervousness. The more complex and formal the information the slower and more deliberate the teacher needs to be. This is especially important where the classroom consists of learners who are not home language speakers of English, as a speech rate which a home language speaker of English may consider appropriate, may be too fast for someone who is not a home language speaker of English. Uys (2006:60) comments that pre-service teachers in the South African context need to be trained to articulate clearly. She continues by stating that such training, 'presupposes knowledge of assimilation, slurring, spelling pronouncing, silent letters, stressed rhythm and reduction' to deliver fluent speech that does not distract the learners' attention.

Learners who are taught by teachers, who successfully use the four language skills, are able to attain academic literacy themselves. However, Elder (2001:162) observes that a better teacher does not necessarily possess a higher level of language proficiency; on the contrary, a teacher who speaks and explains in simple terms to second-language learners may achieve better results. To learners, simplicity, clarity and sensitivity are more important traits. Darling-Hammond and Bransford (2005:161) suggest that language education should be an inherent part of the professional development of all teachers and should inform students on how language is used in everyday life and in the particular learning areas in which they specialise.

Language proficiency and the roles of the teacher

Teachers operate in different contexts, which include a personal level, the classroom and school environment, and the community (Dippenaar & Peyper, 2011:35). On a personal level, the teacher needs language proficiency and competence to prepare lessons and teaching resources, design activities and set tests/examinations. In the school environment, the teacher needs language to communicate with learners and manage teaching and learning in the classroom. Teachers need a high language proficiency level to communicate with colleagues, government officials, parents and members of the community. Language proficiency of teachers is related to the seven roles of the teacher, as identified by the norms and standards for teachers (Department of Higher Education and Training, 2015:51). These roles are briefly discussed in the paragraphs that follow in relation to language proficiency.

As *mediator of teaching and learning*, teachers have to demonstrate innovative ways to ensure effective communication in the classroom and to overcome communication barriers. Interactive classroom discussions, correct and clear use of language when giving instructions, asking questions and giving feedback to answers all contribute to successful mediation of teaching and learning. Language is used to implement successful group work, pair work, using mind maps, summaries or brainstorming techniques.

As *learning area specialist*, teachers have to be proficient enough to interpret visual information, which includes graphs, bar charts, pictograms, diagrams and tables in their specific learning area. They need to be proficient in the language to understand and explain subject-specific jargon in a specific learning area.

As *interpreter and designer of programmes and materials*, teachers have to be able to read, analyse and interpret appropriate learning material in their own content area, as well as prepare and present lessons, using language correctly. They have to be able to demonstrate how to use teaching resources such as newspapers and brochures. In addition they need language to write minutes, faxes, notices, memos, notes, formal and informal letters, and organise events in the community.

As *leader, administrator and manager*, teachers need to be able to manage their own contexts, which includes the ability to apply for jobs, use electronic mail, keep records, file documents, organise school functions, make announcements, draft advertising brochures, pamphlets, notices, correspondence, transactional writing, official documents, and conduct meetings. As *scholar, researcher and lifelong learner*, teachers have to be able to conduct valid research in their subject area, write research reports and incorporate findings in the classroom. They need to demonstrate the ability to reflect on their own teaching practices and apply research findings.

In a *pastoral role*, teachers have to be able to act responsibly and empathetically towards self, learners and colleagues, and they have to be able to communicate with learners and colleagues in an appropriate way in a school and community setting.

As *assessor*, teachers have to be able to set curricula accurately, assess learners, and reflect on the learners' results. However, to be able to realise these roles, it might require that teachers are more aware of the language diversity experienced in the South African classroom. Garcia and Flores (2012:232) argue that learners should be taught in a way that supports and develops their diverse language practices. That is the only way to ensure meaningful participation in education, and thus a transformed society. Multilingual classroom practices are at the centre of education and teachers should aim to enhance meaningful student participation.

One way to achieve this is to make code switching part and parcel of every teaching and learning opportunity. Code switching occurs when an individual alternates between two or more languages (Cook & Singleton, 2014:9). It is a valuable tool in mediating learning; especially when learners have limited language proficiency in the medium of instruction, as is the case in many South African classrooms. Garcia (2009:296) differentiates between random and responsible code switching. Random code switching refers to a spontaneous or intuitive switch from one language to another by competent bilinguals, whereas responsible code switching is where students are guided in understanding content by translating concepts in the learners' mother tongue for clarification. It is thus deliberate and serves a particular purpose. Research has shown that teachers' ability to speak, general language competence and knowledge of the medium of instruction impact on the effectiveness of their teaching and the learner's understanding of the content being presented. It is clear that 'regardless of the particular context, language is the thread that ties teacher, text, activity, use of space and learner together in the overall process of meaning-making' (Evans & Cleghorn, 2010:142).

Conclusion

Language in the South African classroom is a complex issue, especially if one considers that English is often the accepted medium of instruction. However, teachers should be urged to assist their learners in achieving BICS/CALP in the medium of instruction in the classroom. In order to achieve an adequate level of language proficiency, pre-service teachers need to be educated, as part of their formal programme, on what communication in the classroom entails and how it is attained. Resources such as the teachers' handbook by Baines, Blatchford and Kutnick (2017) promote effective group work and provide activities for teachers to develop learners' skills in speaking, listening, asking and answering questions, brainstorming and using language to express their opinions. Such activities teach learners skills such as asking questions, showing and telling.

Learners can be encouraged to participate in debates where they have to collaborate and develop vocabulary to provide answers or request reasons. Teacher discourse impacts on student participation and can limit or enhance students' opportunities for participation. When teachers ask students questions without providing adequate time for responses, it limits interaction. This is especially true when teachers only require short answers to lower level questions where students need to recall facts, and they do not provide opportunities for students to draw conclusions or synthesise ideas. Teachers can enhance student participation by creating opportunities for interactive class discussions and debates. A teacher's own discourse habits and requirements for learners are related. If teachers frequently encourage learners' participation and the sharing of ideas, learners accept that as part of their learning, in contrast to classrooms where teachers require little learner input, or accept learners' answers without asking for elaboration or critical thinking to be evidenced. When teachers ask questions about what learners are thinking, it sends a message to the learners to challenge others and to explain and justify their thinking instead of merely passively accepting transmitted knowledge (Webb, Nemer & Ing, 2006).

In conclusion, teachers' ability to communicate confidently influences interactive communication in the classroom. Teachers' practices in their classrooms, which include their interpersonal discourse, negotiations on learner participation, and creating a stimulating classroom climate, are important factors for successful communication in the classroom. Teachers who demonstrate interaction and communicate their thinking to one another are more successful than teachers who merely give general instructions. Communication is the essence of any educational interaction.

 Individualised learner support

ANNALENE VAN STADEN

But the fact is, no matter how good the teacher, how small the class, how focused on quality education the school may be, none of this matters if we ignore the individual needs of our students. (Roy Barnes)

Introduction

The Department of Education (2001:15) describes learner support as any form of help, assistance and guidance given to individual learners or groups of learners who experience barriers to learning to support them in overcoming their barriers to learning (Learner Support, 2011; Erradu, 2012). Individualised learner support can be categorised into low, moderate or high intensive levels of support, depending on the individual needs of the learner or group of learners (Erradu, 2012). Within the South African education context, researchers define 'learning difficulties', as being caused by extrinsic or intrinsic barriers to learning. Thus 'learning difficulties' may arise from environmental, cultural or economic challenges, or as mentioned, intrinsic factors such as visual, hearing, motor, and physical impairments, and also include learners with emotional problems (Nel, Nel & Hugo, 2016) (see also Chapter 29). With regard to the current chapter that deals with individualised learner support, the majority of children in South Africa experience learning difficulties as a result of problems related to language, ie, both spoken and written language. These include challenges or limited abilities to listen, speak, read, write, spell, and think, and mathematical difficulties (Nel et al, 2016). At the heart of developing effective learning support programmes is ongoing identification of the learners' needs, and to address these needs accordingly. In supporting the needs of the learner with learning difficulties, the core aim of learning support programmes should be to make the curriculum accessible for all learners. With regard to this chapter, the core focus of individualised (or group) support will be on reading, spelling and mathematical support.

Reading

Proficient reading is a highly multifaceted task that requires extensive knowledge and a broad range of skills. These inter alia include the following:

- Rapid, sequential processing of visual symbols to recognise letters and word forms (also known as rapid-automatised naming);
- Forming virtually instantaneous associations between visual word forms and oral word forms;
- Understanding vocabulary;
- Drawing upon linguistic knowledge to attain meaning from the word order;
- Mastery of writing conventions to know the significance of punctuation;
- Gathering and holding sufficient basic material in working memory to access the ideas being expressed; and
- Collecting and holding the ideas to facilitate comprehension (Saskatchewan Learning, 2004; Paananen, February, Kalima & Kirk, 2011).

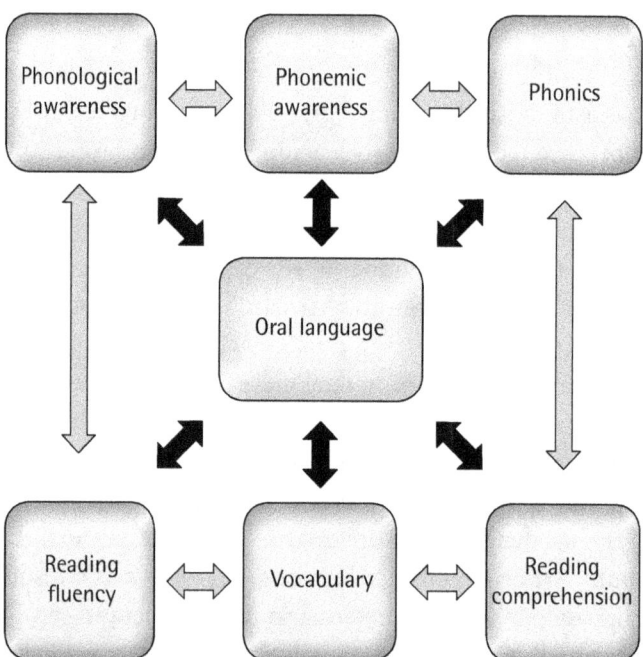

FIGURE 22.1 Important elements of reading instruction
Source: Adapted from Bos & Vaughn, 1994

Individualised learner support

Focusing on the specific skills that are important for reading development, Figure 22.1 illustrates the interrelatedness of these skills or elements, all of which should be considered during the development of a reading support programme.

From the above it is clear that a single method or approach to reading development cannot guarantee reading success. One should rather consider a multi-strategy approach (also known as a balanced or integrated approach) to support reading development (Burns, 2006). In the next section, the focus will be on how to develop effective reading skills, such as word decoding, word reading and reading fluency; vocabulary and reading comprehension, followed by an overview of spelling difficulties and strategies to support spelling development.

- The singing of songs, chanting of rhymes, phonemic and word games, exploring language and listening to adults read word-play books;
- Using the tapping technique can help learners to identify speech sounds before they spell words (for example by touching the thumb to successive fingers as they segment and pronounce the speech sounds);
- Phonics instruction should focus learners' attention on letter-sound patterns to develop sound-letter relationships. This can be achieved via:
  - Activities that focus on phonological tasks such as rhyming and blending exercises;
  - Sound deletion and substitution exercises;
  - Counting syllables;
  - Adding and deleting syllables;
  - Phonemic tasks, such as matching beginning consonants in words; and
  - Substituting sounds in words.
- Mnemonics (ie, cognitive strategies that help learners remember information) can also help learners to remember complex spellings of word families. These can include both visual and auditory activities or strategies, for example rhymes, songs or picture images to support the recall of reading and spelling of words;
- Use exercises to increase learners' awareness of word families (or word patterns) both in reading and spelling—these include activities to *emphasise prefixes, roots and suffixes*, beginning with inflections that change the spelling of a base word (eg *fine, finest; begin, beginning; study, studied*); and
- Link meaning and spelling. For example the words designate, signal and assignment, share a root (the root word being 'sign'). Utilising this technique helps learners to identify spelling patterns which they can use as a tool to read and write new words.

FIGURE 22.2 Activities to improve word decoding and fluency

Decoding skills

Word decoding is a developmental process that relies on foundational skills, such as phonological awareness and orthographical knowledge (ie, phonological and orthographic codes) to access or decipher words (Van Staden, 2017). In practice, this implies that problems related to word decoding will ultimately affect the child's potential to efficiently and fluently read words, and thus also negatively affect word automaticity, and reading comprehension. In order to improve word decoding, the activities explained in Figure 22.2 can be considered (see Saskatchewan Learning, 2004; Paananen, et al, 2011).

Word reading and reading fluency

As discussed previously, reading skills such as word decoding, word reading and reading fluency are all interrelated. Activities to further enhance word reading and reading fluency can be explained as follows:

- It is important to create rich literacy environments via labelling (also known as environmental print), already among early childhood learners. This includes composing word walls of high-frequency words or key words to enhance learners' awareness of word families.
- Irrespective of the learners' age or grade, it is imperative that the ability to recognise words (especially high frequency words) be practiced on a daily basis (ie, the learner should be able to read words fluently on sight/or at an automatic response level). This can be practised by using flash cards, playing fast-word-recognition games, such as *Bingo* and *Snap*, matching words, etc. Numerous online versions and printed lists are also available that entail high frequency word lists. Some examples are the Dolch sight word lists, 1st- and 2nd-hundred words, etc. These word lists can be included in the individualised support programme of the child, while all learners in the class should also practice these words daily.
- Also include words with irregular spelling patterns, such as 'physical' and 'know', or 'said' and 'one' as part of learners' high frequency word lists.
- Introduce visual imagery strategies to learn and store visual images of phonological irregular words in learners' long-term memory mental lexicons (see Table 22.1).

As mentioned earlier, the aim of fluency is not only to read fluently, but also to enhance comprehension. Nel and Nel (2016) recommend the following reading strategies to increase reading fluency:

- Echo reading: teacher reads and the groups repeat after the teacher (reread aloud);
- Choral reading: teacher and learners read together (aloud)—can also be practised with a peer or older learner/buddy;
- Partner or paired reading: learners read in pairs, taking turns to read aloud;

Individualised learner support

- Whisper reading: independent reading (aloud but in a quiet voice); and
- Fluency should be practised daily, for approximately 10 to 15 minutes per day.

TABLE 22.1 Important visual concepts to support memory and learning

Visual concept(s)	Definition
Visual imagery	Involves cognitive imagery which inter alia constitutes the sense of having 'images' in the mind. Visual imagery is utilised for different reasons, for example to cope with unpleasant experiences, to enhance performances, etc. With regard to academic performance and learning, it can be used as an information processing strategy, for example to enhance spelling performance by 'seeing the word in one's minds eye' (Van Staden, 2010).
Mnemonics	Mnemonics are strategies used to remember (or recall) a longer string of information. For example, it can include word associations, images, acronyms, and songs—thus anything that helps you to remember a fact, word, etc. It is a useful strategy to learning the spelling of more challenging words or to remember facts, for example the names of the different planets ('My Very Educated Mother Just Served Us Nachos' to remember the order of the planets Mercury, Venus, Earth, Mars, Jupiter, Saturn, Uranus, Neptune) (Belleza, 1981).

Some other suggestions to practice reading fluency include the following:
- Repeated reading: The re-reading of the same paragraph(s) occurs daily, for a week. (As the learner's fluency improves, increase the difficulty of the reading text.)
- Provide opportunities for learners to listen to recordings (audio or computer-generated voice) of books while reading along.
- Include strategies such as 'reading theatres'. This is a fun activity that develops reading fluency and also boosts the self-confidence of weaker readers (see Burns, 2006).

Vocabulary

Reading research emphasises the important role that vocabulary plays in reading success. Accordingly, children with larger vocabularies are more successful readers, read more fluently and with understanding, and are therefore more likely to read more independently than children with smaller vocabularies (Van Staden, 2016). Thus, to develop reading comprehension, it is imperative to include activities to enhance learners' vocabulary such as the following:

- Learners need to be taught oral and written vocabulary in order to enhance their reading abilities—this is also crucial for developing reading comprehension (National Reading Panel, 2000).
- The National Reading Panel (NRP) (2000) identified the following five basic approaches to teaching vocabulary, namely:
  - Explicit instruction (ie, of difficult words; words that are not part of a learner's everyday experience);
  - Indirect instruction (exposure to different reading materials);
  - Multi-media methods (ie, going beyond the text—include multi-media texts, such as a visual stimulus, using the computer or sign language) (Van Staden, 2017);
  - Capacity methods (focus on how to make reading an automatic activity); and
  - Association methods (encouraging learners to draw connections between unfamiliar words with what they know—ie, activating their prior knowledge).
- Other suggestions entail the following:
  - Word study is very important: this includes exploring word meanings and talking about how words are used and providing multiple exposure to words in a variety of contexts;
  - Creating word-walls with high-frequency words and theme words—paste these on the wall, or in front of the classroom; as well as 'portable word-walls'—this can be pasted or written in learners' individual dictionaries that they design themselves;
  - Assist the learner with understanding the definitions and functions in a sentence or phrase, until the learner knows the word and is comfortable with the way the word is used;
  - Words are taught in the context of a selection or unit; and
  - Include context clue types to enhance word meaning, for example, a definition of the word, synonyms and antonyms, playing word games, etc.
- Relationships are drawn between new words and known words and concepts (ie, the activation of learners' prior knowledge).
- Learners are taught to use context clues and reference resources such as dictionaries to enhance their word knowledge.
- Learners are encouraged to interact with the words so they are able to process them more deeply.

Reading comprehension

- Reading comprehension skills and strategies should be taught explicitly, especially in the case of learners with reading difficulties (these skills do not develop automatically—it should be practiced via effective scaffolding and guided practice).
- Even among early childhood learners comprehension can be practised via picture stories and colourful books. Various questions can be asked about the picture(s) or characters in the pictures. These include questions about the content or questions which stimulate creative thought (ie, open-ended questions); 'why?' questions are valuable and promote thinking and reasoning abilities (Nel & Booysen, 2015).
- The teacher can scaffold the following reading strategies to enhance learners' meta-cognitive abilities and support reading comprehension:
    - Summarising;
    - Predicting;
    - Developing effective questioning techniques;
    - Clarifying;
    - Encouraging learners to relate the content of the text to their personal experience(s) and knowledge (ie, activating prior knowledge);
    - Guiding learners to construct mental representations of the text (eg, utilising visual imagery);
    - Monitoring learners' understanding of the text; and
    - Determining and connecting important ideas to construct meaning.

- Reciprocal questioning procedure (ReQuest): http://www.readingeducator.com/strategies/request.htm;
- Guided reading procedure: http://literacy.kent.edu/eureka/strategies/manzo.pdf;
- SQ3R reading technique: http://www.studygs.net/texred2.htm;
- K-W-L (Know–Wonder–Learn)—entails teaching learners how to generate questions about a text. Learners can generate questions before they read, such as in a K-W-L (Know–Wonder–Learn) chart helping learners relate a passage to an experience, another book, or other facts: http://schoolnet.org.za/teach10/resources/dep/prior_knowledge/kwl_charts.htm;
- Teaching the 'Think-Pair-Share' strategy (after learners spend a minute thinking about a particular topic, they pair with another learner to discuss their ideas, and then share their ideas with the larger group): http://www.readwritethink.org/professional-development/strategy-guides/using-think-pair-share-30626.html.

FIGURE 22.3 Some specific reading methods or strategies to support reading comprehension development

- Include shared-reading activities, where the teacher and learner(s) read together, often from a *big book* (Block, Gambrell & Pressley, 2002).

In Figure 22.3, there are some additional reading methods or strategies to improve reading comprehension.

Supporting spelling development

In developing support strategies for learners who struggle with the spelling of words, it is important to distinguish between a writing impairment (also known as dysgraphia) and spelling difficulties. A learner with dysgraphia needs more specialised support, for example occupational therapy to support his/her motor difficulties, and special adaptations should be considered to remove learning barriers in an inclusive classroom setting, such as oral examinations, also known as amanuensis (Bornman & Rose, 2010; Paananen, et al, 2011).

Learners with spelling difficulties may struggle to notice, remember and recall the features of language that letters represent. This includes the ability to analyse and remember the individual sounds in the words (phonemes), such as the sounds associated with *f, sh*, or *p*, syllables, such as *cas, mem, neg*, and meaningful parts of longer words (morphemes), such as *re-, -ment* or *-est* (Paananen, et al, 2011). In Figure 22.4, strategies to support spelling are suggested. These strategies can be used in individual support programmes, while all learners in the classroom will also benefit from these strategies (Saskatchewan Learning, 2004; Paananen, et al, 2011; Van Staden & Purcell, 2016).

- Teach reading and spelling together. This gives a context for language and meaningful practice.
- Discuss word structures, origins and meaning of words and morphemes.
- Encourage hands-on practice with spelling words via multi-sensory learning activities, for example:
  - Trace words in salt; colour glue; sand; sand paper letters and modelling clay to make words;
  - Practice word building with clay letters, plastic letters, magnetic letters, etc; and
  - Print a spelling word on a strip of paper, cutting the letters out and have learners rearrange the letters to recreate the word.
- Use box-words that mirror the shape of letters in words, eg, m-o-t-h-e-r would look like this:

(Learners then have to match the word to the blank boxes and use the blank boxes to guide encoding or to guide sorting a list of words into word families.)

- The well-known 'look-cover-write-check' spelling strategy has also been used with great success both in empirical studies and in inclusive classroom settings (ie, *look at the word, cover the word, write the word from memory and check your spelling*).
- The efficacy of teaching spelling via the orthographic route, namely through strategies such as visual (or mental) imagery and storing images of spelling words in learners' long-term memory, has also demonstrated to be very successful (see Van Staden & Purcell, 2016).
- Make correctly spelled words easily accessible by:
  o Keeping a list of most-commonly misspelled words or having learners create a personal dictionary for reference;
  o Having learners regularly re-practising and using challenging words;
  o Brainstorming with students before they write, in order to generate and provide correct spelling of pertinent words; and
  o Making word prediction software available.
- Provide adaptations to ensure learners feel successful by:
  o Reducing the number of spelling words a learner needs to master, focusing on quality not quantity; and
  o Ensuring that spelling tasks are at a level where learners experience success, gradually increasing the degree of difficulty as the learners' spelling abilities improve.

FIGURE 22.4 Strategies to support spelling development

Supporting mathematical development

In the literature, a clear distinction is being made between mathematical difficulties that stem from neurological or cognitive challenges, also known as dyscalculia, and mathematical difficulties, for example, problems or challenges learners have with regard to numeracy development, number concept, basic operations, etc. Although they may share some common attributes, there are many different types of mathematical difficulties. Emanating from the above, the following characteristics or behaviour of learners with mathematical difficulties may be visible in the classroom.

Learners may struggle with:
- Acquiring and remembering mathematical vocabulary;
- Acquire competency and confidence in number concepts;
- Distinguishing right from left and problems related to spatial and three-dimensional aspects;
- Using the mathematical calculation signs;
- Calculations entailing multiple steps, such as long division;
- Confusing basic operations and facts;

- Applying logic, but not accurately completing calculations;
- Understanding and solving word problems;
- Being hesitant, refusing or experiencing anxiety when asked to engage with mathematical concepts;
- Remembering and applying mathematical functions in various ways;
- Recalling math rules, formulas or sequences;
- Being able to perform an operation one day, but not the next;
- Understanding abstract concepts like time and direction;
- Checking change, reading analogue clocks, keeping score during games, budgeting, estimating;
- Remembering dance step sequences or rules for playing sports;
- Visualising the face of a clock or places on a map;
- Recalling dates, addresses, schedules and sequences of past or future events;
- Organise the steps required for problem solving;
- Develop a repertoire of mathematical techniques; and
- Making meaningful connections within and across mathematical experiences.

The strategies in Figure 22.5 to support learners with mathematical difficulties can be considered both for individual learners and the whole class (Saskatchewan Learning, 2004; Paananen, et al, 2011).

- It is imperative to provide exact instruction in small groups. However, teachers need to make sure that their instructions are understood. Be careful to only ask: 'Do you understand?' Use various teaching methods with different techniques and tools.
- Learners should be given clear models of how to arrive at a solution.
  - Give them the opportunity to apply the solution strategies to multiple examples;
  - Provide immediate feedback on their accuracy; and
  - Allow them to ask questions and think aloud about the decisions they make while solving mathematical problems.
- Encourage learners to represent the information in math problems in a variety of ways.
- Include activities that facilitate the learners' concept of numbers and operations, starting on a concrete level (eg using counters); then move to iconic forms (ie semi-concrete activities), such as drawings and mathematical worksheets, and then to symbolic representations using standard mathematical notations (ie thinking on an abstract level).
- Have learners verbalise discussions and solutions to a mathematics problem.
- Make use of web-based and software technology to provide a variety of ways to represent numbers and operations while increasing learners' abilities to create mental representations of concepts.

- Represent numbers and operations in visual format, for example use concrete, plastic or magnetic numbers, number building cards, etc.
- Provide a talking calculator which will say each number and symbol aloud as entered, enabling continuous self-checking of work.
- Provide organisational assistance by:
    - Using graph paper for mathematical computations if learners experience difficulties aligning their work;
    - Assigning manageable amounts of practice work as skills are learned; and
    - Assigning a peer (or 'buddy') to work along with the learner demonstrating ways to organise mathematics work.

FIGURE 22.5 Specific strategies to support mathematical development

Conclusion

The Education White Paper 6 (Department of Education, 2001) advocates for an inclusive approach to education and entails a paradigm shift as far as the education of learners who experience barriers to learning are concerned. Notwithstanding the objectives clearly delineated in White Paper 6, numerous South African learners still experience 'exclusion', specifically learners who require higher levels or individualised support. It is hoped that the suggestions included in this chapter, will assist educators working with individuals and groups of learners with learning difficulties, and empower them to support these learners, so these learners' full potential can be realised.

6

Health and well-being

23 Teacher well-being and the role of positive psychology

BEVERLEY FELDMAN

Educating the mind without educating the heart is no education at all.
(Aristotle)

Introduction

'How are you?' This simple question is shared millions of times among millions of people around the world every minute of every day. In some cultures, particularly in Africa, 'How are you?' is the greeting. Clearly, this is a very significant question, reflecting the prominence of well-being in our lives. Typical responses to the question reveal something about the respondent's state of well-being.

Well-being exists when there is congruence between one's thoughts, words and feelings when one responds, 'I am well, thank you.' This suggests a state of happiness. This state of happiness, or well-being, researchers agree, is what humans have been pursuing since the beginning of time and which Aristotle considered the overarching goal of all human actions.

In the 21st century, our lives have become very busy as we are overloaded with information, work and have many challenges and obstacles to navigate on a daily basis. Sometimes these stressors may make us feel worn out and beaten. When we feel that the problems we face overshadow our joy, we are not coping and our feelings of ease and happiness are eroded; we may be said to be in a state of 'dis-ease' or 'ill-being' and we become psychologically, emotionally, physically and often even spiritually unwell.

If, however, we feel capable of withstanding the problems and we have enough resources, internally and externally, to protect us from the pressure and we are able to retain our joy and sense of task ease, then we are more likely to experience a sense of well-being, to cope and flourish.

In South Africa, the scope of educational psychology is to optimise functioning in the broad context of learning and development (Department of Health, 2011). Since teachers play such a critical role in the process of learning and development in society, this chapter focuses specifically on teacher well-being and how the principles of positive psychology can be used to promote such well-being.

One definition of well-being as proposed by Dodge, Daly, Huyton and Sanders (2012) describes it quite simply as the balance point between the psychological, social and physical challenges one experiences and the psychological, social and physical resources one has. This means that if the challenges outweigh the resources, well-being will decrease, but will increase as the resources increase. Challenges include demands on one's life, such as pressure relating to work, time, family, finances, crime and other psychosocial issues, and resources may include internal (resilience) and external (support system) buffers.

Beltman, Mansfield and Price (2011) similarly define resilience as 'the outcome of the dynamic relationship between individual risk and protective factors'. To enable people to thrive, the risk factors need to be reduced and the protective factors enhanced. Both well-being and resilience, therefore, are promoted when there is balance between positive and negative factors influencing one's life, and increase when positive factors outweigh negative ones.

The importance of teacher well-being

The influence that teachers have in the lives of the learners they engage with on a daily basis is well documented in research. It is illustrated in films such as 'Stand by Me' and 'Dangerous Minds' and can probably be testified to in our own lives. We all remember the teachers who made a positive difference in our lives, and those who did not. The ones in between, we hardly remember. Teachers, who have an inner reservoir of happiness, enjoy their work, have positive relationships with the learners they teach and who are good at what they do, are more likely to impart some of that to their learners and in turn promote the well-being of their learners. By contrast, teachers who have little within, have little to share with their learners resulting in learners' experiences in their classrooms being impoverished and uninspiring in terms of the 'hidden curriculum', ie, what we teach unintentionally. Learner achievement is directly proportional to teacher input; therefore, teacher well-being is a matter of critical importance.

People, who are in caring and civic professions such as teaching ought to have enough resources for themselves as well as the people they work with, eg, learners. Imagine a tank that provides water and nutrients for a garden. If the tank runs empty, the flowers and plants in the garden may not be nourished sufficiently to grow well and flourish. This metaphor illustrates the role teachers play in the learning and development of learners. If the teacher, who is the nurturing tank, is running on empty, there will be little left to give to the learners in his/her care. A common analogy related to emotional and psychological well-being is that of a tank of internal resources. We can give much if our emotional tanks are full, not so if they are empty. The stronger our resilience, the greater our ability to withstand the pressure and the better our well-being. High levels of teacher stress, work overload and adverse conditions in many schools erode teacher well-being, and are a leading cause of low levels of teacher resilience and well-being, and a leading cause of teachers leaving the teaching profession.

Prominent theories of well-being and the role of positive psychology

Even though the issue of human happiness and well-being is an age-old question, the following brief history highlights one or two of the popular theories in more recent years.

People generally seem inclined to focus on the problems in society, in others, in themselves, their places of work, their governments and the world. This is called a deficit-based view of life. Perhaps it is the way we have been conditioned, or perhaps it is symptomatic of the medical model that looks at 'what is wrong with people?', but this perspective is not conducive to the promotion of well-being. This view has been evident in the discipline of psychology too, which appears to hinge on psychopathology, the study of the disease (pathology) of the psyche.

Relatively recently, a much needed shift in focus occurred as scientists and researchers sought a different approach to the study of people and their well-being. This shift brought a more optimistic, positive view of the human condition and sought to focus on the strengths and wellness (fortology) of humans, rather than their illness (pathology).

These theories are examples of an asset-based approach, which means looking at the strengths, as opposed to a deficit-based approach that focuses on the weaknesses or problems. An asset-based approach in psychology focuses on the strengths in people and seeks ways to enhance those strengths and to promote well-being and flourishing.

In 1969, Bradburn's research on psychological well-being marked a shift away from diagnosing psychiatric cases to exploring the psychological reactions of ordinary people and how they coped with difficulties on a daily basis. He suggested that people with more positive than negative affect would have higher levels of well-being, and people that are more negative would be lower in well-being. In 1979, Antonovsky's influence on this important change in thinking was his concept of 'salutogenesis' (the origins of health) as opposed to the focus on what causes disease.

In South Africa, Strümpfer (1995) later extended this idea into the idea of fortology, which focuses on the origins of strength, not only in terms of health, but also at other end points such as psychological well-being. Wissing and Van Eeden (1997, 2002) further extended this concept into psychofortology, focusing on the 'nature, manifestations and ways to enhance psychological well-being and develop human capacities'.

In 1998, Martin Seligman, in his opening speech as President of the American Psychological Association (APA) introduced the term 'positive psychology' as a new field of psychology, bringing together the shift in focus from 'what is wrong with people?' to 'what can people do that is right?' and seeking to promote well-being. This earned him the title as the founder of positive psychology, even though these ideas had been growing in many parts of the world.

Well-being and positive psychology

In this chapter, we look specifically at positive psychology as useful in the promotion of well-being and look at how it can be beneficial in the context of education settings to promote teacher well-being, and consequently learner well-being. Eloff (2013) speaks of a 'natural affinity between positive psychology and education, enhanced by the fact that positive psychology can be taught and deep learning about the field can be facilitated'. Seligman promotes the idea that humans are designed for much more than just coping or surviving; instead they are designed to flourish.

> *I used to think that the topic of positive psychology was happiness. I now think that the topic of positive psychology is well-being, that the gold standard for measuring well-being is flourishing, and that the goal of positive psychology is to increase flourishing.* (Seligman, 2011:13)

Based on this idea, he developed a theory of well-being called PERMA theory. More recently, following continuing research and input from fellow researchers, Seligman has adapted the PERMA model to PERMA Plus (+). PERMA is an acronym for the five pathways that lead to the state of well-being. It stands for positive emotion, engagement, relationships, meaning and accomplishment, and is described more fully in the sections that follow.

P—Positive emotion

Every person needs and yearns to experience positive emotions such as hope, interest, amusement, joy, love, compassion, contentment, gratitude, pride and very importantly, optimism. Our genetics can determine the extent to which we experience positive emotion, for example, what researchers call our 'happiness set point' or nature (some people are more positive than others are). Each person, however, has the ability to 'purposefully experience more positive emotion' (Seligman, 2011). This means that well-being can be improved by the deliberate creation of moments and experiences that ignite these emotions in us.

E—Engagement

When we are so absorbed in an activity we enjoy or are good at that time seems to stand still, we are engaged. 'We are living in the present moment and entirely focused on the task at hand' (South Australian Health and Medical Research Institute, 2017). In positive psychology, this is referred to as 'flow'. Csikszentmihalyi (2002) (pronounced 'cheeks-sent-me-high') believes that we experience flow when we use our highest strengths or skills to engage in challenging tasks. Petersen and Seligman (2004) identified 24 universal human strengths. Their view is that when the work we do correlates or uses our highest strengths, we are more likely to be engaged and experience well-being relating to our work. One can identify one's signature strengths by taking the Values in Action (VIA) Signature Strengths test (Petersen & Seligman, 2017) on the website, www.authentichappiness.com.

R—Relationships

Positive relationships are central to well-being. These include relationships with family and friends, relationships at work and the broader community. This includes our social and professional networks and support systems. It is in our relationships with others that we experience love, joy, acceptance, belonging, compassion and many other positive emotions so important to our well-being. This links well with resilience research done by Ebersöhn (2012), who found that fight or flight were not the only responses when faced with threat or challenges. She found that people also flock together, as a protective factor in adversity. This means that people connect with or create a network of positive relationships with others to support them and increase their resilience. This is one way to promote well-being—by creating balance between our resources and the challenges we experience.

M—Meaning

Victor Frankl (1969:31) declared that people's hearts are restless until they have found, and fulfilled, meaning and purpose in life. Such meaning can come from different sources that make us feel that we are doing something valuable and worthwhile. Seligman (2012) suggests that this involves belonging to or serving something that we believe is greater than we are, and that people are generally altruistic by nature. Kashdan and McKnight (2009) found that people, who have discovered purpose in their lives, generally live longer, are healthier and have greater life satisfaction than people who have not. Seligman proposes that a strong sense of purpose or meaning improves confidence, feelings of self-efficacy and feelings of resilience in the face of obstacles and challenges. Finding meaning and purpose in our lives, whether in the service of others, for a worthy cause, in a caring profession, a religious or spiritual belief, a hobby, creative endeavour or anything else that gives meaning and purpose to our lives, strengthens us in times of adversity, builds our resilience and improves our well-being.

A—Accomplishment

Accomplishment, also known as achievement, competence or mastery is equally important in promoting our sense of well-being. It gives us a sense of success in achieving goals we may have set for ourselves and enables us to appreciate our own efforts, skill, self-discipline and perseverance. It builds our self-efficacy and strengthens our belief that we are capable. Every person needs to experience success in accomplishing something, however small it may be. Such experiences enhance well-being over time (Brunstein, 1993).

PERMA Plus (+)

As multi-dimensional beings, aspects of our being include mind, body, spirit and emotions, the whole of which is greater than the sum of its parts. This means that in order to attain well-being, we need to cultivate and develop well-being in all the aspects of our being. PERMA Plus (+) therefore seeks to include pathways to well-being that embrace a more holistic approach to building our resilience and well-being.

Four pathways have been added to the PERMA model as follows:

Optimism

Optimism easily fits under the positive emotion pathway of PERMA, yet its significance in the promotion of well-being requires a notable mention. A commonly depicted difference between optimism and pessimism is that optimists are likely to see a glass as half full, whereas the pessimist will view the same glass as being half empty.

Physical activity

To enhance our psychological well-being it is important to take care of our physical health too. Engaging in physical activity reduces our chances of acquiring conditions such as type 2 diabetes, high blood pressure and obesity. Physical activity also improves cardiac health and increases our feel good chemicals, serotonin, thus reducing depression. Furthermore, participation in sport, for example, creates opportunity for experiencing positive emotions, being engaged in the activity of our choice, building relationships with others through social engagement, finding meaning and purpose in our physical pursuits and experiencing a sense of accomplishment when goals related to our activity of choice are achieved. The Sports Science Institute of South Africa (SSISA) has initiated the Teachers on the Move programme, to get teachers moving through exercise, particularly in vulnerable schools and communities. The aims of the programme include improving teacher well-being as well as motivating learners to engage in physical activity in an effort to keep them otherwise engaged and off the streets.

Nutrition

In an age of genetically modified and fast food, it becomes critically important to nourish our minds and bodies with nutrient rich, wholesome food. Since the food security of the majority of people in South Africa is often compromised, it has become important for people to learn how to grow their own fruit and vegetables.

Sleep

Natural sleep, playfully called 'The mother of all calm' is critical to well-being. It gives the mind and body a chance to reprocess the day, recharge and rejuvenate. Hillman and Lack (2013) found that disruptions in mood, concentration, thinking, memory, vigilance learning and reaction times could all be associated with a lack of sleep. People have different sleep needs, but generally, adults need between 7 and 9 hours of sleep to be fully rested. Skimping on sleep over an extended period is detrimental to our health and well-being. Sleep is a gift and should be valued and enjoyed to promote our psychological, emotional and physical well-being.

Relevance to South African schools and classrooms

The challenges experienced by teachers and learners alike, in the majority of South African schools is a matter of concern. A growing body of research finds teachers to be highly stressed and many are leaving the profession at an alarming rate. Well-being among teachers is generally found to be low, and teacher illness is found to be relatively high in comparison with people in other professions. The concern is that when teacher well-being is low, their personal and professional efficacy is likely to be impacted negatively, compromising optimal teaching and learning experiences. Consequently, learners are likely to be affected. Current research finds South African learners to be underperforming when measured against their counterparts in other countries and studies have found a large percentage of school leavers to be illiterate. In acknowledgement of this critical issue, the Department of Basic Education (DBE) has adapted the Care and Support for Teaching and Learning (CSTL) Framework developed for the SADC Countries to address barriers to teaching and learning. The CSTL policy framework identifies nine strategic care and support priority action areas, including psychosocial support for teachers and learners in an effort to promote their emotional, mental and social well-being (Department of Basic Education & MIET Africa, 2010).

Given the situation in South African schools and the low morale experienced by many teachers, the question that arises is whether teacher well-being can be promoted, and how. The answer lies in understanding that each person has the ability to increase their reservoir of resources, which can be done in interesting and resourceful ways, such as:

- Giving priority to self-care;
- Knowing what one needs psychologically, emotionally, socially, physically and spiritually;
- Intentionally creating more opportunity for getting more of what one needs, eg, watching a film that makes one feel good, going for a walk, spending time in the company of loved ones and good friends, praying, gardening, taking up a sport or hobby, volunteering in a community organisation or practising mindfulness, meditation or yoga; and
- Using the pathways in the PERMA (+) framework to enhance one's life on each of the proposed pathways.

Conclusion

Csikzsentmihalyi (2002) persuades us that happiness and well-being does not just happen, but that 'it is a condition that must be prepared for, cultivated, and defended privately in the hands of each person'. People therefore have the power and responsibility to create happiness and well-being in their lives. Equally encouraging, is the realisation that well-being can be cultivated by the intentional pursuit of activities and experiences that enhance and promote well-being. When contemplating the brutality and hardship that life can bring, Frankl (1984) reminds us of 'the defiant power of the human spirit', encouraging us to

three-tier education system, piloted 412, 415–417
TIMSS *see* Trends in International Mathematics and Science Study
training and development units, at universities 386
Trends in International Mathematics and Science Study (TIMSS) 107, 294
trust 183
TVE *see* technical and vocational education
TVET *see* technical and vocational education and training

U

ubuntu 220
UDHR *see* Universal Declaration of Human Rights
'ugly laws' 288
UNCRC *see* United Nations Convention on the Rights of the Child
unemployment 287, 288, 289, 393–394, 418
UNESCO *see* United Nations Educational, Scientific and Cultural Organisation
UNICEF *see* United Nations Children's Emergency Fund
uniqueness of learners 104, 397–398
United Nations Children's Emergency Fund (UNICEF) 213, 261
United Nations Convention on the Rights of the Child (UNCRC) 29, 31–32, 259, 261
United Nations Educational, Scientific and Cultural Organisation (UNESCO) 261, 262, 340, 416
United Nations Psychosocial Working Group 217–218
Universal Declaration of Human Rights (UDHR) 259, 261
Universal Design for Learning 289
university student protests 9, 17, 390
university student support services
    coordination of *383*, 385–389
    debates in higher education 389–391
    definition of 382
    functions of 385
    importance of 382, 384–385, 391

V

values 217–218
violence
    and aggression in schools 330–336
    children's rights 30–31
    psychosocial well-being and 215–216
    against women and girls 337–344
visual imagery *195*
voice skills 187
volunteering 302, 305
Vygotsky, Lev
    giftedness 347–348
    language development 176, 179
    mediation 130–138, *132*, *133*
    social constructivism 73
    sociocultural theory 62–68, 105–106
    theory of learning and human development 40

W

welfare grants 327
well-being
    definition of 204
    positive psychology and 203–211
    psychosocial 212–220, *214*
    relationship-focused approach 221–228, *226*
    of teachers 203–211
    theories of 205–206
    of university students 386–387, 390–391
Wernicke's area 141, 379
whole child development *see* holistic education
word decoding 193–194, *193*
working memory 114–116, 119, 121
World Conference on Special Needs Education 260
World Declaration on Education for All 259
World Education Forum conferences 259–262
writing 136, 138

Y

youth 288, 289, 412–413, 414, 418

Z

zone of proximal development (ZPD) 65–66, 68, 135, 137–138, 156

'short list' 239–240, *240*
SIAS *see* Screening, Identification, Assessment and Support (SIAS) policy
SIFs *see* subjective identity forms
simultaneous multisensory instruction (SMI) 86–93
skills shortages 107
Skinner, B.F. 19, 23–24, 71, 176
sleep 209
SMI *see* simultaneous multisensory instruction
SNT *see* social network theory
social and emotional learning 106, 108–109
social capital 284–285
social constructivism 73
social ecology 217, 239–241, *240*
social interactions 59, 130–138, *132*, *133*, 366–367, 370, 372
social learning theory 45–51
social network theory (SNT) 283–285
social self 249–250
sociocultural approach 62–68, 137
socioecological model 273
socio-educational context 230–231, 331–332
socio-emotional learning 213, 215
Socrates 12
soft skills 384–385 *see also* non-cognitive skills
South African Council for Educators (SACE) 2, 46, 220
South African Higher Education Act 387
South African National Youth Risk Behaviour Survey (3rd) 413
South African norms and standards for educators 220
South African Schools Act 217, 264, 305, 325, 328, 372, 414
special educational needs (SEN) 266, 267–268 *see also* persons with disabilities
special schools as resource centres (SSRC) 273–274, 278
spelling development 198, *198–199*
spontaneous concepts 66
sports 388–389

SSFASNE *see* Salamanca Statement and Framework for Action on Special Needs Education
SSRC *see* special schools as resource centres
stability 121–123
stigma 325, 326, 334
stories 94–101, 398
strength-based assessment *see* deficit model vs strength-based model
stress 54, 60, 106, 108
structuration theory 339
subjective identity forms (SIFs) 394, 398
'Success for All' 294–295
support structures *244*, 271–278, 304
Sustainable Development Goals (SDG) 261, 416
systemic theory of giftedness 349
systems theory 293, 394

T
taxonomies of learning 72
teachers
 collaboration 279–285
 education programmes for 24–26, 40, 105, 405–406, 412
 emotional intelligence of 52–60
 identity of 36–44
 language proficiency of 184–189
 learning support 277
 relationship with learners 164
 as role models 45–51
 roles of 187–189, 216
 teaching styles 42, 78, 83, 87–88, 165–166
 well-being of 203–211, 217–218
 well-being of learners 218–219
Teachers on the Move programme 209
teaching, definition of 42–44
technical and vocational education (TVE) 411–418
technical and vocational education and training (TVET) 411, 413–414, 417
technical high schools 412
technology 69–76, 83, 91, 148, 304, 335
'teenage pregnancy' 323–329
'*theory* theory' 159–162
Thorndike, Edward L. 20, 27, 71

positive psychology 203–211, 229–236, 290
positron emission tomography (PET) scans 140–141
postmodern social constructionists 37
post-traumatic stress 108, 216, 380
poverty 326, 331–332
power 225, *226*, *245–246*, 340–341
pregnancy *see* 'teenage pregnancy'
private self 249–250
problem solving 233, 234, *244*
professional skills 53–54
Progress in International Reading Literacy Study (PIRLS) 107, 294
Promotion of Equality and Prevention of Unfair Discrimination Act 325, 328
'psychological first aid' 405
psychology and education 10–18, 401–402
'psychology of education', use of term 11, 15
psychometric testing 3, 275–276
psychosocial development, theory of 106

Q
quick fixes 297–298

R
racism 329, 390
reading development 143–144, 192–198, *192*, *193*, *195*, *197*, 294–295
Realism 12–13
reasoning 114–116
receptionists 304
receptive language development 172, *172–174*
recreational activities 388–389
relationships 164, 207, 221–228, *226*, *245*, 367
remedial intervention 273, 403–404
resilience
    adversity and 237–238
    beating odds vs changing odds 238
    case study 241–242
    championing of 218, 242–243, *244–246*, 246
    importance of 237
    resources 243, *244–246*
    social ecology 239–241, *240*

respect 224, 226–227, *226*
responsibility 31–32, 224–225, *226*
Revised policy on minimum requirements for teacher qualifications 53–54
revisionists 324, 326–327, 329
Rogers, Carl 43–44, 250–251, 253–254
role models, teachers as 45–51
rootedness *see* belonging
rote learning 145, 158

S
SACE *see* South African Council for Educators
safe psychosocial environments 218–219, 334–335
safe sex behaviours 317, 319–320, 342
Salamanca Statement and Framework for Action on Special Needs Education (SSFASNE) 260
same-sex sexual relationships 319, 320, 322
SBST *see* school-based support teams
scaffolding 50, 66–67
school-based support teams (SBST) 274–275, 279–285, 305
scientific concepts 66
Screening, Identification, Assessment and Support (SIAS) policy 275–277, 368, 372, 404
SDG *see* Sustainable Development Goals
self-actualisation 43, 397–398
self-determination theory 164, 166–167
self-employment 289, 290
self-esteem 250–254
self-evaluation 247, 250, 251
self-knowledge 165, 166, 167–168, 249–251
self-regulation 165, 167, *246*, 247–254
self-reliance 351
self-talk 247–254
Seligman, Martin 206, 208, 231–232, 233, 234
SEN *see* special educational needs
Sesotho proverbs 230, 231, 232, 233–234, 235
'seven tensions' 239–240, *240*
sexuality education 316–322, 328
sexual violence *see* violence

National Reading Panel (NRP) 196
National School Violence Study (NSVS) 215
nature vs nurture debate 174–175, 176, 349–351
NCESS *see* National Committee on Education Support Services
NCS *see* National Curriculum Statement Grades R-12
NCSNET *see* National Commission on Special Needs in Education and Training
NEET *see* not in education, employment or training
Neisser, Ulrich 151
Networks 4 Change project 337, 343
neuroscience
    brain anatomy and function 375–378, *376*, 379
    cognitive psychology and 152
    creativity and 146–147
    debates within field 379–380
    definitions 374–375
    Gardner's multiple intelligence theory 379
    giftedness 347–348, 353
    history of 140–142
    implication for educationists 139–140, 148–149
    language development 142–143, 146, 378–379
    learning and 378
    mathematical development 144–146, 378–379
    'Mind, Brain and Education' 139
    neurons 89, 111–112, 120–121, 141–142, 147, 378, 380
    reading development 143–144
    relevance to SA schools 380–381
    simultaneous multisensory instruction 89
non-cognitive skills 106–107 *see also* soft skills
Norms and standards for educators 53
not in education, employment or training (NEET) 287
NRP *see* National Reading Panel
NSVS *see* National School Violence Study
nurture vs nature debate 174–175, 176, 349–351
nutrition 209, 360

O

OBE *see* outcomes-based education
object tracking system (OTS) 145
observational learning 45, 46–48
OTS *see* object tracking system
outcomes-based education (OBE) 64, 107

P

parental partnerships 299–307, *301*, *302*, 361
parenting styles 360
patriarchy 339–343
pedagogy 12, 63, 64–66, 286
people with disabilities *see* persons with disabilities
perception 117, *117*
PERMA theory 206–209
'personal is political' 338–340, 344
personal skills 53–54, 56, 58–59
persons with disabilities
    employment of 286–291
    inclusive education 256–262, 263–270
    learning support 271–278
    policies 7
    simultaneous multisensory instruction 87
    teacher collaboration 280, 281
    university student support services 388
perspective-taking 252–253
PET scans 140–141
philosophy 8, 10–18
phonological awareness 144
physical activity 209, 380
Piaget, Jean 73, 120–129, *125*, *127*, 151, 153, 172
piloted three-tier education system 412, 415–417
PIRLS *see* Progress in International Reading Literacy Study
placeholder structures 158
plasticity in brain 141, 378
Plato 12, 53, 401
poor academic performance of learners 87, 107, 210, 294, 332–333, 389–390

features of language 175–176
forms of language 171
functions of language 175
importance of 171, 182
neuroscience and 142–143, 146
process of 174–176, *175–176*, *177*
relevance to SA schools 177–178
role of educational psychologists 181–182
stages of 171–172, *172–174*
strategies for enriching 179–181
vocabulary development 195–196
Vygotsky, Lev 135–136, 138
language diversity 83, 177–178, 184, 189
language processing 378–379
language proficiency 183–190
languages, indigenous 96, 101
languages, official 83, 177, 184
layering 121–123
leadership 188, 386
learner-centred approach 50, 64, 74–75
'learner with special educational needs' (LSEN) 266, 267–268, 272
learning
    emotions and 58–60
    at home 302–303
    process 26
    sociocultural approach 62–68
    styles 77–85, *80–81*, 91–92, 165–166
    support 271–278, 403–404
    technology and 69–76
    theories 41–44, 69–76
    well-being and 221–228, *226*
learning support teacher (LST) 274, 275, 406–407
LeDoux, Joseph 55
legal support for learners 216–217
life construction theory 395, 396
life design 393–399
life goals 165, 168
Life Orientation (LO) 32, 107–108, 316, 318–319
Life Skills 107–108, 316
listening 43–44, 232–233
'little scientists', children as 159–162
LO *see* Life Orientation
long-term memory 116–117, 119
LSEN *see* 'learner with special educational needs'
LST *see* learning support teacher
Lui, Siyuan 146–147
Lurie, David 311–312, *312*

M

magnetic resonance imaging (MRI) 140
Mandela, Nelson 29, 49, 256, 382, 384
Manifesto on Values, Education and Democracy 217
masculinity 341–342
Master's degree in educational psychology 5–6, *22–23*, 402, 407–409
mathematical development 63–64, 144–146, 199–200, *200–201*, 378–379
MBE *see* 'Mind, Brain and Education'
meaning 164–165, 167–168, 208
mediated learning experiences, theory of 106
mediation 65–68, 131–135, *132*, *133*, 137
medical deficit model *see* deficit model vs strength-based model
Meltzoff, Andrew 159–161
memorising 116–117
mental networks 120–129, *125*, *127*
metacognitive thinking 249, 380
mimicry 147
'Mind, Brain and Education' (MBE) 139
mindset, theory of 349
mnemonics *193*, *195*
modelling 45–51
mother tongue 96, 177–178
motivation 163–168
MRI *see* magnetic resonance imaging
multiple intelligences theory 55, 80–85, *80–81*, 89, 106, 379, 380

N

National Action Plan 390
National Commission on Special Needs in Education and Training (NCSNET) 7, 264
National Committee on Education Support Services (NCESS) 7, 264
National Curriculum Statement Grades R-12 (NCS) 108
National Policy Framework for Teacher Education and Development in South Africa 39

Higher Education South Africa
 (HESA) 390
HIV/AIDS 216, 276, 390–391
holistic education 7, 102–109
home language 96, 177–178
homophobia 319, 320, 322
housing for university students 387, 391
HPCSA *see* Health Professions Council of South Africa
human capacity 217
'Human Potential' movement 54–55
human rights 29–34, 216–217, 259, 264, 288, 324–325, 352

I

IDE *see* Incheon Declaration for Education
Idealism 12–13
identity 36–41, 44, 97, 163–168, *245–246*, 248, 251–252, 254
IDP *see* individual developmental programme
IE *see* inclusive education
ignorance hypothesis 327
imitation learning 45, 46–47
Incheon Declaration for Education (IDE) 261–262
inclusive education (IE)
 autism spectrum disorders 364–365, 372
 barriers to learning 267–268
 development of 4, 7
 diversity and 235–236
 focus on 23, 403–404
 giftedness 352
 global movement of 256–262
 learner responses to exclusion 334–335
 SA context of 263–270
 simultaneous multisensory instruction 87
 social inclusion 257, 258–259, 263
 terminology 266–268
incommensurability 155–157
India 104
indigenous knowledge 94–101, 103, 291
individual developmental programme (IDP) 369, 373
individualised learner support
 definition of 191

Education White Paper 6 201
 identification of needs 191–192
 mathematical development 199–200, *200–201*
 reading development 192–198, *192*, *193*, *195*, *197*
 spelling development 198, *198–199*
inequality 288–289, 316, 320–321, 331–332, 340–341, 343–344, 351, 393
inhibitory control 118
Integrated Quality Management Systems (IQMS) 227
intelligence quotient (IQ) 25, 231, 347
intelligences 77–85, *80–81*
internalisation 132, *132*, 135–137
international *see* global context, education in
internet *see* technology
internship programmes 6, 23, 28, 402, 408
interpersonal language 184–186
intersectionality 288–289, 341
interventions 293–298, 370, 396, 398
intuitive theories 158–159
IQ *see* intelligence quotient
IQMS *see* Integrated Quality Management Systems

J

Japan 103–104
Jomtien World Declaration on Education for All 260–261
justice *244–245*
justness 167

K

'kaleidoscope' metaphor of disability 287–288
KiVa anti-bullying programme 296–297
knowing 41–43
Kuhn, Thomas 153, 155, 159
Kwanele! Enuf is Enuf! Initiative 338

L

labelling 334, 349–351
language development
 challenges of 178–179, *179*
 definition of 170
 disorders 178–179, *179*

477

Education White Paper 6 (EWP6) 88, 109, 201, 230, 264–267, 269, 273, 279, 352
educators *see* teachers
EFA movement 257, 262, 287, 416
efficacy of teachers 16
egocentric speech 134
EI *see* emotional intelligence
Eisner, Elliot 309, 310, 311, 313
emotional intelligence (EI) 52–60
employment for persons with disabilities 286–291
empowerment 245–246, 317, 322
engagement 166, 207 *see also* disengaging of learners
entrepreneurship 290
environmental concerns 105, 108
epilepsy 91, 374, 375–376, 380–381
Epstein, Joyce 299, 302–303, *302*
Erikson's theory of psychosocial development 106
evaluation of others 251
Evans, Kate 310, 313
everyday concepts 66
EWP6 *see* Education White Paper 6
exclusion, learner responses to 334–335
exercise *see* physical activity
expressive language development 172, *172–174*
externalisation 135–136

F

failure 128–129
families 7, 299, 305
Fees Must Fall campaigns 9, 17, 390
femininity 341
feminist theory 288–289
FET phase 414, 417
financial aid for university students 388
first language 96, 177–178
Fischer, Norman 311, 315
five steps of teaching 20
fMRI *see* functional Magnetic Resonance Imaging
fortology 206
Foucault, M. 225
Framework for Action to Meet Basic Learning Needs 259
Frankl, Victor 208, 210–211

frontal lobe 359, 377, 379
full-service schools (FSS) 274, 278
functional Magnetic Resonance Imaging (fMRI) 140–141, 144, 145, 146–147, 152
funding for higher education 389
further education and training (FET) phase 414, 417

G

Gage, Phineas 377, 379
games, indigenous 94–101
gangs 335–336
Gardner, Howard 55, 77, 80–85, *80–81*, 89, 106, 379, 380
gender
    inequality 329, 340–341, 343–344
    regimes 339
    sexuality education 317, 318, 320–321, 322
    violence and 335–336, 337–344
general education and training (GET) phase 414, 417
giftedness 345–353, *348*
Ginott, Haim 373
global context, education in 105, 256–262, 283
goals of learners 165, 168
Goleman, Daniel 55, 56–57, 58–59
Gopnik, Alison 159–162
governance 301, 303, 386
Greek era 11–12

H

healing of divisions 234–235
health *see* well-being
Health Professions Act 2
Health Professions Council of South Africa (HPCSA) 2, 3, 5, 23, 24, 402, 404–405, 407–408
Hebbian model 378
HEI *see* higher education and training institutions
hemispheres of brain 146, 378, 380
Herbart, Johann Friedrich 20
HESA *see* Higher Education South Africa
higher education and training institutions (HEI) 414

cultural-historical activity theory
    (CHAT) 37, 40
cultural values 33, 217–218, *246*, 306, 375,
    399
curriculum
    CAPS 64, 83, 107, 276
    children's rights 32, 34
    Curriculum 2005 64
    giftedness 350, 353
    language proficiency 183–190
    role of educational psychologists 26
    for teacher education 27
    technical and vocational
        education 411–418

D

Dakar Framework for Action 260–261
DBE *see* Department of Basic Education
DBST *see* district-based support teams
decoding skills 193–194, *193*
decolonisation 9, 17, 248
deep learning 314–315
deficit model vs strength-based model 3,
    7–8, 203, 205, 231, 272, 278, 375, 404
Department of Basic Education (DBE) 2,
    39, 107, 210, 275, 278, 293, 404, 412,
    416, 417
Department of Education (DoE) 215, 217,
    328–329
Department of Higher Education and
    Training (DHET) 24, 417
depression 108, 209, 216, 360
developing countries 17, 396
development, stages of, Piaget's 123–124,
    127–128
developmental psychology 153
Dewey, John 40
DHET *see* Department of Higher
    Education and Training
*Diagnostic and statistical manual of mental
    disorders* (DSM-5) 178, 354
dialogical approaches to learning 137
dialogical self-construction theory 394
disabilities *see* persons with disabilities
discrimination 257–258, 272
disengaging of learners 78, 330, 332, 333,
    334, 336 *see also* engagement
disequilibration 153

disposition modelling 48–49, 51
district-based support teams (DBST) 274,
    275, 372
diversity
    inclusive education 256
    indigenous knowledge 94
    intelligences 77–85, *80–81*
    language 83, 177–178, 184, 189
    learning styles 77–85
    positive psychology and 229–236
    role of educational psychologists 25–26
    simultaneous multisensory
        instruction 87–88
    university student support services 382
    violence and 332–333, 336
    well-being and 219–220
divisions, healing of 234–235
DoE *see* Department of Education
domain-general thinking structures 153
domain-specific knowledge systems
    153–154, 157
dropout rates in schools 324
DSM-5 *see Diagnostic and statistical
    manual of mental disorders*
Dweck's theory of mindset 349

E

early reproduction 323–329
ecological systems theory 106, 213–215,
    214, 300, 375
education
    definition of 23–24
    philosophy and 11–13
    psychology and 14–17, 401–402
educational psychology
    debates within field 27
    definition of 19
    education and 10–18
    history of 3–4, 20
    importance of 20–21, *21*, 27–28
    philosophy and 10–18
    as profession 2–9
    psychology and 10–18
    role of 4–5, 23–26, *24*
    as science 2–9, 16
    theories in 6–7
    way forward for 9
education for all (EFA) movement 257,
    262, 287, 416

475

Bradburn, N.M. 206
brain
    ADHD 359
    anatomy and function of *376*, 377–378
    -body system 120–121
    cognition 111–112, 118–119, 374–381
    emotions and 55
    learning styles and 166
    multiple intelligence theory and 379
    neuro-physical impairment 374–381
    plasticity 141, 378
    simultaneous multisensory instruction 89
    see also neuroscience
Broca's area 141, 378–379
Bronfenbrenner, Urie 106, 213–215, *214*, 300, 375
Bruner, J.S. 63, 67, 72, 176
bullying 215–216, 296–297
burnout 54

C

C2005 (Curriculum 2005) 64
CALP *see* Cognitive Academic Language Proficiency
CAPS curriculum 64, 83, 107, 276
Care and Support for Teaching and Learning (CSTL) 210, 217, 276, 293
career paths within educational psychology
    career possibilities 5–6, 400–401, *401*, 405–410
    importance of knowledge of 401–403
    major debates 403–405
    map metaphor 400–401, *401*, 409
    paradigm shifts 403–405
    training programmes 21–23, *22–23*, 24
career psychology 8, 288 *see also* life design
caring 224, *226*, 277, 291
'causal loop' of thinking and action 112–113, *112*, *113*, *114*, 119
cellphones *see* technology
Centre for Justice and Crime Prevention (CJCP) 215
chaos theory 394
character, developing of 104
CHAT *see* cultural-historical activity theory
Children's Act 216

Chomsky, N. 176
CJCP *see* Centre for Justice and Crime Prevention
classed assumptions 329
code switching 189
cognition 111–119, *112*, *113*, *114*, *117*, 374–381, *376*
Cognitive Academic Language Proficiency (CALP) 184
cognitive psychology
    Carey, Susan 154–159
    conceptual change 152–155, 157
    definition of 150–151
    Gopnik, Alison 159–162
    history of 13, 151–152
    learning and 150
cognitivist learning theory 72–73
coherence 42, 122
collaboration in schools 279–285
communication 134, 183–190, 225, *226*, 302, 304, 369
communities 181, 303, 304–305
commuter learners 331–332
complexity theory 222
conceptual change 152–155, 157
confidentiality 302, 368
connectedness 223–224, *226*
connectivist learning theory 74–76
Constitution of RSA 45, 216, 230, 264, 352
constructivist learning theory 73–74
context, importance of 297
Convention for the Rights of Persons with Disability (CRPD) 257, 259, 287, 288
Convention on the Rights of the Child (CRC) 29, 31–32, 259, 261
correspondence theories 42
counselling 216, 219, 387, 407–408
CRC *see* Convention on the Rights of the Child
creativity 146–147, 313 *see also* aesthetic learning
Crenshaw, K. 288, 341
critical feminist perspective 324, 326, 327–328, 329
critical theorists 43
CRPD *see* Convention for the Rights of Persons with Disability
CSTL *see* Care and Support for Teaching and Learning

Index

A

ABCD acronym 317
abortion 321
abused children 30–31, 106, 215 *see also* violence
access to institutions of learning 166, 389
accommodation 126–127, *127*, 128–129, 153
achievement (accomplishment) 163–168, 208
activity theories 137
ADHD *see* attention deficit hyperactivity disorder
adult learning 286
aesthetic learning 309–315, *311*, *312*
African Charter on the Rights and Welfare of the Child 259
African proverbs 230, 231, 232, 233–234, 235, 279
agency 37, 41, *245*–246, 335, 342–343
aggression *see* violence
AIDS *see* HIV/AIDS
alternative formal schooling systems 103
American Psychological Association (APA) 20, 206
ANAs *see* annual national assessments
andragogy 286
annual national assessments (ANAs) 107, 415
ANS *see* approximate number sense
APA *see* American Psychological Association
apartheid 3–4, 68, 264, 325, 339, 347, 351, 404, 411–413, 417
approximate number sense (ANS) 145
Arendt, Hannah 314
Aristotle 12–13, 203, 401
ASD *see* autism spectrum disorders
assimilation 124–126, *125*, 128–129
attention 118
attention deficit hyperactivity disorder (ADHD)
  causes of 358–360
  debates within field 358
  diagnosing of 355, *356–357*
  impact of 354–355
  importance of understanding of 357–358, 363
  intervention 357, 360–361
  recommendations 362
  relevance to SA schools 361–362
auditory system 174–175
authenticity 43–44, 277
autism spectrum disorders (ASD)
  assessment 365–366, 368–369
  characteristics of 365, 366–368
  debates within field 366–372
  individual developmental programme 369, 373
  relevance to SA schools 372
  simultaneous multisensory instruction 91
  support 368–373
autonomy 164
awareness 114–116

B

Bandura, Albert 47, 249–250, 251, 252, 253
Basic Interpersonal Communication Skills (BICS) 184
Behaviourist Learning Theory 42, 71–72
behaviourist psychology 13, 151, 360–361
belief systems 251–252
'bell-curve theory' 25, 403
belonging 224, 313
BICS *see* Basic Interpersonal Communication Skills
Bill of Responsibilities for the Youth of South Africa 31–32
Bill of Rights 45, 264
bio-ecological model *see* ecological systems theory
bio-psychosocial model 375
Bloom, Benjamin 72
bootstrapping 157
Botswana 294, 415

Zunker, V.G. 1998. *Career counseling: Applied concepts of life planning.* 5th ed. Pacific Grove, CA: Brooks/Cole Publishing.

Zuze, T.V.R., Juan, A., Hannan, S., Visser, M. & Winnaar, L. 2016. *Safe and sound? Violence and South African education.* [online] Available from: http://www.hsrc.ac.za. Accessed: 23 March 2016.

Wissing, M.P. & Van Eeden, C. 1997. *Psychological well-being: A fortigenic conceptualisation and empirical clarification.* Paper presented at the Annual Congress of the Psychological Society of South Africa, Durban, South Africa.

Wissing, M.P. & Van Eeden, C. 2002. Empirical clarification on the nature of psychological well-being. *South African Journal of Psychology,* 32:32–44.

Wong, D. 2006. Beyond control and rationality: Dewey, aesthetics, motivation, and educative experiences. *Teachers College Record,* 109(1):192–220.

Wood, D., Bruner, J.S. & Ross, G. 1976. The role of tutoring in problem solving. *Journal of Child Psychology and Psychiatry,* 17:89–100.

Wood, L. & Goba, L. 2011. Care and support of orphaned and vulnerable children at school: Helping teachers to respond. *South African Journal of Education*:275–290. [online] Available from: http://www.scielo.org.za/pdf/saje/v31n2/v31n2a10.pdf. Accessed: 8 June 2017.

Wood, L. & Meyer, L. 2016. Collaborated Understandings of Context-Specific Psychosocial Challenges Facing South African School Leavers: A Participatory Approach. *Educational Research for Social Change (ERSC),* 18–34.

Woolfolk, A. 2010. *Educational Psychology.* 11th ed. London: Pearson Education.

Woolfolk, A. 2014. *Educational Psychology.* 10th ed. Boston, MA: Pearson Education, pp 334–335.

Woolfolk, A. 2014. *Educational Psychology.* 12th ed. Boston, MA: Pearson Education, pp 14–15.

Woolfolk, A. 2016. *Educational Psychology.* 13th ed. Boston, MA: Allyn & Bacon.

World Health Organization, War Trauma Foundation & World Vision International. 2011. *Psychological first aid: Guide for field workers.* Geneva: WHO, pp 1–64.

Wynn, K. 1992. Children's acquisition of the number words and the counting system. *Cognitive Psychology,* 24:220–251.

Xu, F. 2011. Rational constructivism, statistical inference, and core cognition (BBS commentary on Carey (2009). *Behavioral and Brain Sciences,* 34(3):151–152.

Yun Dai, D. 2005. Reductionism versus emergentism: A framework for understanding conceptions of giftedness. *Roeper Review,* 27(3):144–151.

Zander, R.S. & Zander, B. 2000. *The art of possibility.* London: Penguin Books.

Zandvliet, D., Den Brok, P., Mainhard, T. & Van Tartwijk, J. 2014. The theory and practice of interpersonal relationships in education. In: D. Zandvliet, P. Den Brok, T. Mainhard & J. Van Tartwijk (eds). *Interpersonal relationships in education: From theory to practice.* The Netherlands, Rotterdam: Sense Publishers, pp 9–24.

Ziegler, A. & Phillipson, S. 2012. Towards a systemic theory of gifted education. *High Ability Studies,* 23(1):3–30.

Ziegler, J.C. & Goswami, U. 2005. Reading acquisition, development dyslexia, and skilled reading across languages: A psycholinguistic grain size theory. *Psychological Bulletin,* 131(1):3–29.

Zimmerman, B.J. 1977. Modelling. In: H. Hom & P. Robinson (eds). *Psychological processes in children's early education.* New York, NY: Academic Press, pp 37–70.

Zipin, L. 2013. Engaging middle years learners by making their communities curricular: A Funds of Knowledge approach. *Curriculum Perspectives*:1–12.

Wehmeyer, M.L. 2017. *Strengths-based approaches to disability: Self-determination and autonomy-supportive interventions to empower people with disabilities* (abstract). [online] Available from: SELF Conference. https://www.self2017.com/keynote-speakers. Accessed: 31 May 2017.

Welsh, M., Parke, R.D., Widaman, K. & O'Neil, R. 2001. Linkages between children's social and academic competence: A longitudinal analysis. *Journal of School Psychology*, 39:463–482.

Werner, E. & Smith, R. 1992. *Overcoming the odds*. Ithaca, NY: Cornel University Press.

Werner, E. 2013. What can we learn about resilience from large-scale longitudinal studies? In: S. Goldstein & R. Brooks (eds). *Handbook of resilience in children*. New York, NY: Springer, pp 87–102.

Wertsch, J. 1991. *Voices of the mind*. Cambridge, MA: Harvard University Press.

Wertsch, J.V. 2007. Mediation. In: H. Daniels, M. Cole & J.V. Wertsch. (eds). *The Cambridge companion to Vygotsky*. Cambridge: Cambridge University Press.

White, M. 2007. *Maps of narrative practice*. New York, USA: W.W. Norton & Company, Inc., pp 3–7.

Whitehead, K.A. 2013. Race-class intersections as interactional resources in post-apartheid South Africa. In: C.M. Pascale (ed). *Social inequality and the politics of representation: A global landscape*. Newbury Park, CA: Sage, pp 49–63.

Wildeman, R.A. & Nomdo, C. 2007. Implementation of inclusive education: How far are we? *IDASA Inclusive Education Occasional Papers*. [online] Available from: http://www.idasa.org.za. Accessed: 5 May 2017.

Williams, D.L. 2010. The speaking brain. In D.A. Sousa (ed). *Mind, brain, & education: Neuroscience implications for the classroom*. Bloomington, IN: Solution Tree Press.

Williams, J. & Mavin, S. 2012. Disability as constructed difference: A literature review and research agenda for management and organization studies. *International Journal of Management Reviews*, 14(2):159–179.

Williamson, N.E. 2013. *Motherhood in childhood: facing the challenge of adolescent pregnancy*. New York, NY: United Nations Population Fund.

Williford, A., Boulton, A., Noland, B., Little, T.D., Kärnä, A. & Salmivalli, C. 2012. Effects of the KiVa anti-bullying program on adolescents' depression, anxiety, and perception of peers. *Journal of Abnormal Child Psychology*, 40(2):289–300.

Willingham, D.T., Hughes, E.M. & Dobolyi, D.G. 2015. The scientific status of learning styles theories. *Teaching of Psychology*, 42(3):266–271.

Wilson, G.B. 2001. *Organizing parent groups: a structured approach to parent involvement*. Atlanta, GA: Humanics Learning.

Wilson, H. & Huntington, A. 2005. Deviant (M)others: The construction of teenage motherhood in contemporary discourse. *Journal of Social Policy*, 35(1):59. [online] Available from: doi: http://doi.org/10.1017/S0047279405009335.

Winner, E. & Hetland, L. 2007. Arts for our sake: School arts classes matter more than ever – but not for the reasons you think. *Boston Globe*. [online] Available from: www.boston.com/news/-globe/ideas/articles/2007/09/02/art. Accessed: 14 May 2017.

Winslade, J. (2003). *Storying professional identity*. [online] Available from: http://dulwichcentre.com.au/articles-about-narrative-therapy/storying-professional-identity/. Acccssed: 19 Scptember 2017.

Vygotsky, L.S. 1978. Mind in society. The development of higher psychological processes. In: M. Cole, V. John-Steiner, S. Scribner & E. Souberman (eds). *Mind in society*. Cambridge, MA: Harvard University Press.

Vygotsky, L.S. 1986. Thought and language. In: E. Hanfmann & G. Vakar (eds). *Thought and language*. Cambridge, MA: MIT Press.

Vygotsky, L.S. 1987. *The collected works of L.S. Vygotsky, Vol 1: Problems of general psychology*. R.W. Rieber & A.S. Carton (eds), N. Minick (translator). New York, NY: Plenum Press.

Wadsworth, B.J. 2004. *Piaget's theory of cognitive and affective development: Foundations of Constructivism*. Allyn and Bacon Classics edition, 5th ed. Boston, MA: Pearson.

Wagner, P. 2014. *Postgraduate students' reflections on the promotion of relational well-being in South African school communities*. Master's dissertation, North-West University, Potchefstroom.

Walker, H.M. 2004. Commentary: Use of evidence-based interventions in schools: Where we've been, where we are, and where we need to go. *School Psychology Review*, 33(3)398–408.

Walton, E. & Rusznyak, L. 2017. Choices in the design of inclusive education courses for pre-service teachers: The case of a South African university. *International Journal of Disability, Development and Education*, 64(3):231-248.

Walton, E. 2015. Global concerns and local realities: The 'Making Education Inclusive' Conference in Johannesburg. *Intervention in School and Clinic*, 50(3):173–177.

Walton, E., Nel, N.M., Muller, H. & Lebeloane, O. 2014. 'You can train us until we are blue in our faces, we are still going to struggle': teacher professional learning in a full-service school. *Education as Change*, 18(2):319–333.

Wartenburger, I., Heekeren, H.R., Abutalebi, J., Cappa, S.F., Villringer, A. & Perani, D. 2003. Early setting of grammatical processing in the bilingual brain. *Neuron*, 37(1):159–270.

Waterhouse, L. 2006. Multiple intelligences, the Mozart effect, and emotional intelligence: A critical review. *Educational Psychologist*, 41(4):207–225.

Watermeyer, B. 2014. Disability and loss: The psychological commodification of identity. *Psychology Journal*, 11(2).

Watson, J.B. 1913. Psychology as the behaviorist views it. *Psychological Review*, 20:158–177.

Watson, M. 2013. Deconstruction, reconstruction, co-construction: Career construction theory in a developing world context. *Indian Journal of Career and Livelihood Planning*, 2:1–12.

Watson, M.B. & Stead, G.B. 2002. Career psychology in South Africa: Moral perspectives on present and future directions. *South African Journal of Psychology*, 32(1):26–31.

Webb, N.M., Nemer, K.M. & Ing, M. 2006. Small-group reflections: parallels between teacher discourse and student behaviour in peer-directed groups. *The Journal of the Learning Sciences*, 15 (1):63–119.

Wehmeyer, M.L. 2013. *The Oxford handbook of positive psychology and disability*. New York, NY: Oxford University Press.

Van Staden, A. 2016. Reading in a second language: Considering the 'simple view of reading' as a foundation to support ESL readers in Lesotho, Southern Africa. *Per Linguam*, 32(1):21–40.

Van Staden, A. 2017. *Cognitive-linguistic correlates of L2 reading: A case study of beginner ESL readers, EduLearn17 Proceedings:* 9th International Conference on Education and New Learning Technologies, Barcelona, Spain. 3–5 July, 2017, pp 4771–4777.

Van Staden, S. & Mihai, M. 2017. *Experiences, challenges and successes: Early reading comprehension practices in resource-constrained settings with children from linguistically diverse backgrounds.* Paper presented at the International Literacy Conference, Cape Town, 3–5 March.

Van Wyk, N. & Lemmer, E. 2009. *Organising parent involvement in SA schools.* Cape Town: Juta and Company Ltd.

Vandeyar, S. & Killen, R. 2006. Teacher-student interactions in desegregated classrooms in South Africa. *International Journal of Educational Development,* 26:382–393.

Vash, C.L. & Crewe, N.M. 2004. *Psychology of disability.* New York, NY: Springer.

Venter, A. 2007. *Die ontwerp, implementering en evaluering van 'n multisensoriese leesprogram vir Graad 3-leerders in Heidedal.* Doktorale proefskrif. Universiteit van die Vrystaat, Bloemfontein. [online] Available from: http://scholar.ufs.ac.za:8080/xmlui/bitstream/handle/11660/2199/VenterA.pdf?sequence=1&isAllowed=y. Accessed: 29 May 2017.

Veresov, N. 2004. Zone of proximal development (ZPD): the hidden dimension? In: A-L. Ostern & R. HeilaYlikallio (eds). *Language as culture tensions in time and space,* vol. 1. Vasa: ABO Akademi, pp 13–30.

Vesely, A.K., Saklofske, D.H. & Leschied, A.D. 2013. Teachers—The vital resource: The contribution of emotional intelligence to teacher efficacy and well-being. *Canadian Journal of School Psychology*, 28(1):71–89.

Viale, R. 2001. Reasons and reasoning: what comes first? In: R. Boudon, P. Demeulenaere & R. Viale (eds). *Explaining social norms: Rationality and cognition.* Paris: Presses Universitaire de France, pp 215–236.

Viviers, A. & Lombard, A. 2013. The ethics of children's participation: Fundamental to children's rights realization in Africa. *International Social Work,* 56(1):7–21.

Vosniadou, S., Vamvakoussi, X. & Skopeliti, I. 2008. The framework theory approach to the problem of conceptual change. In: S. Vosniadou (ed). *International handbook of research on conceptual change.* New York: Routledge, pp 3–34.

Vygotsky, L. 1978. *Mind in society: The development of higher psychological processes.* Cambridge, MA: Harvard University Press, pp 1–140.

Vygotsky, L. 1986. *Thought and Language.* (A. Kozulin, ed. & translator). Cambridge, MA: MIT Press.

Vygotsky, L. 1997. Interaction between learning and development. In: M. Gauvain & M. Cole (eds). *Readings on the development of children.* 2nd ed. New York, NY: W.H. Freeman & Co.

Vygotsky, L.S. 1931. *Genesis of higher mental functions.* The open access Vygotsky archive. [online] Available from: https://www.marxists.org/archive/vygotsky/. Accessed: 1 July 2017.

United Nations. 2006. *Convention on the Rights of Persons with Disabilities.* [online] Available from: http://www.un.org/disabilities/documents/convention/convoptprot-e.pdf. Accessed: 5 May 2017.

United States Department of Education. 2017. *Issue brief: Student support teams. Office of Planning, Evaluation and Policy Development.* [online] Available from: https://www2.ed.gov/rschstat/eval/high-school/student-support-teams.pdf. Accessed: 22 August 2017.

Universities South Africa. 2016. *Universities funding in South Africa: A fact sheet.* [online] Available from: https://www.uct.ac.za. Accessed: 18 May 2017.

University of Edinburgh, Moray House School of Education. 2016. *Inclusive pedagogy.* [online] Available from: http://www.ed.ac.uk/education/election-briefings/inclusive-pedagogy, pp 2–4. Accessed: 30 May 2017.

University of Zululand Revised Rules. 2012. *Registration management-intake and graduation processes and procedures.* Kwa-Dlangezwa: University of Zululand.

Uys, A.H.C. 2006. *A proposed model for training English medium of instruction teachers in South Africa.* Doctoral thesis, North-West University, Potchefstroom.

Uys, M., Van der Walt, J.L., Van den Berg, R. & Botha, S. 2007. English as a medium of instruction: a situation analysis. *South Africa Journal of Education*, 27(1):69–82.

Valle, M.F., Huebner, E.S. & Suldo, S.M. 2006. An analysis of hope as a psychological strength. *Journal of School Psychology*, 44(5):393–406.

Van Breda, A. 2017. A comparison of youth resilience across seven South African sites. *Child & Family Social Work*, 22(1):226–235.

Van der Merwe, A., Dawes, A. & Ward, C. 2011. The development of youth violence: An ecological understanding. In: A. van der Merwe, A. Dawes & C. Ward. (eds). Cape Town: UCT Press.

Van der Merwe, M. 2004. Onderrigkommunikasie in die klaskamer: 'n Uitnodigende perspektief. *Acta Academica*, 36(3):82–202.

Van der Venter, K. 2009. Perspectives of teachers on the implementation of Life Orientation in Grades R–11 from Selected Western Cape schools. *South African Journal of Education*, 29(1):127–145.

Van Dijk, M.P.A., Branje, S., Keijsers, L., Hawk, S.T., Hale, W.W. & Meeus, W. 2014. Self-concept clarity across adolescence: Longitudinal associations with open communication with parents and internalizing symptoms. *Youth Adolescence*, 43(11):1861–1876. [online] Available from: doi: http://10.1007/s10964-013-0055-x.

Van Niekerk, P.A. 1986. *Die opvoedkundige sielkundige. 'n Handleiding in die Opvoedkundige Sielkunde* (The educational psychologist. A manual in Educational Psychology). Stellenbosch/Grahamstown: Universiteitsuitgewers en Boekhandelaars.

Van Rensburg, E. & Barnard, C. 2005. Psychological resilience among sexually-molested girls in the late middle-childhood: A case study approach. *Child Abuse Research in South Africa*, 6(1):1–12.

Van Staden, A. & Purcell, N. 2016. Multi-sensory learning strategies to support spelling development: a case study of second-language learners with auditory processing difficulties. *International Journal on Language, Literature and Culture in Education*, 3(1):40–61.

Van Staden, A. 2010. Improving Grade 3 learners' spelling abilities through visual imaging teaching strategies. *Per Linguam*, 26(1):13–28.

UNESCO. 2015b. *Fixing the broken promise of education for all.* Montreal: UNESCO.

UNESCO. 2016. *Technical vocational education and training.* [online] Available from: http://www.unesco.org/new/en/newdelhi/areas-of-action/education/technical-vocational-education-and-training-tvet/. Accessed: 28 May 2017.

UNESCO. nd. *Priority gender equality at UNESCO.* [online] Available from: http://www.unesco.org/fileadmin/MULTIMEDIA/HQ/BSP/GENDER/GEHandoutFinalUpdatedVersion.pdf. Accessed: 4 June 2017.

UNESCO-UNEVOC. nd. *Promoting learning for the world of work, UNESCO.* [online] Available from: http://www.unevoc.unesco.org/go.php. Accessed: 28 May 2017.

Ungar, M. 2011. The social ecology of resilience: Addressing contextual and cultural ambiguity of a nascent construct. *American Journal of Orthopsychiatry,* 81(1):1–17.

Ungar, M. 2012. Social ecologies and their contribution to resilience. In: M. Ungar (ed). *The social ecology of resilience: Culture, context, resources and meaning.* New York, NY: Springer, pp 13–32.

Ungar, M., Brown, M., Liebenberg, L., Othman, R., Kwong, W.M., Armstrong, M. & Gilgun, J. 2007. Unique pathways to resilience across cultures. *Adolescence,* 42(166):287–310.

Ungar, M., Theron, L., Liebenberg, L., Tian, G., Restrepo, A., Sanders, J., Munford, R. & Russell, S. 2015. Patterns of individual coping, engagement with social supports, and use of formal services among a five-country sample of resilient youth. *Global Mental Health,* 2:1–10. [online] Available from: https://www.cambridge.org/core/services/aop-cambridge-core/content/view/638BB9899BEDE1F226EC678C986679AB/S2054425115000199a.pdf/patterns_of_individual_coping_engagement_with_social_supports_and_use_of_formal_services_among_a_fivecountry_sample_of_resilient_youth.pdf. Accessed: 4 July 2017.

Ungerer, A. 2012. *'n Verkennende ondersoek na die bevordering van die verhouding tussen opvoeders en leerders in vaardigheidskole [An exploratory inquiry into the promotion of the relationship between educators and learners in schools of skills].* Master's dissertation, North-West University, Potchefstroom.

UNICEF. 1999. *The African Charter on the Rights and Welfare of the Child.* [online] Available from: http://www.unicef.org/esaro/African_Charter_articles_in_full.pdf. Accessed: 5 May 2017.

UNICEF. 2009. *Guide to the evaluation of psychosocial programming in emergencies.* [online] Available from: http://resourcecentre.savethechildren.se/sites/default/files/documents/6454.pdf. Accessed: 8 June 2017.

UNICEF. 2015. *Developing social and emotional learning (SEL) in schools: Guidance for UNICEF country and regional offices.* Northampton: The University of Northampton, Northampton Centre for Learning Behaviour.

United Nations. 1948. *Universal Declaration of Human Rights.* [online] Available from: http://www.jus.uio.no/lm/un.universal.declaration.of.human.rights.1948/portrait.a4.pdf. Accessed: 5 May 2017.

United Nations. 1989. *Convention on the Rights of the Child.* [online] Available from: http://www.ohchr.org/EN/ProfessionalInterest/Pages/CRC.aspx. Accessed: 5 May 2017.

United Nations. 1993. *Declaration on the Elimination of Violence against Women.* [online]. Available from: http://www.un.org/documents/ga/res/48/a48r104.htm. Accessed: 3 June 2017.

Townsend, S.B. 2007. *The need for a remedial qualification within inclusive education.* Master's dissertation, Nelson Mandela Metropolitan University, Port Elizabeth (unpublished).

Truitt, M., Biesecker, B., Capone, G., Bailey, T. & Erby, L. 2012. The role of hope in adaptation to uncertainty: The experience of caregivers of children with Down syndrome. *Patient Education and Counseling,* 87(2):233–238.

Tulving, E. 1962. Subjective organization in free recall of 'unrelated' words. *Psychological Review,* 69:344–354.

Twum-Danso, A. 2009. Reciprocity, respect and responsibility: The 3Rs. Underlying parent-child relationships in Ghana and the implications for children's rights. *International Journal of Children's Rights,* 17(3):415–432.

Twum-Dansoh, A. 2011. Searching for a middle ground in children's rights in Ghana. *The Journal of Human Rights,* 10(3):376–392.

Uitzinger, C. & Ragpot, L. (under review). How to bring mathematical cognition theory to bear on psycho-educational assessment: a group case study of dyscalculia. *South African Journal of Psychology.*

UK Answers. 2011. *Opportunity and freedom to read and grow.* [online] Available from: http://uk.answers.yahoo.com/question/index?qid=20070314162158AAlvlFC. Accessed: 16 May 2017.

UN Department of Economics and Social Affairs. 2016. *The Sustainable Development Goals Report 2016.* [online] Available from: doi: http://dx.doi.org/10.18356/3405d09f-en.

UNESCO, 2010. *Education for all Global Monitoring Report 2010: Reaching for the marginalized.* Paris: UNESCO.

UNESCO, UNICEF, World Bank, UNFPA, UNDP, UN Women & UNHCR. 2015. *Education 2030 Incheon Declaration towards inclusive and equitable quality education and lifelong learning for all.* [online] Available from: http://www.uis.unesco.org/Education/Documents/education_2030_incheon_declaration_en.pdf. Accessed: 5 May 2017.

UNESCO. 1994. *The Salamanca Statement and Framework for Action on Special Needs Education. Adopted by the World Conference on Special Needs Education: Access and Quality. Salamanca, Spain, 7-10 June.* [online] Available from: http://www.unesco.org/education/pdf/SALAMA_E.PDF. Accessed: 5 May 2017.

UNESCO. 2000. *Inclusion in education: The participation of disabled learners. Executive summary for World Education Forum.* Dakar, Senegal: UNESCO.

UNESCO. 2003. *Gender Mainstreaming Framework.* Paris: UNESCO. [online] Available from: http://www.unesco.org/fileadmin/MULTIMEDIA/HQ/BSP/GENDER/PDF/1.%20Baseline%20Definitions%20of%20key%20gender-related%20concepts.pdf. Accessed: 3 June 2017.

UNESCO. 2004. *Changing teaching practices, using curriculum differentiation to respond to students' diversity.* Paris: UNESCO.

UNESCO. 2007. *A human rights-based approach to education for all. A framework for the realisation of children's right to education and rights within education.* New York, NY: UNICEF/UNESCO.

UNESCO. 2015a. *Education for All. 2000-2015: Achievements and challenges.* Paris: UNESCO. [online] Available from: http://unesdoc.unesco.org/images/0023/002322/232205e.pdf. Accessed: 5 May 2017.

Theron, L. & Engelbrecht, P. 2012. Caring teachers: Teacher-youth transactions to promote resilience. In: M. Ungar (ed). *The social ecology of resilience: Culture, context, resources and meaning.* New York, NY: Springer, pp 265–280.

Theron, L. & Malindi, M. 2010. Resilient street youth: A qualitative South African study. *Journal of Youth Studies,* 13(6):717–736.

Theron, L. & Theron, A. 2010. A critical review of Studies of South African youth resilience, 1990–2008. *South African Journal of Science,* 106(7/8). [online] Available from: http://www.sajs.co.za/critical-review-studies-south-african-youth-resilience-1990%E2%80%932008/theron-linda-theron-adam. Accessed: 4 July 2017.

Theron, L. & Theron, A. 2014. Education services and resilience processes: Resilient black South African students' experiences. *Child and Youth Services Review,* 47(3):297–306.

Theron, L. 2016a. Towards a culturally- and contextually-sensitive understanding of resilience: Privileging the voices of black, South African young people. *Journal of Adolescent Research,* 31(6):635–670.

Theron, L. 2016b. The everyday ways that school ecologies facilitate resilience: Implications for school psychologists. *School Psychology International,* 37(2):87–103.

Theron, L., Cameron, C., Didkowsky, N., Lau, C., Liebenberg, L. & Ungar, M. 2011. A 'Day in the lives' of four resilient youths: A study of cultural roots of resilience. *Youth & Society,* 43(3):799–818.

Theron, L., Liebenberg, L. & Malindi, M. 2014. When schooling experiences are respectful of children's rights: A pathway to resilience. *School Psychology International,* 35(3):253–265.

Theron, L., Theron, A. & Malindi, M. 2012. Towards an African definition of resilience: A rural South African community's view of resilient Basotho youth. *Journal of Black Psychology,* 39(1):63–87.

Theron, L.C. & Dalzell, C. 2006. The specific Life Orientation needs of Grade 9 learners in the Vaal Triangle region. *South African Journal of Education,* 26(3):397–412.

Theron, L.C. & Engelbrecht, P. 2012. Caring teachers: Teacher-youth transactions to promote resilience. In M. Ungar (ed). *The social ecology of resilience: Culture, context, resources and meaning.* New York, NY: Springer, pp 265–280.

Theron, L.C. 2016. The everyday ways that school ecologies facilitate resilience: Implications for school psychologists. *School Psychology International.* 37:87-103. doi:101177/0142723713503254.

Theron, L.C. & Donald, D.R. 2013. Educational psychology and resilience in developing contexts: A rejoinder to Toland and Carrigan (2011). *School Psychology International*: 34–51, originally published online 2 February 2012. [online] Available from: doi: http://journals.sagepub.com/doi/abs/10.1177/0143034311425579.

Thomas, J.B. 2007. Psychology of education in the UK: Development in the 1960s. *Educational Studies,* 33(1), 53–63.

Tomlinson, C.A. 2005. Grading and differentiation: Paradox or good practice? *Theory into Practice,* 44(3):262–269.

Tonjes, M. 1988. Metacognitive modelling and glossing: two powerful ways to teach self responsibility. In: C. Anderson (ed). *Reading: The ABC and Beyond.* Basingstoke: Macmillan.

Topping, K. 2012. Conceptions of inclusion: Widening ideas. In: C. Boyle & K. Topping (eds). *What works in inclusion?* Berkshire: Open University Press, pp 9–19.

Stead, G. & Watson, M.B. 2017. *Career psychology in the South African context*. Pretoria: Van Schaik Publishers.

Stead, G.B. & Watson, M.B. 2006. Indigenisation of career psychology in South Africa. In: G.B. Stead & M.B. Watson (eds). *Career psychology in the South African context*. Pretoria: Van Schaik Publishers, pp 181–190.

Stetsenko, A. & Arievitch, I.M. 2004. The self in cultural-historical activity theory. Reclaiming the unity of social and individual dimensions of human development. *Theory & Psychology,* 14(4):475–503.

Stetsenko, A. 2005. Activity as object-related: Resolving the dichotomy of individual and collective planes of activity. *Mind, Culture and Activity,* 12(1):70–88.

Stevenson, L.M. & Deasy, R.J. 2005. *Third space: When learning matters*. Washington, DC: Arts Education Partnership.

Stroh, D.P. 2015. *Systems thinking for social change: A practical guide to solving complex problems, avoiding unintended consequences, and achieving lasting results*. White River Junction, VT: Chelsea Green Publishing.

Strümpfer, D.J.W. 1995. The origins of health and strengths: From 'salutogenesis' to 'fortigenesis'. *South African Journal of Psychology,* 25:81–89.

Subotnik, R., Olszewski-Kubilius, P. & Worrell, F. 2011. Rethinking giftedness and gifted education: A proposed direction forward based on psychological science. *Psychological Science in the Public Interest,* 12(1):3–54. [online] Available from: doi: 10.1177/1529100611418056.

Suchman, A.L. 2006. A new theoretical foundation for relationship-centered care. *Journal of General Internal Medicine*, 21(1):40–44.

Sugai, G. & Horner, R.H. 2009. Responsiveness-to-intervention and school-wide positive behavior supports: Integration of multi-tiered system approaches. *Exceptionality*, 17(4):223–237.

Suid-Afrikaanse Onderwysersunie Kurrikulumdienste. 2006. *Raamwerk vir die ontwikkeling van 'n fasebeleid (Grade R-3), Leerareabeleid (Grade 4–9) of vakbeleid (Grade 10–12)* (Ongepubliseerd).

Swart, E. & Pettipher, R. 2016. A framework for understanding inclusion. In: E. Landsberg, D. Krüger & E. Swart (eds). *Addressing barriers to learning: A South African perspective*. 3rd ed. Pretoria: Van Schaik Publishers, pp 3–27.

Swart, E. & Phasa, T. 2016. Family and community partnerships. In: E. Landsberg, D. Krüger & E. Swart (eds). *Addressing barriers to learning: A South African perspective*. 3rd ed. Pretoria: Van Schaik Publishers, pp 265–287.

Swarts, S. 2011. *iKASI*. Johannesburg: Wits University Press.

Szpringer, M., Kopik, A. & Formella, Z. 2014. 'Multiple intelligences' and 'minds for the future' in a child's education. *Journal Plus Education*, Special issue, 2014:350–359.

Task Team. 2012. May. [online] Available from: http://sites.google.com/site/epttsa/home.

Thapa, A., Cohen, J., Guffey, S. & Higgins-D'Alessandro, A. 2013. A review of school climate research. *Review of Educational Research*, 83(3):357–385.

Theron, L. & Dunn, N. 2010. Enabling white, Afrikaans-speaking adolescents towards post-divorce resilience: Implications for educators. *South African Journal of Education*, 30(2): 231–244.

Spaull, N. 2011. *A preliminary analysis of SACMEQ III South Africa.* Working Paper 11/11. Stellenbosch University: The Department of Economics and the Bureau for Economic Research.

Speizer, I.S., Pettifor, A., Cummings, S., MacPhail, C., Kleinschmidt, I. & Rees, H.V. 2009. Sexual violence and reproductive health outcomes among South African female youths: A contextual analysis. *American Journal of Public Health*, 99S:S425–S431. [online] Available from: doi: http://doi.org/10.2105/AJPH.2008.136606. Accessed: 2 June 2017.

Spelke, E. 2012. Natural number and natural geometry. In: S. Dehaene & E.M. Brannon (eds). *Space, time and number in the brain. Searching for the foundations of mathematical thought.* Amsterdam: Elsevier, pp 287–317.

Spelke, E.S. & Kinzler, K.D. 2007. Core knowledge. *Developmental Science*, 10(1):89–96.

Spelke, E.S., Phillips, A. & Woodward, A.L. 1995. Infants' knowledge of object motion and human action. In: D. Sperber, D. Premack & A.J. Premack (eds). *Causal Cognition.* Oxford: Oxford University Press, pp 44–78.

Sperling, G. 1960. The information available in brief visual presentations. *Psychological Monographs*, 74:1–29.

Squire, L.R. & Kandel, E.R. 1999. *Memory: From mind to molecules.* New York, NY: WH Freeman.

Srivastava, M., De Boer, A. & Pijl, S. 2015. Inclusive education in developing countries: a closer look at its implementation in the last 10 years. *Educational Review*, 67(2):179–195. [online] Available from: doi: 10.1080/00131911.2013.847061.

Stacey, R. 2007. The challenge of Human Interdependence. Consequences for thinking about the day to day practice of management in organisations. *European Business Review*, 19(4):292–302.

Stacey, R.D. 2001. *Complex responsive processes in organisations: Learning and knowledge creation.* London: Routledge.

Stacey, R.D. 2003. *Complexity and group processes: A radically social understanding of individuals.* New York, NY: Brunner-Routledge.

State Secretariat for Education, Research and Innovation. 2014. *Facts and Figures. Vocational Education and Training in Switzerland.* Bern: State Secretariat for Education, Research and Innovation (SERI).

Statistics South Africa, National Department of Health, South African Medical Research Council (2017). *South Africa demographic and health survey 2016: Key indicators.* Pretoria. [online] Available from: http://www.statssa.gov.za/publications/Report%2003-00-09/Report%2003-00-092016.pdf. Accessed: 23 August 2017.

Statistics South Africa. 2012. *Census 2011: Statistical release.* [online] Available from: http://www.sttssa.gov.za/publications/P03014/P030142011.pdf. Accessed: 18 June 2017.

Statistics South Africa. 2016. *National and provincial labour market Youth.* Pretoria: Government Printer, p xx. [online] Available from: http://www.statssa.gov.za/publications/P0211/P02111stQuarter2016.pdf. Accessed: 15 April 2017.

Staunton, T. 2015. *Mark Savickas and life design – theories every careers adviser should know.* [online] Available from: https://runninginaforest.wordpress.com/2015/03/08/marksavickasandlifedesigntheorieseverycareersadvisershouldknow/. Accessed: 24 September 2016.

Stavredes, T. 2011. *Effective online teaching: Foundations and strategies for student success.* San Francisco, CA: John Wiley & Sons.

Siemens, G. 2005. Connectivism: A learning theory for the digital age. *International Journal of Instructional Technology & Distance Learning.* [online] Available from: http://www.itdl.org/Journal/Jan_05/article01.htm. Accessed: 20 May 2017.

Singer, W. 1995. Development and plasticity of cortical processing architectures. *Science,* 270(5237):758–764.

Singh, P. 2009. Trawling through language policy: Practices and possibilities post-1994. *Language Learning Journal,* 37(3):281–291.

Skinner, B.F. 1950. Are theories of learning necessary? *Psychological Review,* 57:193–216.

Skinner, B.F. 1953. *Science and human behavior.* Cambridge: B.F. Skinner Foundation, Simon and Schuster. [online] Available from: https://scholar.google.co.za/scholar?hl=en&q=Skinner%2C+B.F.+1953.+Science+and+human+behavior.+Cambridge%3A+B.F.+Skinner+Foundation%2C+Simon+and+Schuster&btnG=&as_sdt=1%2C5&as_sdtp=. Accessed: 10 August 2017.

Skutnabb-Kangas, T. & Dunbar, R. 2010. Indigenous children's education as linguistic genocide and a crime to against humanity? A global view. *Journal of Indigenous People's Rights,* 1:1–128.

Slavin, R.E., Madden, N.A., Chambers, B. & Haxby, B. 2008. *2 million children: Success for All.* Thousand Oaks, CA: Corwin Press.

Smeyers, P. & Depaepe, M. 2013. Making sense of the attraction of psychology: On the strengths and weaknesses for education and educational research. In: P. Smeyers & M. Depaepe (eds). *Educational Research: The attraction of psychology.* Dordrecht: Springer.

Smith, A.B. 2002. Interpreting and supporting participation rights: Contributions from sociocultural theory. *International Journal of Children's Rights,* 10(1):73–88.

Smith, C., Carey, S. & Wiser, M. 1985. On differentiation: A case study of the development of size, weight, and density. *Cognition,* 21(3):177–237.

Smith, C.L. 2010. *Conceptual change.* [online] Available from: http://www.education.com/reference/article/learning-conceptual-change/. Accessed: 30 May 2017.

Smylie, M. & Evans, A. 2006. Social capital and the problem of implementation. In: M.I. Honig (ed). *New directions in education policy: Confronting complexity.* Albany, NY: State University of New York Press, pp 187–208.

Snowman, J. & Biehler, R. 2006. *Psychology applied to teaching.* Boston, MA: Houghton Mifflin Company.

Society for Neuroscience. 2012. *Brain facts: A primer on the brain and nervous system.* [online] Available from: http://www.brainfacts.org/book. Accessed: 1 July 2017.

Solberg, M.E. & Olweus, D. 2003. Prevalence estimation of school bullying with the Olweus Bully/Victim Questionnaire. *Aggressive Behavior,* 29(3):239–268.

Somr, M. & Hrušková, L. 2014. Herbart's philosophy of pedagogy and educational teaching. *Studia Edukacyjne,* 33:413–429.

Sontag, S. 1969. The aesthetics of silence. In: S. Sontag (ed). *Styles of radical will.* New York, NY: Piccador, pp 3–34.

Sousa, D.A. 2006. *How the brain learns.* 3rd ed. Thousand Oaks, CA: Corwin Press.

South Australian Health and Medical Research Institute (SAHMRI). *The well-being and resilience Centre. PERMA+.* [online] Available from: at www.well-beingandresilience.com. Accessed: 13 May 2017.

Sowetan Live. 2013. *One hundred quoted from Nelson Mandela.* [online] Available from: https://www.sowetanlive.co.za. Accessed: 18 April 2017.

Schunk, D. 2012. *Learning theories: An educational perspective.* 6th ed. Boston, MA: Pearson.

Schunk, D.H. 1987. Peer models and children's behavioural change. *Review of Educational Research,* 57:149–174.

Schunk, D.H. 2012. *Learning theories: An educational perspective.* 6th ed. Upper Saddle River, NJ: Pearson.

Schwab, K. 2016. *The Fourth Industrial Revolution: what it means, how to respond.* [online] Available from: http://www.weforum.org/agenda/2016/01/the-fourth-industrial-revolution-what-it-means-and-how-to-respond. Accessed: 27 September 2016.

Schwarz, N. 2012. Feelings-as-information theory. In: P. Van Lange, A. Kruglanski & T. Higgins (eds). *Handbook of theories of social psychology,* pp 289–308.

Schweik, S.M. 2009. *The ugly laws: Disability in public.* New York, NY: NYU Press.

Scott, J. & Carrington, P. 2011. *The Sage handbook of social network analysis.* London: Sage.

Seccombe, K. 2002. 'Beating the Odds' Versus 'Changing The Odds': Poverty, resilience, and family policy. *Journal of Marriage and Family,* 64(2):384–394.

Secker, E. 2013. Witchcraft stigmatisation in Nigeria: Challenges and successes in the implementation of child rights. *International Social Work,* 56(1):3–6.

Sefotho, M.M. 2015. A researcher's dilemma: Philosophy in crafting dissertations and theses, *Journal of Social Sciences,* 42:1-2, 23-36.

Seifert, K. & Sutton, R. 2011. *Educational Psychology.* 3rd ed. [online] Available from: https://www.saylor.org/site/wp-content/uploads/2012/06/Educational-Psychology.pdf. Accessed: 31 May 2017.

Seifert, K. & Sutton, R. 2009. *Educational Psychology.* 2nd ed. Zürich: The Saylor Foundation.

Seligman, M. 2004. *The new era of positive psychology.* [online] Available from: TED Talks. http://ted.comtalks/martin_seligman_on_the_state_of_pisitive_psychology. Accessed: 31 May 2017.

Seligman, M.E. 2011. *Flourish: A visionary new understanding of happiness and well-being.* New York, NY: Atria Paperback, division of Simon & Schuster Inc.

Semali, L.M. & Kincheloe, J.L. 2011. What is indigenous knowledge and why should we study it. In: L.M. Semali & J.L. Kincheloe (eds). *What is indigenous knowledge?: Voices from the Academy.* New York, NY: Routledge.

Shams, L. & Seitz, A.R. 2008. Benefits of multisensory learning. *Trends in Cognitive Sciences,* 12(11):411–417. [online] Available from: doi:10.1016/j.tics.2008.07.006.

Shaw, P. 2002. *Changing conversations in organisations: a complexity approach to change.* London: Routledge.

Shea, N. 2011. New concepts can be learned, review essay on Susan Carey, *The origin of concepts. Biology & Philosophy,* 26:129–139.

Shefer, T. & Macleod, C. 2015. Life Orientation sexuality education in South Africa: Gendered norms, justice and transformation. *Perspectives in Education,* 33(2).

Shein, P.P. & Chiou, W. 2011. Teachers as role models for students' learning styles. *Social Behavior and Personality,* 39(8):1097–1104. [online] Available from: doi: http://dx.doi.org/10.2224/sbp.2011.39.8.1097.

Shuell, T.J. 1996. The role of Educational Psychology in the preparation of teachers. *Educational Psychologist,* 31(1):5–14.

Shultz, J.M. & Forbes, D. 2014. Psychological first aid. *Disaster Health,* 2(1):3–12.

Rutter, M. 2013. Annual research review: Resilience – Clinical implications. *Journal of Child Psychology and Psychiatry,* 54(4):474–487.

Ryan, R.M. & Deci, E.L. 2006. Self-regulation and the problem of autonomy: Does psychology need choice, self-determination, and will? *Journal of Personality,* 74(6):1557–1586.

Salmivalli, C., Garandeau, C.F. & Veenstra, R. 2012. KiVa anti-bullying program: Implications for school adjustment. In: A.M. Ryan & G.W. Ladd (eds). *Peer relationships and adjustment at schools.* Charlotte: Information Age Publishing, pp 279–307.

Sapon-Shevin, M. 2007. *Widening the circle.* Boston, MA: Beacon Press.

Saskatchewan Learning. 2004. *Teaching students with reading difficulties and disabilities: A guide for educators.* [online] Available from: https://www.edonline.sk.ca/bbcswebdav/library/Curriculum%20Website/English%20Language%20Arts/Resources/Additional/Reading-Difficulties-Disabilities.pdf. Accessed: 3 June 2017.

Sastre, A. 2014. Towards a radical body positive: Reading the online 'body positive movement'. *Feminist Media Studies,* 14(6):929–943.

Savickas, M.L. 1997. Career adaptability: An integrative construct for life-span, life-space theory. *Career Development Quarterly,* 45**:**247–259.

Savickas, M.L. 2002. Career construction: A developmental theory of vocational behavior. In: D. Brown (ed). *Career choice and development.* 4th ed. San Francisco, CA: Jossey-Bass, pp 149–205.

Savickas, M.L. 2005. The theory and practice of career construction. In: S. Brown & R.W. Lent (eds). *Career development and counseling: Putting theory and research to work.* New York, NY: John Wiley & Sons, pp 42–70.

Savickas, M.L. 2010. Re-viewing scientific models of career as social constructions. *Revista Portuguesa de Pedagogia Psychologica, Numero Conjunto Comemorativo,* 30:33–43.

Savickas, M.L. 2011. *Career counselling.* Washington, DC: American Psychological Association.

Savickas, M.L. 2013. The theory and practice of career construction. In: S.D. Brown & R. W. Lent (eds). *Career development and counseling: Putting theory and research to work.* 2nd ed. Hoboken, NJ: John Wiley & Sons, pp 147–186.

Savickas, M.L. 2015. *Life-design counselling manual.* Rootstown, OH: Author.

Savickas, M.L., Nota, L., Rossier, J., Dauwalder, J.P., Duarte, M.E., Guichard, J. & Van Vianen, A.E.M. 2009. Life designing: A paradigm for career construction in the 21st century. *Journal of Vocational Behavior.* [online] Available from: doi: 10.1016/j.jvb.2009.04.004.

Sayed, Y. & Ahmed, R. 2015. Education quality, and teaching and learning in the post-2015 education agenda. *International Journal of Educational Development,* 40:330–338.

Schau, C.G., Phye, G.D., Hudgins, B.B., Theisen, G.L., Arnes, C. & Ames, R. 1983. *Educational Psychology.* Itasca, IL: FE Peacock Publishers Inc.

Scherf, K.S., Sweeney, J.A. & Luna, B. 2006. Brain basis of developmental change in visuospatial working memory. *Journal of Cognitive Neuroscience,* 18:1045–1058.

Schiller, F. 2016. *On the Aesthetic Education of Man.* London: Penguin Random House.

Schlegel, A., Kohler, P.J., Alexander, P., Konuthula, D. & Tse, P.E. 2013. Network structures and dynamics of mental workspace. *PNAS,* 110(40):16277–16282. [online] Available from: doi: 10.1073/pnas.1311149110, http://www.pnas.org/content/110/40/16277.abstract. Accessed: 10 May 2017.

Richards, J.C. 2010. Competence and performance in language teaching. *RELC Journal*, 41(2):101–122.

Richmond, S. 2009. Art's educational value. *The Journal of Aesthetic Education*, 43(1):92–105.

Rindermann, H., Sailer, M. & Thompson, J. 2009. The impact of smart fractions, cognitive ability of politicians and average competence of peoples on social development. *Talent Development & Excellence*, 1(1):3–25.

Rizzolatti, G. & Craighero, L. 2004. The mirror-neuron system. *Annual Review Neuroscience*, 27:169–192.

Roffey, S. & McCarthy, F. 2013. Circle Solutions, a philosophy and pedagogy for learning positive relationships: What promotes and inhibits sustainable outcomes? *The International Journal of Emotional Education*, 5(1):36–55.

Roffey, S. 2008. Emotional literacy and the ecology of school wellbeing. *Educational and child psychology*, 25(2):29–39.

Roffey, S. 2010. Content and context for learning relationships: A cohesive framework for individual and whole school development. *Educational and Child Psychology*, 27(1):156–167.

Roffey, S. 2012. Introduction to positive relationships: Evidence-based practice across the world. In: S. Roffey (ed). *Positive relationships: Evidence-based practice across the world*. New York, NY: Springer, pp 145–162.

Roffey, S. 2015. Becoming an agent of social change. *Educational and Child Psychology*, 32(1):21–30.

Roffey, S. 2016. Building a case for whole-child, wholeschool wellbeing in challenging contexts. *Educational and Child Psychology*, 33(2):30–42.

Rogers, C. 1951. *Client-centered therapy*. Boston, MA: Houghton-Mifflin, p 2.

Rogers, C. 1959. A theory of therapy, personality and interpersonal relationships as developed in the client-centered framework. In: S. Koch (ed). *Psychology: A study of a science*. New York, NY: McGraw Hill, pp 59–71.

Rogers, C.R., Lyon, H.C. & Tausch, R. 2014. *On becoming an effective teacher*. New York, NY: Routledge, pp 1–179.

Rooth, E. 2005. *An investigation of the status and practice of life orientation in South African schools in two provinces*. Doctoral Thesis, University of Western Cape, Cape Town.

Rosenthal, T.L. & Bandura, A. 1978. Psychological modeling: Theory and practice. In: S.L. Garfield & A.E. Bergin (eds). *Handbook of psychotherapy and behavior change: An empirical analysis*. 2nd ed. New York, NY: John Wiley & Sons, pp 621–658.

Röthlisberger, M., Neuenschwander, R., Cimeli, P., Michel. E. & Roebers, C.M. 2011. Improving executive functions in 5- and 6-year-olds: Evaluation of a small group intervention in prekindergarten and kindergarten children. *Infant and Child Development*, 21(4):411–429.

Rudge, L.T. 2008. *Holistic education: An analysis of its pedagogical application*. Doctoral Thesis, The Ohio State University, Columbus, OH.

Rudge, L.T. 2016. Holistic pedagogy in public schools: A case study of three alternative schools. *Other Education: The Journal of Educational Alternatives*, 5(2):169–195.

Rutter, M. 1989. Isle of Wight revisited: Twenty-five years of child psychiatric epidemiology. *Journal of the American Academy of Child and Adolescent Psychiatry*, 28(5):633–653.

Pretorius, E.J. & Currin, S. 2010. Do the rich get richer and the poor poorer? The effects of an intervention programme on reading in the home and school language in a high poverty multilingual context. *International Journal of Educational Development*, 30:67–76.

Pretorius, E.J. 2002. Reading ability and academic performance in South Africa: Are we fiddling while Rome is burning? *Language Matters: Studies in the Languages of Southern Africa*, 33(1):169–196.

Pretorius, G. 2012. Reflections on the scope of practice in the South African profession of psychology: A moral plea for relevance and a future vision. *South African Journal of Psychology*, 42(4):509–521.

Price, M. 2011. The little-known roots of the cognitive revolution. *Monitor*, 42(8):26–28. [online] Available from: http://www.apa.org/monitor/2011/09/otto-selz.aspx. Accessed: 31 June 2017.

Psychosocial Working Group. 2003. *Psychosocial intervention in complex emergencies: A conceptual framework*. Working Paper. Edinburgh: Queen Margaret University College.

Purdie-Vaughns, V. & Eibach, R.P. 2008. Intersectional invisibility: The distinctive advantages and disadvantages of multiple subordinate-group identities. *Sex roles*, 59(5):377–391.

Ragpot, L. 2013. *Student learning in a course on cognitive development in childhood*. Doctor of Educational Psychology thesis, University of Johannesburg, Johannesburg.

Rashid, A.M. 2011. Career development interventions in technical and vocational schools in Malaysia. *The Journal of Human Resource and Adult Learning*, 7(2):23–33.

Rawatlal, K.V. & Petersen, I. 2012. Factors impeding school connectedness; a case study. *South African Journal of Psychology*, 346–357.

Razer, M. & Friedman, V.J. 2013. Non-abandonment as a foundation for inclusive school practice. *Prospects*, 2013:361-375.

Reddy, S. & Dunn M. 2007. Risking it: Young heterosexual femininities in South African context of HIV/AIDS. *Sexualities*, 10(2):159–172.

Reddy, S.P., James, S., Sewpaul, R., Sifunda, S., Ellahebokus, A., Kambaran, N.S. & Omardien, R.G. 2013. *Umthente Uhlaba Usamila: the 3rd South African National Youth Risk Behaviour Survey 2011*. Cape Town: South African Medical Research Council.

Republic of South Africa. 1996a. The South African Schools Act No. 84 of 1996. *Government Gazette*. Pretoria: Government Printer.

Republic of South Africa. 1996b. The Constitution of the Republic of South Africa, 1996. *Government Gazette*. Pretoria: Government Printer.

Republic of South Africa. 1996c. The South African Schools Act No. 84 of 1996. *Government Gazette*. Pretoria: Government Printer.

Republic of South Africa. 1997. Higher Education Act No. 101 of 1997. *Government Gazette*. Pretoria: Government Printer.

Republic of South Africa. 2000. Promotion of Equality and Prevention of Unfair Discrimination Act No. 4 of 2000. *Government Gazette*. Pretoria: Government Printer.

Republic of South Africa. 2000. South African Council for Educators Act No. 31 of 2000. *Government Gazette*. Pretoria: Government Printer.

Republic of South Africa. 2005. Children's Act No. 38 of 2005. *Government Gazette*. Pretoria: Government Printer.

Piaget, J. 1955. *The child's construction of reality*. London: Routledge.

Piaget, J. 1968. The mental development of the child. In: J. Piaget. *Six psychological studies*. Vintage Books edition. New York, NY: Random House, pp 3–76.

Piaget, J. 1977. The essential Piaget. In: H.E. Gruber & J.J. Vonèche (eds). *The essential Piaget: An interpretive reference and guide*. New York, NY: Basic Books.

Piaget, J. 1983. Piaget's theory. In: P. Mussen (ed). *Handbook of child psychology*, Vol. 1. New York, NY: John Wiley & Sons, pp 103–128.

Piazza, M. 2010. Neurocognitive start-up tools for symbolic number representations. *Trends in Cognitive Sciences,* 14(12):542–551.

Pickering, S.J. & Howard-Jones, P. 2007. Educators' views on the role of neuroscience in education: Findings from a study of UK and international perspectives. *Mind, Brain, and Education,* 1(3):109–113.

Pienaar, A., Swanepoel, Z., Van Rensburg, H. & Heunis, C. 2011. A qualitative exploration of resilience in pre-adolescent AIDS orphans living in a residential care facility. *Journal of Social Aspects of HIV/AIDS,* 8(3):128–137.

Pilarska, A. 2016. How do self-concept differentiation and self-concept clarity interrelate in predicting sense of personal identity? *Personality and Individual Differences,* 102:85–89. [online] Available from: doi: http://dx.doi.org/10.1016/j.paid.2016.06.064.

Pillay, J. & Nesengani, R.I. 2006. The educational challenges facing early adolescents who head families in rural Limpopo Province. *Education as Change,* 10(2):131–147.

Pillay, J. 2012. Experiences of learners from child-headed households in a vulnerable school that makes a difference: Lessons for school psychologists. *School Psychology International,* 33(1):3–21.

Pillay, J. 2014a. Advancement of children's rights in Africa: A social justice framework for school psychologists. *School Psychology International,* 35(3):225–240.

Pillay, J. 2014b. Challenges educational psychologists face working with vulnerable children in Africa. In: T. Corcoran, (ed). *Psychology in Education: Critical theory practice*. Rotterdam: Sense Publishers, pp 95–111.

Pillay, J. 2014c. The role of educational psychologists in promoting ethical research conducted with children: An exploratory study. *Journal of Psychology in Africa,* 24(6):520–525.

Pillay, J. 2016. Children's rights in South African families. In: M. Makiwane, M. Nduna, & N.E. Khalema (eds). *Children in South African families: lives and times*. Cambridge Scholars Publishing, pp 1–23.

Porteus, K. 2008. Decolonising inclusion. In: N. Muthukrishna (ed). *Educating for social justice and inclusion in an African context: Pathways and transitions*. New York, NY: Nova Science Publishers, Inc.

Posner, G.J., Strike, K.A., Hewson, P.W. & Gertzog, W.A. 1982. Accommodation of a scientific conception: Toward a theory of conceptual change. *Science Education*, 66:211–227.

Posner, M.I. 2010. Neuroimaging tools and the evolution of educational neuroscience. In: D.A. Sousa (ed). *Mind, brain, & education: Neuroscience Implications for the classroom*. Bloomington, NY: Solution Tree Press.

Potgieter, J.R. & Malan, J. 1987. *Crows and cranes*. Stellenbosch: University Publishers and Booksellers.

Ozmon, H.A. & Craver, S.M. 2012. *Philosphical foundations of education.* Upper Saddle River, NJ: Pearson.

Paananen, M., February, P., Kalima, K., Möwes, A. & Kariuk, D. 2011. Learning disability assessment. In: T. Aro & T. Ahonen (eds). *Assessment of learning disabilities. Cooperation between teachers, psychologists and parents. African edition.* [online] Available from: https://www.nmi.fi/fi/kehitysyhteistyo/materiaalit/learning-disabilities-book.pdf. Accessed: 1 December 2016.

Parliamentary Monitoring Group. 2011. *Access to Higher Education: Challenges; Higher Education SA briefing by USAf.* [online] Accessed from: https://pmg.org.za. Accessed: 17 May 2017.

Patrick, H., Anderman, L.H., Bruening, P.S. & Duffin, L.C. 2011. The role of educational psychology in teacher education: Three challenges for educational psychologists. *Educational Psychologist,* 46(2):71–83.

Pattman, R. & Chege, E. 2003. *Finding our voices: Gendered and sexual identities and HIV/AIDS in education.* Nairobi: UNICEF.

Patton, W. & McMahon, M. 2006. *Career development and systems theory: connecting theory and practice.* 2nd ed. Rotterdam: Sense Publishers.

Payne-Van Staden, I. 2015. *Exploring Full-Service School teachers' self-efficacy within an inclusive education.* Doctoral thesis, North-West University, Potchefstroom (unpublished).

Peckham, H. 2013. Epigenetics: The Dogma-defying discovery that denes learn from experience. *International Journal of Neuropsychotherapy,* 1:9–20. [online] Available from: doi: 10.12744/ijnpt.2013.0009-0020, http://www.neuropsychotherapist.com/epigenetics-the-dogma-defying-discovery-that-genes-learn-from-experience/.

Perold, M., Louw, C. & Kleynhans, S. 2010. Primary school teachers' knowledge and misperceptions of attention deficit hyperactivity disorder (ADHD). *South African Journal of Education,* 30(3):457–473.

Peterson, C. & Seligman, M.E.P. 2004. *Character strengths and virtues: A handbook and classification.* Washington, DC: American Psychological Association.

Peterson, C. & Seligman, M.E.P. 2017. Values in action (VIA) Signature strengths test. University of Pennsylvania authentic happiness website. [online] Available from: https://www.authentichappiness.sas.upenn.edu.

Peterson, P.L., Clark, C.M. & Dickson, W.P. 1990. Educational psychology as a foundation in teacher education: Reforming an old notion. *Teachers College Record,* 91(3):322–346.

Phasha, N., Mahlo, D. & Dei, G.J.S. 2017. Inclusive schooling and education in African contexts. In: N. Phasha, D. Mahlo & G.J.S. Dei (eds). *Inclusive education in African contexts.* Rotterdam: Sense Publishers, pp 1–17.

Phasha, T. 2010. Educational resilience among African survivors of child sexual abuse in South Africa. *Journal of Black Studies,* 40(6):1234–1253.

Phelan, S.K. 2011. Constructions of disability: A call for critical reflexivity in occupational therapy. *Canadian Journal of Occupational Therapy,* 78(3):164–172.

Phillippo, K. & Stone, S. 2006. School-based collaborative teams: An exploratory study of tasks and activities. *Children and School,* 28(4):229–235.

Philpott, S. & McLaren, P. 2011. *Hearing the voices of children and caregivers: Situation analysis of children with disabilities in South Africa.* Pretoria: Department of Social Development/UNICEF.

Noble, T., McGrath, H., Roffey, S. & Rowling, L. 2008. *A scoping study on student wellbeing*. Canberra: Department of Education, Employment and Workplace Relations (DEEWR).

Noddings, N. 2002. *Educating moral people: a caring alternative to character*. New York, NY: Teachers College Press.

Noddings, N. 2010. Moral education in an age of globalization. *Educational Philosophy and Theory*, 42(4):390–396.

Norwich, B. 2002. *Education and Psychology in Interaction*. London: Routledge.

Nsamenang, A. 2008. (Mis)Understanding ECD in Africa: The force of local and global motives. In: M. Garcia, A. Pence & J. Evans (eds). *Africa's future, Africa's challenge: Early childhood care and development in sub-Saharan Africa*. Washington, DC: World Bank, pp 135–149.

Nsamenang, A.B. 2005. The intersection of traditional African education with school learning. In: L. Swartz, C. De la Rey & N. Duncan (eds). *Psychology*. Cape Town: Oxford University Press.

Nsubuga, Y. 2011. A research tool for analyzing and monitoring the extent to which environmental issues are integrated into teachers' lessons. *Southern African Journal of Environmental Education*, 28:105–117.

Nyika, A. 2015. Mother tongue as the medium of instruction at developing country universities in a global context. *South African Journal of Science*, 111:33–37.

Oberle, E., Domitrovich, C.E., Meyers, D.C. & Weissberg, R.P. 2016. Establishing systemic social and emotional learning approaches in schools: A framework for schoolwide implementation. *Cambridge Journal of Education*, 46(3):277–297.

O'Donnell, A.M. & Levin, J.R. 2001. Educational psychology's healthy growing pains. *Educational Psychologist*, 36(2):73–82.

OECD. 2010. *Learning for jobs, OECD reviews of vocational education and training*. [online] Paris: OECD Publishing, p 16. [online] Available from: https://www.oecd.org/edu/skills-beyond-school/Learning%20for%20Jobs%20book.pdf. Accessed: 22 May 2017.

Ogawa, S., Lee, L.M., Kay, A.R. & Tank, D.W. 1990. Brain magnetic resonance imaging with contrast dependent blood oxygenation. Proceedings of National Academy of Sciences, 87:9868–9872.

Orey, M. 2012. Educational Media & Technology Yearbook, 2012, Vol. 37. In: M. Orey, S.A. Jones & R.M. Branch. (eds). *Educational media and technology yearbook*. New York, NY: Springer, pp 225–357.

Ornstein, A.C., Levine, D.U., Gutek, G.L. & Vocke, D.E. 2017. *Foundations of Education*. Boston, MA: Cengage Learning.

Oswald, M. & Swart, E. 2008. How teachers navigate their learning in developing inclusive learning communities. *Education as change*, 12(2):91–108.

Oswald, M. & De Villiers, J-M. 2013. Including the gifted learner: Perceptions of South African teachers and principals. *South African Journal of Education*, 33(1):1–21.

Oswald, M. & Rabie, E. 2016. Rethinking gifted education in South Africa: The voices of gifted grade 11 students. *Gifted Education International*:1–13. [online] Available from: doi: 10.1177/0261429416642285.

Oswald, M. & Swart, E. 2011. Addressing South African pre-service teachers' sentiments, attitudes and concerns regarding inclusive education. *International Journal of Disability, Development and Education*, 58(4):389–403.

Nel, M., Engelbrecht, P., Nel, M. & Tlale, L. 2013. South African teachers' views of collaboration within an inclusive education system. *International Journal of Inclusive Education,* 18(9):903–917. [online] Available from: doi: 10.1080/13603116.2013.858779.

Nel, M., Nel, N. & Lebeloane, O. 2016. Assessment and learner support. In: M. Nel, N. Nel & A. Hugo (eds). *Learner support in a diverse classroom: A guide for foundation, intermediate and senior phase teachers of language and mathematics.* 2nd ed. Pretoria: Van Schaik Publishers, pp 59–91.

Nel, M., Nel, N.M. & Hugo, A. 2016. Inclusive education: An introduction. In: M. Nel, N.M. Nel & A. Hugo (eds). *Learner Support in a Diverse Classroom.* 2nd ed. Pretoria: Van Schaik Publishers, pp 3–34.

Nel, N. 2011. Second language difficulties in a South African context. In: E. Landsberg, D. Krüger. & E. Swart (eds). *Addressing barriers to learning: A South African perspective* 2nd ed. Pretoria: Van Schaik Publishers, pp 167–185.

Nel, N., Muller, A. & Rheeder, E. 2011. Support services within inclusive education in Gauteng: The necessity and efficiency of support. *Mevlana International Journal of Education,* 1(1):38–53.

Nel, N., Nel, N. & Hugo, A. (eds) 2013. *Learner support in a diverse classroom: A guide for Foundation, Intermediate and Senior Phase teachers of language and mathematics.* Pretoria: Van Schaik Publishers.

Nel, N.M., Tlale, L.D.N., Engelbrecht, P. & Nel, M. 2016. Teachers' perceptions of education support structures in the implementation of inclusive education in South Africa. *KOERS — Bulletin for Christian Scholarship,* 81(3). [online] Available from: doi: https://doi.org/10.19108/ KOERS.81.3.2249.

Nelson, G. & Prilleltensky, I. 2010. *Community psychology: In pursuit of liberation and wellbeing.* 2nd ed. New York, NY: Palgrave Macmillan.

Neser, J., Ladikos, A. & Prinsloo, J. 2004. Bullying in schools: An exploratory study. *Child Abuse Research in South Africa,* 5(1):5–18.

Net-industries. 2017. *Attitudes and Behaviour.* [online] Available from: https://www.psychology.jrank.org/pages/52/Attitudes and Behaviour. Accessed: 18 May 2017.

Newell, A., Shaw, J.C. & Simon, H.A. 1958. Elements of a Theory of Human Problem Solving. *Psychological Review,* 23:342–343.

Ngũgĩ wa Thiong'o. 1986. *Decolonising the mind: The politics of languages in African literature.* Nairobi: James Currey and Heinemann.

Ngũgĩ wa Thiong'o. 1992. *Decolonising the mind: The politics of language in African literature.* London: James Currey, p 16.

Nieman, M. 2006. Using the language of learning and teaching (LoLT) appropriately during mediation of learning. In: M. Nieman & R. Monyai (eds). *The educator as mediator of learning.* Pretoria: Van Schaik Publishers.

Nigg, J., Lewis, K., Edinger, N. & Falk, M. 2012. Meta-analysis of attention deficit/hyperactivity disorder or attention deficit/hyperactivity disorder symptoms, restriction diet, and synthetic food color additives. *Journal of the American Academy of Child & Adolescent Psychiatry,* 51(1):86–97.

Nikku, B.R. 2013. Children's rights in disasters: Concerns for social work: Insights from South Asia and possible lessons for Africa. *International Social Work,* 56(1):51–66.

Muthukrishna, N., Morojele, P., Naidoo, J. & D'Amant, A. 2016. Access to education: experiences from South Africa. In: E.G. Iriarte, R. McConkey & R.H. Gilligan (eds). *Disability and human rights: Global perspectives.* London: Palgrave, pp 133–149.

Mwamwenda, T.S. 2004. *Educational Psychology – an African perspective.* 3rd ed. Cape Town: Heinemann.

Mweli, M. 2016. *Three-tiered education system planned for 2017, Pretoria, Department of Basic Education.* [online] Available from: http://www.education.gov.za/Newsroom/MediaRelease/tabid/347/ctl/Details/mid/3963/ItemID/3920/Default.aspx. Accessed: 22 May 2017.

Mwoma, T. & Pillay, J. 2015. Psychosocial support for orphans and vulnerable children in public primary schools: challenges and intervention strategies. *South African Journal of Education,* 35(3). [online] Available from: doi: 10.15700/SAJE.V35N3A1092.

Nabi, A.U., Ahmad, T. & Khan, M.I. 2016. Hope and psychological well-being among diabetes patients: A correlational study. *The International Journal of Indian Psychology,* 3(4–63):97.

Naicker, S.M. 1999. *Curriculum 2005: A space for all.* Cape Town: Renaissance Publishers.

Naidoo, P., Maja, P.A., Mann, W.M., Sing, D. & Steyn, A.J. 2011. Employing people with disabilities in South Africa. *South African Journal of Occupational Therapy,* 41(1):24–33.

Nakagawa, Y. 2000. *Education for awakening: An Eastern approach to holistic education* (vol 2), Foundations of Holistic Education Series. Brandon, VT: Foundation for Educational Renewal.

National Action Plan. 1995. *Draft for public consultation to combat racism, racial discrimination, Xenophobia and Related Intolerance, 2016–2021.* Pretoria, South Africa.

National Reading Panel. 2000. *Teaching children to read: An evidence-based assessment of the scientific research literature on reading and its implications for reading instruction.* Rockville, MD: National Institute of Child Health and Human Development.

National Research Council. 2001. *Educating children with autism.* Washington, DC: The National Academies Press. [online] Available from: doi:10.17226/10017.

Naudé, M. & Davin, R. 2017. *Assessment in the Foundation Phase.* Pretoria: Van Schaik Publishers.

Neeta, N.C. & Klu, E.K. 2013. Teachers' professional knowledge competence and second language education in South Africa. *International Journal of Educational Sciences,* 5(3):255–262.

Neisser, U. 1967. *Cognitive psychology.* New York, NY: Appleton-Century-Crofts.

Neisser, U. 1997. The roots of self-knowledge: Perceiving self, it, and thou. In: J.G. Snodgrass & R.L. Thompson (eds). *The self across psychology.* New York, NY: New York Academy of Sciences, pp 5–18.

Nel, M. & Booysen, R. 2015. Support strategies and activities for BICS and CALP. In: M. Nel (ed). *How to support English second Language learners.* Pretoria: Van Schaik Publishers, pp 17–18.

Nel, M. & Nel, N.M. 2016. English language. In: M. Nel, N.M. Nel & A. Hugo (eds). *Learner support in a diverse classroom.* Pretoria: Van Schaik Publishers, pp 79–116.

Nel, M. 2013. Understanding inclusion. In: A. Engelbrecht, H. Swanepoel, M. Nel & A. Hugo (eds). *Embracing diversity through multilevel teaching.* Cape Town: Juta and Company Ltd., pp 1–32.

Mokhele, P.R. 2006. The teacher-learner relationship in the management of discipline in public high schools. *African education review*, 3(1–2):148–159.

Mokitimi, M.T. 1997. *The voice of the people.* Pretoria: Unisa Press.

Molemane, S.N. 2000. *Caring as an aspect of school climate: Implication for school effectiveness.* Doctoral thesis, University of Johannesburg, Johannesburg.

Moll, L.C. 1990. Introduction. In: L.C. Moll (ed). *Vygotsky and education: Instructional implications and applications of sociohistorical psychology.* New York, NY: Cambridge University Press, pp 1–27.

Monetta, L. & Joanette, Y. 2003. Specificity of the right hemisphere's contribution to verbal communication: The cognitive resources hypothesis. *Journal of Medical Speech-Language Pathology,* 11(4):203–212.

Moody, J. & White, D. 2003. Structural cohesion and embeddedness: A hierarchical concept of social groups. *American Sociological Review,* 68(1):103–127.

Moore, K.A. 2006. Research-to-Results. *Child Trends,* 12:1–3.

Moore, K.A., Vandivere, S. & Redd, Z. 2006. A sociodemographic risk index. *Social Indicators Research Series,* 27, pp. 45–81.

Morgan, H. 2014. Maximizing learner success with differentiated learning. *The Clearing House,* 87:34–38.

Morrison, K. 2002. *School leadership and complexity theory.* London: Routledge.

Morrow, W. 2009. *Bounds of democracy: Epistemological access in higher education.* Cape Town: HSRC Press.

Morton, V. & Watson, D.R. 2001. The impact of impaired vocal quality on children's ability to process spoken language. *Logopedics Phoniatrics Vocology,* 26(1):17–25.

Mosimege, M.D. & Onwu, G. 2004. Indigenous knowledge systems and science education. *Journal of Southern African Association for Research in Mathematic, Science, and Technology Education,* 8:1–12.

Mullis, I.V.S., Martin, M.O., Foy, P. & Drucke, K.T. 2012. *PIRLs 2011 International Results in Reading.* International Association for the Evaluation of Educational Achievement (IEA). Chestnut Hill, MA: USA: TIMSS and PIRLS International Study Center, Lynch School of Education, Boston College.

Mullis, I.V.S., Martin, M.O., Kennedy, A.M. & Foy, P. (2007). *PIRLS 2006 international report: IEA's study of reading literacy achievement in primary schools.* Chestnut Hill, MA: Boston College.

Munn, P. 2000. Social capital, schools and exclusions. In: S. Baron, J. Field & T. Schuller (eds). *Social capital: Critical perspectives.* Oxford: Oxford University Press, pp 168–181.

Munongi, L. 2016. *An investigation of children's rights and responsibilities as known by Grade 9 learners and their significant adults.* Doctoral Thesis, University of Johannesburg, Johannesburg.

Murphy, G.L. & Medin, D.L. 1985. The role of theories in conceptual coherence. *Psychological Review,* 92(3):289–316.

Murphy, P.K. 2003. The philosophy in thee: Tracing philosophical influences in educational psychology. *Educational Psychologist,* 38(3):137–145.

Mutanga, O. 2017. Students with disabilities' experience in South African higher education —a synthesis of literature. *South African Journal of Higher Education,* 31(1).

McCandliss, B.D., Cohen, L. & Dehaene, S. 2003. The visual word from area: Expertise for reading in the fusiform gyrus. *Trends in Cognitive Sciences,* 79(7):293–299.

McCoy, M. 2013. *Knowledge is power.* [online] Available from: https://www.quora.com. Accessed: 18 May 2017.

McCubbin, L.D., McCubbin, H.I., Zhang, W., Kehl, L. & Strom, I. 2013. Relational well-being: An indigenous perspective and measure. *Family relations,* 62(2):354–365.

McLauglin, C. & Clarke, B. 2010. Relational matters: A review of the impact on school experiences on mental health in early adolescence. *Educational and Child Psychology,* 27(1):91–103.

McLennan, D.M.P. 2008. The benefits of using socio-drama in the elementary classroom: Promoting caring relationships among educators and students. *Early Childhood Education Journal,* 35(5):451–456.

McMahon, M., Watson, M. & Bimrose, J. 2012. Career adaptability: A qualitative understanding from the stories of older women. *Journal of Vocational Behavior,* 80:762–768.

McNamara, A., Tegenthoff, M., Hubert, D., Buchel, C., Binkofski, F. & Ragert, P. 2007. Increased functional connectivity is crucial for learning novel muschel synergies. *NeuroImage,* 35:1211–1218.

McWhirter, J., McWhirter, B., McWhirter, E. & McWhirter, R. 2007. *At risk youth.* 4th ed. Belmont, CA: Thomson Higher Education.

Meerder, H. 2006. *Globalization 3.0: Why career clusters matter more than ever!* Adel, IA: Visions Unlimited.

Meier, D. & Wood, G. 2004. *Many children left behind: how the no child left behind act is damaging our children and our schools.* Boston, MA: Beacon Press.

Miller, G.A. 1956. The magical number seven, plus or minus two. *Psychological Review,* 63:81–97.

Miller, J. 2005. Holistic learning. In J.P. Miller, S. Karsten, D. Denton, D. Orr & I.C. Kates, (eds). *Holistic learning and spirituality in education: Breaking new ground.* New York, NY: State University of New York Press, pp 1–6.

Miller, J. 2006. Ancient roots of holistic education. *Encounter: Education for Meaning and Social Justice,* 19:55–59.

Miller, J. 2007. Holistic education in Japan: A Gaijan's (foreigner's) journey. *Education for Meaning and Social Justice,* 20(1):28–31.

Miller, R. 1997. *What are school for? Holistic education in American culture.* 3rd ed. Brandon, VT: Holistic Education Press.

Miller, R. 2002. *What is holistic education?* [online] Available from: http://www.psicopolis.com/Psicomunita/learncomm/miller5.htm. Accessed: 20 May 2017.

Mitei, J.K. 2015. *Teachers' perception of vocational education in the primary school curriculum in Kenya: A case of Sotik district, Bomet County.* Doctoral thesis, Moi University, Nairobi.

Mkhwanazi, N. 2006. Partial truths: Representations of teenage pregnancy in research. *Anthropology Southern Africa,* 29(3):96–104.

Mkhwanazi, N. 2014. Revisiting the dynamics of early childbearing in South African townships. *Culture, Health & Sexuality,* 1058(March):1464–5351. [online] Available from: doi: http://doi.org/10.1080/13691058.2014.930512.

Marshall, P. 2015. Neuroscience, embodiment, and development. In: R. Lerner, W. Overton and P. Molenaar (eds). *Handbook of child psychology and developmental science: Theory and method.* 7th ed. Hoboken, NJ: John Wiley & Sons, pp 244–283.

Martin, A. 2014. Interpersonal relationships and students' academic and non-academic development in interpersonal relationships in education. In: D. Zandvliet, P. Den Brok, T. Mainhard & J. Van Tartwijk (eds). *Interpersonal Relationships in Education: From Theory to Practice.* Rotterdam, The Netherlands: Sense Publishers, pp 9–24.

Martindale, C. 1990. *Cognitive psychology, a neural network approach.* Pacific Grove, CA: Brooks/Cole.

Martinez, M. 2010. *Learning and cognition: The design of the mind.* Upper Saddle River, NJ: Pearson, pp 233–271.

Martlew, J., Stephen, C. & Ellis, J. 2011. Play in the primary school classroom? The experience of teachers supporting children's learning through a new pedagogy. *An International Research Journal,* 31:71–83.

Mason, M. 2008. Complexity theory and the philosophy of education. *Educational philosophy and theory,* 40(1):4–18.

Masonga, M. 2005. South African research in indigenous knowledge systems and challenge of change. *Indilinga: Journal of Indigenous Knowledge Systems,* 4:74–88.

Masten, A. & Wright, M. 2010. Resilience over the lifespan: Developmental perspectives on resistance, recovery and transformation. In: J. Reich, A. Zautra and J. Hall (eds). *Handbook of adult resilience.* New York: Guilford, pp 213–237.

Masten, A. 2001. Ordinary magic: Resilience processes in development. *American Psychologist,* 56(3):227–238.

Masten, A. 2014a. *Ordinary magic. Resilience in development.* New York, NY: Guilford.

Masten, A. 2014b. Global perspectives on resilience in children and youth. *Child Development,* 85(1):6–20.

Masten, A. 2016. Resilience in developing systems: The promise of integrated approaches. *European Journal of Developmental Psychology,* 13(3):297–312.

Mayer, J.D. & Salovey, P. 1997. What is emotional intelligence? In: P. Salovey & D. Sluyter. *Emotional development and emotional intelligence: implication for educators.* New York: Basic Books, pp 3–31.

Mayer, J.D., Salovey, P. & Caruso, D.R. 2008. Emotional intelligence: New ability or eclectic traits? *American psychologist,* 63(6):503.

Mayer, R.E. 2014. Incorporating motivation into multimedia learning. *Learning and Instruction,* 29:171–173. [online] Available from: doi:10.1016/j.learninstruc.2013.04.003.

Mazzocco, M.M.M., Feigenson, L. & Halberda, J. 2011. Impaired acuity of the approximate number system underlies mathematical learning disability (dyscalculia). *Child Development,* 82(4):1224–1237.

McAdams, D.P. 2001. The psychology of life stories. *Review of General Psychology,* 5(2):100–122.

McCabe, D.P. & Castel, A.D. 2008. Seeing is believing: The effect of brain images on judgments of scientific reasoning. *Cognition,* 107:343–352.

McCall, L. 2005. The complexity of intersectionality. *Signs: Journal of Women in Culture and Society,* 30(3):1771–1800.

scholar.google.com/citations?view_op=view_citation&hl=en&user=4r1KpT4AAAAJ&citation_for_view=4r1KpT4AAAAJ:u5HHmVD_uO8C. Accessed: 2 June 2017.

Malindi, J. & Machenjedze, N. 2012. The role of school engagement in strengthening resilience among male street children. *South African Journal of Psychology,* 42(1):71–81.

Mampane, R. & Huddle, C. 2017. Assessing the outcomes of school-based partnership resilience intervention. *South African Journal of Education,* 37(1):1–13.

Manfreda, P. 2016. The reasons for the Arab Spring: The root causes of the Arab awakening in 2011. [online] Available from: https://www.thoughtco.com/the-reasons-for-the-arab-spring-2353041. Accessed: 23 September 2016.

Mangold, S.V. 2002. Transgressing the border between protection and empowerment of domestic violence victims and older children: Empowerment as protection in the foster care system. *New England School of Law,* 36(1):67–127. [online] Available from: http://www.nesl.edu/userfiles/file/lawreview/vol36/1/mangold.pdf. Accessed: 8 April 2015.

Maree, J.G. & Beck, G. 2004. Using various approaches in career counselling for traditionally disadvantaged (and other) learners: Some limitations of a new frontier. *South African Journal of Education,* 24(1):80–87.

Maree, J.G. & Molepo, M. 2017. Implementing a qualitative (narrative) approach in cross-cultural career counselling. In: M. McMahon (ed). *Career counselling: Constructivist approaches.* 2nd ed. Rotterdam: Sense Publishers, pp 65–78.

Maree, J.G. 2009. Career counselling in the 21st century: South African institutions of higher education at the crossroads. *South African Journal of Higher Education,* 23(3):429–435.

Maree, J.G. 2011. Brief overview of the advancement of postmodern approaches to career counseling. *Journal of Psychology in Africa,* 20(3):361–369.

Maree, J.G. 2013. *Counselling for career construction: Connecting life themes to construct life portraits. Turning pain into hope.* Rotterdam Sense Publishers.

Maree, J.G. 2013. Latest developments in career counselling in South Africa: Towards a positive approach. *South African Journal of Psychology,* 43(4):409–421.

Maree, J.G. 2015. Research on life design in (South) Africa: A qualitative analysis. *South African Journal of Psychology,* 45:332–348.

Maree, J.G. 2016. *Manual for the Maree Career Matrix (MCM).* Randburg: JvR Psychometrics.

Maree, J.G. 2017a. Applying the narrative approach in career counselling and related research. In: A. Fynn, S. Laher & S. Kramer (eds). *Social science research in South Africa: Theory and applications.*

Maree, J.G. 2017b. Utilizing career adaptability and career resilience to promote employability and decent work and alleviate poverty. In: J.G. Maree (ed). *Handbook of career adaptability, employability, and resilience.* New York, NY: Springer.

Maree, J.G. & Van der Westhuizen, C.N. 2011. Profession of counseling in South Africa: A landscape under construction. *Journal of Counseling & Development,* 89(1):105–112.

Maree, K. (ed). 2011. *Shaping the story. A guide to facilitating narrative career counselling.* Rotterdam: Sense Publishers.

Marshall, C. 1991. Teachers' learning styles: How they affect student learning. *The Clearing House,* 64:225–227.

Marshall, K. 2016. Rethinking differentiation: Using teachers' time most effectively. *Phi Delta Kappan,* 98(1):8–13.

Lucas, B. 2006. *Involving parents in school.* London: Network Continuum.

Ludbrook, R. 2000. *Victim of tokenism and hypocrisy: New Zealand's failure to implement the United Nations Convention on the Rights of the Child in advocating the children.* Dunebin, NZ: University of Otago Press.

Luker, K. 2006. *When sex goes to school: Warring views on sex—and sex education—since the sixties.* New York, NY: Norton.

Macleod, C. 2003. The conjugalisation of reproduction in South African teenage pregnancy literature. *PINS*, 29:23–27. [online] Available from: http://www.pins.org.za/pins29/pins29_article03_Macleod.pdf. Accessed: 2 June 2017.

Macleod, C. 2011. *'Adolescence', pregnancy and abortion: Constructing a threat of degeneration.* London: Routledge.

Macleod, C. 2013. Teenage pregnancy. In: T. Teo (ed). *Encylopaedia of Critical Psychology.* New York, NY: Springer. [online] Available from: http://www.springerreference.com/docs/html/chapterdbid/304961.html. Accessed: 4 June 2017.

Macleod, C., Seutlwadi, L. & Steele, G. 2014. Cracks in reproductive health rights: Buffalo City learners' knowledge of abortion legislation. *Health SA Gesondheid*, 19(1):1–10. [online] Available from: doi: doi.org/10.4102/hsag.v19i1.743.

Macleod, C. & Tracey, T. 2010. A decade later: Follow-up review of South African research on the consequences of and contributory factors in teen-aged pregnancy. *South African Journal Of Psychology*, 40(1):18–31. [online] Available from: http://proxy.antioch.edu/login?url=http://search.ebscohost.com/login.aspx?direct=true&db=a9h&AN=48480774&site=ehost-live&scope=site. Accessed: 5 June 2017.

Maddux, J. 2012. Stopping the 'madness': Positive psychology and deconstructing the illness ideology and the DSM. In: S.J. Lopez & C.R. Snyder. *The Oxford Handbook of Positive Psychology.* Oxford: Oxford University Press, pp 21–22.

Mafisa, P.J. & Van der Walt, J.L. 2002. Grammatical competence of ESL teachers. *Per Linguam*, 18(10):15–26.

Magliocco, S. 2010. *Witching culture: Folklore and neo-paganism in America.* Philadelphia, PA: University of Pennsylvania Press.

Magson, N.R., Craven, R.G., Munns, G. & Yeung, A.S. 2016. It is risky business: can social capital reduce risk-taking behaviours among disadvantaged youth? *Journal of Youth Studies*, 2016:569–592.

Mahadev, R. 2015. Making silent voices heard: Using participatory video to address sexual violence, *Agenda*, 29(3):13–21.

Mahlo, D. 2017. Rethinking inclusive education in an African context. In: N. Phasha, D. Mahlo & G.J.S. Dei (eds). *Inclusive education in African contexts.* Rotterdam: Sense Publishers, pp 1–17.

Mahmoudi, S., Jafari, E., Nasrabadi, H.A. & Liaghatdar, M.J. 2012. Holistic education: An approach for the 21st century. *International Education Studies*, 5(2):178–186.

Makhalemele, T. & Nel, M. 2016. Challenges experienced by district-based support teams in the execution of their functions in a specific South African province. *International Journal of Inclusive Education*, 20(2):168–184.

Makiwane, M., Desmond, C., Ruchter, L. & Udjo, E. 2006. *Is the child support grant associated with an increase in teenage fertility in South Africa? Evidence from national surveys and administrative data.* Pretoria: HSRC Press. [online] Available from: http://

Lemmer, R. 2009. *Die assessering van 'n leerder in Graad R met Asperger-Sindroom.* Meestersgraad in onderwys proefskrif, Universiteit van Suid-Afrika, Pretoria.

Lerner, J. & Johns, B. 2015. *Learning disabilities and related mild disabilities: strategies for success.* 13th ed. Boston, MA: Houghton Mifflin.

Lerner, R. 2006. Resilience as an attribute of the developmental system: Comments on the papers of Professors Masten & Wachs. In: B. Lester, A. Masten & B. McEwen (eds). *Resilience in children.* Boston: Blackwell, pp 40–51.

Lewis, M. 1997. The self in self-conscious emotions. In: J.G. Snodgrass & R.L. Thompson (eds). *The self across psychology.* New York, NY: New York Academy of Sciences, pp 119–142.

Lidz, C. & Macrine, S. 2001. An alternative to the identification of gifted culturally and linguistically diverse learners. *School Psychology International,* 22(1):74–96.

Lindberg, L.D. & Maddow-Zimet, I. 2012. Consequences of sex education on teen and young adult sexual behaviors and outcomes. *Journal of Adolescent Health,* 51(4):332–338. [online] Available from: doi: doi.org/10.1016/j.jadohealth.2011.12.028.

Lindsay, G. 2003. Inclusive education: A critical perspective. *British Journal of Special Education,* 30(1):3–12.

Lindsay, G. 2007. Educational Psychology and the effectiveness of inclusive education/mainstreaming. *British Journal of Educational Psychology,* 77(1):1–24.

Linley, P.A. & Joseph, S. 2004. *Positive psychology in practice.* Hoboken, NJ: John Wiley & Sons.

Liu, S., Chow, H.M., Xu, Y., Erkkinen, M.G., Swett, K.E., Eagle, M.W., Rizik-Baer, D.A. & Braun, A.R. 2012. Neural Correlates of Lyrical Improvisation: An fMRI Study of Freestyle. *SciRep,* 2:834. [online] Available from: http://www.nature.com/articles/srep00834.

Lomofsky, L. & Lazarus, S. 2001. South Africa: First steps in the development of an inclusive education system. *Cambridge Journal of Education,* 31(3):303–317.

Longa, C. 2011. Social aggression in children and adolescents: A meta-analytic review. Miami, FL: University of Miami Scholarly Repository.

Lopes, M. 2008. *South African educator's experiences of learners who may have ADHD in their classrooms.* Doctoral thesis, University of Pretoria, Pretoria.

Lord, J.E., Suozzi, D. & Taylor, A.L. 2010. Lessons from the experience of UN Convention on the Rights of Persons with Disabilities: Addressing the democratic deficit in global health governance. *Journal of Law, Medicine and Ethics,* 38(3):564–580.

Loubser, J. 2005. Unpacking the expression 'Indigenous knowledge system'. *Indilinga: African Journal of Indigenous Knowledge Systems,* 4:74–88.

Lowe, P., Lee, E. & Macvarish, J. 2015. Biologising parenting: Neuroscience discourse, English social and public health policy and understandings of the child. *Sociology of Health & Illness,* 37(2):198–211. [online] Available from: doi: http://dx.doi.org/10.1111/1467-9566.12223.

Lu, Z.L. & Dosher, B.A. 2007. Cognitive Psychology. *Scholarpedia,* 2(8):2769.

Lubbe, C. & Eloff, I. 2004. Asset-based assessment in Educational Psychology: Capturing perceptions during a paradigm shift. *The California School Psychologist,* 9:29–38. [online] Available from: https://link.springer.com/article/10.1007/BF03340905http://link.springer.com/article/10.1007/BF03340905?sa_campaign=email/event/articleAuthor/onlineFirst. Accessed: 23 July 2017.

Kosher, H., Ben-Arieh, A. & Huebner, X. 2014. Advances in children's rights and well-being in schools: Implications for school psychologists. *School Psychology Quarterly,* 29(1):1–20.

Kovelman, I., Baker, S.A. & Petitto, L.A. 2008. Bilingual and monolingual brains compared: A functional magnetic resonance imaging investigation of syntactic processing and a possible 'neural signature' of bilingualism. *Journal of Cognitive Science,* 20(1):153–169.

Kozleski, E.B. & Siuty, M.B. 2016. Understanding the complexities of inclusive education from a comparative perspective: How cultural histories shape the ways that teachers respond to multiple forms of diversity. *Equity Centered Capacity Building Network, Essential approaches for excellence & sustainable school system transformation.* [online] Available from: http://capacitybuildingnetwork.org/article6. Accessed: 10 August 2017.

Kozulin, A. 1990. *Vygotsky's Psychology: A biography of ideas.* Cambridge, MA: Harvard University Press.

Krüger, D. 2017. Inclusive physical education. In: S. Krog & R. Naidoo (eds). *Teaching physical education and sports coaching: Theory and practice.* Cape Town: Oxford University Press.

Kuhn, D. 1989. Children and adults as intuitive scientists. *Psychological Review,* 96(4):674–689.

Kunda, Z. 1999. *Social cognition: Making sense of people.* Cambridge, MA: Bradford.

Lake, L. & Pendlebury, S. 2009. *Children's right to basic education.* Cape Town: South African Child Gauge. Children's Institute, University of Cape Town.

Lamb, S. 2011. TVET and the poor: Challenges and possibilities. *International Journal of Training Research,* 9(1–2):60–71.

Landsberg, E., Krüger, D. & Swart, E. (eds). 2016. *Addressing barriers to learning: A South African perspective.* 3rd ed. Pretoria: Van Schaik Publishers.

Larsen, D. & Stege, R. 2010. Hope-focused practices during early psychotherapy sessions: Part I: Implicit approaches. *Journal of Psychotherapy Integration,* 20(3):271–292.

Lassen, N.A., Ingvar, D.H. & Skinhoj, E. 1978. Brain function and blood flow. *Scientific American,* 238:62–71.

Lau, U. & Van Niekerk, A. 2011. Restorying the Self: An exploration of Young Burn survivors' narratives of resilience. *Qualitative Health Research,* 21(9):1165–1181.

Lave, J. & Wenger, E. 1991. *Situated learning: legitimate peripheral participation.* Cambridge, MA: Cambridge University Press.

Leach, F. & Humphreys, S. 2007. Gender violence in schools: Taking the 'girls-as-victims' discourse forward. *Gender and Development,* 15(2):51–65.

Leadbetter, J. & Arnold, C. 2013. Looking back: A hundred years of applied psychology. *The Psychologist,* 26(9), 696–698.

Learner Support. 2011. [online] Available from: http://www.thedataservice.org.uk. Accessed: 10 November 2016.

LeDoux, J.E. 2014. Comment: What's basic about the brain mechanisms of emotion? *Emotion Review,* 6(4):318–320.

Legg, M.J. 2011. What is psychosocial care and how can nurses better provide it to adult oncology patients. *The Australian Journal of Advanced Nursing,* 28(3):61–67.

Leisman, G., Mualem, R. & Mughrabi, S.K. 2015. The neurological development of the child with educational enrichment in mind. *Psicología Educativa,* 21:79–96.

Kershner, R. & Farrell, P. 2009. *Psychology for inclusive education: new directions in theory and practice.* London: Taylor & Francis.

Khanare, F.P. 2009. *School management teams' response to learners who are orphaned and vulnerable in the context of HIV and AIDS: A study of two senior secondary schools in KwaZulu-Natal.* Masters of education dissertation, University of KwaZulu-Natal, Durban.

Khanare, F.P. 2015. *Rethinking care and support of 'vulnerable' learners in the age of HIV and AIDS: An arts-based approach.* Doctoral thesis, Nelson Mandela Metropolitan University, Port Elizabeth.

Khoo, S.L., Tiun, L.T. & Lee, L.W. 2013. Unseen challenges, unheard voices, unspoken desires: Experiences of employment by Malaysians with physical disabilities. *Kajian Malaysia*, 31(1):37–55.

Kihlstrom, J.F. & Klein, S.B. 1997. Self-knowledge and self-awareness. In: J.G. Snodgrass & R.L. Thompson (eds). *The self across psychology.* New York, NY: New York Academy of Sciences, pp 5–18.

Killian, M., Tendayi, G. & Augustine, T. 2009. An assessment of partnerships between technical vocational education and training and its stakeholders in the development of Ethiopian SMEs. *Economia, Seria Manage*, 12(2):39–56.

Kirby, D. 2011. Sex education: Access and impact on sexual behavior of young people. Department of Economic and Social Affairs, United Nations, New York. [online] Available from: http://www.un.org/esa/population/meetings/egm-adolescents/p07_kirby.pdf. Accessed: 21 April 2017.

Kisirye, R. 2007. *Rapid assessment report on trafficking of children into worst form of child labour, including child soldiers in Uganda.* Kampala: ILO.

Kitching, A.E. 2010. *Conceptualising a relationship-focused approached to the co-construction of enabling school communities.* Doctoral thesis, North-West University, Potchefstroom.

Kitching, A.E., Roos, V. & Ferreira, R. 2011. Ways of relating and interacting in school communities: Lived experiences of learners, educators and parents. *Journal of Psychology in Africa*, 21(2):247–256.

Kitching, A.E., Roos, V. & Ferreira, R. 2012. Towards an understanding of nurturing and restraining relational patterns in school communities. *Journal of psychology in Africa*, 22(2):187–199.

Knowles, M.S. 1970. *The modern practice of adult education: Andragogy versus pedagogy.* New York, NY: Association Press.

Knowles, M.S. 1984. *Andragogy in action.* San Francisco, CA: Jossey-Bass.

Koch, R. & Lockwood. G. 2010. *Superconnect: Harnessing the power of networks and the strength of weak links.* New York, NY: W.W. Norton.

Konu, A. & Rimpelä, M. 2002. Well-being in schools: A conceptual model. *Health Promotion International*, 17(1):79–87.

Kop, R. & Hill, A. 2008. Connectivism: Learning theory of the future or vestige of the past? *The International Review of Research in Open Distance Learning. E-journal*, 9(3). [online] Available from: http://www.irrodl.org/index.php/irrodl/article/view/523/1103. Accessed: 18 May 2017.

Jewkes, R., Dunkle K., Koss M.P., Levin J.B., Nduna M., Jama N. & Sikweyiya, Y. 2006. Rape perpetration by young, rural South African men: Prevalence, patterns and risk factors. *Social Science & Medicine*, 63(11):2949–2961.

Jewkes, R.K., Dunkle, K., Nduna, M. & Shai, N. 2010. Intimate partner violence, relationship power inequity, and incidence of HIV infection in young women in South Africa: A cohort study. *The Lancet*, 376(9734):41–48. [online] Available from: doi: http://doi.org/10.1016/S0140-6736(10)60548-X.

Johnson, B. & Lazarus, S. 2008. The role of schools in building resilience of youth faced with adversity. *Journal of Psychology in Africa*, 18(1):19–30.

Johnson, D. 2009. Commentary: Examining underlying paradigms in the creative arts therapies of trauma. *The Arts in Psychotherapy*, 36(2):114–120. [online] Available from: doi: http://dx.doi.org/10.1016/j.aip.2009.01.011.

Jokela, P., Karlsudd, P. & Östlund, M. 2008. Theory, method and tools for evaluation using a systems-based approach. *Electronic Journal of Information Systems Evaluation*, 11(3):197–212.

Jonassen, D.H. 2006. *Modeling with technology: Mindtools for conceptual change.* Upper Saddle River, NJ: Pearson Education Inc.

Jones, B.F. 1985. Educational psychologists—Where are you? Reflections of an educational psychologist. *Educational Psychologist*, 20(2):83–95.

Jones, H.M.F. 2002. Respecting Respect: Exploring a Great Deal. *Educational Studies*, 28(4):341–352.

Jones, S.R. 1996. Toward inclusive theory: Disability as social construction. *NASPA Journal*, 33(4):347–354.

Josselson, R. 1996. *The spaces between us. Exploring the dimensions of human relationships.* Thousand Oaks, CA: Sage.

Jörg, T. 2009. Thinking in complexity about learning and education: A programmatic view. *International Journal of Complexity and Education*, 6(1):1–22.

Kadushin, C. 2012. *Understanding social networks: Theories, concepts, and findings.* Oxford: Oxford University Press.

Kahneman, D. 2003. Maps of bounded rationality: A perspective on intuitive judgment and choice. In: T. Frangsmyr (ed). *Les Prix Nobel, The Nobel Prizes 2002*. Stockholm, Nobel Foundation, pp 416–499. [online] Available from: http://www.nobelprize.org/nobel_prizes/economic-sciences/laureates/2002/kahnemann-lecture.pdf. Accessed: 1 July 2017.

Kashdan, T.B. & McKnight, P.E. 2009. Origins of purpose in life: Refining our understanding of a life well lived. *Psychological Topics*, 18:303–316.

Kashdan, T.B. 2007. New developments in emotion regulation with an emphasis on the positive spectrum of human functioning. *Journal of Happiness Studies*, 8:303–310.

Keil, F.C. 1989. *Concepts, kinds, and cognitive development.* Cambridge, MA: MIT Press.

Kekae-Moletsane, M. 2008. Masekitlana; South African traditional play as a therapeutic tool in child psychology. *South African Journal of Psychology*, 38:367–375.

Kelly, A.M.C. & Garavan, H. 2005. Human functional neuroimaging of brain changes associated with practice. *Neuroimage*, 15:1089–1102.

Kendall, J., Wagner, C. & Ruane, I. 2011. The experiences of primary school teachers of ADHD in their classrooms. *New Voices in Psychology*, 7(1):19–34.

Human-Vogel, S. & Morkel, J. 2017. Teacher and learners beliefs in a just world and perspectives of discipline of Grade 4–8 learners in South African schools. *Educational Studies*, 43(3):343–353.

Human-Vogel, S. & Rabe, P. 2015. Measuring self-differentiation and academic commitment in university students: A case study of education and engineering students. *South African Journal of Psychology*, 45(1):60–70.

Human-Vogel, S. 2008. The role of identity in commitment: When do students cope and when do they commit? *Journal of Psychology in Africa*, 18(1):115–122.

Inter-Agency Network of Education in Emergencies. 2016. *Background paper on psychosocial support and social and emotional learning for children and youth in emergency settings.* New York, NY: International Rescue Committee, Inc.

International Association for the Evaluation of Educational Achievement (IEA). 2015. *IEA's trends in international mathematics and science study – TIMSS 2015.* [online] Available from: http://timss2015.org/download-center/. Accessed: 11 July 2017.

Iriarte, E.G., McConkey, R. & Gilligan, R.H. 2016. Disability and human right: global perspectives. In: E.G. Iriarte, R. McConkey & R.H. Gilligan (eds). *Disability and human rights: Global perspectives.* London: Palgrave Macmillan, pp 1–9.

Jackson, R.M. 2017. *Down so long ...: The puzzling persistence of gender inequality.* [online]. Available from: http://personalitycafe.com/critical-thinking-philosophy/767074-down-so-long-puzzling-persistence-gender-inequality-robert-max-jackson.html. Accessed: 3 June 2017.

Jacobs, A. 2011. Life Orientation as experienced by learners: A qualitative study in North West Province. *South African Journal of Education*, 31(2):212–223.

Jansen, J. 1997. Why outcomes based education will fail: An elaboration. In: J. Jansen & P. Christie (eds). *Changing curriculum: Studies on outcomes based education in South Africa.* Cape Town: Juta and Company Ltd., pp 3–17.

Jaycox, L.H., McCaffrey, D.F., Ocampo, B.W., Shelley, G.A., Blake, S.M., Peterson, D.J., Richmond, L.S. & Kub, J.E. 2006. Challenges in the evaluation and implementation of school-based prevention and intervention programs on sensitive topics. *American Journal of Evaluation*, 27(3):320–336.

Jearey-Graham, N. & Macleod, C.I. 2017. Gender, dialogue and discursive psychology: A pilot sexuality intervention with South African high-school learners. *Sex Education*:1–16. [online] Available from: doi: doi.org/10.1080/14681811.2017.1320983.

Jewell, P. 2005. Gifted education in democracy: refuting the critics. *Gifted Education International*, 19(2):107–113.

Jewkes, R. & Morrell, R. 2010. Gender and sexuality: Emerging perspectives from the heterosexual epidemic in South Africa and implications for HIV risk and prevention. *Journal of the International AIDS Society*, 13(1). [online] Available from: doi: https://doi.org/10.1186/1758-2652-13-6.

Jewkes, R. & Morrell, R. 2012. Sexuality and the limits of agency among South African teenage women: Theorising femininities and their connections to HIV risk practises. *Social Science and Medicine*, 74(11):1729–1737. [online] Available from: doi: https://doi.org/10.1016/j.socscimed.2011.05.020.

Jewkes, R. & Morrell, R. 2012. Sexuality and the limits to agency among South African teenage women: Theorising femininities and their connection to HIV risk practices. *Social Science & Medicine*, 74(11):1729–1737.

Hodgkin, R. & Newell, P. 2007. *Implementation handbook of the Convention on the Right of the Child*. New York, NY: UNICEF.

Hoeft, F., Ueno, T., Reiss, A.L., Meyer, A., Whitfield-Gabrieli, S., Glover, G.H., et al. 2007. Prediction of children's reading skills using behavioral, functional, and structural neuroimaging measures. *Behavioral Neuroscience,* 121(3):602–613.

Hofmann, W., Luhmann, M., Fisher, R.R., Vohs, K.D. & Baumeister, R.F. 2014. Yes, but are they happy? Effects of trait self-control on affective well-being and life satisfaction. *Journal of Personality,* 82(4):265–277. [online] Available from: doi: http://dx.doi.org/10.1111/jopy.12050.

Honeyford, M.A. & Boyd, K. 2015. Learning through play. *Journal of Adolescent & Adult Literacy,* 59:63–73.

Hopper, L.M., Flynn, E.G., Wood, L.A. & Whiten, A. 2010. Observational learning of tool use in children: Investigating cultural spread through diffusion chains and learning mechanisms through ghost displays. *Journal of Experimental Child Psychology,* 106(1):82–97.

Horner, V., Whiten, A., Flynn, E. & De Waal, F.B.M. 2006. Faithful replication of foraging techniques along cultural transmission chains by chimpanzees and children. *Proceedings of the National Academy of Sciences,* 103(37):13878–13883.

Howe, R.B., Covell, K. & McNeil, J.K. 2010. Implementing children's human rights education in schools. *Improving Schools,* 13(2), 117–132. [online] Available from: doi: 10.1177/1365480206061994.

Howe, R.B., Covell, K. & McNeil, J.K. 2008. If there's a dead rat, don't leave it. Young children's understanding of their citizenship rights and responsibilities. *Cambridge Journal of Education,* 38(30):321–339.

Howie, S., Van Staden, S., Tshele, M., Dowse, C. & Zimmerman, L. 2012. *PIRLS 2011: South African children's reading literacy achievement (Summary Report)*. Pretoria: Centre for Evaluation and Assessment, University of Pretoria. [online] Available from: http://www.ecexams.co.za/2012_Exam_Results/Reading%20Literacy%20Achievement%202011.pdf. Accessed: 29 May 2017.

Howson, R. 2006. *Challenging Hegemonic Masculinities*. New York, NY: Routledge.

Hudziak, J., Derks, E., Althoff, R., Rettew, D. & Boomsma, D. 2005. The genetic and environmental contributions to attention deficit hyperactivity disorder as measured by the Conners' Rating Scales—Revised. *The American Journal of Psychiatry,* 162(9):1614–1620.

Hughes, B. 2009. Wounded/monstrous/abject: A critique of the disabled body in the sociological imaginary. *Disability and Society,* 24(4):399–410.

Huitt, W. & Hummel, J. 2003. Piaget's theory of cognitive development. *Educational Psychology interactive*. Valdosta, GA: Valdosta State University. [online] Available from: http://www.edpsycinteractive.org/topics/cognition/piaget.html. Accessed: 20 May 2017.

Human Rights Watch. 2015. *'Complicit in exclusion' South Africa's failure to guarantee an inclusive education for children with disabilities*. [online] Available from: https://www.hrw.org/report/2015/08/18/complicit-exclusion/south-africas-failure-guarantee-inclusive-education-children. Accessed: 7 July 2017.

Human-Vogel, S. & Mahlangu, P.P. 2009. Commitment in academic contexts: First year Education students', beliefs about aspects of the self, the lecturer, and instruction. *South African Journal of Higher Education*, 23(2):309–328.

Health Profession Council of South Africa. (nd). *Professional Board of Psychology, List of accredited universities in South Africa*. Pretoria: HPCSA. [online] Available from: http://www.hpcsa.co.za/uploads/editor/UserFiles/downloads/psych/psycho_education/LIST%20OF%20ACCREDITED%20UNIVERSITIES%20IN%20SA.pdf. Accessed: 28 June 2017.

Health Profession Council of South Africa. 2017. *Professional Board of Psychology: Scope of practice guidelines for educational psychologist*. Pretoria: HPCSA. [online] Available from: http://www.hpcsa.co.za/Uploads/editor/UserFiles/downloads/psych/guidelines_for_Educational%20_PsychologistFinal_31Jan2017.pdf. Accessed: 10 August 2017.

Heckman, J.J., Humphries, J.E., Urzua, S. & Veramendi, G. 2011. *The effects of educational choices on labor market, health, and social outcomes*. Human Capital and Economic Opportunity Working Group, Working Papers No. 2011–002.

Hedegaard, M. 1998. Situated learning and cognition: Theoretical learning and cognition. *Mind, Culture and Activity*, 5(2):114–126.

Heilman, K.M., Nadeau, S.E. & Beversdorf, D.O. 2003. Creative innovation: Possible brain mechanisms. *Neurocase*, 9:369–379.

Hen, M. & Goroshit, M. 2016. Social-emotional competencies among teachers: An examination of interrelationships. *Cogent Education*, 3:1151996. [online] Available from: doi: doi.org/10.1080/2331186x.

Henning, E. & Ragpot, L. 2013. Pre-school children's bridge to symbolic knowledge: First literature framework for a learning and cognition lab at a South African university. *South African Journal of Psychology*, 45(1):71–80.

Henslin, J.M. 1997. *Sociology. A Down-to-earth approach*. 3rd ed. London: Allyn and Bacon.

Heslep, R. 2001. Habermas on Communication in Teaching. *Educational Theory*, 51(2):191–207.

Heugh, K. 2009. Contesting the monolingual practices of bilingual policy. *English Teaching Practice and Critique*, 8(2):96–113.

Hewitt, S. 2005. *Specialists support approaches to autism spectrum disorder students in mainstream settings*. London and Philadelphia: Jessica Kingsley Publishers.

Hicks, S.D. 2011. Technology in today's classroom: Are you a tech-savvy teacher? *The Clearing House*, 84:188–191.

Hill, W.F. 1985. *Learning: A survey of psychological interpretations*. 4th ed. New York, NY: Harper and Row.

Hillman, D.R. & Lack, L.C. 2013. Public health implications of sleep loss: the community burden. *The Medical Journal of Australia (MJA)*, 199:S7–S10. [online] Available from: doi: 10.5694/mja13.10620.

Hirschmann, N.J. 2013. Queer/fear: Disability, sexuality, and the other. *Journal of Medical Humanities*, 34(2):139–147.

Hirshfield, J. 1997. *Nine gates – Exploring the mind of poetry*. New York, NY: HarperCollins Publishers.

Hlalele, D. 2012. Psychosocial support for vulnerable rural school learners: in search of social justice! *Journal for New Generation Sciences*, 10(2):63–76.

Hlatshwayo, M. & Vally, S. 2014. Violence, resilience and solidarity: The right to education for child migrants in South Africa. *School Psychology International*, 35(3):266–279.

Guttorm, T.K., Leppänen, P.H.T., Poikkeus, A.M., Eklund, K.M., Lyytinen, P. & Lyytinen, H. 2005. Brain event-related potentials (ERPs) measured at birth predict later language development in children with and without familial risk for dyslexia. *Cortex,* 41(3):291–303.

Haberland, N.A. 2015. The case for addressing gender and power in sexuality and HIV education: A comprehensive review of evaluation studies. *International Perspectives on Sexual and Reproductive Health,* 41(1):31–42. [online] Available from: doi: https://doi.org/10.1363/4103115.

Hajii. 2006. *Respect and the at-risk learner: implications for academic achievement and the formation of positive attitudes toward school and self.* Doctoral thesis, Seattle University, Seattle.

Hall, A. & Theron, L. 2016. How school ecologies facilitate resilience among adolescents with intellectual disability: Guidelines for teachers. *South African Journal of Education,* 36(2):1–13.

Hall, D.T. 1996. Protean careers of the 21st century. *Academy of Management Executive,* 10:8–16.

Hancock, A.M. 2007. When multiplication doesn't equal quick addition: Examining intersectionality as a research paradigm. *Perspectives on Politics,* 5(1):63–79.

Hanich, L.B. & Deemer, S. 2005. The relevance of educational psychology in teacher education programs. *The Clearing House,* 78(5):189–191.

Hanisch, C. 2006. *The Personal is Political: The Women's Liberation Movement Classic with a New Explanatory Introduction. Women of the world, Unite.* [online] Available from: http://www.carolhanisch.org/CHwritings/PIP.html. Accessed: 29 June 2017.

Harasim, L. 2012. *Learning theory and online technologies.* New York, NY: Routledge.

Hardman, J. 2011. The developmental impact of communicative interaction. In: D. Hook, B. Franks & M. Bauer (eds). *Communication, Culture and Social Change: The Social Psychological Perspective.* London: Palgrave, pp 25–45.

Hardman, J. 2007. Towards a methodology for using Activity Theory to explicate the pedagogical object in a primary school mathematics classroom. *Critical Social Studies*(1):53–69.

Harpur, P. 2012. Embracing the new disability rights paradigm: The importance of the convention on the rights of persons with disabilities. *Disability and Society,* 27(1):1–14.

Hart, A., Gagnon, E., Eryigit-Madzwamuse, S., Cameron, J., Aranda, K., Rathbone, A. & Heaver, B. 2016. *Uniting resilience research and practice with an inequalities approach. SAGE Open,* 6(4), 2158244016682477. [online] Available from: doi: http://journals.sagepub.com/doi/full/10.1177/2158244016682477. Accessed: 4 July 2017.

Hartung, P.J. 2011. Career construction: Principles and practice. In: K. Maree (ed). *Shaping the story: A guide to facilitating narrative counselling.* Rotterdam: Sense Publishers, pp 103–120.

Hassan, N., Jani, S.H.M., Som, R.M., Hamid, N.Z.A. & Azizam, N.A. 2015. The relationship between emotional intelligence and teaching effectiveness among lecturers at Universiti Teknologi MARA, Puncak Alam, Malaysia. *International Journal of Social Science and Humanity,* 5(1):1–5.

Hattie, J. 2011. *Visible learning for teachers: Maximizing impact on learning.* New York, NY: Routledge.

Ghassemzadeh, H. 2005. Vygotsky's mediational psychology: A new conceptualization of culture, signification and metaphor. *Language Sciences,* 27:281–300.

Giangreco, M., Carter, E., Doyle, M. & Suter, J. 2010. Supporting students with disabilities in inclusive classrooms: Personnel and peers. In: R. Rose (ed). *Confronting obstacles to inclusion: International responses to developing inclusive schools.* Abingdon, Oxfordshire: Routledge, pp 247–263.

Giddens, A. 1984. *The Constitution of society.* Cambridge, UK: Polity Press.

Giddens, A. 1990. *The Consequences of modernity.* Cambridge, UK: Polity Press.

Gilligan, R.H. 2016. Children's rights and disability. In: E.G. Iriarte, R. McConkey & R.H. Gilligan (eds). *Disability and human rights: Global perspectives.* London: Palgrave Macmillan, pp 115–132.

Gillum, J. 2012. Dyscalculia: Issues for practice in educational psychology. *Educational Psychology in practice,* 28(3):287–297.

Ginott, H.G. 1972. *Teacher and child: A book for parents and teachers.* New York, NY: Macmillan.

Global Alliance of Transforming Education (GATE). 1991. *Education 2000: A Holistic Perspective,* pp 240–241. [online] Available from: http://www.ties-edu.org/GATE/Education2000.html. Accessed: 4 June 2017.

Glover, J. & Macleod, C. 2016. *Rolling out comprehensive sexuality education in South Africa: an overview of research conducted on Life Orientation sexuality education.* Unpublished policy brief document, Critical Studies in Sexualities and Reproduction, Rhodes University, Grahamstown.

Goleman, D. 1995. *Emotional intelligence.* New York, NY: Bantam.

Goleman, D. 1998. *Working with emotional intelligence.* London: Bloomsbury.

Gopnik, A. & Meltzoff, A.N. 1997. *Words, thoughts, and theories.* Massachusetts: MIT Press.

Gopnik, A. 1993. How we know our minds: The illusion of first-person knowledge of intentionality. *Behavioral and Bran Sciences,* 16(1):29–113.

Gopnik, A. 2003. The theory theory as an alternative to the innateness hypothesis. In: L. Anthony & N. Hornstein (eds). *Chomsky and his critics.* New York, NY: Basil Blackwell, pp 238–254.

Gore, J.S. & Cross, S.E. 2014. Who am I becoming? A theoretical framework for understanding self-concept change. *Self and Identity,* 13(6):740–764. [online] Available from: doi: https://doi.10.1080/15298868.2014.933712.

Graham, A.M., Pfeifer, J.H., Fischer, P.A., Lin, W., Gao, W. & Fait, D.A. 2015. The potential of infant fMRI research and the study of early life stress as a promising exemplar. *Developmental Cognitive Neuroscience,* 12:12–39.

Grandin, T. 2008. *The way I see it. A personal look at autism & Asperger's.* Arlington, TX: Future Horizons Inc.

Greenberg, M.T. 2004. Current and future challenges in school-based prevention: The researcher perspective. *Prevention Science,* 5(1):5–13.

Guichard, J. 2005. Life-long self-construction. *International Journal for Educational and Vocational Guidance,* 5:111–124.

Guichard, J. 2009. Self-constructing. *Journal of Vocational Behavior,* 78:251–258.

Gutheil, G. 1999. Scientists as children. Words, thoughts and theories. Alison Gopnik and Andrew Meltzoff. *Applied Cognitive Psychology,* 13(6):585–586.

Gaillard, W.D., Grandin, C.B. & Xu, B. 2001. *Developmental aspects of pediatric fMRI: Considerations for image acquisition, analysis, and interpretation.* Neuroimage, 13:239–249.

Galguera, M.P. 2015. UNESCO (2015). *Education for all 2000–2015: Achievements and challenges. EFA Global Monitoring Report 2015*: Paris, France. Publication by the United Nations Educational Scientific and Cultural Organization. *Journal of Supranational Policies of Education* (JOSPOE), 3:328–330.

Garcia, E. 2014. *The need to address non-cognitive skills in the education policy Agenda.* EPI Briefing Paper 386, December 2014. Economic Policy Institute, Washington, DC. [online] Available from: http://files.eric.ed.gov/fulltext/ED558126.pdf. Accessed: 12 May 2017.

García, O. & Flores, N. 2012. Multilingual pedagogies. In: M. Martin-Jones, A. Blackledge & A. Creese (eds). *The Routledge handbook of multilingualism.* New York, NY: Routledge, pp 232–246.

García, O. 2009. *Bilingual Education in the 21st century: A global perspective.* Oxford: Blackwell.

Garcia-Moreno, C., Heise, L., Jansen, H.A., Ellsberg, M. & Watts, C. 2005. Violence against women. *Science*, 310(5752):1282–1283.

Gardner, H. & Moran, S. 2006. The science of multiple intelligences theory: A response to Lynn Waterhouse. *Educational Psychologist*, 41(4):227–232. [online] Available from: https://pdfs.semanticscholar.org/7a12/3a77c89308f8f58fd66d9c753212fd86bade.pdf. Accessed: 9 June 2017.

Gardner, H. 1983. *Frames of mind: The theory of multiple intelligences.* New York, NY: Basic Books, pp 3–12.

Gardner, H. 2006. On failing to grasp the core of MI theory: A response to Visser, et al. *Intelligence*, 34:503–505.

Gardner, R.A. 2002. *Sex abuse trauma?: Or trauma from other sources?* New York, NY: Creative Therapeutics.

Gasque, G. 2016. Seven glimpses into the emotional brain. *PLoS biology*, 14(12):1/4-4/4.

Gelderblom, D. 2003. *Social Institutions, Introduction to Sociology.* Cape Town: Oxford University Press.

Gelman, S.A. & Wellman, H.M. 1991. Insides and essences: Early understandings of the non-obvious. *Cognition*, 38:213–244.

Gerace, A., Day, A., Casey, S. & Mohr, P. 2015. Perspective taking and empathy: Does having similar past experience to another person make it easier to take their perspective? *Journal of Relationships Research*, 6(e10):1–14. [online] Available from: doi: https://doi.org/10.1017/jrr.2015.6.

Gergen, K. 2009. *Relational being: Beyond individual and community.* New York, NY: Oxford University Press.

Geronimus, A.T. 1997. Teenage childbearing and personal responsibility: An alternative view. *Political Science Quarterly*, 112(3):405–430.

Geronimus, A.T. & Thompson, J.P. 2004. To denigrate, ignore or disrupt: Racial inequality in health and the impact of a policy-induced breakdown of African American communities. *Du Bois Review: Social Science Research on Race,* 1(2):247–279. [online] Available from: doi: http://doi.org/10.1017/S1742058X04042031. Accessed: 3 June 2017.

Florian, L. 2015. Conceptualising inclusive pedagogy: The inclusive pedagogical approach in action. In: J.M. Deppeler, T. Loreman, R. Smith & L. Florian (eds). *Inclusive pedagogy across the curriculum*, vol. 7. Edinburgh: Emerald Group Publishing Limited, pp 11–24.

Florian, L., Young, K. & Rouse, M. 2010. Preparing teachers for inclusive and diverse educational environments: Studying curricular reform in an initial teacher education course. *International Journal of Inclusive Education*, 14(7):709–722.

Flynn, E. & Whiten, A. 2008. Cultural transmission of tool use in young children: A diffusion chain study. *Social Development,* 17(3):699–718.

Forbes, S.H. 2003. *Holistic education: An analysis of its ideas and nature.* Brandon, VT: Foundation for Educational Renewal.

Forlin, C. 1995. Educators' beliefs about inclusive practices in Western Australia. *British Journal of Special Education*, 22(4):179–185.

Foucault, M. 1982. The subject and power. *Critical inquiry*, 8(4):777–795.

Fourie, J. 2017. *School-based collaborative support networks fostering inclusive education in selected South African schools.* Doctoral thesis, University of Johannesburg, Johannesburg. [online] Available from: http://hdl.handle.net/10210/232384. Accessed: 22 August 2017.

Francis, D.A. 2012. Teacher positioning on the teaching of sexual diversity in South African schools. *Culture, Health & Sexuality*, 14(6):597–611. [online] Available from: doi: doi.org/10.1080/13691058.2012.674558.

Frankl, V.E. 1969. *The doctor and the soul. From psychotherapy to logotherapy.* New York, NY: Bantam Books.

Frankl, V.E. 1984. *Man's search for meaning.* Revised and updated. New York, NY: Washington Square Press.

Fraser, B.J. 2007. Classroom learning environments. In: S.K. Abell & N.G. Lederman (eds). *Handbook of research on science education.* Mahwah: Lawrence Erlbaum Associates, pp 103–124.

Freedman, J. & Combs, G. 1996. *Narrative therapy. The social construction of preferred realities.* New York, NY: W.W. Norton & Company, pp 19–41.

Freedman, J. 2017. *Emotional what? Definitions and history of EQ* (2017 update). [online] Available from: http://www.6seconds.org/articles/. Accessed: 2 June 2017.

Freeman, M. 2000. The future of children's rights. *Children and Society,* 14(4):277–293.

Freire, P. 2005. *Pedagogy of the oppressed. 30th Anniversary Edition.* New York, NY: Continuum.

Freud, S. 1924, 1956. Further remarks on the defense neuropsychoses. In S. Freud. *Collected Papers by Sigmund Freud,* Vol. 1. London: Hogarth, pp 155–182.

Fritz-Stratmann, A., Balzer, L., Herholdt, R., Ragpot, L. & Ehlert, A. 2014. A mathematics competence test for Grade 1 children migrates from Germany to South Africa. *South Journal of Childhood Education*, pp 114–133.

Fuller, A. 2001. A blueprint for building social competencies in children and adolescents. *Australian Journal of Middle Schooling*, pp 40–48.

Gabrieli, J., Christodoulou, J.A., O'Loughlin, T. & Eddy, M.D. 2010. The reading brain. In: D.A. Sousa (ed). *Mind, brain, & education: Neuroscience implications for the classroom.* Bloomington, IN: Solution Tree Press.

Faulstich Orellana, M., Johnson, S.J., Rodriguez-Minkhoff, A.C., Rodriguez, L. & Franco, J. 2017. An apprentice teacher's journey in 'seeing learning'. *Teacher Education Quarterly*, Spring, pp 7–26. [online] Available at: http://go.galegroup.com.ez.sun.ac.za/ps/retrieve.do?tabID=T002&resultListType=RESULT_LIST&searchResultsType=SingleTab&searchType=AdvancedSearchForm&currentPosition=5&docId=GALE%7CA492996025&docType=Report&sort=Relevance&contentSegment=&prodId=AONE&contentSet=GALE%7CA492996025&searchId=R2&userGroupName=27uos&inPS=true. Accessed: 6 June 2017.

Feigenbaum, P. 2009. Development of communicative competence through private and inner speech. In: A. Winsler, C. Fernyhough & I. Montero (eds). *Private speech, executive functioning, and the development of verbal self-regulation*. Cambridge: Cambridge University Press, pp 105–120.

Feigenson, L., Dehaene, S. & Spelke, E. 2004. Core systems of number. *Trends in Cognitive Sciences*, 8(7):307–314.

Fendler, L. 2013. Psychology in teacher education: Efficacy, professionalization, management, and habit. In: P. Smeyers & M. Depaepe (eds). *Educational Research: The Attraction of Psychology*. Dordrecht: Springer.

Ferguson, D.L. 2008. International trends in inclusive education: The continuing challenge to teach each one and everyone. *European Journal of Special Needs education*, 23(2):109–120.

Ferguson, L. 2013. Not merely rights for children but children's rights: The theory gap and the assumption of the importance of children's rights. *International Journal of Children's Rights*, 21(2013):177–208.

Ferraina, S. 2012. Analysis of the legal meaning of Article 27 of the UN CRPD. *Key Challenges for Adapted Work Settings*. BAG: WfbM & UNAPEI, March 2012.

Ferreira, R. (ed). 2016. *Psychological assessment*. Cape Town: Juta and Company Ltd.

Firat, H. 2013. Turkish education and children's rights. *International Journal of Academic Research*, 5(4):412–419.

Fischer, K.W., Daniel, D., Immordino-Yang, M.H., Stern, E., Battro, A. & Koizumi, H. 2007. Why mind, brain, and education? Why now? *Mind, Brain, and Education*, 1(1):1–2.

Fischer, K.W. & Heikkinen, K. 2010. The future of educational neuroscience. In: D.A. Sousa (ed). *Mind, brain, & education: Neuroscience implications for the classroom*. Bloomington, IN: Solution Tree Press.

Fischer, N. 2001. Do you want to make something out of this? *Grantmakers in the Arts Reader*, 12(3):1–10.

Flavell, J.H. 1996. Piaget's legacy. *Psychological Science*, 7(4):200–203.

Fleming, N.D. & Mills, C. 1992. Not another inventory, rather a catalyst for reflection. *To Improve the Academy*, 11:137–155. [online] Available from: http://digitalcommons.unl.edu/cgi/viewcontent.cgi?article=1245&context=podimproveacad. Accessed: 17 May 2017.

Florian, L. & Black-Hawkins, K. 2011. Exploring inclusive pedagogy. *British Educational Research Journal*, 37(5):13–828.

Florian, L. 2012. Preparing teachers to work in inclusive classrooms: Key lessons for the professional development of teacher educators from Scotland's inclusive practice Project. *Journal of Teacher Education*, 63(4):275–285. [online] Available from: doi: 10.1177/0022487112447112.

Engelbrecht, P., Nel, M., Smit, S. & Van Deventer, M. 2016. The idealism of education policies and the realities in schools: the implementation of inclusive education in South Africa. *International Journal of Inclusive Education*, 20(5):520–535.

Engelbrecht, P., Green, L. & Naicker, S. 1999. *Inclusive Education in action in South Africa*. Pretoria: Van Schaik Publishers.

Engelbrecht, P., Oswald, M., Swart, E. & Eloff, I. 2003. Including learners with intellectual disabilities: stressful for teachers? *International Journal of Disability, Development and Education,* 50(3):293–308.

Engeström, Y. 1999. Activity theory and individual and social transformation. In: Y. Engeström, R. Miettinen & R.L. Punamaki (eds). *Perspectives on activity theory.* Cambridge: Cambridge University Press, pp 19–38.

Epstein, J.L. 2011. *School, family, and community partnerships: preparing educators and improving schools.* 2nd ed Thousand Oaks, CA: Corwin.

Erradu, J. 2012. *Learner support to Foundation Phase learners who are intellectually impaired: A case study.* Master's dissertation, University of South Africa, Pretoria.

Ertmer, P.A. & Newby, T.J. 2013. Behaviorism, cognitivism, constructivism: Comparing critical features from an instructional design perspective. *Performance Improvement Quarterly,* 26(2):43–72. [online] Available from: doi: 10.1111/j.1937-8327.1993.tb00605.x.

European Commission. 2013. *TVET and skills development in EU development Cooperation 2012/308055/1,* Final Report, European Commission, p 66. [online] Available from: http://ec.europa.eu/europeaid/sites/devco/files/tvet-study-aets-2012-final-report_en.pdf. Accessed: 20 May 2017.

Evans, J.S.B. 2011. Dual-process theories of reasoning: Contemporary issues and developmental applications. *Developmental Review,* 31:86–102.

Evans, K. 2016. A/R/T(HERAPIST)-OGRAPHY – Examining the Weave. In: K.T. Galvin & M. Prendergast (eds). *Poetic inquiry II – Seeing, caring, understanding: using poetry as and for inquiry.* Rotterdam: Sense Publishers, pp 41–50.

Evans, R. & Cleghorn, A. 2010. 'Look at the balloon blow up': Students teacher-talk in linguistically diverse Foundation Phase classroom. *Southern African Linguistics and Applied Language Studies,* 28(2):141–151.

Eye Witness News. 2017. Opinion: *What decolonized education should & shouldn't mean.* Eye Witness News. [online] Available from: https:/www.youtube.com/user/ewnonline. Accessed: 18 May 2017.

Fair, D., Cohen, A.L., Poer, J.D., Dosenbach, N.U.F., Church, J.A., Meizin, F.M., et al. 2009. Functional brain networks develop from a local to distributed organisation. *Public Library of Science,* 5(5):871–882.

Fakaye, D.O. & Sonyika, A. 2009. Indigenous languages in pre-primary and primary education in Nigeria. *European Journal of Social Sciences,* 10:565–573.

Farganis, J. 1996. *Readings in social theory: The classic tradition to post-modernism.* New York, NY: McGraw-Hill, p 9.

Farkas, R.D. 2003. Effects of traditional versus learning-styles instructional methods on middle school students. *The Journal of Educational Research,* 97(1):42–51. [online] Available from: doi:10.1080/00220670309596627.

Ebersöhn, L. 2016. Enabling spaces in education research: an agenda for impactful, collective evidence to support all to be first among un-equals. *South African Journal of Education*, 36(4): Art #1390, 12 pages. [online] Available from: doi:10.15700/saje.v36n4a1390.

Ebersöhn, L. 2017. A resilience, health and well-being lens for education and poverty. *South African Journal of Education,* 37(1):1–9.

Ebersöhn, L. 2017. A resilience, health and well-being lens for education and poverty. *South African Journal of Education.* 37(1), Art. # 1392, 9 pages. [online] Available from: doi: 10.15700/saje.v37n1a1392. http://www.scielo.org.za/scielo.php?script=sci_arttext&pid=S0256-01002017000100002.

Ebersöhn, L., Loots, T., Eloff, I. & Ferreira, R. 2015. Taking note of obstacles research partners negotiate in long-term higher education community engagement partnerships. *Teaching and Teacher Education*, 45:59–72.

Education Labour Relations Council. 2003. Collective Agreement No 8 of 2003: Integrated Quality Management System.

Edwards, P.A. 2009. *Tapping the potential of parents: a strategic guide to boosting student achievement through family involvement.* New York, NY: Scholastic.

Eggen, P. & Kauchak, D. 2001. *Educational Psychology: Classroom Connections.* 5th ed. New York, NY: Macmillan.

Eisner, E.W. 1985. Aesthetic modes of knowing. In: E.W. Eisner (ed). *Learning and teaching the ways of knowing: 84th yearbook of the National Society for the Study of Education.* Chicago, Il: University of Chicago Press, pp 23–36.

Eisner, E.W. 2001. The role of the Arts in educating the whole child. *Grantmakers in the Arts Reader,* 12(3):1–2.

Eisner. E.W. 2003. The arts and the creation of mind. *Language Arts,* 80(5):340–344.

Elder, C. 2001. Assessing the language proficiency of teachers: are there any border controls? *Language Testing,* 18(2):149–170.

Elliott, S.N. & Travers, J.F. 1996. *Educational psychology: Effective teaching, effective learning.* Madison, WI: Brown & Benchmark.

Eloff, I. & Ebersöhn, I. 2004. *Keys to Educational Psychology.* Cape Town: Juta and Company Ltd.

Eloff, I. 2013. Positive psychology and education. In: M. Wissing (ed). *Well-being research in South Africa. Cross-cultural advancement in positive psychology.* Dordrecht: Springer.

Eloff, I. 2015. Reflections on educational psychology in an emerging democracy. *International Journal of Educational Psychology,* 4(3):226–251.

Engel, G. 1980. The clinical application of the biopsychosocial model. *The American Journal of Psychiatry,* 137(5):535–544. [online] Available from: doi:http://dx.doi.org/10.1176/ajp.137.5.535.

Engelbrecht, P. 2004. Changing roles for educational psychologists within inclusive education in South Africa. *School Psychology International,* 25(1):20–29.

Engelbrecht, P. 2006. The implementation of inclusive education in South Africa after ten years of democracy. *European Journal of Psychology of Education,* 21(3):253–264.

Engelbrecht, P. 2009. Inclusive psychology and social transformation: Responding to the challenges of the new South Africa. In: P. Hick, R. Kershner & P. Farrell (eds). *Psychology for inclusive education: New directions in theory and practice.* Abingdon: Routledge, pp 108–116.

Donald, D., Lazarus, S. & Moolla, N. 2014. *Educational psychology in social context. Ecosystemic applications in southern Africa*. 5th ed. Cape Town: Oxford University Press.

Donaldson, M. 1978. *Children's minds*. London: Croom Helm Ltd.

Dondolo, L. 2005. Intangible Heritage: The production of indigenous knowledge in various aspects of social life. *Indilinga: African Journal of Indigenous Knowledge Systems*, 4:110–126.

Donohue, D. & Bornman, J. 2014. The challenges of realizing inclusive education in South Africa. *South African Journal of Education:* 34(2):1–14. [online] Available from: http://www.sajournalofeducation.co.za/index.php/saje/article/view/806. Accessed: 28 August 2017.

Dryden, G. & Vos, J. 2005. *The new learning revolution*. Great Britain: Bloomsbury.

Dunbar-Krige, H. & Pillay, J. 2010. Community psychology in educational contexts. *Education as Change*, 14:S1–S2. [online] Available from: doi.org/10.1080/16823206.2010.517908. Access: 28 August 2017.

Dunn, R., Dunn, K. & Price, G.E. 1984. *Learning style inventory*. Lawrence, KS: Price Systems.

Duplass, J. 2006. *Middle and high school teaching: Methods, standards, and best practices*. Boston: Houghton Mifflin Company.

Durlak, J.E., Dymnicki, A.B., Taylor, R.D., Weissberg, R.P. & Schellinger, K.B. 2011. The impact of enhancing students social and emotional learning: A meta-analysis of school-based universal interventions. *Child Development*, 82(1):405–432.

Dweck, C. 2015. Teachers' mindsets: Every student has something to teach me. *Educational Horizons*, December 2014/January 2015:10–15.

Ebersöhn, L. & Eloff, I. 2006. *Life skills and assets*. 2nd ed. Pretoria: Van Schaik Publishers.

Ebersöhn, L. & Eloff, I. 2006. Identifying asset-based trends in sustainable programmes which support vulnerable children. *South African Journal of Education*, 26(3):457–472.

Ebersöhn, L. & Ferreira, R. 2011. Coping in an HIV/AIDS-dominated context: Teachers promoting resilience in schools. *Health Education Research*, 26(4):596–613.

Ebersöhn, L. & Ferreira, R. 2012. Rurality and resilience in education: place-based partnerships and agency to moderate time and space constraints. *Perspectives in Education*, 30(1):30–42. [online] Available from: http://repository.up.ac.za/bitstream/handle/2263/18597/Ebersöhn_Rurality(2012).pdf. Accessed: 14 July 2017.

Ebersöhn, L. & Loots, T. 2017. Teacher agency in challenging contexts as a consequence of social support and resource management. *International Journal of Educational Development*, 53:80–91.

Ebersöhn, L. (ed). 2008. *From micro-scope to kaleidoscope. Reconsidering educational aspects related to children in the HIV & AIDS pandemic*. Rotterdam: Sense Publishers.

Ebersöhn, L. 2007. Voicing perceptions of risk and protective factors in coping in a HIV & AIDS landscape: Reflecting on capacity for adaptiveness. *Gifted Education International*, 23(2):1–27.

Ebersöhn, L. 2012. Adding 'flock' to 'fight and flight': A honeycomb of resilience where supply of relationships meets demand for support. *Journal of Psychology in Africa*, 1:29–42.

Ebersöhn, L. 2015. Making sense of place in school-based intervention research. *Contemporary Educational Psychology*, 40:121–130.

Devlin, K. 2010. The mathematical brain. In: D.A. Sousa (ed). *Mind, brain, & education: Neuroscience implications for the classroom*. Bloomington, IN: Solution Tree Press.

Dewey, J. 1904. The relation of theory to practice in education. In: J. Boydston (ed). *Essays on the new empiricism 1903-1906: The middle works of John Dewey 1899-1924*, 3. Carbondale, IL: Southern Illinois University Press, pp 249–272.

Dewey, J. 1934. *Art as experience*. New York, NY: Perigree.

Di Fabio, A. & Maree, J.G. 2011. Group-based life design counseling in an Italian context. *Journal of Vocational Behavior*, 80:100–107.

Diale, B.M. 2016. Life Orientation teachers' career development needs in Gauteng: Are we missing the boat? *South African Journal of Higher Education*, 30(3):85-110. [online] Available from: http://www.journals.ac.za/index.php/sajhe/article/view/670. Accessed: 22 May 2017.

Diale, B.M. Pillay, J. & Fritz, E. 2014. An exploration of the dynamics in the personal and professional development of Life-Orientation teachers in the Gauteng province in South Africa, *Journal of Social Sciences*, 38(1):83-93. [online] Available from: http://www.krepublishers.com/02-Journals/JSS/JSS-00-0-000-000-1997-Web/JSS-00-0-000-000-1997-1-Cover.htm. Accessed: 10 January 2015.

Dillon, R.S. 2007. Respect: A philosophical perspective. *Gruppendynamik*, 38(2):201–212.

Dipale, M.P. 2013. *Exploring the game of masekitlane as a narrative therapeutic intervention tool with children in Grade four*. Johannesburg: University of Johannesburg.

Dippenaar, A.J.F. 2004. *The Vista University English language proficiency course: An evaluation*. Doctoral thesis, North-West University, Potchefstroom.

Dippenaar, H. & Peyper, T. 2011. Language awareness and communication as part of teacher education at the University of Pretoria, Pretoria. *Journal for Language Teaching*, 45(2):32–46.

Dispenza, J. 2016. *Change from the inside out*. [online] Available from: http://www.drjoedispenza.com/index.php?page_id=Live_Neurons_Connecting_Pruning. Accessed: 20 November 2017.

Dlamini, K. 2016. Kwazi Dlamini for *Vox Newsletter*, March. [online] Available from: http://Voxnewsletter. Accessed: 17 April 2017.

Dodge, R., Daly, A., Huyton, J. & Sanders, L. 2012. The challenge of defining well-being. *International Journal of Well-being*, 2(3):222–235. [online] Available from: doi:10.5502/ijw.v2i3.4b.

Dodge, R., Daly, A., Huyton, J., & Sanders, L. 2012. The challenge of defining wellbeing. *International Journal of Wellbeing*, 2(3):222–235. [online] Available from: doi:10.5502/ijw.v2i3.4b.

Domitrovich, C.E., Bradshaw, C.P., Poduska, J.M., Hoagwood, K., Buckley, J.A., Olin, S., Romanelli, L.H., Leaf, P.J., Greenberg, M.T. & Ialongo, N.S. 2008. Maximizing the implementation quality of evidence-based preventive interventions in schools: A conceptual framework. *Advances in School Mental Health Promotion*, 1(3):6–28.

Donald, D., Lazarus, S. & Lolwana, P. 2001. *Educational psychology in social contexts*. 2nd ed. Cape Town: Oxford University Press.

Donald, D., Lazarus, S. & Lolwana, P. 2010. *Educational psychology in social context: Ecosystemic applications in southern Africa*. 4th ed. Cape Town: Oxford University Press.

Department of Education. 2001. *Opening our eyes: Addressing gender-based violence in South African schools—A manual for educators, Department of Education.* [online] Available from: www.unicef.org/southafrica/SAF_request_openingoureyes.pdf. Accessed: 7 June 2017.

Department of Education. 2007. *Measures for the prevention and management of learner pregnancy.* Department of Education. [online] Available from: http://www.naptosa.org.za/index.php/doc-manager/40-professional/46-general/105-sgb-dbe-pregnancy-2007/file. Accessed: 4 June 2017.

Department of Education. 2014a. *Revised National Curriculum Statement Grades R to 9 (Schools) Policy: Overview.* Pretoria: Department of Education. [online] Available from: http://www.education.gov.za/Curriculum/NationalCurriculumStatementsGradesR-12.aspx. Accessed: 7 July 2017.

Department of Education. 2014b. *Policy on Screening, identification, Assessment and Support.* Pretoria: Department of Education. [online] Available from: http://www.naptosa.org.za/index.php/whatsnew/1168-policy-on-screening-identification-assessment-and-support-sias-2014. Accessed: 7 July 2017.

Department of Health. 2011. Health Professions Act No. 56 of 1974. *Government Gazette* No. R. 704. Pretoria: Government Printer.

Department of Health. 2011. R 704 Regulations defining the scope of the profession of psychology. No. 34581 *Government Gazette*, 2 September 2011. *Education and Training: Building an expanded, effective and integrated post school system,* Pretoria: Government Printer, p xii.

Department of Health. 2011. Regulations defining the scope of the profession of psychology form R. 704. *Government Gazette* (No. 34581). Pretoria: Government Printer: 4–5.

Department of Higher Education and Training. 2015. *Revised policy on the minimum requirements for teacher education qualifications (MRTEQ).* [online] Available from: http://www.dhet.gov.za/Teacher%20Education/National%20Qualifications%20Framework%20Act%2067_2008%20Revised%20Policy%20for%20Teacher%20Education%20Quilifications.pdf. Accessed: 10 August 2017.

Department of Higher Education and Training. 2010. Draft policy on minimum requirements for teacher education qualifications. *Government Gazette* (No 33788). Pretoria: Government Printer.

Department of Higher Education and Training. 2013. *White Paper for Post School.*

Department of Higher Education and Training. 2015. National Qualifications Framework Act (67/2008): Revised policy on the minimum requirements for teacher education qualifications. *Government Gazette* (No 38487), 596, February. Pretoria: Government Printer.

Department of Social Development. 2012. *White Paper on families in South Africa.* Pretoria: Department of Social Development.

Department of Social Development. 2016. *White Paper on the rights of persons with disabilities.* Pretoria: Department of Social Development.

Departments of Health and Basic Education. 2012. *Integrated school health policy.* Pretoria: Sol Plaatjie House. [online] Available from: https://www.health-e.org.za/wp-content/uploads/2013/10/Integrated_School_Health_Policy.pdf. Accessed: 5 May 2017.

Department of Basic Education. 2010. *Guidelines for inclusive teaching and learning: Education White Paper 6, Special Needs Education, Building an inclusive education and training system.* [online] Available from: www.thutong.org.za/Learningspaces/InclusiveEducation.aspx. Accessed: 22 May 2017.

Department of Basic Education. 2010. *The status of the language of learning and teaching (LOLT) in South African schools: A quantitative overview.* Pretoria: Government Printer.

Department of Basic Education. 2011. *Curriculum and Assessment Policy Statement. Life Orientation. Further Education and Training Phase Grades 10–12.* Pretoria: Government Printer.

Department of Basic Education. 2012. *Curriculum, Assessment and Policy Statements (CAPS).* Pretoria: Government Printer.

Department of Basic Education. 2012. *National Curriculum Statement Grade R–12.* [online] Available from: http://www.education.gov.za/Curriculum/NationalCurriculumStatementsGradesR-12.aspx. Accessed: 2 August 2017.

Department of Basic Education. 2013. *Education statistics in South Africa 2013.* [online] Available from: https://www.education.gov.za/Portals/0/Documents/Publications/Education%20Statistic%202013.pdf . Accessed: 2 August 2017.

Department of Basic Education. 2014. *Policy on screening, identification, assessment and support* (SIAS). Pretoria: Sol Plaatjie House.

Department of Basic Education. 2015. *Action plan to 2019: Towards the realisation of schooling 2030.* Pretoria: Government Printer, p 28.

Department of Basic Education. 2015. *White Paper 6 on inclusive education an overview for the period: 2013–2015.* Pretoria: Sol Plaatjie House.

Department of Basic Education. 2016. *Education Department briefs portfolio committee on 'skills revolution'.* [online] Available from: http://www.education.gov.za/Newsroom/MediaRelease/tabid/347/ctl/Details/mid/3963/ItemID/3920/Default.aspx. Accessed: 22 May 2017.

Department of Basic Education. 2017. Information for teachers, initial teacher education. Department of Basic Education official website. Available at: http://www.education.gov.za/Informationfor/Teachers/InitialTeacherEducation/tabid/416/Default.aspx. Accessed: 7 June 2017.

Department of Basic Education & MiET Africa. 2010. *Care and Support for Teaching and Learning Programme*, Durban: MiET Africa.

Department of Education. 1997. *Quality education for all. Overcoming barriers to learning and development. Report of the National Commission on Special Needs in Education and Training (NCSNET) National Committee on Education Support Services (NCESS).* Pretoria: Government Printer.

Department of Education. 2000. Norms and standards for educators. Notification regarding National Education Policy Act, 1996. *Government Gazette*, pp 12–14. [online] Available from: http://www.gov.za/sites/www.gov.za/files/20844.pdf. Accessed: 7 June 2017.

Department of Education. 2001. *Education White Paper 6: Special needs education. Building an inclusive education and training system.* Pretoria: Department of Education.

Department of Education. 2001. *Manifesto on values, education and democracy.* Pretoria: Government Printer. [online] Available from: http //www.dhet.gov.za/LinkClick.aspx?fileticket=2vv9jRcRMOQ%3D&tabid=92&mid=495. Accessed: 1 June 2017.

De Bellis, M.D., Keshavan, M.S., Clark, D.B., Casey, B.J., Giedd, J.N., Boring, A.M., Frustaci, K. & Ryan, N.D. 1999. Developmental traumatology. Part II: Brain development. *Biol. Psychiatry,* 45:1271–1284.

De Houwer, J., Barnes-Holmes, D., & Moors, A. 2013. What is learning? On the nature and merits of a functional definition of learning. *Psychonomic Bulletin & Review*, 20(4):631–642.

De Klerk, R. & Le Roux, R. 2003. *Emosionele intelligensie vir kinders en tieners: 'n praktiese gids vir ouers en onderwysers.* Kaapstad: Human & Rousseau.

De Lange, N., Moletsane R. & Mitchell C. 2015. Seeing how it works: A visual essay about critical and transformative research in education. *Perspective in Education*, 33(4):151–176.

De Villiers, J. 2017. *Courtney Pieters was raped twice before being murdered, court hears.* [online] Available from: http://www.news24.com/SouthAfrica/News/courtney-pieters-was-raped-twice-before-being-murdered-court-hears-20170517. Accessed: 2 June 2017.

Deb, S. & Mathews, B. 2012. Children's rights in India: Parents' and teachers' attitudes, knowledge and perceptions. *International Journal of Children's Rights,* 20(2):241–264. [online] Available from: http://booksandjournals.brillonline.com/content/journals/10.1163/157181811x616022. Accessed: 17 October 2017.

Dede, C. 2008. Theoretical perspectives influencing the use of information technology in teaching and learning. In: J. Voogd & G. Knezek (eds). *International Handbook of Information Technology in Primary and Secondary Education.* New York, NY: Springer, pp 43–59.

Dednam, D. 2011. First language: Difficulties in spoken language. In: E. Landsberg, D. Krüger & E. Swart (eds). *Addressing barriers to learning: A South African perspective* 2nd ed. Pretoria: Van Schaik Publishers, pp 126–142.

Dednam, D. 2011. First language: Difficulties in reading, spelling and writing. In: E. Landsberg, D. Krüger & E. Swart (eds). *Addressing barriers to learning: A South African perspective.* 2nd ed. Pretoria: Van Schaik Publishers, pp 143–166.

Dehaene, S. & Cohen, L. 2011. The unique role of the visual word form area in reading. *Trends in Cognitive Sciences,* 15(6):254–262.

Dehaene, S. 1997, 2011. *The number sense: How the mind creates.* Oxford: Oxford University Press.

Dehaene, S. 2010. The calculating brain. In: D.A. Sousa (ed) *Mind, brain, & education: Neuroscience implications for the classroom.* Bloomington, IN: Solution Tree Press.

Dehaene-Lambertz, G., Dehaene, S. & Hertz-Pannier, L. 2002. Functional neuroimaging of speech perception in infants. *Science,* 298(500):2012–2015.

Depaepe, M. 2013. Struggling with the historical attractiveness of psychology for educational research illustrated by the case of Nazi Germany. In: P. Smeyers & M. Depaepe (eds). *Educational research: The attraction of psychology.* Dordrecht: Springer.

Department of Basic Education official website. [online] Available from: http://www.education.gov.za/Informationfor/Teachers/InitialTeacherEducation/tabid/416/Default.aspx. Accessed: 7 June 2017.

Department of Basic Education. 2010. *Guidelines for inclusive teaching and learning.* Pretoria: Government Printer.

D'Mello, S.K., Strain, A.C., Olney, A. & Graesser, A. 2013. Affect, meta-affect, and affect regulation during complex learning. In: R. Azevedo & V. Aleven (eds). *International handbook of metacognition and learning technologies*, New York: Springer, pp 669–681.

Dai, D.Y. & Chen, F. 2013. Three paradigms of gifted education: In search of conceptual clarity in research and practice. *Gifted Child Quarterly*, 57(3):151–168.

Daily Mail Online. 2013. World's most racist countries. *Daily Mail Online*. Article, 2325502. [online] Available from: www.dailymail.uk. Accessed: 17 May 2017.

Daily, M. 2005. *Inclusion of students with autism spectrum disorders*. Baltimore, MD: Johns Hopkins, School of Education.

Dalton, E.M., McKenzie, J.A. & Kahonde, C. 2012. The implementation of inclusive education in South Africa: reflections arising from a workshop for teachers and therapists to introduce Universal Design for Learning: Original research. *African Journal of Disability*, 1(1):1–7. [online] Available from: http://dx.doi.org/10.4102/ajod.v1i1.13.

Daly, A. 2012. Data, dyads, and dynamics: Exploring data use and social networks in educational improvement. *Teachers College Record*, 114(11):1–38.

Damons, L.N. 2014. *Enhancing a sense of self in a group of socially marginalised adolescent boys through participatory action research*. Doctoral thesis, Stellenbosch University, Stellenbosch.

Daniels, B., Collair, L., Moolla, N. & Lazarus, S. 2007. School psychology in South Africa. In: S.R. Jimerson, T.D. Oakland & P.T. Farrell (eds). *The Handbook of International School Psychology*. Thousand Oaks, CA: Sage, pp 361–372.

Darling-Hammond, L. & Bransford, J. 2005. *Preparing teachers for a changing world*. San Francisco, CA: John Wiley & Sons.

Dass-Brailsford, P. 2005. Exploring resiliency: Academic achievement among disadvantaged black youth in South Africa. *South African Journal of Psychology*, 35(3):574–591.

Davids, J. 2010. Book review: The philosophical baby: what children's minds tell us about truth, love, and the meaning of life, by Alison Gopnik. *Infant Observation*, 13(2):247–253.

Davin, R.J. 2003. *'n Uitkomsgebaseerde assesseringsmodel vir die ontvangsjaar*. Doktoraal in onderwys-proefskrif, Universiteit van Suid-Afrika, Pretoria.

Davis, B., Sumara, D. & Luce-Kapler, R. 2008. *Engaging minds*. 2nd ed. New York, NY: Routledge, pp 1–226.

Davis, G.A. 1983. *Educational Psychology: Theory and practice*. London: Addison Wesley Publishing Company.

Davis, J. 2001. Conceptual Change. In: M. Orey (ed). *Emerging perspectives on learning, teaching, and technology*. [online] Available from: http://epltt.coe.uga.edu/. Accessed: 20 May 2017.

Davis, K. 2008. Intersectionality as buzzword: A sociology of science perspective on what makes a feminist theory successful. *Feminist Theory*, 9(1):67–85.

Dayton, T. 2007. Emotional repair through action methods: The use of psychodramatic, sociometry, psychodramatic journaling and experiential group therapy with adolescents. In: V. Camilleri. *Healing the Inner City Child: Creative Arts Therapies with At-risk Youth*. London: Jessica Kingsley Publishers, pp 197–211.

Conley, L., De Beer, J., Dunbar-Krige, H., Du Plessis, E., Gravett, S., Lomofsky, L., Merckel, V., November, I., Osman, R., Petersen, N., Robinson, M. & Van der Merwe, M. 2010. *Becoming a teacher*. Cape Town: Pearson Education South Africa, pp 1–196.

Connell, C. & Elliott, S. 2009. Beyond the birds and the bees: Learning inequality through sexuality education. *American Journal of Sexuality Education*, 4(2):83–102. [online] Available from doi: doi.org/10.1080/15546120903001332.

Connell, R.W. & Messerschmidt, J.W. 2005. Hegemonic masculinity. Rethinking the concept. *Gender & Society*, 19(6):829–859.

Connell, R.W. 1987. Hegemonic masculinity. In: S. Jackson & S. Scott (eds). 2002. *Gender: A Sociological Reader*. London: Routledge.

Connell, R.W. 2002. *Gender*. Cambridge, UK: Polity Press.

Cook, V. & Singleton, D. 2014. *Key topics in second language acquisition*. Toronto: Multilingual matters.

Cook, W. 2013. *Vocational education protecting options for pre-16 pupils*. London: Institute for Public Policy Research.

Cooper, D., De Lannoy, A. & Rule, C. 2015. *Youth health and well-being: Why it matters: South African child gauge 2015*. School of Public Health, University of the Western Cape, Cape Town.

Cooper, R.K. & Sawaf, A. 1997. *Executive EQ: Emotional intelligence in the business*. London: Orion.

Corey, G. 2009. *Theory and practice of counseling and psychotherapy*. 8th ed. Belmont, CA: Thomson Brooks/Cole.

Cozolino, L. 2010. *The neuroscience of Psychotherapy: Healing the social brain*. 2nd ed. New York, NY: WW Norton & Company.

Creese, A., Daniels, H. & Norwich, B. 2012. *Teacher support teams in primary and secondary schools*. UK: David Fulton Publisher.

Crenshaw, K. 1989. Demarginalizing the intersection of race and sex: A black feminist critique of antidiscrimination doctrine, feminist theory and antiracist politics. *University of Chicago Legal Forum*:139.

Crenshaw, K. 1994. Mapping the margins: Intersectionality, identity politics, and violence against women of color. In: M.A. Fineman & R. Mykitiuk (eds). *The Public Nature of Private Violence*. New York, NY: Routledge, pp 93–118.

Crossley, M. 1999. The disability kaleidoscope. *Notre Dame Law Review*, 74:621–1737.

Crothers, L.M. & Levinson, E.M. 2004. Assessment of bullying: A review of methods and instruments. *Journal of Counseling & Development*, 82(4):496–503.

Crozier, W.R. 2011. The psychology of education: Achievements, challenges and opportunities. In: J. Furlong & M. Lawn (eds). *Disciplines of Education: Their Role in the Future of Education Research*. Oxon: Routledge.

Csikzsentmihalyi, M. 2002. *Flow: The psychology of happiness: The classic work on how to achieve happiness*. London: Rider, Random House Group.

Cummins, J. 1999. *BICS and CALP: Clarifying the distinction*. [online] Available from: http://files.eric.ed.gov/fulltext/ED438551.pdf. Accessed: 7 May 2017.

Cummins, J. 2000. *Language power and pedagogy: Bilingual children in the crossfire*. Clevedon, England: Multilingual Matters Ltd.

Chia, N.K.H. & Kee, N.K.N. 2013. The 2-Triple-E framework of inclusive employment for people with disabilities in Singapore. *Academic Research International*, 4(5):469.

Chisholm, L. 2004. *The quality of primary education in South Africa*. Background paper prepared for UNESCO Education for All Global Monitoring Report, April 2004.

Chisholm, L., et al. 2000. *A curriculum for the twenty first century: Report of the Review Committee on Curriculum 2005* (presented to Prof Kader Asmal, Minister of Education, 31 May 2000).

Chohan, Z. & Langa, M. 2011. Teenage mothers talk about their experience of teenage motherhood. *Agenda: Empowering Women for Gender Equity, 950* (March):87–95. [online] Available from: http://doi.org/10.1080/10130950.2011.610993.

Chomsky, N. 1959. Review of verbal behavior, by B.F. Skinner. *Language*, 35:26–57.

Chomsky, N. 1980. *Rules and representations*. New York: Columbia University Press.

Christiaans, D.J. 2006. *Empowering teachers to implement the Life Orientation Learning Area in the Senior Phase of the General Education and Training Band*. Masters of education dissertation, University of Stellenbosch, Stellenbosch.

Christy, T.C. 2013. Vygotsky, cognitive development and language: New perspectives on the nature of grammaticalization. *Historiographia Linguistica*, 40:199–227.

Cilliers, P. 1998. *Complexity and postmodernism: understanding complex systems*. London: Routledge.

Clarebout, G., Elen, J., Juarez Collazo, N.A., Lust, G. & Jiang, L. 2013. Metacognition and the use of tools. In: R. Azevedo & V. Aleven (eds). *International handbook of metacognition and learning technologies,* New York, NY: Springer, pp 187–195.

Cluver, L., Fincham, D.S. & Seedat, S. 2009. Posttraumatic stress in Aids orphaned children exposed to high levels of trauma: The moderating role of perceived social support. *Journal of Traumatic Stress*:1–7.

Coalition to Stop the Use of Child Soldiers. 2008. *Child soldiers global report, 2008*. London: Coalition to Stop the Use of Child Soldiers.

Cobbett, M. 2014. Beyond 'victims' and 'heroines': Constructing 'girlhood' in international development. *Progress in Development Studies*, 14(4):309–320.

Coetzee, M. & Jansen, C. 2007. *Emotional intelligence in the classroom*. Cape Town: Juta.

Coffey, H. nd. *Modeling*. [online] Available from: www.learnnc.org/lp/pages/4697. Accessed: 1 June 2017.

Coffield, F., Moseley, D., Hall, E. & Ecclestone, K. 2004. *Should we be using learning styles? What research has to say to practice*. London: Learning and Skills Research Centre.

Cohen, J, Pickeral, T. & McCloskey, M. 2008. The challenge of assessing school climate. *Educational Leadership*, 66(4). [online] Available from: http://www.ascd.org/publications/educational-leadership/dec08/vol66/num04/toc.aspx. Accessed: 18 October 2017.

Cole, E.R. 2009. Intersectionality and research in psychology. *The American Psychologist*, 64(3):170–180.

Coleman, L. 2014. Studying ordinary events in a field devoted to the extraordinary. *Journal of the Education of the Gifted*, 37(1):81–93. [online] Available from: doi: 10.1177/0162353214521521.

Coleman, M. 2013. *Empowering family-teacher partnerships: building connections within diverse communities*. Los Angeles: SAGE.

Camilleri, B. & Law, J. 2007. Assessing children referred to speech and language therapy: Static and dynamic assessment of receptive vocabulary. *International Journal of Speech-Language Pathology,* 9(4):312–322.

Camilleri, V.A. 2007. At-risk children. In: V. Camilleri, *Healing the inner city child: Creative arts therapies with a-risk youth.* London: Jessica Kingsley Publishers, pp 17–20.

Campbell, C. & Ungar, M. 2004. Constructing a life that works: Part 1: Blending postmodern family therapy and career counselling. *The Career Development Quarterly,* 53:16–27.

Canonici, N.N. 1993. *Izinganekwane: An anthology of Zulu folktales.* Durban: University of Natal.

Carastathis, A. 2014. The concept of intersectionality in feminist theory. *Philosophy Compass,* 9(5):304–314.

Carey, S. & Sarnecka, B. 2004. The development of human conceptual representations: A case study. In: Y. Munakata & M.H. Johnson (eds). *Processes of Change in Brain and Cognitive Development.* London: Oxford University Press, pp 473–496.

Carey, S. & Spelke, E. 1994. Domain-specific knowledge and conceptual change. In: A. Lawrence, S. Hirschfeld & A. Gelman (eds). *Mapping the mind: domain specificity in cognition and culture.* Cambridge: Cambridge University Press, pp 169–199.

Carey, S. 1988. Conceptual differences between adults and children. *Mind and language,* 3(3):168–181.

Carey, S. 2009. *The origin of concepts.* New York: Oxford University Press.

Carlson, S.M. 2005. Developmentally sensitive measures of executive function in pre-school children. *Developmental Neuropsychology,* 28:595–616.

Carr, A. 2000. *Family therapy: Concepts, process and practice.* Chichester: John Wiley & Sons.

Carr, A. 2006. *The handbook of child and adolescent clinical psychology: A contextual approach.* 2nd ed. London: Routledge.

Carrim, N. & Keet, A. 2005. Infusing human rights into the curriculum: The case of the South African. *Revised National Perspectives in Education,* 23(2):99–110.

Cefai, C. 2007. Resilience for all: A study of classrooms as protective contexts. *Emotional and Behavioural Difficulties*:119–134. [online] Available from: doi: 10.1080/13632750701315516.

Centre for Development and Enterprise. 2012. *Vocational education in South Africa: Strategies for improvement.* The Centre for Development and Enterprise, 3:113. [online] Available from: http://www.cde.org.za/. Accessed: 2 August 2017.

Centre for Justice and Crime Prevention. 2015. *Optimus Study Research Bulletin: The Optimus study on child abuse, violence and neglect in South Africa.* [online] Available from: http://www.saferspaces.org.za/resources/entry/the-optimus-study-on-child-abuse-violence-and-neglect-in-south-africa. Accessed: 12 May 2017.

Chataika, T., McKenzie, J.A., Swart, E. & Lyner-Cleophas, M. 2012. Access to education in Africa: Responding to the United Nations Convention on the Rights of Persons with Disabilities. *Disability and Society,* 27(3):385–398.

Chepkemei, A., Watindi, R., Cherono, K.L., Ng'isirei, R.J. & Rono, A. 2012. Towards achievement of sustainable development through technical and vocational education and training (TVET): A case of middle level colleges-Kenya. *Journal of Emerging Trends in Educational Research and Policy Studies,* 3(5):686–690.

Bornman, J. & Rose, J. 2017. *Believe that all can achieve: Increasing classroom participation in learners with special support needs.* 2nd ed. Pretoria: Van Schaik Publishers.

Bos, C.S. & Vaughn, S. 1994. *Strategies for teaching students with learning and behaviour problems.* Boston: Allyn and Bacon.

Bradburn, N.M. 1969. *The structure of psychological well-being.* Chicago: Aldine.

Bright, J.E.H. & Pryor, R.G.L. 2005. The chaos theory of careers: A user's guide. *The Career Development Quarterly,* 53(4):291–305.

Broadbent, D.E. 1957. A mechanical model for human attention and immediate memory. *Psychological Review,* 64:205–215.

Brodie, K. 1997. A new mathematics curriculum: Reflecting on outcomes in process. *Pythagoras,* 43:29–37.

Bronfenbrenner, U. & Morris, P. 2006. The bioecological model of human development. In: R. Lerner & W. Damon (eds). *Handbook of child psychology. Volume 1: Theoretical models of human development.* 6th ed. New York, NY: John Wiley & Sons, pp 793–828.

Bronfenbrenner, U. 1986. Ecology of the family as a context for human development: Research perspectives. *Developmental Psychology,* 22(4):723–742.

Brown, T.H. 2006. Beyond constructivism: Navigationism in the knowledge era. *On the Horizon,* 14(3):108–120. [online] Available from: doi: 10.1108/10748120610690681.

Bruer, J.T. 1997. Education and the brain: A bridge too far. *Educational Researcher,* 26(8):4–16.

Brunstein, J.C. 1993. Personal goals and subjective well-being: A longitudinal study. *Journal of Personality and Social Psychology,* 65:1061-70.

Bruwer, P. 2003. Autism misunderstood. *Rekord,* 12(5):4.

Burden, R. & Taylor, W. 2014. Applying educational psychology in a changing world: Some lessons from Mongolia. *School Psychology International.* 35(4):341–356.

Burke, K. & Dunn, R. 2010. Style-based teaching to raise minority student test scores there's no debate! *The Clearing House: A Journal of Educational Strategies, Issues and Ideas,* 76(2):103–106. [online] Available from: doi: 10.1080/00098650209604959.

Burman, E. 2012. Deconstructing neoliberal childhood: Towards a feminist antipsychological approach. *Childhood,* 19(4):423–438. [online] Available from: http://doi.org/10.1177/0907568211430767.

Burnette, C. & Sierra, J. 2003. Cultural dimensions of children's games and play behaviour in the Northern Cape Province, South Africa. *African Journal for Physical, Health Education, Recreation and Dance.* October 2003 (Supplement):15–25.

Burns, B. 2006. *How to teach balanced reading and writing.* California, CA: Corwinn Press Incorporated.

Burton, P. & Leoschut, L. 2012. *School violence in South Africa: Results of the 2012 National School Violence Study.* Cape Town: Centre for Justice and Crime Prevention.

Butterworth, B. 1999. *The mathematical brain.* Basingstoke, UK: Macmillan.

Butterworth, B. 2010. Foundational numerical capacities and the origins of dyscalculia. *Trends in Cognitive Sciences,* 14(12):534–541.

Calvo-Merino, B., Glaser, D.E., Grèzes, J., Passingham, R.E. & Haggard, P. 2006. Seeing or doing: Influence of visual and motor familiarity in action observation. *Current Biology,* 16(19):1905–1910.

Cameron, R.J. 2006. Educational psychology: The distinctive contribution. *Educational Psychology in Practice,* 22(4):289–304.

Benadé, D.A. 2013. *Educational psychological guidelines for parents based on the lifeworld of the high-achieving young adolescent.* Masters in education dissertation, University of South Africa, Pretoria.

Benner D.G. (ed). 1993. Development of guilt. In: *Baker encyclopedia of Psychology.* 5th ed. Grand Rapids, MI: Baker.

Berger, K.S. 2008. *The developing person through childhood and adolescence.* London: Worth Publishers.

Berger, M. 2013. *The role of the educational psychologist in supporting inclusion at school level.* Masters in education dissertation, University of Pretoria, Pretoria (unpublished).

Berk, L.E. 2000. *Child development.* 5th ed. Boston: Allyn and Bacon.

Berliner, D.C. 1993. The 100-year journey of educational psychology. *Exploring applied psychology: Origins and critical analyses,* 1–33.

Bezuidenhout, H. 2017. *Development of early numerical competence: Number talk and executive function as data for children's input analyzers.* Doctorate seminar, University of Johannesburg, Johannesburg.

Bhana, D. 2012. Understanding and addressing homophobia in schools: A view from teachers. *South African Journal of Education,* 32(3):307–318.

Bhardwaj, A. 2016. Importance of education in human life: A holistic approach. *International Journal of Science and Consciousness,* 2(2):23–28. [online] Available from: http://www.ijsc.net/docs/issue4/importance-of-education-in-human-life.pdf. Accessed: 7 May 2017.

Bill of Responsibilities for the Youth of South Africa. 2011. [online] Available from: http://www.education.gov.za/LinkClick.aspx?fileticket=QX%2FfCO6lKM0%3D&tabid=454&mid=425. Accessed: 12 February 2012.

Bing, E., Van Staden, J. & Tabane, R. 2016. *My child has ADHD! Help!* Pretoria: Traecan.

Blair, C. & Raver, C.C. 2015. *School readiness and self-regulation: A developmental psychobiological approach.* New York: New York University.

Blignaut, S. 2017. *Two decades of curriculum transformation: What have we learnt and where do we go from here?* Unpublished Inaugural lecture, Nelson Mandela Metropolitan University.

Block, C.C., Gambrell, L. & Pressley, M. 2002. *Improving comprehension instruction.* San Francisco: Jossey-Bass.

Blustein, D.L. 2006. *The psychology of working: A new perspective for career development, counseling, and public policy.* Mahwah, NJ: Erlbaum.

Booth, T. 2011. The name of the rose: Inclusive values into action in teacher education. *Prospects,* 41:303–318.

Borek, J.A. & Thompson, S.M. 2003. Multisensory learning in inclusive classrooms. *Academic Exchange Quarterly,* 7(3):244–249.

Boring, E.G. 1950. *A history of experimental psychology.* 2nd ed. New York: Appleton-Century-Crofts.

Bornman, J. & Donohue, D.K. 2013. South African teachers' attitudes toward learners with barriers to learning: Attention-deficit and hyperactivity disorder and little or no functional speech. *International Journal of Disability, Development and Education* 60(2):85–104.

Bornman, J. & Rose, J. 2010. *Believe that all can achieve: Increasing classroom participation in learners with special support needs.* Pretoria: Van Schaik Publishers.

Bandura, A. 1977. *Social learning theory*. Englewood Cliffs, NJ: Prentice-Hall.

Bandura, A. 1986. *Social foundations of thought and action: A social cognitive theory*. Englewood Cliffs, NJ: Prentice-Hall.

Bandura, A. 1991. Social cognitive theory of self-regulation. *Organizational behavior and human decision processes,* 50:248–287.

Bandura, A. 2004. Health promotion by social cognitive means. *Health Education & Behaviours*:143–163.

Bandura, A. 2006. Guide to the construction of self-efficacy scales. In F. Pajares & T. C. Urdan (eds.). *Self-efficacy Beliefs of Adolescents*. Greenwich, CT: Information Age Publishing, pp 307–337.

Banks, D. 2016. What is brain plasticity and why is it so important? *The conversation: Academic rigour, journalistic flair*. [online] Available from: http://theconversation.com/what-is-brain-plasticity-and-why-is-it-so-important-55967. Accessed: 18 May 2017.

Barab, S. & Plucker, J. 2002. Smart people or smart contexts? Cognition, ability, and talent development in an age of situated approaches to knowing and learning. *Educational Psychologist,* 37(3):165–182.

Barkley, R. 2013. *Taking charge of ADHD: The complete, authoritative guide for parents*. 3rd ed. New York, NY: The Guilford Press.

Barner, D. & Baron, A.S. 2016. An Introduction to core knowledge and conceptual change. In: D. Barner & A.S. Baron (eds). *Core Knowledge and Conceptual Change*. New York, NY: Oxford University Press, pp 1–10.

Barnes, C. 1992. Disability and employment. *Personnel Review,* 21(6):55–73.

Barnes, M.K. & Duck, S. 1994. Everyday communicative contexts for social support. In: B.R. Burleson, T.L. Albrecht & I.G. Sarason (eds). *Communication of social support: Messages, interactions, relationships, and community*. Thousand Oaks, CA: Sage, 175–194.

Barsalou, L.W. 2008. Grounded cognition. *Annual Review of Psychology,* 59:617–645. [online] Available from: doi:10.1146/annurev.psych.59.103006.093639.

Bartolo, P.A. 2010. Why school psychology for diversity? *School Psychology International,* 31(6):567–580.

Beddoe, L. & Joy, E. 2017. Questioning the uncritical acceptance of neuroscience in child and family policy and practice: A review of challenges to the current doxa. *Aotearoa New Zealand Social Work,* 29(1):65–76. [online] Available from: http://dx.doi.org/10.11157/anzswj-vol29iss1id213.

Bell, F. 2011. Connectivism: Its place in theory–informed research and innovation in technology-enabled Learning. *The International Review of Research in Open and Distance learning,* 12(3):98–118.

Bell, N.J., Wieling, E. & Watson, W. 2004. Self-reflecting in developmental context: Variations in level and patterning during the first 2 university years. *The Journal of Genetic Psychology,* 165(4):451–465. [online] Available from: doi: https://10.3200/GNTP.165.4.451-465.

Belleza, E.S. 1981. Mnemonic devices: Classification, characteristics and criteria. *Review of Educational Research,* 51:247–275.

Beltman, S., Mansfield, C. & Price, A. 2011 Thriving not just surviving: A review of research on teacher resilience. *Educational Research Review,* 6(3):185–207.

Ansari, D. & Coch, D. 2006. Bridges over troubled waters: Education and cognitive neuroscience. *Trends in Cognitive Sciences,* 10(4):146–151.

Ansari, D. 2010. The Computing Brain. In: D.A. Sousa (ed). *Mind, brain, & education: neuroscience implications for the classroom.* Bloomington, IN: Solution Tree Press.

Ansari, D. 2017. *Why should educators care about cognitive neuroscience?* Learning & the brain conference, San Francisco, February 2017. San Francisco, CA: Numerical Cognition Laboratory at the Department of Psychology & Brain and Mind Institute at the Western University.

Antonovsky, A. 1979. *Health, stress, and coping.* San Francisco, CA: Jossey Bass Inc.

Archard, D.W. 2011. Children's rights. In: E.N. Alta, (ed). *Stanford Encyclopedia of philosophy.* Summer, 2011 edition. [online] Available from: http://plato.stanford.edu/archives/sum2011/entries/rights-children/. Accessed: 15 June 2015.

Arendt, H. 1958. *The human condition.* Chicago, Il: The University of Chicago.

Arfo, E. 2015. *A comparative analysis of technical and vocational education and training policy in selected African countries.* Doctor of Philosophy thesis, University of KwaZulu-Natal, Durban.

Arrows, F. & Miller, J. 2012. Holistic and indigenous education: A dialogue. *Encounter: Education for Meaning and Social Justice,* 25(3):44–54.

Arsalidou, M. & Pascual-Leone, J. 2016. Constructivist developmental theory is needed in developmental neuroscience. *Science of Learning,* 1:16016. [online] Available from: http://www.nature.com/articles/npjscilearn201616. Accessed: 2 June 2017.

Artiles, A.J. & Kozleski, E.B. 2016. Inclusive education's promises and trajectories: Critical notes about future research on a venerable idea. *Education Policy Analysis Archives,* 24(43):1–29.

Arts, K. & Popvoski, V. 2006. *International criminal accountability and the rights of children. From peace to justice series.* London: Cambridge University Press.

Atkinson, R. & Shiffrin, R. 1968. Human memory: A proposed system and its control processes. In: K. Spence & J. Spence (eds). *The psychology of learning and motivation: Advances in research and theory (Vol. 2).* New York, NY: Academic Press, pp 13–113.

Autism South Africa. 2015. *Outisme: Praktiese riglyne.* [online] Available from: www.autismsouthafrica.org. Accessed: 6 April 2017.

Baddeley, A. 2000. The episodic buffer: a new component of working memory? *Trends in Cognitive Sciences,* 4(11):417–423.

Badjanova, J. & Iliško, D. 2014. Holistic philosophy based teaching approaches in Latvian primary schools: Primary education teachers' view. *Rural Environment Education Personality* (REEP). Proceedings of the International Scientific Conference, (vol. 7), March 7th–8th February 2014, LLU, Jelgava, Latvia. 271:22–28.

Badjanova, J. & Iliško, D. 2015. Holistic approach as viewed by the basic school teachers in Latvia. *Discourse and Communication for Sustainable Education,* 6:132–140.

Baines, E., Blatchford, P. & Kutnick, P. 2017. *Promoting effective group work in the primary classroom: A handbook for teachers and practitioners.* London: Routledge.

Banda, D. & Morgan, W.J. 2013. Folklore as an instrument of education among Chewa people of Zambia. *International Review of Education,* 59:197–216.

Bandura, A. 1969. *Principles of behavior modification.* New York, NY: Holt, Rinehart and Winston.

References

Acevedo, V.E. & Hernandez-Wolfe, P. 2014. Vicarious resilience: An exploration of teachers and children's resilience in highly challenging social contexts. *Journal of Aggression, Maltreatment and Trauma*: 473–493. [online] Available from: doi: 0.1080/10926771.2014.904468.

African National Congress. 2017. *5th National policy conference: Social transformation discussion document.* Pretoria, South Africa.

Agianse, D.U., Williams, J.J., Dunnamah, A.Y. & Tumba, D.P. 2015. Conceptual change theory as a teaching strategy in environmental education. *European Scientific Journal*, 11 (35):1857–7881.

Ainscow, M. 2014. Struggling for equity in education: The legacy of Salamanca. In: F. Kiuppis & R.S. Hausstatter (eds). *Inclusive education: Twenty years after Salamanca.* New York: Peter Lang, pp 41–56.

Akoojee, S. 2007. *Private technical and vocational education and training (TVET) and national development: The South African reality.* Doctor of Philosophy thesis, University of Witwatersrand, Johannesburg.

Akoojee, S., Gewer, A. & McGrath, S. 2005. *Vocational education and training in southern Africa: A comparative study.* Cape Town: Human Sciences Research Council.

Alexander, P. 2003. Coming home: Educational psychology's philosophical pilgrimage. *Educational Psychologist*, 38(3), 129–132.

Alicke, M.D., Dunning, D.A. & Krueger, J.I. (eds). 2005. *The self in social judgment.* New York: Psychology Press.

Alidou, H. & Brock-Utne, B. 2006. Teaching practices: Teaching in a familiar langauge. In: H. Alidou, A. Boly, B. Brock-Utne, Y.S. Diallo, K. Heugh & E. Wolff. (eds). *Optimizing learning and education in Africa–The Language Factor.* Paris: ADEA, pp 85–100.

Allinson, C. & Hayes, J. 1996. The cognitive style index. *Journal of Management Studies*, 33:119–135.

American Psychiatric Association. 2013. *Diagnostic and statistical manual of mental disorders.* 5th ed. Arlington, VA: APA.

American Psychiatric Association 2013. *Diagnostic and statistical manual of mental disorders.* 5th ed. Washington, DC: American Psychiatric Association. [online] Available from: https://www.autismspeaks.org/what-autism/diagnosis/dsm-5-diagnostic-criteria. Accessed: 7 July 2017.

An, D. & Carr, M. 2017. Learning styles theory fails to explain learning and achievement: Recommendations for alternative approaches. *Personality and Individual Differences*, 116:410–416. [online] Available from: doi:10.1016/j.paid.2017.04.050.

Anderman, E.M. 2011. Educational Psychology in the twenty-first century: Challenges for our community. *Educational Psychologist*, 46(3):185–196.

Anderman, E.M. 2014. *Classroom motivation.* Boston, MA: Pearson, p 157.

Ansah, S.K. & Ernest, K. 2013. Technical and vocational education and training in Ghana: A tool for skill acquisition and industrial development, *Journal of Education and Practice*, 4(16):172–180.

Lessons for South Africa

There are several areas for development within the education sector that can be strengthened to improve TVE:

- Distinct and connecting pathways for learners entering higher education through the different education programmes can be highlighted;
- Public–private integration in policy, educational programme development, curriculum delivery and school–industry–community partnerships;
- Creating good balance between national and local policies and standards;
- Notable articulation between programmes and qualifications;
- Quality teacher education, eg, well qualified and knowledgeable teachers who know the workplace and its demands; and
- Potential to develop a special policy framework for expanding TVE in South Africa, particularly at identified schools of specialisations.

The focus on TVE is essential to help unemployed youth at risk. Furthermore, it is most likely to result in a steady increase in artisan and technical skills in the country which is currently a serious problem. With the focus on TVE, the South African government expects the number of youth in TVE to increase from 650 000 in 2013 to 'one million by 2015 and 2, 5 million by 2030' (Department of Higher Education and Training, 2013:xii).

Conclusion

Globally, the need for relevant technical and vocational skills has risen with the advent of technology. This is particularly true in many African countries, including South Africa. We need to prepare youth who can compete in a global society. It is in this context that this chapter highlighted how South Africa could do well by investing in TVE at an early age to address its critical shortage of technical and artisan skills. TVE could also provide better learning and work opportunities for youth at risk and thus close both the skills development and youth unemployment gaps, finally addressing the many socio-economic challenges mentioned earlier in this chapter. The South African government, the private sector and NGOs can actively become part of the process of better preparing future artisans and technicians for the realities that they will face in the evolving technological world. In this way, private companies can become part of the quest towards social justice for at-risk youth and contribute towards better preparing them for the world of work.

knowledge in local contexts, while being sensitive to global imperatives' through 'facilitating the transition of learners from education institutions to the workplace' (Department of Basic Education, 2012:1). This will give employers sufficient learner profiles that show their competences (Department of Basic Education, 2010). In turn, the process can promote social transformation by ensuring that past imbalances are redressed, and that equal educational opportunities are provided for all groups of our population (Department of Basic Education, 2010). In addition, Rashid (2011) suggests career development interventions to support individuals attempting to deal more effectively with the influence of work. While there are various factors that can keep such a needed intervention from succeeding, the advantages of fully implementing such initiatives nationally outweigh the challenges. It is, however, important to highlight the envisaged challenges so as to develop an intervention that will effectively address them.

Potential challenges in implementing the three stream system

The potential challenges in implementing the three stream system may be:
- Balancing the legacy created by the apartheid system to equalise the quality of TVE for all South African learners. Stigmatisation of TVE as a 'poorer' and 'inferior' form of education still haunts South Africa today.
- Many parents view artisan training as unsuitable for further education of their children. It is perceived as too 'non-academic'.
- Current TVET Colleges cater for children 15 years and above. Many parents want their children to study with learners their own age.
- TVET Colleges do not provide extra-curricular activities, like culture and sport, causing a gap in the holistic development of its learners.
- There is no smooth transition from Grade 9 into TVET Colleges.
- There is insufficient subject choice. Learners cannot choose particular combinations suited to the vocational field they want to pursue.
- The subjects mathematics and physical sciences still remain academic rather than addressing the needs of learners who may be interested in TVE.
- TVET Colleges are managed by the Department of Higher Education and Training, while GET and FET are managed by the Department of Basic Education. The lack of continuity in education and conspicuous articulation between these two departments present a challenge.

However, not all is doom and gloom. There are some valuable lessons for TVE in South Africa.

and technical drawing, and will be aimed at learners who want to study trades like boiler making and fitting and turning after school. **The technical occupational stream** is aimed at producing learners who can leave matric and immediately enter the workplace, with skills like spray painting, woodwork, and hairdressing (Mweli, 2016).

While the Department of Basic Education has classified these as three streams in their pilot, this chapter refers to the latter two streams as TVE. All these efforts are geared towards meeting the goal of universal primary education—stimulated by goal four of the Sustainable Development Goals (UN Department of Economics and Social Affairs, 2016) and the Education for All initiative led by UNESCO, thus increasing the demand for vocational education and training that leads to innovation and lifelong employability (Chepkemei, Watindi, Cherono, Ng'isirei & Rono, 2012; European Commission, 2013; UNESCO, 2016).

Although TVE has the potential to develop skills that are essential for socio-economic growth, national development, employment and job creation in South Africa (Ansah & Ernest, 2013), the negative historical view, poor policy and lack of cohesion between education and industry can lead to its failure (Killian, Tendayi & Augustine, 2009). Further, Arfo (2015) argues that TVE programmes fail due to poor planning. In addition, selecting the wrong personnel involved within the planning poses a potential threat to the success of this much needed programme in South Africa.

Meeder (2006) argues that integrating TVE into school programmes can re-engage youths by encouraging active learning that offers them pathways to re-imagine their future aspirations and goals (cited in Lamb, 2011:64). This shows that TVE can ensure school completion because it provides important programmes that will, according to Lamb (2011), re-engage potential and early school leavers. Therefore, introducing TVE early in the learners' education system can benefit the youth who drop out of school before Grade 9 as they would have acquired the skills needed to find rewarding employment and therefore be self-reliant (Chepkemei, 2012).

Relevance of TVE to South African schools and classrooms

Considering the above discussions, the need to develop a comprehensive TVE framework that will provide an integrated structure in the senior phase of schooling in the South African curriculum cannot be underestimated. This framework will further inform theory, practice and policy to ensure that the curriculum fulfils what it is meant to do; that is 'to promote the idea of grounding

countries are known to be high-income countries, TVE is an ongoing research project that seems to be needed all over the world, as it can benefit all countries in wonderful ways. The importance of vocational education in schools has been identified as the key link between education and employment (OECD, 2010).

TVE and its system has always been heavily influenced and shaped by a country's history, with South Africa not being an exception to this trend (Akoojee, Gewer & McGrath, 2005). Just as the educational system was influenced by the colonisation of South Africa as well as the social and discriminatory policies implemented under apartheid, so was its TVE system. Around the world, there has always been competition for work-related vocational skills, knowledge and expertise in the market, with vocational education yielding vocationally skilled and trained workers for the global world of work (Kipkemoi, 2015).

In African countries such as Kenya, vocational subjects have been found to be extremely useful at the primary school level (Kipkemoi, 2015). It is argued that vocational education at the primary school level enables learners to appreciate vocational skills in the world of work and the dignity of manual work, as well as equipping them for further education. In a study by Akoojee, Gewer and McGrath (2005) it was found that the reputation of TVE in Botswana was poor. Similar to the South African context, in Botswana TVE was perceived to produce poor quality learners, staff, curricula and resources. The study also revealed that the community regarded TVE as a second rate educational option and that it was considered a dumping ground for failures. Botswana also had a Brigades programme, which provided practical skills training to the youth to improve self-reliance. The programme offered skills such as auto mechanics, bricklaying, plastering, carpentry, electrical, forestry, general agriculture, plumbing and textiles/dressmaking, bookkeeping, sewing, horticulture, computer skills, farming, gardening, non-formal education, business skills, knitting and textiles (Akoojee, Gewer & McGrath, 2005). However, since this programmes did not lead to certification, it appeared to be almost non-operational.

In transforming the education system in South Africa, more emphasis has been placed on maths, science and English as reported in ANA results (Department of Basic Education, 2016), while little has been said about the importance of TVE as a vehicle to grow the economy. The currently piloted three-tier education system will hopefully see about 60% of learners completing technical qualifications. According to the department, the plan is currently implemented in 58 schools.

The system will diversify the options in terms of subjects and include academic, technical vocational and technical occupations choices. **The academic stream** will resemble the current schooling system, with a focus on academic studies. **The technical vocational stream** will include subjects like engineering

2. None of the generic primary school subjects at Grades 4–7 focus on introducing TVE and training to learners. This exclusion leaves a huge gap in terms of skills development in the country.

Currently, the education system comprises of three main phases, namely: the general education and training (GET) phase, which caters for learners from Grades 1–9. This is followed by the further education and training (FET) phase from Grades 10–12, then higher education and training institutions (HEI) (Department of Basic Education, 2013). According to the South African Schools Act No. 84 of 1996 (Republic of South Africa, 1996) the GET phase is compulsory for children aged 7–15 years and it is assumed that by this age learners will have passed their Grade 9. However, the reality is that approximately 15% of learners around the age of 15 do not reach Grade 9, due to a myriad of challenges such as repeating grades, dropping out of school and socio-economic conditions (Department of Basic Education, 2015; Statistics South Africa, 2016).

While primary education is aimed at preparing learners for general life as well as for higher education studies, FET and HEI is aimed at preparing learners for entering the world of work. It is during the FET phase that technical vocational education and training (TVET) is introduced through TVET Colleges, preparing learners to be skilled in specific occupations so that they can be immediately productive in the workplace (Department of Higher Education and Training, 2013). However, a gap exists in the system as TVET seems not to work according to policy, especially considering the myriad of socio-economic challenges experienced by a majority of South African learners long before they can reach the FET phase.

These challenges have a negative impact not only on the economy of the country, but also on the education of children and youth in general and leads to many of these children being categorised as youth at risk (Moore, 2006; Pillay, 2012). To address this gap while keeping to the promise of quality education for all, we need to strengthen teacher continuous professional development and capacity building in TVE. This will then provide the learners with a sense of hope in their schooling and curtail them from falling prey to a variety of social ills, including crime, teenage prostitution, teenage pregnancies and substance abuse.

Trends in technical and vocational education

The debate on TVE has a long standing history in the world. Many countries such as Australia, Netherlands, Switzerland, Germany, Canada and Singapore have a strong focus on TVE in their school curriculum (Cook, 2013; State Secretariat for Education, Research and Innovation, 2014). Although the above-mentioned

more susceptible to risk and this was evident in the 3rd South African National Youth Risk Behaviour Survey (Reddy, James, Sewpaul, Sifunda, Ellahebokus, Kambaran & Omardien, 2013) where it was found that the youth experienced significant levels of sadness and hopelessness. While this finding is alarming, it is not surprising, since this could be one of the devastating consequences of the apartheid legacy. As scientists, we should take care not to consistently point to causal links between apartheid and current-day challenges for our youth, yet the negative impact that the legacy of apartheid has on the youth which still seems to prevail twenty years down the road of democracy (Pillay, 2012) cannot be denied. The challenges of poverty, crime, drug and substance abuse, unemployment, inequality, HIV/AIDS, child and youth headed households, and school violence prevail in South Africa, negatively affecting national development, and in turn, the learning and development of learners (Diale, 2016; Diale, Pillay & Fritz, 2014). These challenges should be viewed from a bio-ecological systems perspective since youth both influence and are influenced by these challenges (Bronfenbrenner, 1986). Akoojee (2007) argues that skills development is an essential strategy to respond to these challenges. Despite Akoojee's (2007) argument for skills development in South Africa, the country's history plays an essential role in understanding the current situation.

Contextualising technical and vocational education in South Africa

In order to understand the importance of TVE in the school curriculum and its influence on the National Development Plan (NDP), we need to first differentiate between technical and vocational education (TVE) and technical and vocational education and training (TVET) as used in this chapter.

TVE refers to technical and vocational related subjects that can be introduced with the general education and training phase which caters for grades one to nine. TVET refers to programmes and qualifications offered at TVET Colleges (formerly known as FET Colleges), catering for students in the further education and training phase which is Grades 10 to 12 and post-school studies.

In addition, the history and background of the South African schooling system is also important. While the post-1994 democratic education system and the new curriculum introduced new subjects at schools which gave more choices to learners, two major downfalls were observed:
1. Vocational subjects such as bricklaying, boiler making and mechanics were excluded in the new curriculum, leading to limited subject choice options for learners presenting with technical and vocational education aptitude (Centre for Development and Enterprise, 2012). These were introduced at TVET Colleges only.

do manual labour as technical or vocational jobs were reserved for their white counterparts (Centre for Development and Enterprise, 2012). Black South Africans who were working in the building construction and motor industries were colloquially called 'dagga boys' meaning those who mixed the mud for the builders, and 'spanner boys' meaning those who gave the technician or mechanic the spanner to do the job, while their white counterparts were technicians and artisans. This black/white divide was further widened by the first democratic government's decision in 1994 to shut down technical high schools, or reduce their subjects from 16 to four—a decision referred to as a 'scandalous mistake' by the government (Mweli, 2016). Unfortunately, this political decision had a disastrous impact on the black communities as most township technical high schools were shut down. Some technical high schools are still functioning, but access to these schools is hampered by issues such as geographical distances and also the language of teaching and learning. In addition, it is becoming increasingly difficult to find qualified teachers for these schools, since many of the teacher education programmes in these fields have been discontinued. It is from this historical background that as a country, more than twenty years into a democracy, the legacy of the apartheid policies still haunt South Africa, leading to many learners still being compromised, and hence being side-lined in the fields of technical and vocational education. The Department of Basic Education is currently working on a three-tier education system to rectify the current situation. This chapter advocates for early introduction of technical and vocational education pathways in the South African school curriculum as a conduit to a quality sustainable and inclusive education for all.

Why is technical and vocational education (TVE) important in the school curriculum?

World-wide, youth are at risk due to social, political, economic, psychological and environmental factors. The term 'at risk' could often be contentious since it has no consistent definition and could sometimes have deleterious effects of stigmatising particular groups (Moore, 2006). Furthermore, some may argue that children themselves should not be seen as being at risk, but it would be more appropriate to view families and communities as at risk (Moore, Vandivere & Redd, 2006). Generally, most definitions of youth at risk highlight their backgrounds which make them vulnerable to some form of victimisation and exploitation as a result of environmental, social and family circumstances. This is most likely to have a negative impact on their personal development and disrupt their smooth transition into the economy and society.

The above definition and contestations of youth at risk succinctly depicts the South African scenario. One may even argue that youth in South Africa are

48 Pathways to technical and vocational education in the school curriculum

BOITUMELO M DIALE

Vocational education programmes have made a real difference in the lives of countless young people nationwide; they build self-confidence and leadership skills by allowing students to utilize their unique gifts and talents.
(Conrad Burns)

Introduction

The field of Technical and Vocational Education and Training, or TVET, requires both definition and differentiation from other designations. Throughout the course of history, various terms have been used to describe elements of the field that are now conceived as comprising TVET. These include: Apprenticeship Training, Vocational Education, Technical Education, Technical-Vocational Education (TVE), Occupational Education (OE), Vocational Education and Training (VET), Career and Technical Education (CTE), Workforce Education (WE), Workplace Education (WE) etc. Several of these terms are commonly used in specific geographic areas.
(UNESCO-UNEVOC, nd)

For many years in South Africa, technical and vocational education (TVE) has been a service available to a privileged minority. The rapidly growing industrial and mining fields in the 19th and 20th centuries saw technical and vocational skills introduced in schools to address the growing need for artisan training (Centre for Development and Enterprise, 2012). Despite this need, the majority of South Africans were never exposed to TVE. Those exposed were made to

hopefully evident, the possibilities are multiple and depend much on individual preferred destinations and routes. The heart-felt personal accounts of the value of educational psychology in practitioners' professional lives may resonate with readers' career plans and dreams, and serve as encouragement to pursue those very dreams.

Regardless of specialisation in either educational support or in the psychological fields, studies in educational psychology also offer the opportunity to do research and engage in scholarly activities in higher education as an **academic**. This may require postgraduate studies up to a PhD level.

After **G** qualified as a teacher in the FET phase, she studied for an honours degree, which allowed her to register as a psychometrist with the HPCSA. This was followed by a Master's degree in educational support, after which she obtained a PhD. These qualifications allowed her to be appointed in an academic department, with research as a special interest. Among other topics she focused on researching macro-systemic interventions within schools. She tells her story in the case study box that follows.

> **CASE STUDY**
>
> Educational psychology is and has always been fundamental to my work as academic specialising in educational support. Knowledge of human learning and development theory and practice, the central foci of educational psychology, is crucial when supporting the development of schools as learning communities, for teacher training to address diverse learning abilities and needs, and for the support of learner education and achievement.
>
> Additionally, educational psychology has also contributed to my teaching responsibilities in this position.
>
> Educational psychology understands human learning and development from a lifelong perspective. Knowledge of learning and developmental theory and practice is therefore vital in many work environments, but especially within the context of education. Knowledge of the social, emotional and cognitive processes involved in learning is imperative for teacher education in higher education settings, but also in schools and classrooms. Teachers cannot develop classrooms as quality learning contexts to ensure good learning without a sound understanding of these theories and practice, and likewise educational psychologists need this knowledge to be able to support teachers, parents and learners.

Conclusion

As a reflective exercise, it might be useful to ponder the following questions:
- What clarity has been gained about routes necessary to consider towards a preferred and attractive destination?
- What new and alternative destinations have come to the fore whilst reading this chapter?

The tentative map provided can hopefully make navigating a career easier. This chapter, however, is not intended as a comprehensive list of all the available employment opportunities after having studied educational psychology. As it is

services, early childhood development centres, technical and vocational education and training institutions, correctional facilities, primary healthcare centres, district hospitals, crisis and trauma centres, places of safety, centres for people with disabilities, faith-based organisations, and non-governmental organisations.

Being able to register with the HPCSA as an **educational psychologist** requires completing a Master's degree in educational psychology, as well as a 12-month full-time internship. This registration allows for private practice, or practice as a school psychologist within departments of education and in schools. Non-governmental organisations (NGOs) delivering service to formal or informal educational settings also employ educational psychologists. The combined stories of **E** and **F** explain their work in private practice.

Both **E** and **F** completed Master's degrees in educational psychology and subsequently registered as educational psychologists with the HPCSA. After **E** was employed at a private mainstream school, a special school and at an institution of higher education, she is currently, as is **F**, self-employed in private practice.

> **CASE STUDY**
>
> Studying educational psychology and gaining knowledge regarding the social, emotional and cognitive processes involved in learning has helped me in applying and recommending specific interventions to improve the learning process in the lives of clients I work with every day. This includes the educational development of children, adolescents and students, but also doing work with a specific focus on barriers to learning, such as attention deficit hyperactivity disorder (ADHD), difficulties with reading, mathematics, written expression, receptive and expressive language, visual perception, auditory processing, fine motor skills, anxiety and other emotional difficulties—to name just a few. Without my knowledge of educational psychology and my academic background as well as ongoing training, I would not be able to assist clients who visit my practice effectively.
>
> Educational psychology encompasses a vast amount and variety of knowledge that enables one to work in private practice—something that requires a high level of expertise. A thorough background in education as well as in psychology is necessary for the work of an educational psychologist.

F elaborates by mentioning that she often consults with teachers and support staff at schools about learners' functioning in the school environment. She states that her initial training as a teacher provided her with the necessary knowledge to have a thorough understanding of how school systems work. This often informs her recommendations after a formal psycho-educational assessment.

> LSEs also facilitate staff training regarding the following topics: learning, life skills challenges, disability challenges, and literacy and numeracy difficulties within the context of the specific school. Different textbooks, readers, online blogs, articles and my own lived experience as a university student enable me to provide this training.
>
> To summarise, educational psychology has provided me with knowledge on how to identify barriers to learning that learners may experience, the ability to support their needs, and made it possible for me to be able to contextually put apt frameworks, programmes and interventions in place.

More career possibilities exist regarding educational support, for instance providing support as a private endeavour, within departments of education or in informal environments. Registered counsellors working within school contexts also practice learning support as a core competency, thereby providing primary preventative psychological care. In the case study that follows, graduates **C** and **D** followed different routes (academic qualifications), although both registered as counsellors with the HPCSA. One has developed her expertise further by obtaining a Master's degree in educational support.

Case study

> Educational psychology as a background has helped us as learning support teachers and counsellors to always view a child holistically. Learners' physical and emotional states, educational environment and social interaction necessitate attention. We like to emphasise what a child can do, rather than what a child cannot do. We focus on building a child's self-esteem by developing strengths and using them as a platform to learn new skills and coping mechanisms in their daily lives. Educational psychology has prepared us to make correct referrals, interpret assessment results and have the ability to communicate these to all the relevant role players.
>
> Studies in education and psychology are complementary fields to educational psychology, allowing a comprehensive understanding of a child. With only education as a background, one tends rather to accept the system and its challenges and forgets to look at each child holistically. Educational psychology also helps us to act in the best interest of the child when compiling intervention plans. The subject matter of educational psychology creates opportunities to work as a counsellor, or as a learning support teacher (and not only in a scholastic way).

The overarching role of the registered counsellor is to make psychological services accessible to the diverse South African population, focusing on the enhancement of well-being in different communities and environments. These environments can include (apart from schools) the police and military

Understanding educational psychology

becoming a teacher and the inner personal changes that occurred during her undergraduate studies.

CASE STUDY

> This subject, educational psychology, gave me (A) a lot of practical insight on how I should teach and support children's learning. I now understand the practical steps in responding to a learning barrier, adhering to the SIAS process. The knowledge that I have of educational psychology is however limited. I do not necessarily have time to think of the correct behavioural response when the children come to me with questions. However, even though my actual knowledge is not as sharp, I do remember the realisations that I had and how my thought patterns changed through the different teachings in this subject. I now see myself as a reflective practitioner who processes all behaviour that takes place in my classroom. I have been shaped into a teacher who constantly wants to bring forth transformation and regularly remind myself to check that my classroom and activities are inclusive.
>
> So, I cannot remember the practical 'book' knowledge of the subject and do not necessarily apply it continuously. The insights and inner transformations that I developed while attending the classes have however changed me. I am a teacher who can respond to all the different challenges that come through teaching.

Being an excellent teacher also creates possibilities, such as advancing to more senior positions in school hierarchies, for instance grade head, head of a phase, vice-principal or principal.

There is another destination that you can reach should you continue on this journey—a career as **a learning support practitioner**. This entails training at a postgraduate level. **B**'s story is illustrated in the case study that follows.

CASE STUDY

> I studied a four-year teaching degree, as well as a one-year postgraduate degree specialising in educational support. I am currently employed in a learning support position at a primary school.
>
> As a learning support educator (LSE), it is of utter importance not just to give support to learners in basic scholastic skills, but also to pay attention to addressing intrinsic and extrinsic barriers to learning, within context. By addressing all barriers, one needs to understand the IE framework and paradigm. Educational psychology, in its multidimensionality, helped and still helps me to address educational barriers in order to optimise learning.
>
> The daily practice of an LSE consists of screening assessments in order to support. This is informed by educational psychology theory and principles. Knowledge on how to practically apply the rationale of policy documents in learning support classrooms and in schools is what attracted me to educational psychology whilst studying at university.

The current scope of practice for registered counsellors can be interpreted as emphasising primary psychological care, preventative work, the promotion of social-culturally appropriate psychological well-being, as well as what the World Health Organization, War Trauma Foundation and World Vision International (2011) and, Schultz and Forbes (2014) refer to as 'psychological first aid'. The scope of practice of registered educational psychologists aims to afford complete educational and psychological services and care within the very broad fields of human learning and development (Department of Health, 2011).

Aspiring to enter the South African education scene

In this section, we will try to describe some of the destinations on the map to which educational psychology allows access, as well as some of the routes that can be taken to reach those destinations. Routes may differ, depending on where and when the journey is started. One of the most important characteristics of the map in Figure 47.1 is that a person can reach one destination, stay there a while and use and apply the knowledge that has been acquired in the field, whilst preparing for a change in direction or, alternatively, gaining additional skills. Different training institutions offer different programmes, so it is important to explore all available options regarding the routes to follow towards a specific destination.

Colleagues and graduates from educational psychology programmes have contributed to this chapter by sending their stories of how the subject prepared them for and still contributes to their career paths/destinations. Their stories will illustrate the different roads they have taken and the career positions to which educational psychology has transported them.

It is assumed that studies in education will include modules in educational psychology, as the subject forms part of all curricula in programmes and/or courses in education. The titles of the modules may differ; some institutions may call it educational psychology, while others may call it psychology in (or of) education. As in the rest of this book, the term 'educational psychology' is used.

The first destination that a person may be transported to might be a position as a teacher in the phase that they specialised in. Knowledge of how physical, behavioural, social, cognitive and moral human development unfolds, learning theories and discourses, assessment and support practices in the classroom, and insight into the environmental and relationship factors against the backdrop of an inclusive pedagogy may enhance a person's teaching in relevant and ethical ways. Preparation as a teacher will be enriched by inputs from educational psychology, and will contribute to professional development in the teaching profession. The story below illustrates one graduate's (**A**) journey towards

address barriers to learning that children may experience as early as possible. This unavoidably implies an assessment process during which not only the barriers to learning are identified, but the support needs are also determined (Nel, Nel & Lebeloane, 2016). In an inclusive pedagogy, the confluence of assessment and support is clear in that it is seen as 'a dynamic, continuous, collaborative process, involving all role players in the learner's ecosystemic environment' (Nel, Nel & Lebeloane, 2016:61). The assets, strengths and abilities of the learner and his/her environment are also identified during the learning support process.

Previously, when the medical model informed educational practices, support of learners who experienced difficulties was aimed at changing the child to 'fit in' by 'fixing' intrinsic deficits. This remedial approach to support generally called for interventions by specialist personnel (Swart & Pettipher, 2016). We subsequently have become aware that biological as well as socioecological factors may influence a child's learning. In 2014, the Department of Basic Education introduced the Screening, Identification, Assessment and Support (SIAS) policy document, which suggests a learning support process that is aligned with an inclusive pedagogy (Department of Basic Education, 2014).

Focusing on the psychology component of educational psychology, a debate often referred to as the 'relevance debate' (Pretorius, 2012) has been discussed and written about since the 1980s. During the previous political dispensation in South Africa, psychological services were only available to certain members of the South African population, which promoted and implicitly supported racial classification and oppression (Pretorius, 2012). In addition, the traditional approach to psychology, informed by a medical and clinical model of the field and with psychologists as the experts, also created a power differential between the service provider and the client and subsequently contributed to an exclusive and expert service that was accessible only to people who could afford the services of professionals. The greater majority of South Africans used to be excluded from professional help, and psychology was seen as belonging to and being relevant to only one group.

Currently there is a lively, continuous debate within the profession of psychology in South Africa regarding the different registration categories of psychologists (clinical, counselling, educational, industrial and research) and registered counsellors, and the respective scopes of practice of the profession. This debate, which includes the Professional Board of Psychology as part of the Health Professions Council of South Africa (HPCSA), the Psychological Society of South Africa (PsySSA) and other associations, all the different medical aids, as well as practitioners in many different fields and settings, contributes to reflective practice, an awareness of micro- and macro-systemic influences, as well as individual, systemic and organisational ethical considerations.

several related qualifications in fields such as learning support, counselling or educational support. This chapter will provide you with a deeper understanding of these routes and options.

Some of the major debates and paradigm shifts in educational psychology

Educational psychology attempts to educate professionals to work within an inclusive education (IE) system. The values of a human rights philosophy and legislation in this regard, as opposed to the practical experiences of some teachers, provide heated debates about the foundational principles of such a system. IE principles are based on the human right to learn and include the assumption that all children can learn. Teachers, on the other hand, are often faced with issues arising from cultural, linguistic, physical and developmental diversity in school communities and classrooms whilst trying to set high academic standards. This leads not only to a divide in paradigms and beliefs about IE, but also in the practice of IE in classrooms.

Inclusive education is discussed in detail in various other chapters in this book. For the purpose of career paths in educational psychology, it is deemed important to mention the concept of an inclusive pedagogy. This is an approach to '… teaching that aims to raise the achievement of all children, whilst safeguarding the inclusion of those who are vulnerable to exclusion and other forms of marginalisation' (University of Edinburgh, 2016). Florian (2015) describes such a pedagogical approach as teachers' ways of responding to differences between children without stereotyping and labelling some children as special or different, and without excluding any children from ordinary learning activities in the classroom, therefore providing an inclusive environment for all learners. An inclusive pedagogy addresses, among other phenomena, what Florian refers to as 'bell curve' thinking in education. The bell curve model depicts the idea that 'most phenomena occur around a middle point while a few occur at either high or low extreme ends' (Fendler & Muzzafar, 2008:63, as cited in Florian, 2015:7). Thinking about learners and their learning according to such a model has traditionally influenced teachers' daily practices and organisational structures. This approach has manifested in teaching as a uniform practice for most children, and then 'special' or 'additional' expertise for the outliers at both ends of the spectrum. Inevitably, this leads to exclusionary and unjust practices, albeit that it also provides opportunities for different opinions regarding the practical application of such a pedagogy.

The above flows into another debate in educational psychology, namely the debate on remedial teaching versus learning support. Learning support aims to

developmental phases, as well as when difficulties arise that may present barriers to learning. He encourages a broad perspective that takes into account interactive processes between children and their environments, rather than a simplistic, linear cause-and-effect view. This thinking was the precursor to current popular theoretical discourses informing an understanding of human development as including person factors, social factors and other environmental factors, as well as the interactive nature of relationships among these factors.

Today the subject of educational psychology in South Africa takes into account that the child and the teaching environment, which includes classrooms and learners' homes, are important to address as a whole, rather than only the child as an individual. The education sector in South Africa faces many challenges, including socio-economic factors, social factors, exclusionary practices, curriculum issues, language and communication practices, limited physical and human resources, as well as various intrinsic barriers that may influence development and learning (Donald, Lazarus & Moolla, 2014).

The content covered in an educational psychology course is therefore often focused on promoting individual and community well-being, as well as addressing the above-mentioned barriers to learning and development. Various career possibilities, like teaching, learner support, counselling and more, as illustrated on the map in Figure 47.1, allow the application of the subject content. Studies of human development, learning and motivation, including literacy and numeracy skills like reading and mathematical reasoning, as well as the social and emotional worlds of individuals, form core components. These components also necessitate knowing about cultural and historical influences on learning, teaching, assessment and support.

Your introduction to, growing awareness of and expanding acquaintance with educational–psychological 'knowledges', ways of thinking and ways of being will not only enrich you as an individual, but also equip you to make a significant contribution to the lives of children within the South African education sector.

Educational psychologists, as such, usually start off with an undergraduate degree, which entails strong foundations in both education and psychology. This can be a four-year education degree, which includes psychology as a major; or a three-year degree majoring in psychology, then followed by a teaching qualification. In general, these undergraduate studies are followed by a postgraduate honours degree in psychology or educational psychology and a Master's degree in educational psychology. A Master's degree in educational psychology is followed by an internship, an entrance examination to the profession and registration at the Health Professions Council of South Africa (HPCSA). Along the way, there are however various exit points and routes towards careers within the broad field of educational psychology. There are also

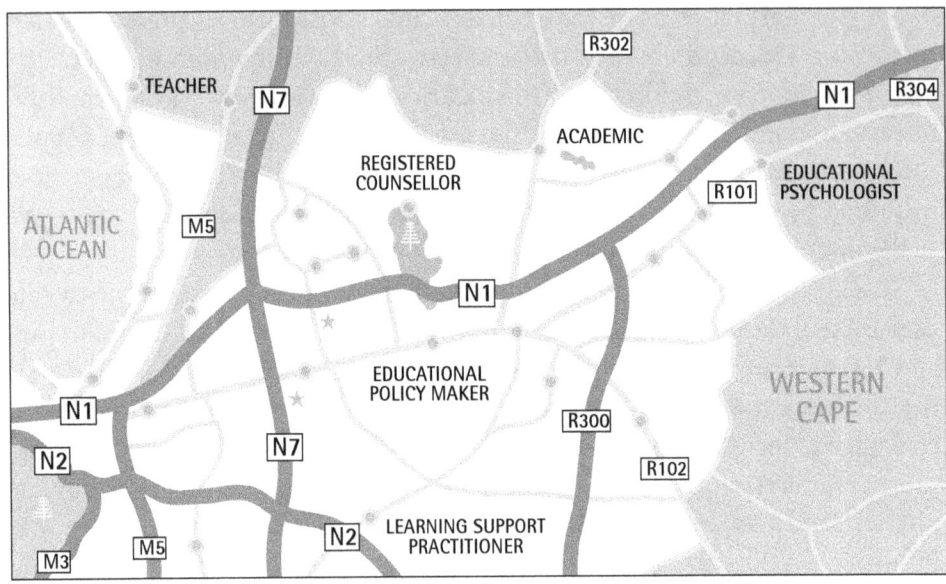

FIGURE 47.1 A map of educational psychology

Different routes to these multiple destinations illustrate the respective subjects, programmes or course choices that can be made. The hope is that this map of educational psychology might enkindle some curiosity, in order to be transported to preferred destinations, or even different potential destinations throughout a career and life.

Why it is important to think about career paths in educational psychology

Historically, the link between psychology and education has existed since the days of the classical philosophers, such as Plato and Aristotle. Among the topics they discussed were '… the role of the teacher, the relationship between teacher and student, … the nature and order of learning, (and) the role of emotion in learning' (Woolfolk, 2014:14).

In the 20th century, educational-psychological researchers focused on themes such as the nature of being human, human development, individual differences, assessment, learning behaviours including memory, cognitive development, intelligence measurement, attention, learning, and how social factors as well as culture affect learning and development processes (Van Niekerk, 1986; Woolfolk, 2014).

Van Niekerk (1986), editor of the first comprehensive text for educational psychologists in South Africa, emphasises the importance of having both educational and psychological insights in order to support children during their

47 A map to career paths within educational psychology

CARLA FEENSTRA & MARIECHEN PEROLD

My lifelong fascination for maps has led me to look at them as a metaphor for my work with people who consult me about a range of concerns. When we sit down together I know that we are embarking on a journey to a destination that cannot be predetermined. I know that we will probably take some extraordinary scenic routes to these unknown destinations. I know that as we approach these destinations we will be stepping into other worlds of experience. (White, 2007)

Introduction

One of the most frequently asked questions at career exhibitions and open days is: With a background in educational psychology, what are the employment possibilities? Maybe this is also on your mind. Does the following question sometimes come up: 'Why should I study educational psychology?'

Within career counselling, theorists popularly refer to the 'ever-changing world of work' and the impact it has on undergraduate students, their programme choices at tertiary level and, ultimately, their career decisions (Maree, 2013:410). This unknown world could be intimidating, but also exciting. White (2007) uses the metaphor of maps for such life situations. 'When I was a young boy it was maps that made it possible for me to dream (about) other worlds ... and imaginatively transport myself to other places.' (White, 2007:3)

In this chapter, the aim is to provide a map highlighting various career possibilities within the field of educational psychology. These are depicted as the various destinations on the map in Figure 47.1.

Conclusion

Our aim as career counsellors should be to enable all people—and not only a privileged few who can afford this often-expensive service—to construct, deconstruct, reconstruct, and co-construct their lives and (re)write their life stories in collaboration with compassionate career counsellors and thereby move forward with hope and confidence. My own research on life design, which was initially based on the first two versions of the life design paradigm and associated models discussed in this chapter, has shown that the life design approach works across cultures. It has shown also that life design counselling for career construction can promote the ability of people from various walks of life and cultures to heal themselves, design and construct successful lives, and make social contributions through their work (Maree, 2015; 2017a; 2017b). Life design counselling can also provide practitioners from different cultures with a viable theoretical and conceptual framework for understanding the unique experiences of disadvantaged people facing career-related crossroads. That said, I encourage readers to conduct research on the applicability of life design in (South) African contexts and report on their findings in order to establish and confirm the value of this exciting approach to career counselling.

'best' ways of collecting career counselling data and with the 'best' ways of administering career counselling. Career counsellors should help learners:

- Identify, understand, and clarify their interests, traits, abilities, and values;
- Identify and relate to their major career-life themes;
- Choose careers that 'fit' their profiles as well as enable them to realise their major life themes;
- Construct themselves in a satisfactory manner; and
- Design successful lives in which they can make meaningful social contributions. (Maree, 2015)

The six-step life design intervention strategy
(Savickas, et al, 2009)

People's idiosyncratic lived experiences shape and inform the six steps of life design counselling. The presenting 'problem' or challenge is identified and articulated jointly by career counsellors and their clients in Step 1. In Step 2, the challenge is contextualised and informed by how clients anticipate they will benefit from life design counselling. Clients are helped to explore their current subjective identity forms (how they see themselves and other people in specific contexts; how they connect with other people—Guichard, 2009; Savickas, et al, 2009). In Step 3, clients' viewpoints are broadened and their career-life stories reviewed and revised. Clients then locate their current challenges in their 'new' stories in Step 4, and in Step 5, clients are encouraged and helped to single out a number of appropriate activities to realise their newly created identity. Step 6 comprises short-, medium-, and long-term follow-ups.

The usefulness of a storied approach to career counselling (parallel to and on a par with 'positivist' approaches) is now generally accepted. In fact, Savickas (2011) and McAdams (2001) stress the importance of harnessing quantitative and qualitative techniques and strategies to elicit and integrate objective information (such as aptitudes and qualities) and subjective information (such as qualitatively elicited life themes) to understand clients better. Early childhood experiences and memories should be factored into any career counselling approach, and the effectiveness of interventions should be evident (Di Fabio & Maree, 2011; Maree, 2013; Savickas, 2012). Most importantly, Savickas (2015) contends that practice leads theory and not the other way around. Researchers and practitioners should not only theorise about what works in career counselling but also conduct research and report on the value and limits of narrative career counselling in one-on-one private settings as well as in small or large group-based contexts, especially non-traditional contexts (Savickas, 2011).

How is life design relevant to South African schools and classrooms?

Career counselling in South Africa

The traditional trait-and-factor method—which is characterised by a top-down 'expert' test-and-tell approach where the learner is 'tested', then receives 'feedback' and is to all intents and purposes 'told' what to study—is still used widely in South African schools today. Learners in under-resourced communities in particular are at a major developmental disadvantage, which further compromises the trustworthiness, reliability, and validity of their choices of subjects and fields of study, contributing to high dropout rates at tertiary level.

From self-actualising to life design, from resemblance to uniqueness

Career counselling as a profession needs to respond to global changes in the occupational world, and the response should not be limited to administering 'vocational guidance' and 'career education' (Savickas, 2011) as had been the case for many decades in the previous century. Rather, career counselling should be aimed at restoring people's belief that they have a future worth living and working for. Life design counselling reflects the global shift in emphasis from a 'self-actualising' approach to one in which life design is promoted; from focusing on resemblance (focusing on how people resemble others and matching them to careers) to uniqueness (focusing on how people make meaning; what makes them unique). Staunton (2015:3–4) argues that:

> ... Savickas draws a distinction between self-actualization approaches to careers interventions and career- and self-construction ones noting that he views the life design approach as being the most pertinent for the post-modern world in which we live.

For South African career counsellors to implement 'best practice', they should post-modernise and restructure their praxis in a way that advances learners' style of choosing and constructing careers, self-construction, and facilitates their life designing in particular (Maree & Molepo, 2017).

A feasible 21st century approach is needed that will enable learners to make meaning in their career-lives, accept authorship of their own career–life stories, and adapt to ever-changing occupational demands. Feedback to learners should be informed by 21st century marketplace realities, and career counselling should help them become employable and adaptable rather than merely finding jobs (Maree, 2009). Career counsellors should familiarise themselves with the life patterns, themes, and subthemes. The ultimate aim of life design counselling is the creation of a space where practitioners and their clients can construct, deconstruct, reconstruct, and co-construct clients' career–life stories to bring about change and forward movement (Savickas, 2011).

Major debates in the field of life design

Maree and Van der Westhuizen (2011) maintain that career counselling in South Africa has always been a contentious issue because of it being embedded in the vocational guidance and career guidance movement in the United States of America and Western Europe. Stead and Watson (2006:181) too urge career counselling researchers in Africa to base career counselling theory and praxis on local conditions, maintaining that Western European and North American perspectives have for far too long been considered the benchmarks for 'contextually appropriate' career counselling theory and praxis. They question the ability of life design (including career construction and life construction) theory and praxis to meet the basic needs of clients in developing country contexts (Watson, 2013).

Watson (2013) argues that the prevailing career and life construction theory, praxis, assessment, and intervention do not cater adequately for the idiosyncratic needs of non-white, non-Western people. Watson (2013) adds that this applies to people in seriously disadvantaged contexts in particular. Maree (2009, 2016, 2017a) warns against the danger of uncritically accepting the validity and reliability of career counselling paradigms, models and practice developed in North America and Europe (including the life design intervention paradigm and associated models) and applying them in developing countries such as South Africa. Maree (2017b) states that little research has been conducted on life design theory and praxis in developing country (including typical African) contexts up till now. Much more research is needed to establish the appropriate and legitimate application of life design counselling in such contexts.

The term 'life design intervention' is unfortunately often used to refer to interventions largely unrelated to what life design actually entails. It should therefore be emphasised that while initial indications (see, for instance, Maree, 2015; McMahon, Watson & Bimrose, 2012) are that life design shows great promise in (South) Africa, it remains a specialist intervention that needs to be studied, researched, practised, and mastered professionally before it can be applied more generally in (South) Africa.

short-, medium-, and long-term assignments, choose careers and construct themselves and their careers satisfactorily, design successful lives, make meaning in their careers, pursue purpose in life, and make social contributions. Three life versions of the design paradigm can be identified.

Three versions of the life design paradigm

In terms of the first version of the life design paradigm (Zunker, 1998), people's meaning-making is promoted via interaction between counsellor and counsellee. They are helped to design their lives by incorporating and drawing on postmodern (narrative) methods such as the lifeline, the collage, and identifying role models. This version emphasises the value of collaborative, group-based dialogues and deliberations but, at the same time, highlights individual (personal) use of life design strategies (Zunker, 1998). In terms of the second version of the paradigm (Campbell & Ungar, 2004), people are helped to proceed through a number of fundamental stages to advance their meaning-making capacity. First, they should determine what they aspire to or want; second, they should take stock of what they already have; third, they should obtain a clear sense of what they are hearing; fourth, they should uncover any limitations that are impeding their ability to make meaning; fifth, they should devise the future they want; sixth, they should 'grow into' their career-life story; and, seventh, they should 'grow out' of their career-life story.

The third version of the life design paradigm has gained global recognition and is being replicated in many contexts, some of them vastly different from the North American/Western European context in and for which it was initially designed and developed. Devised by Savickas, et al (2009), this paradigm is based on the view that how work is structured and organised socially in the 21st century poses serious challenges to career counsellors in their attempts to help clients advance their work–life stories. Based on two career counselling theories that cover career-related performance namely career construction theory (Savickas, 2005) and life construction theory (Guichard, 2005), life design is shaped in a way that renders it holistic, life-long, contextual, and preventive. Five basic beliefs or assumptions direct or govern the notion of life design counselling (Savickas, 2015). First, life design counselling (also referred to as life design for career construction, life designing, or career construction counselling—Savickas, 2015) is premised on the belief that contextual possibilities can advance life design counselling. Second, it is believed that dynamic processes are involved in life design counselling. Third, it is believed that life design counselling proceeds in a non-linear manner. Fourth, it is believed that life design counselling is based on multiple perspectives and, fifth, it is believed that life design counselling uncovers and draws on personal career-

help workers develop a protean approach to work–life ('protean careers' refer to the Greek god Proteus who could shape-shift or transform himself at will) and the resilience needed to deal with work-related transition and trauma (Hall, 1996). Life design counselling offers a viable strategy to achieve these objectives.

Why is life design important?

Background

The concept 'career maturity' has fallen out of favour over the past 20 years or so, with Savickas (1997) suggesting that it be replaced with the term 'career adaptability'. Career counsellors themselves need to adapt and, at the same time, help their clients become more adaptable in terms of the four dimensions of career adaptability (Savickas, 2011), namely concern, control, curiosity, and confidence. They should encourage their clients to show concern about their career lives, demonstrate control over their career lives, show interest in (be curious about) future developments in the world of work, and exhibit confidence in their ability to achieve their career aspirations in rapidly changing occupational environments (Savickas, 2002).

What is life design?

Life design (the first-ever integrated theory of career counselling (Savickas, 2013) comprises 'a 're-view' of career theory and techniques envisioned from different perspectives and elaborated from new premises' (Savickas, 2010:33). The life design paradigm comprises a broader paradigm (Mark Savickas, personal communication, 16 September, 2015) that includes career construction counselling (Hartung, 2015; Savickas, 2011), dialogical self-construction theory (Guichard, 2005), chaos theory (Bright & Pryor, 2005), and systems theory (Patton & McMahon, 2006). Each of these theories is associated with a specific assessment technique and intervention strategy. Whereas, for instance, career construction counselling (Savickas, 2011) is associated with the career construction interview (CCI), the dialogical self-construction theory (Guichard, 2005) is associated with the exploration and exploitation of clients' current system of subjective identity forms (SIFs). Guichard (2005) also underlies the notion of an integrated or blended, qualitative+quantitative approach to career counselling—an approach that complements logical positivism (the 'test-and-tell' approach) with a storied, narrative approach rooted in socio-constructionism (Savickas, 2013) and proposes a contemporary theoretical and conceptual framework for facilitating 'best practice' in career counselling. Here, 'facilitating best practice' (based on life design principles) is defined as empowering people to decide on suitable careers, navigate career-related transitions, navigate

46 Life design: The essence of helping people live successful lives and make social contributions

KOBUS MAREE

The other day I dreamed that I was at the gates of heaven. And St. Peter said, 'Go back to Earth. There are no slums up here.' (Mother Teresa)

Introduction

Today, more than ever before, workers' sense of identity, purpose, usefulness, and meaning-making is being taken away from them by circumstances beyond their control (Maree, 2011). Rising unemployment, the ever-present threat of another financial meltdown, spiralling levels of poverty, and an increase in global instability are some of the reasons for this state of affairs. While rapid changes (brought about largely by information communication technology advances in the world of work over the past two decades in particular) have brought prosperity to some, the situation of low-paid workers has deteriorated. The wage gap between high-paid and low-paid workers has widened, and the socio-economic position of indigent people has weakened. Schwab (2016:3) argues that '(i)n addition to being a key economic concern, inequality represents the greatest societal concern associated with the Fourth Industrial Revolution'.

Maree (2015) encourages career counselling professionals to conduct research and to collect and analyse the data to help them revise the theory and practice of career counselling with a view to planning and executing appropriate strategies to deal with change and its impact on workers—and to facilitate sustainable decent work *for all*. It should be remembered that 'widespread discontent over unemployment and low living standards' (Manfreda, 2016:1) was the second biggest reason for the Arab Spring uprising. An approach is needed that will

10

Careers

Healthy lifestyle and free health screening campaigns

For over four decades, HIV and AIDS has received international attention and as such it is recognised as a global problem. In South Africa, the pandemic impacted negatively on the workforce including university students and graduates. Through using health screening and know-your-status campaigns, the Sefako Makgatho Health Sciences University of South Africa reduced the HIV infection rate from 8% in 2008 to 1.5% in 2015. Changing attitudes and behaviour of people requires a multipronged approach. The more psychologists can understand the relationship between attitude and behaviour and factors that influence both, the better they will become at treating different psychological disorders, thus contributing more to understanding world challenges and complexities (Net-industries, 2017). The growing empirical literature on HIV and AIDS informs student support services at South African universities.

Residences as living and learning spaces

South African universities have actively sought to integrate living and learning spaces on and off campus to improve students' academic performance and success rates. Students are increasingly using social spaces for learning, and the use of technology platforms for learning is also multiplying. These trends impact on the way in which living and learning spaces for students are designed and structured.

The chapter affirms the ideal that students should be afforded the opportunity and freedom to read and grow to become whatever they wish (UK Answers, 2011).

Conclusion

Universities that invest in student support services tend to improve student retention, success and throughput. This chapter presented the view that student support services are an essential and critical part of teaching and learning in tertiary institutions. Students have different needs and can benefit from a variety of support services that are provided. While some of the support services may focus on soft skills and emotional intelligence that increase chances of success at a university, other services focus on both academic and adjustment needs that enhance the quality of student life and experiences, health and wellness, living and learning spaces and sports and recreation. Information provided is presented generically in order to be applicable to all universities in South Africa, with the assumption that the emphasis will be different in various university arrangements. Last but not least, the need for the student support services is a universal one, as universities around the globe provide student support services on a large scale. Student support services are an essential part of higher education in that they enhance teaching and learning and can ensure student retention and success. Students are encouraged to use student support services and achieve according to the best of their abilities and efforts.

Preparedness of school leavers entering tertiary education

Some academics, educationists and universities in the country question the validity of a matric pass as an adequate preparatory certificate for university entrance and as a barometer for undergraduate success. A briefing by the then unit of Higher Education South Africa (HESA) to the Education Portfolio Committee in 2011 acknowledged under-preparation of learners in basic education phases in South Africa as a challenge. Although students are admitted to university on the basis of their matric pass as per government requirement, some institutions do further student assessments on their own in order to plan for early intervention and support of students at risk. There are, however, many people opposed to this view, who see such practice as potentially exclusive, demeaning and even racially motivated.

Free decolonised education (FDE)

This is an education system advocated strongly by students in the Fees Must Fall campaigns. FDE refers to non-payment to the universities and a non-colonial, independent acquisition of knowledge, skills, values, beliefs and habits by students as supported by democratic South Africa (Eye Witness News, 2017). While the above-mentioned description is meaningful and acceptable to some, there are individuals who in turn believe that the current education system has to be completely overthrown to give room to FDE. Some scholars see the latter as non-progressive, dangerous and as misguided views (Eye Witness News, 2017).

Racism in tertiary institutions

It somehow caught South Africans by surprise when racial tensions erupted among students in some universities in the country in 2015, twenty-one years into democracy. As a result, higher education institutions in the country were advised to implement the National Action Plan (NAP, 2015), which is a policy of driven and guided intervention against racism, racial discrimination, xenophobia and related intolerance in higher education. Despite South Africa's history of institutionalised racial segregation and active movements towards redress, the understanding is that racial discrimination exists in almost all countries the world over and very few, if any, are totally free from racism (Daily Mail Online, 2013). After the dismantling of apartheid in 1994, there have been sporadic eruptions of racial tensions in South Africa, not only in universities, but also in the country. It is, however, encouraging to observe that universities are relatively quiet after the adoption of the NAP and sentiments in the country are publicly critical and unsympathetic to people who harbour racist tendencies and practices.

Sports and recreation

Sports and recreation in universities play an important role as an extension of student life into extracurricular activities. Many students play or watch sports as a means of relaxation after a hard day's work. Others participate in sports internationally and dedicate major portions of their time on training and preparation for key sporting events. Sport in universities is therefore played at both competitive and recreational levels. There are numerous sporting activities for students in South Africa. They can include athletics, aikido, archery, aquatics, badminton, basketball, chess, cycling, fencing, gymnastics, soccer, rugby, netball, hockey, lifesaving, cricket, tennis, table tennis, canoeing, rowing, judo, trampolining, volleyball, water polo, wrestling, triathlon, karate and boxing for both male and female students. On the cultural side, students can, for instance, participate in debating, serenading, music performances, choirs, art weeks and multilingual storytelling events. Recreational activities can include hiking, mountaineering, student-bashes, 'Miss and Mr University' competition, poetry reading and recitations, music appreciation and gospel singing. It is important for students to balance their academic studies with involvement in sports and recreation in order to create sufficient opportunities for relaxation.

Major debates

The sections highlight the major debates in higher education currently being discussed.

Access to higher education in South Africa: A major concern

Sentiments about the poor quality of education in general and inadequate funding for students in higher education, rank very high on the list of education challenges in South Africa. Basic education, that is Grades R to 12, has to improve in order to ensure meaningful access and success of students in higher education (Parliamentary Monitoring Group, 2011). Furthermore, the inadequacy of funds provided by the national government to higher education (Universities South Africa, 2016) and to the majority of students, particularly the previously disadvantaged students, is another area of concern (Parliamentary Monitoring Group, 2011). The current allocation procedures seem to increase student debt and reduce psychological and emotional well-being as students accumulate huge debt by the time they graduate. Whilst Universities South Africa (2016) empathises with the plight of students on exorbitant university fees, the freezing of fee increment to universities by government in 2016 will have long-term consequences to the universities' budgets and plans.

within the confines of the residences. There has been major success in some of the innovation around residences providing living and learning spaces. Some of the universities that have enjoyed success in the said area are the University of Pretoria, Stellenbosch University, and Tshwane University of Technology.

Financial aid and bursaries

The financial aid division is responsible for administration and management of the financial aid scheme. Operations involve student applications, processing and distribution of loans from the government of South Africa. At the time of publication, student loans in South Africa are equivalent to a bursary of 40 % off total fees, or a bursary for the total fee if the student passes all modules at first- or second- (or third) year in a four-year degree. If the student passes all modules in their final year and they are graduating in that year, the full loan, specifically for the final year, is convertible to a full bursary. The financial aid division also manages students' bursaries and sponsorships from the private sector. Students, who cannot afford timeous payments, are encouraged to take loans or make payment plans with the university in order to pay off their university fees and reduce their outstanding debt, which should be paid in full before graduation.

Special needs

International students

International students are foreign students who have study permits and have been admitted to study at universities in South Africa. Because of their unique and special needs, most institutions open a unit and provide dedicated staff to take care of the well-being of international students. The needs of international students are many. They may vary from feelings of homesickness to failure to relate to different students. They may also be perplexed by the new culture and their own challenges to adjust to and accommodate new changes in a foreign country.

Students with disabilities

Similar to most countries around the world, South Africa has also legislated access and support for students with disabilities and special needs in higher education institutions. While some progress has been made, there are still gaps between policy directives, infrastructure and provision of quality education to all in South Africa, and the students with disabilities are often at the receiving end (Mutanga, 2017). The ideal is that all students, including those with disabilities, should be fully catered for and supported according to their needs and abilities.

Student health and wellness

This support section consists of the medical health clinic and guidance and counselling sections. Other subsections may include peer counselling and education, career assessment and counselling. The medical clinic provides primary health care, HIV/AIDS counselling and emergency services. The medical clinic often operates with professional nursing sisters and fulltime or part-time medical practitioners and emergency medical officers. All staff need to be registered with their respective boards in the Health Professional Council of South Africa (HPCSA). In addition to the provision of their specific professional services, all health and wellness staff are expected to provide first aid and run first-aid training to students and staff. Counselling is provided by qualified psychologists who often work with peer counsellors. The latter provide an essential service by students to other students on issues students find uncomfortable to discuss with adults. Peer counsellors are always supervised by professional counsellors and psychologists. Career guidance, assessment and counselling are also provided by qualified staff. Junior staff are supported with regular consultations by senior staff and usually have referral procedures to follow when faced with challenges and in need of support.

Student housing

Student housing includes off-campus accommodation and its oversight management.

The South African Higher Education Act No. 101 of 1997 (Republic of South Africa, 1997) regulates student housing in public universities through its policy on the minimum norms and standards that provide specifications for higher education institutions in South Africa. As students come from different parts of South Africa and from other countries in Africa and abroad, most students require on-campus accommodation. Students frequently wish to reside on campus or close to the residences under the direct control of the university. Others prefer to stay in accredited privately owned residences close to and collaborating with universities. These facilities are usually of better quality, but cost a little more than campus accommodation. In rural settings where student accommodation is limited, some private owners are noncompliant to set policies, but given time, legislation will eventually close the gap. Off-campus student accommodation plays an important role as many universities cannot provide sufficient student residences within their premises. Most universities and private owners often cooperate to upgrade residences to be conducive to teaching and learning. Unlike in the past where residences were usually noisy and remotely controlled by staff, the intention currently is to convert them into living and learning spaces where students can actually carry out university studies with little or no disruption

- Student governance and leadership;
- Student training and development;
- Health and wellness;
- Student housing;
- Financial aid and bursaries;
- Students with special needs; and
- Sports and recreation.

The next sections give a brief discussion of the roles and functions of each subdivision.

Student governance and leadership

This subdivision works directly with the student leadership structures and trains students in good governance and leadership. Some of the important structures are the Students' Representative Council (SRC), student parliament, political formations, academic societies and social clubs. The SRC is the students' voice and mouthpiece that links all student formations through their respective subdivisions to its strategic officer, advocate and policy advisor in the office of the dean of students. Student parliament usually presides over the student political formations, academic societies and social clubs. This may take various forms at different universities. The South African Student Union (SAUS) is a national student structure that represents all SRCs in the country.

Student training and development

Students' needs analysis is an ongoing process that is aimed at providing effective and relevant support services to students. The training and development unit is responsible for all in-house student training and workshops. At some universities, this unit may reside under student support services, while at others, it may perhaps be found under the broader academic umbrella of teaching and learning. They also provide essential support to the first-year experience (FYE), which is student training, support and development specifically designed for new first-year students as they enter the university system. This support extends up to the end of their first year of study. Also forming an integral and essential part of the FYE is student orientation (SO) which takes two to four weeks of intensive information sessions of guided support and instruction on essential and critical resources such as facilities, programmes, services, venues, personnel, sport and recreational, academic, curricular and extra-curricular activities on campus. In areas where the training and development staff of the university may not have the relevant capacity, training may be outsourced to competent service providers.

New students often find too many activities competing for their attention and they may be unable to deal with such challenges. Training in appropriate soft skills such as prioritising, communication, time management, adaptability, adjustment, and teamwork become essential in a stressful university environment. It is safe to say that most students require support with regards to their academic work, personal, interpersonal, and sociocultural challenges. If students know what type of help is available, they can empower themselves and take advantage of the services on offer. As pointed out by Sir Francis Bacon in 1597, 'Knowledge is power' (McCoy, 2013), and the saying still enjoys currency today.

What then are functions of student support services in universities?

Critical functions of student support services in institutions of higher learning worldwide are to:

- Improve the quality of student life and enhance student experience;
- Train and develop students in soft skills for survival in tertiary institutions;
- Empower capable students to help other students in distress and support those at risk;
- Help institutions not only to provide, but also manage, their living and learning spaces to be conducive to teaching and learning;
- Ensure that student success and retention are maximised;
- Facilitate engagement and participation in extracurricular activities; and
- Provide information to prospective students, parents, sponsors and other stakeholders.

Coordination and provisioning of student support services

Figure 45.1 illustrates the typical student support services available at a university. Student support services involve an intricate network of connected entities that all seek to serve the students. Institutions that invest in quality student support services that are student centred optimise their potential to improve student performance and success across all academic years. The structure of the organogram will differ from institution to institution. The example that is used in this chapter is therefore only a guideline that can be adjusted to various tertiary environments.

Office of the Dean of Students

In most institutions, the head of student support services is the Dean of Students. The division is further managed by senior staff in middle management that may lead the following subdivisions:

South African universities face a vast challenge of supporting and helping students as the majority come from previously disadvantaged backgrounds. Student support services run training and development programmes, which start at the beginning of the first academic year, soon after registration and continue to the end of the year. Beyond the first year, there are usually ongoing support programmes for senior students who struggle to cope and who are in need of academic support in specific areas. Often these students experience a medley of problems in the academic realm and may run the risk of dropping out if help is not forthcoming. Students at risk are identified through various assessment programmes. In many universities student support services may overlap with student academic development. While the former focuses on orientating new students, assisting them to adjust to the tertiary environment and offering ongoing support, the latter deals with all students, the academic skills training and development that render students at risk if such skills are underdeveloped. The student support services are usually set up to enhance student adjustment and to develop 'survival' and learning skills, with the aim of increasing the chances of academic retention and success. Nelson Mandela highlighted in his conversations the importance of education and the fact that it is the most powerful weapon to change the world (Sowetan Live, 2013). It is in this spirit that student support services at South African universities often operate.

> **NOTE**
> This division is informed by and aligned to the real needs of the students and may be hampered by budgetary constraints.

Why are student support services important?

Without a fully functioning division of the student support services at universities, the majority of students would struggle to complete their studies and attrition rates would certainly be higher. Universities may also fail to graduate the majority of students within the stipulated time. The university's student throughput as well as output can be significantly compromised if students in need are not supported effectively. The negative effects when the free flow of incoming and outgoing students are hindered, have been recognised (University of Zululand Revised Rules, 2012). In monetary terms, skewed relationships between intake and graduation rates of students at university are seen as wasteful expenditure. It will impact negatively on a university's financial sustainability (Universities South Africa, 2016), as well as the national skills development and economic growth of the country (African National Congress, 2017).

Efficacy of the student support services

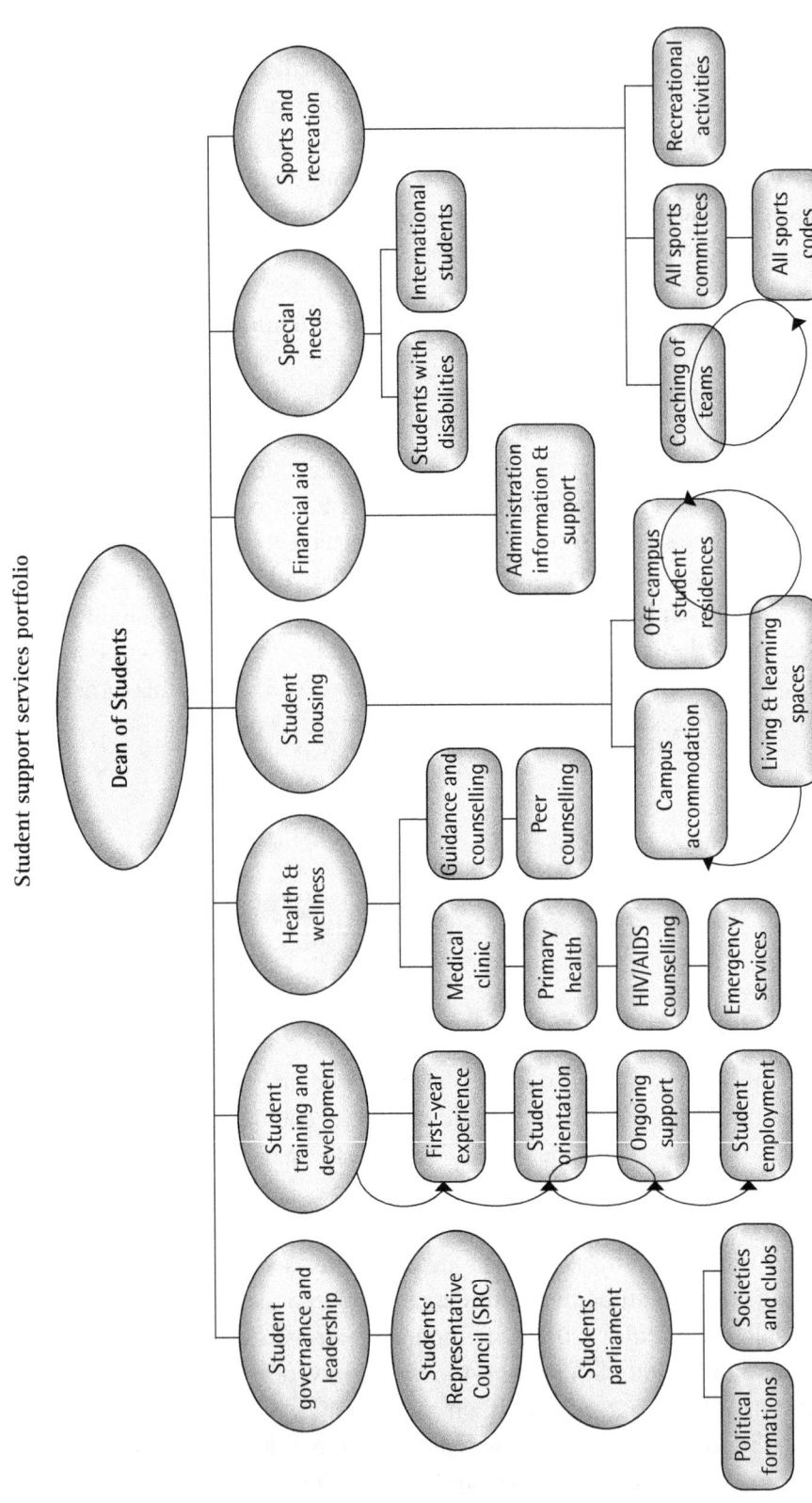

FIGURE 45.1 A typical student support services division at a university

45 Efficacy of the student support services

MANDLA MORRIS HLONGWANE

Our children are the rock on which our future will be built, our greatest asset as a nation. They will be the leaders of our country, the creators of our national wealth, those who care for and protect our people. (Nelson Mandela, 3 June 1995)

Introduction

Student support services are constituent divisions of universities. This chapter seeks to explicate what these support services are and to foreground the dire need for such critical, strategic university structures. The student population at any university is usually the largest, most diverse component of the university community. Students may differ in respect of culture, language, age, gender, experiences, ability, learning potential, home background and scholastic and academic history. Common among students is that they all meet the minimum requirements to enter tertiary institutions despite their differences. For many, personal and group differences may be vast. Given such differences, teaching students without adequate preparation and support would compromise optimum intellectual development, independent thinking and self-actualisation. Environmental factors include significant levels of cumulative under-preparedness in some students, depending on the situational factors at play and the subsequent dynamics of these factors. While universities generally adhere to the good practice of helping students to adjust to challenging, complex university environments, conditions should ultimately be conducive to learning and independent studies.

- Implement safety measures in and out of class such as not seating the learner close to a window (to prevent him/her from falling against the window during a seizure);
- Support and advise parents of learners with epilepsy through knowledge of neuroscience and neuropsychology;
- Promote social inclusion by demystifying myths about epilepsy;
- Collaborate with health care professionals involved with the learner with epilepsy; and
- Translate knowledge of neuroscience and neuropsychology to other neuro-physical impairments such as cerebral palsy. A certain type of cerebral palsy (ataxia) could be caused by damage to the cerebellum that regulates balance and coordination.

Conclusion

A human brain can be viewed as an organ with functional regions, but it is so much more. It crowns the human race with endless potential although ongoing research still has to unlock many of its mysteries. The brain cannot be confined to absolute terms as illustrated by the case of Phineas Gage who was not expected to walk and talk shortly after his brain injury.

life, ie, the integration of body, brain, mind and social-cultural context (Lowe, Lee & Macvarish, 2015).

The rise of the neuroscience paradigm is also not without problems in the psychotherapies. According to Johnson (2009), a neuroscientist who specialises in post-traumatic stress disorder, the neural (or 'brain') basis of therapies is often based on simplified presentations of highly complex research. For example, data about the hormone cortisol that largely regulates stress reactions are quite inconsistent. Therefore, stressful events do not necessarily impact brain development negatively. Another example is left/right brain functioning that refers to the two 'halves' or hemispheres of the brain. Popular psychology often attributes creativity, for example, to right brain functioning, whereas neuroscience researchers have established that both sides of the brain are involved in creativity (see also Chapter 17).

Exercise is considered key to learning and development (Krüger, 2017) as there are strong neural links between areas in the brain involved in movement and those involved in cognitive activity. However, learners with impaired mobility and who use wheelchairs also learn and develop.

How is cognitive neuroscience and neuropsychology relevant to South African schools and classrooms?

Teachers can:
- Rely on the brain's ability to respond to new challenges and to acquire new skills and knowledge;
- Use the frontal lobes' executive functions of monitoring and control to actively promote metacognition (an awareness of one's thinking and learning or thinking about thinking and learning);
- Apply Gardner's multiple intelligences to design workstations in the learning environment according to the following cognitions: naturalist, musical, logical-mathematical, interpersonal, bodily-kinaesthetic, linguistic, intra-personal and spatial;
- Understand how neurons that 'misfire' while transmitting electrical impulses create abnormal brainwave activity that affects the functioning of brain regions during an epileptic seizure;
- Appreciate that the learner with epilepsy performs like all other learners once the neurons cease to misfire and brainwave activity returns to normal;
- Accommodate learners during and after an epileptic seizure depending on the kind of seizure;

articulation of spoken words (see the left frontal lobe in Figure 44.1). Damage to Broca's area causes difficulty with the pronunciation of words or fluent speech although the person can understand language. This condition is called Broca's aphasia; it affects expressive language. Wernicke's area (named after Karl Wernicke) is located towards the back of the left temporal lobe and is considered to be the language comprehension centre. Damage to Wernicke's area destroys the ability to understand language and to produce coherent and meaningful speech. Although the speech is fluent, it is meaningless. This condition is called Wernicke's aphasia; it affects receptive language. Broca's and Wernicke's areas are connected by a bundle of nerve fibers.

Brain regions and Gardner's multiple intelligence theory

The brain is usually associated with intelligence. Howard Gardner (1983) postulated a theory about multiple intelligences as opposed to a single general intelligence. Multiple intelligences portray human cognition to the fullest and are uniquely blended in individuals. Naturalist intelligence, for example, is the human ability to distinguish between, classify and use features of natural environments (such as plants) or artificial environments (such as archaeological artefacts). Gardner used brain research to map certain areas of the brain to eight distinct intelligences. With reference to the frontal lobe case study of Phineas Gage, Gardner argued that the frontal lobes play a prominent role in interpersonal knowledge. He formulated interpersonal intelligence as the ability to discern and respond appropriately to the intentions, motivations and desires of other people. The field of educational psychology requires interpersonal intelligence as part of the individual's unique blend of intelligences.

Major debates within the field of cognitive neuroscience

Nowadays some countries suffer from 'neuromania' that frequently constitutes excessive and unscientific application of neuroscience. Their policies on early childhood and child protection rely heavily on neuroscience in relation to childhood, parenting, abuse and maltreatment. Although the role of the parent in the child's brain development cannot be negated, policy makers should bear in mind that neuroscientific knowledge is limited. Many of the popular claims being made today are not based on scientific evidence. Care should be taken especially when causation is implicated, such as that stressful events could impact brain development negatively or a stimulating environment during the early years boosts brain power for a lifetime (Beddoe & Joy, 2017). The shift to 'neuroculture' reduces the child to a brain and overlooks the child's embodied

plays a key role in the body's spatial awareness (proprioception), for example, sitting down on a chair and not falling off. The **temporal lobe** (at the side of the head) processes auditory information, especially understanding language. Substructures in the temporal lobe are also involved in facial recognition, object recognition and emotional reactions. The **occipital lobe** (at the back of the head) processes visual information. The seemingly 'visual activity' of writing illustrates the functional connections between associative areas in the brain. When a learner is sitting at the desk (proprioception) and writing (fine motor control), the eyes fixate and move across the paper (visual) while holding the pen (touch) and ignoring background noise (auditory).

The brain consists of a magnitude of nerve cells or **neurons**. Although neurons have different functions, they are primarily involved in the generation and transmission of impulses through electrical and chemical signals.

Neuroscience and learning

Cognitive neuroscientists use images of the brain (neuroimaging) to map brain regions to cognitive functioning. However, knowledge is distributed widely over the brain in ways that are still not fully understood. Martinez (2010) refers to the Hebbian model which essentially states that neurons that fire together, wire together, ie, the neurons form a circuit or pathway to facilitate learning. Brain plasticity or **neuroplasticity** is the ability to form new neural pathways and superimpose them over the old pathways. The brain's ability to make new connections with other neurons supports learning, memory, behaviour modification and recovery after brain injury.

Mathematical reasoning and language processing

As mentioned earlier, the brain is divided in two symmetrical halves or hemispheres. The left and right hemispheres are connected. The most important connection is the corpus callosum which permits the exchange of information between the two hemispheres. Although the left hemisphere generally specialises in language processing and the right hemisphere in spatial information, it is a gross oversight to label a person as left-brained or right-brained suggesting that the person processes information either analytically (left-brained) or holistically (right-brained). In fact, mathematical reasoning activates different areas in neuroimaging depending on the *kind* of mathematical activity (Martinez, 2010). Calculation relies on areas associated with language in the left hemisphere. Comparison activates areas associated with spatial information in the right hemisphere (see also Chapters 17 and 18).

Two important areas in the brain for language processing are Broca's area and Wernicke's area. Broca's area (named after Pierre Paul Broca) helps with the

The brain, cognition and neuro-physical impairment

The simplified brain anatomy exposes basic functions of the human brain as illustrated in Figure 44.1. (The separation between brain regions is arbitrary and indicated by imaginary lines in the drawing.) The brain consists of a forebrain, midbrain and hindbrain. The midbrain is hidden deep in the middle of the brain and not discussed in this chapter. The brain consists of two halves, a left and a right hemisphere. The cerebral cortex—the outer wrinkled surface of the two hemispheres of the brain—is the largest structure of the forebrain and involved in reasoning and cognition. The cerebellum and brainstem are components of the hindbrain. The cerebellum is at the back of the skull and regulates mainly balance and coordination. The brainstem connects the brain to the spinal cord. Information is relayed to and from the brain via the spinal cord. The brainstem is the most primitive component and sometimes also called the 'reptilian' brain. It controls vital body functions such as breathing, heart rate and consciousness.

The brain has four lobes that are housed and protected by the bony skull. Although certain functions are assigned to each lobe, they are also associated with other areas in the brain. Brain regions are not yet fully understood and researchers are still discovering how the brain works. The **frontal lobe** (in the front of the head) controls attention, reasoning, planning, problem solving, decision making, speech, personality and voluntary movement among others.

> **CASE STUDY**
>
> **Frontal lobe case study—Phineas Gage**
> Phineas Gage, 25 years old, became one of the famous case studies in neuroscience. He was a railway worker and in charge of explosives to blast away rock to build the railroad. On 13 September 1848, he used a tamping iron to compact the explosive powder into a hole. The powder accidentally ignited and launched the iron rod of approximately 1 meter long and 3 cm in diameter, right through Gage's left cheek and out of his skull before landing some meters away. Despite severe damage to his left frontal lobe, Gage walked and recounted the accident the same day. Although Gage miraculously survived his injuries, his personality changed for the worse afterwards. His behaviour was erratic, disrespectful and impulsive. He used socially offensive language and could not control his emotions. He died more than a decade later of epileptic seizures that resulted from his injury. Later his body was exhumed to be studied (Gage's skull and the tamping iron are on display at the Harvard University School of Medicine today). The case of Phineas Gage helped scientists to better understand how the frontal lobe plays an important role in emotional processing, reasoning and decision making.

The **parietal lobe** (on top of the head) integrates sensory input, such as taste, hearing, sight, touch and smell. A large area of the parietal lobe is dedicated to the fingers and hands to receive and process sensory data. The parietal lobe also

Understanding educational psychology

impaired. Applied knowledge improves educational psychology practices as illustrated in the case study on the next page.

CASE STUDY

A teacher wrote the following in her observation notes about a learner, named Rami, in her class:

- Achievements fluctuate—especially an inconsistent memory. What he knows one day, he forgets the next and the day after he suddenly remembers again.
- Signs of confusion without any reasonable cause. Rami suddenly appears disorientated; it looks as if the familiar environment of the class is strange to him.
- Sometimes he stops writing. After a while, when he continues, his handwriting is very untidy.
- He often does not finish assignments.
- He battles to read and still sounds the words.
- He daydreams and fails to concentrate.
- He is a loner and often fights with other children.

The teacher thought that Rami is disobedient, aggressive and into mischief. His behaviour should thus be modified. She also questioned his intellectual potential. However, all the observations above are actually indicators of *possible* abnormal brainwave activity, also known as 'soft' neurological signs. Rami suffered from undiagnosed absence epilepsy. His epilepsy was invisible to the naked eye, but wrecked havoc on his learning and behaviour. Once his brainwave activity was normalised by anti-convulsive medication, he was able to concentrate and achieve according to his potential. His behaviour also improved.

Brain anatomy and function

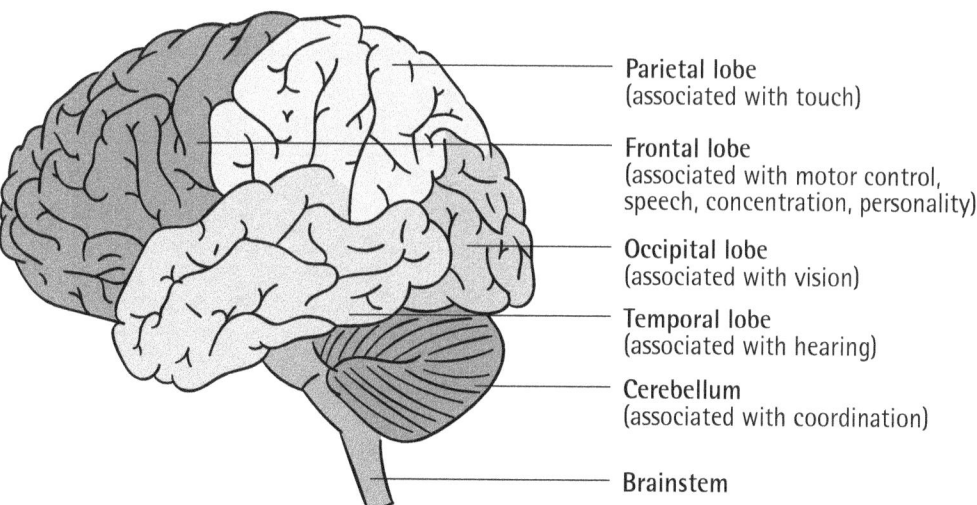

FIGURE 44.1 Lateral view of brain lobes, structures and functional areas—anterior/front (left) to posterior/back (right)

cognitive psychology. However, cognitive neuroscience and neuropsychology are closely related. A cognitive neuroscientist could, for instance, also be a neuropsychologist.

Terminology such as **neuroanatomy** (or anatomy of the brain) and impairment is often associated with the medical deficit model that focuses on the diagnosis and treatment of the condition or disease. The scientific reductionist understanding of health conditions and disease often comes across as impersonal, for example, a person with epilepsy could experience that the doctor, usually a neurologist, reduces him/her to brain activity only. Epilepsy is caused by abnormal brain activity that is measured in waves by an electroencephalogram or EEG. The person could be made to feel like he/she is 'just a brain' and not a whole person in a contextual life-world. Although scientific medical knowledge is essential to diagnose and treat neuro-physical impairment, the medical field has already gone beyond the brain as the only cause of neuro-physical impairments in the 1980s when the bio-psychosocial model proposed that every cell, organ, person, family, community and nation is part of a system that is influenced by the configuration of the environment, ie, a hierarchy of other systems (Engel, 1980). Closer to the field of educational psychology, the bio-ecological model of Bronfenbrenner includes brain function under person characteristics (Bronfenbrenner & Morris, 2006). Brain development is promoted in early childhood development. Culture also plays an important role in learning (Nsamenang, 2008) throughout a lifespan. Nowadays, cognitive neuroscience uses 'embodiment' to show the integration of body, brain, mind and social-cultural context (Marshall, 2015). This shift is known as social-cognitive neuroscience which acknowledges that the brain is embodied in social interaction although social interaction is not specifically located in the brain. (Note also the importance of social context and interaction in Chapter 41 in relation to giftedness.) Some functions that are located in the brain are briefly introduced in this chapter.

Neuro-physical impairment is a physical impairment that is neurologically related, ie to the brain or the spinal cord. Examples are epilepsy, cerebral palsy or spina bifida.

Why is basic knowledge of brain functioning important?

Educational psychology is mainly concerned with learning and development in social contexts. Cognitive neuroscience and neuropsychology explore the relationship between the brain and learning and development albeit typical or

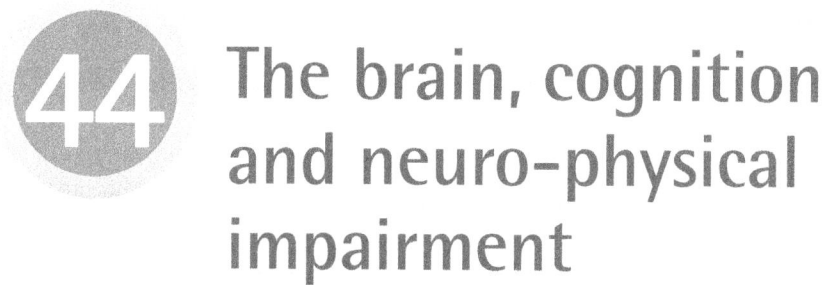
The brain, cognition and neuro-physical impairment

Deirdré Krüger

We are nothing without a brain, but with a brain, we are so much more than just a brain. (Anonymous)

Introduction

This chapter deals with the basic anatomy of the human brain and its relation to learning, which is referred to as **cognitive neuroscience**. In Chapter 17, an overview of neuroscience in the classroom is provided. This chapter, in turn, provides practical examples and discusses some of the neuro-physical *impairments* that teachers may encounter in learners in their classrooms and the ways in which they can provide support. Epilepsy, for instance, is the most common neuro-physical impairment that could affect learning. This broad field can be referred to as **neuropsychology**.

What is the difference between cognitive neuroscience and neuropsychology? 'Cognitive' refers to human mental processes such as rational thought, perception, memory and reasoning. 'Neuro' relates to nerves of the nervous system that are controlled by the brain. Therefore, cognitive neuroscience is the study of the intersection of the biological functions of the brain and the mind. Cognitive neuroscience is considered a subfield of neuroscience. Neuropsychology studies people with impaired cognitive functioning. For example, when a person sustains a brain injury, a neuropsychologist can determine whether the person's memory, attention, thinking, etc have been affected. In neuro-psychology the focus is on the mind instead of the brain and therefore, it is a subfield of

Conclusion

> *Teachers learn according to the same principles as the learners in their classrooms. Multiple exposures, opportunities to practice, and active involvement in learning are all important aspects of learning for teachers, as well as learners. Many provinces and community organisations have invested substantial funding in teacher preparation through workshops and large-audience lectures by well-known speakers. While such presentations can stimulate enthusiasm, they do not substitute ongoing consultation and hands-on opportunities to observe and practice skills in working with learners with ASD.* (National Research Council, 2001:226)

Knowing how learners with autism learn and perceive their world guides us toward being more effective teachers. We should modify our classrooms to adapt to the children's individual strengths and weaknesses. These adaptations include environmental changes, as well as modifying our teaching methods.

If a child exhibits some traits that could be characteristic of ASD spectrum disorders, he/she should be referred for screening by a specialist. After diagnosis, a teacher should plan for that child in their class, set up an IDP with the help of the supporting team, and assess the learner according to the IDP and in collaboration with the SBST and DBST teams.

Working with learners with ASD in a mainstream school is a great challenge, but to a teacher with a passion for teaching, no challenge will be too big, or too hard, to overcome. The wise words of Haim Ginott (1972:13) appropriately summarise a teacher's role:

> *I've come to a frightening conclusion that I am the **decisive element in the classroom**. It's my personal approach that creates the climate. It's my daily mood that makes the weather. As a teacher, **I possess a tremendous power** to make a child's life miserable or joyous. I can be a tool of torture or an instrument of inspiration. I can humiliate or heal. In all situations, it is my response that decides whether a crisis will be escalated or de-escalated and a child humanized or dehumanized.*

- Warn child before touching him/her; and
- Be careful; sometimes a hug could be very painful.
• Auditory:
- Use noise cancelling earphones; and
- Close windows and doors.

As a teacher, you will learn to be an active observer and a creative teacher when you work with learners with ASD (National Research Council, 2001; Autism South Africa, 2015).

How is assessment and support of learners with autism spectrum disorder relevant to South African schools and classrooms?

The South African Schools Act No. 84 of 1996 declares that public schools must allow and accept all learners with their educational needs without any discrimination. The Act declares that, where reasonable, the state will provide special needs education in public schools, as well as appropriate educational support services. The school principal and the head of department should take the parents' rights and wishes into consideration, and the principle of what is best for the learner must be borne in mind (Lemmer, 2010).

In the context of inclusive education, delays in learning might be a great challenge for learners and all the parties involved in the learning process (Hewitt, 2005). According to SIAS (Department of Education, 2014b) the different levels of the system should be involved in the assessment process eg, school-based support teams (SBSTs) and district-based support teams (DBSTs) need to work closely together, ensuring that assessment processes are smoothly pursued.

The primary challenge for learners with ASD is social development. Learners with ASD will most probably experience problems as adults in their workplace because of their communication and social difficulties. Teachers and other support staff should therefore intentionally teach social skills.

Assignments should be more structured and shorter. Lessons can be adapted to fit their learning needs. Most teachers are not formally qualified to work with learners with ASD, yet most teachers will, in all likelihood, encounter a learner with ASD at some point during their teaching careers. Inclusion, however, is about inclusion of *all learners.*

- Create individual workstations.
- Communication skills:
  - Use short, specific instructions;
  - Give oral instruction with visual supports; and
  - Make use of the picture exchange communication system.
- Body language:
  - Incorporate skills to help these learners learn when they violate a person's personal space; and
  - Demonstrate nonverbal cues and facial expressions.
- Visual learner:
  - Pair oral instructions with visuals (for example, objects, pictures);
  - Use visual supports and visual schedules; and
  - Use sunglasses if light is too bright.
- Routine structure:
  - Provide routine—keep to the same routine;
  - Set up a strong reward system—instruction, behaviour, reward; and
  - Use Grandma's rule: first you do X, then you get Y.
- Transitions:
  - Prepare child in advance;
  - Cue with visual as well as auditory information (for example, use visual schedules); and
  - Keep individual schedules on their desks.
- Identify key details:
  - Highlight key details;
  - Make information stand out; and
  - Break tasks into smaller steps.
- Behavioural differences:
  - Identify behaviour;
  - Generate possible functions;
  - Teach replacement skills—an alternative behaviour or a new way to communicate; and
  - Increase social motivation by encouraging self-awareness.
- Gross-motor development:
  - Use swings, roundabout, trampoline and see-saw.
- Fine-motor development:
  - If standing too close to peers, mark a line on the floor and help them learn to stand an arm's length from their peers;

2. Social instructions should be used in different settings throughout the day, using age appropriate, individual social goals in specific activities and intervention plans.
3. Teaching the social skills for playing with friends, with additional instructions to use toys and other materials in an appropriate way.
4. Instructions, which are focused on the cognitive development, should be in context with the skill used, with generalisation and maintenance of the natural context which is as important as the new skill acquired. New skills should be acquired before they are generalised. Methods of instruction for new skills may vary in teaching strategies to support generalisation and maintenance.
5. Intervention strategies, which address challenging behaviour, should include information of the context in which the behaviour took place, positive, proactive approaches and the series of techniques which support the experimental (for example, functional assessment, functional communication education, reinforcing alternative behaviour).
6. Functional academic skills should be addressed when skills and the child's needs are appropriate'. (National Research Council, 2001)

Since family members have the greatest impact on the lives and development of these children, they too must have the necessary skills and knowledge to help learners with ASD. These skills and knowledge should be about supporting their healthy development and helping these learners to reach the IDP's outcomes and goals.

Learners with ASD need daily individual attention so that they can reach their individual goals effectively. Individual attention may include individual therapy, developmentally appropriated group instructions and direct one-on-one contact with their teachers.

Modifications in the classroom

Looking at the core features and common characteristics of learners with ASD, we know that there are areas of strength and challenges faced by them. We must make adaptations to help them.

These modifications help ensure that the child with ASD is able to attend and learn, grow and develop.

- Concentration:
  - Decrease distraction;
  - Make eye contact;
  - Work at a child's level;
  - Do not let them sit near the door or windows; and

1. Baseline assessment: Baseline assessment is used to determine what the learner already knows, can do and values about the new learning content. For learners with ASD, baseline assessment can be conducted in consultation with school-based support teams (Department of Education, 2014b) (see also Chapters 31 and 32).
2. Formative assessment: Formative assessment is developmental—it assists the teacher in planning assessment daily, enhancing the day-to-day teaching and learning. It also helps teachers to improve the learning outcomes so that they can see the learners' progress.
3. Summative assessment: Summative assessment gives an overall picture of learners' progress at a specific time, for example, at the end of the semester or end of the year. It is usually conducted after the completion of a learning activity, a study unit, semester or year. It is always planned and makes use of different assessment instruments and strategies.
4. Diagnostic assessment: Diagnostic assessment is used to assess learners' strengths and weaknesses, and to identify the nature and causes of specific learning disabilities. This is followed by appropriate strategies for support or intervention (Suid-Afrikaanse Onderwysersunie Kurrikulumdienste, 2006:6).

Individual developmental programme

When developing an individual developmental programme (IDP), it is important that the teacher considers the learners' holistic development, as well as supports them in reaching their full potential. An IDP includes the learners' cognitive development, their communication skills, social development, as well as play development, emotional development and the behavioural patterns of learners with ASD that present challenges within the learning environment.

Support

Learners with ASD need different levels of additional support from their teachers (Department of Education, 2014b). An array of strategies is available to teachers. This may range from providing structure and routines, adapting the environment, implementing noise reduction strategies, celebrating strengths and communicating expectations at the learner's developmental level. The following six interventions are helpful:

1. Functional, spontaneous communication should be the main focus of teaching in the early years. Effective teaching strategies for both spoken language and alternative communication skills of functional communication should be implemented throughout the school setting. Every young child should be able to learn to talk.

ASD can become more functional and learn to adapt to the world around them. (Grandin 2008:12)

Autism experts told Human Rights Watch:

> ... *'highly functioning' children with autism, such as children with Asperger's Syndrome, currently do not receive adequate support in mainstream schools but could be accommodated with the right level of support and dedicated attention to avoid their being left unaccompanied, which increases the risk of bullying and anxiety.* (Human Rights Watch, 2015)

Screening, identification, assessment and support

The assessment policy (*Government Gazette* No. 19640 of 1998) in South Africa defines assessment as the process whereby information about a learner's achievements is identified, collected and interpreted, according to nationally agreed outcomes for a specific learning phase. More recently, the Policy on Screening, Identification, Assessment and Support (Department of Education, 2014b), more commonly known as SIAS, provides a policy framework for the procedures to first identify and assess and then to provide programmes for all South African learners who require additional support in school. In this way it is envisioned that the participation of learners with disabilities in education can be increased.

Principles of true and reliable assessment

Every child is unique and must thus be assessed in totality. For reliable assessment to take place, different situations and different methods of assessment can be utilised. During assessment, both the learning process and the outcomes are relevant. The assessment process itself must be credible and reliable, and the results must also be credible, true and reliable. The most important aspect of assessment is that it should be confidential (Davin, 2003; Naudé & Davin, 2017).

The principle underlining inclusive assessment is that, as far as possible, all learners will be assessed within the same curriculum and assessment framework. Barriers to learning are not only impairments; they are also systemic (challenges in the system), community aspects (poverty, backlogs) and teacher relevance (unqualified teachers) (see also Chapter 30).

The main rationale for assessment is to develop and allow learners to grow individually, to monitor their improvements and to facilitate their learning experience. It takes many different forms, depending on the goal of the assessment. It includes the following (Department of Education, 2014a):

1. *Deficits in social-emotional reciprocity, ranging, for example, from abnormal social approach and failure in ordinary back-and-forth conversation to reduced sharing of interests, emotions, or affect to failure to initiate or respond to social interactions.*

2. *Deficits in nonverbal communicative behaviours used for social interaction, ranging, for example, from poorly integrated verbal and nonverbal communication to abnormalities in eye contact and body language or deficits in understanding and use of gestures to a total lack of facial expressions and nonverbal communication.*

3. *Deficits in developing, maintaining and understanding relationships, ranging, for example, from difficulties in adjusting behaviour to suit various social contexts to difficulties in sharing imaginative play or in making friends to absence of interest in peers'* (American Psychiatric Association, 2013:50).

The stage at which functional impairment becomes obvious will vary according to individual characteristics and his or her environment; every person is unique, with different strengths and challenges. Core diagnostic features are evident in the developmental period, but intervention, compensation and current supports may mask difficulties in at least some contexts. Manifestations of the disorder also greatly vary, depending on the severity of the autistic condition, developmental level and chronological age. (American Psychiatric Association, 2013:56; Grandin, 2008)

Individuals with ASD have a normal lifespan, excluding accidents. In 2012, an estimated 7 665 children were born in South Africa with autism. That means that 23 children with autism are born daily (Autism South Africa, 2015; Human Rights Watch, 2015). It is four times more common in boys than girls, and is consistently prevalent around the globe within different racial, social and ethnic communities. It is regarded as the third most general developmental disorder.

It is difficult to diagnose ASD, because it is unlike Down's syndrome where a chromosome test may be conducted. The diagnosis is based on the different patterns seen in typical development, and it can only be diagnosed by experienced health care practitioners, eg, psychologists, psychiatrists and other medical practitioners.

Autism is a different way of thinking and learning. People with autism are people first; autism is only one part of who they are. Autism spectrum disorder is no longer viewed strictly as a behavioural disorder, but one that affects the whole person on various fronts: biomedical, cognitive, social and sensory. With individualised and appropriate intervention, learners with

teacher plan intervention strategies so that all learners with disabilities will be identified as soon as possible and that their specific learning needs are addressed. Assessment tasks must therefore be developed and adapted to include learners with ASD.

It must be determined whether assessment, from the perspective of the learners' learning characteristics, is well planned and applied, implying that sensory needs as well as academic, cognitive, loco-motor, emotional and social behaviours are taken into account and understood. The total development of all learners, as well as learners with learning and developmental disabilities such as ASD, should be taken into account.

Current debates within the field of assessment and support of learners with autism spectrum disorder

The definitions and characteristics of learners with ASD and assessment and support are discussed next.

Autism spectrum disorder (ASD)

Autism spectrum disorder is a lifelong, complex neurodevelopmental disorder which manifests during early childhood, from birth or in the first two years of life. Autism spectrum disorder refers to a continuum of mild to severe impairments in the two domains of social communication and also repetitive patterns of behaviour, restrictive interests and insistence on sameness (American Psychiatric Association, 2013). It apparently has a genetic origin and has many consequences. 'Current research suggests there may be different subsets arising from genetics, environmental insults, or a combination of both' (Grandin, 2008:52). It leads to disruption of brain development and brain functioning.

> *ASD encompasses disorders previously referred to as early infantile autism, childhood autism, Kanner's autism, high-functioning autism, atypical autism, pervasive developmental disorder not otherwise specified, childhood disintegrative disorder, and Asperger's disorder.* (American Psychiatric Association, 2013:50)

Most learners with ASD appear to function normally, but their days are filled with difficult and distracting behaviour, remarkably different from their peers. This behaviour includes: daydreaming for hours, throwing uncontrollable emotional tantrums, having no interest in other people, and doing strange repetitive activities without any explicit goals (Bruwer, 2003).

> *Persistent deficits in social communication and social interaction across multiple contexts, as manifested by the following:*

In this chapter, we examine learners with autism spectrum disorder (ASD) so that you may gain the necessary insight into the lives of learners with ASD so that we can learn to recognise the disorder and learn how to organise the learning environments of these learners so that they can also develop to their full potential.

Successful inclusion of learners with ASD in a mainstream school setting depends on the level of impairment, the teacher's attitude and training, and the cooperation of all the educational parties involved. Inclusivity is apparently the best arrangement for many learners with ASD, but it is not always the most productive situation for all learners (Daily, 2005).

Autism Spectrum Disorder (ASD) is a neurodevelopmental (brain development) disorder. Its primary characteristics include:

- *Severe and pervasive impairments in reciprocal social communication and social interaction (verbal and nonverbal); and*
- *Restricted, repetitive patterns of behaviour, interests and activities.* (American Psychiatric Association, 2013:50).

Autism spectrum disorder affects learners' rate and pattern of development. This disorder is general, and may affect learners on many different levels. They experience problems with communication, social interaction and have repetitive behavioural problems. Learners with ASD are sometimes confused, unpredictable and can present a great challenge to a teacher. Conversely, they can also be fun and it can be especially rewarding working with them when they succeed (Grandin, 2008). It furthermore becomes evident that learners with ASD have many learning and developmental challenges. To understand the effect of ASD on learners and on their environment, supporting structures must be planned for their unique learning style to help them learn.

Why are assessment and support important for learners with autism spectrum disorder?

The principles of the curriculum must ensure that the needs of learners with learning disabilities are met. This may be achieved through thoughtful design and implementation of learning activities which include appropriate and learner-friendly content. Learners are intended to develop as lifelong learners having self-confidence, independence, literacy, numeracy, multipurpose respect for their environment and being actively involved in services in their community (Department of Education, 2014a).

Continuous assessment of learning ensures that all learners will benefit from the curriculum. It is important to develop assessment tasks to help the

43 Assessment and support of learners with autism spectrum disorders

Rina Lemmer

For autistic individuals to succeed in this world, they need to find their strengths and the people that will help them get to their hopes and dreams. In order to do so, ability to make and keep friends is a must. Amongst those friends, there must be mentors to show them the way. A supportive environment where they can learn from their mistakes is what we as a society need to create for them. (Bill Wong, Autistic Occupational Therapist)

Introduction

Inclusive teaching is defined as instruction in a learning environment that improves the personal and academic development of every learner in totality, regardless of race, class, gender, impairment, religion, culture, sexual preferences, learning styles and language. (Department of Education (DoE), 2001:2) (see also Chapter 29).

In the current South African education system, all learners must be included in mainstream schools, regardless of their impairment. Inclusive education is based on the principles that all learners have the right to learn and that all learners need support to learn. Inclusive education acknowledges that every learner is different and has different needs. Owing to the diversity within a classroom, it is important that teachers employ various learning and teaching methods to create inclusive classroom environments. The curriculum should also accommodate learners with different needs.

- Anticipate ADHD symptoms; however, work hard on catching the best-desired **behaviour** and rewarding it.

The similar age appropriate pointers can be considered for adults who suffer from ADHD.

Conclusion

Attention deficit hyperactivity disorder is a neurodevelopmental disorder but it is treatable. ADHD does not have to limit an individual's life, academic progress or functioning. It is important that educational psychologists and teachers understand this disorder, especially as it tends to be present with other behavioural, mood and psychological disorders.

Role players such as parents and teachers should be encouraged to learn about this disorder. For teachers, knowledge about ADHD can assist their teaching and classroom management. It is only through proper diagnosis that people may be assisted to function at their optimal best.

highlights the important role of the educational psychologist plays within the educational system.

A classroom containing learners suffering from ADHD may interfere with classroom management and may disrupt teaching. Be aware that the other learners in the classroom may also get distracted which could affect their learning. All learners in the classroom have the right to learn, not just those perceived as being intelligent or well-behaved. Teachers should therefore have a helicopter view and a holistic understanding of their classrooms.

Learners with ADHD can also affect the teacher's teaching style, can test his/her patience and thus affect his/her mood. Teachers often need to exercise extreme self-control and ensure that they do not prejudice learners with ADHD by victimising them through calling them names, ignoring them or deliberately side-lining them (exclusion) and emotionally abusing them.

In terms of learner, teacher and classroom support, educational psychologists can recommend the following to teachers:

- Work hard on minimising distractions in the classroom (physical, auditory, visual, etc).
- Involve parents (or caregivers), as they are your allies.
- Involve other teachers like the Life Orientation or sport/physical education teacher, as their experiences with the learner might differ from what teachers observe in their classroom. Share best practices.
- Schedule challenging work for first thing in the morning.
- Establish and agree on rules and routines for the classroom (no exceptions). Develop visual and auditory cues to remind the affected learner to pay attention.
- Teacher should align their teaching style with the learners' learning styles.
- Catch a learner's attention—align academic demands to the learner's level of interest and keep them stimulated. Ensure that instructions are clear.
- Work should be brief but cover all the content required. It is important for work to match the learner's attention span.
- Change monotonous teaching to active, energetic and engaging class activities. Bring in music and art and include age-appropriate physical activities if needed.
- Place the learner in a desk where he/she will benefit. It will not benefit the learner who is easily distracted to sit next to a window facing a busy road.
- At times, learner with ADHD might require a safe time-out place. Create such a space during class and teaching time. This will also work as part of classroom management.

learning how and when to perform certain expectations. Thus a dysfunctional environment may encourage some symptoms of ADHD.

There are various programmes that can be devised to assist an individual with ADHD, be it in the school or at work. Parental programmes include scheduling or coming up with a timetable to assist the children to produce desirable behaviour. A reward system works very well in this regard, where parents focus on highlighting and rewarding good behaviour rather than focusing on punishing an unwanted behaviour.

In the school context, the same is also true; teachers can learn to schedule their teaching and plan their lesson around the learner's needs. In teacher programmes a reward system also works well. Unfortunately, in South Africa, most schools focus more on the demerit system where an unwanted behaviour receives more attention than the behaviour that deserves the merits (rewards).

Medication

There are growing concerns about the use of medication in the treatment of ADHD, especially when the individual is still a young child. Thus, it is important to refer and consult with other health professionals in this regard.

In South Africa, the main medication used for ADHD contains methylphenidate, which is a key ingredient of medication brands like Ritalin® and Concerta®. Educational psychologists work closely with psychiatrists and/or paediatricians who prescribe this medication so that the individual's progress on this medication can be closely monitored. It is always important to have a collegial relationship with the different health and mental health professionals, teachers, parents and the individual as the purpose is to assist the individual diagnosed with ADHD optimally.

How is attention deficit hyperactivity disorder relevant to South African schools and classrooms?

Parents', teachers' and learners' knowledge and understanding of ADHD is essential, as it will guide the type of support necessary for learners, parents and teacher programmes. Various studies (Lopes, 2008; Perold, Louw & Kleynhans, 2010; Kendall, Wagner & Ruane, 2011) conducted in South Africa cover teacher knowledge and experiences with ADHD. A study by Kendall (2008) found that most teachers obtained ADHD knowledge through their teaching experience and at workshops and, in affluent areas, professionals like educational psychologists and/or school therapists. Educational psychologists are the first line of the psychological profession that parents, schools and departments of education encounter. This

Environmental causes

Some researchers believe that disturbances in the family resulting from factors such as divorce, abuse and poor parental management or discipline are the cause of symptoms of ADHD in children. As an educational psychologist it is important to understand that while some parenting styles might seem 'unacceptable', many parents are doing the best they can to raise a fully functioning child. Children who are continuously exposed to substance abuse, depression or high levels of stress could, however, show symptoms similar to ADHD. Other factors that are associated with such symptoms include parental neglect, problems with peer relationships, low socio-economic status and academic difficulties.

Permissive parenting styles that do not set rules and boundaries and where the child may do as they like, can lead to a child who does not follow instructions, for instance, and this can also be linked to other behavioural disorders. Similarly, authoritarian parents who do not allow the child to be creative or voice an opinion may result in a reserved child who may be perceived to be suffering from the inattentive ADHD. Proper diagnosis by a professional like an educational psychologist is however important.

The debates around the link between ADHD and nutrition and diet are endless, with sugar and food colourants cited in particular. Some research suggests that diet may contribute to the symptoms of ADHD, however, it does not cause ADHD. However, more studies should be undertaken (Nigg, Lewis, Edinger & Falk, 2012).

Intervention

The cost of ADHD is not only financial due to expensive medication and specialised programmes or other interventions sought by those diagnosed with it; it also affects significant others who have to deal with and address the challenges that ADHD presents for the whole family. While ADHD cannot be cured, it is treatable and an individual suffering from ADHD can lead a productive and fulfilling life.

Behavioural therapy

Behavioural therapy, also referred to as behaviour modification, requires commitment from individuals diagnosed with ADHD and their significant others. Parents and teachers need to work together so that learners receive the help and attention they deserve. An adult with ADHD will also need support from their significant others, employers or employees among others.

Structure is important when dealing with ADHD. Such structure includes routine, where teaching involves repetition with an individual with ADHD

school of thought that maintains that biological or heredity factors are the main cause. However, there are also those who believe that the cause is to be found in the environment (eg, diet, upbringing), in other neurodevelopmental disorders and/or in behavioural disorders.

Biological or heredity

In most cases, when children are brought for educational psychology assessment and diagnosed with ADHD and often if children are diagnosed with ADHD, their parents are also found to have the disorder. In many cases, this disorder has been found to be intergenerational; that is, it can be traced back in the family tree. Individuals with a family history of ADHD are therefore often born with a predisposition, although multiple genes may be responsible for the disorder (Carr, 2006).

Studies conducted on identical twins also support this argument, because research has shown that if one twin suffers from ADHD, there is an almost 90% chance that the other twin will also have this disorder. Genetic analysis studies have found that ADHD is predominantly influenced by genetic factors (Hudziak, Derks, Althoff, Rettew & Boomsma, 2005).

Brain research

The brain has to process a lot of information and various imaging studies have shown alterations in the brain structure of people diagnosed with ADHD. The frontal lobe of the brain is affected in people with ADHD and they consequently have difficulty regulating their executive functions, such as concentration, impulse control and delayed gratification, as well as planning and decisiveness (Carr, 2006; Bing, Van Staden & Tabane, 2016).

Today, with different computer programmes and social media platforms, individuals are flooded with masses of information that the brain needs to make sense of and organise. Distracting information finds its way through brain processing and can negatively affect individual performance.

Research on brain chemicals further indicates that the brain releases different chemicals for different functions through the neurotransmitters (a substance that sends signals between nerve cells). For inattention ADHD it is associated with norepinephrine (also called noradrenaline) and for predominantly hyperactivity-impulsive ADHD, dopamine. These chemicals are released between synapses (small gap) between brain cells (neurons). In people with ADHD, the brain does not release enough dopamine, for instance, to assist the brain to pass the message which results in the individual's thoughts about any outside activity distracting them. Noradrenaline plays a critical role in the high-level cognitive functions in people with ADHD.

Attention deficit hyperactivity disorder is a complex disorder, as it is often associated with other disorders; hence it may be referred to as a co-morbid condition. It is not uncommon for an individual diagnosed with ADHD to also present challenges with the following disorders:

- Other **neurodevelopmental disorders** such as a specific learning disorder (SLD), for example difficulties with reading, spelling, writing, language and mathematics; as well as dyslexia, Tourette's and tic disorders, and autism spectrum disorder (ASD);
- **Disruptive behavioural disorders** (DBD), for example conduct disorder (CD), and oppositional defiant disorder (ODD);
- **Mood disorders**, for example depression; and
- **Psychotic disorders**, for example schizophrenia spectrum.

Thus, knowledge and understanding of what ADHD is, is necessary to make a proper diagnosis. It will also help to draw a distinction between ADHD and any other co-morbid disorders because this has implications for treatment and intervention.

Major debates within the field of attention deficit hyperactivity disorder

In some quarters, there is debate on whether ADHD does in fact exist or whether it is merely a disorder of 'convenience'. It was initially believed to be only a childhood disorder, but we now know that the disorder persists, with the symptoms changing from adolescence to adulthood. Needless to say, most studies on ADHD have been conducted in the Western world and thus arguments about whether ADHD exists in other parts of the world continue.

Attention deficit hyperactivity disorder is a neurological disorder and has for some time gone undiagnosed owing to differences in beliefs and cultures. For instance, in some communities, girls are expected to be more reserved and boys overactive and dominant. Thus, it is unlikely that children in such communities who display these behaviours will be referred for assessment. Nevertheless, ADHD is a serious condition that affects individuals on various levels of functioning.

What causes attention deficit hyperactivity disorder?

Researchers and practitioners still do not agree on what causes ADHD. According to Carr (2016), the causation factors of ADHD can be explained in terms of three theories, namely, biological, heredity or genetic; brain development; and environmental or psychosocial factors. There is a strong

Present with the following symptoms	Present with the following symptoms	Present with the following symptoms
• Forgetfulness in daily activities (eg missing appointments, forgetting to bring lunch). • Failure to complete tasks such as homework/chores/reports/work assignments/meet the due dates etc. • Frequently loses things necessary for tasks or activities (eg school materials, pencils, calculator etc).		

Why is understanding attention deficit hyperactivity disorder important?

Educational psychologists specialise in the learning and/or development of individuals across their life span. Parents, for instance, consult with educational psychologists to assist with their children's learning and/or developmental issues. Such issues may cover intelligence, personality, neurodevelopmental challenges, as well as emotional, behavioural, learning and career guidance. Adults may have challenges at work, for instance, with meeting deadlines or submitting rushed and poor quality work. Educational psychologists clinically diagnose ADHD and develop interventions. They can also develop intervention programmes that may include, among others, therapy, psycho-education, parental support, individualised education programmes (IEP), and teacher support programmes. In the process, educational psychologists collaborate with relevant professionals such as psychiatrists, who prescribe relevant pharmacotherapy (medication) where necessary.

An accurate and clinical diagnosis of ADHD by a professional like an educational psychologist, psychiatrist or other relevant health-care practitioner can benefit an individual, especially at an early age. Thus, early intervention is paramount and educational psychologists are trained to work with childhood disorders and to contribute to learning and/or development across an individual's life span.

TABLE 42.1 Criteria for attention deficit hyperactivity disorder

Inattentive	Hyperactivity	Impulsivity
Lack of ability to focus on the task or sustain attention or concentrate on the task.	Lack of ability to monitor and control one's body movements and execute them at one's will.	Lack of ability to control one's impulses. Simply put, monitoring and controlling one's reflexes and executing at one's will.

Present with the following symptoms

Inattentive:
- Difficulty paying attention to detail and tendency to make careless mistakes in school or other activities; producing work that is often messy and careless. Appears to be drifting off into space.
- Easily distracted by irrelevant stimuli happening around him/her.
- Inability to sustain attention and/or focus on tasks or activities.
- Difficulty finishing schoolwork or paperwork or performing tasks that require sustained concentration.
- He/she is restless. Attention jumps or shifts from one uncompleted activity to another.
- Procrastination.
- Uncoordinated and disorganised work habits.

Hyperactivity:
- Cannot sit still: constant fidgeting, squirming when seated.
- Frequently getting up to walk or run around (disruptive behaviour in class like standing and going outside the class regularly; approaching classmates' desks without permission).
- Going to colleagues workstation and not able to stay long at own desk.
- Running or climbing excessively in places that are inappropriate (in teens and adults this may appear as restlessness).
- Having difficulty playing quietly or engaging in quiet leisure activities.
- Described as always being 'on the go', 'too much energy', 'does not get tired'.
- Talking continuously.
- Poor coordination.

Impulsivity:
- Being impatient.
- Difficulty delaying responses.
- Blurting out answers before a question is completed.
- Difficulty waiting his/her turn.
- Frequently interrupting.
- Intruding on others.
- Taking too many risks.
- Taking shortcuts.
- Not thinking decisions through.
- Instability: demand, interrogate, does not know when to stop.

Attention deficit hyperactivity disorder is therefore a disorder of self-control and comprises problems with attention span, impulse control and activity level (Barkley, 2013). The resulting behaviour hinders the individual's age-appropriate functioning and development. Furthermore, according to Bing, Van Staden and Tabane (2016), the behaviour also affects the individual's behavioural, emotional and academic functioning, as well as the quality of the individual's relationships with family, authority, and the peer group.

Diagnosing attention deficit hyperactivity disorder

A better understanding of ADHD can lead to timeous identification, diagnosis and support in different contexts, including schools. Teachers play an important role in identifying ADHD, which is important as it affects children's learning. They should therefore know when and how to refer children for assessment and support and also how to make adaptations for them in the classroom (see also Chapter 32).

Psychologists, psychiatrists and other relevant professionals are trained to assess, diagnose and treat ADHD. Before making a clinical diagnosis, psychologists do the following:

- Take a proper and detailed developmental history. This includes getting a better picture of the family medical history.
- Eliminate any other disorders and establish whether this behaviour presents across multiple contexts.
- Conduct a thorough assessment, make a diagnosis and, where indicated, refer the child to other professionals like paediatricians and psychiatrists.

Individuals with ADHD are usually diagnosed with one of the following types:

1. Inattentive type.
2. Impulsive and hyperactive type.
3. Combined type.

An ADHD diagnosis can only be made if the DSM-5 criteria are met (American Psychiatric Association, 2013) (six or more in children/five or more in late adolescents and adults). These symptoms should not be a manifestation of oppositional behaviour, defiance, hostility, or a failure to understand tasks or instructions (American Psychiatric Association, 2013). Teachers should be able to identify and support learning problems that are often associated with the inattentive type, and manage behavioural disorders with impulsivity and hyperactivity. Table 42.1 lists the criteria for diagnosing ADHD according to the DSM-5 (2013).

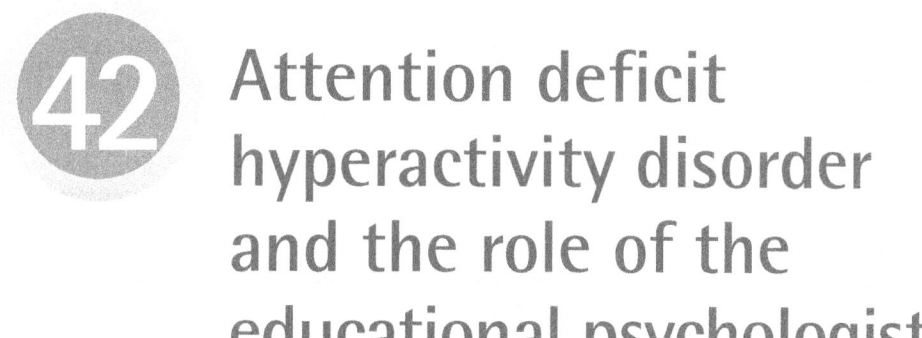 Attention deficit hyperactivity disorder and the role of the educational psychologist

RAMODUNGOANE TABANE

The biggest atrocity of all is to indoctrinate our children into a system that does not value their creative expression, nor encourage their unique abilities.
(Benjamin Greene)

Introduction

Attention deficit hyperactivity disorder (ADHD) is one of the most common conditions first diagnosed in infancy, childhood, adolescence and, in recent research, adulthood. According to the *Diagnostic Statistical Manual-5* (DSM-5) (American Psychiatric Association, 2013), it is classified as a neurodevelopmental disorder because it manifests in early childhood (before the age of 12 years) and affects development in personal, academic, social and/or occupational functioning. Attention deficit hyperactivity disorder affects about 5% of the population with more boys being diagnosed than girls, with a ratio of 4:1. The majority of boys present with over activity whereas girls are more often diagnosed with inattentiveness. Attention deficit hyperactivity disorder is a chronic disorder that manifests differently across the life span.

Attention deficit hyperactivity disorder is often referred to as an 'invisible disability' as it does not present with physical signs. However, it interferes with and affects the individual's day-to-day ability to:
- Attend to the task at hand (inattention);
- Regulate activity level (hyperactivity); and
- Inhibit behaviour (impulsivity).

of giftedness should be considered in a review on teacher training. Currently, the notion of giftedness as innate and static is in question, while emergent and multidimensional views on giftedness have gained ground. Recent discoveries in neuroscience emphasise the neuroplasticity of the brain. The neuro-system can change in those regions of the brain involved with learning, suggesting that giftedness is more open to development than had previously been thought (Cozolino, 2010). The accent today is therefore on the conditions which encourage the emergence of gifted performance. Good learning happens predominantly in smart contexts which allow giftedness to emerge through the active relations between the learner and the learning context. Research has found that greater attention to the educational needs of gifted learners can reveal hidden potential and improve the education of all learners. Curriculum differentiation for education of the gifted, as propagated by education documents, is but one option in a smart classroom. Several other methods could unleash potential. New developments in gifted education could contribute to a rise in the general standard of education in South Africa.

Given the extent of both diversity and poverty in South Africa, offering viable educational opportunities for gifted learners from all cultures and contexts, however challenging, is a fundamental necessity.

Inclusive education in South Africa embodies a strong human rights perspective fundamental to the Constitution, with an emphasis on the inclusion and support of all learners in quality learning settings. Education White Paper 6 of 2001 (Department of Education, 2001) upholds the wider interpretation of inclusive education, that is, the inclusion and support of all learners. Giftedness was not mentioned in this White Paper, and has only lately been recognised as a category of exceptionality and linked to curriculum differentiation (eg, Department of Basic Education, 2010). Recent international measurements reveal that learners, including the gifted, are not doing well on global comparisons (Spaull, 2011). Smaller qualitative studies (Oswald & De Villiers, 2013; Oswald & Rabie, 2016) highlight that gifted learners were often neglected in the classroom. It seems as if instruction was aimed at average or underperforming learners, and that gifted learners were absent from the agenda of education authorities.

Given a systemic understanding of giftedness (Ziegler & Phillipson, 2012), a refocus on the gifted learner in South Africa would call for an intervention on several system levels. Representatives from the Department of Basic Education, Provincial Departments of Education, higher education institutions, teachers, parents and the broader community need to reconsider their position on the learning pathways of gifted learners. New incentives should be implemented with the support of education departments and schools, while classroom teachers should adopt innovative approaches to giftedness. Teachers should recognise and honour the rights of all learners, help them to flourish and to achieve their goals in life.

Research has shown a serious need for meaningful teacher education at both pre- and in-service levels (Oswald & De Villiers, 2013). Given the paucity of research on giftedness in South Africa, resources should be allocated to larger research projects, grounded in the more recent interpretation of giftedness, to inform teacher training initiatives. Such training should be a shared initiative of the Department of Basic Education and higher education institutions. It should be directed at creating good learning opportunities in smart contexts for the benefit of all learners, including the gifted.

Conclusion

This chapter argued for a refocus on giftedness in South African schools and classrooms. Research has shown that these learners are often at the end of the queue for educational provision. Recent developments in the understanding

them ownership of learning activities, and allowing them time to work on self-sustaining tasks demanding high levels of concentration (Marshall, 2016).

Building the self-reliance of gifted learners is crucial. As with any other child, they need to master the ability to self-assess, to know their own strengths and weaknesses, and to deal with difficulty and failure (Marshall, 2016). Gifted children also need to believe they can develop their abilities through hard work and good learning strategies. Children 'who learn that they can grow their brains (make new, stronger neural connections when they stretch themselves to learn hard things) show greater motivation to learn and earn higher grades' (Dweck, 2015:10).

Labelling children as gifted can harm their motivation and their performance in several ways. They may avoid effort and challenges in order not to appear dumb. Praise should be given, not simply for being gifted, but for their efforts and for what they accomplish through practice, study, learning from their mistakes, persistence and effective learning strategies (Dweck, 2015).

The relevance of giftedness to South African schools and classrooms

Internationally, the 1990s witnessed a crisis of confidence in gifted education (Ziegler & Phillipson, 2012). This coincided with a period of radical political and educational transformation in South Africa. Before the advent of democracy in 1994, this was the only sub-Saharan country to record significant developments in gifted education. It received particular attention in the 1980s. After 1994, the debate focused on the needs of the historically disadvantaged. At the same time, an effort was made to offer all children equal education of an acceptable standard. This was not easy to accomplish. Given South Africa's troubled history, traditional views of giftedness which singled out a group of learners with advanced abilities were seen as exacerbating still existing inequalities, catering to a minority who were already privileged (Oswald & De Villiers, 2013).

It is important to be clear about how equal educational provision is understood. Equal should not be confused with identical, as this denies learners' individual identities and dehumanises them (Oswald & De Villiers, 2013).

> [D]enying the need, on the ground that the gifted are already privileged, or because of ideas about [equality], is misguided and counterproductive. Denying the need is most damaging to the prospects of poorer or minority children. (Jewell, 2005:112)

cognitive performance and more on 'what' conditions allow the emergence of such performance. The learning environment will need to be adapted to gifted learners' unique abilities, allowing them to learn through interaction with individually tailored environments. The emphasis is on doing and on the making of giftedness in smart contexts (Yun Dai, 2005). The ability of the individual is situation-specific. Learners can perform differently in different settings, even while doing the same problems. This suggests that giftedness can be taken out of the hands of the few, and that talent can be developed in those schools which support the development of all learners to reach their potential (Barab & Plucker, 2002). In South Africa, however, gifted learners are largely taught in mainstream classrooms where talent 'comes in different packages' and is 'often masked by indifference, aggression, boredom and apathy' or 'by poverty and illiteracy in certain communities' (Oswald & De Villiers, 2013:16).

Outstanding achievement depends upon well-developed levels of performance. It calls for many learning steps that without support would be challenging to navigate. A learning pathway for the gifted is built of a series of essential learning incidents which require the active involvement of teachers, parents and other professionals. Teachers need to be ready to help map out such incidents, as well as to accompany their learners down these pathways. Clear goals and long-term, high-quality feedback are vital. Once learning is completed, the environment needs to be redesigned to ensure future learning activities at the appropriate level of difficulty and with the relevant feedback (Ziegler & Phillipson, 2012).

Marshall (2016) claims that differentiating the curriculum is only one way to address giftedness in the classroom. Contrary to expectations, it can encourage labelling in the classroom, lowering the expectations of certain learners. In smart contexts, the teacher will find ways through different modalities to make content accessible to all learners, including the gifted. These could include demonstrations, hands-on experiments, well-conducted lectures, a challenging textbook passage, a film, a field trip with well-set goals for learner' feedback, a visiting speaker, an internet search with links to learners' interests and experiences, novel experiences to spark long-term passions, and thoughtful use of whole-class, small-group, and individual work. Additionally, Barab and Pucker (2002) argue for authentic learning contexts which transcend the classroom. The focus should be on aiding learners to develop an appreciation of those situations in which they could show talent. Good teaching entails gaining the willing cooperation of learners and showing them how school and classroom activities can be relevant to their broader lives. Lessons for gifted learners should address the integration of higher order thinking skills and creative thinking, with open-ended activities to increase opportunities for problem solving, giving

Dweck's (2015) theory of mindset is also based on the malleability of the brain. Gifted individuals with an entity theory of intelligence believe that their ability is fixed and unrelated to effort. Those with an incremental theory, however, believe that intelligence is malleable and that they can grow smarter with increased effort. In turn, this has a profound effect on their levels of motivation.

Subotnik, Olszewski-Kubilius and Worrell (2011), despite a more individualistic approach, also honour new developments concerning the malleability of the brain. They see giftedness as the manifestation of potential at the upper end of the distribution of a talent domain ('hardware'). Opportunities for development in domain-specific skills ('software') offered by the environment are, however, also crucial for future eminence. Psychosocial variables play an essential role in the manifestation of giftedness at every stage of development. Both intelligence and psychosocial variables are malleable and need to be deliberately nurtured.

Ziegler and Phillipson (2012) prefer a systemic theory of giftedness, combining the individualistic with the holistic perspective. For them, systemic thinking is always contextual. A child's intelligence, interests, capabilities and personality reflect the environment in which he/she is acting. Each child is a combination of various subsystems, while the child's environment comprises several systems. Given the interconnectedness of the systems, a change in any system can affect a series of secondary changes, the developmental potential of the child being highlighted in interaction with a dynamic context. Giftedness is 'a label granted to individuals for whom we can identify a learning pathway that leads to eminence' (Ziegler & Phillipson, 2012:196). In the educational context, this raises the question whether a systemic environment offers a gifted child the kind of learning challenges and support needed to guarantee future eminence.

The systemic approach focuses not on issues of selection and placement, but on smart contexts (Barab & Plucker, 2002) that enable good learning (Coleman, 2014). The issue is not to identify and label the gifted child; such labelling comes with a range of risks, including 'social isolation, development of egocentric attitudes and behaviours, endangering or disturbing personality development and self-concept through extreme pressures or too much responsibility' (Ziegler & Phillipson, 2012:25). Talent needs to be carefully nurtured in the classroom, and in this process giftedness will show itself. This occurs through the active relations of the individual and the environment. It is only by carefully studying learners as they change in a particular knowledge domain that teachers can discover and identify giftedness (Coleman, 2014).

Contrary to what was hitherto believed, giftedness is a complex social phenomenon. The accent now is less on 'who' is capable of exceptional

system to change in those regions of the brain involved with learning. Learning in response to experiences in the child's environment is reflected in neural changes such as the connectivity between neurons, new neural pathways, the expansion of existing neurons, and the growth of new neurons (Cozolino, 2010) (see also Chapters 14 and 17).

Table 41.1 Metatheoretical frameworks for understanding giftedness

Reductionist framework	Emergentist framework
Focus on basic elements and lower level explanations.	Focus on complexity and higher-level explanations.
	Giftedness cannot fully be explained by biological and psychological theories.
Biological and psychological level theories: • Giftedness innate to the individual, stable and fixed. • Fully explained in terms of brain structures and functions and genetic differences. • Measured by psychometric tests.	Intentional-level and activity-level theories: • Intentional properties are consciously available mental constructs such as desires, intentions, interest, individual goals, motivation, self-awareness and self-knowledge. • Focus on the functional context of the child: everything in own environment that allows for experience and activity. Giftedness develops within a dynamic interaction between child and an activity tailored to the child's needs.

Source: Compiled from Yun Dai, 2005

Vygotsky rejected 'the explanation of intelligence as residing in the head, locked within the impermeable skin,' although he recognised that 'the human brain ('hardware') provides the necessary apparatus for higher mental functions' (Yun Dai, 2005:144). He argued that instruction should provide:

> ... rich content-related resources for the mind ('software') responsible for our intelligent behaviour. Moreover, culturally engendered activities can lead to biological adaptations in the form of micro-evolution in individual development. The hardware of the brain changes along with the software of the mind in the face of adaptive challenges and through experience and practice. (Yun Dai, 2005:144)

This resulted in his well-known claim that learning pulls development. Thus, development follows learning, whereas traditionally it was thought that for learning to happen, the child needed to be developmentally ready. The child will also have agency and can take an increasingly active role in his/her own development (Coleman, 2014).

them from reaching their potential (Dweck, 2015). The belief that, on the results of a single IQ measurement some children are destined for success while others are not, also needs addressing. New developments in neuroscience show that giftedness is much more open to development over time than had previously been thought (Cozolino, 2010). Tests scores and measures of achievement tell you where a learner is, but not where he/she could end up (Dweck, 2015).

The accomplishments of gifted learners are often downplayed because of incorrect societal stereotypes about them. They are often incorrectly labelled as 'bookish, nerdy, socially inept, absentminded, emotionally dense, arrogant and unfriendly, and that they are loners' (Subotnik, Olszewski-Kubilius & Worrell, 2011:10). These stereotypes can affect their decision whether to strive for achievement or merely to aim for acceptance by their peer group. This is especially so with children from challenging circumstances, but also with females of all backgrounds. Research is needed on the true manifestations of giftedness, rather than those resulting from environmental factors. The development of psychological strength programmes should be considered for gifted children (Subotnik, Olszewski-Kubilius & Worrell, 2011).

Giftedness is found across all cultures and contexts, rather than in any one segment of society. In South Africa, the perception of giftedness by society and educationalists tends to be directly related to the historical, cultural and political context of the country. Given South Africa's troubled history, singling out a group of learners with advanced abilities may exacerbate still existing inequalities, favouring a minority who are already perceived as privileged. This group is often stereotyped as an elite because of the special provisions accorded them during the apartheid era (Oswald & De Villiers, 2013). Research is needed into how talent develops within knowledge domains and over time, why many talented learners fail to achieve at high levels or only enter specific fields of work, and what experiences and activities can promote development (Subotnik, Olszewski-Kubilius & Worrell, 2011).

The major debates in the field of giftedness

There is no agreed-upon unified definition of giftedness. Yun Dai (2005) presents two broad and contrasting metatheoretical frameworks, namely reductionist and emergentist. Table 41.1 shows these frameworks.

Lately emergent and multidimensional views on giftedness have gained ground. Several theories have been presented to better understand giftedness. Some are based on Vygotskian concepts. Vygotsky's understanding of learning and development can be aligned with new discoveries in neuroscience, more specifically neurogenesis. Recent research has revealed the ability of the neuro-is a dynamic system made up both of the individual and his/her environment (Ziegler & Phillipson, 2012).

This altered perspective holds important implications for understanding giftedness, and for policy development and instruction for the gifted learner. Although we need to remain sensitive to local contexts when considering global shifts in gifted education, we cannot ignore recent educational developments. This chapter will investigate these new shifts in gifted education.

Why is a focus on giftedness important?

Cognitive giftedness is a contested and complex phenomenon, challenged by many controversies. Society is often ambivalent or even negative about the idea of giftedness. However, there are many reasons why a focus on giftedness is necessary for educational psychology. One of the primary reasons is evident in Subotnik, Olszewski-Kubilius and Worrell's (2011) argument that an increase in the number of individuals who develop their talents to extraordinary levels will result in an advance for all mankind. A study by Rindermann, Sailer and Thompson (2009) confirms the importance of the gifted for the cognitive development of nations. Development of talent will be beneficial not only for the gifted individual but even more through its general effects on the development of society, including the wealth, health, politics, ethics, science and technology. It is important, therefore, that we invest in understanding how we can nurture the talents of such individuals.

Educational professionals need to be informed about recent developments in gifted education, as the understanding of giftedness has shifted towards an accent on reciprocal interactions between the individual and his/her environment, highlighting the pivotal role of the learning context in the progress of gifted learners (Ziegler & Phillipson, 2012). When a school offers meaningful opportunities for its gifted learners, hidden or masked abilities are often uncovered. The expectations and achievements of the whole school and class are also raised (Subotnik, Olszewski-Kubilius & Worrell, 2011). This is especially relevant in South Africa as the country struggles to raise the general standard of education.

The belief that gifted learners will make it on their own, no matter in what educational environment they are placed, needs to be dispelled, since it leads to minimal attention being paid to these children in today's classrooms. The notion that they require little effort or input from a teacher to be successful is a myth. The appearance of effortlessness disguises the commitment of time and dedication the gifted learner needs to achieve. The faith in an innate potential can result in learners holding harmful beliefs about the role of effort, hindering

41 Giftedness

MARIETJIE OSWALD

Educators, researchers, and policy makers [need] to more equitably apply the labels of gifted or talented, realizing the value of the perspective that nobody has talent, yet everybody can engage talented transactions. (Barab & Plucker, 2002:179)

Introduction

Globally speaking, systematic research into giftedness was established more than 100 years ago. Despite this, scholars have struggled to understand giftedness and to identify those young individuals who will make outstanding contributions as adults. The inability to correctly identify future eminence is one of the main reasons why gifted education is in a crisis. Research into giftedness traditionally focused on an exclusive group of children with the potential for outstanding achievement in one or more areas. Today, measures for identifying cognitive giftedness are often still oriented on the selection and labelling of children. It remains a struggle to find suitable educational placements for them and to establish methods which are sufficiently robust to ensure their maximum achievement (Ziegler & Phillipson, 2012).

While giftedness is evident across many talent domains, this chapter will focus on cognitive giftedness as it is relevant to the field of education. Recent approaches to gifted education have begun to question the notion of giftedness as an individual characteristic, one which remains fixed and stable. Instead, learning contexts are seen not only as crucial for the development of potential, but also as making up an essential part of what giftedness actually is. Thus, it

when the educators 'make the pedagogical more political and the political more pedagogical' inequalities can be challenged and VAWG be can addressed.

Conclusion

In this chapter, I have provided a picture of VAWG as a pervasive problem that pivots around structural gender inequality, which is framed by patriarchy and informed by hegemonic masculinity. While VAWG seems an insurmountable problem, often hidden in the realm of the personal and the private, the consciousness raising can indeed enable the personal and private to become the public and the political. It is everyone's concern—both men and women, and boys and girls in all arenas of life—to work towards gender equality and to speak out when violence is witnessed, heard of, or experienced. It is indeed a social problem that affects the learning and development, and the health and well-being of girls. It is time for all of us to say: Kwanele! Enuf is Enuf!

> **Acknowledgement**
> I wish to acknowledge Relebohile Moletsane for her generosity to act as critical reader.

of a gender forum, new measures to ensure safety on campus, and a proposal for a women's centre. Similar work with schoolgirls took place, and they too engaged with their school management team and school governing body and made their voices on safety at school heard.

What has violence against women and girls got to do with schooling?

School has always been seen as a key site for the advancement of society through education. Leach and Humphreys (2007:52) point out that the fact that 'schooling leads to social and economic betterment, initially obscured the fact that schools may in reality reinforce gender inequalities and constitute unsafe sites for students'. As pointed out earlier, society and the school are structured in a masculine way that perpetuates the inequalities between girls and boys— often with both girls and boys thinking that such inequalities and behaviour is normal. It is therefore necessary to understand gender relations within schools in order for it to be transformed (Pattman & Chege, 2003). In this regard, the work of the school and its educators should be to ensure that inequalities are not perpetuated in and through the school structures, and that school is not a site of VAWG.

Within the school structure, it then becomes imperative to raise consciousness of gender inequalities and to challenge myths and stereotypes of VAWG. Moreover, schools should, as Reddy and Dunn (2007) argue, engage with the constructions of femininity and masculinity and, therefore, the educators themselves should understand the working of gender, gender identity, gender inequality and VAWG, and teach in a gender sensitive way to disrupt the oppressions of women and girls within the structures of the school (UNESCO, nd). This needs to start in the early childhood development and foundation phases, where the educator could lay the foundation for gender equality through teaching in a gender sensitive way, a gender responsive way and, importantly, a gender transformative way (UNESCO, nd).

In this regard, awareness raising of inequalities and how they are linked to violence against women and girls could also come from girls-as-agents. In our Networks 4 Change project referred to earlier, the secondary schoolgirls we were working with to address VAWG, made a cellphilm entitled, *Stop Taking Sides*, which called educators out for taking the side of the boys in the class. The girls could clearly identify the unequal treatment they were receiving in the class and were able to articulate the inequality and also suggest ways of how educators should treat them equally. According to Blignaut (2017), referring to Giroux,

a grim picture of hegemonic and aggressive masculinities, and evoking hash tags such as #MenAreTrash. Howson (2006:279) makes an interesting argument for change, for a de-gendered world with women not only 'assuming equality through sameness to men' but with men 'involving themselves in new relations and configurations of practice that break down traditional cathetic and sexual imperatives, division of labour, and power.'

One sees initiatives by men, such as the counter hash tag, #NotAllMenAre Trash, which show how men are trying to counter their positioning as violent and are instead showing themselves as a contingent who could contribute to changing the experiences of women and girls—not for them, but in alliance with them. Men who counter hegemonic and aggressive masculinities are successful role models for boys and men on how to perform masculinity which is nonviolent.

Girls-as-victims versus girls-as-agents

Within the VAWG literature, girls are often constructed as victims (or survivors, which has a positive connotation) but seldom as having agency. Leach and Humphreys (2007:51) raise a further important point that most research on VAWG focuses on women and girls being victims within a heterosexual context —the 'normal' context—ignoring other forms of VAWG such as homophobic and girl-on-girl violence. This they attribute to 'unequal and antagonistic gender relations,' which are normalised by existing structures and processes in society, also in schools. It is problematic to overlook VAWG that falls outside a heterosexual context because that limits understanding, and will hamper an inclusive programmatic intervention addressing VAWG. This is why the voices of all women and girls should be heard—enabling relevant interventions within specific contexts.

Cobbett (2014), and Jewkes and Morrell (2012) bring the agency of girls and women into the current debate, arguing that they do indeed show agency in, for example, choosing and attracting partners, choosing to have sex—in other words, they do have sexual and emotional agendas but their agency is limited where condom use is concerned because insisting on condom use might put them at risk. Girls-as-agents can also be seen in terms of intervention. One example of young women taking action from the ground up to address VAWG, comes from university teacher education students who drew on their own insider knowledge of VAWG in a university context to produce a set of visual artefacts (cellphilms, policy posters and action briefs), which they used to engage in dialogue with university policy makers to push for creating a safer university space for women (De Lange, Moletsane & Mitchell, 2015). They had several dialogues with various policy makers that resulted in the establishment

When women and men and girls and boys are not valued equally, the potential for oppression and violence against women and girls emerges and is sustained by the structures and systems of society. Hence, Jackson (2017:28) argues that 'gender inequality, as an instance of status inequality, must be embedded in systems of positional inequality to persist ... and ... [be] sustained across generations'. Gender inequality has a long history, is experienced in the lives of women and girls, varies in intensity, and forms across time and place, and is sustained by positional inequality (Jackson, 2017).

To explain the complexity of the inequalities of women, Crenshaw (1994) coined the word 'intersectionality' to describe the lived experiences of women's inequalities, and which, according to Davis (2008:67), shows 'the interaction of multiple identities and experiences of exclusion and subordination'. So, it is not only the gender difference that contributes to inequality, but also race and class and an intersection of these, for example, being a woman who is black, or being a woman, who is black and poor, will contribute to different experiences of inequality as privilege and power diminish.

Masculinity and femininity

The social constructions of masculinity and femininity are very important in understanding VAWG, because the latter is about gender and power, and not about sex. It is about a strong, aggressive, powerful and dominant masculinity and a need to demonstrate power over women and girls. Such masculinity has social and cultural nuances and expectations that deepen the complexities of violence against women and girls. Emphasised femininity, as a social construction, also has social and cultural nuances and expectations, to which women and girls aspire to meet the criteria of being a 'good' woman (Jewkes & Morrell, 2012). It is when, as Cobbett (2014) points out, an ideal or successful femininity requires them to be heterosexually desirable and in a relationship, that it is difficult for women and girls to break out of a relationship that becomes violent. Such normative constructions of femininity could also make women and girls give up power to meet the criteria of being a 'good' woman (Jewkes & Morrell, 2012:1736) and accept risky and coercive sexual practices.

Hegemonic masculinity

Hegemonic masculinity, according to Connell (1987:61), 'is constructed in relation to women and subordinated masculinities' and legitimises the dominant position of men and the subordination of women and men with different masculinities, underpinning the violent behaviour against women and girls and other men who do not fit into the normalised male identity. More often than not, men are positioned only as the perpetrators of VAWG, painting

In order to facilitate or deepen our understanding of patriarchy and its role in VAWG, it is necessary to understand the current discourses among scholars and activists in this field.

Discourses around patriarchy and violence against women and girls

In this section, we take a brief look at four discourses important to understanding violence against women and girls, namely gender, gender inequality and power; masculinity and femininity; hegemonic masculinity; and girls-as-victims versus girls-as-agents.

Gender, gender inequality and power

It is important to look at how we come to identify as a girl and being feminine, or as a boy and being masculine, and how we come to behave within the norms of a specific gender regime (Connell, 2002). The difference between three concepts—biological sex, sexual orientation, and gender—are important in this discussion. A person is born with a biological makeup as male, female or intersex. A person will also express a certain sexual orientation (ie, heterosexual, bisexual or homosexual), which refers to whom a person is sexually attracted. Gender (ie, masculine, transgender or feminine) is taught and learned or engendered through a process of socialisation, and refers to the psychological makeup of the person. The learning of gender occurs in various ecologies (family, school, community, society), which are framed by the structures of society referred to earlier, such as patriarchy, and which influence the development of hegemonic and aggressive masculinities and emphasised and compliant femininities (Connell & Messerschmidt, 2005; Leach & Humphreys, 2007), leaving girls in a vulnerable position.

The inequality between men and boys, and women and girls, is often positioned at the centre of violence against women and girls (Garcia-Morena, Heise, Jansen, Ellsberg & Watts, 2005). Inequality is a complex phenomenon that we can begin to understand by looking at what gender equality, according to UNESCO (2003:2), means:

> *Gender equality means that women and men have equal conditions for realising their full human rights and for contributing to, and benefiting from, economic, social, cultural and political development. Gender equality is therefore the equal valuing by society of the similarities and the differences of men and women, and the roles they play. It is based on women and men being full partners in their home, their community and their society.*

that has to be addressed. It is through such political action that the lived experiences of women and girls can be improved.

A challenge, however, lies with making the violence public, reporting the violence, telling the stories in a society where keeping silent is often the only way women and girls deal with the violence against them (Mahadev, 2015). For example, research suggests that only one in nine cases of violence against women ever reaches official police records (Jewkes, Dunkel, Koss, Levin, Nduma, Jawa & Sikweyiya, 2006). It is therefore important to agitate for a safe and supportive space in which to report the violence enacted against women and girls without their being re-traumatised, but assisted in getting access to counselling and support at individual level. Such support should be easily accessible to all women and girls in all socio-economic contexts. It is, however, not adequate to stop there—at the reporting level, and bringing the perpetrator to book—when it is structural gender inequalities (Leach & Humphreys, 2007) that enable such violence to occur.

Giddens (1984), in his structuration theory, refers to 'systems' to describe the patterns of the social structure of society. People have created structures that are used to shape behaviour, for example, Connell (2002) refers to gender regimes—regimes that determine how men should behave, and how women should behave. Such structures are usually enabling for some, and constraining for others because the structures can be manipulated by people who have the power to get what they want. In South Africa, the way in which the apartheid system structured society is an example of how such structuration enabled one group of people and constrained and oppressed other groups of people, using a position of power to manipulate the behaviour and movement of the constrained and oppressed groups. While apartheid was abolished in 1994, the deep-seated racial inequalities still linger and the effects of the oppression are still embedded in the psyches of people, which are oftentimes drawn on to explain the violent behaviour of some men. In a similar way, patriarchy has structured society, positioning women and girls as unequal to men and boys, and giving men and boys power over women and girls—shaping their behaviour in terms of a gender regime, limiting their opportunities, and policing their behaviour (also producing homophobia and violence against members of the lesbian, gay, bisexual and transgender (LGBT) community). As such, the patriarchal structure is at the heart of the inequalities that women and girls of all cultures and ethnicities experience. In order to change the way women and girls are treated, consciousness should continually be raised about the effects a patriarchally structured society has on women and girls. According to Giddens (1990:53), 'reflexive approaches to knowledge' are required and are seen as a starting point for raising awareness—by ensuring that the personal is political —and by calling out the powerful influence of patriarchal structures on society.

in, and contribute to, community and society. Moreover, it leads to negative health and educational outcomes.

While VAWG is a concern worldwide, it is the South African context that is often in the spotlight. Recently, a spate of violence perpetrated against women and girls has made news headlines and has pushed to the fore the question of why this is happening—why there is so much violence directed against women and girls in a country that boasts a rights-based constitution (Republic of South Africa, 1996a) that includes the right to safety for all. Several national initiatives over the years have ranged from Chapter 9 institutions, such as the Commission for Gender Equality, developing policies to protect girls and women to the commissioning of interventions that include education and training materials —such as Opening our Eyes (Department of Education, 2001) for teacher development—and using them to conduct professional development with teachers in addressing VAWG. Furthermore, community-based participatory projects working in a 'from-the-ground-up approach', drawing on the voices of women and girls about their experiences of violence to generate local and relevant solutions, have been implemented. These have focused on enabling agency among girls and women to take a stand and to say 'Kwanele! Enuf is Enuf!'

> **NOTE**
> The Kwanele! Enuf is Enuf! Initiative, founded by Andy Kawa, aims to break the chain of silence protecting rape and sexual violence—and their perpetrators—by urging every man, woman and child to take a continuous and proactive stand against these crimes.

Yet, the issue of VAWG does not go away; indeed, it seems to be worsening. The question thus arises about why this is so. What are the underlying causes of the continued VAWG? And, more importantly, how can we deepen our understanding thereof so that everyone can address it.

'The personal is political'

The origin of the phrase, 'The personal is political', is believed to have emerged in the late 1960s in feminist circles, but who coined the phrase is not exactly clear. The phrase, often restated as 'The private is political', is interpreted to refer to the intersection of women and girls' personal struggles with the social and political structures that frame their oppression. In other words, raising consciousness about women and girls' personal dilemmas is a form of political action (Hanisch, 2006). It is therefore important to see VAWG not only as an individual's problem and as a personal problem but, indeed, as a public concern

40 Gender and violence against women and girls

NAYDENE DE LANGE

'We are unsafe out on the streets; at home, we are not safe at all.'
(Grade 9 schoolgirl)

Introduction

The words above from a Grade 9 schoolgirl in our Networks 4 Change project sum up the experiences of most, if not all, girls and women of all age groups across all cultures and all ethnicities in South Africa.

> **NOTE:** Networks for Change and Well-being: Girl-Led 'From the Ground up' policy making to address sexual violence in Canada and South Africa is a six-year Social Sciences Humanities Research Council-funded project led by Claudia Mitchell and Relebohile Moletsane (see http://www.networks4change.ca/).

The girl is referring to violence against women and girls (VAWG)—the focus of this chapter. Violence against women and girls is 'any act of gender-based violence that results in, or is likely to result in, physical, sexual or psychological harm or suffering to women' (United Nations, 1993:line 62), and includes domestic violence, intimate partner violence, rape, sexual exploitation, sexual harassment, sexual homicide and sexual coercion. A constant worry about not feeling safe and always vulnerable takes away from the opportunity to celebrate girlhood and womanhood, and affects the way in which girls and women engage

of this is that girls who have access to these often dangerous men may threaten or harass their educators and peers with them.

Young men are often targeted for recruitment into gangs or as drug and weapon mules. The increasing threat, exposure to and experience of violent acts have also resulted in an increasing number of learners bringing some kind of weapon with them to school. (Van der Merwe, Dawes & Ward, 2012; Zuze, Juan, Hannan, Visser & Winnaar, 2016)

Conclusion

According to Van der Merwe, Dawes and Ward (2012:58), 'the earlier a child develops an aggressive pattern of behaviour, the more likely she/he is to continue to be aggressive'. Disengaging increases the learner's vulnerability to social isolation and limits the young person's access to resources, such as additional academic support to address specific barriers to learning, and psychosocial support services to address intrinsic or familial or environmental challenges (Bandura, 2004, 2006; Van der Merwe, Dawes & Ward, 2012).

Increased sensitivity to working with diverse learners implies not having a too narrow focus on race and class. Within these foci there are multiple and often subtle nuanced differences. Governance, management, educators and learners should be encouraged to engage in reflexive praxis that allows them to be responsive to an ever-changing dynamic within school populace. Training that stimulates and supports reflexive praxis among management, staff and educators should be given. This is important, as it will help to interrupt negative self-talk that may influence individuals and permeate the school culture. Reflexivity should therefore not only relate to curriculum-based practices, but educators should also take time to focus on themselves and their learners and individuals in relationship with one another in a specific context at a specific time. It is important that teachers understand how their experiences, expectations and values may create potential bias towards learners or the contexts from which they originate.

No school is immune to the influence and experience of aggression and violence, yet we have a tendency to continue to act as if it only happens in communities plagued by violence. The changing dynamic of how violence manifests within the school, on the way to school and within the broader community means that schools have to be creative and proactive in developing strategies that ensure the safety and well-being of the educators and learners. Schools should strive to be spaces that acknowledge the lived realities of all and seek to put in place interventions that promote the holistic development of learners and staff.

miss cues that point to learners being on a trajectory to delinquency, and they hence miss an opportunity to intervene in this negative risk chain (Fuller, 2001).

It is important for educators to understand the complex network of stressors learners experience and how the stressors occur in relation to one another, which often results in learners feeling a strong sense of abandonment by the adults in their worlds. This increases their sense of vulnerability in the multiple contexts they navigate on a daily basis.

Confused, conflicted, frustrated and angry young people feel increasingly misunderstood and marginalised in both their school and their community contexts. As they progress through the stages of development, they increasingly stop looking to adults for guidance and support and create their own peer support networks. In these networks, they may often willingly surrender their personal agency, because they have witnessed incidents where 'walking alone' makes you 'a target'. This faith in the collective agency of a cluster group or gang association often makes them feel more secure and these social spaces then become communities of support, validation and protection. It is, however, important to note that not all learners who belong to or associate with groups are on a trajectory to delinquency. These are not homogeneous entities and function on a continuum from prosocial or aspirational to antisocial tendencies and foci (Damons, 2014). According to Dayton (2007), young people often gravitate towards one another because they have had similar experiences or experience similar challenges in a context. These groups are complex social entities that expect their members to conform to their values and practices. These values and practices may actively encourage members to disengage from school culture and conform to the group values. While learner members may not agree with all the practices of the group, their experiences of compromised efficacy in the school or community context often result in them developing a high tolerance for anti-establishment behaviour, such as aggression towards other peers, educators, and the school culture.

Shifting gender dynamics in school violence

Increasingly larger numbers of girls are participating in acts of physical violence. These incidents are either fights with other female peers or bullying incidents. These violent encounters often take place with an audience and are recorded with cellphones. These recordings are then often uploaded onto the internet as live feeds. It is interesting to note that there is often very little regard for the consequences of these acts or that the recordings serve as evidence implicating them in a crime. According to current research, vulnerability and association with older men are a dynamic that affords these girls increased access to drugs, alcohol and social spaces that normalise violent activities. Another consequence

to these learners as 'hostile stay-in-school youths' and point to the fact that they come to school to learn life skills that have very little to do with the mainstream curriculum (Longa, 2011; McWhirter, et al, 2007).

Learner responses to feeling unsafe and excluded

Each of the communities with which the learner engages has different and often conflicting values, norms, expectations and practices. These are often implicit rather than explicit in some contexts; dominant and contextual discourses on what is acceptable and expected are often in direct conflict and result in confusion and frustration. So, for example, when a teacher chastises a learner for verbal aggression, this could be in direct contradiction to the message received in his/her community that if someone challenges you, you need to stand up for yourself; otherwise you will be viewed as a weakling. While it may not be the educator's intention, the learner may experience this as disrespecting his/her family and community values and practices.

Learners' aspirations often do not align with that of their parents, so going to school outside their community or being limited to attending school within the confines of their families' socio-economic capacity presents the learners with unique, often unimagined challenges. This often leads to frustration at not being able to make decisions and being forced into spaces that may not welcome them and that expose them to a set of experiences that may be very different to those of their friends and family in their communities of origin.

The trajectory to increasingly aggressive behaviour within the school context often begins with bi-directional attitudinal aggression between educators and learners and is often related to enforcing compliance with how things should be as opposed to how they could be. Learners' perceptions of educators' lack of empathy for or insight into the complex nature of the stressors they are exposed to and teachers' perceptions of learners' disrespect and lack of cooperation often lead to increasingly aggressive behaviour, with educators' authority often being openly challenged.

Youth culture is fluid, and too narrow a focus on race, class, gender and culture differences may lead us to missing cues of learner disengagement and may result in labelling and stigmatising. It should be accepted that some learners may not be interested in learning for entrance into the traditional economies, but may come to learn the informal curriculum that teaches them how to navigate the spaces they occupy outside of the school context (Damons, 2014).

The relational distance then often means that learners do not access the social and educational support services they need. According to Razer and Friedman (2013), teachers often unconsciously disengage when their sense of efficacy is compromised. In addition, this inhibited interaction also means that educators

malaise of behavioural responsive styles that may be reflective of or mimic what is common in their context of origin. This diversity of values and behavioural styles make inclusive school cultures and classroom management particularly challenging. This, according to the literature creates particular challenges for educators, who are being exposed to behaviour and response styles beyond their experience. In an effort to manage this phenomenon, educators often attempt to coerce learners to conform to traditional school culture; any resistance to this may result in learners from specific contexts being labelled as problematic and having limited access to academic and psychosocial support they may need.

Responses to challenging behaviour

Many vulnerable children disappear in the education system because of a tendency among teachers and school administrators to focus too much on presenting behaviours. This complexity in defining at-risk behaviour, McWhirter, et al (2007) argue, means that the narrow symptomatic focus may cause us to miss the less visible challenges that the learner may not be able to articulate. Exposure to cumulative stressors over time could place young people on a trajectory of risk. Stressors are classified as either chronic (eg, environmental factors such as violence in the community or socio-economic status) or discrete (eg, more personal such as domestic violence). Both these categories are considered complex in that their influence is reciprocal and a product of time and context (Camilleri, 2007). It is imperative that we acknowledge the impact these stressors may have on educators, as they are in close relationship with the learners and are tasked with creating environments that encourage learning. Failure to take into account the effect that exposure to these stressors may have on learners, educators and overall school culture can translate into increased feelings of frustration, anger and aggressive behaviour in both educators and learners (Wood & Meyer, 2016).

Having too narrow a focus on the manifesting behaviour in the classroom and dealing with the learner only in terms of the presenting acting-out behaviour, may escalate the levels of aggression displayed (McWhirter, et al, 2007; Longa, 2011). This results is less academic contact time, labelling and stigmatisation and further limits access to learning and psychosocial support services at the school. The learner becomes increasingly marginalised within the school context and eventually disengages. This alienation and resultant academic underachievement have been found to increase vulnerability to recruitment into antisocial groupings that can set learners on a trajectory to delinquency. Current research points to a high correlation between academic performance and engaging in acts of aggression and violence at school (Magson, Craven, Mums & Young, 2016; Rawatlal & Petersen, 2012). Some of the literature refers to the aspirations of parents and learners and, more recently, to safety at school. Failure to create schools as a safe space that is responsive to the educational, physical and psychosocial aspirations of the learners negatively impacts the quality and quantity of teaching and learning that takes place. The literature cites perceptions of unresponsive school cultures as one of the primary reasons that learners disengage from school (Magson, Craven, Mums & Young, 2016; Rawatlal & Petersen, 2012; McWhirter, McWhirter, McWhirter & McWhirter, 2007). The end result is the 'acting out' behaviour we see in class. A too-narrow focus on the acting out behaviour without exploring the factors that may be contributing to it often leads to tensions in interactions and relationships or feelings of inclusivity. Traditional responses of punitive action include exclusion (eg, visits to the principal's office, and being physically excluded during contact time) or more subtle bi-directional attitudinal aggression between the learner and educator.

The link between aggression and poor academic performance

The link between aggression and poor academic performance is well documented, and is ascribed to a number of factors, such as the fact that children who are aggressive are disruptive and this disruption itself means less on-task behaviour, which in turn may lead to less concentration on learning tasks and independent study. In addition, disruptive young people are often physically absent from the class because of referrals to the principal's office, inclusion in diversion programmes or suspension (Damons, 2014). Limited academic achievement contributes to learners' negative self-perception, which encourages more negative behaviour, which in turn leads to even more limited academic achievement, often trapping the learner in a cycle of negative engagement and outcomes (Damons, 2014; McWhirter, et al, 2007; Swarts, 2016).

The findings of multiple studies suggest that the aggression of alienated youths appears to have an interpersonal meaningfulness that is directed specifically against people or institutions from which they experience rejection (Longa, 2011). This rejection may not be purposeful, but is often related to failure of schools to adapt to changing learner demographics. Institutional responses vary, with some rigidly sticking to traditional ways of being, while others mirror the structural neglect of the communities in which they are situated. Learners from various contexts bring with them the challenges of their contexts of origin. Some of these include gang or neighbourhood cluster group affiliation, navigating risky commuter routes, which increase their vulnerability, and exposure to harassment and various forms of aggression. It also introduces into the school context a

contexts that impact or influence them. Recent research commissioned by the Human Sciences Research Council (HSRC) (Zuze, Reddy, Juan, Hannan, Visser & Winnar, 2016) found that almost 50% of children of school-going age will experience some form of aggression or violence during their school career. The type, severity and frequency of the acts of aggression and violence learners are exposed to, are however significantly influenced by where they attend school, their socio-economic status and their gender.

While school is considered by most as the pathway to hope for the future, it is often fraught with tension and conflict (Swartz, 2009). For some learners, school has become more than a space for the acquisition of conventional learning for the job market; it has become a space in which learners seek to acquire skills for living (Zipin, 2013).

This chapter will consider some of the factors that may influence the choices learners make and how the dynamic interplay of these factors influences their experiences with educators and schools. It by no means posits to be a comprehensive exploration, but instead presents the view that in order to navigate the increasingly aggressive school terrain, we need to reflect on the factors discussed here.

The changing socio-educational landscapes of schools

Education is about building relationships and creating safe spaces for interaction so that learning can take place. One of the significant factors that contribute to the increasing number of challenges experienced in the South African educational context is that we continue to be confronted with structural inequalities that have kept some communities trapped in a cycle of poverty and has seen increased strain being placed on schools that are perceived to be better resourced. These experiences of inequality have created a number of social challenges related to increased learner mobility, changing demographics of learner populations and perceptions of increasingly dysfunctional and disorganised schools in certain contexts. Physical location can no longer be considered the primary determinant of the sociocultural or socio-economic composition of the learner populace. The impact of learner mobility is that it introduces lived realities and ways of navigating spaces that are often foreign to the schools that commuter learners attend. The phenomenon of commuter learners also presents schools with increasing challenges to create a culture that reflects the diverse lived realities of their learner population.

The increasing number of commuter learners who attend schools outside of their community of origin is attributed to perceptions of the ability or inability of community-based schools to provide a learning space that speaks

# Exploring the complexity of aggression and violence within the school context

LYNNE DAMONS

If we desire a society of peace, then we cannot achieve such a society through violence. If we desire a society without discrimination, then we must not discriminate against anyone in the process of building this society. If we desire a society that is democratic, then democracy must become a means as well as an end. (Bayard Rustin)

Introduction

Schools are social worlds that often mirror broader societal challenges. It is therefore important to take cognisance of the social environment in which young people are embedded so that we are able to understand the environmental factors and social networks that influence their lived realities, behaviour and risk for engagement in challenging behaviour (Magson, Craven, Munns & Young, 2016). Violence is a subcategory of aggression and it is important to know that it usually escalates from relational aggression to physical acts of violence over time. In the school context, a cycle of bi-directional aggression sets youths on a trajectory that sees both teacher and learner disengaging and withdrawing their cooperation (Wood & Meyer, 2016).

South African history and continued structural disparity contribute significantly to the nature and complexity of violence in schools (Van der Merwe, Dawes & Ward, 2012). The interplay between the contexts of the school and community of origin impacts the experience of all learners, whether the schools are based in economically challenged communities or in suburbia. It is therefore important that experiences of school violence not be viewed in isolation of the

that learners may be required to take a leave of absence for up to two years to 'exercise full responsibility for parenting' (Department of Education, 2007:5). These extremely punitive stipulations are in contradiction to the stated aim to encourage schools to 'strive to ensure a climate of understanding and respect in regards to unplanned pregnancies' (Department of Education, 2007:6). Subsequent research has shown that these measures were not clear and still left too much to the discretion of the educators, principals and school governing bodies to apply their own morals and values about teenage sexuality. These guidelines were under review at the time of writing this chapter.

Revisionists and critical feminist authors argue that it is not only the bureaucratic processes of access that require attention, but also the social norms within which pregnant women find themselves, in schools and society. Revisionists argue that the cultural practices that render teenage pregnancy manageable within particular milieus need attention (Mkhwanazi, 2014). Critical feminist authors point to the need to deconstruct the raced and classed assumptions that underpin common understandings. For example, pregnant teenagers with working-class families of origin are often assumed to transfer disadvantage more easily out of ignorance or individual deficits than young women from middle-class families of origin. The latter young women are described in more positive terms as engaging in age-appropriate behaviour by experimenting, making mistakes and rebelling against their families (Wilson & Huntington, 2005).

Revisionists and critical feminists are more likely to consider the deficiencies of the social context in which the pregnancy takes place as opposed to individuals or families involved. For example, they point to the fact that unsupportable pregnancies occur more often in communities with high levels of sexual violence (Speizer, Pettifor, Cummings, MacPhail, Kleinschmidt & Rees, 2009). It is gender inequality which connects these variables and gives men considerable relational power over women's reproductive health outcomes (Jewkes & Morrell, 2012).

Conclusion

There is more than one way of understanding and responding to the phenomenon of 'teenage pregnancy'. The debates which continue among researchers indicate that this is a controversial and contested issue. Schools, teachers and psychologists have an important role to play in advancing social justice and transformation to facilitate greater understanding, support and accommodation of pregnancy and mothering in those spaces. In this way, women can complete their schooling and reduce the risk of childbearing limiting their adult work lives and future ambitions.

teenager is neither child nor adult, but paradoxically both. As such, she is prone to 'storm and stress' as the 'primitive' urges of childhood compete with the mature, 'civilised' traits of adulthood. This has been termed the adolescent-in-transition discourse (Macleod, 2011). Critical feminists ask: 'What if the "transitional stage of adolescence" is not universal, not self-evident or necessarily part of human nature? What if there is no developmental blueprint? What if ways of being teen-aged have more to do with social, cultural and temporal understandings than with the physiological, psychological or cognitive processes that occur within individuals?' (Macleod, 2011:16). There is already a substantial body of research that critiques the dominant assumptions which underlie developmental psychology (Burman, 2012).

What kinds of educational solutions or social support should be provided?

Educational solutions to early reproduction have focused mainly on prevention, in particular through sexuality education. Since democratisation in South Africa, there have been some formal commitments to the rights of pregnant teenagers. Before 1994, exclusion of pregnant and mothering learners was common. With the adoption of the South African Schools Act No. 84 of 1996, compulsory attendance of all learners is mandated which curtails a school's ability to expel learners. In addition, the Promotion of Equality and Prevention of Unfair Discrimination Act No. 4 of 2000 stipulates that school learners who become pregnant may not be unfairly discriminated against which supports their right to complete their schooling.

However, these rights are not guaranteed. In most cases the implementation of protections has been patchy, contradictory and sometimes resulted in punitive actions being meted out to pregnant or mothering learners. In 2007, *Measures for the Prevention and Management of Learner Pregnancy* was published by the Department of Education so as to address the issue of an implementation vacuum of the legislation. The approach of this document was very much in keeping with the standard research approach on teenage pregnancy in that it focused on pregnancy prevention, opening with the phrase 'Children should abstain from engaging in sexual intercourse' (Department of Education, 2007:1).

Despite an attempt to be explicit about the steps that should be taken by management and educators in the event of learner pregnancy, the document errs instead on the side of imposing responsibilities on learners. These responsibilities include learners informing educators of any suspicions they may have regarding pregnancy among other learners. Perhaps the most contradictory guidelines are the stipulations that 'no learner should be readmitted in the same year that they left due to the pregnancy' (Department of Education, 2007:5) and

What are the contributing factors, and are these important?

Much research conducted on the contributing factors to 'teenage pregnancy' has taken a deficit-finding focus on the individual young woman or her family. Pregnant teenagers are often spoken of as disadvantaged victims of poor individual choices and dysfunctional families. These deficits have included lacking physical attributes, information, knowledge, maturity, psychological well-being, assertiveness, and normative family relationships to sustain childbearing.

The most common contributory factor has become known as the ignorance hypothesis. This is the idea that teenaged pregnancy happens because teenagers do not have the information they need about reproductive health, conception and contraception. Researchers have also investigated the following aspects:

- The association between early menarche or early sexual debut and teenage pregnancy;
- Knowledge about contraception;
- Risk-taking sexual behavior;
- Psychological problems resulting from childhood abuse, trauma or loss;
- Cognitive deficiencies;
- Peer influence; and
- Dysfunctional family patterns (Macleod & Tracey, 2010).

A key contributory factor bandied about in public is that welfare grants called the child support grant (CSG) in South Africa function as perverse incentives for poor young people to have children. The CSG was first introduced in 1998 and the amount provided is small (R380 per month per child in 2017). There is no evidence in South Africa, however, to suggest a positive association between the grant and the trend in teenaged childbearing (Makiwane, Desmond, Richter & Udjo, 2006).

Revisionists argue that the concentration on the 'causes' of 'teenage pregnancy' is misplaced. The focus on the 'causes' would only be of interest if the negative consequences are shown absolutely to be associated with age rather than other variables. Instead, they argue, that the focus should not be on preventing *teenage* pregnancy per se, but rather on unsupportable pregnancies across the board, and providing more support to all pregnant women. These researchers focus on different contributory factors, such as the causes of poor health care for young women and teachers' responses to learners who are pregnant or mothering.

Critical feminist authors point out that the search for contributory factors draws on the dominant understanding of adolescence as a natural, inevitable and universal developmental stage of human growth. In this stage, the pregnant

Researchers in the revisionist category, however, point out that these negative consequences may not be associated with age per se. They indicate that when well-designed research is conducted that compares the outcomes of early reproduction with the outcomes of reproduction among older women of the same social circumstances (eg, socio-economic status, access to health care facilities, family structure, marital status, and parity), the differences tend to disappear. Indeed, socio-economic status appears to be the biggest contributor to negative pregnancy outcomes (Macleod, 2011).

With this in mind, revisionists do research that shifts the focus to the social context in which pregnancy happens. For example, revisionists argue that much of the standard approach is motivated by particular cultural assumptions: the middle-class, nuclear-family experience as a universal aspiration (Geronimus, 1997), even when it is clear that it does not reflect the values, environmental contingencies or life expectations of all people (Mkhwanazi, 2014). Their research conducted with pregnant young women has focused on how early childbearing could represent a rational choice for those in situations of poverty and lead to positive outcomes. There seems little sense in delaying childbearing since these young women have better access to family support and their pregnancies often strengthen relational bonds. If your life is foreshortened owing to health deterioration as a consequence of inequities, then early childbearing ensures a longer and healthier parenting time (Geronimus & Thompson, 2004).

In the South African context where tertiary education and appealing employment options are very limited, pregnancy and motherhood offer some opportunity for status to young women in the absence of middle-class resources. If further education or meaningful employment is denied to you, then becoming a mother could represent a successful lifespan progression. Revisionist researchers have conducted studies, which highlight how the impact of early childbearing has been positive for young women by improving their status and creating a heightened sense of maturity and motivation to complete schooling (Chohan & Langa, 2011).

The critical feminists note that the very term 'teenage pregnancy' has had a very short history. Before the 1980s in South Africa, pregnant adolescents were treated as a moral problem and described routinely as 'unwed mothers' giving birth to 'illegitimate children'. When these moralising labels were no longer socially acceptable, there was a shift to talking about pregnant teenagers as needing medical and scientific attention (Macleod, 2003). Pregnant teenagers are not the only category of women who have been identified as unfit to mother. In South Africa many poor black women, lesbian, single, HIV-positive and women with disabilities have faced significant social stigma with regards to their desire to experience pregnancy and motherhood. Critical feminists point to the raced, classed and heteronormative power relations on which these judgements are based.

since many categories of women were excluded from claiming sexual and reproductive rights under apartheid. A number of empowering policies and legislation have been put in place to break with past discriminatory practices, such as the South African Schools Act No. 84 of 1996 and the Promotion of Equality and Prevention of Unfair Discrimination Act No. 4 of 2000. However, these rights-based documents (which are discussed further in the section 'What kinds of educational solutions or social support should be provided?' later on in this chapter) may be at odds with the hierarchical spaces in which young women have to negotiate with teachers and school managers who have the power to exclude them. A human rights approach to pregnant and mothering young women is often met with resistance from learners, teachers and school management (although, this resistance may be understandable in schools which are over burdened and under-resourced).

The prevention of teenage pregnancy (along with the prevention of HIV, STIs and sexual violence) is a key objective in public health and school interventions (see the chapter on school-based sexuality education in this book). These interventions tend to cast pregnancy as a personal calamity and social problem, which can only lead to damaging consequences. This rendition adds to the stigma around early reproduction, fails to connect with the lived realities of young people, and is not necessarily accurate. In the following sections, we outline the debates on 'teenage pregnancy' that need to be considered.

The major debates

There are three major approaches to 'teenage pregnancy': standard, revisionist and critical feminist. The debates tend to cohere around the following questions: Is 'teenage pregnancy' really a problem? What are the contributory factors, and why are they important? What kinds of solutions or social support should be provided to young pregnant or mothering women?

Is teenage pregnancy really a problem?

Researchers utilising a standard approach problematise 'teenage pregnancy' as having multiple and ongoing negative consequences. The starting point for these researchers is that owing to the teenager's developmental status, she is physically, emotionally, economically and socially unsuited to pregnancy, childbearing and parenting. Unsurprisingly then, there is a fairly long list of negative consequences, including disruption of schooling, the perpetuation of poverty, poor parenting practices, poor outcomes for the children, obstetric problems for the woman, breakdown in family and partner relations, and associations with HIV.

revisionists and the critical feminists (Macleod, 2013; Mkhwanazi, 2006). In this chapter, we outline why the question of 'teenage pregnancy' is important, what the debates are between researchers, and locate these debates within the South African context. Readers will note that we use the term 'teenage pregnancy' in inverted commas (in line with the critical feminist perspective) which will be explained further below.

Why is 'teenage pregnancy' important?

Teenage pregnancy is not rare: about 20 000 teenagers give birth every day across the world (Williamson, 2013). In all regions of the world, impoverished, poorly educated and rural teenagers are more likely to become pregnant than their wealthier, better educated, urban counterparts. In addition, young women from ethnic minorities or marginalised groups (who have few opportunities and poor access to sexual and reproductive health care) are more likely to choose pregnancy or experience unsupportable pregnancy owing to lack of access to adequate sexual and reproductive health care. About 95% of teenage pregnancies occur in low- to middle-income countries, with 90% of these occurring within marriage (Williamson, 2013).

Early reproduction is a factor in the disruption of schooling. While some studies suggest causal links between teenage pregnancy and school dropout, others have argued that school dropout often precedes pregnancy. The failure to return to school often has more to do with the unsupportive circumstances as opposed to a desire to end schooling. Ultimately the evidence related to whether pregnancy delays or terminates schooling prematurely is not clear-cut.

Nevertheless, it is incumbent upon educators and psychologists to provide personal and social support to teenagers so as to reduce any potential disruptions to the young woman's return to, and continued attendance of, school. This is in line with the rights of all women of reproductive age to receive support in the workplace (or in this case the learning space). This support can take a range of forms including:

- Home visits to ascertain familial support and to supplement this where necessary;
- Assisting in making child care arrangements, including the possibility of the young woman having a space to breastfeed while at school; and
- Systemic work with other members of the school to reduce stigma and to provide a positive environment for the young woman.

The attainment of sexual and reproductive rights, which includes the right to reproductive decision-making and support during and after pregnancy, is considered especially important within the historical context of South Africa,

38 'Teenage pregnancy' or early reproduction

TRACEY FELTHAM-KING & CATRIONA IDA MACLEOD

Why, despite evidence to the contrary, does the narrative of the negative consequences of teenage pregnancy, abortion and childbearing persist? (Macleod, 2011)

Introduction

'Teenage pregnancy' is a topic that receives a lot of sensationalised media attention. Headlines proclaim an increase in learner pregnancies, with dramatic figures drawing attention to supposedly worrying numbers. This is despite the fact that in South Africa the rate of teenage pregnancy has been estimated by researchers to have been declining since the 1980s and remaining stable from end of the 1990s (Statistics South Africa, National Department of Health, South African Medical Research Council, 2017).

Teenagers who reproduce are constantly blamed for contributing to a range of social problems, most notably the transfer of poverty from one generation to another. The common view is that 'teenage pregnancy' demonstrates a failure on the part of the girl, her family and her community. However, not all researchers agree with this sentiment and the issue continues to be debated.

There are three major approaches to understanding the issue of 'teenage pregnancy'. The standard approach in social science research is to try to understand the consequences of early reproduction, to look for the causes and to investigate preventive interventions. This approach has, however, been vigorously contested by other researchers who fall into two groups, namely the dialogical group approach where learners can freely discuss and debate issues that are pertinent to their own lives is far more effective. However, such an approach cannot work unless the teacher is able to model a respectful and non-judgemental attitude, and to ensure that such an ethos prevails during discussions. Varied participatory learning methods are also recommended, such as role plays, drama, and art work.

Second, sexuality education needs to be comprehensive and empowering in the broadest possible terms, not only with regards to reproductive issues (such as including discussions on abstinence, contraception, pregnancy and abortion), but also in terms of gender. Sexualities (gay, lesbian, straight, bisexual, asexual) and gender (cisgender/transgender, gender binary/non-binary, gender power relations) need to be discussed openly and non-judgementally. Where there are conservative views in a community or school (eg, homophobia (Bhana, 2012)), it is sometimes helpful to provide personal stories of the struggles of people who identify with a minority sexuality/gender. Dominant heterosexual gendered ideals (such as males needing to 'score' with females, and females needing to attract males) should be openly discussed and critiqued, and gendered power inequities need to be exposed.

Finally, the challenges of teaching such a value-laden and personal topic such as sexuality need to be acknowledged. It requires self-awareness, strong interpersonal skills, knowledge of varied participatory teaching styles, and an understanding of the socially constructed nature of gender on the part of the educator. Furthermore, such teachers are often the ones to whom learners turn when faced with sexual difficulties. Specific training in providing sexuality education is required, and some form of external support can be of great assistance to sexuality education teachers. Having an outside facilitator run dialogical groups (Jearey-Graham & Macleod, 2017) may work better than leaving sexuality education to the sole responsibility of the LO teacher.

Conclusion

We hope that it is clear from the above discussion that sexuality education is able to reduce one or more risky sexual behaviours if it is conducted in a participatory and empowering manner, where learners are encouraged to engage, debate, discuss, and challenge 'normal' sexual and gendered behaviours, and if it is comprehensive in the broadest possible way. Given the distressingly high levels of adverse sexual outcomes in South Africa, high quality sexuality education is a key learning priority.

Merely tagging on a sentence or two about the need for mutual respect in relationships and basic equality is not sufficient to empower young people and transform inequitable gendered norms. CSE programmes rather need to be fundamentally geared to empowering young people in the areas of gender and power. This needs to be done through varied dialogical and participatory methods, where learners are encouraged to debate and discuss some of the relational, gendered and sexual issues and difficulties that are prevalent in their own contexts (Jearey-Graham & Macleod, 2017). This allows for taken-for-granted gendered behaviours to be brought into the open and critiqued.

Addressing abortion in sexuality education classes

Abortion (also referred to as termination of pregnancy, or TOP) can be a highly emotive topic. Some people believe that abortion is tantamount to murder, while others believe that abortion is a necessary provision to promote women's reproductive health, rights, and justice. People in the latter camp point out that unsupportable pregnancies often arise through structural, relational, gendered and economic injustices, and that safe abortion services are important in the fight against these injustices. South Africa has among the most liberal abortion laws in the world, allowing women, including minors, to request a termination of pregnancy up to 12 weeks of gestation, and thereafter under specified conditions. Despite these liberal laws, the actual provision of safe abortion services throughout the country is patchy, with rural areas being typically under-resourced.

There is evidence that many young people are unaware of their legislative rights to abortion (Macleod, Seutlwadi & Steele, 2014) which may result in their turning to illegal, 'back-street' abortionists when faced with an unsupportable pregnancy. Therefore, regardless of one's personal views, it is important to give young people factual information about abortion and how to access it safely. As with providing other sexual information, discussing abortion openly is unlikely to increase the rates of abortion or unsupportable pregnancies, and it may save some young women from the high risks of illegal abortions.

Recommendations for school-based sexuality education

In the light of the above, what are our recommendations for sexuality education? First, we urge that sexuality education be conducted in a dialogical and participatory manner, with learners divided into small groups. 'Chalk and talk' teaching is particularly ineffective when educating about sexualities, where values and social norms affect behaviour far more than knowledge. Rather, a

Fortunately, South Africa does not face the same kinds of wranglings at a political level, and CSE has been firmly encoded in educational policy documents for the last two decades. However, at the grassroots level, South Africa is a very 'value-diverse' country, with widely disparate views on sexuality and how (and whether) young people should learn about sexual issues. Some people feel that discussing sex openly with children or adolescents will incite their curiosity, and trigger their sexual debut earlier than if they had merely been told to 'stay away from sex'. Some people believe that it is important to scare young people away from sex by focussing only on the risks, and they fear that informing young people about safe sex methods like contraceptives and condoms will give them 'permission' to engage in sex. Some teachers feel that talking about sex openly with learners undermines their authority. Furthermore, there are strongly homophobic attitudes in many South African communities, with same-sex activity viewed as disgusting, un-Godly, un-African, and unnatural. All of these factors can make it very difficult for teachers to teach CSE in an open and non-judgemental way (Francis, 2012).

However, regardless of one's personal values, the weight of research is increasingly favouring CSE. Well-designed CSE programmes generally perform better than abstinence-only programmes, which in turn may or may not perform better than no sexuality education at all (Lindberg & Maddow-Zimet, 2012) terms of delaying sexual debut and increasing condom and contraceptive use.

Addressing gender in sexuality education classes

A growing body of research over the last two decades has shown that worse sexual outcomes (increased STI rates, more unsupportable pregnancies, and higher levels of gender-based violence and sexual coercion) occur in contexts where there is a more unequal distribution of power between genders (for example, Jewkes, Dunkle, Nduna & Shai, 2010). Unequal gendered behaviours typically revolve around males exerting control over females, and lauding male strength, toughness, and sexual 'conquests', with females acquiescing to such behaviours, and needing to be desirable to men in order to prove their womanhood (Jewkes & Morrell, 2010).

There has therefore been an increasing emphasis on addressing gender and power issues in sexuality education, and recent research has shown that CSE programmes that address such issues in a comprehensive manner are significantly more likely to positively affect one or more reproductive health outcomes (Haberland, 2015). Such programmes have been given a range of labels, including 'rights-based', 'sex-positive', 'gender-transformative', and 'empowerment sexuality education' (Haberland, 2015).

Sadly, studies have highlighted major deficiencies in many of the sexuality education classes in South African schools. Glover and Macleod's (2016) overview of this research indicates the following:

1. There is an over-emphasis on negative messages about sex ('danger, disease and damage'), with a general silence around the positive aspects of sexuality, such as pleasure, relationships, and connection.
2. There is a disconnection between the classes' construction of the 'ideal' young person who is responsible and risk-averse, and learners' situated realities.
3. Classes are conducted in a primarily non-relational and teacher-centred manner.
4. Rigid gender categories tend to be reinforced, with males positioned as dominant, predatory, and sexualised, and females as submissive, lacking sexual desire, and potential victims, yet simultaneously needing to take primary responsibility for sexual practices.
5. Homophobia is frequently implicitly or explicitly upheld, with teachers often avoiding addressing issues of sexual diversity, and LO manuals maintaining a general silence about same-sex sexual relationships.
6. Teachers often find teaching sexuality education to be very challenging: sexuality is a value-laden topic, and teachers may find themselves caught between the conflicting values of the national curriculum, the school, the parents, the learners, their own beliefs, and their other roles within the school.

Abstinence-only versus comprehensive sexuality education

The debate over whether sexuality education should promote only abstinence, or should address other safe sex methods as well, has become a central battle ground in the United States between conservative and liberal interests (Connell & Elliott, 2009). Conservative groups promote abstinence-only programmes, which teach that the only acceptable context for sexual activity is within a monogamous heterosexual marriage relationship. Liberal approaches favour comprehensive programmes which discuss a range of sexual options, and try to resist promoting the view that there is only one acceptable context for sexual expression. Despite mounting evidence that comprehensive sexuality education (CSE) first does not lower the age at which young people first start having sex, and second generally delivers better outcomes in terms of reducing unsupportable pregnancies and STIs (sexually transmitted infections) than abstinence-only programmes (Kirby, 2011) the battle over which type of sexuality education should be delivered in schools remains a hot political issue in the United States.

The major debates within the field of sexuality education

Does sexuality education 'work'?

Sexuality education is now an almost universal aspect of school education in the West, and also in large parts of the developing world (Luker, 2006). It has been a compulsory aspect of the South African school curriculum since the late 1990s. Despite this, the adverse sexual outcomes mentioned above continue unabated. So, does it work?

The broad answer to the question of whether sexuality education programmes can reduce risky sexual behaviours is, 'Yes, but ...' To be effective, they must be well designed and well implemented by a skilled facilitator or teacher, and for a reasonable length of time. They also need to address issues of gendered power.

Kirby's (2011) meta-analysis of studies of sex or STI/HIV education programmes which were both curriculum- and group-based indicated that the most effective programmes had a modest positive effect on one or more risky sexual behaviours. These programmes lowered the risky behaviour by about one quarter to one third. This effect may seem small, but sexual behaviours are influenced by a large number of factors. A modest positive effect for such an 'over-determined' behaviour is therefore not to be sniffed at, and can lead to 'meaningful reductions in pregnancy and STI rates' (Kirby, 2011:5) (read also Chapter 38).

Factors which Kirby (2011) identified as characteristic of effective programmes included:

- Expert design that is sensitive to community values and available resources and is pilot-tested;
- A focus on specific risk and protective factors;
- The use of participatory, active, and varied teaching methods;
- Being group-based rather than classroom-based;
- Addressing values and peer norms;
- Building self-efficacy for safe sex behaviours;
- Providing training and support for the teachers/facilitators; and
- Having at least 12 sessions.

It is thus clear that a great deal more than simply providing learners with some factual information is necessary for sexuality education to be effective. A number of qualitative studies of the sexuality education that is provided in South African schools through the LO subject have been conducted (see, for example, the special issue of *Perspectives in Education* (Shefer & Macleod, 2015)).

In this chapter, we examine the importance of sexuality education and discuss some of the major debates within the field. We provide some recommendations for conducting sexuality education classes and conclude by noting the urgency of providing high quality sexuality education throughout all South African schools.

Why is sexuality education important?

South Africa is beset with high levels of adverse outcomes from risky and abusive sexual behaviours. The obvious ones are HIV and other sexually transmitted infections, unwanted and unsupportable pregnancies, gender-based violence, rape, sexual coercion and sexual abuse. However, there are also less obvious negative consequences from some sexual behaviours. Sex is primarily relational: it occurs and is expressed between people using the most intimate parts of our bodies and psyches, and much relational hurt occurs when sex is used for essentially selfish reasons: to exert control, to numb pain, or to boost one's status.

Sexuality and gender are also primary means through which we perform our identities and express who we are to others and to ourselves. We are categorised as 'female' or 'male' at birth (or earlier) and we are socialised as such from that time onwards. Adolescence is often a time when young people are trying to understand who they are and how they should relate to others. It is also a time when sexual maturity is attained. Thus, working out how to relate successfully as a sexual and gendered being can be a major occupation for adolescents. It is, therefore, important to address issues of sex and sexuality with young people before they become sexually active, both to assist them with understanding identity and relational struggles, and to help them choose which sexual behaviours they would like to engage in or abstain from.

A public health model (which is the dominant model guiding health interventions) views sexuality education as important because of its preventative potential. At its best, it can help prevent adverse sexual outcomes by helping young people to practice safe sex behaviours (generally defined according to the ABCD acronym—sexual Abstinence, Being faithful to one partner, Condom use, and Delayed sexual debut) and promoting respect in sexual relationships.

Another view of sexuality education is from an empowerment perspective. This approach takes the view that, whilst it is important to educate young people about sexual risks and how to avoid them, and to alert them to the potential for abuse in sexual relationships, it is more important to assist young people to understand and own their bodies and their desires, to know their rights, and to empower them to relate to themselves and to others in a mutually respectful, enjoyable, and healthy manner.

37 Sexuality education

NICOLA JEAREY-GRAHAM & CATRIONA IDA MACLEOD

It's not so much sexuality **education** *that young people need, as sexuality* **dialogues**. (Jearey-Graham & Macleod, 2017:14)

Introduction

'I am a virgin but I always act as if I'm not a virgin in front of my friends'; 'I'm so not into boys but I'm 15!'; 'My secret is with my girlfriend, we had sex...'; 'I want to have sex without a condom'; 'I was dumped because I failed Grade 9'; 'I dated my friend's lover'; 'One day after school I was on my way home and a girl was raped in front of me.'

How, when, where and with whom sex should be expressed are subjects that occupy many political, academic, public and personal debates. The struggles of many young people as they try to negotiate such contested terrain is highlighted in the above 'post-secrets', written by some Grade 9 learners. Ideally, sexuality education provides an opportunity to address some of these contestations in an open and non-judgemental manner. However, research shows that often it fails to connect with the lived experiences of young people, and unwittingly becomes a conduit where gendered, raced and classed inequities are reinscribed.

Sexuality education is an umbrella term that has been applied to a wide range of interventions, aimed primarily at young people, which address issues of human sexuality. The most common form of sexuality education in South Africa today is provided through the compulsory school subject Life Skills (intermediate phase) and Life Orientation (LO) (senior phase), which have modules on various aspects of sexuality.

persistent desire and anxious restlessness for more effectiveness, improvements, and not being left out. As eloquently stated by Fischer, 'art making is anti-making' (Fischer, 2001:2), meaning to 'unpile' (Fischer, 2001:4) the piled *up doing*—the unmaking of thoughts and perceptions. During such a process, one question un-does time and again, allowing life to enter itself fully: How am I in *this* moment in *this* world? It is a truly aesthetic experience.

4. Another entry place would be to provoke anticipation and imagination grounded in the present situation as a counterpart of prediction and expectation based on what is already known. As suggested by Wong (2006), introduce 'what if,' 'what could be,' and 'what might happen' experiences.

5. Deliberate practising of what we do, the discipline of educational psychology as our art, is essential in learning how to attend and come into unwavering presence (Hirshfield, 1997) because the aesthetic aptitude takes effort and this is the effort of artful learning. Just as the musician practices scales, the dancer repeats movements, and the poet revises a poem, the student and practitioner will need to read, re-read, formulate and reformulate, visit and re-visit, write and re-write incessantly as a way of continued honing deeper levels of connected learning.

Conclusion

In a modern, non-communication time characterised by utility, newsfeed fetishism, immediateness, and nonstop information, the aesthetic disposition that allows receptive experiencing, is seriously neglected. Undone and unmade spaces are regarded as voids and filled up with sounds, images, and distractions. How can the training student or practitioner craft conditions that would evoke and cultivate attributes of attentiveness, sensitive awareness of irony, ambivalence, and metaphor, thus encouraging deep engagement?

This chapter attempted to provide and explain ways in which the very much needful aesthetic nature of any professional practice can be understood and explored deliberately as a way of artful engagement. The resemblance between studying and practising any artistic discipline and any other form of deep learning is based on intellectual skills such as perceiving and exploring multiple relationships, surprising possibilities, nuance, metaphor, and being attuned attentively. These skills constitute the aesthetic disposition, the clarification and magnification of everything that is already implicated, as well as an elegant awareness for enlarging transitions—*of what may be known, what may be felt, what may be done*. Poignant discoveries await students in training and practitioners who are willing to hold up a mirror for themselves. The effort of aesthetic learning, which is the very being of artistry in any discipline, is indeed an impressive undertaking.

How can we practise aesthetic openness to stimulate deep learning?

Aesthetic openness comprises an innermost awareness distinguished by a shift of being, knowing, and understanding. In the understanding of philosopher Hannah Arendt, aesthetic openness is a way of being reborn, a miraculous insertion into the world again through imaginative wonder (Arendt, 1958). This presence of existential awakening, or Arendt's concept of natality, depicts a pre-linguistic nature where mysterious wonder comes before defining, descriptive language. As mentioned earlier in the chapter, it indicates receptiveness to what it means to exist, and human existence mapped by irony, ambivalence, ecstasy, and vulnerability.

In the process of natality, reflective inquiry and contemplative dwelling necessitate 'putting yourself at play and risk' (Arendt, 1958) in order to be pushed towards the boundaries of that which seems to be certain and known. Students in training and practitioners should continuously create places of entry into aesthetic experiences. Suggestions for crafting such places could perhaps include the following:

1. The Bohm Dialogue, which is based on physicist David Bohm's theory of free dialogue, can be used to playfully stimulate an attentive state where awareness is focussed and unified, yet permeable and open. This specific dialogue is characterised by a free-flowing, non-judgemental group conversation with no predefined purpose or agenda. It is to be used in a self-justified manner, emphasising exploration of the movement of complex thought processes, and exercising the capacity to embrace the fullness of different qualitative experiences. The Bohm Dialogue acts as an entrance *token* (Hirshfield, 1997) to new and deeper levels of understanding.

2. On relational silence (acknowledging the surrounding environment of sound and language) as opposed to absolute silence, the writer Susan Sontag (1969) advises the reader to craft a space where selfless and unselfconscious attention can be paid to the world. Such a space (activity, exercise) would be regarded as silent, characterised by creative concentration and unreactive contemplation where willed effort drops away, as opposed to a Twitter and Facebook culture characterised by reactive tossing of opinions.

3. Encourage musing and dwelling on feelings and thoughts, the pure sensation of *un-madeness*, by consciously resisting the need to justify, explain, and verbalise pre-linguistic experiences immediately, for we want to be out of words (to be swept away, inspired), not to have no words (grounded in attenuated intellect and a lack of vocabulary characterised by richness and range). It involves being undone, unmade, and undefined without the

- What do you need to do after you have pondered this photograph? How is it the same as or different from what you have done before you have pondered the photograph?

The educative function of art lies in its aesthetical value, which is the inspirational experience with which students and practitioners are stimulated. At the basis of the aesthetical experience, certain intellectual skills that are necessary for deep and meaningful participation on the side of any practitioner must be identified. Based on the work of Richmond (2009) and Evans (2016), the following skills are stimulated by way of the aesthetical experience:

- Responsiveness of mind and body, and because of this, a sensitive awareness of affective experiences (feelings, emotions, moods), cognitive experiences (thoughts, ideas), and behaviour (actions) are all experiences that are forms of intelligible responses when looking at the person as a whole.
- Attentiveness (paying attention, listening, and responding) concerning the occurrence and exploration of possible relationships, subtleties, needs, ambivalence, challenges, choices, patterns, processes, preferences, and recurring themes.
- Appreciation of phenomena, events, and narratives peculiar to *la condition humaine*. Evans (2016:44) speaks of witnessing as a way of beholding something; therefore, recognising its effect and often complex and sometimes delicate unfolding nature without immediate evaluation. At the heart of this appreciative response is the ability to imagine, relate empathically to, and become immersed in the possible inner life of another appreciatively. As an outcome of this, according to Eisner (2001), 'surprise' might therefore just as well be the reward of your knowledgeable imagination at work.

Intellectual creativity, referring to:
- A richly variegated and extensive frame of reference;
- Critical propensity characterised by the capacity to analyse, evaluate, and establish relationships between seemingly non-related matters, and creating associations; and
- The capacity to apply existing knowledge resourcefully in new and innovative ways.

Perhaps Richmond's (2009:104) notion of creativity as a clear expression of a unique sensibility steers us in making sense of this ability of artful practice in any discipline, albeit educational psychology, teaching, engineering or other professional disciplines.

- The connected and interdependent nature of aesthetic experiences also furnishes us with a sense of rootedness (belonging) as an imperative in a consumer society characterised by utility and media marketing.

me; while recording what is seen, what is shown invokes what or who is not shown. They are at the centre of this narrative: the true subjects of the photographs are, in this sense, invisible, yet contained within the photographs.
(Morning after Dark exhibition by David Lurie, Stellenbosch University Museum, August 2015)

FIGURE 36.2 Cape Town train station, from N2 Motorway, 2013
Source: David Lurie

Ponder the photograph in Figure 36.2 taken by South African artist David Lurie and answer the following questions:

- What do you experience? Try to describe your responses.
- What does the photograph or image do to you? What went through your mind, body, and perhaps total being while you were looking at the photograph?
- How does this experience or sensation compare with anything else in your life? How may it even be different?
- If you would look at yourself standing in front of the installed photograph in an art gallery, what would your observations and conclusions be?
- What did you notice in the photograph? Of what does it remind you?
- What is perhaps not visible in the photograph but certainly present?
- What have you realised about yourself/others/the world?
- What are you unsure, scared, or excited about at this current moment?

Educational psychology and aesthetic learning

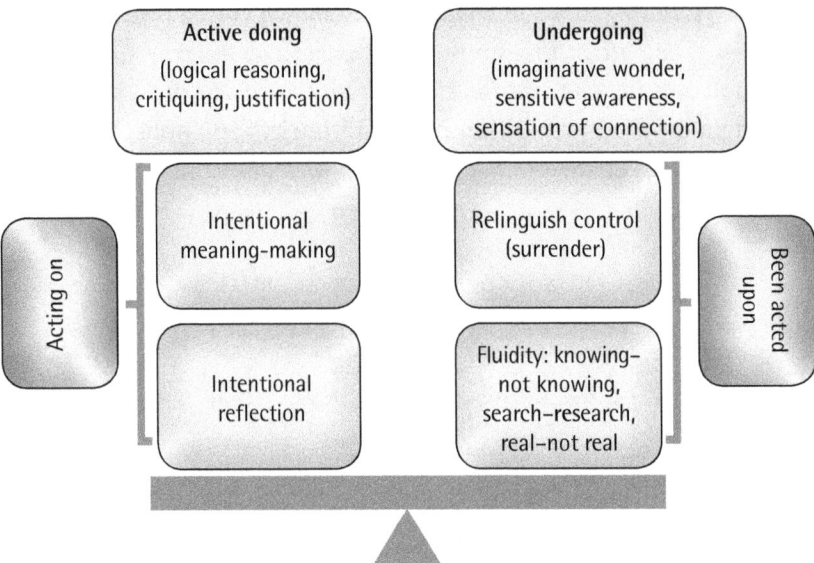

FIGURE 36.1 The aesthetic learning experience

For Dewey (1934), Eisner (1985), Hirshfield (1997), and Wong (2006), educationalists and writers from whom much have been gleaned about aesthetic learning experiences, deep engagement requires both active doing and receptive undergoing in a mutually determined way. This implies students and practitioners need not only construct meaning intentionally and reflectively in the light of that which emerges, which resonates much with constructivist philosophy. Apart from controlled interaction, students and practitioners also need to surrender and relinquish control when they plunge into the wondrous fluidity of back-and-forth movement between knowing and not knowing, here and there, real and not real, familiar and strange, search and re-search. According to Wong (2006:205), 'deeply engaged learners have the capacity to be both active and receptive'. **Active doing**, which is by nature intentional (**acting on**), refers to the rational and logical reasoning, analysing, and justification of ideas and consequences based on what is already known. **Receptive undergoing** refers to an immediate, spontaneous sense—**to be acted upon**—without it becoming a functional object of construction and reflection. This resonates with poet Norman Fischer's (2001:5) point on beauty: 'Beauty is not necessarily pretty; it is, rather, this accidental sensation, before we think about it and therefore make something of it, of connection, unmadeness … freedom.' The photographer-artist, David Lurie, perhaps alludes to this capacity for receptive undergoing when he speaks of some of his photographic images as follows:

The moments I have chosen to isolate, when the protagonists of the photographs are absent, was deliberate and something of a departure for

The aesthetic disposition subscribes to a continuous process of propulsion into an ever more comprehensive understanding and rethinking of the temporary, fictional nature of being and knowing. This principle of not knowing and the incompleteness of everything, together with a creative surge, might lead us to curiously ponder and imagine a labyrinth of richly chequered ideas, insights, and practices. The creative surge denotes a profound, compelling encounter that activates and necessitates a deeper consciousness, more than just thought and theory, when being swallowed up by and absorbed into the object of focus or subject matter. We enter a state of aesthetic openness to be perfused with a feeling of 'heightened vitality' (Dewey, 1934:19). Aesthetic openness is brought to fruition when we release ourselves to imaginative wonder, courageously venture into the unknown, and respond with awakened interest, exuberance, and compassion. While we are so used to the colonisation of our experiences by semantics of language that wishes to describe, explicate, and separate between the self and others, aesthetic openness allows us to reach the state where everything becomes an extension of something else. By way of the creative surge, we find ourselves in a pre-linguistic state where we can experience a deeply felt connection with the root matter of all things. Kate Evans (2016:45), a writer and psychotherapeutic counsellor, speaks about this embodied consciousness as follows: 'When it happens, it is a precious and critical resonance of myself with another self.' Evans's description of this impregnated awareness depicts the pre-linguistic experience of receptive undergoing, of being acted upon, even before language describes and defines in functional and predetermined ways. We come to ask ourselves the following: 'How can my being, knowing and acting as a counsellor or an educational psychologist, become a mirror in which I can identify myself as a practitioner with an aesthetic disposition for not knowing, non-certainty, therefore learning?'

Why are aesthetical learning experiences important?

The way in which any artistic discipline is studied and practised, serves to be an analogy for receptive engagement that is an aesthetic experience. Writers like Hirshfield (1997) and Eisner (1985, 2003) suggest that the existence of a clear resemblance between *ars poetica* and any other form of deep learning is based on intellectual skills such as perceiving and exploring multiple relationships, surprising possibilities, nuance, metaphor, and being attentive. It is not surprising that one of the often-neglected aspects in the major discourses on education and training refers to the evocative nature of learning.

36 Educational psychology and aesthetic learning

KARLIEN CONRADIE

What is essential is invisible to the eye. (Antoine de Saint-Exupéry in *The Little Prince*)

Introduction

Where do you currently focus your attention, time, and energy? What are you busy doing? Perhaps it is your profession, your academic studies, your family relationships or other fundamental life tasks. How would you describe the way in which you attend to, participate in, and complete these tasks and activities? What are the essential attributes necessary for deliberate practice *within* a task or activity? These questions are echoed somewhat in the works of eminent scholars like Friedrich Schiller (1759–1805) (Schiller, 2016) and Elliot Eisner (1933–2014) who emphasised the aesthetic disposition as a necessity for deep, wholehearted engagement.

What does the aesthetic disposition look like?

The aesthetic disposition refers to a contemplative way of being in and sensing the world, an ultimate state of openness or sensitive receptiveness to the realities and qualities of what it means to exist. It embraces human existence often mapped by subtleties, irony, ambivalence, ecstasy, and vulnerability. An aesthetic orientation towards the world and others is concerned with the underlying moral question of humanity, which is: How should we be in this world (how should we live)?

9

Educational psychological support

Conclusion

Parents are not always aware that their involvement in their child's school has a positive impact for the child, school and themselves, and therefore schools need to convey this message more effectively. Parents are willing to participate in a relationship with the school if they are treated like adults and if they are made to believe that they can contribute to the well-being of children—their own and others. This cooperation also causes them to get better at their own parental skills. Making sure that parents experience these interactions in a positive light, is a challenge that many schools are dealing with. In conclusion, parental partnerships start at school.

especially important when working with the minority groups in the school. It is not uncommon for teachers to be hesitant to work with parents who differ in language, race, culture, etc, or to feel unsure of how to address the differences. Gathering information about the parent's culture is not the only way to empower oneself. Cultural competence, according to Bornman and Rose (2017:16), includes showing respect and honouring the family's values and beliefs with an open mind and without judgement, prejudice or bias. Cultural competence will ensure that families experience teachers' care. Edwards (2009:56) suggests 'differentiated parenting' and 'parentally appropriate' actions to connect with the diverse parents. Actions to ensure acceptance of all families include for example to ask parents of the different languages represented in the school, to translate newsletters or the bulletin boards, or an interpreter in the class to explain what is verbally and nonverbally communicated.

Although there is a diversity in South African parents, research shows that all the different family groups gain from parental partnerships with schools, irrespective of the family's race, ethnic group and income group (Coleman, 2013:55). Keep in mind that the 'family structure in itself is not predictive of parenting quality' (Pryor, cited in Coleman, 2013:29).

Negative influences on parental partnerships

Although this chapter focuses on the positive outcomes of parental involvement, there are two sides of this coin. Partnerships between schools and families can be compromised and negatively influenced, which can be problematic for all the stakeholders involved.

The school can be the negative influence that compromises the partnership, when teachers take a back seat and rely on the parents to uphold the partnership alone, make all the decisions or expect parents to be solely responsible for fundraisers. Criticism and a judgemental attitude towards parents can also terminate the partnership. It is important for schools to realise that not all parents are able to be involved. Schools should respect and understand the parents' situation when they are unable to form a partnership due to workload or health impairments.

On the other hand, parents can jeopardise the partnership when they get too involved with the running of the school and feel it is their right to dictate all the decisions being made. Parents can intrude in the teachers' domain and this may lead to conflict and to the termination of the partnership.

It is therefore clear that mutual respect, a healthy balance of power and adaptations by both parties, are essential for partnerships between schools and families.

difficulties (Donald, Lazarus & Lolwana, 2010:342). Address topics such as homework support, literacy or numeracy support, parenting styles, or behaviour management. Organise social events for parents to meet one another.

Make use of parents' expertise and start a parent mentorship programme where skilled parents work with disadvantaged, talented, troubled or difficult children. Involve parents as assistants in the classroom. As volunteers they can help in a wide variety of ways—doing administration, reading to small groups or individuals, helping with homework, supporting children with special needs, coaching sport, or serving in the school management team.

To achieve these goals schools need to have a positive mind-set about working together with parents. Focus on the family strengths and avoid negative stereotyping. Keep in mind that families do care and are doing the best they know. Therefore reinforce the families' efforts and not only their successes (Coleman, 2013). The reason for family partnerships must always be to reach the end goal, namely to support learners' education and invest in social capital where the learner and the family gains.

In conclusion, for successful parental partnerships 'parents must feel it, believe it and see it happen' (Wilson, 2001:8). Schools need to think creatively and explore new ways to involve parents in order for them to buy into this partnership.

Parental partnerships in South African schools

The South African Schools Act No. 84 of 1996 (Republic of South Africa, 1996a), as well as the South African inclusive education system (Department of Education, 2001) acknowledge the rights of parents and the important role they play in the education of their child. Parents of learners, who experience barriers to learning and require additional support, are therefore encouraged to be part of the school-based support team (SBST) who develops strategies to address these barriers to learning (Department of Basic Education, 2014).

South African schools have a rich diversity of different languages, religions, races, cultures, and socio-economic backgrounds. Modern families may be single-parent families, child headed families, unwed teenage mothers, same sex marriages, unmarried couples, extended and blended families. These factors seem to be a challenge for schools to remain inclusive and to involve all parents of all the diverse groups. Schools can benefit from the parent surveys to determine the diversity in their school's demographic and plan differentiated parental involvement accordingly.

Effective cooperation with parents means showing respect, appreciation and sensitivity for parents, their culture or language and their family values. This is

very important role as they are the parents' first encounter with the school. Not only is it a role of a friendly, well-informed host of the school, but also an administrative manager.

It is necessary to keep the relationship and participation ongoing by updating parents with regular newsletters—weekly, monthly or quarterly. Newsletters developed for each grade can inform parents about the curriculum followed, which gives them the opportunity to become more connected with the curriculum. They are now more than just homework overseers—they are actively involved in their child's schoolwork and how the child progresses or where more work is needed. Welcoming letters at the start of the new year, or during the year to new parents, convey the message of their importance to the school. These letters can include a year programme, upcoming important events, workshops, parent–teacher conferences, the school organisation and contact information. The different grades in the school can develop their own welcoming letter, which can include the academic year programme for the grade and tips on how to help the learner with homework, studying, projects and activities for the home that is linked to the academic programme. By using multimedia, the school is able to give regular updated news. Make use of a school web page, Facebook and WhatsApp group, and send emails or SMSs where parents have access. Use technology and make video clips available for parents about homework and parenting or give them the links for good tutorial YouTube clips. Inform parents about the schools homework policy and how they can help with homework or projects, by making tip sheets available electronically.

Communication includes having regular parent evenings—monthly or quarterly—where parents can personally meet the teacher and discuss the child's work or barriers to learning. Explain the academic report and answer questions about the learner's general progress. Have comfortable adult-sized chairs for these meetings and ensure that classroom doors have the name of the teacher on. Offer free coffee, tea or water at these meetings. When meetings are held, be sure to use accessible language and avoid or explain education jargons. Communication should not only take place in times of trouble, but staff members can contact parents to share good news about their child. Lucas (2006:23) suggests that each family should receive at least two of these 'sunshine calls' or WhatsApp messages during the year.

Parents need support to improve their parental skills on different levels. Establish support groups for parents at school, eg, support groups for attention deficit hyperactivity disorder, single parents, bullying, depression or a group for those who experienced trauma. Get the community involved by asking a professional in the community to facilitate these meetings. Have regular workshops to empower parents, especially parents of the learners with learning

5. Parents can be involved in the management and governance of the school by including them in **decision making**.
6. The **involvement of the community** in education is imperative for the school system to provide the best education and services to learners. Resources from within the community can help schools deliver quality education.

These six types of partnerships between the school and the home can benefit the learner, the family, the school and the community.

Getting and keeping parents involved

Parental partnerships start at school. It is important for the school to cultivate a welcoming environment for parents and to create a warm, inviting and inclusive atmosphere where parents feel comfortable and at ease. Schools can create such an environment by planning purposefully and allocating a specific staff member with the portfolio of parental involvement. Although this colleague acts as the organiser of parental involvement, the whole staff acts as the face of the school and is involved in all the interactions with parents. When planning family involvement programmes remember to start small and let it develop and grow organically. This way parents aren't forced and overwhelmed, which can lead to them feeling uninterested in any other further collaboration.

Start off by conducting a parent survey and gather valuable information about the parent's occupation, areas of expertise, hobbies, available resources, home language, best day and time for attending parent evenings, how they would like to be communicated with and in what language. Convey the importance of school–parent partnerships as parents are not always aware of the positive impacts and do not know how to get involved and on what level. Arrange parent focus group meetings where they can voice their opinion on school matters. These opinions can help to make the school more welcoming.

Schools should convey the message to parents that they are appreciated and important. Welcoming signs, banners and information-rich bulletin boards for the parents, as well as for the learners (Edwards, 2009:18), communicate publicly the schools' values, organisation, announcements and events and other important information. Presenting it in an interesting and colourful way attracts parents' attention to read more. Parents often feel educated, involved and important when reading this information.

The school's foyer where parents enter the building, can be used to display trophies, rewards, achievements or photos of the school or the learners. Have named photos of all the staff in the foyer. Lucas (2006:5) suggests having a child's drawing of each staff member next to the photo. Receptionists play a

Understanding educational psychology

The different types of parental partnerships

> Definition of parental involvement; Parental involvement is the parent's participation in all the different facets of the child's education and development throughout all the stages of the child's life. This includes school-based as well as home-based activities.

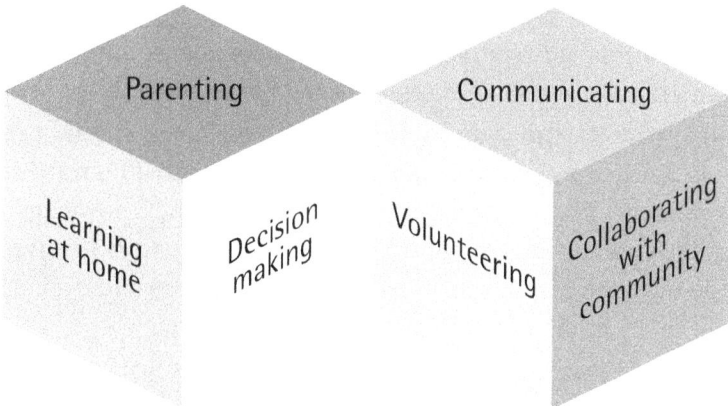

FIGURE 35.2 Joyce Epstein's six types of involvement for parents

There are different types of parental involvement. Joyce Epstein (2011) describes six equally important types of involvement for parents and community members. According to Swart and Phasha (2016:269) these six types include parenting, communicating, volunteering, learning at home, decision making and community collaboration.

The six types can be described as:

1. **Parenting** is difficult and during partnerships teachers can assist parents with this difficult task by empowering them with parenting skills, strategies and knowledge.
2. Open **communication** is imperative in any partnership. Schools should be transparent and communicate clearly and frequently with parents regarding their child's well-being, academic work and social-emotional skills. Respect, trust and confidentiality are the keywords during communication, whether it is to be school–home communication, or home–school communication.
3. The most well-known form of a partnership, **volunteering**, not only includes the traditional way of helping at school functions and fund raisers, but are extended to parents offering their talents and expertise to help run and support the school in every aspect.
4. Although parents might be eager to help their child with school work at home, they are not always sure how to be of assistance. Schools can lead in this process by giving parents information to equip them with this task. **Learning at home** can strengthen and support learning at school.

tertiary level, but it was also associated with a higher income as young adult. Better reading skills, significantly lower school dropout numbers and higher numbers in school completion were found where schools form partnerships with the parents. Coleman (2013:51–55) states that in addition to better academic achievements, parental partnerships impact the children in all aspects of their lives. Studies show a positive influence on the learner's classroom behaviour and less incidents of disciplinary problems are reported. Even school attendance improved. Learners developed emotionally and showed greater academic responsibilities.

In return, parents also gain by being involved in their child's education. Parents learn new parenting skills and enrich themselves with knowledge about child development. The result is that they now have the knowledge and self-confidence to advocate for their child's education. Being more involved in their child's academic work inspires them to have bigger dreams and expectations for the future of their child.

The school and teachers also benefit from the parents being involved in their child's academic lives. Teachers get to know the family better and understand the world that defines the child. This expanded knowledge of the child, together with a stronger relationship with the parents, improve the teacher–learner relationship, which in turn can improve teachers' self-efficacy (Coleman, 2013:78; Van Wyk & Lemmer, 2009:16). Schools also benefit from the expert knowledge they gain from parents being involved in the governance of the school, and sometimes welcome all the help they receive from parents giving their time to work at the school during fund-raising events or in classes as teacher assistants.

All the stakeholders are influenced by the positive impact of parental partnerships between the school, the home and the community. Figure 35.1, illustrates how the learner gains the most out of parental partnerships—a strengthened academic future.

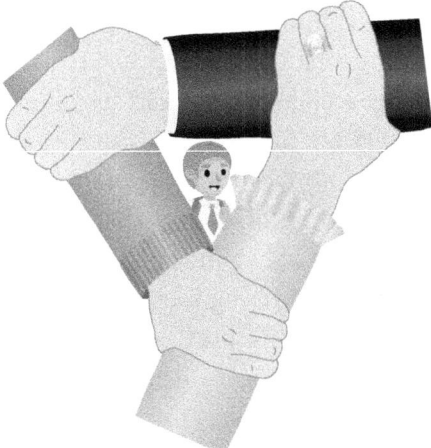

FIGURE 35.1 Parental partnerships between the school, the home and the community strengthens the future of a child

Theoretical background

Theories and models are used to describe and understand our world (Swart & Pettipher, 2016:10). Urie Bronfenbrenner's bio-ecological model describes different systems that have a direct or an indirect influence on a learner's development. These nested and interrelated systems are factors that contribute to the learner's education and development and give the teacher a total picture of the learner's world.

The microsystem includes the family, the school and the peers of the learner. These systems have a direct influence on the learner. The interaction between the microsystems is called the mesosystem and refers to the impact it has when the three microsystems interact—in this case when the school and the home work together. The microsystems are influenced and modified by the mesosystem, eg, the impact of the relationship that develops between the school and the home influences the learner's academic achievements directly (Swart & Pettipher, 2016:15).

The exosystem is an indirect influence on the learner's development and refers to environments such as the education system, the media or the parents' work. While the macrosystem represents the indirect influence of the values, beliefs and attitudes of the society, the chronosystem refers to the dimensions of time in which the other systems influence the development of the learner (Swart & Pettipher, 2016:15).

For a teacher to have insight and understand all the facets of the learner, it is necessary to understand the direct or indirect influence these systems have on the development of the learner. This gives insight on the importance of the relationship (mesosystem) between the school (microsystem) and the home (microsystem).

The importance of parental partnerships

The value of partnerships between parents and teachers is well recognised. Research indicates that parent partnerships with the school leads to student achievement (Coleman, 2013:52; Swart & Phasha, 2016:265; Van Wyk & Lemmer, 2009:14). The cycle repeats itself when a positive school climate will encourage parents to become involve, which in turn improves teaching and leads to learners' academic achievement. In return, learners' achievement cultures a positive school climate, and the circle continuous. Partnerships between the school and the home not only help parents to be better parents and teachers to be better teachers, but also encourage the learner to be positively involved in his/her learning and the community to take ownership of education and to become involved.

Studies show that parental partnerships impact on children throughout their lives (Coleman, 2013:52). Not only does it have a positive effect on learners' academic achievement during pre-school, primary school, high school and on

35 Strengthening parental partnerships

DEBBIE CILLIERS

There are many reasons for developing school, family, and community partnerships. The main reason to create such partnerships is to help all youngsters succeed in school and in later life. (Joyce Epstein)

Introduction

The old saying, 'it takes a village to raise a child', can have more meaning and impact if all the villagers work together more closely. It is clear that a partnership between the school and the home is not a new idea, but as society develops and changes, the idea of partnerships also changes and we therefore need to look at it differently. School–home partnerships form an integral part of a learner's academic success and therefore needs to be investigated. The South African inclusive school system requires greater involvement of parents and the community. This chapter addresses the importance of school–parental partnerships, different types of parental involvement, how to get parents involved and partnerships in the South African context.

> **Definition of parents:** The word parent refers to the adults in the child's life who are primarily responsible for the child's upbringing, well-being and education. This includes biological parents, extended parents (eg, grandparents, adult siblings) and sociological parents (eg, guardians, adoptive parents, stepparents) (Coleman, 2013:3,4).

> **Definition of family:** The South African Department of Social Development (2012:3) describes a family as 'a societal group that is related by blood (kinship), adoption, foster care or the ties of marriage (civil, customary or religious), civil union or cohabitation, and go beyond a particular physical residence'.

Furthermore, areas of innovation and development have been identified to ensure that prevention and intervention delivery is maximised in school settings. According to Walker (2004:402), the first area includes implementation and treatment integrity, meaning that the implementation process and careful assessment of variables that affect the quality of the intervention are systematically studied. Data or information about the context or problem is analysed in detail to establish measures that can monitor performance or progress over time (Sugai & Horner, 2009:223).

A second area is scaling up, diffusing and sustaining interventions. Regarding sustainability, Greenberg (2004:6) believes that instead of approaching schools for permission to test new interventions, schools must become collaborators to understand what support and structures are needed to create sustainable change.

Walker's (2004:403) third area of innovation and development pertains to the transportability of interventions from efficacy to effectiveness. Domitrovich, Bradshaw, Poduska, Hoagwood, Buckley, Olin, Hunter Romanelli, Leaf, Greenberg and Ialango (2008:7) define delivery of an intervention as the frequency, duration, timing and mode of delivery of the core components, including the individuals who take responsibility for the implementation of the intervention. Developing from efficacy to effectiveness ideally means that the intervention should develop from mechanical implementation to routine implementation, and ultimately to a stage of refinement.

Conclusion

Working in education is perhaps the call to assist in, at times, dire circumstances that cannot be ignored. It is, however, important to take the whole system into account. When we intervene in a system, we expect that some changes should take place. However, this has to be undertaken with care, as when we implement a programme there may be competing feedback loops that actually cancel out any good that we intended. Worse still, we do not always think in the long term, or of interventions over a sustained period. Usually when we are confronted with a problem, we need to solve the problem soonest, inevitably resulting in a quick fix. When working with schools, it is important to have a long-term view, to work within the system, and to get stakeholders to realise that they have the power of change agency.

> Second, the next lessons to be given are presented. Ongoing in the discussions is the issue of culturally appropriate content. Learners in the intermediate phase also complete questionnaires to ascertain current views and attitudes on bullying and overall well-being within the school.
>
> Based on these two examples, we provide some theoretical insights on making the most of the implementation of interventions.

Theoretical insights on maximising the implementation quality of interventions

During the implementation of our interventions, we encountered some problems. For example, while schools thought our interventions were a good idea, getting the participants actively involved, ensuring that motivation levels were sustained and that the interventions were implemented consistently, posed a challenge. Similar to other projects (see for example Ebersöhn & Eloff, 2006; Ebersöhn, 2015; Ebersöhn, Loots, Eloff & Ferreira, 2015) the problems and our observations have forced us to rethink our approach. We needed to think about the system as a whole and not just about the part that we wanted to influence (see also Chapters 25 and 27).

Thus, it is important to realise that when implementing an intervention the context in which you work is crucial. It is true that organisations and the social systems within them have a life of their own. While the intentions behind the intervention may be noble, good intentions are not enough to ensure change within the system (Stroh, 2015:7). It is about seeing the system as a whole and of getting stakeholders to see how they may be unintentionally contributing to the very problem they would like to solve. Thus, it is important to begin where the greatest impact on others will be achieved. It is about getting stakeholders mobilised to take action that increases the effectiveness of the whole system over time, instead of looking at the immediate needs. Several principles become important when thinking regarding systems (Stroh, 2015:17):

1. The relationship between the problem and the cause is not always obvious or direct.
2. We unconsciously create our problems and have significant control over solving them through changing our behaviour.
3. Most quick fixes have unintended consequences. Quick fixes may make things worse in the long run.
4. To make sure that the whole functions efficiently, the relationships between the parts have to be improved.
5. Only a few key coordinated changes sustained over a period produce significant system changes.

CASE STUDY 2

The KiVa anti-bullying programme

Bullying is one of the most underestimated problems, taking place at both primary and secondary schools. Bullying is a worldwide phenomenon (Salmivalli, Garandeau & Veenstra, 2012:279) and has been receiving more and more attention from the academic world as well as the media. The focus is perhaps not surprising as there seems to be an increase in the occurrence of bullying as an indication of societal changes (Solberg & Olweus, 2003:240). In the past, bullying has been viewed as harmless or a phase some children go through, thereby downplaying the serious implications of bullying behaviour. However, bullying is one of the hidden aspects of a culture of violence that ultimately contributes to different manifestations of violence within societies (Neser, Ladikos & Prinsloo, 2004:6). Bullying is not teasing, nor a mere disagreement, but rather repeated acts of aggression with the intention to harm a victim who is weaker in physical size, social status, or other aspects. The consequences of bullying, for both the victim and the bully, are severe in both the short- and long term. The effects may include physical and psychological stress, in addition to maladaptive social skills that result in reduced adult adjustment (Crothers & Levinson, 2004:496), which is why there is a need for intervention.

The KiVa anti-bullying programme was developed at the University of Turku, Finland. The word KiVa in the Finnish language means 'against bullying'. Thus positive changes in the behaviour of the group and what is acceptable should contribute to the reduction in bullying behaviour. The idea behind the programme is that bystanders often contribute to the emergence and maintenance of bullying behaviour (Salmivall, Garandeau & Veenstra, 2012:287). Both universal and indicated actions are included in the programme. The KiVa anti-bullying programme comprises curricula, the universal actions, designed to increase anti-bullying attitudes in the group by targeting the bystanders to increase self-efficacy (Williford, Boulton, Noland, Little, Kärnä & Salmivalli, 2012:290). The ten lessons, spanning one calendar year, are fun for the children and include a variety of activities such as class discussions, group work, short films about bullying, and role playing exercises. One of the most potent activities included is the self-reflection exercises at the end of each lesson. Each teacher that presents the KiVa programme receives a teacher manual, each with lessons prepared, and suggested materials and activities. Each lesson takes a double period to complete. KiVa also includes an indicated intervention component, a targeted approach, that addresses identified cases of bullying. With the indicated actions, a team of three school staff members in each school works with the classroom teacher to resolve the issue through individual and group discussions with the victims and bullies. Bullies are challenged to put forward suggestions on how the situation can be remedied and prevented in the future while the victim also identifies friendly classmates and then classmates who are challenged to provide support for the victim (Williford et al, 2012:291).

Currently, ten schools are participating in the KiVa programme. In South Africa the intermediate phase is targeted as the contents of KiVa aligns well with the Life Skills curriculum. There are four teacher workshops annually where the lessons are discussed. The workshops serve two purposes. First, teacher experiences of the lessons presented are discussed in the group. Thus we learn from each other.

Overall, 'Success for All' is based on multidimensional intervention theory, meaning that vulnerable learners who are at risk to fail in school require intervention on many fronts. 'Success for All' would follow a goal focused implementation process to determine the school's goals, analyse their current state and analyse their achievement data. 'Success for All' reading lessons takes place for 90 minutes every morning. Reading comprehension is aimed at getting children to provide evidence for what they are reading. Children are grouped according to reading ability of good, average or poor. Poor readers and average readers are paired, while average readers and good readers are paired. Good readers and poor readers are never paired since the gap in ability is too large for them to work effectively as a team. Ability grouping also means that for the 90 minutes reading lesson each morning means young children (6 or 7 years) may share a classroom with older children (8- or 9-year-olds).

Teachers do a minimal amount of talking during the reading lesson, and most talking is done by the children in explaining their thoughts and ideas on what they have read. 'Success for All' emphasises the use of clear targets—in their teams, children know exactly what they are supposed to do and how they should engage with activities. Targets are set using immediate feedback (eg, a teacher holds her hand up for silence, and the team that responds quickest is rewarded). Children are taught from early on to respond in full sentences. This teaches them to think through their answers and practice newly acquired vocabulary. Furthermore, management of the classroom is done collaboratively. This means that the teacher never spends time asking children to sit down, keep quiet or listen. Instead, she uses hand gestures and relies on partners to keep each other focused. The intervention is aimed at ensuring individual success through team success, while the principle of no competition between teams mean that opportunities exist for social problem solving.

While the goals of any intervention need to be met, it has to be kept in mind that interventions occur within a context. So, for example, did the present context of the participating schools present reading specific and resource specific challenges. Reading specific challenges included what teachers referred to as 'cramming' or the reliance on memory to 'read'. In these cases, cramming was made easy as a result of a lot of repetition in readers. Those learners who presented some skill in reading, but who do not read with understanding, often resort to 'reading' pictures when flashcards were shown and did not know how to construct sentences. Teachers frequently complained that the pace of prescribed lesson plans was too fast and that ready-made assessments provided by the Department of Basic Education provided little evidence of skill mastery (Van Staden & Mihai, 2017:10). Resource specific challenges included learners with home environments that are characterised by poverty, with little access to basic amenities such as water and electricity, occurrences of abusive family structures, and lack of parental support. In addition, schools presented with little to no electronic resources for use when teaching, large classes, and language barriers between teachers and learners. These challenges compound an already complex social context where learners come from varied linguistic backgrounds. Added to this complexity, teachers' inability to teach directed reading instruction successfully and with a wide repertoire of skills and strategies to monitor learners' reading progress puts learners at a double deficit—not only are learners socially at a disadvantage in attempts to make academic progress, but are also at an instructional disadvantage in being taught basic reading abilities ineffectively that could have ensured early success and ultimately academic progress and achievement in later grades (Van Staden & Mihai, 2017:19).

In this chapter, we describe two examples of school-based interventions in primary schools in Gauteng which are aimed at the department's priority areas of safety and protection and co-curricular support. Based on these cases, theoretical issues are discussed on how to ensure that the implementation quality of school-based interventions is maximised. Here, evidence-based programmes are defined as programmes that have a positive impact on targeted outcomes in an empirical study by observation or experimentation (Jaycox, McAffrey, Ocampo, Shelley, Blake, Peterson, Richmond & Kub, 2006:321).

CASE STUDY 1

Success for All

In South Africa, grave concerns about low levels of learner achievement pervade research initiatives and educational debates. South African learners perform poorly in international comparative assessment studies such as the Trends in International Maths and Science Study (TIMSS) and the Southern and Eastern African Consortium for the Monitoring of Educational Quality (SACMEQ). South African learners' poor performance in reading literacy was first evidenced by the Progress in International Reading Literacy Study (PIRLS) 2006 results. South African Grade 5 learners achieved the lowest score of the 45 participating education systems of 302 (SE=5.6) (Mullis, Martin, Kennedy & Foy 2007:37). Grade 4 learners achieved on average 253 points (SE=4.6). Average achievement for both these grades was well below the fixed international reference average of 500 points. Even when administering an easier reading assessment in the 2011 cycle of PIRLS, the prePIRLS results point to continued underperformance by South African learners with little evidence of improved reading literacy scores. More specifically, South African Grade 4 learners obtained the lowest reading achievement score in comparison to the international centre point of 500 at 461 (SE=3.7), compared to 463 (SE=3.5) as achieved by learners from Botswana, and 576 (SE=3.4) as obtained by learners from Colombia (Mullis, Martin, Foy & Drucker, 2012:39).

Depending on the medium of instruction at each school, reading skills in South African schools are developed during the Foundation Phase of schooling using mother tongue basal readers (Pretorius, 2002:189). Much emphasis is placed on the teaching of decoding skills, but this is often done in a superficial, haphazard and decontextualised fashion. Children may read lists of syllables or words aloud from the chalkboard. Singing along sounds and words in a chorus-style is another favourite reading activity teachers expect learners to participate in, resulting in the minimal monitoring of those learners who fail to 'sing' the correct words or phrases. As teachers assume that when learners can decode, they will be able to comprehend, little attention is given to reading comprehension, therefore the transition from decoding syllables or words on a chalkboard to meaningful reading activities using extended texts does not happen easily (Pretorius & Currin, 2010:68).

Against this background, a pilot intervention at two schools in Gauteng started in 2016. Called 'Success for All', findings of research on effective school instruction, curriculum, school and classroom organisation, assessment, accommodation for struggling learners, parent involvement, and professional development are put into practice (Slavin, Madden, Chambers & Haxby, 2008:8).

34 Considering school-based interventions: What do you need to think about?

SURETTE VAN STADEN & VANESSA SCHERMAN

It is unconscionable to continue using ineffective practices if effective ones are readily available and capable of serving any school that is prepared to dedicate itself to quality implementation. (Robert Slavin)

Introduction

Children in South African schools have been on the receiving end of research-supported, school-based interventions on a broad range of issues. Policy emphasis on evidence-based practices over the last two decades has meant an increased availability of opportunities for intervention. So, for example, is the Department of Basic Education's (DBE) mandate to create enabling environments to improve learning outcomes. This directorate takes the form of its Care and Support for Teaching and Learning programme (CSTL). Currently, the policy mandate states that the DBE must ensure that primary schooling is compulsory, accessible and available to all children, that attendance is encouraged to protect vulnerable children and that education provides advancement of all children to their full potential. The goals of the CSTL programme are to realise the education rights of all children through schools becoming inclusive centres of learning, care and support.

When thinking about enabling environments, it is important to look at the system as a whole. Inevitably, systems that deal with human interaction are complex. Within systems thinking, a framework is provided in order to examine the parts within the whole, and thus provides a holistic perspective (Jokela, Karlsudd & Östlund, 2008:197).

8

Schools

2004:xi). Teaching disability in educational psychology could focus on human responses to disability in order to enhance understanding and care and putting the person first.

Psychosocial caring

Psychosocial caring support 'involves the culturally sensitive provision of psychological, social and spiritual care' (Legg, 2011:62). Educational psychology is helping humanity to understand ecologies of care, and these have to form part of indigenous knowledge systems that inform teaching and learning. African cultures have indigenous systems of care from which educational psychology can benchmark teaching about psychosocial care and support for adaptation. Psychosocial caring in contexts of educational psychology can provide for hope and psychological well-being for all learners, but perhaps mostly for learners with disabilities (Nabi, Ahmad & Khan, 2016).

Psychosocial adaptation

Central to psychosocial adaptation is hope that leads to resilience. Valle, Huebner and Suldo (2006) perceive hope as a psychological strength that fosters healthy development. Teaching about hope in educational psychology could strengthen the willpower and promote the resilience of learners with disabilities. Psychosocial adaptation '… has been described generally as psychological well-being in living with a condition' (Truitt, Biesecker, Capone, Bailey & Erby, 2012:233). In the context of disability, psychosocial adaptation can be perceived to equally lead to psychological well-being.

Conclusion

This chapter reviewed disability and inclusive employment within the field of educational psychology. Social construction of disability was highlighted, and Article 27 of the CRPD and the intersectionality that is at play within this field was foregrounded. The chapter reviewed teaching about psychosocial aspects of disability from the psychology of disability, and discussed psychosocial caring and adaptation. From these discussions, it is evident that inclusive employment is complex and intricate, and closely linked to the creation of inclusive learning environments throughout an education system.

The intensification of curriculum differentiation in order to address diverse learning needs in view of the transition to inclusive employment is important for classroom practice in South Africa. One of the most critical areas of classroom practice is to cater for students who may not be academically inclined and help them to nurture their entrepreneurial aptitude. Differentiating the curriculum towards entrepreneurship addresses self-employment issues at early stages of learning and instils in the learners a sense of independence. The real challenge is to include '… everybody, everywhere and all the time' (Ferguson, 2008:109).

'"Differentiated instruction" is a philosophy of teaching, purporting that students learn best when their teachers effectively address variance in students' readiness levels, interests and learning profile preferences' (Tomlinson, 2005:263). Generally, once content is differentiated, the teacher has to consider that he/she is working within the frame of 'the needs-based "differentiation" paradigm' (Dai & Chen, 2013:154) with a focus on 'methods of presentation, methods of practice and performance, and methods of assessment' (UNESCO, 2004:15).

Teaching about the psychosocial aspects of disability

Disability is inherently a complex phenomenon and a subsection of diversity. Human beings often assume that they know and understand disability. However, continuously learning about disability in all its complexities and diversities may go a long way in assisting learners in school to accept and support one another in society. The classroom may be a safe space where learners can engage in understanding different disabilities and how to support one another. The place of educational psychology in society is ideal for creating an environment of care, support, advocacy and encouragement 'to improve the educational, psychological and social well-being' (Ebersöhn, 2017:1) (see also the section on health and well-being). Teaching may start with the psychology of disability, proceed to psychosocial caring, and then psychosocial adaptation.

Psychology of disability

Psychology is historically known for its emphasis on preventing psychopathology (Valle, Huebner & Suldo, 2006). Psychology generally approached disability from a deficit medical perspective, to '… rely heavily on grief and bereavement theories' (Watermeyer, 2014:101). Current discourses of acceptance and acknowledgement in positive psychology (Ebersöhn, 2017) and inclusive education emphasise the importance of the human person over disability. The psychology of disability entails '… the study of how human organisms respond to a set of stimulus conditions associated with disability' (Vash & Crewe,

Although the concept has been used and widely acknowledged as a feminist paradigm (Hancock, 2007); McCall (2005) regards it as complex. Nonetheless, intersectionality is helpful in understanding '… systems of oppression which construct our multiple identities' (Carastathis, 2014:304). In this case, it helps to understand disability as constructed difference (Williams & Mavin, 2012).

Educational psychology is positioned to play a critical role in understanding the differences and their implications to teaching and learning, and the transition to the world of work. In order to change the status quo, it is important that society embraces disability for inclusion in education and employment. Intersectionality operates on the basis of '… categories of identity, difference and disadvantage' (Cole, 2009:170). Persons with disabilities mostly struggle with identity issues as they are often stigmatised and labelled, based on their disability. Disability renders them different, and the majority are disadvantaged. Educational psychology has made some inroads in explaining these categories, but less so as they relate to disability.

The relevance of inclusive employment for South African schools and classrooms

Youth unemployment keeps rising in South Africa, and youth with disabilities are no exception. The post-independence South African school should be a school that is poised to inculcate innovation, self-employment and employment creation early on in the education system, especially for persons with disabilities. The Universal Design for Learning is critical in the era of inclusive schools, and South African schools can play a critical role in addressing the diverse needs of learners.

> *Universal Design for Learning (UDL) is a relatively new model for designing all aspects of the learning environment to address the wide-ranging variation of students' needs that exist in an inclusive educational system.* (Dalton, McKenzie & Kahonde, 2012:3)

All learners should feel accommodated in South African schools, and all learners must embrace hope for their future world of work. The responsibility for understanding inclusion rests on a number of factors, including the 'conceptual and contextual considerations … choices to be made in teacher education for inclusive education … inclusion as an issue of students and their diversity … inclusion as an issue of teachers and their competence … inclusion as an issue of schools and society' (Walton & Rusznyak, 2017:232). Thus, within the school, students would have opportunities to learn about diversity, teachers will hone their skills for inclusive teaching, and schools will sharpen their implementation skills for inclusion.

monstrous/abject' (Hughes, 2009:399). These types of social constructions are negative and can lead to unfortunate legislations such as 'ugly laws' (Schweik, 2009). These laws '…barred disabled individuals from appearing on the streets and other public spaces in the 19th and early 20th centuries' (Hirschmann, 2013:142). During the latter part of the 20th century, 'a call for critical reflexivity' (Phelan, 2011:164) to change negative attitudes 'towards a radical body positive' (Sastre, 2014:929) appeared globally. This call led to disability being regarded as a human rights issue that covered all aspects of life, including education and employment (Lord, Suozzi & Taylor, 2010). Thus, the protection afforded people with disabilities began to slowly change in some contexts.

Article 27 of the Convention for the Rights of Persons with Disability and the right of inclusive employment

The CRPD, adopted on 13 December 2006, has become a beacon of hope and a critical advocacy instrument to safeguard and promote the rights of persons with disabilities (Lord, Suozzi & Taylor, 2010). Article 27 of the CRPD is about work and employment, and Article 27(e) is specific to the promotion of employment opportunities and career advancement for persons with disabilities in the labour market, as well as assistance in finding, obtaining, maintaining and returning to employment (Ferraina, 2012).

Through the psychology of working, Blustein (2006:275) advocates for an '… inclusive psychological practice that effectively embraces work-related issues'. Within the field of educational psychology, work- and employment-related issues are generally addressed under career psychology (Watson & Stead, 2002), specifically career guidance and counselling or career development, depending on the context. In South Africa, there seems to be a drive towards career development, although it needs more articulation for South African society.

Given the historical background of South Africa, it makes more sense to promote inclusive employment to address high rates of unemployment among youth, especially those who were traditionally disadvantaged (Maree & Beck, 2004). Inclusive employment takes a broad perspective within the South African context and should not only be confined to disability. Employment inclusion emerges as a condition without which the South African labour market cannot be sustainable, based on the intersectional nature of its population (Whitehead, 2013).

Intersectionality

Intersectionality emerged as a political feminist theory coined by Crenshaw (1989), with a central focus on promoting the interaction of human differences and diversity through addressing relationships of inequality (Whitehead, 2013).

Since the commencement of the Education for All (EFA) movement in the early 2000s, several attempts were made to attain access to education for all children by 2015. However, Galguera (2016:328) notes that the *Education for all 2000–2015: Achievements and Challenges. EFA Global Monitoring Report 2015* shows that only a third of countries reached all the EFA goals with measurable targets. Specifically, after many decades, education still does not include many learners with disabilities. These learners have been identified as being not in education, employment or training (NEET). Educational psychological services thus become more and more critical to address socio-emotional and economic issues related to non-participation in education of people considered as NEET, as well as those in education, but who are negatively affected by a lack of pro-poor, pro-disability services such as career guidance and counselling for inclusive employment.

Disability unemployment continues to be problematic, even after efforts to include persons with disabilities started in earnest after the take-off of EFA in 2000. Disability employment is confronted with '… a complex system of hostile environments and disabling barriers referred to as institutional discrimination' (Barnes, 1992:55). Education, as a social institution, and educational psychology should be geared towards addressing disability and inclusive employment issues. An inclusive labour market has the propensity to grow if persons with disabilities are included in employment to contribute to the building of society (Naidoo, Maja, Mann, Sing & Steyn, 2011). Educational psychology, as a mental health profession, is predisposed to address the 'unseen challenges, unheard voices and unspoken desires' (Khoo, Tiun & Lee, 2013:37) of learners with disabilities during this time of 'inclusive and diverse educational environments' (Florian, Young & Rouse, 2010) and inclusive employment (Chia & Kee, 2013).

Some of the major debates within the field of disability and inclusive employment relate to the social construction of disability, Article 27 of the United Nations Convention for the Rights of Persons with Disability (CRPD) (Harpur, 2012), and also the right to inclusive employment and intersectional visibility (Purdie-Vaughns & Eibach, 2008). These are discussed in the sections that follow by examining them through the lens of educational psychology.

Social construction of disability

The 'kaleidoscope' metaphor of disability used by Crossley (1999) points to the diverse nature of the social constructions of this concept. Disability, as a social construct, has its roots in the social '… contexts, relationships, institutions or situations that define and shape the meaning of disability' (Jones, 1996:349). The social constructions are claimed to be made by people without disabilities, sometimes describing disability through 'the sociology of the body' as 'wounded/

33 Disability and inclusive employment through the lens of educational psychology

MAXIMUS MONAHENG SEFOTHO

Inclusive employment for the disabled can enhance the well-being of all in society. (Monaheng Sefotho)

Introduction

The field of educational psychology is important in understanding behaviour in relation to teaching and learning. Educational psychology is a branch of psychology that is concerned with behaviour in relation to teaching and learning. It therefore is 'a foundation' in teacher education (Peterson, Clark & Dickson, 1990:3).

Educational psychology as a field of study generally concentrates on the teaching of children, referred to as pedagogy, but under the scope of lifelong learning. Educational psychology also considers adult learning, technically referred to as andragogy. Learning takes place throughout life, but there is a distinction between children's learning and adult learning. The Greek etymology of pedagogy: παιδαγωγία (paidagōgia), from παιδαγωγός (paidagōgos), means 'to lead a child'. Andragogy is a sub-branch within educational psychology that is concerned with adult learning. It comes from the Greek word *anere*, which means 'adult', and *agogus*, which means 'the art and science of helping students to learn' (Knowles, 1970; Knowles, 1984). In educational psychology, teaching and learning cover a whole continuum, from infancy to old age, envisioning *all* who participate in education. Educational psychology also studies families, peers and communities as they are part of children's life–world.

Open networks show dynamic fluidity as the network changes with regards to variable factors such as time, personnel, and the nature of their work (Daly, 2012). SBSTs are open in establishing ties with many other agencies and the nature of their work is dependent on the unique context, situation and setting of the school. Generally schools with complex, open, dynamic networks between educators, multi-disciplinary teams and outside agencies are better at supporting learners' diverse needs, than schools with closed, limited networks (Fourie, 2017). The power of the collaborative network seems to lie in the complexity of the relationship ties, rather than in the personal attributes of the individual agents. More connections, even if relatively weak, increase the social capital of the network. Open networks with many connections offer more opportunities and resources for the teacher team in supporting diverse learning needs.

Conclusion

Support teams network internally with educators in identifying learning barriers, designing support plans, implementing inclusive pedagogical practices, and differentiating the curriculum. Teams network externally when guiding parents and involving specialist support personnel. Teams network with other government sectors such as social workers, welfare, feeding schemes, and safe houses. Effective teams network with support groups, for example in South Africa, FamiliesSA, Autism SA, SA Association for Learning and Educational Differences, Read for Africa, and the SA Depression and Anxiety Group.

Social network theory provides a useful frame for understanding teacher collaboration as it focuses on how the structure of the ties affects agents' behaviour and the network's functioning. The power of a social network lies in the strength of the ties, connections and relationships. Unlike traditional social scientific studies with the focus on individuals and the assumptions that people's attributes, such as personality and intellect, are influential in actions, social network theory provides an alternative view. Within this theory, the attributes of agents or individuals are less important than their relationships and the ties with other agents within the network. Individual agency alone is viewed as limiting, whereas social capital is empowering. The power of the support team lies within the complex structure of the network, rather than in the personal attributes, skills or knowledge of any one individual team member (see also Chapters 25 and 27).

formal, workplace organisations. Ties between agents imply an exchange of some nature between the nodes. The agents within social networks are tied by cohesive forces or interdependencies that may take varying forms of shared values, visions, friendship or exchange. Network structures enhance resource flow if the necessary relationships are in place, but resource flow may also be impeded with insufficient connectivity between agents (Moody & White, 2003).

In this framework, the people within a school community are considered actors or agents who interact with one another in various relationships. SBSTs function as sociocentric networks, which have a distinct, well-defined boundary of belonging as there is a clear core of team members. The members of the SBST are agents who are tied with other agents such as teachers, therapists and parents by various relationships where there is an exchange of ideas and services between the agents. SBSTs network with the express purpose of supporting diverse learning needs. Intra-school ties are formed between teachers within the same school. Inter-organisational ties are formed between the school and other outside agencies such as specialist professional personnel and the knowledge networks of district teams, which support the entire educational system (Daly, 2012).

Agents within social networks build social capital in the network. Social capital refers to the person's ability to draw on resources, knowledge and power in order to resolve a problem or meet the goals of the team. A person's position in the network influences his/her social capital and agents with multiple ties have more social capital (Smylie & Evans, 2006). Generally, small and tight, closed networks with weak, loose or redundant connections are less useful as closed groups are prone towards similar opinions, common ideas, and continually sharing similar resources and knowledge. More open, intricately woven networks with many connections, even if they are weak, are more likely to offer new opportunities and ideas to their members (Koch & Lockwood, 2010). Since an average person may only be able to establish a few strong ties due to physical constraints such as time and energy, the establishment of numerous weak ties are more effective in providing the group with insights, innovation and information —'the strength of weak ties'.

Complex, open networks are more likely to be useful in addressing the diverse needs of the school community. Team members with many connections to outside agents have more access to broader resources and ranges of information. Such networks support children's well-being and development which is powerfully shaped by the social capital inherent in the people with whom they interact. Furthermore, schools are often the driving forces in building social capital for inclusive and respectful societies (Munn, 2000).

Professional barriers relate to difficulties arising due to lack of training, skills and knowledge. Teachers who have difficulty working together could compromise the quality of school projects and the collaborative process in supporting learning. Educators should develop sophisticated skills and strategies in the collaborative processes to enhance school-based reforms.

Educator collaboration internationally

Educators working collaboratively to support the needs of all learners in schools are an international occurrence. In America, the purpose of the support team is to promote individual learner success in the 'regular classroom' using specific assessment and intervention techniques to address barriers to learning. In these teams there is a dedicated support teacher who helps coordinate, assess, train, and assist the staff in meeting the specific instructional needs of struggling learners. These support teachers conduct curriculum-based assessments, consulting with teachers and facilitate intervention techniques (United States Department of Education, 2017). Teacher support teams meet the special educational needs of learners in the United Kingdom. These teams support teachers with concerns relating broadly to special educational needs and follow comprehensive functioning guidelines (Creese, Daniels & Norwich, 2012). The teams play a crucial role in enhancing service efficiency and provide opportunities for teachers' professional development. The teams plan programmes for individual cases, check for accountability, and provide teacher training. The teams attend to both individual students' psychosocial needs and school systemic issues (Phillippo & Stone, 2006).

A collaborative theoretical framework

The SBST in South Africa and the teacher support teams in other countries are similar support structures, whose primary purpose is to increase learning success. Since these teams perform a vital role in addressing barriers to learning, their functioning and effectiveness is vital in the transformation towards inclusive schools.

Social network theory (SNT) provides a useful theoretical framework for understanding the effective functioning of teacher collaboration in supporting diverse learners in inclusive schools. A social network is a virtual structure consisting of nodes or agents, which may be individuals or organisations that are tied by one or more types of relationships or interdependencies (Kadushin, 2012). SNT attempts to explain complex social relationships in terms of networks formed by individuals or organisations, which are characterised by the type of content that is exchanged between the agents (Scott & Carrington, 2011). Networks explain information exchange and knowledge transfer in

coordination and management of educational resources is more efficient and sustainable with high levels of collaboration. Support personnel are used more effectively as staff negotiates the boundaries of their professional roles. Schools with well-functioning support teams have less referrals to specialised psychology services and report fewer problem behaviours and improved parent involvement.

Difficulties in collaboration

Although various types of educator teams are common in schools, they are fraught with difficulties regarding implementation, maintenance and leadership. These multiple obstacles to collaboration can be classified as conceptual, pragmatic, attitudinal and professional. Conceptual barriers prevent role expansion or modification with team members exhibiting rigid ideas of appropriate responsibilities and tasks for individuals which greatly limit their collective action. Support personnel might operate in isolation from the broader teaching staff as different professional cultures create barriers and active resistance to meaningful engagement. Parallel working and compartmentalisation may evolve. Teachers often prefer to learn from each other, which may reinforce existing habits and isolate them from new ways of thinking.

Pragmatic barriers deal with resources such as funding, time, space, and materials, which make team action difficult. Challenges of collaboration between educators may arise around basic constraints such as scheduling of meetings. Donahue and Bornman (2014) note the most significant constraints to implementation of inclusive education lie in ambiguity and lack of clarity regarding procedures and unaccountable authorities who do not assume responsibility and control the implementation process. In a study in Gauteng, Nel, Muller and Rheeder (2011) reported that learners with special needs and disabilities, 'never' or 'seldom' received specialised support. School management teams and teachers often struggle with what constitutes an effective teacher support team, and how to support learners who are experiencing barriers to learning (Nel, Engelbrecht, Nel & Tlale, 2013). Furthermore, in reviewing inclusive education in developing countries, Srivastava, De Boer and Pijl (2015) found there is often a serious gap in policy vision and implementation practices.

Attitudinal barriers refer to beliefs and expectations of team members. For instance, beliefs that certain learners should not be included in mainstream schools or that change should happen immediately and be relatively effortless. Such beliefs may limit team members' investment in and support of the team's collective efforts. However, if educators have actively experienced the implementation of inclusive programmes they have more positive attitudes towards learner diversity.

Goals of collaboration

The goal of educator collaboration is broadly to provide pedagogical support for optimising learners' participation and academic performance. Educators collaborate to support all learners and specifically those identified as having additional or special support needs. SBSTs need a clear common, shared goal when working with learners as opposed to fragmented and disjointed programmes that leave learners with inappropriate educational plans (Giangreco, Carter, Doyle & Suter, 2010). This focus on providing cohesive, individualised programmes for diverse learning needs can be fostered by effective teacher teamwork.

Support in education may take many forms and can be thought of as the scaffolding around a building. The scaffold provides a firm structure and pillars of strength while the walls are being built. In educational terms—the developing child is scaffolded by caring educators while the child is growing and maturing. Support may involve modifying the physical school environment to ensure that buildings are accessible for learners with physical impairments. Support may relate to individualising the curriculum content and pace for learners with cognitive difficulties. Support may require concessions in the ways that learners are assessed and graded. Support may include specialised technology and assistive devices for learners with sensory impairments. Support could be individualised and tailored to suit the specific needs and requirements of the learner at that particular time. For instance, a learner who is visually impaired may need intense support initially in order to learn to read in Braille. As the learner's competence improves, less support is needed until the learner is fully independent as a Braille reader and writer. Educators thus work together in providing this individualised and dynamic support.

Benefits of collaboration

When educators work together, there are multiple benefits. Educators working together actualise school policies, protocols, and processes in building caring, sensitive schools. When educators work closely together, they build mutual trust which enhances both teacher commitment and retention. The exchange of expertise between educators enhances professional development and the reliance on outside experts is minimised. Joint decision making is crucial for individualised support planning. Collaboration allows educators to take ownership of creatively solving problems as educators support one another with particular difficulties. With peer support confidentiality must be respected as educators share ideas to solve problems on equal terms. No one is seen as the expert with all the answers. Educators interacting professionally and sharing their knowledge enhances learners' academic outcomes. The

and caregivers would be part of the discussions. Proceedings can be augmented by expertise from the local community, professional support personnel (school counsellor, psychologist, speech therapist, occupational therapist, learning support educators, school nurse, physiotherapist, dietician) and district-based support teams to assist with particular challenges (Department of Basic Education, 2014).

School-based support teams are the collective mechanism that teachers use in identifying learners who experience barriers to effective learning and implementing appropriate interventions. These teams can be highly effective when the members' roles are clearly defined and when teachers are well informed and motivated to help learners. The SBST works collaboratively with all teachers to improve the whole school. The team should be led by a dedicated teacher who coordinates the activities of the team. Collaborative teamwork and joint planning are essential as these teams assist with differentiating the curriculum, adapting teaching methods, modifying learning environments and incorporating assistive devices and e-learning into schools.

The importance of collaborative teacher teams

The segregated, marginalising discourse of special needs education has moved towards conversations focusing on systemic, contextual, individualised education. This conceptual shift places most of the special needs debate outside of the special school sector implying that many more learners are actually part of the inclusion debate than in the previous deficit conceptualisation (Porteus, 2008). Learners need support for a plethora of extrinsic socio-economic issues, language challenges, and intrinsic psychological and health conditions.

With specific regard to disability in Africa, it has been estimated that only 10% of such children attend school (United Nations, 2006). In South Africa, it is estimated that up to 70% of school-age children with disabilities are not in school (Department of Education, 2001) even though school is compulsory between the ages of seven and 15 years. Thus, many children are potentially eligible for supportive education and this lends impetus to the need for basing support services directly within the school itself, and so the requirement for a well-functioning school-based support team arises.

These conceptual changes have impacted greatly on schools that have taken up the challenge to reorganise and become more supportive of diversity. Whereas mainstream schools traditionally referred learners to specialist education support personnel, these schools now coordinate internal support services. In order for these teams to perform their supportive role adequately, they need to establish strong links with various agents in the school community.

32 Teacher collaboration and working with school-based support teams

JEAN FOURIE

A single bracelet does not jingle. (Congolese proverb)

Introduction

Collaboration in schools is one of the key strategies in developing an inclusive education system. The African saying—'a single bangle does not jingle'—captures the essence of people working together to achieve a greater goal than an individual working alone. The South African movement towards an inclusive education system is set against the international background call of 'Education for All', where schools accommodate all learners regardless of their race, gender, physical, intellectual, social, emotional or linguistic differences (see also Chapter 29). Modern classrooms are increasingly diverse in their cultures, languages and developmental abilities thus demanding the implementation of collaborative school practices (Florian, 2012).

School-based support teams

Education White Paper 6 (Department of Education, 2001) outlined the framework for developing an integrated education system where special needs are infused throughout the system and support services are available to all learners with the establishment of school-based support teams (SBST). The school principal is mandated to establish the team and ensure its functionality. The SBST is a group of core teachers who are tasked to institute well-coordinated learner and educator support services. Where appropriate the learner, parents

adequately trained in supporting learners who experience barriers to learning, and they consequently believe in general that they don't have the capacity (Engelbrecht, Nel, Smit & Van Deventer, 2016; Makhalemele & Nel, 2016; Nel, Tlale, Engelbrecht & Nel 2016; Nel, Engelbrecht, Nel & Tlale, 2014). As a result, when looking at current learning support praxis in South Africa, the medical model still prevails (Swart & Pettipher, 2016; Nel, Engelbrecht, Nel & Tlale, 2014).

Including learners, who experience barriers to learning in their classroom, especially intrinsic barriers give rise to higher stress levels for teachers (Engelbrecht, Oswald, Swart & Eloff, 2003). They would therefore rather refer these learners to health professionals, who they believe are better equipped to provide support, and have them placed in special education (Nel, Engelbrecht, Nel & Tlale, 2014.). Since support systems are not fully functional to ensure high quality support (Department of Basic Education, 2015) it is very difficult for mainstream or Full-service schools to include learners who have more severe disabilities. Consequently, according to the Department of Basic Education (2015), there is an increase of special schools built, from 295 in 2002 to 453 in 2014. The number of learners who gained access to these schools have also escalated from 64 000 in 2002 to 117 477 in 2014, and there are still long waiting lists of learners who have requested access to these schools. Full-service schools are also not effectively functioning as fully inclusive schools mainly due to teachers not feeling adequately trained and experiencing a sense of self-inefficiency to implement inclusive education (Engelbrecht, Nel, Smit & Van Deventer, 2016; Payne-van Staden, 2015; Walton, Nel, Muller & Lebeloane, 2014). The Department of Basic Education also recognises that the majority of children with severe to profound disabilities, who function at the lowest level of development, have not had access to public funded education and support, leaving them vulnerable and excluded from the network of available support services. This is currently being addressed with the introduction of a draft policy where a specially designed learning programme will be made available for these learners, special needs teachers and caregivers will be trained to teach and support these learners, and health professionals will be giving more individualised support (Department of Basic Education, 2016).

8. Curriculum support.
9. Co-curricular support.

The role of the teacher within learning support

A central feature of the teacher within a learning support process should be that of authentic caring. Authentically caring about learners implies not labelling learners, but motivating all of them to succeed in learning, as well as allowing them to experience a sense of belonging and well-being. This requires that they do not make assumptions and judgements based on observable behaviour and achievement in the classroom. Teachers need to be thorough in making time to understand their learners' learning barriers, but also learn about their contexts (ie, backgrounds, home situations, communities, cultures, etc). It is thus critical that teachers have an in-depth conceptual understanding of inclusion and the diverse needs of learners, as well as about barriers to learning. This is important since the SIAS policy (Department of Basic Education, 2014) emphasises that the uncovering of barriers to learning must be based on sound information. This requires:

- Observation of the learner during all teaching, learning and assessment activities. This includes formative actions. Decisions and assumptions about learning difficulties should not be made on formal assessments (such as tests and exams) only. Keeping record of these observations is essential.
- Interviews and consultation with various role players (eg, parents, other relevant teachers, even the learner and maybe health professionals).
- Reflection on appropriate teaching, learning and assessment strategies, ie, was the learner's unique needs addressed?
- Looking at previous records (consult the learner profile).

Supporting the learner entails the ability to differentiate and adjust content, learning material as well as teaching, learning and assessment strategies. Knowledge and skills to implement a flexible curriculum is therefore vital for the teacher. Being able to apply the necessary accommodations in assessment and examinations is also necessary.

Conclusion

As reported in the previous chapter, the implementation of inclusive education still has many challenges, including a sound functioning support system. Challenges such as large classroom numbers and too wide a diversity of learning needs contribute to teachers not being able to apply good learning support practices. However, a crucial factor is that most teachers have not been

process in respect of the nature and level of educational support the learner needs (Department of Basic Education, 2014). It is emphasised in this policy that the assessment of a learner who experiences barriers to learning also has to take socio-environmental factors into consideration. Thus, barriers that are experienced by the individual need to be assessed, but also barriers impacting on the learner located within the curriculum, school, family, community and social context levels. Different forms of assessment (including curriculum-based assessments) from a variety of perspectives should therefore be employed.

The teacher is primarily responsible to apply the SIAS process and should assume the role of case manager to drive the support process. Yet, the knowledge and wishes of the parents/caregivers must carry the ultimate weight in any decision-making process (Department of Basic Education, 2014).

Keeping in mind the emphasis on a socio-ecological model and supporting the learner holistically, the SIAS also integrated several other governmental strategies. This includes the Integrated School Health Policy (ISHP), Care and Support for Teaching and Learning (CSTL) Framework, School Nutrition Policy, the National Curriculum and Assessment Policy Statements (CAPS), and the HIV and AIDS in Education Policy (Department of Basic Education, 2014). The ISHP affirms that schools provide an ideal opportunity for health education and interventions (Departments of Health and Basic Education, 2012). This could address health and socio-economic factors impacting on learners' learning. The CSTL Framework envisions to uphold the educational rights of vulnerable children in South Africa through schools becoming inclusive centres of learning, care and support (Department of Basic Education & MIET Africa, 2010). For this to realise, the framework will coordinate all existing services, including other government departments, community services, private professionals, non-government organisations (NGOs), disabled people organisations (DPOs), early intervention providers and community-based rehabilitation services. Factors that could have a negative impact on the enrolment, retention, performance and progression of vulnerable learners in schools will be prevented and mitigated through the CSTL programme. Nine priority areas have been identified to address the afore-mentioned. This includes:

1. Nutritional support.
2. Health promotion.
3. Infrastructure for water and sanitation.
4. Safety and protection.
5. Social welfare services.
6. Psychosocial support.
7. Material support.

incorporated. Although appointed in the district office, the learning support teacher (LST) is also part of the SBST (Department of Basic Education, 2014).

Functions of the school-based support teams

The teacher is usually the first person to identify a learner in need of additional support. This is after various measures have been attempted to ensure the learner's progress in the classroom. These measures include using a variety of teaching, learning and assessment strategies, investigating the learner's background, talking to the parents as well as all teachers, who were and are involved with the learner. When all of these measures still do not provide the desired learning outcomes, the learner is referred to the SBST, who then assesses what kind of support is needed and develop a programme for the teacher and parents (see Chapter 35). This programme must be continuously monitored and evaluated (Department of Basic Education, 2014).

In addition to individual support, these teams must also support the teaching and learning process of the school. This includes coordinating all learner, teacher, curriculum and school development support in the school, identifying school needs and, in particular, barriers to learning at learner, teacher, curriculum and school levels, developing strategies to address these needs and barriers to learning, drawing in the resources needed, from within and outside the school, to address these challenges, and monitoring and evaluating the work of the team within an 'action-reflection' framework. Although the DBST can provide support and advice throughout, they usually only become involved when all resources and efforts have been exhausted in providing these support programmes and progress has not been made (Department of Basic Education, 2014).

Policy on screening, identification, assessment and support (SIAS)

This policy was introduced in 2014 by the Department of Basic Education. The purpose is to standardise procedures to identify, assess and provide support programmes for all learners, who require additional support to ensure their participation and inclusion in education (Department of Basic Education, 2014:1). Although medical model practices are incorporated in the SIAS policy, the socioecological perspective is applied as fundamental operating principle. Health professionals (such as psychologists, audiologists, speech-, occupational- and physiotherapists) play a significant role in the SIAS process and are used to conduct more formal assessments. Consequently, standardised scholastic and psychometric tests (such as intelligent quotient (IQ) tests) are allowed as part of a range of assessment strategies, and may not be used to classify and categorise. These tests must be culturally fair and only inform the teaching and learning

neighbouring mainstream and full-service schools. Placement in these schools must be a last resort and should not be seen as permanent. If a learner's support needs can be accommodated in an ordinary/mainstream or FSS near to his/her home, this learner may not be admitted to a SSRC (Department of Basic Education, 2014).

Full-service school (FSS)

The objective of a FSS is to increase participation and diminish exclusion by admitting all learners from a particular area, regardless of their disabilities, in an ordinary/mainstream school. These schools should become flagship inclusive schools, as well as provide a range of appropriate support services (Department of Basic Education, 2014, 2015). All learners are therefore welcomed in terms of their cultures, policies and practices. The knowledge and expertise with regard to teaching, learning, assessment and support activities of staff attached to these schools should also be made available to neighbouring mainstream schools. Mainstream schools are increasingly being converted into FSSs: from 30 in 2007 to 787 in 2014 (Department of Basic Education, 2015).

District-based support teams (DBST)

The DBST, situated at district offices, is responsible to coordinate and promote inclusive education by providing training, support curriculum delivery, coordinate the distribution of resources and infrastructure development, as well as handling the identification, assessment and addressing of barriers to learning. Ultimately the DBST must support schools to ensure that they function as inclusive centres of learning, care and support (Department of Basic Education, 2014).

Personnel attached to these DBSTs includes psychologists, therapists, remedial/learning support teachers, special needs specialists (relating to specific disabilities), and other health and welfare professionals (Department of Basic Education, 2014). Recently learning support teachers (LSTs) have been appointed at district offices as members of the DBST. They are assigned to a few schools where they provide assistance with regard to the identification and support of learners experiencing barriers to learning (Nel, Tlale, Engelbrecht & Nel, 2016).

School-based support teams (SBST)

These teams are situated at schools as a school-level support mechanism and mainly comprises of the management and teachers at the school. Their primary function is to put coordinated school, learner and teacher support in place. However, community members and health professionals may also be

Socio-ecological model

In an inclusive education system, a more socio-ecological collaborative approach to learning support is emphasised. This perspective acknowledges that a diversity of learning needs exist that result from individual, as well as societal and systemic factors. Therefore, in this approach, the intricacy of influences, interactions, and interrelationships between the individual (learner) and several other systems are acknowledged (Nel, Nel & Hugo, 2016; Swart & Pettipher, 2016). These systems can be in direct (eg, parents, teachers and peers) or indirect (eg, community, socio-economic circumstances, parent's work circumstances, education policies) interaction with the learner. Consequently, besides medical concerns, contextual factors and influences are also investigated and taken into consideration during the *assessment and learning support process* by different role players (such as health professionals, teachers, parents, learners, school and district based support teams) working together in collaborative partnerships. Moreover, in this model, it is also essential that stumbling blocks within society and the system (such as those referred to in the previous chapters) should be removed (Florian in Swart & Pettipher, 2016). Within a human rights and social justice perspective the socio-ecological model is thus the more appropriate model.

> **NOTE:** The term learning support is endorsed by policy in South Africa, emphasising a socio-ecological approach. However, it is important to note that in the colloquial mouth, as well as internationally, terms such as remediation and remedial intervention are also still used, although this ratifies a more medical model approach.

Support structures envisioned by EWP6 to promote a more inclusive education system include special schools as resource centres (SSRC), full-service schools (FSS), district-based support teams (DBST), school-based support teams (SBST) and a Policy on Screening, Identification, Assessment and Support (SIAS).

Support structures

Special schools as resource centres (SSRC)

Special schools as resource centres (SSRCs) must be fully equipped to provide access to and accommodate learners who need high-intensity educational support programmes and services. This can include learners with severe cognitive and/or physical disabilities, visual and hearing impairments, as well as behavioural difficulties such as autism spectrum disorders. Staff and support personnel attached to these schools should also offer support services to

Understanding learning support

There are two predominant models that are important to understand with regard to the support of learners who experience barriers to learning. They are the medical-deficit model and the socioecological model.

Medical-deficit model

Before the transformation to a more inclusive education system in South Africa, a medical model was used as framework when learners with disabilities (ie, intrinsic barriers to learning) were identified. In a medical model, the primary focus of *intervention* is to diagnose and remediate the 'deficit-within-the-child'. Education support staff, who were mainly health professionals (eg, psychologists, speech- and occupational therapists, and social workers), employed by the government, applied a battery of psychometric tests and made the final decisions regarding placements and suggested interventions. These learners were then categorised, given a Learner with Special Education Needs (LSEN) number, as well as a weighting based on their medical/biological conditions and/ or cognitive disability and subsequently placed in an applicable, but separate special education environment. For example, a learner who was placed in a class/ school for the learning disabled counted for two learners, or a learner placed in a school for learners with a severe cognitive disability counted for five learners. They were consequently excluded from what was seen by society as 'mainstream normal' and also followed a different curriculum (Swart & Pettipher, 2016). In this model, health professionals (employed by government or in private practice) were inclined to believe that their services were indispensable and that they are the predominant experts on their distinctive fields (Engelbrecht, 2009). Parents, teachers and learners, therefore, could not really influence this decision. This was therefore a very individualistic, remedial intervention approach and mostly ignored systemic and socio-environmental influences.

From a human rights discourse, the medical model perspective results in discriminatory practices. This is based on the following reasons:
- Unique human beings cannot be classified into simple medical-disability diagnoses;
- Learners may have different medical disabilities, but similar educational needs; and
- Diagnoses are often a way of social control (and not necessarily as effective as it purports to be) (Naicker, 1999:48).

However, it is important to note that the medical data gained from this practice adds valuable information in the assessment and learning support process of learners experiencing barriers.

31 Learning support in South Africa

MIRNA NEL

Every student (learner) can learn, just not on the same day or in the same way. (George Evans)

Introduction

Learning support is an embedded feature of an inclusive education approach. Being a good teacher infers being able to provide appropriate support, whether it is to learners, who struggle with some aspects of a subject, or who experience more serious barriers to learning. All learners can experience some learning difficulties at a time in their school careers, which does not necessarily mean that they have a learning disability. These difficulties can be, for example, as a result of poorly constructed explanations and instructions, not learning in one's mother tongue or simply not being interested in a subject. Usually when teachers reflect on their teaching and choose alternative teaching methods and/or allow for flexibility in assessment and give some additional support the learner progresses well. This implies learning support in a broader sense where supporting all learners during teaching and learning in general ensures effective learning. However, in the context of this chapter, the focus will be more on supporting learners, who struggle continuously with learning as a result of intrinsic and/or extrinsic barriers to learning.

as of equal value and worth implies acceptance and respect, without stereotyping and/or labelling someone simply because he/she looks, thinks and believes differently (Nel, 2013).

- Poor language proficiency in the Language of Learning and Teaching (LOLT) as a consequence of learners not learning in their mother tongue;
- Poor socio-economic circumstances of learners, resulting in social problems and inadequate resources;
- Too many problematic home circumstances as a result of poverty, social problems, illnesses (such as HIV and AIDS and tuberculosis) and other reasons;
- Poor parental support;
- Inappropriate and/or insufficient resources and learning materials, especially for learners with disabilities (such as Braille material for the visually impaired, hearing aids for learners with hearing impairments and mobility support for the physically disabled);
- Inadequate training of teachers who need to deal with diverse learning needs and barriers to learning;
- Restricted financial resources;
- Limited and poor functioning support structures;
- Continuous curriculum changes;
- Too many administrative duties for teachers; and
- Discipline and behaviour problems in classes.

In a report on the Implementation of Education, White Paper 6 on Inclusive Education (Department of Basic Education, 2015) it is stated that although there has been a large increase of learners with disabilities enrolling in schools it is estimated that there are still more than 500 000 children with disabilities between five and 18 years old out of school, which is more than double the number that was initially identified in 2001. The reasons for this seem to be limited resources with regard to personnel provisioning (support staff and teachers) and finance, inadequate access to specialist support services, insufficient processes and procedures to identify children with disabilities early and a large number of drop-outs before these learners complete schooling (Department of Basic Education, 2015; Muthukrishna, Morojele, Naidoo & D'Amant, 2016).

Conclusion

There are obvious practical challenges to the implementation of inclusive education in South Africa. However, based on a human rights belief integrating and applying inclusive values to ensure equal education opportunities for all learners should be an integral principle and practice in all classrooms. This includes equality, social justice, respect for and acceptance of diversity, participation, as well as compassion and care (Booth, 2011). Treating everyone

Hugo, 2014) although this is not acknowledged by policy (Department of Basic Education, 2014).

> **NOTE**
> The possible abuse of scientific terminology to exclude or label learners has been mentioned above. However, in many instances unacceptable idiomatic labels are attached by educationist (including teachers and specialist professionals such as psychologists and therapists) as well as society to learners who struggle. This could be:
> - 'The lazy child';
> - 'The problem child';
> - 'The child will never achieve anything in life';
> - 'The special child';
> - 'The slow child';
> - 'The retarded child';
> - 'The mad child'; and
> - 'Our inclusive kids'.

Challenges in implementing inclusive education successfully

Although South African policies outline specific guidelines, requirements and procedures to affect an inclusive education system, numerous research studies and reports have found that schools find it very difficult to enact inclusive education. This is specifically applicable to learners who have a disability or multiple disabilities. Including these learners in a mainstream classroom are seen by many people in the South African society as still challenging and only an ideology. Bornman and Rose (2010:7) assert that '[a] general lack of support and resources, as well as the prevailing negative attitudes toward disability, all contribute to the general bewilderment in South African schools towards inclusion'.

Besides the continuous exclusion of learners with disabilities, the most significant challenges that have been reported within the South African context include the following (Engelbrecht, Nel, Smit & Van Deventer, 2016; Makhalemele & Nel, 2016; Nel, Nel & Hugo, 2016; Sayed & Ahmed, 2015; Walton, 2015; Nel, Tlale, Engelbrecht & Nel, 2016; Berger, 2013; Bornman & Donohue, 2013; Chataika, McKenzie, Swart & Lyner-Cleophas, 2012; Oswald & Swart, 2011; Wildeman & Nomdo, 2007):

- Negative attitudes of society (including teachers);
- Large class sizes;
- Learning needs that are too diverse in one class (eg, different abilities, disabilities, languages, cultures, religions, socio-economic circumstances, etc);

Extrinsic barriers to learning and development

Extrinsic barriers to learning and development are circumstances outside of the learner that result in learning difficulties. These extrinsic barriers can be caused by the societies in which learners live or by the school system itself. This includes socio-economic barriers, for example:

- Poverty;
- A dysfunctional family;
- Abuse, crime, gangs, and violence in the neighbourhood and/or at home;
- A lack of basic amenities such as water, electricity, proper housing, and ablution facilities; gender issues in cultural groups and in society as a whole; and
- A home language that differs from the language of learning and teaching.

Within the school system, extrinsic barriers to learning can refer to a lack of basic and appropriate learning support materials, inadequate facilities at schools, overcrowded classrooms, and a dysfunctional management system. Learners can also experience barriers to learning as a consequence of poor teaching and/or teachers that are not properly trained, insufficient support from teachers, inappropriate and unfair assessment practices, an inflexible curriculum (eg, not relevant to learners' pace, prior knowledge, learning styles), teachers not being able to deal with a diversity of learning needs, and poor classroom management (Nel, Nel & Hugo, 2016).

Intrinsic barriers to learning and development

Intrinsic barriers to learning and development correspond to conditions within the learner. This refers to medical conditions and disabilities. These barriers can be genetic, neurological, occur as a consequence of pregnancy or birth complications, or they could be the result of accidents or illnesses. These intrinsic barriers to learning and development include cognitive disabilities, sensory impairments such as visual and hearing impairments, physical impairments (eg cerebral palsy), and neurological conditions (eg, epilepsy or dyslexia) (Nel, Nel & Hugo, 2016).

EWP6 (Department of Education, 2001) recognises that the terms 'special educational needs', 'disability' and 'impairments' are still internationally used, and for that reason, these terms are retained when referring specifically to those learners whose barriers to learning and development are rooted in intrinsic organic/medical causes. It also needs to be mentioned that SEN and LSEN continues to be used in colloquial educational conversations about learners who experience barriers to learning. Learners who are being referred and placed in special education also seem to still be classified as LSEN (Nel, Nel &

Inclusive education:

- *Is about acknowledging that all children and youth can learn and that all children and youth need support;*
- *Is accepting and respecting the fact that all learners are different in some way and have different learning needs which are equally valued and an ordinary part of our human experience;*
- *Is about enabling education structures, systems and learning methodologies to meet the needs of all learners;*
- *Acknowledges and respects difference in children, whether due to age, gender, ethnicity, language, class, disability, HIV status, etc;*
- *Is broader than formal schooling, and acknowledges that learning occurs in the home, the community, and within formal and informal modes and structures;*
- *Is about changing attitudes, behaviours, methodologies, curricula and environments to meet the needs of all children; and*
- *Is about maximising the participation of all learners in the culture and the curriculum of educational institutions and uncovering and minimising barriers to learning.*

The use of appropriate terminology within the South African context

Since South Africa has a history of discriminatory and exclusionary practices the use of words/terminology can have a significant impact. It can either harm, label and stereotype or carry over a message of inclusion and belonging. Terminology such as special educational needs (SEN), disabilities and impairments are generally used to label and categorise learners. As soon as the label 'learner with special educational needs' (LSEN) is awarded to a learner, he/she is categorised according to the disability/impairment the child has and then separated from mainstream education and placed in special education settings. Alas, the so-called 'normal' community then believes that these learners will not be able to achieve success in a mainstream academic and working world since these disabilities are judged as arising from within the learner (Department of Education, 1997; Nel, 2013; Swart & Pettipher, 2016). Because of these negative connotations to the term 'learner with special educational needs' or 'special educational needs', it was replaced by EWP6 with 'learners experiencing barriers to learning and development' as an official term (Department of Education, 2001). A barrier to learning can be defined as 'anything that stands in the way of a child being able to learn'. These barriers can be experienced as a result of intrinsic or extrinsic factors.

emphasised the principles that should be given prominence to in an inclusive education system, namely:
- Human rights and social justice for all learners;
- Participation and social integration;
- Equal access to a single, inclusive education system;
- Access to one curriculum;
- Equity and redress; and
- Community responsiveness (Department of Education, 1997, 2001).

EWP6 acknowledges that diverse learning needs can arise as a result of intrinsic barriers to learning including:

> ... *physical, mental, sensory, neurological and developmental impairments, psycho-social disturbances, differences in intellectual ability, particular life experiences or socio-economic deprivation,*

but also emphasises that the following extrinsic (societal and systemic) barriers to learning can result in learning difficulties:

- *Negative attitudes to and stereotyping of difference;*
- *An inflexible curriculum;*
- *Inappropriate languages or language of learning and teaching;*
- *Inappropriate communication;*
- *Inaccessible and unsafe built environments;*
- *Inappropriate and inadequate support services;*
- *Inadequate policies and legislation;*
- *The non-recognition and non-involvement of parents; and*
- *Inadequately and inappropriately trained education managers and educators.* (Department of Education, 2001:7)

An important fact that you need to take cognisance of is that EWP6 puts emphasis on the fact that barriers to learning do not only reside within the learner, but can also be a result of barriers that the education system, as well as socio-environmental issues, cause.

Defining inclusive education within a South African context

Although there are different interpretations by researchers and practitioners of what inclusive education entails, the following definition as given in EWP6 should be used as the foundation (Department of Education, 2001:6).

Background to inclusive education in South Africa

Since South Africa participated in and undersigned all the international conventions (as discussed in the previous chapter), it contributed largely to South Africa's move to inclusive education in the last few decades. However, the predominant motive for implementing an inclusive education system was driven by South Africa's poor human rights history. In the previous political dispensation, discriminatory policies and practices segregated learners based on race and disability. Different races were in different schools and learners with disabilities (also called special needs) were placed in special classes and schools. These special schools mostly accommodated white learners and were well-resourced. Only a few under-resourced special schools for black learners with disabilities were nationally available. As a consequence, many black learners, who had special needs were included by default into mainstream education. Access to special schools was also rigidly controlled. After a battery of tests by different health professionals (eg, doctors, psychologists, speech- and/or occupational therapists or social workers) only learners with organic or medical disabilities and severe behaviour problems were allowed to attend special schools. There were also a large number of learners with disabilities not in schools at all. In 2001, it was determined that nearly 240 000 learners with disabilities were out of school (Department of Education, 2001). After the democratic political transformation, impelled by the Constitution (Republic of South Africa, 1996b) and more specifically the Bill of Rights, several education policies affirmed that there should be equal rights and social justice for all learners by accommodating them into one integrated education system.

The South African Schools Act No. 84 of 1996 (Republic of South Africa, 1996c) was the first legal educational document that affirmed the obligation to redress past injustices in education and uphold the rights of all learners by eradicating unfair discrimination and intolerance. However, the most important policy that is fundamental to all educational decisions and practices in South Africa is Education White Paper 6 (EWP6) on special needs education, building an inclusive education and training system (Department of Education, 2001). This policy was developed and accepted in 2001 after an investigation into all aspects related to special needs and support services by the National Commission on Special Needs in Education and Training (NCSNET) and the National Committee on Education Support Services (NCESS). The findings of this investigation affirmed that there were two distinct categories of learners—the majority with ordinary needs, and then a minority of learners with special needs, who were taught and received remedial intervention in special schools. These learners were deemed by the education departments and society as not being able to fit into mainstream education. In response to this report, EWP6

30 Inclusive education in the South African context

MIRNA NEL

Inclusive, good quality education is a foundation for dynamic and equitable societies. (Desmond Tutu)

Introduction

Although inclusive education is a global approach, it remains a contextual issue. Every continent and country has its own sociocultural, political, historical and economic contexts and challenges. Inclusion within an African perspective has a specific meaning. There is a saying in Sepedi: A person is a person because that person exists among others, not in isolation (Mahlo, 2017). Or alternatively, you have heard the adage: It takes a village to raise a child. With regard to inclusive education, this means that the whole school community, including parents, elders, wider families and cultural custodians must ensure that all children receive quality and equal education. This constitutes a togetherness, sharing and reciprocity as well as an acknowledgement of every child's identity, history, cultures and experiences that they bring to school (Phasha, Mahlo & Dei, 2017; Mahlo, 2017). The given in South Africa is that classrooms are diverse with regard to race, ethnicity, culture, religion, language and abilities. This in itself represents inclusivity. The focus of inclusive education in South African can therefore not only be disability-centred, but should have a broader purpose of social inclusion and addressing diverse learning needs.

The following values are also immersed in the IDE 2030:
- Human rights and dignity;
- Social justice;
- Inclusion;
- Protection;
- Cultural, linguistic and ethnic diversity; and
- Shared responsibility and accountability.

It is acknowledged by IDE 2030 that education is the only strategy to achieve full employment and the eradication of poverty. This includes access, equity and inclusion, as well as quality learning outcomes, within a lifelong learning approach (UNESCO, UNICEF, World Bank, UNFPA, UNDP, UN Women and UNHCR, 2015).

Conclusion

It is evident from the above discussions that inclusive education is taken seriously by most countries, but the implementation thereof seems to remain challenging. The United Nations Educational, Scientific and Cultural Organisation (UNESCO) is the central global organisation that works with governments and partners to ensure that the implementation of inclusive education progresses to address exclusion from and inequality in educational opportunities (see http://www.unesco.org/new/en/inclusive-education/). Every year UNESCO publishes an Education for All global monitoring report to give an account on the progress of the EFA movement. The 2015 report accounted that great improvement was made internationally to implement more inclusive education systems and provide education for all. Apparently 34 million more children are attending schools than in 2000 (UNESCO, 2015a). However, in this and another 2015 report by UNESCO named 'Fixing the Broken Promise of Education for All' it was claimed that the progress to provide all children with access to basic education has stalled since 2007 (UNESCO, 2015b). The causes of this are reported as increasing poverty, war and conflict in countries, gender discrimination, child labour, language challenges, as well as social, institutional and environmental barriers linked to disability. Apparently, there are also still 58 million children, more or less between the ages of six and 11, out of school globally. An estimate of 30 million of these children is in sub-Sahara Africa. A large number of children with disabilities continue to have no access to education and a stigma that keeps them hidden away in many communities still persists. It is obvious therefore that many vulnerable children continue to be marginalised worldwide, despite efforts to achieve education for all and promote inclusion.

the Jomtien World Declaration on Education for All (Jomtien, 1990) as well as the Universal Declaration of Human Rights and the Convention on the Rights of the Child were reaffirmed at this conference. The thread of equal and equitable access as well as quality education for all children was supported in the goals of this framework. Particular areas of concern that were identified included HIV and AIDS, early childhood education, school health, education of girls and women, adult literacy, and education in situations of crisis and emergency (UNESCO, 2000:3). It was asserted that high quality educational opportunities must neither exclude nor discriminate.

Acknowledgement was given to the fact that the pace, style, language and circumstances of learning will never be uniform for all, and therefore room should be provided for diverse formal or less formal approaches. Additionally, free, compulsory and good quality primary education was a key emphasis of this framework. The Dakar framework also illuminated that despite the 1990 Jomtien EFA framework, little progress was made from 1990 until the year 2000 with regard to the following:

- More than 113 million children still had no access to primary education;
- 880 million adults were illiterate;
- Gender discrimination was evident in education systems; and
- The quality of learning as well as the acquisition of human values and skills did not meet the needs of individuals and societies.

It was emphasised that, if these concerns were not addressed, poverty reduction and sustainable development would not be achieved and inequality among countries and within societies would remain (UNESCO, 2000). In this framework, sub-Saharan Africa and South Asia were prioritised for the advancement of the EFA goal.

Another World Education Forum in Incheon, Republic of Korea was held in 2015. This conference was organised by UNESCO, together with the United Nations Children's Emergency Fund (UNICEF), the World Bank, the United Nations Populations Fund (UNFPA), the United Nations Development Programme (UNDP), UN Women, and the United Nations High Commissioner for Refugees (UNHCR), and over 1 600 participants from 160 countries attended. The Incheon Declaration for Education (IDE) 2030 was agreed upon with a 15-year vision to transform lives through education. It was acknowledged that a renewed agenda focusing on leaving no one behind was necessary. The Sustainable Development Goal (SDG) 4 of UNESCO, namely, 'Ensure inclusive and equitable quality education and promote lifelong learning opportunities for all' (UNESCO, UNICEF, World Bank, UNFPA, UNDP, UN Women and UNHCR, 2015:iii) was used as the foundational principle for this declaration.

- Refugees;
- Those displaced by war; and
- People under occupation.

Children with disabilities were also expressly identified and it was asserted that equal access to education to every category of disabled persons should be provided. In this document, attention was also brought to the more than 100 million school-going age children without access to a formal education setting at the primary phase of schooling, as well as those dropping out and then not being able to re-access the schooling system (UNESCO, 2000).

After the Jomtien conference, the World Conference on Special Needs Education in Salamanca, Spain took place in 1994. This conference made significant strides to endorse inclusive education with the adoption of the Salamanca Statement and Framework for Action on Special Needs Education (SSFASNE) and was signed by 92 countries (including South Africa) (UNESCO, 1994). It was emphasised in this framework that: 'Every child has a fundamental right to education, and must be given the opportunity to achieve and maintain an acceptable level of learning' (UNESCO, 1994:viii), and that 'schools should accommodate all children regardless of their physical, intellectual, social, emotional, linguistic or other conditions' (UNESCO, 2000:6). This includes disabled and gifted children, street and working children, children from remote or nomadic populations, from linguistic, ethnic or cultural minorities and from other disadvantaged or marginalised areas or groups (UNESCO, 2000:6).

The uniqueness of children is also acknowledged, which requires that education must consider their diverse needs and characteristics:

Inclusive schools must recognise and respond to the diverse needs of their students, accommodating both different styles and rates of learning and ensuring quality education to all through appropriate curricula, organisational arrangements, teaching strategies, resource use and partnerships with their communities. (UNESCO, 1994:11–12)

In addition, the SSFASNE explicitly puts emphasis on granting children with special educational needs access to mainstream schools where all children can learn together and at the same time, and where their individual differences and learning needs are catered for through the provision of additional support (Swart & Pettipher, 2016). The most significant impact of the SSFASNE is that it provided the foundational narrative of how inclusive education should be understood globally.

In 2000, a World Education Forum conference was held in Dakar, Senegal. During this conference, 164 countries adopted the Dakar Framework for Action, 'Education for All: meeting our collective commitments'. The vision of

child according to these within-child-deficits. Even if academic challenges are experienced because of a disability, there are always multiple contextual societal and systemic factors that contribute to these academic challenges (such as living in poverty, parents' poor education levels, inadequately qualified teachers, inefficient support, etc).

After gaining an understanding of how inclusive education is viewed globally, the following sections will present several important international conventions over the last two centuries, which attempted to change education to become more inclusive. You will most probably recognise that the broader second viewpoint has more emphasis in these developments.

Historical global conventions

As can be concluded from the above discussion, access to basic education is internationally regarded as a basic human right. It is therefore important to note the following conventions, which played a pivotal role in the initiation of the movement to inclusive education. This includes the Universal Declaration of Human Rights (UDHR) in 1948 after World War II (United Nations, 1948), the Convention on the Rights of the Child (CRC) aged 0 to 18 years in 1989 (United Nations, 1989), the African Charter on the Rights and Welfare of the Child in 1999 (UNICEF, 1999), and the Convention on the Rights of People with Disabilities (CRPD) (United Nations, 2006), which was adopted in 2006 and ratified by South Africa in 2007. All of these aforementioned conventions emphasise the principle that inherent dignity of all people, as well as their equal and inalienable rights, should be recognised as the foundation to freedom, justice and peace (United Nations, 1948).

However, the specific focus on inclusive education started in 1990 at a World Education Forum conference in Jomtien, Thailand, where a World Declaration on Education for All and the Framework for Action to Meet Basic Learning Needs were adopted by 155 countries at the conference (UNESCO, 2000). This framework emphasised that basic education of quality should be provided to all children, youth and illiterate adults to reduce disparities. The following groups were specifically mentioned:
- Girls and women;
- The poor;
- Street and working children;
- Rural and remote populations;
- Nomads and migrant workers;
- Indigenous peoples;
- Ethnic, racial, and linguistic minorities;

(Philpott & McLaren, 2011; Gilligan, 2016). In many societies, there is a belief that these children are some sort of 'punishment' or 'bewitchment'. They are consequently rejected by some parents and communities and are hidden away.

People with disabilities assert that prejudicial attitudes of people towards them are one of the hardest things that they regularly encounter (Gilligan, 2016; Philpott & McLaren, 2011). They feel that people tend to only see them *as a disability* and ignore *the person behind the disability*. As a result, the label of disability disregards who they are as a person (Donald, Lazarus & Lolwana, 2010:283). The whole child is then seen as 'abnormal', and as a rule, abnormal behaviour is expected of the child.

Generally, it is also mindlessly assumed that any disability results in intellectual impairments. Consequently, it is believed that it is better for this child to be separated from the mainstream and placed in special education settings, where specially qualified teachers can work with them. Contrariwise, even when children with disabilities are mainstreamed or integrated, they are still required *to fit into* the classroom, because they are the *'abnormal ones'* that must adapt to *'normalness'*.

In mainstreaming or integration, the school society and system do not always purposefully adapt to fully include these learners in all activities (Swart & Pettipher, 2016; Sapon-Shevin, 2007). One must therefore be careful to think of this as inclusion. In an inclusive education setting children with disabilities, like any other person, are seen as unique human beings with their own personal attributes (such as background, ethnicity, gender, religion, political beliefs, values and principles), and are provided equal opportunities to participate in all formal and informal learning activities.

Second viewpoint: Social inclusion

Without disregarding the disability emphasis, it is important to understand that inclusion needs to be addressed as a societal and systemic issue as well. In this viewpoint, 'inclusion' is not seen as referring to one group (those with disabilities) only, while 'social inclusion' refers to a different group, since *'all inclusion and exclusion are socially created'* (Booth, 2011:307). Social inclusion recognises that intrinsic (special needs/disabilities) and societal and systemic (extrinsic) factors interact in creating barriers to learning. Children can experience learning difficulties and consequent exclusion as a result of various societal and systemic factors, such as poverty, abuse, racial discrimination, limited proficiency in the Language of Learning and Teaching (LOLT), poor quality of teaching, ineffective support systems, insufficient infrastructure, inadequate policies, and more recently immigrant status. One must therefore take care not to seek deficits only within a single child and consequently label and categorise such a

the fundamental educational approach and philosophy accepted by many governments to counter exclusion and discrimination.

Understanding inclusive education in a global context

Defining inclusive education is quite complex. Currently, it seems that there are two leading viewpoints globally: one that primarily focuses on the inclusion of learners with different kinds of disabilities (also called special needs) in mainstream education, and the broader view that inclusion is a societal issue (ie, social inclusion) where inclusivity deals with diversity with regard to race, religion, social class, socio-economic disadvantages, ethnicity, gender and academic achievement, as well as disabilities (Ainscow, 2014; Topping, 2012). Within the broader view, the emphasis is therefore on education for all (EFA) (see also the section on historical global conventions further on in this chapter). Both these perspectives are based on the belief that education is a basic human right for all learners, and a quality inclusive education system will foster a more just society.

First viewpoint: Including children with disabilities

According to the Convention on the Rights of People with Disabilities (CRPD) people with disabilities can be identified as those:

> ... *who have long-term physical, mental, intellectual or sensory impairments which in interaction with various barriers may hinder their full and effective participation in society on an equal basis with others.* (United Nations, 2006:4)

This CRPD was adopted in 2006 to protect the rights of people with disabilities internationally (United Nations, 2006). The purpose of the CRPD is:

> ... *to promote, protect and ensure the full and equal enjoyment of all human rights and fundamental freedoms by all persons with disabilities, and to promote respect for their inherent dignity.* (United Nations, 2006:2)

However, despite the CRPD and several other interventions, children with disabilities remain some of the most vulnerable populations excluded from society and from fully enjoying their basic human rights. This is therefore the reason why many inclusion activists, as well as research and governmental policies, still primarily focus on this viewpoint.

Children with disabilities continue to have poor access to education, health services and future employment (Iriarte, McConkey & Gilligan, 2016). In addition, these children experience social, cultural and attitudinal obstacles and are particularly vulnerable to victimisation, violence, abuse and exploitation

Inclusive education: The global movement

MIRNA NEL

Inclusion is a right, not a privilege for a select few. (Judge Geary, Oberti vs Board of Education (D.N.J., 1992))

Introduction

We live in a world where human rights abuses are rife and prejudices against diversity are commonplace. So if asked to think about the following statements, what would your response be? Excluding (and discriminating against) someone simply because he/she looks, thinks and believes differently is regular practice. In most societies people who have a different religion, skin colour and/or sexual orientation, live in a different socio-economic area, wear different clothes, have a disability and/or illness generally creates a sense of discomfort and inharmoniousness. Alternatively, being with someone who is more or less the same as you generates more comfort and familiarity.

In an attempt to end discriminatory and exclusionary practices against difference, the principle of inclusion, and more specifically social inclusion, has been increasingly embraced by societies all over the world. These societies regard education as the critical tool through which:

- Inclusionary values can be identified and learned to be respected; and
- Diversity can be regarded as something to learn from and enrich one's own way of thinking and believing.

As Nelson Mandela said: 'Education is the most powerful weapon which you can use to change the world.' Consequently, inclusive education became

Inclusion

which contradicts the self-concept. Furthermore, people do not always accurately identify the source of their feelings, thereby limiting its informational values (Schwarz, 2012). Negative self-talk is extremely incapacitating in the sense that it keeps the status quo in place. Resulting in continued negative self-concept and low self-esteem, it may lead to disqualifying behaviour which may, for example at school, discourage learners to venture and initiate new learning. Fear to venture and initiate new learning may contribute to academic performance anxiety and poor personal functioning (Anderman, 2014). Negative feedback from others, for example from teachers, may further be interpreted as confirming original negative self-appraisals (Kunda, 1999).

On a wider scale in South Africa, South Africa's population, and South Africa's youth in particular, are faced with various complicated societal challenges which may have an impact on their self-esteem. In addition to the heritage of South Africa's political past and the frequent political unrest, South Africa's youth struggle with unemployment and socio-economic problems such as poverty and poor education. Western narratives which continue to be part and parcel of society and education create questions about identity. Imposed values in the past required all South Africans to adapt and adjust to one way of thinking and one way of being. Any alternative way of looking at the world and at personhood was considered as deviating. This resulted in 'dissociation of self from the own cultural identity' (Ngũgĩ wa Thiong'o, 1992:16).

The negative and self-defeating self-talk that we often hear, confirms that fundamentally there is a search for identity in South Africa. It is a good time for teachers and educational psychologists to promote identity formation through reflexive teaching. This may inform a new, more positive realistic kind of self-talk. In this respect Brandtstadter (as cited in Bell, Wieling & Watson, 2004) found a correlation between increased self-reflection and self-regulation.

Conclusion

The quality of self-talk was argued in this chapter as essential for identity development and therefore central to the development of self. In addition to its influence on the private identity, self-talk influences social interaction, social relationships and social identity. The fact that we sometimes evaluate others and see them as we see ourselves, teaches us that the key to understanding others, is often understanding ourselves first. Our youth need to learn a self-criticism style which is beneficial and constructive and through which they can create useful problem formulations, not only for themselves, but for the way in which they look at others. To undergo a change in self-concept—admittedly a profound and long-term process—a good place to start would be to become aware of how self-talk plays a role in self-regulation.

reversal (Feigenbaum, 2009), children are enabled to see themselves as authority figures see them. In other words, the authority figure's perspective becomes the child's own self-perspective (Gore & Cross, 2014). In agreement with the authority figure, the self then becomes an additional authority figure. During perspective-taking children also internalise their parents' corrective attitudes as a part of their new self-perspectives. If these attitudes are severely punitive or rejecting, they may also be internalised and children may begin to inflict similar punishments on themselves when they fall short of their internalised ideals (Benadé, 2013). According to Benner (1993), such punitive and self-rejecting self-talk forms the core of neurotic guilt feelings.

Notwithstanding the influencing variables in self-talk, people are not necessarily completely subject to these influences. This is because they possess self-reflective, self-reactive, metacognitive and meta-affective capabilities that enable them to exercise some control over their thoughts, feeling, motivation and actions. Bandura (1991:249) refers to this as 'standards of behavior' that people employ in the exercise of self-directedness. Self-reflection includes meta-affect, or 'how we think about the feelings we experience' (D'Mello, Strain, Olney & Graesser, 2013:675). According to Schwarz (2012), feelings are also a source of information. A learner may for example experience frustration while facing a cognitive challenge, and think (self-talk): 'This isn't working.' This may motivate the learner to find a new strategy that may work. Meta-affect, or monitoring our feelings, may therefore add to the quality of our self-talk and help us to consider new behavioural options. Just as metacognition, it may help us to monitor and manage our problem solving strategies and our behaviour. The quality of our self-talk therefore influences the choices we make, the effort we put into goals and how long we persevere. This reminds us of the high premium Bandura (1991) placed on people's belief in their capabilities and its importance for self-regulation.

Educational implications of the quality of self-talk in schools in South Africa

While various self-structures and cognitive tasks intersect during self-regulation, self-talk concerns the evaluative components of the self-structure (Van Dijk, et al, 2014). This means that what we say to ourselves has major personal and social implications: the quality of our self-talk influences self-esteem, which has an impact on our self-efficacy.

Still, attitudes, which are usually based on the belief system, do not change that easily, nor does behaviour. Rogers (1959) argued that even if the self-concept may be unrealistic and self-defeating, people may reject incoming information

important in evaluative self-talk. According to Bandura (1991:254), such standards are not adopted automatically, but 'are constructed through reflective processing of multiple sources of direct and vicarious influence'. Children normally start out by adopting their parents' belief system and values but as they go through transitions, they are exposed to new information, form new relationships and are faced with differing backgrounds and beliefs. This has a great impact on self-talk as the belief system constitutes the norm against which people measure their thoughts and actions, and ultimately their identity. For each role we assume in life, for example as student, parent, friend, spiritual person, cultural member, we have a value against which we compare how we fare. When I evaluate myself as a religious person, I will take lessons which I learnt from my religious teachings as my measure. When I think of myself as an employee, I will compare my work to the expectations of my employer and the ethics of my workplace. When I think about myself as a friend, I will compare my friendships against identification figures from whom I learnt lessons in integrity and friendship. Although values are generally lasting, they may change throughout the lifespan.

Our existing self-esteem and self-descriptive statements

In addition to our existing knowledge and self-knowledge, and our belief system, we have an existing self-esteem which, as explained above, is mostly affectively constituted and may change depending on analysis of new information. This perceived self-image leads to the establishment of another influencing variable in self-talk, namely self-descriptive statements. Self-descriptive statements are core beliefs about the self which are used to endorse new incidents (Kunda, 1999). They function almost like a stereotype or default attitude about ourselves and usually play a role when we interpret new information. To say for example 'I always say the wrong thing' or 'I always find a way to get through difficult times' not only refers to what people know and believe about themselves but to how they may react in the face of new circumstances.

Our perspective-taking as a cognitive skill

Perspective-taking is a cognitive skill which may further impact self-talk. It is described as the ability to view a situation (or the self) from another's point of view (Gerace, Day, Casey & Mohr, 2015), but it is more than empathy. As explained earlier, the ability for joint attentional behaviour later leads to a shift from focusing joint attention on objects, to focusing joint attention on the child herself. The child not only learns to focus on herself as the object of her attention, but moreover, to adopt the perspective of the parent when she focuses on herself. By learning the cognitive tasks of reciprocal imitation and role

may make self-esteem more stable (Pilarska, 2016). In the case of a failure in one area in the life of a person with high self-complexity, the person may accept the failure in this one area, but will not allow it to affect other areas of self and will therefore retain his/her sense of self-esteem. Bandura (1991) says that a firm sense of identity and strong orientation toward fulfilling personal standards display a high level of self-directedness in people. The opposite is also true. When self-complexity is low and self-aspects are highly interrelated, enmeshed and dependent, a failure in one area may be perceived by the person as incompetence in all areas (Kunda, 1999). Therefore, although subject to change, the pursuit of consistency is an essential manifestation of self and a significant indicator of effective adaptation and mental health (Rogers, 1959, as cited in Pilarska, 2016). The complexity and clarity of our self-knowledge also has relevance for how we see other people, in other words, for our social judgement. This will be further explained as one of the variables that may influence information processing. Numerous variables may play a role when we interpret new information.

Variables that may play a role when we interpret new information

What follows below explains how our tendency to self-evaluate and to evaluate others, our existing belief system, our self-descriptive statements, our existing self-esteem and our cognitive ability of perspective-taking may influence our self-talk.

Our tendency to self-evaluate and to evaluate others

Humans have an inborn tendency to evaluate the self and others. From the moment that the child can conceive rules and goal messages from his/her environment, in other words, as soon as the child gets an idea of what is appropriate, self-talk starts to be evaluative with regard to others, but also with regard to the self (Lewis, 1997). It has been recognised for many years how perceptions of others influence perceptions of self, and vice versa. While Freud (1924/1956) explained it as projection, Horney (as cited in Alicke, Dunning & Krueger, 2005:5) understood it as a 'naïve belief' that others think and feel the same way as we do. Later, Rogers (1951) assumed that people's social experiences are organised into a structure of self. In the same way, people also make predictions about others according to their own self-understanding (Alicke, Dunning & Krueger, 2005).

Our existing belief system

Our existing knowledge further includes our belief system. The belief system constitutes the values one acquires through acculturation and is extremely

said that self-regulation consists of self-monitoring, self-judgement and affective self-reaction. In so doing, he linked environment, behaviour and cognition. Self-regulation is therefore the conscious awareness, analysis and regulation of one's own thoughts, behaviour and feelings. It manages the functional and dynamic interaction between the self and the environment and is facilitated through self-talk.

Having various representations of self—or at least a private and a social self as explained above—means that each person has to possess a store of existing factual knowledge, whether social or private. Still, our existing factual knowledge is not always altogether factual, but can be highly subjective, limited and even biased (Alicke, Dunning & Krueger, 2005). This means that situations and incidents are often interpreted not as they actually happened; our 'biased self-reference processes' (Bandura, 1991:253) often result in our processing information in a subjective way so that we may end up with fiction rather than fact or with 'perceived constructs' (Anderman, 2014:57). Bandura (1991) is not of the opinion that we are predetermined always to process information subjectively, but he argues that behaviour is highly resistant to change and therefore more than self-monitoring is necessary for behavioural change to occur. This means that if we learn to be overly critical in our self-evaluation in childhood, we may tend to keep on doing it. In distinguishing between self-concept and self-esteem (*what I know about myself and what I think about myself*) some authors divide the processing of incoming information into at least two phases.

Both self-concept and self-esteem are often used to refer to the perception of self (Van Dijk, Branje, Keijsers, Hawk, Hale & Meeus, 2014) and include self-perception and self-evaluation. In his famous definition, Rogers (1951:2) defined the self-concept as 'the organized, consistent set of perceptions and beliefs about oneself'. Although this definition describes the self-concept as the dynamic view according to which one perceives oneself, some recent distinctions make a cognitive-affective division in the processing of information. Recently the self-concept is regarded as being more informative, namely the objective knowledge which a person has about him-/herself, while self-esteem is described as more evaluative, or the subjective perception of a person about him-/herself (Pilarska, 2016). According to this line of argumentation self-esteem is the affective evaluation of the information in the self-concept, a general attitude about the self (Anderman, 2014). This definition draws the meaning of self-knowledge and the self-concept closer together, although for the purposes of this chapter this difference will not be further investigated. Roger's (1959) definition of 'organised' and 'consistent' can be useful in considering the impact that clarity of self-knowledge has on self-esteem.

Clarity of self-knowledge implies that different aspects of self are complex, organised and distinguishable (Gore & Cross, 2014). Clarity of self-knowledge

followed by thoughts on the relevance and necessity of enhancing the quality of self-talk in South African schools and classrooms.

Clarification of self-talk and related constructs

Humans have many ways of adding to their self-knowledge. They receive information from the environment, which usually contains ecological and social rules. New information is processed by relating it to existing knowledge and self-knowledge. Additional processes and constructs such as self-evaluation and social judgement, the belief system, self-descriptive statements and perspective-taking also play a role in self-talk. In this process, which is known as self-regulation, self-talk functions as a conscious, often verbal, mediating cognitive task. As a conscious cognitive activity, it may involve metacognitive thinking—thinking about our thoughts—to understand our behaviour or our ways of approaching a problem (Clarebout, Elen, Juarez Collazo, Lust & Jiang, 2013:187). Metacognitive thinking may then facilitate self-regulation as it helps us to peruse our own cognitive problem-solving strategies. But let us first focus briefly on the development of the self as a conceptual structure.

Around the first year after birth, following first perception, conceptual thought begins where children learn concepts from a parent or caregiver (Neisser, 1997). During shared attention, the object of joint interest may be the child him-/herself (Feigenbaum, 2009). When the parent speaks to the child about the child, the child now takes him/herself as an object of his/her subjective thought. Children begin to think of themselves as having traits, attributes, worth and value. Authors have identified various aspects of self, of which the most notable are the private and the social self. These aspects of self or are not alien people inside us, taking control over us, but ways of positioning ourselves to react and respond to different situations and people in our lives and to integrate information from those situations with our already existing knowledge and self-knowledge.

As children grow up, they start to distinguish between the various aspects of self. When they evaluate themselves with regard to their role in their family and school, they will be evaluating their social identity or social self. When they reflect on their private conception of self, for example their unique features, they will be reflecting on their private self. These are not loose-standing constructs. When a new event is experienced consciously, the social self, as embedded in its environment, intersects with the private experience part of the self (Kihlstrom & Klein, 1997). These ongoing representations of the self, derived from ongoing conscious experience of events in our lifeworld, are linked to the existing way in which we represent ourselves in our own minds. Bandura's (1991) suggestion of three processes, which are encompassed by self-regulation, is helpful here. He

belief system and social rules, and allowing it to influence self-talk, self-esteem, behaviour and relationships.

Why is it necessary to take note of self-talk in educational psychology?

Self-talk plays a crucial role in identity formation and has enormous consequences for quality of life and happiness. The quality and content of one's self-talk influences self-esteem and in its turn self-esteem informs identity. How is this relevant for South Africans today? In the political past of our country the idea of one absolute truth, the promotion of scientific knowledge at the cost of subjective knowledge and the assumption that reality as a construct can be accessed, were imposed on all South Africans. This led to considering other ways of seeing the world, such as subjective experience, as 'non-reasoned' (Farganis, 1996:9). Considering alternative narratives as deviating from the required norm has resulted in socially and politically marginalised groups being subjected to doubt their way of existence and in dissociating children from their natural and social environment (Ngũgĩ wa Thiong'o, 1992). When we peruse printed and social media reporting on calls for decolonisation in various areas of society, including education, it may therefore be agreed that identity is at the heart of current discourses in South Africa today.

In school, learners are still developing towards identity clarity. They may take incoming information containing social values and hidden narratives as the truth and may use this information in their self-talk to evaluate themselves and others in an unrealistic way (Anderman, 2014). The role of the teacher and the educational psychologist who seek to discourage destructive self-criticism and promote quality of mental, emotional and physical life by facilitating positive and realistic self-talk can therefore not be overestimated.

The quality of self-talk in self-regulation is an important element in private and social identity development and necessitates a discussion of the related theoretical constructs that underpin self-talk. To gain understanding of the self as conceptual structure, the development of self-awareness and the social and private self are considered in this chapter. Self-knowledge, self-concept and self-esteem as three important constructs in self-regulation are defined and briefly compared. A few variables which play a role in the quality of self-talk during self-regulation are discussed. These variables are linked to the human tendency to evaluate the self and others, the belief system, self-descriptive statements and perspective-taking. Ways of controlling and managing clarity of self-knowledge to enhance a complex and differentiated self-structure which may enable people to develop a realistic positive self-esteem are discussed in the next sections,

28 The role of self-talk in self-regulation

RIENIE VENTER

The struggle young people face these days is being lost; most of us don't know where we come from and we don't know where we are going. We have no direction ... Even our elders have given up on us; they understand that we are a lost cause (Anonymous young South African, interviewed by Kwazi Dlamini for Vox Newsletter, March, 2016)

Introduction

Reflect for a moment on the remarkable phenomenon of self-consciousness and on humans' ability to reflect on their own thoughts. This self-directed communication—the 'I' who is talking to, and is able to think about 'me'—takes place by means of silent self-speak or out loud, sometimes aided by the use of language (Feigenbaum, 2009:105). While reflecting on our own self-talk, it may become clear that our self-talk often has an evaluative aspect. Are we not constantly evaluating ourselves in terms of work, studies and relationships, in terms of the merit of our decisions? The construct which is described here is self-regulation, our ability to monitor and manage our own thoughts, behaviour and feelings (Schwarz, 2012:290). An important part of self-regulation is self-evaluation. What is the measure that we use when we evaluate ourselves and how does it influence our self-esteem?

What is described here is at the heart of educational psychology, namely the continuous awareness of self while surveying and processing messages from the environment, relating it to existing knowledge, past experience, a personal

Resilience Process	Examples from South African studies
Agency and mastery and the beginnings of a powerful identity *(continued)*	**Teachers encourage dreams about a better future** For example, resilient university students from disadvantaged backgrounds reflected that their teachers had actively drawn their attention to their academic potential, celebrated children doing well in tests/trying hard, and encouraged them to go to university (and in some instances, even helped them pay for registration or informed them about bursaries) (Ebersöhn, 2007; Theron & Theron, 2014).
Cultural and/or religious adherence in support of self-regulation	**Teachers instil relevant values** When asked to comment on what they believed buffered rural children from communities challenged by poverty, HIV and AIDS, and violence, a group of local adults noted that when teachers purposefully taught children to value traditional and spiritual principles, then they were promoting children's resilience (Theron, Theron & Malindi, 2012). Similarly, when children reflected on their resilience they noted that teachers who encouraged them to pursue education as a pathway to a better future, and concomitantly urged diligence and excellence, had been instrumental to their beating the odds (Dass-Brailsford, 2005; Malindi & Machenjedze, 2012; Theron & Malindi, 2010).

Conclusion

In summary, for you (as teachers, educational psychologists, other school-based staff) to facilitate good developmental outcomes in the children you interact with, you need to understand that resilience processes need systemic (social ecological) support because resilience is about more than a child's strengths. This entails active partnerships with children in which children's strengths are acknowledged and drawn on, but which also provide children with protective resources that are relevant to South African contexts/cultures. Ultimately, to champion resilience requires acceptance and enactment of communities' (also school communities') duty to support children to engage in constructive resilience processes and to change the odds that threaten children.

Resilience Process	Examples from South African studies
Social justice *(continued)*	One sexually abused girl recounted that some of her teachers hid her when local boys who had raped her came to her school to taunt her, and how their keeping her physically safe had nurtured her resilience (Phasha, 2010). **School systems are fair to children** In contexts of adversity, children's schooling is often interrupted and/or children come late to school. Some school systems understand this and make exceptions to support these children to progress/complete their education, despite the challenges that keep them away from school. For example, resilient young people have reported that their schools allowed them to skip grades (when they returned to school and were much older than their cohort), provided they had demonstrated academic competence, or adapted curriculum choices, or were lenient about late-coming (Theron & Theron, 2014). Others drew attention to the value of schools accepting refugee children and to teachers supporting older learners to access bursaries (Hlatshwayo & Vally, 2014).
Constructive relationships	**Positive teacher–child connections** For example, in Johnson and Lazarus's (2008) study of children who had been placed at risk for poor developmental outcomes by their communities, children reported that friendly, approachable teachers were supportive of their resilience. The AIDS-orphans who participated in Pienaar, et al's 2011 study provided details of how supportive teachers treated them in ways that encouraged them to feel valued. Other at-risk children (eg, those from divorced homes, or marginalised communities, or visibly scarred burn victims, or living on the street) also reported that teacher encouragement and unconditional support of them, buffered the difficulties they faced (Dass-Brailsford, 2005; Lau & Van Niekerk, 2011; Malindi & Machenjedze, 2012; Mampane & Huddle, 2017; Theron & Dunn, 2010; Theron & Engelbrecht, 2012; Theron & Theron, 2014).
Agency and mastery and the beginnings of a powerful identity	**Teachers model resilience** For example, children living on the street, and those from impoverished, marginalised communities reported that their teachers inspired them to develop powerful identities and to do well in life (Dass-Brailsford, 2005; Malindi & Machenjedze, 2012; Theron, 2016a; Theron & Engelbrecht, 2012). What encouraged them most was the fact that their teachers came from similar backgrounds, but had turned their lives around and become educated, respected members of society. Likewise, when teachers disclosed that they had faced similar hardships to those confronting children, then children were motivated, by their teachers' examples, to resile (Theron & Engelbrecht, 2012).

Table 27.1 Differentially valued resilience resources

Resilience Process	Examples from South African studies
Pragmatic support (including access to material resources and problem-solving)	**Teachers make food and clothing available** For example, an orphaned boy reported that his teachers were aware of his troubles and therefore helped him fulfil basic needs, by providing food and clothing (Theron, et al, 2011), as well as for AIDS-orphans (Pienaar, Swanepoel, Van Rensburg & Heunis, 2011), street children (Malindi & Machenjedze, 2012), and children from poor or uncaring homes (Theron & Engelbrecht, 2012). In many of these instances, this meant that teachers fed and clothed children out of their own pockets, even when they did not have much themselves. In resource-poor communities, teachers developed school gardens and use the produce to help local families to supplement their food supplies (Ebersöhn & Ferreira, 2011; Ebersöhn & Loots, 2017). **Trustworthy teachers give advice** For example, girls who had been sexually abused explained that they experienced resilience-supporting teachers as adults whom they could trust to listen to their problems and to provide advice (Van Rensburg & Barnard, 2005). Similarly, children from poor homes (Theron, 2016a; Theron & Engelbrecht, 2012; Theron, Liebenberg & Malindi, 2014) and those living on the street (Malindi & Machenjedze, 2012) reported that teachers supported their adjustment to daily hardship when they treated them respectfully, and listened sympathetically, before offering meaningful advice. Children challenged by intellectual disability reported that their teachers were trustworthy and helped them solve social and other problems (Hall & Theron, 2016). **Teachers use systems of identification and referral to get help for children** For example, in HIV-challenged, resource-poor communities, teachers assisted children and their families to access health and social development services (Ebersöhn & Ferreira, 2011). Teachers found practical ways of supporting such access, including involving health-care providers in school-based support groups or asking school nurses to visit learners' homes (Ebersöhn & Loots, 2017).
Social justice	**Teachers keep children safe from prejudice and harm** For example, resilient street children described how their teachers took active steps to prevent other school children from excluding them and so ensured their physical access to local schools (Theron & Malindi, 2010) and their safety at school (Malindi & Machenjedze, 2012).

knowledge (summarised in Table 27.1) will provide you with a starting point of what you can do to facilitate resilience in the young people you work with. I exclude international studies, given the understanding that resilience processes are relative to culture and context (Ungar, 2011) and so it would be dangerous to generalise the findings of non-local studies. At the same time, however, what we currently know is incomplete and so I encourage you to consider additional ways that teachers and other school staff, educational psychologists, and school-based service providers could support children's resilience.

You will notice that Table 27.1 makes no mention of educational psychologists or school-based service providers (eg, school nurses, speech therapists, school-based support teams). This does not mean that these people cannot facilitate resilience processes, but it does raise questions about why they are absent from studies of resilience (particularly as the studies cited in Table 27.1 were not limited to understanding how teachers support resilience). Might it mean that educational psychologists or school-based service providers are typically inaccessible to children who are at risk? Might it mean that educational psychologists or school-based service providers are so involved in other activities (eg, screening for learning difficulties) that they have no time to support resilience? Whatever the reason, Table 27.1 highlights that educational psychologists or school-based service providers need to become more involved in children's resilience processes and that we need to acknowledge the important role that many teachers play in children adjusting well to adversity (Theron, 2016b). Enacting the resilience processes summarised in Table 27.1 and adding other relevant ways of facilitating resilience should spare South African children from experiencing teachers (and other school-related staff) as unhelpful of children's resilience as reported, sadly, in a handful of South African studies (eg, Johnson & Lazarus, 2008; Krüger & Prinsloo, 2008; Pillay & Nesengani, 2006; Theron & Theron, 2014).

Perhaps the most important lesson from Table 27.1 is that teachers and school systems support children's resilience using 'ordinary magic' (Masten, 2001:227). Put differently, teacher facilitation of resilience requires some very ordinary things (eg, initiating referrals, or celebrating academic achievement). It also requires actions that go beyond the call of everyday duty (eg, hiding children from rapists, or feeding and clothing children using personal resources). In other words, facilitating resilience in school contexts is very doable, but will sometimes demand selfless, case-specific responses (Theron & Theron, 2014).

> She also allows Tulani to work in her classroom after school. This is helpful because it gives him a quiet place with good lighting to do his homework and to study. At home, they mostly use candles for lighting and his cousins are noisy.
>
> Walking home in the early evening is a bit risky for Tulani, because he must walk almost two kilometres along a poorly lit path. On one occasion some unemployed young men who were quite drunk tried to beat him up, but he managed to run away from them. To avoid this happening again, Tulani makes sure that he walks home before the sun begins to set. He also follows the advice of his Life Orientation teacher, who knows that it can be dangerous for pupils walking to and from school, and so encourages pupils to walk in groups—if there are other pupils leaving school at that time, he makes sure to walk with them.
>
> Tulani is excited about university, but also a little nervous. He wonders how he will cope and he does not really know what to expect. Nobody in his family has ever been to university or college. None of his neighbours have either. What comforts him a little is that he knows his ancestors and God (whom he believes in strongly) will protect him and support him to do well in his new life. His Mathematics teacher is very approachable and so Tulani asks him to tell him what university is like and give him some tips on how to succeed there. The teacher spends his break time talking about this with Tulani. In the past, this same teacher invited local entrepreneurs to come and talk to pupils about the importance of entrepreneurial skills to survive the harsh realities of high levels of youth unemployment and economic disadvantage. In response to Tulani's question, this teacher invites some of the school's ex-pupils to come and talk to the Grade 12s about life at college and university and to share some strategies for success. Tulani is hugely encouraged when he realises that youths from his own community, who have similar backgrounds to him, are coping well at university.

Championing resilience in relevant ways in the South African classroom

Tulani's example alerts us to the possibility that resilience should never be understood as static or fixed for all time. For example, what might happen to how well Tulani copes with adversity if he does not get a bursary to go to university? Or, if he succeeds at university, but struggles to find employment once he graduates? Or, if his grandmother should die while he is at university and he has to shoulder the responsibility for his younger cousins? The uncertainty of resilience means that as adults who serve children we need to constantly search for ways to facilitate and/or sustain resilience processes.

To this end, let's take a look at what South African resilience studies teach us about how teachers and other school staff, educational psychologists, school-based service providers, and school systems have supported South African young people, who were placed at risk for negative life outcomes, to do well in life. This

To help you understand all of the above better, let's consider a case study. Careful reading should show you that developing positively in the midst of hardship:
- Is more than a personal quality;
- Fluctuates over time and is complex; and
- Draws on multiple systemic resources that are relevant to the context of the child, as well as a child's personal resources (Masten, 2016; Ungar, 2011).

CASE STUDY

The case of Tulani

Tulani is a Sesotho-speaking boy. He is in Grade 12 at a Quintile 1 school in QwaQwa. He lives with his elderly grandmother who has raised him since his mother died when he was six years old. He does not know his father, or even if his father is still alive, because his father left the family to work on the mines in Johannesburg when Tulani was a couple of months old. He sent a little money home in the beginning, but stopped after a while. His family never heard from him again and there were rumours that he had been killed in a hostel fight, but his body was never found.

Tulani's grandmother receives a small government pension. She uses this to support Tulani and four other younger grandchildren whom she parents. To help them survive, she grows spinach and sells her produce by going from door-to-door in Puthaditjaba. On weekends, Tulani helps her hawk the spinach.

Tulani does not help sell spinach during the week because he spends every available minute in the afternoons and evenings to study. He is a dedicated student and determined to matriculate so well that he will qualify for a bursary that will support him to study engineering at a university. His grandmother encourages him to be committed to his schoolwork. She always tells him that a good education will be the answer to their financial problems because with a good education Tulani should be able to get a well-paying job.

His teachers also encourage him. They praise him for working hard, and they tell him he has become a role model to local children. He was not always devoted to his studies. Around the middle of primary school, he became disillusioned. He was angry that nobody could answer his questions about his father. He hated that some nights there was so little food in the house that they all slept hungry. He wanted to play soccer on weekends instead of hawking spinach with his grandmother. Sometimes he bunked school and he never learned for school tests. His grandmother asked the pastor of their church to talk to Tulani and to help him accept that a good education would turn his life around. Over the next couple of months, the pastor spent many hours with Tulani and also introduced Tulani to a slightly older boy who headed his household, but who was optimistic and committed to schooling, despite the many challenges in his life. The two boys connected and in time Tulani's attitude and behaviour became more positive.

His English teacher, in particular, is very supportive of Tulani. She sometimes brings him food to eat, because she is aware that Tulani has little food, other than the daily meal his school provides as part of the National School Nutrition Programme.

safe neighbourhoods, a pro-social network of peers) and broader systems (eg, effective health care systems, pro-poor government policies, meaningful cultural rituals). Although the resilience literature provides detailed lists of protective resources (eg, Kumpfer, 1999; Werner, 2013), we do not include these protective resources for you for two reasons. First, the presence of protective resources does not predict resilience (Rutter, 1989); if children and social ecologies do not draw on resources to support resilience processes, then they are meaningless. Second, not all resources will be equally meaningful to all children. The usefulness of resources depends on the child's developmental stage and sociocultural context (Ungar, 2011; Masten, 2014a). However, if you are interested in the protective resources that are most typically reported in South African studies of resilience, read Theron and Theron (2010) or Van Breda (2017). As you read these, consider how applicable they are to the young people you work with and how this summary needs to be updated.

The short list (Masten & Wright, 2010)	The seven tensions (Ungar et al, 2007)
Attachment, or constructive connections.	Constructive relationships.
Meaning-making, or re-interpreting hardship in positive/hopeful ways.	Sense of cohesion, or a sense of belonging and/or that life has meaning.
Agency and mastery, or taking action and experiencing success.	A powerful identify, or a sense of purpose and of personal competence, and others' acknowledgement thereof. Social justice, or experiences of fair treatment.
Culture and religion, which support belonging, pro-social behaviour, and identity.	Cultural adherence, or identification with group's beliefs/norms.
Problem-solving.	Access to material resources, or support to obtain sufficient food, clothing, education, employment, etc. Experiences of power and control, or being able to affect positive change.
Self-regulation, or adjusting behaviour and emotion to fit pro-social expectations.	
A foundation of protective resources	

FIGURE 27.1 Commonly occurring resilience processes

Which matters more: Children's contributions to the resilience process or those of the social ecology?

Another debate in the resilience field relates to whether resilience is defined as a static characteristic of an individual child or as a systemic process that supports individual children to be functional, even though they are challenged by life events or circumstances that predict dysfunctional outcomes. In response to the question, 'Is there a trait of resilience?' Ann Masten (2014b:14), a leading global resilience scholar, responded 'The answer is no.' Believing that resilience is not a child-centered construct is very important because it means that societies cannot blame children if they 'fail' to be resilient. In fact, understanding that resilience is a process that draws on constructive, contextually-meaningful resources that children and their relational, social, organisational, and cultural environments bring (see, for example, Masten, 2001, 2014a, 2016; Lerner, 2006; Rutter, 2013; Ungar, 2011, 2012; Werner & Smith, 1992) means that we can no longer talk about a 'resilient' child. Instead we need to talk about resilience processes that support children to do OK even when they are challenged by adverse life circumstances or events. And, it means that as adults who serve children we have a huge responsibility to facilitate these processes. In fact, Ungar, et al (2015) have suggested that at higher levels of risk, what adults who serve children do to facilitate resilience (eg, providing access to resources or services) is probably even more important than how children contribute to the resilience process (eg, being hopeful or not giving up).

There are multiple ways that social ecologies and children can partner to facilitate functional outcomes in the presence of risk. There is not space in this chapter to refer to them all. Instead, be aware of what Ann Masten and Margaret Wright call the 'short list' (2010:222). This list refers to the most commonly occurring ways in which social ecologies (including education departments, teachers and other school staff, educational psychologists, and other school-based service providers) can support young people who are vulnerable to do well in life. This list is similar to what Ungar, et al (2007:295) call the 'seven tensions'. These seven mechanisms were the commonly occurring ways that social ecologies across 11 very diverse countries (Canada, United States, China, India, Israel, Palestine, Russia, Gambia, Tanzania, South Africa, Colombia) supported young people to do well in life. Figure 27.1 summarises the 'short list' and the 'seven tensions' and shows where they seem to overlap.

The processes summarised in Figure 27.1 are complex and draw on protective resources. Protective resources can be found in children (eg, a sense of humour, determination, social skill), families (eg, supportive grandparents, educated, caring parents, family traditions), communities (eg, health-promoting schools,

we cannot talk about resilience when children experience very little adversity, or levels of stress that are quite common to everyday life (such as exam pressure, or being stuck in traffic, or having an occasional argument with a friend). We can talk about resilience when children are well-adjusted (however that might be defined by a child's community at a given point in time) even though they are chronically and seriously ill or disabled, or live in poor or dysfunctional families or disadvantaged communities, or have mentally ill, chronically or terminally ill, and/or substance-abusing parents, or experience violent crime or war or terrorism, or are picked on by bullies (also cyber-bullies), or abused, or experience the death of significant loved ones or friends, and so on. If you look closely at the examples just mentioned to illustrate significantly negative circumstances or events, you will notice that the risks that threaten the well-being of children are mostly outside of the child, or socially constructed. Children are often at risk for negative life outcomes because their social ecologies (their relational, social, organisational, and cultural environment) are harmful. Educational psychologists, teachers and other school staff, school-based service providers, and school systems should therefore not just facilitate resilience processes, but should also purposefully advocate for South African societies that advantage children.

Beating the odds versus changing the odds

A major debate in the resilience field is whether it is helpful enough to understand how children overcome adversity (ie, how they beat the odds). There is a sense that if we promote resilience, then governments and societies can get away with not facilitating constructive social change and putting an end to the conditions (such as violence against children or structural disadvantage) that force children to demonstrate resilience. In the light of this argument, some resilience researchers are calling for the focus to shift from what facilitates children to beat the odds to a focus on how societies can change the odds that make children vulnerable (Seccombe, 2002; Hart, et al, 2016). I encourage you to avoid arguing for either position. In post-colonial, resource-constrained contexts like South Africa where the pace of social change is slow, we need both foci. It is really important for adults who serve children (including educational psychologists) to better understand how some children have beaten the odds and use this evidence base to champion resilience in greater numbers of children. At the same time, it is also really important for adults who serve children (including educational psychologists) to advocate for social change that will result in fewer children needing to beat the odds.

 School-based championship of resilience

LINDA THERON

Children's resilience is intertwined with teacher actions and attitudes.
(Linda Theron)

Introduction

This chapter focuses on the process of resilience, or why and how some children adjust well to harmful circumstances and/or events that would usually predict negative life outcomes. In particular, I want you to grasp that educational psychologists, teachers and other school staff, school-based service providers, and school systems can, and *should*, champion resilience processes. With the ever-increasing numbers of vulnerable children in South Africa (and elsewhere) it is non-negotiable for adults who serve children (eg, educational psychologists or teachers) to understand resilience and know how to be resilience champions. To this end, I end this chapter with examples from South African resilience studies to guide how you might facilitate and sustain the resilience processes of the children you work with.

Please remember that resilience processes only come into play when children are challenged by circumstances and/or events that are significantly negative, and when these circumstances and events do not result in outcomes that would be defined as dysfunctional, or negative, by the child's community (Masten, 2014a). For example, at this point in history, most South African communities would consider criminal behaviour, or disengagement from school, or suicide, or substance abuse as evidence that a child is not doing well in life. In other words, when diversity advanced without inclusion when we do not craft environments where learners, in particular, those from marginalised backgrounds feel like they fully belong and thrive, then, we miss the benefits of diversity. A key issue to consider is a habit in the context of conscious positive learning ... *Are we all ready to contribute to our well-being? Then I will begin...*

person brings. We can learn even from the learners…you will be surprised how much knowledge they have. They are the ones who know all the corners in this school unlike us…all we do is sit in the staffroom … (Teacher Lungi)
(Khanare, 2009)

The benefits and challenges of positive psychology in a diverse society: Thinking forward

Positive psychology perspectives are multiple and have huge potential for improving lives and repairing challenging contexts that inhibit people from living a full, rich live. Diversity is a nebulous concept which is open to many interpretations and entails various diversities such as intelligence, culture, religion, class, sex, beliefs, physical appearance, race, disabilities and so on. The topic (from the most recent South African policies) is Embrace Diversity and Increase Unity (Department of Basic Education, 2014; Department of Social Development, 2016). That view, is however, short-sighted if we do not advance inclusion at the same time.

When choosing a diversity topic, you may find some tensions in the classroom, but the richness that can emerge from the facilitated discussions can enhance inclusive learning environments for all. Positive psychology within the emergence of strengths-based approaches to teaching and learning is a purposeful and healing approach to employ in a diverse classroom or school.

Conclusion

The potential for teaching and learning in diverse classroom contexts is significant. Teachers routinely come to learn new things as they struggle to make sense of the unfamiliar diverse ideas and practices that they may encounter. This chapter has highlighted the use of positive psychology in teaching diversity and utility in diverse classrooms. This notion of connecting diversity with positive psychology via the vehicle of Sesotho proverbs challenges the hegemonic accounts where diversity is constructed as a mere form of addressing divisions brought by the apartheid schooling system in South Africa prior to 1994. Diversity provides an opportunity to identify and craft more alternatives in order to make people's lives fulfilling and rich. As such, diversity promotes the use of hidden or untapped resources such as proverbs (as shown in this chapter), particularly with regard to improving lives. This chapter, therefore, invites the employment of positive psychology as a form that makes diversity open and widely accessible with multiple opportunities to learn and thrive. Our country, like many others, has made great improvements in increasing diversity. But

From Teddy Bear's excerpt presented learners have gained prominence as 'builders' of positive schools by identifying skills to amplify them and not just being passive in the school context. But what is interesting is the identification of the conditions that inhibit a positive school environment. In a context of diversity learners from previously marginalised backgrounds and communities are not only 'accommodated', but rather fully included. Positive psychology scholars remind us that we (teachers) should 'recraft work' (Seligman, 2004). As indicated in the previous excerpt, the unhealthy school which seems to be full of gossiping could be turned into a supportive environment where school members (learners, teachers and school leadership and management) could live full, rich lives (Linley & Joseph, 2004; Wehmeyer, 2017). This may include making conscious efforts to be open and widely accessible to others, sharing signature strengths and talking positively about one another.

Nurturing diversity to heal divisions

A positive psychology perspective points out that we should be 'as concerned with making the lives of normal people fulfilling and with nurturing high talent as with healing pathology' (Linley & Joseph, 2004; Seligman, 2004). Seligman reminds us that people require a sense of nurturing and healing if they are to live a fulfilling life. There are many proverbial expressions which invoke nurturing and healing, such as, *Leihlo le fahloa le shebile* (open eyes also fail to dodge dirt). This proverb tries to explain that there is no person, solution or situation which is perfect. We would like to see our teachers provide a nurturing environment when learners are confronted with problems and dilemmas. Diversity, therefore, requires an individual teacher or teachers as a collective to reflect on, evaluate, modify, recraft and carry forth to future applications what they have learned.

Some teachers in South Africa have been familiar with the challenges and dilemmas learners face for a number of years, but it is only recently that those challenges created a mind shift for teachers. They no longer need to find the challenges daunting. They can be thinking like a positive psychologist, identifying alternative pathways to problem solving, thinking about every person as an asset, and as a problem solver, not just a problem to be solved. Certain schools have also adopted a whole-school approach. So it is no surprise that teachers demonstrate through their expressions presented below that they are open to diversity and continuous learning in order to improve the knowledge, skills and well-being of their learners. Below is an example of how teachers, though not trained in positive psychology, apply this approach in an attempt to improve.

> *[A]s teachers, in fact the whole school, need a refresher course about how we can learn from each other instead of always looking for the mistake one person has done. We have to learn from each no matter how small one*

to another person, empathise with them, and understand their point of view is one of the highest forms of intelligent behaviour. Being able to listen to learners' diverse ideas, detecting indicators of their potential as they speak about issues of diversity, problems and alternative viewpoints, are all indicators of unique strengths.

Under any circumstances, children or learners could provide a repertoire of alternative ideas of strategies for problem solving. The following proverbial expression explains the importance of children's voices when a child is calling for a repair of a bad situation which might hamper his/her well-being—the expression is: *Ngoana sa lleng o shoela tharing* (child who does not cry, will die on his mother's back—children must speak about their demands). As children speak, we could say that the teacher becomes aware of their strengths, while at the same time, attending to their needs and demands. Diversity increases opportunity of listening to many unique voices, and may contribute towards the teacher becoming aware of each learner's individual strengths and similar or collective strengths and challenges. These strengths could be a vehicle of building and strengthening indigenous oral traditions that may arguably be overlooked in academic discussions of educational psychology.

Building diverse classrooms

Use in the service of something larger than you. (Seligman, 2004)

In a classroom, an initial description of stories of learners' ideas or experiences provide material for further exploration of alternative or possible solutions during problem solving. After allowing the learners to speak or explicate their individual ideas, it could be applied to different situations and embody the distilled and collective experience of the whole class. These are didactic moments which can suggest a course of action to be taken.

The Sesotho proverb, *Hlaahlela le lla ka le leng* (a lamp shines another lamp) concur with this idea to communicate how differing practical life experiences may also contribute towards the richness of life. The young people already perceive an increased understanding of the importance of a diversity of voices in the school. The following excerpt taken from a study of rural school children's constructions of care and diversity is illustrative:

> ... we are saying let's talk important things in our school. We need people to talk to, like Heads of Departments, principals, and teachers because among teachers there are counsellors. We need to know more about the people around because you can be surprised how teachers and learners know and have different skills. Open communication is needed in the school about what good things people do not only too much gossiping which kills us, said, Teddy Bear, girl aged 19. (Khanare, 2015)

with weakness', 'be as interested in building the best things in life as in repairing the worst', and 'be as concerned with making the lives of all people fulfilling and with nurturing high talent as with healing pathology' (Seligman, 2004).

Given the various backgrounds that make up a diverse classroom in many schools in South Africa, the teacher and learners may draw from each other's strengths and build resources to deliver curriculum content. Building enabling classrooms and contributing towards resources for learning is part of learners, is likely to have a positive impact on their development and they may succeed in reaching their full potential. This change of attitude could also be traced in some of the Sesotho proverbs on a variety of occasions. The Sesotho proverb that reads: *Bohlale ha bo ahe ntlong e le nngoe* (wisdom is found in the counsel of many) endeavours to create a sense of consciousness that even in many age-old wisdoms still exist in many of the South African communities. Diversity and sharing of ideas could be used and maximised to create a more effective community. Within a diverse classroom, we can add as many examples as possible so that the perspective of positive psychology becomes diverse, visible and localised.

The influence of positive psychology on diversity

The typical classroom in South Africa is often overcrowded with learners whose futures lie in the hands of the teachers. Positive psychology reminds us that every learner that we see in our classroom has a dream, potential and/or untapped potential that could change his/her family status and the whole community. These potentials (existing and/or hidden) need to be nurtured both as individuals and as a collective. The teacher might be the only newcomer (in a learner's life) to an already established group of friends, peers, classmates or even religious mates.

Ways of enhancing positive diversity in the classroom

Combining a positive psychology perspective (identifying strengths, building the best things and nurturing talents) with diversity (differentiated identities) is not impossible. However, it requires thorough planning and precise classroom organisation which are seldom performed in isolation.

Being aware of the strengths

Learning to listen, listen to learn. (Khanare and Marina)

It is often easy for teachers to be the first one to talk in class, defining and explaining issues or topics. Some psychologists believe that the ability to listen

reality. The stance that the author takes in this chapter is drawn from the work of Martin Seligman, which is then utilised in synergy with African proverbs, especially, Sesotho proverbs. In this instance, the author wishes to illustrate that proverbs can be an indication that diversity is a resource. It also shows how recent developments in scientific research can connect with age-old wisdoms within oral traditions.

Positive psychology perspective

The positive psychology perspective (Seligman, 2004) is gaining momentum in the South African education system. A number of studies have expressed the value of positive psychology, and the needs for educational processes to be properly contextualised within enabling learning environments (school, home and wider community of schools) in South Africa (Eloff, 2013). In 2000, Martin Seligman made a particular shift towards children's development and learning (Linley & Joseph, 2004). Seligman discovered the need to study the development of internal strength, a sense of self-worth and how to support children to live full, rich lives (Wehmeyer, 2017). In particular, the important role of self-worth is to move away from pathology-based practices or models to strengths-based approaches and supportive interventions (Wehmeyer, 2017). This part of psychology is now known as positive psychology (Seligman, 2004; Wehmeyer, 2017).

The question might well be asked: Was/Is there a negative psychology? For more than six decades, psychology worked within a 'disease'-model or 'deficit'-model, whereby, the focus was about finding what is wrong with people (Seligman, 2004). Furthermore, learners were classified according to their cognitive abilities, popularly known as IQ. Those with lower IQ were often regarded negatively and in need of treatment. I remember when I was in primary school, my teacher used to point at some learners' foreheads and say 'what is wrong upstairs?' Though anecdotal, these kinds of incidents pointed to the 'deficit'-approach, where shortcomings were emphasised to the detriment of individual strengths. However, the application of positive psychology points out that many of the functional disorders in children may take an alternative pathway with the emergence of strength-based approaches aimed at improving people's lives by rather focusing on their strengths.

To guide teachers through such a perspective of positive psychology, Seligman (2004) proposes a set of principles towards full and rich lives and livelihoods. Though there are many principles and ideas about positive psychology, I opted to adhere to those that could help teachers to view diverse classrooms as an opportunity to learn and share knowledge. He noted different principles for analysing diverse classrooms which include 'be as concerned with strengths as

in Western perspectives and might seem rather distant from the many people in remote areas in the African context. However, in order to understand the importance of positive psychology and diversity, the integration of selected African proverbs (Mokitimi, 1997), in particular, Sesotho proverbs (one of the eleven official languages in South Africa) are used as concepts applicable for explaining the practices of Africans in their endeavours to mould and shape the well-being of children. Integrating these proverbs could also be seen as advancing positive psychology 'beyond the reactionary phase' (Eloff, 2013). The theoretical underpinnings or principles of positive psychology could be explained as a specific way to promote diversity as an asset or resource that promotes learning, not only for academic purposes, but also—and even more importantly—for the ultimate moral purpose of creating environments for all learners to thrive in life as enshrined in human rights and children's rights laws and policies. The chapter will conclude by highlighting the benefits and challenges of positive psychology in a diverse and unequal society in South Africa.

A socio-educational context

The educational landscape has seen enormous changes since the establishment of a democratic dispensation in South Africa. It has diverse learners from a variety of cultural groups and backgrounds—all of who have the potential to learn and thrive. The Constitution (Republic of South Africa, 1996a) supports the principle of the best interest of the child. Hlalele (2012) explains why learners' success in school is important for South Africa's emerging economy. He argued that all children 'represent the economic lifeblood of the economy' (Hlalele, 2012). While the Constitution indicates messages of hope for all the children, it is also problematic because it seems to portray a utopian kind of a classroom, school or even a community. That is, although children's success is crucial for their well-being, the well-being of schools, families, and the whole community, it is insufficient to explain children's success in isolation from their interactions with the diverse people and environments in their everyday lives.

Diversity, as the author of this chapter perceives it, relies on interaction with self, other people, and geographies for social negotiation of the possible. In today's education, especially in an African setting, hope for the children as 'future leaders' seem to be increasingly a collective effort. Thus, we understand children's success as including active participation in their classrooms as well as forming partnerships with their teachers, parents and whole school-community partnerships—especially since the implementation of the Education White Paper 6 (Department of Education, 2001). People are, after all, social beings and much development would be impossible without drawing from a diverse social

26 Positive psychology and diversity: Accumulation of strengths

FUMANE PORTIA KHANARE

As for the future, it remains unwritten. Anything can happen, and often we are wrong. The best we can do with the future is prepare and savor the possibilities of what can be done in the present. (Todd Kashdan)

Introduction

Listen my child! You are smart but other children are smart too in their own ways. (Annacleta 'Maqhaola Ntlhoi, 1978)

Annacleta Ntlhoi was my grandmother who did not have any formal education or teaching qualification. Her comment, which she used to make about my siblings too, make a good theme for this chapter—and even for teaching in general. Children differ in various ways, both individually and because of their association with families, communities or cultural groups. All of us, including teachers, have a particular way of moulding a child. Sometimes, diverse backgrounds through which the children live can make classroom teaching more challenging, but other times, as Annacleta Ntlhoi implied, children simply enrich classroom life. Or to put it another way: it is important to support children by instilling positive images about themselves where possible, but also make them aware that the existence of other children is important for everyone.

This chapter outlines a perspective that is a prerequisite for diversity. It begins by introducing the socio-educational context in South African schools. It then examines a positive psychology perspective as a dynamic approach that includes diversity. The perspectives of positive psychology are grounded

Conclusion

A relationship-focused approach is proactive and encompasses ongoing conversations, informed by key elements relevant to the co-construction of relational spaces in which the development of learning and well-being are optimised. The approach implies the involvement of all role players in school communities as equal partners in the co-construction of these relational spaces. The commonly accepted focus on individuals as bounded beings and the sole agents of social change is, therefore, challenged and the attention shifts towards relationships among people with the conviction that when we focus on relationships in our classrooms and schools, we ensure a future for all involved (Gergen, 2009).

and interacting with reference to respect and reprimand the learners for not respecting fellow learners and influencing the atmosphere in classrooms negatively. If more of these incidents occur on a regular basis, they must be able to address the patterns of disrespectful engagement in the classroom as a relational space in a more proactive way.

If a group of learners, for example, support other learners who have limited resources, teachers can identify this effort as a way of relating and interacting that nurtures the co-construction of enabling spaces—through the learners caring for each other. This pattern can be strengthened by encouraging learners to act in supportive ways on a more regular basis.

It is critically important to understand that this process is ongoing— teachers should maintain these conversations. Teachers should keep in mind that both nurturing and restraining ways of relating and interacting are always present in a space. The co-construction of relational spaces that will enhance learning and well-being therefore, have to be viewed as a fluid process in which teachers should continually engaged to ensure that the relationships on all the levels of interrelatedness are nurturing rather than restraining. By applying a relationship-focused approach, the co-construction of relational spaces for the optimal development of learning and well-being becomes a concerted effort of all those involved—teachers, learners and parents.

Why is the application of a relationship-focused approach relevant in a South African context?

The relevance of applying a relationship-focused approach in a South African context is evident if we consider the emphasis on relationships as a critical competency of teachers as indicated in performance standard 6 of the Integrated Quality Management Systems (IQMS) for school-based educators (Education Labour Relations Council, 2003). Unfortunately, policies and practices that deal with the relational dimension of human behaviour in schools do not consider the complex nature of human interactive dynamics and are, therefore, not always effective in improving relationships and promoting relational well-being in South African school communities. This state of affairs clearly emphasises the need for the introduction of an alternative approach to enhance relationships between teachers, learners and parents as a basis for changing schools into humanised relational spaces where people can flourish.

In the graphic representation depicted in Figure 25.1, a relationship-focused approach is represented visually.

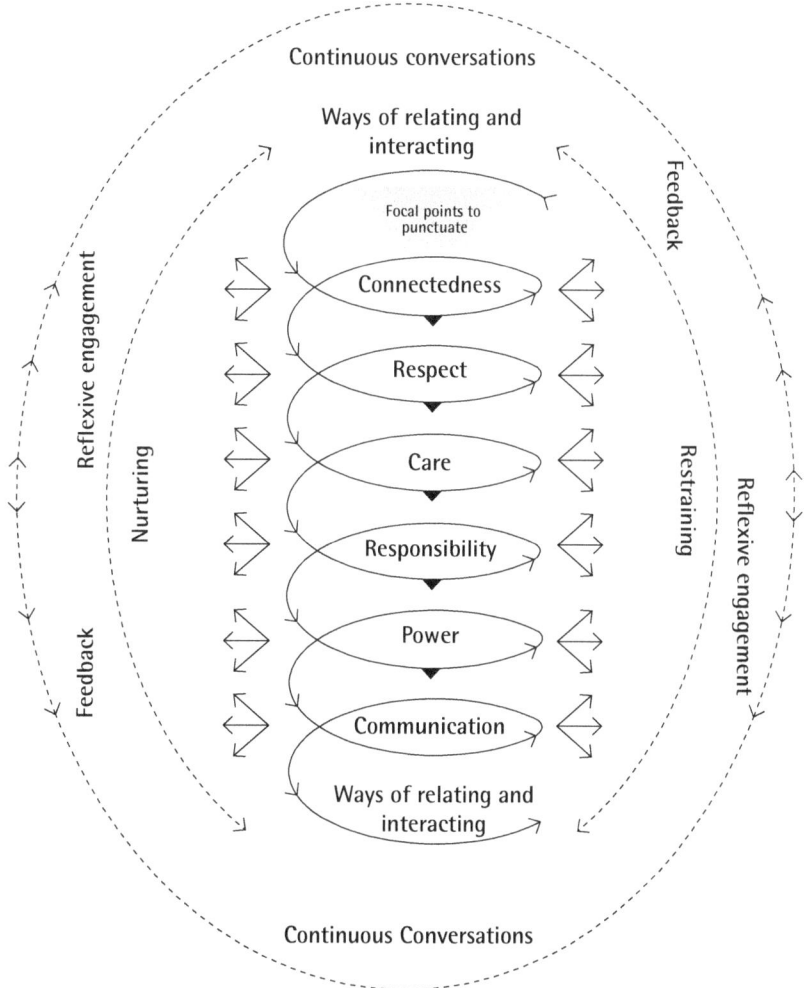

FIGURE 25.1 Graphic representation of a relationship-focused approach

In the graphic representation, the discussed key elements are indicated as focal points in ongoing conversations among teachers, learners and parents. These elements are always present as part of the complex interactive dynamics that are created when people interact with one another. Teachers can use these key elements to determine whether the ways in which role players relate and interact are restraining or nurturing the co-construction of relational spaces that will enhance the optimal development of learning and well-being.

If a group of learners keep shouting derogatory remarks at another learner, for example, a teacher should not merely identify the behaviour of learners as unacceptable, but identify these remarks as a restraining way of relating

as a core duty of teachers but viewed from a complexity perspective, teachers as individuals cannot construct a relational space on their own. Ongoing conversations should emphasise the role of every role player involved. Shared responsibility can best be illustrated by thinking of relational spaces as a web of threads that connect all involved in a particular space—movement in any part of the web influences the whole web. This implies that teachers, learners and parents should understand that they, for example, cannot blame others for existing tension in a relational space, without taking responsibility for their own role in creating tension in the first place.

5. **Power** as a key element of ongoing conversations implies that teachers have to understand that power is present in all relationships and that they cannot disregard the role of power in the co-construction of enabling spaces. Foucault (1982) describes power relations as a set of actions that induces others to act in a manner that makes it either easier or more difficult for them to act in a particular context. An in-depth understanding of these two sides of power and power relations is critical for the co-construction of supportive relational spaces. Teachers often become engaged in power plays due to a lack of understanding—power forms part of all relationships. When teachers do not understand these two sides of power, they might become engaged in power struggles with colleagues, learners and parents that will create interactive dynamics that can disrupt the co-construction of relational spaces that enhance learning and well-being. However, when teachers understand power dynamics, they will be able to allow learners and parents to have a voice in the co-construction of classrooms and schools into such supportive relational spaces (Nelson & Prilleltensky, 2010).

6. **Communication** is a key element of ongoing conversations and encompasses more than sending and receiving messages and information. Communication implies a process of making sense of what happens in a particular space and sharing that with others (Suchman, 2006). Through this process people co-construct inter-subjective spaces in which they encounter one another as individuals and explore challenges together (Heslep, 2001). Teachers should, therefore, make sure they facilitate open and honest communication about their own experiences and the experiences of learners and parents of how they function together in classrooms and school communities. In practice, this implies that conversations among teachers, learners and parents should move beyond merely discussing academic work. The conversations should also include reflections on the way they relate and interact with one another across all levels of interrelatedness and the identification of strategies for creating relational spaces in which all involved, are included.

of connectedness is described in research literature as getting acquainted on a more personal level within and beyond the boundaries created by a system (McLauglin & Clarke, 2010). To facilitate a sense of connectedness, teachers, learners and parents should become more visible to one another as human beings, regardless of their capacity and status. In this way a deep sense of understanding for one another, that will facilitate what Roffey (2015) refers to as inclusive belonging, as opposed to exclusive belonging where only certain groups are connected.

2. **Respect** as a key element of ongoing conversations encompasses a mutual process of respect due and respect earned (Dillon, 2007; Hajii, 2006). Teachers, learners and parents should be encouraged to view each other as equals and show consideration for one another by accepting one another and appreciating one another. Input should be valued with regard to the process of co-constructing enabling spaces. Teachers—by default—often accept that respect is an intrinsic value that should be displayed by all involved. However, research conducted by Jones (2002) found that respect is not necessarily linked to intrinsic worth but based on the nature and quality of relationships between people. People show respect if it is shown to them, but, if they perceive another person as dismissive, inattentive or unaware, no respect is awarded. It is, therefore, of the utmost importance that teachers emphasise the mutual, reciprocal character of respect. Van der Merwe (2004) concurs that persons, who would like to be respected, should show respect. In relationships with learners, the responsibility to initiate and maintain respect rests on the shoulders of adults.

3. **Care** as a key element of ongoing conversations implies the acceptance of the unique capabilities and characteristics of all individuals (Roffey, 2012). Furthermore, care involves an emphatic engagement between these individuals. The love for fellow human beings and a willingness to serve others and to address legitimate needs in formal and informal support networks form the basis of this emphatic engagement (Barnes & Duck, 1994). An emphasis on the principle of love and kindness as a basis for serving and supporting others should hence be emphasised on a continuous basis to counter rigorous academic standards and high performance expectations that can dehumanise people (McLennan, 2008). Teachers should also model a deep sense of care in their interactions with colleagues, learners and parents while encouraging other role players to be caring, kind and supportive towards one another (Noddings, 2002, 2010).

4. **Responsibility** as a key element of ongoing conversations emphasises the shared responsibility of all involved in a relational space for changing it into a space for optimal learning and well-being. Responsibility is often perceived

What does a relationship-focused approach to the optimal development of learning and well-being encompass?

Human behaviour is too complex to design a blueprint programme with a set of rules that teachers can apply to facilitate relational spaces in their classrooms and school communities (Cilliers, 1998). The facilitation of such supportive relational spaces, necessitates an understanding that the teachers, learners and parents form a web of interrelatedness through their interactions with one another (Josselson, 1996).

In this web of interrelatedness, patterns of relating and interacting develop: A restraining relational pattern may be, for example, the exclusion of certain learners or parents through name-calling and gossiping, while caring for fellow learners or colleagues by assisting them with an assignment or complimenting them indicates a nurturing relational pattern. Teachers should be able to recognise these relational patterns and associated interactions to be able to give voice to the relational dimension of being together. This implies that teachers have to be equipped to observe and reflect on interactions among themselves, learners and parents on a continual basis. Teachers should also be able to engage with one another, learners and parents in spontaneous dialogue about how they relate and interact with one another. These dialogical conversations should be reflexive and ongoing in nature, which means that teachers should be able to reflect on their own experiences as well as guide learners and parents to reflect on their experiences of being together in a specific context. Through these reflexive engagements with one another, they can obtain a deeper understanding about what they should do together to co-construct relational spaces that will contribute to the optimal development of learning and well-being.

In the next section, six key elements identified through research conducted in South African school contexts (Kitching, 2010; Kitching, Roos & Ferreira, 2011, 2012; Ungerer, 2012; Wagner, 2014), that should be incorporated in the ongoing conversations between teachers, learners and parents, are presented. The brief discussions indicate how each key element might contribute to the co-construction of relational spaces in which learning and well-being could be developed:

1. **Connectedness** as a key element of ongoing conversations implies the enhancement of a sense of connectedness across all levels of interrelatedness, ie, between teacher–teacher, teacher–learner, learner–learner, teacher–parents, learner–parent, and parent–parent. Enhancing a sense of connectedness implies more than merely telling people to reach out to one another by greeting one another or knowing the names of individuals. A sense

Why a relationship-focused approach?

Teachers are often trained to perceive people as individuals, who can function independent of one another. Gregen (2009), challenges this perception and argues that, as human beings, we are relational beings who cannot exist without others. From the perspective of complexity theory on human behaviour, schools and classrooms are complex, interactive and dynamic processes of relating and interacting (Jörg, 2009; Mason, 2008; Shaw, 2002; Stacey, 2001, 2003, 2007). These complex interactive ways of relating and interacting influence how those involved experience these spaces (Morrison, 2002). Teachers should, therefore, be equipped to apply a relationship-focused approach to ensure that they effectively deal with the complexity of human relating and interacting in their classrooms, as a basis for optimising learning and well-being.

The critical role of relationships in the optimal development of learning and well-being

Research literature in the field of educational psychology strongly emphasises the importance of the relationships as a basis for the optimal development of learning and well-being. Meier and Wood (2004) argue that schools are transformed and through human relationships. The role of relationships is emphasised in school climate literature (Cohen, Pickeral & McCloskey, 2008; Thapa, Cohen, Guffrey & Higgins-D'Alessandro, 2013). Positive and supportive relationships enhance the healthy functioning and development of both teachers and learners (Zandvliet, Den Brok, Mainhard & Van Tartwijk, 2014). The positive impact of warm and supportive relationships on learner motivation and engagement is evident as relationships facilitate a productive learning environment (Fraser, 2007; Martin, 2014). Konu and Rimpelä (2002) include social relations as an important category in the evaluation of well-being in schools. Roffey (2008, 2010) argues that a focus on relationships on all levels has a positive ripple effect on well-being and on the motivation and performance of learners. Individuals in school communities should, therefore, be embedded in networks of positive and supporting relationships in order to flourish (McCubbin, McCubbin, Zhang, Kehl & Strom, 2013). According to Molemane (2000), a web of caring relationships contributes to a school climate that fosters school effectiveness. Trusting, respectful and cooperative relationships also promote the maintenance of discipline (Mokhele, 2006).

25 A relationship-focused approach to the optimal development of learning and well-being

ANSIE ELIZABETH KITCHING

When relational well-being is at the centre of our concern we approach a life-giving future. (Gergen, 2009)

Introduction

Human beings are relational beings who cannot develop optimally without the presence of others. Relationships therefore play a significant role in the co-construction of positive learning environments (Roffey, 2012). From this position, schools and classrooms can be perceived as relational spaces in which the interactions between teachers, learners and parents will contribute to the achievement of academic outcomes and the promotion of children's well-being. The co-construction of relational spaces, that presents a basis for the development of learning and well-being, are a concerted effort between all role players. However, teachers, due to their position, play a significant role in the co-construction of the process and should therefore be equipped to guide the process.

Educational psychology as a discipline, that applies the understanding of the processes of human interaction in contexts of learning and well-being, is positioned to equip teachers to facilitate such positive learning environments in their classrooms and schools. In this chapter, a relationship-focused approach is presented to guide teachers to incorporate six key elements, identified through research conducted in schools from an educational psychology perspective, to facilitate the co-construction of relational spaces, that are conducive for the optimal development of learning and well-being.

environments. The roles and responsibilities for teachers, as illustrated in the *South African norms and standards for educators* (Department of Education, 2000), do not require teachers to become therapists, but they do require teachers to have the knowledge and skills to screen, identify and assess, as well as to render first-level support to any school community.

The multidisciplinary team members should include not only professionals trained within the western medical model, such as psychologists and social workers, but also traditional healers, faith-based leaders and organisations, as well as community elders and leaders. The skilled teacher should be able to identify and appreciate contributions made by different role players in the interests of the individual's and the school community's well-being.

In order to be able to screen, identify and assess, and to render first-level psychosocial support, teachers should have a thorough understanding of child development and learning theories and be sensitive to cultural differences within diverse contexts. In South Africa, the South African Council for Educators (SACE) recognises that an educational institution serves the community and also that there will be various customs and belief systems in that community (Landsberg, Krüger & Swart, 2016). Respect for tribal and traditional belief systems is a crucial element for any successful counselling process. The principles of ubuntu are therefore crucial for understanding and upholding these systems as well as for enabling teachers to bridge cultural differences by using different cultural lenses as prescribed by or in a particular cultural context (see also Chapters 3, 6 and 12).

Conclusion

In this chapter, we explored the psychosocial factors that can inhibit or promote the well-being of learners and teachers in educational environments within the framework of Bronfenbrenner's ecological systems theory. We discussed the teacher's role in creating a safe psychosocial educational environment, which includes various teaching and learning contexts. We ascertained that teachers should consider how an ecology of resilience-risk factors such as poverty, HIV/AIDS and other adverse social factors can be mediated and serve as assets by using available protective resources from the micro- to the macro level. Skills related to counselling, in which teachers play a vital role should also be honed and employed to foster and promote psychosocial well-being in educational environments.

Swart, 2016). Literature has highlighted the following skills for teachers which play a vital role in fostering well-being, resilience and coping (Acevedo & Hernandez-Wolfe, 2014; Cefai, 2007; Masten, 2014; Theron, 2016).

For example, teachers should:
- Develop warm, respectful connections by conveying the message that they are 'there' for the learners in all circumstances, thereby showing compassion and empathy, irrespective of the negative behaviour learners may exhibit;
- Communicate achievable, consistent expectations by recognising existing strengths and competencies and using their strengths to overcome challenges and problems;
- Facilitate the learning of other life skills such as anger management, assertiveness, communication skills, goal setting and conflict resolution;
- Engage and develop learners as active, capable agents by allowing them to participate in all school activities, even curriculum planning and evaluation strategies;
- Develop learners' creativity in dealing with any classroom or school-related problems so as to promote a physically and psychologically safe teaching and learning environment; and
- Develop networking and collaborative relationships with appropriate stakeholders.

Taking the above aspects into consideration, it is important to point out that rendering psychosocial care does not belong to the Life Orientation teacher and the school-based support team alone. All teachers have a major role to play in providing life orientation skills to learners. Training all teachers in life orientation would also enable them to cope with the large numbers of orphans and vulnerable children (OVC) in public schools (Wood & Goba, 2011). It is thus every teacher's responsibility to render psychosocial support and to create and maintain an enabling teaching and learning environment. One can, therefore, recommend basic counselling skills as a strategy that could be employed to equip teachers with the knowledge and expertise to identify learners with psychosocial needs and refer them to the right services, especially the OVC (Mwomai & Pillay, 2015).

Promoting psychosocial well-being within diverse teaching and learning contexts

Teachers should understand their roles and responsibilities as active multidisciplinary team members in rendering psychosocial support and promoting psychosocial well-being in various education and learning

Both culture and value systems play a major role in psychosocial well-being in that they influence individual and social aspects of functioning. This system may affect the way a particular society sees the teaching profession, and ultimately how a teacher is respected and supported.

These three domains simultaneously reflect areas in which teacher resilience can be strengthened and developed to improve their psychosocial well-being. A closer look indicates how these domains align with the macro systems of Bronfenbrenner's ecological systems theory and how one system can affect the other either positively or negatively.

The teachers' role in creating a safe psychosocial environment

School ecologies or systems are by nature filled with protective factors that support children to adjust constructively to various challenges (Theron, 2016). According to resilience-focused literature, schools can be regarded as mesosystemic resources that are, or can be, instrumental to the process of resilience. Consequently, by using the protective resources available, one can mediate an ecology of resilience risk factors (here poverty-related). Furthermore, teachers' socio-emotional competence is equally important for promoting positive learning environments for the learners they teach (Hen & Goroshit, 2016).

Now, reimagine the thirteen-year-old girl we mentioned earlier. Irrespective of her social challenges, she may have had a loving and nurturing caregiver, a caring teacher, traditional and religious surroundings and supporting community-based centres. Her context could, therefore, serve as resilience-building factors, thereby becoming assets (Landsberg, Krüger & Swart, 2016). These aspects may, from an African perspective, also incorporate a spiritual domain, which includes spiritual and traditional healers. All these affirming factors can contribute to her psychosocial well-being.

Teachers are uniquely positioned to support positive psychosocial outcomes for children living in adverse contexts, as their position within the children's social ecologies allows them to reach out to children living difficult lives (Theron & Engelbrecht, 2012). However, they should be aware that they are only a part of the collection of any ecology's protective resources that are involved in facilitating resilience in children. It is therefore crucial for schools to identify others who can offer resources that are beyond the school's capability in promoting psychosocial well-being in teaching and learning environments from an inclusive and holistic perspective.

Research further indicates that teachers may be the only social, emotional, material and spiritual refuge that a learner encounters (Landsberg, Krüger &

rights are also stipulated in the Manifesto on Values, Education and Democracy (Department of Education, 2001), as well as the South African Schools Act No. 84 of 1996 (Republic of South Africa, 1996c).

Additionally, the Care and Support for Teaching and Learning (CSTL) Programme is a Southern African Development Community (SADC) initiative to realise the educational rights of all children, including those who are most vulnerable, through schools becoming inclusive, caring and supportive. To realise its goal by 2015, the Department of Education identified nine priority areas, of which psychosocial support is one. In this regard, school-based support entails the school acting as the primary service provider or as the vehicle for other service providers to reach vulnerable children and youth. This programme highlights the prominent role that schools and teachers have to play in creating safe and caring psychosocial teaching and learning environments.

The importance of the teacher's psychosocial well-being

For a better understanding of teachers' psychosocial well-being, a definition proposed by the Psychosocial Working Group (2003) of the United Nations is useful. This definition views the psychosocial well-being of individuals and communities through three core domains which are described in the sections that follow.

Human capacity

Human capacity refers to teachers' mental and physical health with specific focus on their knowledge base, capabilities and skills. It may be thought of as the teachers' awareness of their strengths and values and being able to draw on them when necessary, especially when confronted by challenges and demands within their personal lives and work environment, as described previously.

Social ecology

Social ecology refers to the network of support surrounding the teacher or the school community. This includes personal and professional support, cohesive relationships, as well as support structures at all levels of the teacher's ecosystem such as the department, district, community, school and personal support and relationships (see also Chapters 25 and 27).

Culture and values

Cultural values relate to the value system that influences the norms and behaviour within every society and links to individual and social expectations.

that is restorative, rather than retributive in how conflicts and code of conduct violations are handled.

Depression and fatigue, two other common results of school violence, can translate to enduring psychosocial effects, which have an influence not only on the individual victim but also on the way victims associate with and adjust to society's norms and values in general. School violence further erodes the ability of casualties to form healthy, pro-social and trusting relationships with peers and adults. Their sense of hope and optimism in their future erodes and, consequently, their ability to cope with any adversity and difficulties they may face (Burton & Leoschut, 2012). Learners may internalise feelings and withdraw from everyday interactions with peers and others. For these reasons, teachers should observe sudden changes in behaviour and moods in their learners and as pastoral caregivers should be supportive when a learner seems to display needs of an emotional or physical nature. For this and other reasons mentioned in this chapter, it is necessary for teachers to develop their skills repertoire to include lay counselling for the benefit of learners in need of such support.

Another study on post-traumatic stress in HIV/AIDS orphaned children found that these children were more prone to symptoms of depression and behavioural problems at school. Such social issues can also affect teachers, learners and the community at large. This in turn can impact on the different subsystems and are illustrated by the systems ecological theory (Donald, Lazarus & Lolwana, 2001). Nonetheless, psychosocial support was considered to have beneficial effects, particularly in buffering responses to such extreme stress (Cluver, Fincham & Seedat, 2009). Teachers, therefore, not only have to play a pastoral or caregiver role but also have a legal responsibility to take on some of the functions and responsibilities of a parent. They need to act in *loco parentis*, a Latin term which means 'in the place of a parent'. There are further constitutional obligations and policies that teachers should take cognisance of that pertain to the psychosocial well-being of learners.

Legal support for psychosocial well-being in learners

The Constitution of the Republic of South Africa, 1996 (Republic of South Africa, 1996b) guarantees the right to a basic education for all children in South Africa, including vulnerable groups, and to take into account the child's best interests. This includes learners who are in conflict with the law, those who have never enrolled in school such as learners living in poverty, children with HIV/AIDS and children with disabilities (Landsberg, Krüger & Swart, 2016). These vulnerable groups are also covered by the Children's Act No. 38 of 2005 (Republic of South Africa, 2005). The right to a basic education further incorporates the right to equality and the right not to be discriminated against; these basic human

The **chronosystem** looks at the developmental timeframes that are involved in the interactions between these systems and their influence on child development. They may be external moments that affect the child's life such as a parent's death, or internal psychological changes such as inferiority complexes, which may also influence the child as he/she gets older.

Learners' psychosocial well-being

In examining learners' psychosocial well-being within the framework of Bronfenbrenner's ecological systems theory, it becomes clear why the thirteen-year-old girl mentioned earlier, who was possibly sexually abused, may eventually experience academic failure and drop out of school. It is also possible that she may come to display violent behaviour. On all levels, her adverse circumstances may influence her psychosocial well-being.

Sexually abused children often suffer from anxiety, post-traumatic stress, guilt, depression and low self-esteem (Carr, 2000; Gardner, 2002). Education provides an opportunity for children to understand that they have the right to be protected from abuse, how to respond in high-risk situations and where to seek help in the event of abuse. The life skills curriculum, for example, provides important socio-emotional lessons on appropriate touching, assertiveness and self-awareness.

There is a thin line between abuse in general and school violence, with abuse generally being the major reason for violence at school. Schools then become sites of violence, and this has become a national concern. Consequently, in 2012, the Centre for Justice and Crime Prevention (CJCP), with the support of the Department of Education (DoE) at that stage, undertook a National School Violence Study (NSVS) focusing on secondary schools in all nine provinces (Burton & Leoschut, 2012:xi). The study sample consisted of 5 939 learners, 121 principals and 239 teachers. The key findings indicated that one in five learners (22.2%) had experienced some form of violence that year while at school. This amounted to 1 020 597 secondary school learners. Certain forms of victimisation, specifically bullying, were found to create vulnerability for other more serious and criminal offences such as alcohol and drug abuse and even murder, as weapons were found to be readily available to many learners. Violent incidents at schools also included violence committed against and by teachers (Burton & Leoschut, 2012). As much as schools are the sites of such violence, they also have the potential to support learners psychosocially through socio-emotional learning experiences that includes conflict resolution, appropriate ways to express and regulate anger and other extreme emotions. In schools, learners may have opportunities to experience basic social justice

Understanding educational psychology

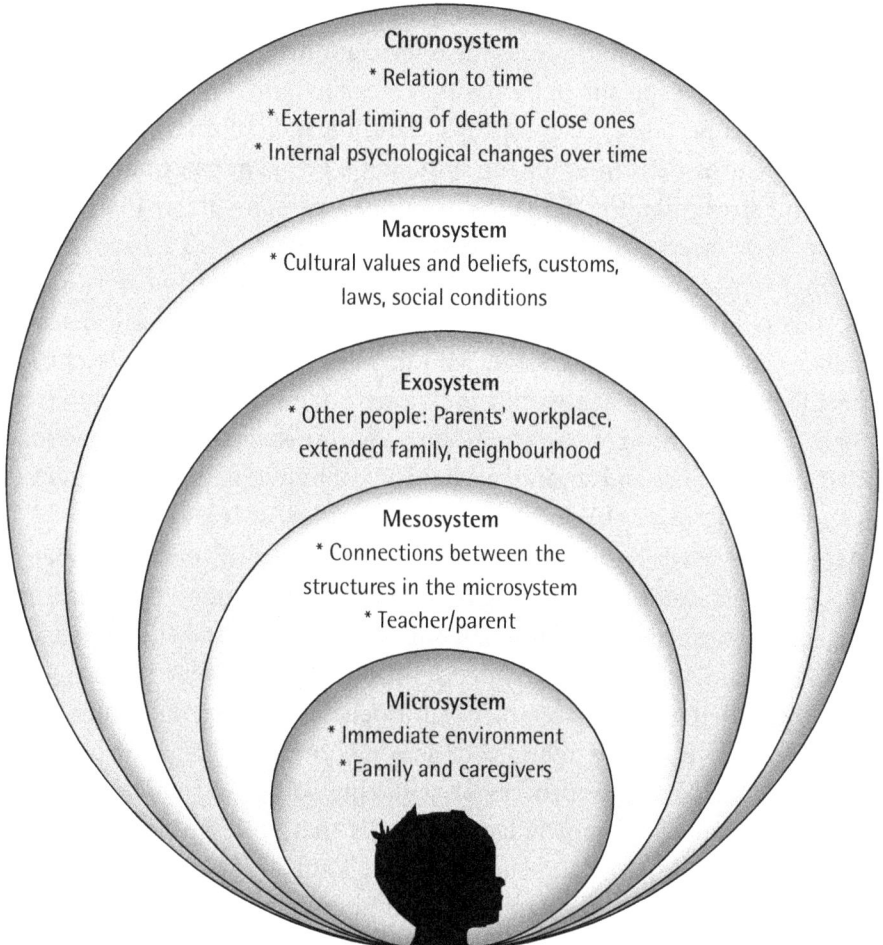

FIGURE 24.1 Bronfenbrenner's ecological systems theory

As illustrated in Figure 24.1, the microsystem is the first level and includes the relationships with family, peers, teachers and caregivers.

The **mesosystem** provides the connections between the structures of an individual's microsystem (Berk, 2000), for example, the interaction between a child's parents and the school and the school's participation in the child's life.

The **exosystem** refers to environments in which the child is not directly involved, but which still play an important part in the child's development, for example, the parents' workplace or the neighbourhood in which they grow up.

The **macrosystem** refers to the attitudes, beliefs and values of a society or culture, which may be further influenced by the other systems that play a part in the child's development, for example, values and beliefs could include democracy, social justice and ubuntu (Nel, et al, 2013).

Understanding the term 'psychosocial well-being'

The term 'psychosocial' emphasises the interrelationship between psychological aspects that involve personal thoughts, emotions and behaviour and social experiences that pertain to relationships, tradition and culture (UNICEF, 2009). Well-being may be defined as having sufficient internal or external resources to balance and strengthen the demands made on a person's life or the challenges that have to be faced (Dodge, Daly, Huyton & Sanders, 2012). Together, these terms imply a state of physical, psychological, mental, social and spiritual well-being, also referred to as psychosocial well-being, which enables learners and teachers to cope with daily stressors and to fulfil their potential. Psychosocial support facilitates resilience within individuals, families and communities. 'It promotes the restoration of social cohesion and infrastructure by respecting the dignity, independence and coping mechanisms of individuals and communities.' (Inter-Agency Network of Education in Emergencies, 2016).

At the heart of psychosocial well-being sits social and emotional competence, which can be developed and taught at school. Education, therefore, is an important psychosocial intervention in building learner resilience, since learners can acquire knowledge, attitudes, decision-making and other skills to enable them to cope better in the face of psychosocial challenges. Learning to cope socially and emotionally is referred to as socio-emotional learning, described by UNICEF (2015) as 'the process of acquiring social and emotional values, attitudes, competencies, knowledge, and skills that are essential for learning, being effective, well-being, and success in life'. Zsolnai (2015) considers socio-emotional competence to be significant in improving an individual's ability to activate the most appropriate skill to handle a given situation.

Bronfenbrenner's ecological systems theory is of particular significance for identifying the complex influences, interactions and interrelationships that can either impede or promote learners' and teachers' psychosocial well-being. It is important for teachers to be familiar with this theory themselves as it will assist them to provide supportive learning and teaching environments in the South African schooling context (Nel, Nel & Hugo, 2013).

Bronfenbrenner's ecological systems theory of human development

Bronfenbrenner's multidimensional model looks at the various interacting systems that affect child development and result in change. Bronfenbrenner identified five levels or systems, which are circular in nature. This means that what happens in one system or level will affect the other systems and may cause a ripple effect for further change. Figure 24.1 illustrates these levels at a glance.

24 Promoting psychosocial well-being in teaching and learning environments

CHERYL FERREIRA, CONNIE HAASBROEK, BEVERLY FELDMAN,
MONKIE MOSEKI & CHANTEL WEBER

What transforms education, is a transformed being in the world.
(Parker Palmer)

Introduction

Imagine a thirteen-year-old girl whose parents have passed away. She has three siblings, lives in a shack in an informal settlement and, because of flooding, she has been left homeless. Their only source of income is a meagre state subsidy. Adding to these devastating circumstances, she is pregnant, has contracted HIV/AIDS and is bullied mercilessly by a group of girls in her school. These are the stark realities of many learners in the South African schooling system. At the same time, in classrooms around the country, many teachers are overwhelmed and often debilitated by overcrowded classrooms, a constantly changing curriculum, mounting administrative tasks and limited resources for assisting and supporting the learners in their classrooms. All these factors can impede on both the learners' and the teachers' psychosocial well-being.

In this chapter, we will be exploring the factors that play a role in the psychosocial well-being of both the learners and the teachers in these demoralising teaching and learning environments. Subsequently, we will suggest ways to promote psychosocial well-being in educational settings.

unleash that power in the face of adversity, in ways that are as gentle and kind as they are powerful and strong. Either teachers can crumble under the weight of the challenges facing education, or they will find the strength and resilience to be their best selves in their service to humanity. Positive psychology promotes asset-based thinking that has the potential to transform the lives of teachers and learners alike, to promote growth, well-being, flourishing and consequently optimise their functioning in learning and development.

www.ingramcontent.com/pod-product-compliance
Lightning Source LLC
Chambersburg PA
CBHW081943230426
43669CB00019B/2910